DATE DUE		
Dec 13 77 H		
Dec 15 78 B		
Apr 25 '80		
Dec 12 '80		

DRAMA ON STAGE

RANDOLPH GOODMAN

Holt, Rinehart and Winston
New York

Copyright Acknowledgments

FOR

Jane and Susan Goodman

————————————————AND A NEW GENERATION
OF PLAYGOERS

Preface

The history of dramatic literature is comparatively rich. We can read plays written in a wide variety of styles for every important period during the past twenty-five hundred years. Our records of theatrical productions, on the other hand, are relatively poor because of the transitory nature of the theater's physical properties. Costumes, scenery, and furnishings have decayed, disappeared, or been destroyed; even stone playhouses have been torn down or have crumbled away. And what of the actor's performance? Powerful though it may be in execution, concluded and applauded it is no more than an insubstantial memory.

Articulate spectators, critics, and members of the theatrical profession have left eyewitness reports, the best of which provide us with highly vivid images of outstanding productions and performances; many of these reports have been made more graphic by the inclusion of sketches, engravings, and photographs. But it is absolutely impossible to re-create a play merely by the use of words and pictures (even *moving* pictures), because the minimum basic requisites for "living" theater are flesh-and-blood actors confronting flesh-and-blood audiences. And all professional playwrights have written for the living theater! A play is born in a manuscript and buried in a printed text; it knows life, like a human being, only in the bright world of action.

Molière was well aware of this fact. With a genius for both dramatic literature and theatrical production, he directed the following words to the readers of the published version of his play *Love Is the Best Doctor:* "There is no need to tell you that many things depend entirely on the manner of the performance. Every one knows well enough that plays are written only to be acted; and I advise no one to read this unless he has the faculty, while doing so, of catching the meaning of the business of the stage."

It is the aim of this book to help the reader catch "the meaning of the business of the stage." This is not an easy assignment. A play is a complex and difficult form of art. As presented in the theater, it is, in fact, a synthesis of all the other arts. The story unfolds in poetry or prose; the action is expressed by voice, gesture, and movement; the scenery involves painting, architecture, and lighting; music and dancing are often integral elements of the work.

If the reader is to keep all of these elements in mind while his attention is fixed on the text of the play, he must have some preparation and assistance. He must be aware of the theatrical conditions under which each work was originally performed, as well as of the varying conditions affecting its later productions. He should be acquainted with the individual, and often conflicting, points of view and practices of the playwright's corps of collaborators—the actors, directors, scene and costume designers, lighting and sound technicians, musicians, dancers, stage managers, and stagehands—whose job it is, collectively, to turn a verbal plan into a viable production.

The interviews with artists and technicians which introduce each of the plays in this volume are intended to stimulate the imagination of the reader and to familiarize him with the procedures of the best professional theater craftsmen. How enlightening it would be if we had Euripides' comments concerning the composition of *Medea* as we have Duerrenmatt's remarks on *The Visit;* and how helpful to an actor if he were able to compare Burbage's interpretation of the character of Macbeth with Olivier's! The collection and preservation of such revelations as these is the task of the theater historian.

The plays offered here were chosen in accordance with two principles: First, each represents an important traditional type—a classical tragedy, a medieval morality play, an Elizabethan tragedy, and a neoclassical comedy (the last-named, the prototype for the comic plays of the Restoration and for the comedy of manners of more recent times). The two modern plays exemplify interesting variations of contemporary style: *A Streetcar Named Desire* is basically realistic or naturalistic, with symbolic and poetic overtones, while *The Visit* is a theatricalist work in which symbolism and expressionism predominate. Read chronologically, the plays provide, in condensed form, a history of western drama. Secondly, each play selected has had numerous and significant productions, particularly during recent years, so that the artists involved have been available for interview.

It is the author's hope that this book will provide at least a clue to the "meaning" of the business of the theater, and that it will, in any case, arouse the reader's interest in drama on stage.

I take special pleasure in expressing my gratitude to those individuals and institutions without whose generous cooperation this book could not have been written. My thanks go first to the professional theater people, mentioned by name in the text, who took time out of busy schedules to talk with me about their work. I am indebted, in addition, to the following:

In New York: To George Freedley, Curator, and to Elizabeth P. Barrett and Paul Myers of the Theater Collection of the New York Public Library, to the staff of the Photographic Division of the Library, and to Gabriel C. Austin of its Information Service; to Anne Minor of the Cultural Division of the French

Embassy and to Daisy J. Lebel of its Library; to the French Institute; to Lisa Basch of the Photographic Services at Columbia University; and to the Austrian, British, French, German, Netherlands, and Swiss information offices.

In New Haven: To Professor Alois M. Nagler of Yale; and to Mary Grahn of the library at the Yale Drama School.

In London: To the British Museum; to the Library of the University of London; to George Nash of the Enthoven Collection, Victoria and Albert Museum; to Sybil Rosenfeld, Phyllis Hartnoll, Ifan Kyrle Fletcher, and David Magarshack.

In Stratford-on-Avon: To the Shakespeare Memorial Library.

In Paris: To the Bibliothèque Nationale; to André Veinstein of the Bibliothèque de l'Arsenal.

In Vienna: To Professor Heinz Kindermann of the University of Vienna; to Gerda Doublier of the Library of the Institut für Theaterwissenschaft.

In Salzburg: To the Festival Information Office.

In Berlin: To Hugo Fetting of the Deutsche Akademie der Künste (*Theatergeschichte*); to the Schillertheater Clipping Files.

In Copenhagen: To the Drama Collection of the Library of the University of Copenhagen.

In Stockholm: To Professor Agne Beijer, Dr. Gustaf Hilleström, Alf Sjöberg, and Per Sjöstrand; to Dr. Karl-Ragnar Gierow, director of the Royal Dramatic Theater; and to the Library of the University of Stockholm.

In Oslo: To Knut Hergel, director of the Oslo National Theater: to Lita Prahl and Christian Stenersen; and to Carl Frederick Engelstad and his family.

In Geneva: To François Simon and Georges Descombes.

In Zürich: To Dr. Kurt Hirschfeld and Ruth Bossard of the Schauspielhaus; to Peter Schifferli of Die Arche Verlag; and to Dr. Elisabeth Brock-Sulzer.

In Spoleto: To the Festival Information Office.

In Rome: To John L. Brown, cultural attaché to the American Embassy; to Dr. Giordano Falzoni of the Cultural Division of the American Embassy; to Maria Theresa de Ruette Scalero of the Library of the United States Information Service; and to Franco Zeffirelli.

Finally, it remains for me to acknowledge my obligations to Robin Leigh III, who started me on the adventure of this book; to Dr. Mildred C. Kuner, who proffered wise advice during the writing process; to Dr. Margarete Bieber, my teacher and friend, who kindly consented to read the chapter on Greek theater; to Professor Otto Reinert, of the University of Washington, who read the entire book in manuscript and offered innumerable and invaluable suggestions; to the Alexander family, Ron Gaskell, and Bernard Michal, dear and helpful friends in London and Paris; and to Jordan Hott, Mrs. Eva Baratta, and Mrs. Evelyn B. Pearlman, who assisted me in the preparation of the manuscript. To those whose names I may inadvertently have omitted, I offer thanks and apologies in equal measure.

                                                                                    R. G.

New York, New York
March 1, 1961

Contents

The Misanthrope—MOLIÈRE

A Streetcar Named Desire—TENNESSEE WILLIAMS

The Visit—FRIEDRICH DUERRENMATT

Medea

〽〽〽〽〽 EURIPIDES

Introduction

Euripides, the son of Mnesarchides, was born in the vicinity of Athens some time between 485 and 480 B.C., presented his first set of tragedies in 455, and won his first victory in 441. He won only four prizes during his lifetime, though another was awarded him posthumously; this is a very unusual record for a man who wrote about eighty-eight plays (twenty-two sets of four) and who was compared even while he lived with Aeschylus and Sophocles. The reason why the judges ignored him is clear: Euripides did not cater to the prejudices of the Athenian crowd.

He did not approve of its superstitions and follies, its social injustices or its moral standards; he objected to its cynicism and its neglect of that human value which he considered highest—love of one's fellow man. And so he dared to write about the decay of the state religion, the disintegration of family life because of the subjection of women, the demoralizing effect of Athenian aggression carried on in the name of democracy, and the false distinction which was made between freeman and slave. His sympathy was reserved for ordinary human beings, including peasants, aliens, and slaves, his scorn for evil-doers and tyrants whether they were men or gods. In fact, he brought the gods, as well as the ancient heroes and heroines, down to the level of the common man, and represented all "not as they ought to be, but as they are." To Euripides the traditional legends implied that the morality of the gods was lower than that of good men.

Such views were revolutionary and objectionable enough, but to make things worse Euripides began to tamper with the very structure of tragedy itself. Greek tragedy, it must be remembered, was nothing like modern drama, for it was not a secular art but a religious one. It was not written primarily to provide entertainment, although that was expected, but to furnish religious instruction and moral inspiration, to effect a purging of the psyche, a catharsis. Even Greek comedy had a ritualistic basis and a didactic purpose.

The modern dramatist may write on any subject he cares to and present it in any form that strikes his fancy, but the Athenian playwright was more or less constrained to select his material from Greek history or legend and to present it in a well-established and highly conventional form. The play had to be written in verse and was accompanied throughout by music; it had to have a chorus, it could use no more than three actors; no violent action could be shown upon the

1

stage, but a messenger might report it; and, finally, a crane-like machine might deposit a god (*deus ex machina*), or several gods, upon the stage, either during or more often at the end of the play, in order to show how the deities were involved in man's life and often settled man's problems. There was even a strict prescription for the use of the verse: The Chorus sang an ode as it entered at the beginning, and as it left at the end of the play; it also sang an ode between each of the five dramatic episodes into which the play was divided. The episodes themselves were written mainly in two kinds of verse, satirical (usually iambic) and lyric, resembling somewhat the recitatives and arias in a modern opera. This traditional and unrealistic form of drama was ideally suited to the mystical visions of Aeschylus and the idealistic views of Sophocles, but it could not properly accommodate the rationalistic and satirical concepts of Euripides. The young playwright, therefore, made a number of changes in the accepted form of tragedy, and earned as a result the general censure of his contemporaries.

Because he wrote plays in which theme and plot were usually more important than character, Euripides introduced long prologues and epilogues which served to announce his thesis, to suggest a pattern for the various episodes, or to supply a moral. He did not hesitate to alter or curtail the use of the Chorus. Aeschylus and Sophocles had written about public conflicts and so a Chorus of Theban Elders might very well take part in the action; but Euripides was concerned about private discords between husband and wife (Jason-Medea) or father and son (Theseus-Hippolytus) and in these a chorus would have little place. The Chorus often actually got in the way of the action, and so we find Euripides apologizing for its presence and limiting its use. Occasionally he brought them on, as a sort of entr'acte, to sing an irrelevant ode between episodes. Euripides also introduced innovations in the musical accompaniment. We do not know exactly what effect was produced, but apparently instead of singing one syllable to a note, so that the meaning of each word would be clear to the audience, the syllables and words were trilled and repeated until they became incomprehensible, as is so much of modern grand opera. Euripides, generally speaking, threw all "classic restraint" to the winds; nor did he write about the fall of a good person brought about by a flaw in his character. The people he chose to write about were driven by sexual passion, anger, revenge, or a desire for power.

The cavalier manner in which the playwright distorted or summarily dismissed the basic elements of tragedy as later enumerated in the *Poetics* makes it impossible for us to classify Euripides' plays as Aristotelian tragedies; not one of his plays, in fact, exactly fits the definition. After careful analysis, we are obliged to refer to them simply as dramas, comedy-dramas, melodramas, romances, and fantasies, while some even approach musical comedy. It is no wonder then that conservative audiences objected, that judges demurred, and that, throughout his life, Euripides was the butt of serious critics and comic poets alike.

In 408 B.C., Euripides left Athens, a voluntary exile because of the ill-will of his fellow citizens, and went to live at the court of Archelaus in Macedonia. He died in exile at the age of 78, in about the year 406, and was buried at Arethusa.

If Euripides was not sufficiently appreciated in his own day, he has been amply vindicated since, for nineteen of his plays are extant, more than double the number of those of all his rivals put together. His *Medea* (431 B.C.) took only third prize, but the plays that placed first and second that year are unknown. As the creator of love-drama, moreover, Euripides was the forefather of Greek New Comedy and of Roman and modern drama as well. He introduced to the stage many forms of intrigue, adventure, and suspense, as well as recognition scenes and psychological probing which have all found their way into the plays that grace our stages and motion picture and television screens. He became the most influential and highly imitated of all the Greek playwrights, and the one whose plays have been most frequently and consistently revived and adapted down to our own time.

In writing the *Medea* Euripides was dealing with one of his favorite myths, one he used as the basis for three separate plays. The love affair between Jason and Medea held strong appeal for the dramatist, for it was a romance fraught with tensions and conflicts.

When Jason claimed the throne of Iolcus, which rightfully belonged to him, his traitorous uncle, Pelias, who occupied it, agreed to give it up on condition that Jason fetch the Golden Fleece from Colchis. Pelias assigned this impossible task believing that the young man would fail in the enterprise and would meet his death at the hands of the barbarians who dwelt in that distant land. Jason coolly set about building the Argo, the first Greek ship, and sailed for Colchis, where at the royal court, he met Medea, a wild, passionate girl who fell deeply in love with him. Medea was the daughter of the king; the grand-daughter of Helios, the sun god; and the niece of Circe, the enchantress; from these forebears she had inherited great powers, both natural and supernatural, and she did not hesitate to put them all at the disposal of the man she loved. She cruelly deceived her father and made it possible for Jason to seize the Golden Fleece; then she boarded the Argo with her lover and fled her own country. Pursued by her brother, Absyrtos, she slew him brutally without any qualms. When they reached Thessaly, Jason and Medea discovered that Pelias had no intentions of giving up the throne, whereupon Medea tricked the king's daughters into causing their father's death. Jason, fearing vengeance, renounced his claim to the throne, hoping, perhaps, to sit upon a richer throne elsewhere. Banished from his own land, Jason took Medea and their two sons to Corinth where the family was granted sanctuary. It seemed as if they would be able to live in peace now; but Creon, the king, having no male heir, was looking about for a mate for his daughter, Glauce, and decided that Jason would be ideal. The king informed Jason that if he agreed to marry the princess, he would be named successor to the throne. Since Medea was an alien, her marriage to Jason was not legally recognized in any Greek city, and her children were considered illegitimate. From a legal point of view, therefore, there was nothing to prevent Jason from leaving Medea to marry Glauce, which is exactly what he did, without informing his wife.

Euripides' play opens shortly after Medea learns that her husband has deserted her. She is in a torment of humiliation and despair, and has become ill and emotionally upset planning revenge. Her Nurse's lament, which serves as a prologue to the play, informs us of the sacrifices that Medea has made in the past for the man who has just left her; we are again reminded of these sacrifices when Medea reproaches and reviles Jason; and we hear of them for the third time from Jason's own lips at the very end of the play. This last touch is a beautiful piece of irony, since Jason clearly remembers his wife's crimes but conveniently forgets that she committed them for his sake. Euripides, however, will allow neither Medea nor the audience to forget that there was strong motivation—even justification, perhaps—for the horrible crimes about to be perpetrated. In Medea love is as ruthless, as brutal, and as destructive a force as hate. Appalling and terrible as she is, Medea is still understandable and real. Where once she dared anything to bring Jason pleasure, she now fears nothing to give him pain.

It is difficult to sympathize with her, but we are forced to admit that Medea was a loyal and devoted wife, who would stop at nothing to advance her husband's welfare. It is Jason who has failed in devotion and fidelity and who, instead of being grateful for the aid his wife has given him, defends himself against her recriminations with insolent and specious arguments. He tells her that it was for her good and for the best interest of their sons that he has married Glauce; he offers her money and letters of introduction to his friends in foreign cities, for she is about to be cast out of Corinth; and he insists that he has adequately repaid her for her services by bringing her from barbarous Asia to civilized Greece. Here Euripides achieves another brilliant piece of irony in making Jason sound like the president of the chamber of commerce congratulating a refugee on reaching God's own country.

But Medea is not so easily taken in; she has dealt with cleverer men than Jason; she has outsmarted princes and kings. She can bend any man to her will because she uses the proper psychological approach to each one. When Creon orders her out of the country at once, she manages by a subtle appeal to his kindness to get one day's grace, which is all she needs to effect her revenge; when Aegeus, the Athenian king, tells her that he is unhappy because he is childless, she sees at once a way to blast Jason's happiness, and in exchange for Aegeus' vow to protect her in his city she promises to cure his sterility. On Jason she practices the greatest deceit and for him she reserves the cruelest punishment, for she not only wrecks his hope of inheriting Creon's throne, but destroys all his loved ones in the bargain.

The manner in which Medea makes her escape from Corinth—in a dragon-drawn chariot sent to her by her grandfather, Helios—has met with the severe disapproval of many critics as an unwarranted intrusion of the supernatural. It certainly would have been easier for the playwright and more credible to the audience simply to have announced Medea's departure, but to a showman and poet of Euripides' caliber the present ending presented at least three distinct advantages: first, it is extremely theatrical and spectacular; then, it better explains how Medea managed to deposit her children's bodies at the temple of Hera at Acrocorinth where, in the dramatist's time, there was a cult involving these children; finally, it was a symbolic means of vindicating Medea, for it was the sun—emblem of reason—that sent the chariot which enabled her to effect her escape.

It is possible to read many themes into the play, but the significance of this work is greater than the sum of all of them. We are shown, for instance, the unfair treatment accorded aliens in Greece; the eternal battle of the sexes; and, most terrifying of all, the oppressed striking back to achieve not justice but revenge.

The odes sung by the Chorus in this play are more closely related to the subject matter of the drama than is generally the case in Euripides. Hearing Medea lament, the Chorus of Corinthian Women enters and in the first ode (called the parados) offers sympathy and cautions her to practice restraint. The next time they sing they mention that the old order is changing: women used to be accused of faithlessness, but now the men have grown deceitful, and Medea has been deserted in a foreign land. After the scene in which Medea hurls her scathing denunciations at Jason, the Chorus again suggests restraint and expresses pity because Medea has no friend to help her; at this point Aegeus, king of Athens, who is passing through Corinth on a journey, meets Medea and promises to give her sanctuary, unaware of the crimes she is planning. Here the Chorus sings an ode in praise of Athens, which must have delighted the audience, although it is not entirely relevant to the action. The Chorus itself wonders how such a sacred city can give protection to a murderess, and begs Medea not to destroy her sons. Here we see the awkwardness of the Chorus in Euripidean drama: All the women in Corinth know that Medea plans to murder her children, but they do not inform Jason, nor do anything else about it, except to advise Medea against it. After Medea sends her children to Glauce with the poisoned gifts, the Chorus expresses sorrow at the fact that the boys will be accomplices in their mother's crime, and weeps again because Medea intends to slay them. When the boys return, Medea, torn between her love for them and her determination to kill them, leads them resolutely into the house, while the Chorus laments that children bring only endless cares. As the women hear the cries issuing from indoors, but are prevented from entering, they pray to heaven to stay Medea's hand. At the end of the play, the Chorus sings a final song (the exodos); here the poet expresses his view of life in words which appear almost verbatim at the conclusion of four of his other plays. Euripides' outlook is not a cheerful one; he stresses the uncertainties of life and points out that those things we count on do not come to pass, while the things we do not dream of are bound to happen. Perhaps because such a viewpoint is based upon feelings of insecurity and anxiety, it has found ready acceptance throughout the ages and is widely held today, as the plays of Tennessee Williams (see pp. 293f.) and many others clearly show.

PRODUCTION IN THE THEATER OF DIONYSUS

The Great Dionysia was an important fertility festival celebrated in Athens in honor of the god Dionysus Eleuthereus. This god was introduced into the city by the tyrant Pisistratus in the sixth century B.C. from the village of Eleutherae. First one temple, then another was built in honor of the god on the southern slope of the Acropolis; beside these temples, on holy ground, the Theater of Dionysus began to take shape and grow until the stage-building hid the temples from the view of the audience, but the drama always retained its religious function.

The Great Dionysia was celebrated each year about the end of March when the skies are clear and the air is warm, for the spring comes early in Greece. As part of the festival, lyric choruses performed, and tragedies and comedies were produced in the Theater of Dionysus. As in most Greek festivals, the presentation of plays took the form of a competition.

The chief religious magistrate of the city, who was in charge of the festival, selected three dramatic poets and three choregoi, rich men who were compelled to finance the plays, to compete. In order to enter the contest, each dramatic poet had to submit a group of four plays, called a tetralogy, consisting of three tragedies (which might or might not be related to each other in subject matter) and a satyr-play, a drama in a lighter vein. The playwright chosen to compete trained his own chorus, directed his play, and served also as costume and scene designer, choreographer, and composer. The choregoi functioned as producers; each one was assigned a poet and had to pay all the expenses involved in putting on that poet's plays. They paid the salaries of the members of the chorus and of the flute-player, and supplied the costumes and scenery. The play might succeed or fail depending upon the generosity or stinginess of the choregos.

Elaborate precautions were taken to insure fairness in the selection of the five judges who awarded first, second, and third prizes to the playwrights at the end of the contest. The verdicts were generally just, but despite all precautions judges were sometimes bribed or influenced. The victorious poet was proclaimed by the herald and was crowned in the theater with a crown of ivy; his choregos also received a crown and a tripod to commemorate the occasion. Plays which failed were often revised by the author and reproduced at less important festivals.

The order of events at the Great Dionysia was roughly as follows: On the day before the festival the audience gathered in the theater to hear the announcement of the names of the plays, playwrights, and leading actors who were to take part. This served in lieu of the printed program. On this day, too, the statue of Dionysus Eleuthereus was paraded in the theater, hymns were sung, and sacrifices offered. The first day of the actual festival started with another procession in which phalloi were carried, then sacrifices were made to the god, and the choregoi appeared in colorful and lavish robes. In the evening a lively performance was put on by revelers who sometimes disguised themselves as animals; this was called a komos, the root of the word comedy. The next three or four days were taken up from dawn till dusk with the presentation of the plays. On the final day of the festival, a special assembly was held in the theater. This assembly inquired into the conduct of the officials and heard all complaints concerning misconduct or injuries connected with the festival.

The Great Dionysia became increasingly important during the Golden Age of Greece not only because of the performances of dramatic contests, but because it was open to the whole Hellenic world and served as an advertisement of Athenian wealth, power, and public spirit, as well as of her artistic and literary leadership. Surplus revenues were displayed in the theater; the sons of veterans were paraded and rewarded; foreign ambassadors attended; prisoners were released on bail; no legal action could be taken; and it was a general holiday.

The Theater

The Theater of Dionysus grew up functionally out of the needs of the people and the contours of the land. Beside the temple on the southern slope of the Acropolis, a large, circular area was leveled off to make a place for the performance of ritualistic dances. The orchestron, or dancing place, consequently, is the oldest element of the theater. Worshipers at first stood around the circle to watch the performers, then moved up the slope to get a better view; there they stood or sat. By the beginning of the fifth century B.C., rows of wooden benches had not only been built up the mountainside but had fanned out in semicircular shape around the northern side of the orchestron. The auditorium, or hearing place, was thus the second element of the theater to appear. The *skene*, or scene-building, which developed into the raised stage, came last. The ritual dances became more pantomimic and dramatic; then actors separated themselves from the chorus and began to speak or chant lines impersonating various characters; soon a need was felt for a scene-building and dressing-rooms, which led to the erection of the *skene*, a wooden structure put up on the southern side of the orchestron facing the auditorium. The three component parts of the theater never achieved complete architectural unity during the fifth century, but improvements were made in each part from year to year: the dancing place was paved and drained; the wooden benches gave way to tiers of stone seats; and the *skene* was replaced each year by a more elaborate one especially designed to improve the stage picture.

The Actors

Thespis is credited with being the first actor; he won that distinction by stepping out of the chorus and assuming a dramatic role. Down to the time of Aeschylus, there appears to have been but one actor in a play and that actor was the poet himself. Aeschylus introduced the second actor. Sophocles took no part in the performance but introduced the third actor; thereafter only three actors were permitted to appear but each played several roles. By the middle of the fifth century the actors were chosen along with the plays and choregoi by the chief magistrate; the three best actors were assigned one each to each of the tragic poets. We know the names of some of the actors of this period; outstanding among them were Kleandros, Mynniskos, Kallipides, Tlepolemos, and probably Kephisophon. Only men were permitted to take part in the performances, as was true later in the Elizabethan and Japanese theaters.

The various parts in the plays were distributed among the three actors, who changed roles by changing masks, costumes, and voice. Children appeared in many of Euripides' plays but they did not speak. In the *Medea,* the parts might very well have been distributed as follows: 1st Actor—Medea; 2nd Actor—Nurse, Jason, Creon; 3rd Actor—Tutor, Aegeus, Messenger; the lines of the children, coming from off-stage, might have been spoken by adult actors.

The actors used words, gestures, and bodily movements. There were three kinds of speech: 1. Speech unaccompanied by music, in dialogue or monologue, which was in iambic trimeters, considered the rhythm closest to prose speech; 2. Speech accompanied by a musical instrument (the flute) called recitative and written in tetrameters and iambics inserted in the midst of lyric systems; and 3. Songs, in lyrics with music.

If the chorus danced while the actors spoke or sang, the flute must have accompanied both. A lyre was used sometimes, as were rattles and various other noisemakers.

The actors' voices were considered very important. The acoustics were good in the theaters, but actors had to speak clearly and correctly. The style of speaking was oratorical, occasionally realistic; vocal tricks, such as imitations of animal cries, bird calls, and other sound effects were also used.

Facial expressions were unalterable because of the masks which the actors wore, but gestures and movements were free in other respects—embracing, kneeling, crawling, and so on. As time went on this freedom grew. The dignified old actor, Mynniskos, nicknamed a younger actor, Kallipides, "The Monkey," because of his excessive use of gesture. In Old Comedy every sort of gesture and movement was used, unrestrained by costume or a sense of delicacy.

The Chorus

The entire performance had originally been put on by the chorus, and the chorus played a part in all Greek drama. In the early plays of Aeschylus it fills the major role, but after the introduction of the second and third actors its importance decreases. It was Agathon, a contemporary of Euripides, who is said to have introduced choral passages that could be transferred from one play to another, as they were merely incidental to the action.

There were twelve men in the chorus of Aeschylus; fifteen in the choruses of Sophocles and Euripides. The members of the chorus were masked, and wore costumes indicative of the characters portrayed. In the *Medea* they represented Corinthian women. The tragic chorus performed in rectangular formation: there were three rows, five men in a row. The leader of the chorus was the choregus. Some of the members of the chorus were said to be mute, that is, they took no vocal part in the action but merely danced. The flute-player entered and left with the chorus.

When the chorus took part in the dialogue, the leader spoke for the entire group; the odes and other choral passages were sung or spoken in unison by full or semichorus.

All dancing was considered mimetic and freely employed expressive and rhythmical gestures. The hands especially were used very pantomimically, and the gestures were intimately associated with the words from moment to moment. After a while the postures and attitudes came to be standardized and named.

The playwrights invented many dances for the chorus; Sophocles and Euripides had themselves been dancers. Various types of dances were done, some slow, some rapid, and some seductive. It is believed that the chorus danced as it sang; or that one part of the chorus danced, while the other part sang. In comedy the dancing was unrestrained, consisting of leaps and kicks, or was obscene, as in the *kordax*, a form of strip-tease sometimes done by an old woman (a man in disguise, of course).

Costumes

The most characteristic aspect of the actors' costumes was the masks. It is believed that masks had their origin in the rites connected with Dionysiac worship. Masks were obligatory for those who took part in the Dionysiac *Komos*, and in the satyr-dances. The chorus from which Thespis detached himself probably was masked, and the actor continued to wear a mask though it probably differed from the others. Thespis is said to have disguised his face originally with white lead, then with leaves, and then with plain linen masks. After that the playwright Choerilus improved the masks and robes, and Phrynichus introduced feminine masks. Later writers of tragedy made further alterations, adapting the masks to the personalities of the characters represented by the actors. It was Aeschylus who first used brightly colored and terrifying masks.

The dresses worn in tragedy were designed to make the characters look more noble, regal, and dignified; the long gowns reached to the ankles, and the sleeves covered the arms to the wrists. The fabrics were rich and highly ornamented and decorated. The chorus was dressed according to its supposed nationality or occupation. Individual characters were also specially dressed, in mourning, for instance, or in rags. Euripides was criticized by Aristophanes for permitting his heroes and heroines to appear in tatters.

Tragic actors wore soft shoes that went up high on the leg; these were called the *kothurnos*. It was not until the Hellenistic period that the soles were made several inches thick; and in the Roman theater the leading actor had thicker soles than the others, the added height showing his greater importance.

The costumes in Old Comedy were more varied and more indecent in order to induce laughter; actors had heavily padded bodies, and very short chitons with exaggerated phalloi showing; on their feet they wore soft, sloppy socks. Their masks were often caricatures of actual celebrities.

Scenery

The *skene*, or stage-building, in front of which the plays were performed generally represented the façade of a palace, a temple, or a house, since these were the locales most frequently called for in the tragedies. As the *skene* was re-erected each year, various improvements and additions were made in its structure. Side wings, called *paraskenia*, as well as platforms and levels, appeared from time to time to intimate the nature of the building which the *skene* was supposed to represent. There were passageways, called *paradoi*, to the right and left of the *skene*, used not only by the spectators for entering and leaving the theater, but also for the entrances and exits of the actors and the chorus. There were additional entrances and exits for the actors in the *skene* itself, for the building had three front doors—a very large center one, and a smaller one on each side of it.

The outdoor theater put a severe limitation upon the playwrights in the choice of scenes which could be convincingly shown as taking place in front of a house, temple, or palace, or in some other open-air setting; it was not possible to present interior scenes realistically. But a mechanical device was introduced during the fifth century which helped partially to overcome the difficulty; it was a platform on wheels, called an *eccyclema,* which was rolled out of the *skene* and on which was represented an action that was supposed to be taking place indoors.

Several other mechanical devices were put to use during the dramatic action. A sort of crane, or derrick, "the machine," lifted a god over the stage-building and brought him down into the midst of the action. When a playwright could not work out his plot, he might bring in a god to wind the play up. This mechanical solution of the problem came to be known as the *deus ex machina* (the god from the machine), a phrase still in use among drama critics. Euripides employed "the machine" frequently; in the *Medea,* for instance, it was by means of this device that the heroine could appear in her chariot on the roof of the *skene* at the end of the play.

Another mechanical apparatus was the *periaktus,* a three-sided prism on each side of which were painted pictures or symbols showing the time or place of the action. There were two *periaktoi,* one on each side of the *skene;* a change of scene could be indicated simply by revolving them.

Painted back-cloths or screens, easily removable, might also have been used during the performance to indicate changes of locale, but positive proof of this is lacking. We do know, however, that many plays called for scene changes both during the action and between separate works. In the bill that included the *Medea,* for instance, some scene changes must have been made, for the *Medea* takes place before a palace, the *Philoctetes* requires a mountain and cave, the *Dictys* probably required a house, while the satyr-play, the *Harvesters,* suggests a field or country region.

The one permanent element in the scenery was the altar situated in the very center of the dancing place. This was not a stage property but a real religious altar, connected with the temples which still stood behind the *skene,* and was part of the sacred ground on which the theater had been erected. Many playwrights took advantage of the presence of the altar, and in their temple scenes required the actors to make use of it.

Music

A great deal of music was used in the drama but not much is known about it because so little of it is extant. It appears to have been very complicated; in addition to being written in modes (varying intervals between notes), it could have diatonic, chromatic, or enharmonic form, and could be sung or played in a number of keys (absolute pitch could be varied). The modes were connected with the emotions: Dorian was considered majestic; Mixolydian, pathetic; Phrygian, sensuous or excited. Aristotle approved of the use of Hypodorian and Hypophrygian modes by the actors when realistic action was called for. The Phrygian mode was considered overemotional; one scrap of this type survives for a passage of Euripides' *Orestes*, lines 338-344.

At first the music was subordinate to the words, but later on, it became more elaborate and florid—a single syllable set to several notes—until the words were unintelligible. Instrumental music apart from words was seldom used, except in special cases in comedy, such as the song of the nightingale imitated in the *Birds* and the twanging of a lyre in the *Frogs*. The coryphaeus (leader of the chorus) gave the chorus the first note.

The Audience

The seating capacity of the great theater of Dionysus in Athens has been estimated to be somewhere between 14,000 and 17,000. Men, women, and children attended. We do not know the price of a seat in the fifth century (in the fourth, it was two obols), but Pericles decreed that those who could not afford to buy a ticket were to be given the money from the theoric fund (a surplus in the treasury). Pericles might have been attempting to win the favor of the people, but the struggle for tickets was so violent and the buying up of seats such an abuse, that the poor only got a chance to attend the theater through the theoric fund. The distribution was not made in cash but in the form of free tickets given out by the authorities of each deme, and only full citizens were entitled to a share.

An official called the Superintendent of Buildings (or Seller of Seats) was in charge of the theater; his salary was paid by the State and it was his duty to see that the theater was kept in good repair and that the seats were properly assigned. Admission to the theater was by ticket or token. Tokens were made of bronze, ivory, bone, lead, clay, and terra cotta. Those of bronze, ivory, and bone were probably for the upper classes, the occupants of the first rows; those of lead, clay, and terra cotta were inexpensive and might have served for most of the audience.

Seats of honor were given by the State to certain priests, officials, and foreign ambassadors. Sixty seats in the front row are inscribed with names of important people for whom the seats were reserved. The center seat in the front row— later a large, elaborately carved, thronelike chair of white marble—was occupied by the priest of Dionysus Eleuthereus; and two seats were provided for priests of Dionysus Melpomenus, for this god was worshiped by the Artists of Dionysus, the actors' union.

Women were seated separately from men, and courtesans apart from other women. The women were placed at a distance from the orchestron. Foreign men and foreign women were seated separately at the extreme left or right of the theater.

The theater was divided into thirteen wedge-shaped blocks; each tribe (there were ten tribes in the fifth century) had its own block of seats and on their tokens were stamped the letter indicating the block and a symbol of the tribe.

Since the performances went on from dawn till dusk, the audience brought re-freshments: food, wine, dried fruits, and candy. These items may also have been sold in the theater. Food was thrown at unpopular actors. The audience had few comforts, but cushions were put on the stone seats.

The audience was very noisy—applauding, hissing, and kicking with their heels —but they could also be extremely attentive. Arguments and fights often devel-oped; and special officials were there to keep order.

Contrary to common belief, not all members of the audience knew the stories of the plays; only the more intellectual ones did. But the audiences were critical: they hissed a line in praise of money and applauded some verses in praise of freedom. They were particularly sensitive to anything that appealed to, or con-flicted with, their moral and political sentiments; their point of view was highly utilitarian. Their ability to follow devotedly day after day three great tragedies, and to enjoy the wit of Aristophanes, shows that they had a high degree of awareness.

THE PRODUCTION RECORD

Euripides' *Medea* received its first performance at the Dionysiac festival in Athens in 431 B.C. Although it won only third prize, the play became so popular and was performed so frequently that its lines were known throughout the ancient world. Many playwrights, both Greek and Roman, borrowed the story from Euripides.

In A.D. 60 Seneca, basing his work on Euripides' play, wrote a *Medea* that lacked the emotional and psychological power of the Greek play, but served nevertheless as a model for many neoclassical playwrights. Seneca departed from Euripides by making Jason a sympathetic character; he also heightened the spectacle and horror by having Medea kill one child on stage and the other on the roof, possibly even flinging their bodies down, in full view of Jason and the audience.

Corneille, whose version of *Medea* appeared in 1634, had two great actors at his disposal for the leading roles: Montdory, the star of the Théatre Marais, and La Villiers, the leading lady, who detested her colleague heartily and as a result gave a very convincing performance as Medea. Corneille based his play on Seneca's version but did not hesitate to rewrite it completely. He omitted the chorus, cut the monologues, built up the dialogues and made them less mechani-cal, and added several complexities to the plot. Since Montdory was the star, his role was enlarged to more than six times the original length, which made Jason almost as important as Medea. There were many other changes, including Aegeus' unreciprocated love for Creusa (Glauce), and the final suicide of Jason. This treatment was well-suited to the tastes of Corneille's audience and proved to be an enormous success.

There have been many *Medeas* in America in original form and in adapta-tion. Maxwell Anderson's *The Wingless Victory* (1937) is an interesting treatment of the story which did not succeed in the theater. Medea here became the African princess, Oparre, who saved the life of a Yankee sea captain and returned with him to New England where, her common-law marriage repudiated, she was estranged and abandoned and slew her children in revenge. In 1946, Jean Anouilh adapted and modernized the play, making Medea a foul-mouthed Russian gypsy, who finally burned to death in her own caravan.

Robinson Jeffers' poetic adaptation of the *Medea* was written at the request of, and dedicated to, Judith Anderson. The play opened in New York on October 20, 1947, and closed on May 15, 1948, after a run of 214 performances. Most of the alterations made in the play were done for the purpose of building up the star's part: Medea's speeches were lengthened; Jason became more insignificant; three women served in place of a chorus; all the supernatural elements were removed from the story, thus highlighting Medea's psychological power; and Medea was given the final lines; she, rather than the poet, has the last word. Miss Anderson's interpretation of the role was as perceptive as it was passionate, and for her efforts she won the Drama League Award for the best acting of the year. Miss Anderson toured with the play almost continuously for the next eight years. During the week of October 12, 1959, a television version of *Medea* was presented for seven performances on Channel 13, WNTA-TV, New York. This was a slightly cut version (air time: 1 hour, 53 minutes, 25 seconds) of the Robinson Jeffers' adaptation with Judith Anderson giving her usual electrifying performance; the star was strongly supported by Aline McMahon as the Nurse and Morris Carnovsky as Creon. The play was produced by David Susskind and Lewis Freedman and directed by Jose Quintero and Wesley Kenney. Note that when *Medea* was produced outdoors in the Theater of Dionysus in Athens it was accounted a play of cosmological and sociocultural scope; later, when it was mounted behind the proscenium arch of an indoor theater, it seemed to be a work of lesser import, dealing merely with the wrath of a vengeful woman; confined to a television screen in a private living-room, its meaning was correspondingly reduced, the play providing the viewer mainly with a magnificent display of virtuoso acting.

This brief notice has of necessity been forced to omit mention of innumerable performances and productions of the *Medea*, both in its original form and in more or less free adaptations, in the two thousand five hundred years of its history, a history which has at the moment no foreseeable end.

BROADWAY PRODUCER
An Interview with Robert Whitehead

Robert Whitehead, one of the busiest and most successful of the theatrical producers on Broadway, is soft-spoken and genial. "He is a man of great singleness of purpose," says Brooks Atkinson, recently retired drama critic for the *New York Times*. "He has taste, skill, and imagination, and he loves the theater as one of the public arts."

Whitehead was born in Montreal, Canada, in 1916. As a child, he took part in living-room theatricals with his cousin, Hume Cronyn, and became dedicated to the stage for life. He arrived in New York at the age of twenty looking for work as an actor, but jobs were not easy to find. He enrolled for a two-year course in acting at the New York School of the Theater (now defunct), studied privately with the well-known coach Benno Schneider, spent a summer with the Barter Theater in Virginia, and found occasional work in New York as a stage-manager or player of "bit" parts.

After his service in World War II Whitehead returned to New York, eager to get back into the theater. The sort of parts he was able to get made acting less and less satisfying, and he began to cast about for another sphere of activity in the theater, possibly producing.

While he was appearing with Bert Lahr in a summer stock version of *Burlesque*, Whitehead met Harold Hecht, who was later to become a film producer. During their conversation, Hecht suggested that Whitehead take a look at Robinson Jeffers' version of *Medea*, a play that the Theatre Guild had had under option but had recently dropped from its schedule. Jeffers' adaptation had been published and Whitehead got hold of a copy. Although he had not been thinking of doing a Greek tragedy, he saw immediately that the play had great theatricality and, in its own terms and with the right cast, would be highly "actable"; it impressed him as being a psychological drama dealing with modern problems. Whitehead decided that he would "go out on a limb and try to put on the show."

Since the Jeffers' play had been written for, and dedicated to, Judith Anderson, Whitehead got in touch with the actress, who lives on the West Coast, and offered her the role, which she eagerly accepted. Then Whitehead took a quick trip to the Coast to talk with Robinson Jeffers. As an unknown and inexperienced producer, he was not sure that Jeffers would consent to his doing the play, but the author agreed. Whitehead explains this by saying, "Jeffers had waited five years to have the *Medea* produced. Four producers had held options on the script, and had given them up. I got the play because nobody else wanted it at that moment; if I'd had any competitors, I'd have lost out." Final business arrangements for the production were handled by the author's agent in New York.

Whitehead had in the meantime acquired as partner Oliver Rea, whom he had met in the army, and who, like himself, was interested in starting a theater with "lofty standards." The two men formed a company, estimated that they would need about $75,000 to do the play, and went about raising the money. Rea was responsible for bringing in two-thirds of it; Whitehead contributed five thousand dollars of his own; and a former actress by the name of Terry Fay, at present Whitehead's casting director, helped to gather money among small investors, such as waiters, secretaries, and switchboard operators. The reaction of a business man, to whom the script had been sent when he expressed an interest in a possible investment in the production, was typical of many received by the producers. The man returned the play, saying, "I think it is beautiful. In fact, so much so that I had my wife read it to me twice. But I don't think you can find an audience for it." Whitehead's puzzled comment was, "I am not sure what made him feel he was in any way more sensitive than an average audience." It took a full year to raise the complete production cost, but the play turned out to be one of the major successes of the season and paid off its backers in seven weeks.

The next task was to find a director able to handle a serious verse drama. There were very few to choose from on Broadway, and these were either not interested in or not available for *Medea*. While watching a performance of *The Importance of Being Earnest* starring the English actor-director John Gielgud, Whitehead was forcibly struck by the star's brilliance and versatility; he was just as expert in handling Wilde's farce as he had been in mounting Shakespearean tragedy. Whitehead went backstage to talk to Gielgud and later sent him a copy of *Medea*. Gielgud liked the script but was planning on returning to England to do a play by Terence Rattigan, and so he rejected Whitehead's offer. The young producer felt that he had reached a dead end, that he would never get the play on. Then, unexpectedly, Gielgud phoned, announced that he had decided to remain in New York, and offered to direct *Medea*.

Gielgud, Whitehead, and Rea spent the summer of 1947 casting the play, keeping in constant touch with Miss Anderson by long-distance telephone. Whitehead soon learned that he had a strong-willed star to deal with, for her intense and definite opinions concerning every aspect of the production caused innumerable and sharp disagreements. One of the most heated arose over the casting of the part of Jason. It was impossible to select a leading man who would satisfy everyone. There is not enough "meat" in the part to interest an important actor, and one of lesser ability or stature would not have Miss Anderson's approval. Rehearsals were scheduled to start in three days and still the cast lacked a Jason. Miss Anderson arrived in New York and was asked to attend a meeting at which Tibor Serly's incidental music for the production was to be discussed; this discussion deteriorated at once into a wrangle as to who would play Jason. Miss Anderson urged Gielgud to undertake the role himself. Whitehead objected because he wanted the director to concentrate on directing and not be distracted by having to double as an actor; Gielgud objected because he felt that he was wrong for the part, never having portrayed what he called a "Butch-type"; but Miss Anderson kept insisting that since she had once seen fit to play Gertrude to Mr. Gielgud's Hamlet, there was no reason why he should not play Jason to her Medea. Nothing was decided finally at that meeting, but a day or so later Gielgud and Whitehead were walking along Madison Avenue, and the producer was startled to hear his director soliloquizing: "There's no reason to refuse to play Jason because I've never played such a part. After all, this would be a good time to try it. Besides, the part's been turned down by so many that *I* might as well do it. And, furthermore, I'll be starting work on *Crime and Punishment* in six weeks, so I won't have to stick with it too long." Little by little, Gielgud sold himself the idea.

In agreeing to play the part of Jason, Gielgud simultaneously solved two other problems for the producer. As a beginner in the field, Whitehead was having trouble booking a theater for his play, but with the names of two stars—Judith

Costs of Broadway Production
As of October 25, 1947

Scenery

Designing	$ 750.00	
Painting	3,937.20	
Building	9,565.00	$14,252.20
Props, Purchases and Rentals		910.31
Costumes		13,478.75
Electrical and Sound Equipment		3,155.95
Director		3,500.00

Rehearsal Expenses

Salaries

Actors	1,214.52	
Stage Managers	770.00	
Company Crew	1,629.40	
Stagehands	1,767.56	
Musicians	599.17	
Theater Expenses and Rent	787.50	
Scripts and Parts	44.00	
Miscellaneous	80.21	6,892.36

Preliminary Advertising

Press Agent, Salary and Expenses	797.00	
Newspaper Advertising	2,090.28	
Photos and Signs	581.87	
Printing	381.48	3,850.63
Miscellaneous, Telephone, etc.		808.37
Music		300.00
Company and General Managers		1,225.00
Office Expense		800.00
Legal Fees and Disbursements		536.68
Auditing		250.00
Payroll Taxes		254.45
Carting		858.41
Insurance		200.00
Transportation		1,836.53
Lighting Show		500.00
Pre-production Expenses		2,000.00
Total Production Costs		**$55,609.64**

Anderson and John Gielgud—on the marquee, he was able to get a theater at once. Gielgud's connections with the production as actor-director also attracted investors who put enough money into the show to bring the total up to $75,000, the amount needed to open.

It was Whitehead's function as producer to engage the scene and costume

RECEIPTS, DISBURSEMENTS, AND EXPENSES
As of October 25, 1947

Receipts

Partners' Capital Contributions			$75,000.00
Less Disbursements and Expenses			
Production Costs	$55,609.64		
Out-of-town Try-out Losses	8,528.10		
	64,137.74		
Less New York Profit (First Week)	5,791.69		
Net Costs to Date		$58,346.05	
Bonds and Deposits			
Actors Equity	8,490.00		
A.T.P.A.M. (Press Agts., Mgrs.)	800.00		
I.A.T.S.E. (Stagehands)	485.00		
Musicians	919.40		
New York Theater	4,000.00	14,694.40	
Total Disbursements and Expenses			73,040.45
Balance Available for Sinking Fund			$ 1,959.55

designers; he employed Ben Edwards, who was young, new, and talented, to do the sets and David Ffolkes, a seasoned and expert theatrical artist, for the costumes. Then endless discussions with the star began: the costume designer was replaced, but Edwards' set remained.

Whitehead is enormously sensitive to the turbulent moods of the theater and on many occasions has demonstrated a remarkable skill for tactfulness. He is not, however, infallible in his dealings. His most notable failure, as he is the first to admit, occurred with Judith Anderson. When Whitehead attempted to suggest to Miss Anderson that she curb some of her exuberant dramatics during her performance, the actress became enraged; and when it came time to seek a replacement for Gielgud who was leaving the cast, the fireworks started again. The result was that for a considerable portion of the run of the play, star and producer were not on speaking terms; they communicated only through an intermediary. Whitehead has, nevertheless, the greatest respect for Miss Anderson as an artist, and realizes now that she was often right in her suggestions and that he was young and headstrong; he has mellowed a great deal since then.

During the very first tryout of the play at the McCarter Theater, in Princeton, New Jersey, Whitehead left the theater in the midst of the performance and actually hid in the bushes. "The play didn't come up to my expectations," he explains. "I thought it was way off base . . . a mess." Later, when more and more people congratulated him, and the box-office returns echoed their opinions, he realized that the play was a great success. "Then I began to feel like a fraud . . . as if I'd fooled everybody . . . because the actual production never comes up to the ideal conception of it. I've had that feeling many times . . . after every success, in fact . . . as if I'd got away with something."

Medea was on the road for two and a half weeks; the text was cut in a few places, but not much else was done to the script; its entire running time was a little over an hour and a half. The play had a starkness that had appealed to Whitehead from the beginning, and there was a definite growth in the characters and increasing tension in the situations. Jeffers had done a masterly adaptation in investing an ancient Greek play with a quality and a tempo that were especially American and contemporary. *Medea* played to full houses on Broadway for seven months, and then toured the country. It was mounted in London by Gielgud, who also played Jason to Eileen Herlie's Medea; the British critics did not take kindly to the play and it closed after three months.

"The success of *Medea* started me on the road to production," says Whitehead. "If the play had failed, I'd probably have gone back to acting."

It is almost impossible to define the job of the producer because it has no limits; the producer must be able to function on every level of the production whenever and wherever his services are needed. Although his job differs with each production, he must constantly and resolutely bolster the weak elements without impeding the strong. A few of the things that a producer must know are how to select a script, how to choose collaborating artists (director, actors, designers), how to finance the play, how to negotiate with the unions (actors', stagehands', musicians'), how to book a theater, when to bring the play in, and how to attract audiences through public relations. All of these skills, naturally, come with experience, are learned by trial and error; but even the most adept and gifted producer is called upon to handle so many details that he can very easily go astray among them and neglect the most important thing—the play itself. The producer's primary concern, always, is to understand precisely what the author is trying to say and precisely what effect the director wants the production to achieve, and to attempt to bring these two factors together in a way that will be best for the play. Whitehead says, "It's a colossal job of diplomacy. You are dealing with creative and artistic people all the time and the idea is to get the job done with the least amount of unnecessary emotion. Everything is fine so long as you are producing winners (the plays I liked best somehow seemed to do best), but if you make too many mistakes, you lose your backers, and you're out of the producing business."

Gielgud Rehearses *Medea**
By Virginia Stevens

The start of the rehearsals for John Gielgud's production of Robinson Jeffers' *Medea* was an occasion of many firsts. It was the premiere of the American poet's free adaptation of the Euripides classic which he wrote expressly for Judith Anderson; it was John Gielgud's first production of a Greek classic; and it was his and Judith Anderson's first appearance in a Greek drama. . . .

* From *Theatre Arts Magazine*, November, 1947, pp. 31-34. Reprinted by permission.

In the house on East Thirty-Eighth Street which serves the youthful producing firm of Whitehead and Rea as headquarters, the cast assembled for the first time on a stifling hot day in September. In a small library on the second floor, before a card table which had been set out for him, John Gielgud sat, promptbook in hand, while the actors gathered in a semicircle about him: Judith Anderson, Albert Hecht (Creon), John Straub (Aegeus), Richard Hylton, Kathryn Grill, Leone Wilson, Grace Mills.

On the mantelpiece in the library stood Ben Edwards' detailed model of the set—the pillared façade of Medea's house with the long steps, a garden at the side, the sea in the background.

The reading began, and the imminence for us today of Robinson Jeffers' version of the prodigious tragedy of passion and revenge was quickly evident. Medea's exile in a strange land, her loneliness and isolation among the alien Greeks, Jason's ruthless drive for power, even the hideous denouement—all are familiarly paralleled in the world we know; indeed we have known even larger, more hideous tragedies. Expanding, vitalizing the text, Gielgud's direction gives the flesh-and-blood reality of today to these legendary people.

The first day every actor was stopped in his reading while his character was described by the director in a few telling phrases. "The tutor is a meek man with a servant's habitual respect." The three actresses representing Chorus, who had been chosen for contrast of body and voice, were immediately personalized. Gielgud did not hesitate to give the actors his own interpretations and in his illumination of the roles the richly dramatic elements of the play were revealed. But when he finished he would tell the actor, "Do what is natural to you." To demonstrate is his own quick, instinctive method of directing. He is first the actor.

No false note escaped his sensitive ear. The actors on this first day had an understandable tendency to read their lines as poetry. He let nothing pass. "Pay no attention to the punctuation. That's one way writers torment actors. It's the meaning you must observe."

He stressed contrast. "You must look for the opposite colors. In a strong person like Creon, for example, find the tenderness. There's too much Goering now. Don't ever be obvious." Again and again he emphasized, "Think out the meanings. The reading will depend on thought and motive."

The youngest member of the cast delivered a full performance, muscles tensed, body quivering. Gielgud's lean face looked quietly amused. Slender and small, Judith Anderson sat utterly relaxed, her black tortoise-shell glasses perched now on her nose, now shoved up on her forehead in a quick little gesture as she turned to the director. "I'd like to get that all in one breath. What do you think, John?" It was startling to hear the passionate speeches, the deep resonant voice coming from the small, quiet figure in the modern easy-chair.

Perspiration was running off the actors' faces. Not a breath of air stirred. There was a break for ice water. Walking over to the model of the set, I saw that little chessmen indicated the actors' positions. "Do you work out all the business beforehand?" I asked Gielgud.

"In no cut-and-dried sense," he answered, "but I have a definite plan even if it's only something to break away from. It's important for the actors to feel that you know precisely what is to be done."

The reading proceeded. With his perfect sense of timing, his unfailing ear for the right emphasis, Gielgud orchestrated the voices, suggested readings for variety and contrast—but never without motivation. He directs with a strong musical sense. "This whole passage is like a song. Diminuendo here, soaring there."

On the second day the play was broken down into scenes, each one taken separately. This day was utterly different from the first. There was complete informality, a gaiety which no doubt the subtle director had created for the relaxation of his cast. (Until the fifth day of rehearsal is passed and his contract thus assured, it is hard for an actor not to work with tension.) Gielgud himself was full of bubbling humor; his ideas poured forth in a stream.

"We must try to marry the two methods, Shakespeare and realism," he pointed out to the actors. "The emotions come out of reality, but in physical terms—in gesture and movement—it is a heightened reality. This is Bach, played with a grand simplicity."

He began to give them the atmosphere. "Here in this first scene there is sunshine and the feeling of the sea, the archaic life. No atom bomb, no noises of today, but the laughter of children, the soft air, light and peace, the beauty of living among simple real people—the whole quality of this first mood is in utter contrast to Medea."

An actress read:

> Never pray for death, never pray for death,
> He is here all too soon.

"Why does she say this?" he interrupted. "Perhaps her own child died last year. It must have some such strong personal meaning for you. Each thought must be clear. The image must come into your brain just a second before you speak—as it would in real life. It is the way all actors must work on Shakespeare. So much of good acting is knowing when and how to pause. You must time to the split second."

With vivid smiles and paraphrases he goaded their imagination. "Here she turns on him like a cobra." "His words are like detectives tracking her down."

With constant change of tempo and key he thrust monotony out. Medea talks to the women of childbirth. They huddle together, soft and intimate in shared experience:

> It is easier to stand in battle three times, in the front
> line, in the stabbing fury, than to bear one child.

But an instant later she has broken the mood completely with her dark hints of revenge.

Gielgud was quick this day to compliment an actor for a correct reading. "Actors are very easily hurt," he explained later. "I should say the ideal approach to them is ruthlessness combined with politeness. (As an actor I'm not very touchy. I like to be told about mannerisms.) But it all depends on the actor. You must study your cast and know how to handle each one.

"You see, an actor's perceptions are delicate and complex," he continued, slumping down in the chair, his long legs swinging over the side. "With one set of feelings he is creating the emotions of the character, he is listening as if he had never before heard the questions and replies of the other actors, as if his own words were new to his ear. At the same time another set of nerves is reacting to the audience, tightening the reins if they are not attentive. Yet it's fatal to become too conscious of an audience. That's when they begin to encourage you in your worst effects. By their quick response to broad effects an audience will tempt you to indulge in cheaper things but you must never allow them to dictate to you."

On the third day there was much excitement among the cast, for Gielgud had agreed to play Jason. This time he put the play on its feet. He was everywhere suggesting movement and gestures. Like the chessmen he had been experimenting with on his model stage, the actors now seemed merely his puppets.

He talked to them of costumes. "We must begin to use the long draped skirts, the flowing sleeves as quickly as possible," he told the women. "Flowing sleeves and drapes will suggest many effective gestures to you. Ellen Terry always wore her dresses longer in front so she could catch up the folds. I remember the unutterably graceful gestures she had!"

The fourth day the actors had taken his suggestions to themselves, they were making them their own. They were no longer puppets.

Judith Anderson would do nothing that did not seem to her to coincide with the thought and feeling of a scene. There is an encounter, for example, between Medea and Aegeus. Having been banished from Corinth by Creon, father of Jason's bride, Medea throws herself on the mercy of Aegeus of Athens. She promises him the use of her occult power if he will help her. Aegeus has just come from the Delphic Oracle. He longs for a son and Medea promises him fulfillment:

> I should need peace and a free mind
> While I prepared the medicines to make you well.

Gielgud suggested that Aegeus rise in his eagerness:

> You'll have them,
> you'll have them, Medea.

"No, no, it isn't right," Judith Anderson said. "The movement makes too much of this. Medea wants to get through with this deal and get on to what is really filling her mind." They tried it her way: a simple pledge with hands, as Aegeus kept his sitting position. Now it was a lesser thing. Gielgud agreed.

Even in the small room, as they worked one could begin to see a suggestion of form, of the pose and movement, the style that was being slowly created.

Whenever Judith Anderson read, the extraordinary power and credibility of her tortured Medea came clear. Her readings indicated long study. "I understand her in modern terms, as modern as I can," the actress told me after the rehearsal. "The words are so beautiful, they speak for themselves. I can forget them and work for the reality of the emotion . . . I see her as the great barbarian, purely animal, all her reactions fiercely primitive in contrast to the smooth and cultured Greeks. I love the part because it is such a challenge. Lady Macbeth with her few telling scenes is simple compared to Medea who must sustain this play."

"What did you mean when you told the actors to marry Shakespeare and realism in this play?" I asked John Gielgud.

"All those—like Laurence Olivier, Maurice Evans and myself—who have successfully produced the classics for modern audiences have found a half-way ground. We must raise young actors to a broader style and the traditional actors must be brought down to a more realistic level. The people in these great plays have the same fundamental emotional reactions that we do, the psychology of emotion is the same. But if one is at all atavistic it is facinating to step into another time. I think an audience should be excited and held by *Medea*. I want them to take out of the theater a feeling of splendor and pity and terror."

On the sixth day the rehearsals moved to the theater. Against the blank walls of the stage, in the bizarre light of rehearsal spots, the figures of the actors took on dramatic dimension. Occasionally a scene came alive. But in the main the actors struggled to coordinate words and movement in the larger space.

Gielgud's tall thin figure strode down the aisle from the back of the theater, leaped on the stage to demonstrate a walk, a gesture. "Simpler. Make it simpler. You're doing too much." Quickly he seized the right movement, the effective grouping. He was continually aware of the stage picture.

And when he stepped in to play Jason, with penetrating and quick intelligence he set the key of the rehearsals; the actors were on their toes to match him.

A scene between Jason and Medea began to suggest the power of the play. Jason has come to chide Medea for her anger, to reason with her. . . . In the rebuke his movement is toward her but her furious reaction drives him back. (The bodies of these two obeyed their thought like well-drilled soldiers while their voices registered every nuance. Their skills were beautifully matched.)

Now she comes to him, dominating him with her passionate reproof, vividly recalling the crimes she has committed for him. Her voice is low in pleading, velvet in remembered tenderness, tense in the moment's pain:

> The world is a little closed to me, ah?
> By the things I have done for you.

But Jason recovers his poise. He will not be moved.

> I see, Medea,
> You have been a very careful merchant of benefits.

He can even tear at her pride.

> As to those acts of service you so loudly boast—whom
> do I thank for them? I thank divine Venus, the goddess

Who makes girls fall in love. You did them because you
had to do them; Venus compelled you; I enjoyed her favor.

In a frenzy of wild fury, Medea drives him from her. . . .

The two actors let the emotions design the movement. At the end of the scene Medea has won the encounter and stands alone, high on the steps of her house, a terrible figure of fury.

From here on the pace quickened, culminating in the opening in Princeton. But the pattern had been set early: the "splendor and pity and terror" of the stars' acting and the director's conception was all there in that first week as this modern retelling of the ancient tragedy unfolded under their expert hands.

THE SCENERY
An Interview with Ben Edwards

As a friend of the producers, Whitehead and Rea, Ben Edwards had an opportunity to see the script of Robinson Jeffers' Medea before the play had actually been bought for production. Edwards was impressed by the work and was delighted when he was offered the opportunity to design the set.

His first task was to read and reread the play until he was thoroughly familiar with the characters, their motivations and their relationships; with the country, its people and its customs; and with the immediate locale—Medea's palace—in all its spatial and temporal dimensions.

It was necessary for the designer to find a unifying concept, a single point of view for the production; conferences with the producers, the director, and the star began. The play calls for just one set—Medea's palace. It was Gielgud's idea that the architectural style of this building should be in keeping with the primitive emotions of the barbarian princess who inhabited it. It was not to have the subtle lines and gleaming whiteness of a palace of the Periclean age, but was to be heavy and archaic, hinting of Mycenaean or Cretan origins.

In Edwards' final design, there were five rough-hewn steps leading up to a large central door, and the palace itself appeared to be situated high up on the rocky coast, allowing a view of the sea and of the distant mountains beyond it. In so placing the palace, Edwards had two things in mind. First, he wished to re-create for modern audiences the feelings of the ancient spectators in the Theater of Dionysus in Athens, who had only to raise their eyes and look above and beyond the skene to see the actual mountains and sea in the distance; secondly, he wanted the location of the palace to provide a physical expression of the theme and mood of the play. Here was a marriage that had gone on the rocks, and a home now standing empty of love and hollow on barren and precipitous ground.

Edwards had an even more subtle idea for heightening the tension of the play in visual terms; he attempted to make the playing areas as straitened and confined as were the souls of the protagonists. He did this by changing the position of the set during the play. For the first act, the façade of the palace stood at an angle to the footlights, allowing the audience a glimpse past the building to the open sea, the sea across which Jason had brought his bride to Corinth; but for the second act, the palace was turned so that it stood parallel to the footlights and the entire building was moved downstage, thus not only cutting off the view and any apparent means of escape, but also giving the impression that Medea was hemmed in and trapped. "Even if an audience is not consciously aware of an altered perspective," Edwards states, "the psychological effect of such a shift of scenery upon the emotional responses of the spectators is unmistakable."

A further assault was made upon the audience's sensibilities by the lighting and costume designers, who worked in close creative collaboration with the scene designer. Peggy Clark, who was responsible for the play's lighting plan, accentuated the coldness and starkness of the palace and of Medea's face by eliminating from her spectrum all the warm colors and using white and steel-blue light exclusively. The achievement of such a symbolic effect by the arbitrary control of light was denied Euripides, for his play was illuminated solely by the brilliant sunlight of Greece. In costumes, too, a symbolism was devised in keeping with the somberness of the play's theme, though contrary to historical accuracy. Euripides' actors wore rich and elaborate gowns in bright and gleaming colors, and such gowns were at first designed for the Jeffers production; then Castillo, Miss Anderson's designer, redid the costumes entirely in grays and black—except for the glistening panoplies of the soldiers—and thus achieved a funereal and muted mood, and an artistic truth greater than the actual.

The technical procedure followed by the scene designer begins with his drawing of sketches embodying his ideas for the set. After the sketches have been approved, the designer makes a miniature model of the set and proceeds to draw detailed construction plans and blueprints from which the builders must be able to construct scenery that will not only stand up and look as sturdy as it is supposed to, but will also support and withstand the life lived in it: the beating of Medea's fists and head against the door and its frames, and the stamping of her feet as she races up and down the steps.

The scenery for *Medea* was built at the Turner Studios in Fort Lee, New Jersey. On several occasions the members of the cast went to the studios and rehearsed on the set while it was under construction to make sure that the acting areas were right and comfortable. Edwards worked in particularly close collaboration with Judith Anderson on the design of the palace steps, for they were meant to represent irregular blocks of stone—some thick, some thin, some narrow, and some wide. It was absolutely necessary that she be able to manage them easily, for she played most of her scenes on these steps.

During the play's tryout period at the McCarter Theater, in Princeton, New Jersey, Edwards worked on such details as checking properties, testing lights against the paint of the scenery, observing the scene-shift, and making sure that every aspect of the physical production worked smoothly. Edwards works at this refining process, as do most other designers, until the curtain goes up at the play's official opening, and sometimes it is necessary for him to make changes during the run of the play.

In the early stages of the production, Edwards sent his sketches to Robinson Jeffers in order to get the poet's reaction to the proposed scenery. In his letter of response, Jeffers told Edwards that he was particularly pleased with the "fiery sky" that was to appear during the final moments of the play. He had called for just such a sky in his script. During the rehearsal period, however, the hot sky was washed out by the lighting designer along with even mildly lukewarm colors, as has already been noted. After seeing the play at its premiere in New York, Jeffers commented especially to Edwards on the absence of the "fiery sky," which apparently disappointed him; he thought, nevertheless, that the scenery was "beautiful and impressive."

THE COSTUMES
An Interview with Antonio del Castillo

The costumes for Judith Anderson, as well as for the other members of the cast of *Medea,* were originally designed in chiffon and brocades in brilliant colors with heavy incrustations of gold. The keynote of these gowns was lavishness and high style, but Miss Anderson disliked their formality and stiffness. The star decided to go for advice to Antonio del Castillo, who had previously designed gowns for her. He advised her to get rid of the chiffon and to use flannel or gray wool, the actual fabrics worn by the primitive Greeks. Miss Anderson agreed, and Castillo molded the cloth to her body. He explained that as she perspired it would cling to her contours more and more and increase in naturalness and beauty. She had to wear these heavy clothes at rehearsals in order to get used to them and to start to make them adhere to her body.

It was at the first performance of the play in Princeton that Castillo saw the gold and brocaded gowns on all the other actors and realized that the entire cast would have to be recostumed. By the time the play reached the Locust Theater in Philadelphia, early in its out-of-town tour, Castillo had arranged with an American designer, Helene Pons, to assist him in replacing the costumes. Miss Pons set up her workshop in the basement of the theater, while Castillo himself draped the cloth on the actors, cut it, pinned it, and basted it by hand with leather thongs. Then he would rush up to the auditorium to see the actor make his entrance on stage in the newly created costume, and dash back to the basement to go on with the clothes for the other actors.

He improvised as he went along. The three women who represented the chorus were on stage practically throughout the play, and yet they had been dressed in brilliant and eye-catching gowns; Castillo felt that since they were almost never absent from the scene, they should not be so "aggressive to the eye," and therefore clothed them in dresses that blended with the scenery and caused them to intrude less into the dramatic action.

The task of recostuming the cast was completed by the end of the week in Philadelphia. In addition to making all the clothes, Castillo made the wigs for

Medea's women attendants, dexterously, with his own hands, creating them out of skeins of ordinary knitting wool.

The gowns, which had never been sewn, but had been pinned or basted with leather thongs, served the members of the cast for the entire run of the play. It is interesting to note that Castillo's method was very close to the original Greek way of making clothes; they were hand-sewn or pinned, and combined a respect for the fabric with a feeling for the beauty of the drapery.

TELEVISING *Medea*
An Interview with Wesley Kenney

"Television drama requires the same basic ingredients as does any other dramatic medium: a good script, good acting, and good production—in the order named," said Wesley Kenney, co-director with Jose Quintero of the television version of *Medea*. Kenney is a graduate of the Drama Department of the Carnegie Institute of Technology; he has acted and directed in summer stock, and has been a television producer-director for the last ten years.

Because a television director must possess an inordinate amount of technical knowledge and skill regarding the handling of camera and sound equipment, Kenney was invited by David Susskind, a producer for WNTA-TV, to work with Quintero, who is primarily a stage director. Kenney accepted the assignment with mixed feelings as he had always worked on his own before. A man of very strong opinions, he had admired Quintero as an artist, but realized that extremely fine diplomacy would be required in any directorial collaboration. The problem in this case was twofold: first, he would have to visualize and project the dramatic values that Quintero saw in the work, at the same time attempting to preserve those values that he himself felt were inherent in the play; and secondly, he would have to take what was basically a stage play and make it visually interesting and "flexible" for television. Compromises would obviously have to be effected. The first difficulty involved the set. The façade of Medea's palace, the steps leading up to it, and the courtyard in front of it were built on a scale usually seen in a theater but seldom in a television studio. The palace was extremely high and wide, and all the action of the play was to take place on the steps in front of it; the scope and dimensions of these steps posed many audio and video problems. If the final decision had been his, Kenney feels that he would have departed radically from the single stage set and would have tried for greater breadth of movement inside the palace as well as around the courtyard. But in this instance, as in many others, he yielded to Quintero and tried to devise unusual ways of handling the camera in order to achieve the flow of action so necessary for the television screen.

The company rehearsed for two weeks before the play was actually taped. During rehearsals, Kenney watched Quintero stage the action and work on characterization with the individual actors, aside from Miss Anderson, who had played the part innumerable times. Once he understood the point his collaborator wished to make in each scene, Kenney was able to suggest the means for obtaining the desired result with camera and sound.

In his staging, Quintero preserved his theatrical approach and put his chief emphasis on character and situation, but in doing so he was sometimes inclined to place the actors in positions which would normally be considered too far apart for a good camera shot, or in relationships natural for the stage but unnecessary in television because of the mobility of the camera.

Miss Anderson was especially concerned about the patterns of her movement on the set because the height and width of the steps and levels differed from those to which she had been accustomed on the stage. Since both directors were determined to retain, wherever possible, Miss Anderson's original interpretation and performance, they permitted her, for the most part, absolute freedom of body movement and gesture and accommodated the camera-work accordingly.

The exact timing which television demands proved troublesome to Quintero, since he had never had to cope with it in directing for the stage. As the play was short and the directors did not wish to add to Jeffers' dialogue, short pieces of business were interpolated into the action to fill up the time. When Jason entered, for example, he was accompanied by a column of soldiers whose movement was followed by the camera; this prolonged the action of the play for several moments, and also added an extra dimension to the scene. Some minor plot and character values were lost, on the other hand, because the two-week rehearsal period was insufficient; but the tempo of the play as a whole was excellent. The camera set-up was the last thing worked out for each scene, because, said Kenney, "pictures can only enhance the quality of the material photographed but cannot create it."

At the beginning of the play, the camera started with a wide-angle shot of the entire palace and moved in slowly to pick up the Nurse, who has the first lines. The opening moments of the action in the television version differed from all stage versions in that Kenney contrived to show Medea lamenting inside the palace; she is seen through the front doors which stand open. In the theater, this lamentation is always done as a "voice off-stage."

The camera-work also helped to create an illusion of movement in a basically actionless and physically static play; cameras zoomed in and out, moving so fast that "the dollies were hot." The problem of integrating classical style and dimensions with the intimacy of the television medium was solved, Kenney feels, by the increased emphasis placed upon Medea's psychological introspection. Medea, as the central figure in the play, was the pivot for every camera shot; during her own scenes she was distinctly in the foreground, while other characters who might be present, such as the Chorus of Women, were seen at a distance; if Medea was on stage during the scenes of other characters, her presence was always noted in the background.

"The camera director," says Kenney, "must always remember to catch reactions as well as actions. He changes his focus, but always keeps the viewer's attention fixed on what is important. The camera is not necessarily restricted, but it is highly selective." In taping *Medea*, Kenney's two cardinal principles were "to keep the camera-work flowing and to preserve good taste by avoiding extreme close-ups"; the latter principle was invoked because of the intensity of emotion displayed in the facial expressions of the star. Seen continuously for almost two hours, such excruciating grimaces might have caused reactions of distaste in the viewer and impaired the dramatic impact of the play.

After two weeks of "dry" rehearsals, the troupe moved into a studio belonging to the American Broadcasting Company and in three days of intensive work video-taped the play. Three cameras were used, one mounted on a pedestal and two mounted on Houston cranes of a type employed in filming motion pictures, which gave Kenney enormous range and flexibility. These were important because of the height and width of the steps which constituted most of the playing area. The director occasionally placed the actors ten, fifteen, and twenty feet apart which necessitated the use of more microphones than are normally required. The set also complicated the lighting arrangements. The limit of the camera's range is ten to fifteen feet, but the constant movement of the actors on several levels called for special planning and made hundreds of light cues necessary. As the camera moved continuously over the playing area, the various lights were "cued" on and off with bewildering rapidity in order to prevent unwanted shadows from being thrown on the actors or the set. These lighting problems were welcomed by Kenney and his technical crew as a challenge to create new values and effects.

The company taped the play over an intensely hot week-end. Work started when a crew arrived at the studio at about 1 A.M. Friday morning to erect the set and mount the basic lights; at 6 A.M. the painters were on hand; at 9 A.M., the set-dressers; and a little while later Kenney arrived with his assistant director and his script girl. The actors appeared at 1 P.M., and everyone worked until 10 that night. The schedule for Saturday was 10 A.M. to 10 P.M., and on Sunday the company worked straight through without a break from 9 A.M. until 5:30 A.M. Monday morning. The play was taped by acts, each act was shot at least twice, and the best print was used.

"Miss Anderson was a dynamo," said Kenney, "not to be believed. She was electric from beginning to end; a fantastic woman. But not long before doing *Medea* she had appeared in a television version of *The Moon and Sixpence* with Laurence Olivier and that complex production had been shot in three crowded days, so she was well prepared." While removing her makeup, after twenty-one hours of continuous work, Miss Anderson, Kenney recalls, remarked wryly: "Well, I think we're good for seven performances!" *Medea* launched a new dramatic series called "The Play of the Week" and was presented on Channel 13, New York, for seven consecutive days starting Monday, October 12, 1959.

The morning after the play was broadcast, the metropolitan television critics hailed the event in such words as those of Kay Gardella in the New York *Daily News*: "The power and emotional range of this tragic tale of revenge were almost too much for a small television screen, but the superb and electrifying performance of Judith Anderson made one grateful for the opportunity to see it. . . ."

The Playbill

Euripides' tragedy was first acted when Pythodorus was Archon, Olympiad 87, year 1 [431 B.C.]. Euphorion [son of Aeschylus] won first prize, Sophocles second, Euripides third, with *Medea, Philoctetes, Dictys,* and the *Harvesters,* a satyr-play.

⁓ *Medea* TRANSLATED BY FREDERIC PROKOSCH

Characters

MEDEA	ATTENDANT
JASON	NURSE
KREON	AEGEUS
MEDEA'S CHILDREN	A MESSENGER
CHORUS OF CORINTHIAN WOMEN	

Scene: Corinth, before the house of Medea.

(*The* NURSE *enters from the house.*)

Nurse. Oh how I wish that famous ship,
The Argo, had never made its way through
The blue Symplegades to the land of Colchis!
How I wish the pine tree had never been felled
In the glades of Pelion, and never   5
Been hewn into oars for the heroes
Who went to fetch the Golden Fleece
For Pelias! For then my mistress, Medea,
Would never have sailed to the towers
Of the land of Iolcos, her heart on fire   10
With love for Jason! Nor would she
Ever have beguiled the daughters
Of Pelias into slaying their father,
Nor have come to live in Corinth with her
Husband and children. For a long time   15
She found favor with the people here
In the land of exile; and she did
All things in complete accord with Jason;
And indeed it is this—when a woman
Stands loyally by a man—which brings   20
To men the only sure savlation. But now
Their love has fallen into decay; and
There's hatred everywhere. For Jason
Has betrayed his children and my mistress;
He has taken a royal bride to his bed,   25
The daughter of Kreon, who is the ruler
Of this land. And poor Medea, scorned
And deserted, can do nothing but appeal
To the vows they made to one another,   29
And remind him of the eternal pledge

They made with their right hands
    clasped.
And she calls upon the gods to wit-
    ness
How Jason is repaying her for her
    love.
She lies half famished; her body is
    bowed
Utterly with grief, wasting away the
    whole   35
Day long. So it has been since she
Learned that he has betrayed her.
Never stirring an eye, never lifting
Her gaze from the ground; and when
    her friends
Speak to her in warning she no more
    listens   40
Than a rock listens, or the surging
    sea wave.
Only now and then she turns her
    snowy neck
And quietly laments, and utters her
    father's
Name, and the name of her land and
    home,
Which she deserted when she fol-
    lowed   45
The man who now brings her such
    dishonor.
Pitiful woman! She has learned at
    last
Through all her sufferings how lucky
Are those who have never lost their
Native land. She has come to feel   50
A hatred for her children, and no
    longer
Wants to see them. Indeed, I fear
She may be moving toward some
    dreadful
Plan; for her heart is violent.   54
She will never submit to this cruel
Treatment. I know her well: her
    anger
Is great; and I know that any man
Who makes an enemy of her

Will have it hard . . . Look;
Here come the children; they have
    been playing.   60
Little they know of their mother's
    misery; little
The hearts of the young can guess of
    sorrow!

(*The* ATTENDANT *brings in* MEDEA's
children.)

Attendant. Why are you standing here,
    in front of the gates?
You've been maid for so many years
    to my mistress;   64
Why have you left her alone, then,
Only to stand outside the gates and
    lament?
Nurse. Listen, old man, who watch over
    Jason's
Sons! It's a sad, sad thing for faithful
Servants like us to see our master's
Fortunes meet with disaster; it stirs
Us to the heart. I am so lost in grief,
Now, that a longing came over me
    to step   72
Outside the gates, and tell the whole
    wide
World and the heavens of my mis-
    tress's sorrows!
Attendant. Poor lady! Hasn't she ceased
    her weeping yet?   75
Nurse. Ceased? Far from it! This is
    only
The beginning; there is far more to
    come.
Attendant. Poor, foolish lady; though I
    shouldn't call her that;
But how little she knows of this latest
    trouble!   79
Nurse. What do you mean, old man?
    Come! Don't be afraid to tell me!
Attendant. Nothing at all; I should
    never have mentioned it.
Nurse. No, no; by your wise old beard
    I beg you,

Don't hide anything from your fellow
servant!

Tell me; and, if you wish, I'll keep it
secret.   85

Attendant. Well, as I was passing the
usual place

Where the old men sit playing
draughts,

Down by the holy fountain of Pirene,

I happened to overhear one of them
saying

That Kreon, king of the land, intends
to send   90

These children, and their mother
from Corinth,

Far away into exile. But whether it
was

The truth he was speaking, I do not
know;

I hope and pray it wasn't the truth.

Nurse. And will Jason allow this thing
to happen to his sons,   95

Even though he is on bad terms with
their mother?

Attendant. Old ties give way to new
ones; and his

Love for this family of ours is dying
away.

Nurse. Oh, it looks dark indeed for us;

New sorrows are being added to old
ones,   100

Even before the old ones have faded!

Attendant. Be still, be still; don't whisper a word of it.

This isn't the proper time to tell our
mistress.

Nurse. O little children,

Do you hear how your father feels
toward you?   105

May evil befall him!

But no; he is still my master. Yet how
cruelly

He has betrayed his dear ones!

Attendant. And which of us has not
done the same?

Haven't you learned long ago, my
dear,   110

How each man loves himself far more

Than his neighbor? Some, perhaps,

From honest motives; some for private gain.

So you see how Jason deserts his
children   114

For the pleasure of his new bride.

Nurse. Go back into the house, children;

All will be well. Try to keep them

Out of the way, old man; keep them
far

From their mother as long as she
feels

This desperate anger. I have already
seen   120

The fire in her eyes as she watched

Them, almost as though she were
wishing

Them harm. I am sure her anger

Won't end till she has found a victim.

Let's hope the victim will be   125

An enemy, and not a friend!

(*Within the house.*)

Medea. Lost, oh lost! I am lost

In my sufferings. I wish, oh I wish

That I could die. . . .

Nurse. My dear children, what did I tell
you?   130

Your mother's mind is filled with the
wildest

Fancies; her heart is wild with anger!

Run quickly back into the house.

Keep out of her sight. Do not

Go near her. Beware of the wild-
ness   135

And bitterness of her heart!

Go, quickly, quickly!

I can feel that her fury will rise

And redouble! I can hear   139

In that cry the rising thunderstorm,

I can feel the approach of thunder
and lightning!
Oh what will she do, in the pride
And torment of her soul? What
Evil thing will she do?

(*The* ATTENDANT *takes the children
into the house.*)
(*Within.*)

Medea. Oh, I have suffered   145
And suffered enough for all these
tears!
I call destruction upon you, all, all
of you,
Sons of a doomed mother, and the
father too!
May ruin fall on the entire house!

Nurse. I am full of pity,   150
Full of deep pity for you! Yet why
Do the children share their father's
crime?
Why should you hate them? O my
poor children,
I fear some outrage will befall you!
Yes, strange and terrible is the temper
of princes.   155
There is none they need to obey;
There is none that can check them:
There is nothing to control
The madness of their mood.
How much better off are the rest of
us   160
Who've been taught to live equally
With our neighbors! All I wish
Is to grow old quietly, not in pride,
But only in humble security.
It's the moderate thing that always
sounds   165
Best to our ears; and indeed it is
The moderate thing that is best in
practice.
For power grows beyond control;
Power brings comfort to no man.
And I say, the greater the power, the
greater   170
The ruin when it finally falls.

(*Enter the* CHORUS *of Corinthian
women. The following lines are
chanted.*)

Chorus. I heard the voice,
I heard the loud lament
Of the pitiful lady from Colchis:
Oh tell me, mother, is she still   175
Unquiet? As I stood
By the house with the double gates
I heard the sound of weeping from
within.
I grieve for the sorrow of this family
Which I have come to love.   180

Nurse. There is no family left; it has
gone,
It has gone forever. The master now
Has a royal bride in the bed beside
him,
And our mistress is withering away
In her chamber, and finds no sol-
ace   185
Or warmth in words
That friends can utter.

(*Within.*)

Medea. Oh how I wish that a stroke of
lightning
Would fall from heaven and shatter
my head!
Why should I live any longer?   190
Death would bring release; in death
I could leave behind me the horror
of living.

Chorus. Did you hear, almighty Zeus?
O earth, O heaven, did you hear
The cry of woe this woman has ut-
tered?   195
Oh why, poor lady, should you long
For that unutterable haven of rest?
Death only can bring it; and death
comes only too soon!
No, no, there is no need to pray for
death.
And if your man is drawn   200
To a new love, remember,

Such things occur often; do not feel
hurt.
For God will be your ultimate friend
the judge
In this as in all matters.
So do not mourn too much,   205
Do not waste away in sorrow
For the loss of the one you loved!

(*Within.*)

Medea. Great Themis, O lady Artemis,
look down
On all I am suffering; and suffering
in spite
Of all the vows my husband made
me.   210
I pray that I may some day see
Him and his bride brought down to
ruin
And their palace ruined for all the
wrong
They dared to do me without cause.
O my own father, my own coun-
try,   215
Shameful it was of me to leave you,
And to have killed my brother be-
fore I left you!

Nurse. Do you hear what she says? Do
you hear
How loudly she cries to Themis, the
goddess of promises,
And to Zeus, whom men think of as
the Emperor of Vows?   220
One thing I know. It is no small
thing
That draws such anger from our mistress!

Chorus. Let her come forth and see us,
Let her listen to our words of warn-
ing,
Let her lay aside the rage and vio-
lence of her heart;   225
Never shall I refuse to help my
friends,
Never shall they turn to me in vain.

Go, go, and bring her from the house
That we may see her; speak kindly
to her!
Hurry, before she does some violent
thing.   230
I feel her passion rising to a new
pitch.

Nurse. Yes; I shall go; but I deeply
doubt
Whether I can persuade my mistress.
Still, I shall gladly go and try;
Though she glares upon her servants,
those   235
That approach and dare to speak to
her,
With the fiery look of a lioness with
cubs!
You would be right, I think,
If you called both ignorant
And trivial those poets of old who
wrote   240
Their songs for festivities and ban-
quets,
Graceful and pleasant sounds for
men
Who lived in gaiety and leisure.
For none of them learned a way
For the song or the musicians   245
To still man's suffering. And suffering
it is
From which all killing springs, and
all calamity
Which falls on the homes of men.
Yet it would be a blessing, surely,
If songs could heal the wounds which
sorrow   250
Inflicts on men! What good is music
And singing at an idle banquet? It
seems to me
That men who are sitting at the ban-
quet table
Have pleasure enough already . . .

(*The* NURSE *goes into the house.*)

Chorus. I heard a cry that was heavy
and sick with sorrow.   255

Loud in her bitterness she cries
On the man who betrayed her mar-
riage bed!
Full of her wrongs she cries
To the gods, to Themis, to the bride
of Zeus,
To the Keeper of Vows, who brought
her away   260
To the shores of Greece which face
the shores of Asia,
Through the straits at night to the
gateway opening
On the unlimited salty sea.

(*Toward the end of this song*, MEDEA
enters from the house.)

Medea. Ladies of Corinth, I have come
forth   264
From my house, lest you should feel
Bitterness toward me; for I know that
men
Often acquire a bad name for their
pride—
Not only the pride they show in public,
But also the pride of retirement;
those who
Live in solitude, as I do, are frequently   270
Thought to be proud. For there is no
justice
In the view one man takes of another,
Often hating him before he has suffered
Wrong, hating him even before he
has seen
His true character. Therefore a for-
eigner   275
Above all should fit into the ways of
a city.
Not even a native citizen, I think,
should risk
Offending his neighbors by rudeness
or pride.

But this new thing has fallen upon
me
So unexpectedly, my strength is
broken.   280
O my friends, my life is shattered;
My heart no longer longs for the
blessings
Of life, but only for death! There was
One man through whom I came to
see   284
The world's whole beauty: and that
Was my husband; and he has turned
out
Utterly evil. O women, of all crea-
tures
That live and reflect, certainly it is
we
Who are the most luckless. First of
all,
We pay a great price to purchase a
husband;   290
And thus submit our bodies to a
perpetual
Tyrant. And everything depends on
whether
Our choice is good or bad—for di-
vorce
Is not an honorable thing, and we
may not
Refuse to be married. And then a
wife is   295
Plunged into a way of life and be-
havior
Entirely new to her, and must learn
What she never learned at home—
She must learn by a kind of subtle
Intuition how to manage the man
who   300
Lies beside her. And if we have the
luck
To handle all these things with tact
And success, and if the husband is
willing
To live at our side without resent-
ment,   304

Then life can become happy indeed.
But if not, I'd rather be dead.
A man who is disgusted with what he
Finds at home, goes forth to put an end
To his boredom, and turns to a friend
Or companion of his own age; while we   310
At home continue to think of him,
And of him only. And yet people
Say that we live in security at home,
While the men go forth to war.
How wrong they are! Listen: 315
I'd rather be sent three times over
To the battlefront than give
Birth to a single child. Still,
My friends, I realize that all this applies   319
Not to you but to me; you after all
Have a city of your own, and a family
Home, and a certain pleasure in life,
And the company of your friends. But
I am utterly lonely, an exile, cast off
By my own husband—nothing but a captive   325
Brought here from a foreign land—without
A mother or brother, without a single
Kinsman who can give me refuge in this sea
Of disaster. Therefore, my ladies, I ask   329
Only one thing of you: promise me
Silence. If I can find some way, some
Cunning scheme of revenge against my
Husband for all that he has done to me,
And against the man who gave away his
Daughter, and against the daughter who   335

Is now my husband's wife; then please
Be silent. For though a woman is
Timid in everything else, and weak, and
Terrified at the sight of a sword: still,
When things go wrong in this thing of love,   340
No heart is so fearless as a woman's;
No heart is so filled with the thought of blood.

Choragus. Yes; I promise this. You will be right,
Medea, in avenging yourself on   344
Your husband. It does not surprise
Me to see you lost in despair . . .
But look!
I see Kreon, our king, approaching:
He will have some news to tell us.

(*Enter* KREON, *with his following.*)

Kreon. Listen to me, Medea! You, with your angry looks
And all that bitterness against your husband: 350
I order you to leave my kingdom! I order you
To go with both your children into exile,
And immediately. This is my decree. And I
Will not return to my house until I have
Hurled you beyond the borders of my kingdom.   355

Medea. Oh, now I am lost indeed! This is the end
Of all things for me! Now my enemies
Are bearing down on me in all their force;
And I have no refuge left in this hour of ruin.
And yet, let me ask you this one thing, Kreon: 360

Why is it, Kreon, you are sending me
away?
Kreon. I am afraid of you. I need no
longer pretend
Otherwise. I am afraid you will do
my daughter
Some mortal harm. And I have many
reasons
For being afraid of this. You are a
cunning   365
Woman, Medea, expert in all kinds
of magic,
So I hear. And you are enraged by
the loss
Of your husband's love. I have also
heard
Them say that you are planning some
kind
Of mischief against Jason and the
bride,   370
And the bride's father, myself, as
well.
It is against these things I take pre-
cautions.
I tell you, Medea, I'd rather incur
your hatred now
Than be soft-hearted and later learn
to regret it.   374
Medea. This is not the first time, Kreon!
Many times before has this strange
reputation
Done me harm. A sensible man
should
Never nowadays bring up his chil-
dren
To be too clever or exceptional. For
one thing,   379
These talents never bring them profit;
For another, they end by bringing
envy
And hatred from others. If you pre-
sent
New ideas to a group of fools, they'll
think you

Ignorant as well as idle. And if your
fame
Should come to exceed the estab-
lished reputations,   385
They'll hate you for it. This has been
My own experience. Some think me
clever,
And resent it; some think me not
So very clever after all, and disap-
prove.   389
And you, Kreon, are somehow afraid
That I may do something to harm
you.
But you need not worry. It isn't for
someone
Like me to quarrel with kings. After
all,
Why should I? You haven't harmed
me.
You've allowed your daughter to
marry   395
As you saw fit. I hate my husband,
certainly;
But as for you, I feel you have acted
Reasonably enough. I don't grudge
you
Your good fortune. I wish you luck
With your daughter's marriage,
Kreon,   400
But beg you only, let me live on in
this
Land. I have been wronged, but I
shall remain
Quiet, and submit to those above me.
Kreon. Your words are gentle enough,
Medea.   404
Yet in my heart I can't help dreading
That you are planning some evil;
And I trust you now even less than
before.
It is easier to deal with a quick-
tempered
Man or woman than with one who is
subtle

And soft-spoken. No. You must go at
once.   410
Make no more speeches. It is settled.
You are my enemy, and there is
nothing
You can do to prolong your stay in
my country.

Medea. I implore you! By your knees,
by your newly wed daughter!

Kreon. You are wasting your words. You
will never persuade me.   415

Medea. Then you'll drive me out without listening to my prayers?

Kreon. I shall; for I love my own family
more than you.

Medea. O my country! How my heart
goes back to you now!

Kreon. I, too, love my country above all
things, except my children.

Medea. How cruelly passionate love
can deal with men!   420

Kreon. And yet, it all depends on the
luck men have.

Medea. O Zeus, never forget the man
who caused this!

Kreon. Go now; go. Spare me this useless trouble.

Medea. No trouble, no pain, nothing
has been spared me!

Kreon. Soon one of my men shall lead
you away by force.   425

Medea. Not that, Kreon, not that! I beg
you, Kreon.

Kreon. It seems you insist on creating
a disturbance.

Medea. I will go. I will go. That is not
what I intended.

Kreon. Why all this commotion, then?
What is it you want?

Medea. Let me stay here just a single
day longer,   430
Kreon. Let me stay and think over
where
I shall go in exile, and how I shall
find

A living for my children, for whom
their father
Has completely failed to provide.
Take pity
On them, Kreon! You too have chil-
dren   435
Of your own; you too must have a
soft place
In your heart for them. What hap-
pens to me now
No longer matters; I only grieve
For the suffering that will come to
my children.

Kreon. I am not a cruel man, Medea. I
have often made   440
Blunders, out of sheer compassion.
Even now
I feel I am making a mistake. All the
same,
Have it your own way. But let me
warn you! If
Tomorrow at sunrise still finds you
and your
Children within the frontiers of my
land,   445
You shall die for it. That is my ver-
dict;
It is final. So stay this one day
Longer, if you must. One day is
Not enough to bring disaster.   449

(*Exit* KREON *with his following.*)

Choragus. Pitiful woman! Oh we pity
The sorrows you suffer!
Where will you turn now? Who can
help you?
What home remains, what land
Is left to save you from destruction?
O Medea, you have been hurled by
heaven   455
Into an ocean of despair.

Medea. Everything has gone wrong.
None can deny it.
But not quite everything is lost; don't

Give up hope, my friends! There still
   are   459
Troubles in store for the young bride,
And for the bridegroom too. Do you
   think
I would have fawned on that old man
   without
Some plan and purpose? Certainly
   not.
I would never have touched him
With my hands. But now, although
   he   465
Could have crushed all my plans by
   instant
Exile, he has made a fatal error;
He has given me one day's reprieve.
One day in which I can bring death
To the three creatures that I loathe:
The father, the bride, my husband.
There are many manners of death.
Which I might use; I don't quite
   know yet
Which to try. Shall I set fire
To the bridal mansion? Or shall I
   sharpen   475
A sword and steal into the chamber
To the wedding bed and plunge it
Into their hearts? One thing
Stands in my way. If I am caught
Making my way into the bridal
   room   480
On such an errand, I shall surely
Be put to death, and my foes will end
By triumphing over me. Better to
   take
The shortest way, the way I am best
   trained in:
Better to bring them down with
   poison.   485
That I will do, then. And after that?
Suppose them dead. What city will
   take me in then?
What friend will offer me shelter in
   his land,
And safety, and a home? None.

Then best to wait a little longer;   490
Perhaps some sure defense will ap-
   pear,
And I can set about this murder
In stealth and stillness. And if no
   help
Should come from fate, and even if
   death
Is certain, still I can take at last   495
The sword in my own hand and go
   forth
Boldly to the crime, and kill. Yes,
By that dark Queen whom I revere
   above   498
All others, and whom I now invoke
To help me, by Hecate who dwells
In my most secret chamber: I swear
No man shall injure me and not re-
   gret it.
I will turn their marriage into sorrow
And anguish! Go now, go forward to
   this
Dangerous deed! The time has come
   for courage.   505
Remember the suffering they caused
   you! Never
Shall you be mocked because of this
   wedding
Of Jason's, you who are sprung from
   a noble
Father and whose grandfather was
   the Sun-God
Himself! You have the skill; what is
   more,   510
You are a woman: and it's always a
   woman
Who is incapable of a noble deed,
Yet expert in every kind of mischief!
                  (Strophe 1)
Chorus. The sacred rivers are flowing
   back to their sources!
The order of the world is being re-
   versed!   515
Now it is men who have grown de-
   ceitful,

Men who have broken their sacred
vows.
The name of woman shall rise to
favor
Again; and women once again
Shall rise and regain their honor:
never   520
Again shall ill be said of women!
                        (Antistrophe 1)
Those poets of old shall cease at last
To sing of our faithlessness. Never
On us did Phoebus, the god of music,
Lavish the talents of the lyre,   525
Else I should long ago have sung
A song of rebuttal to the race
Of men: for the years have many
things
To tell of them as well as of us!
                        (Strophe 2)

You sailed away from your father's
dwelling   530
With your heart on fire, Medea! And
you passed
Between the rocky gates of the seas;
And now you sleep on a foreign
shore,
In a lonely bed: now you are driven
Forth, and far away from the land
Once more you go in exile and dis-
honor!   536
                        (Antistrophe 2)

Gone is the dignity of vows,
Gone from great Hellas the sense of
honor.
It has flown and vanished in the
skies.   539
And now no father's dwelling house
Stands as a refuge from this storm!
Now another princess lies
In the bed which once was yours,
and rules your home!

(*As the* CHORUS *approaches the end
of the song,* JASON *enters.*)

Jason. This is not the first time I have
noticed
How difficult it is to deal with a vio-
lent temper.   545
Ah, Medea, if you had patiently ac-
cepted
The will of our ruler, you might have
stayed on
Quietly in this land and this house.
But now your pointless complaints
Are driving you into exile. Not that
I   550
Minded them myself; I didn't mind
it at all
When you called Jason an evil man.
But,
Considering your references to the
King
Himself, you may count yourself
lucky
That your punishment is exile. Per-
sonally,   555
I have always done my best to calm
The King's anger, and would have
liked
To see you stay on here. But you
refused
To give up this sort of folly, and kept
on
Slandering him; with the result that
you   560
Are facing banishment. Nevertheless,
In spite of your behavior, I feel in-
clined
To do you a favor; I have come to
make
Some sort of provision for you and
the children,
My dear, so that you won't be pen-
niless   565
When you are in exile; for I know
that exile
Will not be easy. And even though
you hate me,

Medea, my thoughts of you will con-
tinue
To be friendly as always.
Medea. You filthy coward!   570
That is the only name I can find for
you,
You and your utter lack of manliness!
And now you, who are the worst of
my enemies,
Now you too have chosen to come
to me! No!   574
It isn't courage which brings you,
Nor recklessness in facing the friends
You have injured; it is worse than
that,
It is the worst of all human vices:
Shamelessness. Still, you did well to
come to me,
For now I can ease my heart by re-
viling you: 580
And perhaps you too will suffer as
you listen.
Let me begin, then, at the very be-
ginning.
I saved your life; every Greek who
Sailed with you on the Argo knows
I saved you, when you were sent to
tame   585
The fire-breathing bulls and to yoke
them,
And to sow the deadly fields. Yes,
And I killed the many-folded serpent
Who lay guarding the Golden Fleece,
Forever wakeful, coil upon coil.   590
And I raised a beacon of light
To bring you to safety. Freely
I deserted my own father and my
own home;
And followed you to Iolcos, to the
hills   594
Of Pelion: and all this time my love
Was stronger than my reason. And I
brought
Death to Pelias by his own daugh-
ters'

Hands; I utterly destroyed the house-
hold.
All of these things I did for you,
Traitor! And you forsook me, and
took   600
Another wife, even though I had
borne
Your children. Had you been child-
less,
One might have pardoned your wish
For a second wedding. But now
All my faith in your vows has van-
ished.   605
I do not know whether you imagine
That the gods by whom you swore
Have disappeared or that new rules
Are now in vogue in such matters;
For you must be aware that you
have   610
Broken your vows to me. Oh this
poor
Right hand, which you so often
pressed!
These knees, which you so often
Used to embrace! And all in vain,
For it was an evil man   615
That touched me! How wildly
All my hopes have fallen through! . . .
Come, Jason, I shall speak to you
quite frankly,
As though we still were friends. Can
I possibly
Expect any kindness from someone
like you?   620
Still, let us assume that I can:
It will only make you appear
Still more ignoble. Very well.
Where shall I go? Home to my fa-
ther?
Home to him and the land I be-
trayed   625
When I followed you? Or back
To the pitiful daughters of Pelias?
What a fine welcome they would
give me,

Who arranged the death of their own
    father!
So this is how it now stands with
    me.   630
I am loathed by my friends at home;
And for your sake I made enemies
Of others whom I need never have
Harmed. And now, to reward me
For all this, look, look,   635
How doubly happy you've made me
Among the women of Hellas! Look
What a fine, trustworthy husband
I have had in you! And now
I am to be cast forth into exile,   640
In utter misery, alone with my chil-
    dren
And without a single friend! Oh,
This will be a shameful shadow upon
    you,
As you lie in your wedding bed! That
Your own children, and their mother,
Who saved your life, should go   646
Wandering around the world like
    beggars! . . .
O Zeus, why have you given us a
    way to tell
True gold from the counterfeit, but
    no way,
No emblem branded on a man's
    body whereby   650
We can tell the true man from the
    false?
Choragus. Dreadful is the anger,
And past all healing,
When lovers in fury
Turn against each other!   655
Jason. The time has come, it seems,
When I must speak, and speak well,
And like a good helmsman
Reef up my sail and weather   659
The tempest of your tongue . . .
And since you dwell so heavily
On all the favors you did me,
Medea, I am certain that I owe
. The safety of my voyage to Aphrodite

Alone among gods and men. Not
    that I   665
Doubt your skill; but all the same,
I prefer not to dwell on this notion
That love, with all its irresistible
Power, compelled you to save my
    life.
I don't think we need go into de-
    tails.   670
I admit that you meant well,
And did your best. But when it comes
To this matter of my safety, let me
Point out that you got rather more
Than you gave. First of all,   675
Instead of living in a barbaric land,
You've come to Greece and enjoyed
Contact with a country where justice
And law prevail, and not brute force;
And what is more, the Greeks
    thought   680
Rather highly of you. You even
Acquired a certain fame here. Where-
    as,
If you had stayed on in that outer
Fringe of the world, your name
Would now be quite unknown.
    Frankly,   685
I'd rather have real fame and distinc-
    tion
Than mighty stores of gold in my
    halls
Or the talent to sing more sweetly
Than Orpheus. That is my answer
To your version of all my labors;
    remember,   690
It was you who brought up this
    matter.
As for your bitter attack on my
    marriage
With the princess, I think I can prove
First of all that it was a shrewd
    move;   694
Secondly, a thoroughly sober one;
And finally, that I did it in your
    interest

And that of your children . . . Wait!
Please remain calm . . . Since I had
  come
From Iolcos involved in every kind
  of trouble,   699
And an exile, what could be luckier
For me than marriage with the king's
Own daughter? It was not—since it
  is
This that seems to rankle in you—
It was not that I grew weary
Of going to bed with you, and be-
  gan   705
To look around for a new wife. Nor
Was it that I was anxious
To have more children. The two
We have are quite enough;   709
I don't complain. No, it was this,
First of all: that we might live
In comfort, and not in poverty.
Believe me, I have learned how
A man's friends desert him
The moment he is penniless . . .
  And then   715
I wanted to bring up my sons
In a manner worthy of my position; I
Even hoped that by having more
  sons,
Who would live as brothers to yours,
We might draw the entire family   720
Into harmony, and all be happy. You
Yourself need no more children;
But I would do well to help
The sons I have through the sons
I hope to have. Do you disagree   725
With all this? You would agree
If it weren't for this matter of love
Which rankles in you. But you women
Have developed such curious no-
  tions:
You think that all is well   730
As long as your life at night
Runs smoothly. But if something
Happens which upsets your way of
  love,

Then all that you once found lovely
And desirable you now find hate-
  ful.   735
Believe me, it would have been better
Far if men could have thought up
Some other way of producing chil-
  dren,
And done away with women; then
No evil would ever have come to
  men.   740
Choragus. O Jason, you have given this
  speech
Of yours a convincing enough air;
  and
Yet I somehow feel, though perhaps I
Shouldn't say so, that you have acted
Wickedly in betraying your wife.
Medea. I suppose I am different in
  many   746
Ways from most people, for I feel
That the worst punishment should
Fall on the man who speaks
Brilliantly for an evil cause,   750
The man who knows he can make
An evil thing sound plausible
And who dares to do so. And still,
Such a man isn't really so very
  wise   754
After all. Listen, Jason. You need
Not bring forth these clever phrases
And specious arguments; for a single
Word from me will destroy you.
  Consider:
Had you not been a coward, Jason,
  you   759
Would have spoken frankly to me
First, and not concealed your wed-
  ding
Plans from the one who loved you.
Jason. And you, no doubt, would have
Done all you could to help
Me, if I had spoken of this   765
Matter: you, who even now cannot
Control the rage in your heart.

Medea. It wasn't this that restrained
you.
No. It was that you thought it might
Not be altogether proper, as you grew
Older, to have a foreign wife.   771
Jason. You may be quite sure of one
thing,
Medea. It was not because of any
Woman that I made this royal   774
Marriage. It was as I said before:
Because I wanted security for you,
And also to be the father
Of royal children bound by blood
To our two children: a thing which
Would have brought welfare to all of
us.   780
Medea. I don't want the kind of welfare
That is brought by suffering. I
Don't want the kind of safety
Which ends in sorrow.   784
Jason. Reflect on that opinion, Medea;
It will make you wiser. Don't
Search for sorrow in prosperity.
Don't keep looking for pain
In a piece of good luck.   789
Medea. Go on; mock me. You at least
Have a home to turn to. But I
Am going into exile, and alone.
Jason. It was you who made this choice;
There is no one else to blame.
Medea. How so? By marrying and de-
serting you?   795
Jason. You called down an evil curse
on the royal house.
Medea. I have brought a curse to your
own house too, I think.
Jason. Well, I don't propose to go
Into this any further. But if
You'd like to take along some   800
Of my money into exile, please
Say so. I am prepared to be
Generous on this point, and even
To give you letters to friends of mine
Abroad who will treat you well. It
would   805

Be madness for you to refuse this
offer.
It will be to your own gain,
Medea, if you give up your anger.
Medea. I will never accept favors
From friends of yours; and I'll   810
Accept nothing from you, so please
Don't offer it. Gifts from a coward
Bring luck to no one.
Jason. Very well then. I call upon
The gods to witness that I   815
Have tried in every way to help
You and the children. It is
You who refuse my offers. It
Is you who are stubbornly rejecting
Your friends. And for this,   820
Medea, you will surely suffer.
Medea. Please go! I can see you are
Longing to be with your new
Sweetheart. Aren't you lingering   824
Too long outside her bedroom? Go,
And taste the joys of your wedding.
Go, and God help you; you may end
By regretting this kind of wedding!

(JASON *goes out.*)

(Strophe 1)

Chorus. When love has passed its
limits
It brings no longer good: 830
It brings no peace or comfort to any
soul.
Yet while she still moves mildly there
is no fire
So sweet as that which is lit by the
goddess of love.
Oh never, upon me, Cypris,   834
Send forth from your golden bow
The unerring arrow poisoned with
desire!

(Antistrophe 1)

Let my heart be temperate: for
that
Is the wisest gift of the gods.
Let not that terrible goddess drive

Me to jealousy or rage! Oh let me
never   840
Be one of those who incessantly are
driven
To some new, forbidden longing!
Let her guide us gently toward the
man we choose;
Let her bless our beds with repose.

         (Strophe 2)
O my country, my own home   845
Let me never leave my city,
Let me never lose my way
In that dark and pitiless life
Where each new day brings sorrow!
O, let me first succumb   850
To death, yes, let me die
Before I suffer the hopeless
Grief of the loss of a home!

        (Antistrophe 2)
I have seen it with my own eyes,
I have heard my own heart tell me:
There is no city, no,   856
No friend who will give you pity
In the hour of your deepest woe.
O, let him perish in darkness
Who is faithless to his friends   860
And lets his heart stay frozen!
Let no such man be my friend!

(MEDEA *has been sitting in despair
on the stairway during this song.*
AEGEUS *enters.*)

Aegeus. Joy to you, Medea! This is the
best
Kind of greeting between old friends!
Medea. And joy to you, Aegeus, son
Of Pandion, king of Athens!   866
How does it happen that you
Have set foot in this country?
Aegeus. I have come from the ancient
oracles of Phoebus.
Medea. And why did you visit that
great center of prophecy?   870
Aegeus. I went to ask how I might
bring fertility to my seed.

Medea. Tell me, has your life been
childless hitherto?
Aegeus. Some divine visitation, I think,
has made me childless.
Medea. Have you a wife, or not?
Aegeus. I have, Medea.   875
Medea. And what did Phoebus tell you
about begetting children?
Aegeus. Words far too subtle for any
man to understand.
Medea. Is it proper for you to tell me
what he said?
Aegeus. Certainly; what I need is clev-
erness like yours.
Medea. Then what were the God's
words? Tell me, if I may hear
them.   880
Aegeus. That I shouldn't loosen the
hanging neck of the wine skin . . .
Medea. Till when? What must you do
first? Where must you go?
Aegeus. Till I have returned again to
my native home.
Medea. Then why have you come sailing to this land?
Aegeus. There is a man called Pittheus,
who is King of Troezen.   885
Medea. A son of Pelops, so they say,
and a man of piety.
Aegeus. I want to discuss this oracle of
the God with him.
Medea. He is a man full of skill and
experience in these matters.
Aegeus. As well as the dearest of my
old spear-bearing friends.
Medea. Good luck to you then! And
success to your wishes!   890
Aegeus. But why do you look so pale
and woebegone?
Medea. O Aegeus, my husband has
turned out to be the vilest of men!
Aegeus. What do you mean? Tell me
what has made you so unhappy.
Medea. Jason is wronging me, and utterly without provocation.

Aegeus. What has he done? Tell me
   more clearly, Medea.   895

Medea. He has taken another wife to
   take my place.

Aegeus. Does he really dare to do such
   a cruel thing!

Medea. He does indeed! He loved me
   once, but no longer.

Aegeus. Has he fallen in love? Has he
   wearied of your bed?

Medea. Ah, he's a great lover! But never
   true to his love. . . .   900

Aegeus. Let him go, then, if he is really
   as bad as you say.

Medea. He's in love with the idea of
   marrying royalty.

Aegeus. And who is the father of this
   princess? Please go on.

Medea. Her father is Kreon, King of
   Corinth.

Aegeus. Indeed, Medea, I understand
   your grief.   905

Medea. I am lost. And there is more: I
   am being banished!

Aegeus. Banished? By whom? This is
   something new you tell me.

Medea. Kreon is driving me from Corinth into banishment.

Aegeus. Does Jason consent? This is a
   contemptible thing.   909

Medea. Not in so many words, but he
   Has not really opposed it.
   O Aegeus, I beg you, I
   Implore you, by your beard
   And by your knees, I beseech you,
   Have pity on me! Have pity   915
   On a friend who is in trouble!
   Don't let me wander about
   In exile! Let me come
   To your land of Athens, let me 919
   Find refuge in your halls! And there,
   With heaven's consent, you may find
   Your love grow fertile and be
   Blessed with children, and your life
   At last end happily. You don't 924

Know, Aegeus, how good your luck
Has been, for I shall end
Your sterility; I shall bring
Power to your seed; for I know
Of drugs that can do this.

Aegeus. There are many reasons, my
   dear   930
   Lady, why I should like to do
   This for you: first, for the sake
   Of the children you promise me
   (For in that matter, frankly,
   I'm at my wits' end). But   935
   Let me state my position. If
   You arrive in Athens, I shall
   Stand by you as I am bound
   To do. But I must warn you
   First, my friend: I won't agree 940
   To take you with me. If you
   Arrive at my halls of your own
   Accord, you shall live there in safety;
   I shan't surrender you to anyone.
   But you yourself must manage 945
   Your escape from this land, for
   I have no wish to incur ill
   Will among my friends here.

Medea. Very well. So be it. Make me a
   formal
   Pledge on this, and I shall be satisfied.   950

Aegeus. Do you distrust me? What is
   it that troubles you?

Medea. I trust you, yes. But the house
   Of Pelias and Kreon as well,
   Both detest me. If you are bound
   To me by an oath, then, 955
   When they come to drag me
   Away from your country, I know
   You will remain true to your
   Vow and stand by me. Whereas,
   If it's only a promise, you might 960
   Not be in a position to resist
   Their demands; for I am weak,
   And they have both money and
   A royal house to help them.

Aegeus. You show considerable fore-
sight   965
In these matters, I must say. Still,
If you insist, I shan't refuse you.
From my own point of view, too,
It might be just as well to have   969
An excuse like this oath to present
To your enemies . . . Now name
your gods.

Medea. Swear by the plain of Earth,
And by my father's father Helios,
The Sun God, and in one sweeping
Phrase by the whole host of the
gods. . . .   975

Aegeus. Swear to do what or not to do
what?
Tell me.

Medea. Swear that you will never cast
Me from your land, nor ever,
As long as you live, allow   98o
An enemy of mine to carry me away,

Aegeus. I swear by the Earth,
And by the holy light of Helios,
The Sun God, and by the entire
Host of the gods, that I will   985
Abide by the terms you have just
made.

Medea. Very well. And if you should
fail,
What curse are you willing to incur?

Aegeus. Whatever happens to such as
disregard the gods.

Medea. Go in peace, Aegeus. All is
well,   990
Now; I shall arrive in your city
As soon as I possibly can—after
I have done what I must do,
And accomplished what I desire.

(AEGEUS *goes out.*)

Choragus. May Hermes, the God of
Travelers,   995
Go with you on your way, Aegeus,
And bring you safely home!
And may you find the thing you have
been seeking

For so long; you seem to be a gener-
ous man.   999

Medea. O Zeus, and Justice who are
The child of Zeus, and light
Of the Sun God! Now, my friends,
Has come the hour of my triumph.
Now I have started on the road;
Now I know that I shall bring   1005
Revenge on the ones I hate. For
At the very moment that my doom
Looked darkest of all, this man
Aegeus appeared, like a harbor for
all
My hopes; and to him I can   1010
Fasten the cable of my ship
When I come to the town and for-
tress
Of Pallas Athene. And now let me
Tell you of all my plans. Listen;
They will not be idle words,   1015
Or pleasant. I shall send
A servant to Jason and ask
For an interview, and when he
Comes, I shall be soft and concil-
iatory;   1019
I shall tell him that I've thought
Better of it; that I agree; that
Even the treacherous marriage
With the princess, which he is
Celebrating, strikes me as sensible,
And all for the best. However,   1025
I shall beg him to let the children
Stay on here: not that I'd dream
Of leaving my babies to be
Insulted in a land that loathes
Me; but purely as a stratagem;   1030
And I shall kill the king's
Own daughter. For I shall
Send them with gifts in their
Little hands, to be offered
To the bride to preserve   1035
Them from banishment; a finely
Woven dress and a golden diadem.
And if she takes these things and
Wears them on her body, she,

And whoever touches her, will 1040
Die in anguish; for I shall
Rub these things with deadly
Poison. That will be that;
But it is the next thing I 1044
Must do which sets me weeping.
For I will kill my own
Children! My own dear children,
Whom none shall take from me.
And when I have brought ruin
On the house of Jason, I shall 1050
Flee from the land and flee
From the murder of my children;
For it will be a terrible deed
To do! It isn't easy, my friends,
To bear the insults of one's 1055
Enemies. And so it shall be.
For what have I left in life?
I have no land, no home,
No harbor to protect me.
What a fool I was to leave 1060
My father's house, to put
My faith in the words
Of a Greek! And for this
He will pay the penalty,
So help me God. Never 1065
Again will he see his sons
Alive; never will he have a son
By this new bride. For she
Is doomed to die, and die
Hideously from the power 1070
Of my poison. Let no man
Think I am a feeble, frail-hearted
Woman who sits with folded
Hands: no, let them know me
For the opposite of that—one 1075
Who knows how to hurt her
Enemies and help her friends.
It is lives like this that
Are longest remembered!
Choragus. Since you have told us all
your plans, 1080
Let me say this to you:
Do not do this thing!
Medea. There is nothing else I can do.

It is forgivable that you should
Say this: but remember, you 1085
Have not suffered as I have!
Choragus. Woman, can you really bring
yourself
To destroy your own flesh and blood?
Medea. I can; for in that way 1089
I can hurt my husband most cruelly.
Choragus. And yourself as well! You
will be
The most miserable of women.
Medea. Then I will; no matter.
No word of warning now can stop
me!

(*The* NURSE *enters;* MEDEA *turns to
her.*)

Go and tell Jason to come to me.
And remember, I send you 1096
On a mission of great secrecy. Say
Nothing of the plans I have
Prepared; don't say a word, if
You are loyal to your mistress 1100
And loyal to the race of woman!
(Strophe 1)
Chorus. Oh listen! We know of a land
Where dwell the sons of Erechtheus,
Fed on the food of wisdom, and
blessed with the blood of gods,
Raised on a soil still holy and still
unconquered; and there 1105
Moving amid that glittering air
where the legends
Say that lovely Harmonia, the
golden-haired,
Brought forth the Sacred Nine, the
Pierian Muses!

(Antistrophe 1)
And where they say that Cypris,
The divine one, sailed to draw the
Water out of the wandering stream of
Cephisus, and the gentle 1111
Winds passed over the land: and
over her glittering

Head the long, sweet-scented rose
   wreaths
Were wound by the Loves, who sit
   by Wisdom's side
And in all virtuous deeds are the
   friends of mortals.

                (Strophe 2)
Then how can this city. O how   1115
Can these scared streams which wel-
   come
Only the ones they love,
O tell, how can they welcome
You who are evil? You   1119
Who are killing your sons? O think
Of the sons you plan to slay,
Of the blood you plan to shed!
We beg, we implore you, Medea:
Do not murder your sons!

            (Antistrophe 2)
Oh where can your hand or your
   heart,   1125
Medea, find the hardness
To do this frightful thing
Against your sons? O how
Can you look on them and yet
Not weep, Medea? How   1130
Can you still resolve to slay them?
Ah, when they fall at your feet
For mercy, you will not be able
To dip your hand in their blood!

(JASON *enters.*)

Jason. I have come at your bidding,
   Medea. For although you are   1136
Full of hatred for me, this small
Favor I will grant you; I will
Listen to you, my lady, and hear
What new favor you are asking.
Medea. Jason, I beg your forgiveness
   for what   1141
I have said! Surely you can afford
To forgive my bad temper; after all,
There has been much love between
   us!   1144

I have reasoned with myself and
Reproached myself. "Poor fool," I
   said,
"Why am I so distraught? Why am I
So bitter against all good advice,
Why am I so angry at the rulers
Of this country, and my husband
As well, who does the best he
   can   1151
For me in marrying a royal princess,
And in having royal children, who
Will be brothers to my own? Why
   not   1154
Stop complaining? What is wrong
With me, when the gods are being
So generous? Don't I have my
Children to consider? Don't I realize
That we are exiles after all, and in
   need   1159
Of friends?" . . . And when I had
Thought all this over, Jason, I saw
How foolish I'd been, and how silly
My anger. So now I agree with you.
I think you are well advised in
Taking this new wife; and I was
   mad.   1165
I should have helped you in your
   plans, I
Should have helped arrange the wed-
   ding.
I should have stood by the wedding
Bed and been happy to wait   1169
On your bride. But we women are—
Well, I shan't say entirely
Worthless; but we are what we
Are. And you men shouldn't stoop
To our level; you shouldn't reply
To our folly with folly. I give in.
I admit I was wrong.   1176
I have thought better of it all. . . .

(*She turns toward the house.*)

Come, come, my children, come
Out from the house, come
And greet your father and then   1180

Say goodbye to him. Give up
Your anger, as your mother does;
Be friends with him again,
Be reconciled!

(*The* ATTENDANT *enters with the
children.*)

Medea. We have made peace now;
Our bitterness is gone. Take   1186
His right hand . . . O God:
I can't help thinking of the things
That lie dark and hidden
In the future! . . . My children,
Hold out your arms—the way   1191
One holds them in farewell after
A long, long life . . . I am close
To tears, my children! I am
Full of fear! I have ended   1195
My quarrel with your father at last,
And look! My eyes are full of tears.

Choragus. And our eyes too
Are filling with tears. O,
Do not let disasters worse   1200
Than the present descend on you!

Jason. I approve of your conduct,
Medea; not that I blame you
For anything in the past. It is
Natural for a woman to be   1205
Furious with her husband when he
Begins to have other affairs. But
Now your heart has grown more sensible,
And your mind is changed for the
better;   1209
You are behaving like a woman
Of sense. And of you, my sons,
Your father will take good care,
And make full provision,
With the help of God. And I
Trust that in due time you   1215
With your brothers will be among
The leading men in Corinth. All
You need to do is grow up,
My sons; and as for your future,
You may leave it safely   1220
In the hands of your father,
And of those among the gods
Who love him. I want to see
You when you've grown to be
Men, tall and strong, towering   1225
Over my enemies! . . . Medea, why
Are your eyes wet with tears?
Why are your cheeks so pale? Why
Are you turning away? Don't these
Happy words of mine make you
happy?

Medea. It is nothing. I was only thinking about these children.   1231

Jason. Take heart, then. I shall look
after them well.

Medea. I will, Jason. It is not that I
don't trust you.
Women are weak; and tears come
easily to them.

Jason. But why should you feel disturbed about the children?   1235

Medea. I gave birth to them, Jason.
And when
You prayed that they might live long,
My heart filled with sorrow to think
That all these things must happen.
Well now; I have told you some of
the things   1240
I called you here to tell you; now
Let me tell you the rest. Since
The ruler of this land has resolved
To banish me, and since I am
Considered an enemy, I know   1245
It will be best for me not to stand
In your way, or in the way of the
king,
By living here. I am going forth
From this land into exile. But these
Children—O let them feel that you
Are protecting them, and beg   1251
Of Kreon not to banish them!

Jason. I doubt whether I can persuade
him; still, I will try.

Medea. Or at least ask your wife
To beg her father to do this,   1255

And give the children reprieve from
exile.

Jason. I will try; and with her I think
I shall succeed.

Medea. She's a woman, after all;
And like all other women.   1259
And I will help you in this matter;
I will send the children to her
With gifts far more exquisite,
I am sure, than any now to be
Found among men—a finely woven
Dress and a diadem of chased gold.
There; let one of the servants   1266
Go and bring me these lovely orna-
ments.

(*One of the* ATTENDANTS *goes into
the house.*)

And she'll be happy not in one way,
But a thousand! With so splendid
A man as you to share her bed,   1270
And with this marvelous gown
As well, which once the Sun-God
Helios
Himself, my father's father, gave his
descendants.

(*The* ATTENDANT *returns with the
poisoned dress and diadem.*)

There, my children, take these wed-
ding   1274
Presents in your hands and take
Them as an offering to the royal
Princess, the lucky bride;
Give them to her; they are
Not gifts to be scorned.   1279

Jason. But why do you give them away
So rashly, Medea? Do you think
The royal palace is lacking
In dresses, or in gold? Keep them.
Don't give them away. If my wife
Really loves me, I am sure she   1285
Values me more highly than gold.

Medea. No, don't say that, Jason.
For I have heard it said
That gifts can persuade even   1289

The gods; and men are governed
More by gold than by words! Luck
Has fallen on your bride, and
The gods have blessed her fortune.
She is young: she's a princess.
Yet I'd give not only gold   1295
But my life to save my children
From exile. Enter that rich palace
Together, children, and pray
To your father's new bride; pray
To my mistress, and beg her   1300
To save you from banishment. Pre-
sent
This garment to her; and above
All let her take the gift from you
With her own hands. Go; don't
linger.   1304
And may you succeed, and bring
Back to your mother the good
News for which she longs!

(*Exit* JASON, *the* ATTENDANT, *and the
children bearing the poisoned gifts.*)

(Strophe 1)

Chorus. No hope now remains for the
children's lives!
No, none. Even now they are moving
toward death;
The luckless bride will accept the
gown that will kill her,   1310
And take the golden crown, and hold
it
In her hand, and over her golden
head will
Lift the garment of Hell!

(Antistrophe 1)

The grace and glitter of gold will enchant her:
She will put on the golden robe and
wear   1315
The golden crown: and deck herself
as the bride
Of death. And thus, pitiful girl,
Will fall in the trap; will fall and
perish.

She will never escape! 1319

(Strophe 2)

You likewise, O miserable groom,
Who planned a royal wedding cere-
mony,
Do not see the doom you are bringing
Upon your sons; and the terrible
death
Now lying in wait for your bride.
Pity 1324
Upon you! O, how you are fallen!

(Antistrophe 2)

And I weep for you too, Medea,
O mother who are killing your sons,
Killing in revenge for the loss
Of your love: you whom your lover
Jason 1329
Now has deserted and betrayed
To love and marry another mistress!

(*Enter* ATTENDANT *with the children.*)

Attendant. My lady, your children are
reprieved
From exile. The royal bride was
Delighted to receive your gifts
With her own hands. And there 1335
Is peace between her and your chil-
dren . . .
Medea! Why are you so distraught
At this lucky moment? Why are you
Turning your head away? Are you
not 1339
Happy to hear this news, my lady?

Medea. Oh, I am lost!

Attendant. That cry does not suit the
news I have brought you, surely!

Medea. I am lost! I am lost!

Attendant. Have I told you of some
disaster, without knowing it?
Was I wrong in thinking that my
news was good? 1345

Medea. You have said what you have
said:
I do not wish to blame you.

Attendant. Then why are you so disturbed? Why are you weeping?

Medea. Oh, my old friend, I can't help
weeping.
It was I, it was I and the gods, 1350
Who planned these things so badly.

Attendant. Take heart, Medea. Your
sons will bring
You back to your home some day.

Medea. And I'll bring others back to
their homes,
Long before that happens! 1355

Attendant. And often before this,
mothers have been
Parted from their sons. Bear your
troubles,
Medea, as all mortals must bear
them.

Medea. I will, I will. Go back into the
house;
And plan your daily work for the
children. 1360

(*The* ATTENDANT *goes into the house,
and* MEDEA *turns to her children.*)

Medea. O my children, my children,
You will still have a city,
You will still have a home
Where you can dwell forever, far
Away from me, far forever 1365
From your mother! But I am
Doomed to go in exile to another
Land, before I can see you
Grow up and be happy, before
I can take pride in you, before 1370
I can wait on your brides and
Make your marriage beds, or hold
The torch at your wedding
Ceremony! What a victim I am
Of my own self-will! It was 1375
All in vain, my children, that I
Reared you! It was all in vain
That I grew weary and worn,
And suffered the anguish and pangs
Of childbirth! Oh pity me! Once

I had great hopes for you; I   1381
Had hopes that you'd look after
Me in my old age, and that you'd
Lovingly deck my body with your
   own hands
When I died, as all men hope   1385
And desire. But now my lovely
Dreams are over. I shall love
You both. I shall spend my life
In grief and solitude. And never
Again will you see your mother
With your own dear eyes; now   1391
You will pass into another
Kind of life. Ah, my dear children,
Why do you look at me like this?
Why are you smiling your sweet
Little smiles at me? O children,
What can I do? My heart gives   1397
Way when I see the joy
Shining in my children's eyes.
O women, I cannot do it! . . .   1400
Farewell to all my plans!
I will take my babies away with me
From this land. Why should I hurt
Their father by hurting them? Why
Should I hurt myself doubly? No:
I cannot do it. I shall say   1406
Good-bye to my plans . . . And
   yet—
O, what is wrong with me? Am I
Willing to see my enemies go   1409
Unpunished? Am I willing to be
Insulted and laughed at? I shall
Follow this thing to the end.
How weak I am! How weak to let
My heart be touched by these soft
Sentiments! Go back into the
   house,   1415
My children . . . And if anyone
Prefers not to witness my sacrifice,
Let him do as he wishes! My poor
Heart, have pity on them, let them
Go, the little children! They'll bring
Cheer to you, if you let them   1421
Live with you in exile! . . . No,

By all the avenging Furies,
This shall not be! Never shall I
Surrender my children to the inso-
   lence   1425
And mockery of my enemies! It is
Settled. I have made my decision.
And since they must die, it is
Their mother who must kill them.
Now there is no escape for the
   young   1430
Bride! Already the crown is on
Her head; already the dress is
Hanging from her body; the royal
Bride, the princess is dying! This
I know. And now—since I   1435
Am about to follow a dreadful
Path, and am sending them
On a path still more terrible—
I will simply say this: 1439
I want to speak to my children.

(*She calls and the children come
back; she takes them in her arms.*)

Come, come, give me your hands,
My babies, let your mother kiss
You both. O dear little hands,
Dear little lips: how I have   1444
Loved them! How fresh and young
Your eyes look! How straight
You stand! I wish you joy
With all my heart; but not here;
Not in this land. All that you   1449
Had here your father has stolen
From you. . . . How good it is
To hold you, to feel your soft
Young cheeks, the warm young
Sweetness of your breath. . . . Go
   now;   1454
Leave me. I cannot look at you
Any longer . . . I am overcome. . . .

(*The children go into the house
again.*)

Now at last I understand the full
Evil of what I have planned.
At last I see how my passion   1459

Is stronger than my reason: passion,
Which brings the worst of woes to
  mortal man.

(*She goes out at the right, toward
the palace.*)

Choragus. Many a time before
  I have gone through subtler rea-
    soning,
  Many times I have faced graver ques-
    tioning
  Than any woman should ever have to
    face: 1465
  But we women have a goddess to
    help us, too,
  And lead us into wisdom.
  Not all of us; perhaps not many;
  But some women there are who are
    capable of wisdom.
  And I say this: that those who have
    never   1470
  Known the fullness of life and never
    had children,
  Are happier far than those who are
    parents.
  For the childless, who never dis-
    cover whether
  Their children grow up to be a cause
    for joy or for pain,
  Are spared many troubles: 1475
  While those who know in their houses
  The sweet presence of children—
  We have seen how their lives are
    wasted by worry.
  First they fret about how they shall
    raise them
  Properly; and then how to leave
    them enough   1480
  Money to live on; and then they con-
    tinue
  To worry about whether all this labor
  Has gone into children that will turn
    out well
  Or turn out ill: and the question re-
    mains unanswered.   1484

And let me tell of one more trouble,
  The last of all, and common to all
    mortals:
  For suppose you have found enough
  For them to live on, and suppose
  You have seen them grow up and
    turn out well;
  Still, if fate so decrees it, Death   1490
  Will come and tear away your chil-
    dren!
  What use is it, then, that the gods
  For the sake of children
  Should pile on us mortals,
  After all other griefs,   1495
  This grief for lost children? This
    grief
  Greater by far than any?

(MEDEA *comes out of the house.*)

Medea. I have been waiting in sus-
    pense,
  Ladies; I have waited long to learn
  How things will happen . . . Look!
  I see one of Jason's   1501
  Servants coming toward us; he is
  Panting; and the bearer of news,
  I think; of bad news . . .

(A MESSENGER *rushes in.*)

Messenger. Fly, Medea, fly!   1505
  You have done a terrible thing, a
    thing
  Breaking all human laws: fly,
  Take a ship for the seas,
  Or a chariot for the plains!
Medea. Why? What reason have you
    for asking me to fly?   1510
Messenger. She lies dead! The royal
    princess
  And her father Kreon too!
  They have died: they have
  Been slain by your poisons!
Medea. You bring me blessed news!
    Now   1515
  And from now on I count you
  Among my friends, my benefactors!

Messenger. What! Are you insane? Are you mad,

Medea? You have done an outrage

To the royal house: Does it make you   1520

Happy to hear it? Can you hear

Of this dreadful thing without horror?

Medea. I too have words to say in reply

To yours. Do not be impatient,

My friend. Tell me: how did   1525

They die? You will make me doubly

Happy if you say they died in anguish!

Messenger. When those two children, your own babies,

Medea, came with their father and entered

The palace of the bride, it gave   1530

Joy to all of us, the servants

Who have suffered with you; for instantly

All through the house we whispered

That you had made up your quarrel

With your husband. One of us kissed   1535

Your children's hands, and another

Their golden hair, and I myself was so

Overjoyed that I followed them in person

To the women's chambers. And there stood   1539

Our mistress, whom we now serve

Instead of you; and she kept her eyes fixed

Longingly on Jason. When she caught

Sight of your children, she covered up

Her eyes, and her face grew pale, and she   1544

Turned away, filled with petulance

At their coming. But your husband tried

To soothe the bride's ill humor,

And said: "Do not look so unkindly

At your friends! Do not feel angry:

Turn your head to me once more, and   1550

Think of your husband's friends

As your own friends! Accept these gifts,

And do this for my sake: beg

Of your father not to let these children   1554

Be exiled!" And then, when she saw

The dress, she grew mild and yielded,

And gave in to her husband. And before

The father and the children had gone

Far from her rooms, she took   1559

The gorgeous robe and put it on;

And she put the golden crown on her curly

Head, and arranged her hair in the shining

Mirror, smiling as she saw herself reflected.

And then she rose from her chair

And walked across the room, stepping   1565

Softly and delicately on her small

White feet, filled with delight at the gift,

And glancing again and again at the delicate

Turn of her ankles. And after that

It was a thing of horror we saw.

For suddenly her face changed its color,   1571

And she staggered back, and began

To tremble as she ran, and reached

A chair just as she was about

To fall to the ground. An old   1575

Woman servant, thinking no doubt that this

Was some kind of seizure, a fit
Sent by Pan, or some other god,
Cried out a prayer: and then, as
she   1579
Prayed, she saw the flakes of foam
Flow from her mouth, and her eye-
balls
Rolling, and the blood fade from
her face.
And then it was a different prayer
She uttered, a terrible scream, and
one   1584
Of the women ran to the house
Of the King, and another to the
newly
Wedded groom to tell him what had
Happened to the bride; and the
whole
House echoed as they ran to and fro.
Let me tell you, time enough for a
man   1590
To walk two hundred yards passed
Before the poor lady awoke from
her trance,
With a dreadful scream, and
opened
Her eyes again. A twofold torment
was
Creeping over her. The golden
diadem   1595
On her head was sending forth a
violent
Stream of flame, and the finely
Woven dress which your children
gave
Her was beginning to eat into the
poor   1599
Girl's snowy soft flesh. And she
Leapt from her chair, all on fire,
And started to run, shaking her
head
To and fro, trying to shake off
The diadem; but the gold still
Clung firmly, and as she shook her
hair   1605

The fire blazed forth with double
fury.
And then she sank to the ground,
helpless.
Overcome; and past all recognition
Except to the eye of a father—
For her eyes had lost their nor-
mal   1610
Expression, and the familiar look
Had fled from her face, and from
the top
Of her head a mingled stream
Of blood and fire was pouring. And
It was like the drops   1615
Falling from the bark of a pine
Tree when the flesh dropped away
From her bones, torn loose
By the secret fangs of the poison.
And terror kept all of us   1620
From touching the corpse; for we
Were warned by what had hap-
pened.
But then her poor father who knew
Nothing of her death, came sud-
denly   1624
Into the house and stumbled over
Her body, and cried out as he
folded
His arms about her and kissed her,
And said: "O my child, my poor
child,
Which of the gods has so cruelly
Killed you? Who has robbed me of
you,   1630
Who am old and close to the grave?
O
My child let me die with you!" And
he
Grew silent and tried to rise to his
Feet again, but found himself
Fastened to the finely spun dress,
Like vine clinging to a laurel   1636
Bough, and there was a fearful
Struggle. And still he tried to lift

His knees, and she writhed and
    clung
To him; and as he tugged, he   1640
Tore the withered flesh from
His bones. And at last he could
No longer master the pain, and
Surrendered, and gave up the ghost.
So there they are lying together:
And it is a sight to send us weep-
    ing. . . .   1646
As for you, Medea, I will say
Nothing of your own problems: you
Yourself must discover an escape
From punishment. I think, and I
    have   1650
Always thought, the life of men
Is a shadow; and I say without
Fear that those who are wisest
    among
All men, and probe most deeply
Into the cause of things—they are
The ones who suffer most deeply!
    For,   1656
Believe me, no man among mortals
    is happy;
If wealth comes to a man, he may
    be
Luckier than the rest; but happy—
    never.

(*Exit* MESSENGER.)

Choragus. It seems that heaven has
    sent, today,   1660
A heavy load of evils upon Jason;
And he deserves them. Alas, poor
    girl,
Poor daughter of Kreon! I pity you
And your anguish; and now you are
Gone, all because of your wedding
    with Jason: 1665
Gone away to the halls of Hades!
Medea. Women, the deed shall be
    done! Swiftly
I will go and kill my children,
And then leave the land: and not

Delay nor let them be killed by
A crueler hand. For die they   1671
Must in any case: and if
They must be slain, it is I,
Their mother who gave them life,
Who must slay them! O my heart,
My heart, arm yourself in steel!
Do not shrink back from this hid-
    eous   1677
Thing which has to be done! Come,
My hand, and seize the sword, take
    it
And step forward to the place
    where   1680
My life's true sorrow begins! Do not
Be a coward . . . do not think
Of the children, and how dear
They are to you who are their
    mother!   1684
For one brief day, Medea, forget
Your children; and then forever
After you may mourn; for though
You will kill them, they were dear
    to you,
Very dear . . . I am a miserable
    woman!

(*With a cry* MEDEA *rushes into the
house.*)

(Strophe)
Chorus. O Earth, and the all-bright-
    ening   1690
Beam of the Sun, look, look
Upon this lost one, shine upon
This pitiful woman before she raises
Her hand in murder against her
    sons!
For lo! these are the offspring   1695
Of thine own golden seed, and I
That divine blood may now be shed
    by men!
O Light flung forth by Zeus,
O heavenly Light,
Hold back her hand,   1700
Restrain her, and drive out

This dark demoniac fury from the house!

(Antistrophe)

Was it all in vain, Medea,
What you suffered in bearing your sons?
Was it utterly in vain   1705
You bore the babes you loved, after you left
Behind you that dark passage through the straits
And past the perilous rocks, the blue Symplegades?
Wretched woman, how has it happened   1709
That your soul is torn by anger
And darkened by the shadow of death?
Heavy will be the price
To pay for kindred blood staining the earth!
Heavy the woe sent down by heaven
On the house of the killer for such a crime!   1715

(A cry is heard from the children within.)

Choragus. Listen! Do you hear? Do you hear the children crying?
Hate-hardened heart! O woman born for evil!

(Crying within.)

1st Son. What can I do? How can I run from mother's hands?

(Crying within.)

2nd Son. I don't know! We are lost, we are lost, brother!

Choragus. Shall I enter the house? Oh surely   1720
I must help! I must save these children from murder!

(Within.)

1st Son. Help, in the name of heaven! We need your help!

(Within.)

2nd Son. Now, now it's coming closer! The sword is falling!

Choragus. Oh, you must be made of stone or steel,
To kill the fruit of your womb   1725
With your own hands, unhappy woman!
I have heard of only one,
Of all the women who ever lived, who laid
Her hand upon her children: it was Ino,
Who was driven insane by the Gods   1730
When the wife of Zeus sent her wandering from her home.
And wild with grief at killing her children,
She flung herself from the sea-battered cliff
And plunged into the sea, and in the sea   1734
Rejoined her two dead children.
Can anything so dreadful ever happen again?
Woe flows forth from the bed of a woman
Whom fate has touched with trouble!
Great is the grief that they have brought on men!

(Enter JASON with his attendants.)

Jason. Ladies, you have been sitting near   1740
This house! Tell me! Is Medea, is
The woman who did this frightful
Thing, still in the house? Or has she
Fled already? O believe me, she'll have
To hide deep under the earth, or fly   1745
On wings through the sky, if she
Hopes to escape the vengeance

Of the royal house! Does she dream,
After killing the ruler of the land,
   that
She herself can escape from these
   halls   1750
Unpunished? But I am thinking of
   her
Far less than of her children; for
   she
Herself will duly suffer at the hands
Of those she wronged. Ladies, I have
Come to save the lives of my   1755
Boys, lest the royal house should
Harm them in revenge for this
Vile thing done by their mother.

Choragus. O Jason, you do not yet
   know
The full depth of your misery,
   or   1760
You would not have spoken those
   words!

Jason. What do you mean? Is she
   planning to kill me also?

Choragus. Your boys are dead; dead
   at their mother's hand.

Jason. What have you said, woman?
   You are destroying me!

Choragus. You may be sure of this:
   your children are dead.   1765

Jason. Oh where did she kill them?
   Was it here, or in the house?

Choragus. Open the doors, and you
   will see their murdered bodies!

Jason. Open the doors! Unlock the
   bolts! Undo
The fastenings! And let me see this
   twofold
Horror! Let me see my murdered
   boys!   1770
Let me look on her whom I shall
   kill in vengeance!

(*His attendants rush to the door.*
Medea *appears above the house in
a chariot drawn by dragons. The
dead children are at her side.*)

Medea. Why do you batter at the
   doors?
Why do you shake these bolts,
In quest of the dead and their
Murderess? You may cease your
   trouble,   1775
Jason; and if there is anything you
Want to say, then say it! Never
Again shall you lay your hand on
   me;
So swift is the chariot which my
Father's father gave me, the Sun
   God   1780
Helios, to save me from my foes!

Jason. Horrible woman! Now you are
   utterly
Loathed by the gods, and by me,
   and
By all mankind. You had the heart
To stab your children; you,   1785
Their own mother, and to leave me
Childless; you have done these fearful
Things, and still you dare to gaze
As ever at the sun and the earth! O
I wish you were dead! Now at
   last   1790
I see clearly what I did not see
On the day I brought you, loaded
With doom, from your barbarous
   home
To live in Hellas—a traitress
To your father and your native
   land.   1795
On me too the gods have hurled
The curse which has haunted you.
   For
You killed your own brother at his
Fireside, and then came aboard our
Beautiful ship the Argo. And that
Was how it started. And then you
Married me, and slept with me, and
Out of your passion bore me chil-
   dren;   1803
And now, out of your passion, you
   have

Killed them. There is no woman in
   all   1805
Of Greece who would dare to do
   this. And
Yet I passed them over, and chose
   you
Instead; and chose to marry my own
Doom! I married not a woman,
But a monster, wilder of heart than
Scylla in the Tyrrhenian Sea!   1811
But even if I hurled a thousand
Insults at you, Medea, I know
I could not wound you: your heart
Is so hard, so utterly hard. Go,
You wicked sorceress; I see   1816
The stains of your children's blood
Upon you! Go; all that is left
To me now is to mourn. I shall
   never   1819
Lie beside my newly wedded love;
I shall never have my sons, whom
I bred and brought up, alive
Beside me to say a last farewell!
I have lost them forever,
And my life is ended.   1825
Medea. O Jason, to these words of
   yours
I could make a long reply; but
Zeus, the father, himself well knows
All that I did for you, and what
You did to me. Destiny has   1830
Refused to let you scorn my love,
And lead a life of pleasure,
And mock at me; nor were the royal
Princess and the matchmaker
Kreon destined to drive me into
   exile,   1835
And then go untormented! Call me
A monster if you wish; call me
The Scylla in the Tyrrhenian Sea.
For now I have torn your heart:
And this indeed was destined,
   Jason!   1840
Jason. You too must feel the pain; you
   will share my grief, Medea.

Medea. Yes; but the pain is milder,
   since you cannot mock me!
Jason. O my sons, it was an unspeak-
   able mother who bore you!
Medea. O my sons, it was really your
   father who destroyed you!
Jason. But I tell you: it was not my
   hand that slew them!   1845
Medea. No; but your insolence, and
   your new wedding slew them!
Jason. And you thought this wedding
   cause enough to kill them?
Medea. And you think the anguish of
   love is trifling for a woman?
Jason. Yes, if her heart is sound: but
   yours makes all things evil.   1849
Medea. Your sons are dead, Jason!
   Does it hurt you when I say this?
Jason. They will live on, Medea, by
   bringing suffering on you.
Medea. The gods are well aware who
   caused all this suffering.
Jason. Yes, the gods are well aware.
   They know your brutal heart.
Medea. You too are brutal. And I am
   sick of your bitter words!
Jason. And I am sick of yours. Oh
   Medea, it will be easy to leave
   you.   1855
Medea. Easy! Yes! And for me too!
   What, then, do you want?
Jason. Give me those bodies to bury,
   and to mourn.
Medea. Never! I will bury them my-
   self.
I will take them myself to Hera's
Temple, which hangs over the Cape,
Where none of their enemies can
Insult them, and where none can
   defile   1862
Their graves! And in this land
Of Corinth I shall ordain a holy
Feast and sacrifice, forever after,
To atone for this guilt of killing.
And I shall go myself to Athens,

To live in the House of Aegeus,
The son of Pandion. And I predict
That you, as you deserve, will
    die   1870
Without honor; and your head
    crushed
By a beam of the shattered Argo;
And then you will know the bitter
End of all my love for you!

Jason. May the avenging fury of our
    sons   1875
Destroy you! May Justice destroy
You, and repay blood with blood!

Medea. What god, what heavenly
    power
Would listen to you? To a breaker
Of oaths? To a betrayer of love?

Jason. Oh, you are vile! You sorceress!
    Murderess!   1881

Medea. Go to your house. Go, and bury
your bride.

Jason. Yes, I shall go; and mourn for
my murdered sons.

Medea. Wait; do not weep yet, Jason!
Wait till age has sharpened your
grief!

Jason. Oh my sons, whom I loved! My
    sons!   1885

Medea. It was I, not you, who truly
loved them.

Jason. You say you loved them; yet you
killed them.

Medea. Yes. I killed them to make you
suffer.

Jason. Medea, I only long to kiss them
one last time.

Medea. Now, now, you long to kiss
    them!   1890
Now you long to say farewell:

But before, you cast them from you!

Jason. Medea, I beg you, let me touch
the little bodies of my boys!   1894

Medea. No. Never. You speak in vain.

Jason. O Zeus, high in your heaven,
Have you heard these words?
Have you heard this unutterable
Cruelty? Have you heard this
Woman, this monster, this murder-
    ess?   1900
And now I shall do the only
Thing I still can do! Yes!
I shall cry, I shall cry
Aloud to heaven, and call on
The gods to witness how you   1905
Killed my sons, and refused
To let me kiss them farewell,
Or touch them, or give them burial!
Oh, I'd rather never have seen them
    live,   1909
Than have seen them slaughtered so!

(*The chariot carries* MEDEA *away.*)

Choragus. Many, many are the things
That Zeus determines, high on the
    Olympian throne;
Many the things beyond men's un-
    derstanding
That the gods achieve, and bring to
    pass.
Many the things we think will hap-
    pen,   1915
Yet never happen.
And many the things we thought
    could never be,
Yet the gods contrive.
Such things have happened on this
    day,
And in this place!   1920

Everyman

~~~~~~~~~~~~~~~~~~~~~~~~~~

INTRODUCTION: THE MEDIEVAL PLAYWRIGHT

The most significant fact about the medieval playwright is his anonymity; the dedicated men who created the tremendous body of medieval drama, like those who built the great cathedrals, did so, not for personal fame, but for the good of the Church, the salvation of men's souls, and the greater glory of God. Though the names of the English dramatists who wrote prior to the sixteenth century have not come down to us, we may be certain that all of them were connected in some way with the Church. From the tenth to the sixteenth century, hundreds of monks, priests, and brothers occupied themselves with the composition and revision of religious plays, from the simple tropes to the technically complex "moralities." These men were not "original" artists; they did not create their own material, but drew upon the stories in the Bible, the legends of the saints, or the dogmas of the Church, which they adapted and dramatized.

For almost a thousand years after the death of Christ, His life story was repeated in the liturgy and in the ritual of all the churches in Christendom. One of the most dramatic stories in the world, it was told in Latin to people who understood no Latin and who knew very little about the Bible, since they could not read. It was the problem of the Church to present to the congregation vivid images to illustrate the story of Christ's birth, passion, and resurrection. The Church began to present spectacles in which action alone revealed the content. Three dramatic essentials—action, costume, and music—were adopted by the Church and the service became more ornate and theatrical. The Easter service and the Christmas service were the most elaborate. By the end of the ninth century, in an elementary form of dramatic dialogue, Latin words were fitted to the special music sung on the high festivals. These brief exchanges of speech, which were introduced into the chanted liturgy, were known as tropes, and the men who wrote them were the forerunners of the playwrights.

By processes of growth and elaboration, the simple dialogue and action of the tropes ultimately resulted in full-length and highly developed dramas. In their first stage, these were called mystery plays and were based mainly on the events set forth in the Old and New Testaments. By the twelfth century practically all of the Bible, from the creation of the World to the Day of Judgment, had been dramatized in well-developed one-act episodes, and the dialogue was no longer written in Latin but in English. The mysteries became enormously popular and attracted great and unruly crowds to the churches.

In response to a demand for greater realism came the miracle plays, a more advanced and more secular form of the drama, which not only dealt with the Scriptures but also presented stories from the lives of the saints. The dramas were embellished with apocryphal and extraneous material, most of which was coarse and farcical; Noah's wife was usually drunk and King Herod ranted and swore.

The great cycle of plays had become so worldly and corrupt by the fourteenth century that it was ordered out of the church, and control over the liturgical drama passed from the hands of the clergy to those of laymen. The plays were taken over by the craft and trade guilds, the most important organizations in the social and economic life of a medieval town, and changed from an indoor cere-monial rite to an outdoor show. Within the church, the plays had been presented at Christmas and Easter, but the cold, wet weather in England at these seasons was unfavorable for outdoor presentations; when they left the church, therefore, the plays were incorporated into the celebration of Corpus Christi Day, a street festival in honor of the Sacrament, in existence since 1316 and occurring yearly late in May or early in June. The miracle plays immediately became the most exciting part of the procession. Although no longer Church-sponsored, the plays were revised, adapted, and elaborated from year to year by ecclesiastical writers especially employed for the purpose. The number of men engaged in this task may be judged by the fact that every important university, cathedral, and market town in England had its own cycle of plays, though only four cycles have come down to us: the York cycle of 48 plays, the Wakefield or Towneley cycle of 32 plays, the Chester cycle of 25 plays, and the Coventry cycle of 42 plays. Usually the cycle was played in one day, from sunrise to sundown, but in some towns the pageants took from three days to a full week. At Chester, they were performed on the Monday, Tuesday, and Wednesday of Whitsun week.

The final development of religious drama was the morality play, which ap-peared about the middle of the fourteenth century. The moralities were more original in invention and more complex in structure than the mystery or miracle plays; their plots were not drawn from Scripture but from well-known allegorical tales, and their characters were personifications of such abstract ideas as Wealth, Lust, and Faith. Virtue and Vice were repeatedly shown struggling for possession of Man's soul. The morality play attempted to furnish answers to the question, "What must I do—what must I believe—to be saved?" In its later development this type of play became dull, narrow, and essentially sectarian, its didacticism relieved only by the scenes of low humor; but the finest example of the morality play is a genuinely profound and moving drama called *Everyman*.

Some scholars believe that *Everyman* is a translation from a Dutch play called *Elckerlyc*, or that both plays have a common source in a Latin work called *Homulus*. It is more likely, however, judging from internal evidence and from the spirit of the piece, that the play is of English origin. It may have been written around 1475 in the reign of Edward IV.

Although we do not know the name of the play's author or a single biographical fact concerning him, it is safe to say that *Everyman* is the work of a priest or theologian. Everyman, for example, puts on the jewel of penance, later wears the robe of contrition, and then takes the seven "blessed sacraments," including "holy and extreme unction." In the final scene of the play, Everyman, holding a small wooden cross, asks his companions to touch the "rodde"; in this symbolic gesture, the various personages who are the abstract concepts of Everyman's own potentialities—his strength, discretion, five wits, beauty, knowledge, and good deeds—signify the full resignation of all the powers of body and soul in the acceptance of death according to God's will. The play is thus a graphic expression of Catholic doctrine relating to sin and contrition, confession, grace, and salvation.

The original source of the story of *Everyman* is the old Buddhist parable of Barlaam and Josaphat in which a man, ordered to appear before his king, applied for help to his three friends; but only one of them, who symbolized his virtue and whom he had always neglected, readily offered to accompany him and plead for him. Further details for the play were borrowed from a Scottish version of Barlaam, in which the virtuous friend was called Good Deeds. This name was particularly useful to the author of *Everyman*, for according to Catholic doctrine, good deeds—consisting chiefly of prayer, fasting, and almsgiving—are necessary to atone for evil and to obtain grace. The writer of *Everyman* also made use of ideas, themes, and actual expressions which had appeared in earlier moralities, *The Pride of Life, The Castle of Perseverance,* and *The Debate of the Body and the Soul,* and in various tales of Chaucer (*Pardoner's* and *Parson's,* for instance) which dealt with religious pilgrimages and repentance. But if this unknown playwright borrowed freely from earlier works, he also made great contributions to later morality plays as well as to the secular drama of the present day.

Everyman has a very simple plot. The strength of the play lies in the skill with which the individual scenes are developed. Although it is an allegory, the story appears to concern itself with an ordinary journey. Death, sent by God, tells Everyman to prepare himself for a long pilgrimage; the language Death uses is poignant and Everyman is struck to the heart with terror. After Death departs, Everyman appeals to his friends (Fellowship), to his close and distant relatives (Kindred and Cousin), and to his worldly possessions (Goods), but they all desert him. Good Deeds alone will accompany him, and she introduces him to her sister, Knowledge, who leads him to Confession. Everyman is advised to surround himself with his most intimate friends, Discretion, Strength, Five Wits, and Beauty, and they remain close by until he approaches the very end of his journey; then one by one they leave him until, at the last, he is sustained by Good Deeds alone.

Although the author of *Everyman* depicts life in this world as a spiritual adventure, he makes this abstract concept convincingly concrete by introducing into his play human situations and vivid figures. By creating characters whose reasoning is psychologically sound and whose behavior is recognizably realistic, the author manages to engage the interest and sympathy of his audiences. Everyman, for instance, lonely and terrified in the face of death, is thoroughly understandable and moving; while the figures who surround him and display various human weaknesses, also evoke pathos and pity. Such characters are not arid personifications but possess genuine and fundamental attributes common to all of us.

The theme and structure of the play are superior to the poetry in which it is written, for the style and language are rugged and rather awkward. This irregularity and clumsiness of the outward form is a natural consequence of the conditions under which the morality was composed. It is evident that the playwright did not aim at producing a pleasing pastime, but rather an unwelcome warning; a dismal, but highly necessary, admonition. That *Everyman* was extremely popular, nevertheless, with early English audiences is attested to by the fact that four different editions of the play are extant. John Skot's edition, believed to have been published about 1530, is reprinted here with modernized spelling and punctuation.

By 1550 the force of religious drama had been spent. Many men who still had religious connections were making names for themselves by writing secular interludes and chronicle history plays. This was the beginning of the literary drama in England; shortly thereafter, the first tragedies and comedies, composed in imitation of ancient classical works, made their appearance and laid the groundwork for the masterpieces of the Elizabethan age.

PRODUCTION IN THE MIDDLE AGES

The decline of the Roman Empire brought with it the degradation of classical tragedy into pantomime, and of classical comedy into farce. The tragic actor became the *pantomimus* who danced out the story of a play to the accompaniment of music, and the comic actor put on vulgar displays for the delight of ignorant audiences. The Christian church preached vehemently against these coarse and sensuous exhibitions to which the multilingual and degraded population flocked; but more important than the opposition of the Church was the contempt of the barbarians of the later invasions. The Church and the barbarians between them dealt the theater in Rome a death blow from which it never recovered, and public entertainment ended with the fall of the Empire.

Between the sixth and the tenth century, wandering mimes, jugglers, and acrobats, who were looked upon as outcasts and vagabonds, roved from town to town and with their comic antics and tricks provided entertainment for the nobleman in his home and for idle crowds in the public squares, while the ancient theater buildings fell into decay. Buildings specially constructed for the performance of plays were not to make their appearance again until the Renaissance.

Paradoxically, it was the Christian church, the formidable adversary of the drama, that actually brought the theater to life again in the Middle Ages. In seeking a way to impress the lessons of the Scriptures more forcefully on the minds of unlettered people, the Church introduced the tropes into the liturgy. The growth and development of these scenes led, as we have seen, to the creation of the mystery, miracle, and morality plays. In mounting these plays effectively, the Church became as great a producing organization as any that had existed in classical times.

The Theater

By the end of the tenth century, the churches were serving as "theaters" during the Christmas and Easter holidays. For the Easter trope, the altar at first symbolized the tomb in which the body of Christ was laid, but not very long afterwards an actual sepulcher with a lid was built of wood or iron and was set up in the north aisle. If more than one locale was required, as for the Christmas drama, Herod's Court was placed in one aisle and the manger in another. This led to the convention of setting up all the scenes of action at one time before the audience. The platform or stalls where the action took place were called *mansions* or houses and these were arranged in regular places in the church. Heaven was usually in the vicinity of the high altar, and nearby were the mansions of the holy characters; while Hell, which served as the abode of the devils, was located at the opposite side of the church building and the houses of the damned were situated near it. The actors moved from station to station around the interior of the church as they presented their long cycle of plays which was a dramatization of the Bible from Creation to Doomsday.

When the drama left the precincts of the church and became part of the Corpus Christi Day procession, the long cycles were broken up into separate scenes, each of which became the property of one of the trade guilds of the town, the members of the guild being made responsible for its production. Some of the guilds chose to produce scenes which were particularly related to their trades; the shipwrights took over *The Building of the Ark*, the fishers and mariners *Noah and the Flood*, and the butchers *The Crucifixion*.

Since the plays were performed as part of a procession, the stationary stage, or *mansion*, was replaced by the pageant-wagon. This was a scaffold on wheels that could be dragged through the streets, something like our modern "floats," but two stories high; the lower story was curtained off and used as a dressing room, while the upper story, reached by a ladder, served as a stage. When the pageant-wagon stopped at the stations in the town where people had gathered to see the plays, the actors performed not only on the upper story of the wagon but descended to the street and used the open area (called the *platea*) in front of the wagon.

It is quite likely that the earliest Morality plays were presented in cyclic form, that is, in a series of scenes on moving pageant-wagons, but by the late fifteenth century, with the appearance of such full-length works as *The Castle of Perseverance* and *Everyman*, the method of production had changed radically. The full-fledged Morality was not performed by the members of a guild but by a troupe of traveling players at one time and at one place, probably the town square or village green. The plays were advertised in advance and audiences gathered at the appointed place on the day of the performance; this was standard practice for the roving acting companies but its major drawback was that the players had to pass the hat for contributions in order to stay in business. The solution to the problem lay in finding a nobleman who would subsidize the company, or an inn yard which could be rented and filled with people who were willing to pay the price of admission. These conditions of production actually came into use during the first half of the sixteenth century and served for the presentation of interludes and chronicle history plays. The inn yard, as we shall see, was the immediate precursor of the Elizabethan theater.

The Audience

It was not for an "audience" that the earliest medieval drama was written but for a church congregation. Very little mention is made of the first spectators since they probably preserved an attitude of silent and serious devotion as the tropes were being enacted. There are a few facts concerning them, however, of which we are quite certain: They were all members of the same religious faith; they represented, socially, a cross-section of the population from prince to peasant; they probably attended services in increasing numbers as a result of the pleasure they took in the literary and dramatic embellishments of the liturgy; and, finally, with the introduction of a great deal of secular material into the plays, their boisterousness and loss of reverence made their presence in the church undesirable.

The miracle plays, which were performed on pageant-wagons that were trundled through the public streets, attracted much more heterogeneous and unruly audiences. The people got up at about four in the morning on Corpus Christi Day and took their places at the city gate, on the village green, and at the various other stations in the town where the wagons were scheduled to stop. Some sat in convenient windows or on wooden "bleachers" erected for the occasion. People of all faiths, or of no faith, were attracted—nobles, clergy, merchants, craftsmen, peasants, and paupers, all joking and jostling, exchanging obscene remarks with the actors and giving vent to ribald laughter. The coarseness and blasphemy that had been kept under a modicum of restraint within the church went completely out of bounds in the market-place.

The audience which later attended the moralities was more subdued and intent, since the plays contained literary, ideological, and theatrical elements that were rather complex; and if admission fees were charged for these performances, the audience was still more select and restrained than the roving street crowds.

The sixteenth century brought an additional refinement of the audience, but even in the heyday of the Elizabethan drama playgoers were not in the habit of listening with rapt attention unless a particular character or scene captivated them. It was much more common practice for them to gape and to gossip and to stuff themselves with food while the play was going on. It was at this time, in fact, that the "private playhouses" were created for the ladies and gentlemen who were willing to pay extremely high prices in order to escape the "noisy rabble" that haunted the public theaters.

The Actors

The medieval actor was primarily an amateur; it was not until the last days of the fifteenth century that semiprofessional and professional acting troupes came into existence. The first "actors," of course, were the priests and minor canons in the churches who chanted the tropes in Latin. By the end of the tenth century they had received specific directions for the enactment of their parts from Bishop Ethelwold of Winchester, who wrote concerning the proper method of performing the *Quem Quaeritis:*

While the third lesson is being chanted, four brethren [of the church] shall costume themselves. One of these, dressed in an alb [a white linen robe], shall enter as though to take part in the service, and, stationing himself at the tomb [altar] without attracting attention, shall sit there quietly with a palm-branch in his hand. Then the other three shall approach dressed in copes [long, flowing garments], bearing in their hands censers with burning incense, and walking carefully as those who seek something, approach the tomb. When he who sits there beholds the three approach, he shall begin to sing in a soft, sweet voice, "Whom do you seek?" And when he has sung it to the end, the three shall reply in unison, "Jesus of Nazareth"; and he shall say, "He is not here . . ." And he shows them the place bare save for the linens from Christ's body . . . and they shall hold them up in the face of the clergy, as if to demonstrate that the Lord has risen and is no longer wrapped in them. They shall sing the anthem, "The Lord is Risen from the Tomb," and shall place the linens upon the altar. Then the priest, sharing their joy at the triumph of Christ over death, shall begin the hymn, "We praise Thee, O Lord," and this begun, all the bells chime out together.

Ethelwold became, in effect, one of our first play directors; and here we see him concerned with principles of staging and acting that have persisted to the present day. The Angel is to enter "without attracting attention," which modern directors would term "stealing" into place; the Three Marys are to pretend they are seeking something, which is the imitation of an action; the properties and costumes help to characterize the actors—the voluminous copes, for instance, heighten the illusion that the three priests, acting the Marys, are women; and, most significantly, there are specific directions for the interpretation, or "reading" of the lines, indicating the emotional and tonal qualities desired.

Since medieval drama was as international as the Church that sponsored it, the techniques of production varied only slightly from country to country. In the French mystery play *The Representation of Adam*, dating from the twelfth century, the text embodies explicit directions to the actor. It says:

Adam shall be trained well to speak at the right moment, so that he may come neither too soon nor too late. Not only he, but all shall be well practiced in speaking calmly, and making gestures appropriate to the things they say; they shall neither add nor omit any syllable of the meter; all shall express themselves in a distinct manner, and say in consecutive order all that is to be said.

And in *Herodes*, an English play of roughly the same period, the actor who was to assume the title role was expressly instructed to "tear a passion to tatters." The directions state:

Then let Herod, having seen the prophecy, kindled with rage, hurl the book to the floor; but let his son, hearing the tumult, advance to calm his father.

When, in the fourteenth century, control over the liturgical drama passed from the Church to the craft guilds, the priests began to withdraw as actors and the members of the guild took over as performers. The great care which the towns took in selecting players for their pageants and in providing beautiful, eye-filling productions was based less on their religious devotion than on their business acumen. The plays attracted great crowds to the towns, where local merchants were eager to receive them, and where high prices were charged for convenient places to view the performances. It was for this reason that the civic authorities involved themselves in the production of the plays; if a town was particularly generous in its treatment of players, people with acting talent would come to it from neighboring towns, from other cycle-towns, and from London. No expense was spared in entertaining the actors. The companies not only paid the actors for their services, but also kept them generously supplied with food and drink. Although the actors were expected to be letter perfect in their parts, a prompter was paid to hold the book and supply the lines when lapses occurred. The actors often rehearsed for weeks before the performance; if their memories failed too often, or they acted carelessly, both they and their companies were fined for the dishonor which they had brought on the town—they by their pageant-masters, and their companies by the town council.

The account-books of the guilds give us some idea of what the actors received for their services. A man who hanged Judas got only fourpence, but he received an additional fourpence for crowing like a cock when Peter denied his Lord; four Saved Souls were paid five shillings and four Damned Souls received an equal amount. A man who played God earned sixpence, while the actors who portrayed Noah and his wife received one shilling and sixpence between them; eleven years later, in 1494, God's salary was raised to tenpence and Noah and Mrs. Noah earned one shilling and eightpence.

The roles that the medieval actors were called upon to portray did not require "characterization" in the modern sense of the word, as the figures in the cycle plays were mainly one-dimensional and fell into one of three well-defined groups. First, there were the serious characters who won the audience's reverence or sympathy: God, Christ, Mary, Abraham and Isaac, the Good Angels, and the Saved Souls. In the second group were the characters who, mainly because of their opposition to Christ, aroused the hatred or scorn of the spectators; these included Judas, Herod, Annas and Caiaphas, and Pilate. The third group consisted of the supporting characters who might be good or evil, serious or comic, depending upon the purpose of the episode in which they appeared; among these were Mrs. Noah, Mak, the Soldiers at Christ's tomb, Lucifer, and a huge assortment of Devils.

The actors in the first group, who strove to evoke awe and respect, were rather restrained in their speech and in their body movements, since they usually expressed the quieter emotions of joy and hope, pity and pain. Those in the second group—the tyrants and the enemies of Christ—used voice, gesture, and grimace with unrestrained violence and passion, which accounts for the indelible impression they made upon the minds of the spectators, and for their enormous popularity. The actors in the third group were mostly comedians who keyed their performances to the taste of the illiterate street crowd; they specialized in knockabout farce seasoned with coarse jests and japes. The expert comic actor had the combined talents of the clown, the dancer, the juggler, and the acrobat, and when he represented a devil or an evil spirit he went to the most extreme lengths in leaping, shouting, and making hideous faces.

With the decline of religious feeling in the fourteenth and fifteenth centuries, people began to lose interest in the long cycle plays, and the guilds no longer found it profitable to support them. But the attraction of the drama still held, and a number of skilled players, aware of the opportunities in a new and uncrowded field, deserted their regular trades and became "strollers." By giving up their memberships in the craft guilds, the players entered the ranks of vagabonds and masterless men, subject to arrest and imprisonment; but that did not deter them from traveling about the country and practicing their art. Morality plays and interludes, which admitted more and more secular and comic elements as time went on, formed the stock in trade of the strolling players.

These companies performed on the village green, in town halls, and in the homes of members of the nobility; the acting troupe usually consisted of only four men and a boy, so that it was often necessary for each of the actors to fill two or three parts in the play. The strollers faced many other difficult conditions. In the first place, they had to work with very poor material; they themselves recognized that their plays were crude, but they did not have the ability to improve them. Then they had to drum up their own audiences; this meant riding around the countryside continually to announce the performances a week in advance of the dates on which they were to be given. Furthermore, since the contributions of the spectators were made on a voluntary basis, the livelihood of the players was extremely precarious. Actors had to resort to tricks and devices of many kinds in order to make audiences part with their money. The appearance of the comic devil, who was always a popular figure, was withheld, for example, until after the collection plate had been passed; and suggestive actions and coarse jokes became standard features of the performance.

Because their financial gains were so small and the manner in which they got them so unconventional, itinerant players found that their reputations were deteriorating rapidly and stringent statutes were being passed against them. These local laws severely hampered the activities of the strolling players. The more talented among them managed to escape from this difficult situation by putting themselves under the protection of important personages, for as "servants" of the great they could no longer be classed as vagabonds. Actors who wore the badges of noble houses could travel about without fear of being molested, and from the fifteenth century on we hear of strolling companies operating under this arrangement. It was not until the sixteenth century, however, when men like the Earl of Leicester and Lord Strange lent their names and their support to companies of players that the greatest troupes of the Elizabethan era developed. Inept and anonymous as he was, the strolling player formed an important link in the chain that led from the old mimes and minstrels to the masters of tragic and comic acting who appeared in the plays of Shakespeare.

Scenery and Lighting

The medieval stage did not lack scenery, but it was usually simple and inclined to be symbolic. The altar of the church originally stood as a symbol for the tomb of Christ; later a simple tomb of wood or iron was built. The various mansions or houses, that were set up inside the church for the dozen or so scenes of action required in the early liturgical plays must have been small and plainly furnished or the aisles could not have accommodated them.

Heaven, in the French mystery play of *Adam*, was to be decorated as follows: "Paradise shall be situated in a rather prominent place, and is to be hung all around with draperies and silk curtains to such a height that the persons who find themselves in Paradise are seen from their shoulders upward. There shall be seen sweet smelling flowers and foliage; there shall be different trees covered with fruit, so that the place may appear very agreeable."

If Heaven was most tasteful and attractive in its décor, Hell was most elaborate and terrifying; for Hell-mouth a great dark hole was necessary into which the capering devils dragged the sinners and from which huge billows of smoke issued forth along with the clash of pots and kettles and shouts of jubilation.

The scenery on the upper level of the pageant-wagon could not have been large or ornate because of the limited space; and yet fountains, arbors, and even clouds were constructed there. Even simultaneous staging was frequently practiced; if two scenes, a forest and a palace, for example, were required for a play, both would be indicated on the pageant-wagon at the same time. At one side of the stage, two trees would represent the forest; at the other side of the stage, a large gilded chair would represent the throne in the palace. The actor, having to make a journey from the forest to the palace, would leave his position near the trees, circle the stage several times, and come to a halt near the chair.

The setting for the Christ child in the manger, which should have been simple, was presented rather lavishly by the mercers of Chester, who decorated their pageant-wagon with yards of velvet, satin, and silk damask in various colors and of silk taffeta of parrot green.

The sets used for the morality plays, which were mounted in open fields or in town squares and which therefore had to be transportable, could not have been any more elaborate than those used on the pageant-wagons. Pageant-wagons, in fact, or two-story scaffolds which resembled them, might very well have served as the settings for *The Castle of Perseverance* and for *Everyman*. The manuscript of the former play merely calls for a castle and close to it a bed for Mankind; *Everyman*, too, could be adequately performed on a two-story scaffold with an open playing space around it. The open space, or *platea*, was an unlocalized stage, which means that it might represent any place. It might be neutral territory, or it might represent a very definite locality made clear to the audience by the words and actions of the characters. This convention of a clearly defined house with an unlocalized stage in front of it was carried over into the Elizabethan theater.

From all accounts, there was a notable absence of realism in the scenery, nor could there have been many realistic lighting effects, as the plays were presented outdoors in ordinary daylight. This made it necessary for the writers of the medieval period, as it did for the Elizabethans much later, to establish time and place by putting such information into the speeches of the actors. In the Towneley *Jacob,* the old patriarch announces:

> The sun is down, what is best?
> Here purpose I all night to rest;
> Under my head this stone shall lie;
> A night's rest take will I.

Special lighting effects, such as burning candles and flaming torches, as well as the more elaborate spectacle of houses or altars being consumed by fire, were much in use.

Costumes and Make-up

If the medieval actor received rather scant help from the scenery, he relied very heavily upon costumes, make-up, and properties to strengthen his characterization. But since the medieval man knew little and cared less about historical accuracy, theatrical costumes might be realistic, symbolic, or fantastic, with all three styles frequently used in a single play.

The priests who took part in the presentation of the tropes, even when representing secular figures, wore lavish church vestments known as albs and copes, and carried palm branches and censers in their hands. The manuscript of the play of *Adam* directs that "the Savior shall appear, robed in a dalmatica [an elaborate ecclesiastical garment]; Adam and Eve place themselves in front of him, Adam dressed in a red tunic, Eve in a white garment and white silk veil."

While the liturgical plays were put on under its sponsorship, the Church provided all costumes and properties; but after the plays were taken over by the trade guilds, the costumes and properties were generally made by guild members. Ecclesiastical gowns and utensils needed for certain scenes might be borrowed, rented, or bought from the Church. Since the aim of each pageant-master was to be ostentatious rather than correct, the productions, on the whole, were rich, gaudy, splendid, and anachronistic.

God was usually represented only by a voice, but when He did appear on stage it was with a gilded face and in a costume of white leather, possibly also gilded; one property list calls for "five sheep-skins for God's coat." Christ, too, was clothed in white leather to symbolize nakedness and purity. Adam and Eve, the only other characters one might expect to see unclothed, apparently wore costumes of some sort. In the property list of the Norwich grocers' *Creation of Eve,* we find "a red rib, a tail for the Serpent, two coats and a pair of dyed stockings for Eve, a coat and dyed stockings for Adam, and two wigs for Adam and Eve."

The Saints and Prophets were generally dressed in church vestments—dalmatics and stoles. Some were further individualized by special costumes and properties: John the Baptist wore a shaggy cloak, had long hair and a beard, and carried a palm-branch; Moses held the Tables of the Law; and Balaam plied his spurs to the ass (made of wood or canvas) upon which he rode.

The "villains" were dressed with equal care, their costumes very often being more intricate and more interesting than those of the holier characters. Herod was an extremely ostentatious figure, who frequently wore armor and a sword. Judas traditionally appeared in a red wig and a red beard. Lucifer as the "angel bright" was dressed in white and gold, but after his fall he became a "devil full dark" and appeared in black. Similarly, the Good Angels and the Saved Souls wore white, while their evil counterparts wore black.

Symbolic and fantastic costumes persisted down to the sixteenth century and were much in evidence in the morality plays. In *The Castle of Perseverance,* the four daughters of God wore cloaks whose colors had symbolic significance: Mercy appeared in white, Righteousness in red, Truth in green, and Peace in black.

The costumes of the devils, particularly of the Vice, or comic devil, were extravagantly fantastic and specially designed, with grotesque animal heads and bodies, to frighten and impress the spectators. A stage property particularly characteristic of the devil, and one of which he made frequent use, was gunpowder—possibly because it suggested fire and brimstone. An extremely interesting description of a performance put on by devils states: "These devils were all clad in skins of wolves, calves, and rams, surmounted with sheep-heads, bullhorns, and cockscombs, with girdles of thick skins, from which hung cows' or mules' bells with horrible noise. Some carried in their hands black rods full of squibs [firecrackers]; others long flaming spars, on which at each turn they threw handfuls of powdered resinous pitch from which issued terrible flame and smoke."

The figure of Death in *Everyman* was made up to look like a skeleton and carried a scythe, or a six-foot length of board to symbolize a coffin.

Such startling and spectacular effects help to account for the popularity of the medieval theater.

Music and Dance

The medieval drama grew out of, and was always closely associated with, music. The chanted liturgy gave birth to the trope and the trope itself was chanted. As the mystery and miracle plays developed, the singing of the church choir supplied background accompaniment to the dramatic action.

There was a general hostility toward the practical use of musical instruments in the medieval Church, perhaps because they had been used by minstrels for many centuries to accompany romantic and bawdy songs; but once the drama left its religious confines, it drew many minstrels and musicians into its own orbit.

The trade guilds hired expert instrumentalists as well as the best available actors to enliven their productions. The musicians supplied background music for the plays; their tones were soft and sweet for certain dramatic moments, loud and furious for others. Music was even introduced on occasions which we would consider most inappropriate for it; for the scene depicting Christ disputing with the doctors in the temple, for example, the Chester smiths were advised to "get minstrels with pipes, tabors, and flutes" to accompany the action.

In addition to instrumental music, there was a great deal of singing, both accompanied and unaccompanied, in the cycle plays. Many of them end with the characters or with a chorus of angels intoning the *Te Deum*. In the Coventry play, *The Magi, Herod, and the Slaughter of the Innocents*, three songs are sung; one of them is a touching lullaby addressed by a chorus of women to their infants in arms.

Music played an even more important part in the productions of the strolling players. To begin with, it was necessary for the strollers to send banner-bearers ahead of the company to announce the plays, present their authority for performing them, and ask that the audience gather on time and create no disturbance. These "advance men" undoubtedly entered the various towns sounding their pipes and drums in order to attract crowds to whom they could make their announcements. Then songs, dances, and incidental music were introduced into the performances not only to heighten the theatrical effectiveness of the dramatic action but for the sheer entertainment of the pleasure-seeking audiences.

The musical element certainly became more pronounced as the plays turned from religious to secular subjects. The musical instruments most commonly used to accompany the speech, the songs, and the dances in medieval drama were lutes, psalteries, viols, trumpets, horns, flutes, pipes, drums, and bells. Music became so integral a part of theatrical production that when the first regular theater was built in 1576 a Music Room was provided for the men who supplied the musical accompaniment for the Elizabethan drama.

THE PRODUCTION RECORD

Everyman was originally produced during the second half of the fifteenth century and was performed with fair regularity for about seventy-five years by semiprofessional and professional acting companies. Although the play was known in Holland as well as in England, no production records regarding it survive from that period in either country.

After a lapse of about four hundred years, William Poel, the founder of the Elizabethan Stage Society, mounted the first modern production of the old morality play on July 7, 1901, in the Great Hall of the Charterhouse in London. Poel directed the play, designed the set and costumes, and, in the role of Death, gave a remarkable and grotesque study of the character; in later productions he took the part of God. The play was acted in strict accordance with the text; there were no cuts, alterations, or transpositions. Poel always insisted upon the rapid and clear speaking of the verse with varied emphasis. The scenery represented the interior of a medieval chapel, but the playing area remained bare. The costumes were copied from those worn by the figures in early-fifteenth-century

Flemish tapestries/ which suggests that Poel was among those who believed that the play was originally Dutch.

After its premiere, the play was repeated on the 13th and the 20th of July, 1901, in the Master's Court of the Charterhouse, in outdoor performances. For the next fifteen years, Poel mounted innumerable productions of the play in theaters, churches, college quadrangles, and public halls, indoors and out, in various sections of London. Many actors who were later to become famous appeared in these early productions; among them were Edith Wynne-Matthison, Charles Rann Kennedy, Lewis Casson, Robert Atkins, and Russell Thorndike. Early in the play's career, Philip Ben Greet, became associated with Poel as co-producer, director, and actor, and it was Ben Greet who brought *Everyman* to America.

In 1911 Max Reinhardt, the great German director, having seen Poel's production of the play, decided to mount his own version of *Everyman*. The script was revised and modernized by the poet and playwright Hugo von Hofmannsthal, and an original musical score was composed for the production by Einar Nilson. The premiere of *Jedermann*, as the play was called in German, took place on December 1 at the Zirkus Schumann in Berlin. Hofmannsthal removed from the old morality play a great deal of the religious ritual and dogma that emphasized Everyman's approaching death, and highlighted instead the protagonist's insatiable lust for life. An elaborate and spectacular banquet scene—involving singing, dancing, feasting, and lovemaking—became the central feature of the German production. The play was done in arena style in a huge old circus building, but Reinhardt had no trouble filling the house.

On March 10, 1913, *Everyman* was revived at the Children's Theatre, New York, by Liebler and Company for a run of twenty-four performances; many members of the cast—headed by Edith Wynne-Matthison and Charles Rann Kennedy—who had appeared in the original production of the play a dozen years before were still in it. The *New York Dramatic Mirror* for March 12 carried an interesting and detailed review, which said in part:

> *Everyman* today is not a warning—it is pathos. We don't derive moral lessons from it at all; we simply are made to feel a certain esthetic sorrow in the spectacle of a healthy, cheerful soul sinking into the grave. Probably when the play was performed before Shakespeare's day, it was taken literally. The mood at the end of the play was one of exaltation—Everyman sat at the right hand of God, the angels rejoiced and were glad; all was well with this world and the next. Nowadays the mood at the end of the play is one of poignant depression. And why? Simply that we are skeptical. . . . We are all of us more or less scientific heathens. . . . We are somewhat at a loss to understand the sacrifice of all wordly things when, after all, the world is everything we have. *Everyman* exalts those who have not lost faith in the soul, and that is why it depressed us.
>
> This mood of poignant sorrow was reinforced by the exquisitely beautiful pathos of Edith Wynne-Matthison's acting in the leading role. When Fellowship deserted her in the journey to the valley of the shadow of death, a very extraordinary thing happened. Real tears welled from her eyes and rolled unchecked down her cheeks. As she walked through the audience in her final pilgrimage to the tomb, with the thin cross held high, a pure white robe lending her the sanctity of those who have per-

formed penance, her tear-stained eyes turned upward and a kind of wistful agony of longing written in her countenance, a rush of tenderness went through the audience like a great communal sigh. One forgot the mellifluous beauty of her voice, almost as one entranced. It was an emotional experience rarely obtained these days in the theater.

After its premiere in 1911, the Reinhardt production of *Jedermann* was done several times in various German-speaking cities. When the Salzburg Festival was inaugurated in 1920, Reinhardt was granted permission by the Austrian Archbishop to set up a platform in front of the Salzburg Cathedral and there to mount his version of the old morality. Temporary bleachers were erected for the audience in the cathedral square and the conditions of a medieval performance were simulated. The simple platform of raw boards on which the actors performed was backed up by the magnificent façade of the great Cathedral and beyond it the spectators, by raising their eyes, could see the peaks of the mountains which surround the city and a medieval fortress outlined against the sky. *Jedermann* was played for the first time at Salzburg on August 22, 1920, and—performed only on Sunday afternoons and special holidays—was repeated four times that season. Reinhardt assembled a brilliant company for the original production: Alexander Moissi was seen as Everyman, Frieda Richard as his Mother, Wilhelm Dieterle as Fellowship, Johanna Terwin as the Courtesan (a character created by Hofmannsthal), Heinrich George as Mammon, Helene Thimig as Good Deeds, Hedwig Bleibtreu as Faith, and Werner Krauss as both Death and the Devil. *Jedermann* immediately became the core and main attraction of the Festival, and drew spectators from all over the world. The play was repeated every year until 1937, when the Nazis forbade its production; performances were resumed, however, in 1946, with Helene Thimig, Reinhardt's widow, in charge. In 1951, Ernst Lothar, who had worked with Reinhardt, took over the directorial chores and made a number of minor alterations in the text, adapting the play "to the needs of the present time by deepening the social approach in amplifying the scenes involving the Poor Neighbor, the Beggar, and Mammon." Although the cast and the costumes have been changed many times since 1920, Reinhardt's concept remains essentially unaltered; the play has been performed about two hundred times in the last forty years.

In 1927 Max Reinhardt decided to bring several of his greatest successes—*Jedermann* among them—to America. The play was presented in German and was produced in association with Gilbert Miller at the Century Theatre, New York, on December 7, for a two-week run. The original musical score of Einar Nilson was used, with the composer conducting, and the brightest stars in the Reinhardt galaxy were present; in the cast were Alexander Moissi, Hans Thimig, Hermann Thimig, Vladimir Sokoloff, Harald Kreutzberg, Tilly Losch, Arnold Korff, and Lili Darvas. Commenting on Reinhardt's treatment of *Jedermann*, Alexander Woollcott, the drama critic for the *New York World*, wrote:

> His matchless resources as a showman, turned loose in a cavernous playhouse, were poured forth without stint for this sumptuous revival. The dread spectral voices that summon the dying Everyman to take up his staff for his last journey seemed to come

out of infinite space. Then choirs invisible invoked the mood for this universal admonition and muted drums, cymbals, and trumpets in some high, unseen loft awakened the panic in the dying man's heart. Great shafts of light curtained the stage with their contrasted darkness when the Voice of the Lord must send the fearful Messenger on earth, a wrathful Voice speaking out of a very tempest of shuddering drums. All these aids did Reinhardt have to enlarge the old play—these and the extraordinary Moissi. . . . I would like to say that his performance last night in the title role of *Jedermann* while it accented sharply some of his shortcomings, only deepened my conviction that here is one of the really great actors of the world's theater. It is quite true that he cannot obey the rhythm of some music outside himself, and his half-hearted little efforts to dance or even to skip in time to the "frolicsome fiddles" was painful to watch. But Moissi is an actor drawn to the scale of a Greek theater. His glorious voice, which can lift the roof of a little shack like the Century apparently without effort, can also fill it with a whisper, and . . . it can be charged at will with a dramatic quality that fills a play with hush and wonder. Then his face is one of the great tragic masks for which the poets write. And finally, in such scenes of dawning fear as those in which the reveling Everyman first hears the ghostly summons from on high, he seems suddenly able to invoke all those powers which make for that great acting of which the gaffers tell in the corner of the hearth at night.

An organization of Roman Catholic girls, known as the Grail, gave an unusual performance of *Everyman* on Sunday, October 29, 1933, at the Royal Albert Hall, London. The various roles were played by groups of girls rather than by individual actors; Everyman, for instance, was played by six girls speaking in unison; Death by a much larger number; Fellowship by thirty; and so on throughout the cast, with the one exception that the Voice of the Lord was heard through loudspeakers. "The choral speaking had a tendency to slow down the play," according to C. B. Mortlock, of the London *Daily Telegraph,* "but there was great beauty and emotional appeal in the liturgical chants which were interpolated, while the ancient plainsong was sung by an angelic choir raised in tiers above the platform-stage where prayer, hope, fear, contemplation were all rhythmically expressed. The beauty of the dresses and the skillful lighting, combined with the perfectly drilled movements of the dancers, went a long way to justify the idea behind this form of representation."

Under the title of *La Leggenda di Ognuno,* an Italian translation of Hofmannsthal's *Jedermann* was magnificently produced in Rome in August, 1944, by the Centro Cattolico Teatrale. The play was presented out of doors in the courtyard of the Sapienza, the historic University of Rome. The title role was played by one of Italy's greatest actors, Ruggero Ruggeri. An American critic who was present wrote of the actor: "He is a man in his sixties, with a profile that you might see on an ancient Roman coin, but his personality is still vibrant. Ruggeri has an amazingly flexible voice, and he is not afraid to use it like a musical instrument."

On Sunday, August 1, 1954, The Catholic Hour, NBC-TV, sponsored Helene Oosthoek, a Dutch actress, in a one-woman performance of *Everyman*. The various characters were represented by large masks held aloft by the actress;

sometimes the masks covered her face, sometimes they were allowed to stand alone against a black backdrop merely suggesting a character as the actress supplied the voice. For the television presentation, Mrs. Oosthoek's seventy-minute stage version of the play was cut to a half hour, which detracted from its meaning. It was actually a tour de force, interesting only as an experiment.

Many revivals of the medieval Dutch morality play called *Elckerlyc* (*c.* 1477), which is thought by some to be the source of the English *Everyman*, were presented in repertory theaters throughout Holland both before and after World War II; but now every summer since 1950, as its contribution to the annual Holland Festival, the Nederlandse Comedie, the most important theatrical company in the country, has mounted the play in the city of Delft, under conditions approximating those of the original production and in a similar style. The play is performed outdoors in the courtyard of the Prinsenhof, the former palace of Prince William of Orange, an area filled with the fresh scent of many trees and shrubs; the nave of a Gothic cathedral serves as background for the action, and the actors, in simple costumes and outlined against the unpretentious red bricks of the building, speak the lines of the play just as they were written more than four hundred fifty years ago. No attempt has been made to modernize or "refine" the work by introducing new characters or incidents, and even a number of minor faults, among them some over-long speeches, have been allowed to remain; but the acting of Han Bentz van der Berg, the celebrated Dutch performer who impersonates Elckerlyc, is, in its freedom from mannerisms, profound and moving, while the direction of Johan de Meester preserves the simplicity and religious aura of the original allegory.

This Dutch production of *Everyman* has, in a sense, offered a challenge to the German one; perhaps that is why there was a complete "rejuvenation" of the Salzburg *Jedermann* in 1960. In addition to a new set and new costumes, a new conception of the old morality play attempted to bring the beauty, power, and truth of the work "closer to the needs of our day."

Producing Everyman
An Analysis by Raymond Williams

The essential elements for the performance of the play are a *platea,* or open playing space . . . although not necessarily circular; and in the center of it, a scaffold, two storeys high, with the lower "room" covered, and the higher open at the top—this scaffold is the "House of Salvation." The lower, covered room represents the grave; the higher is heaven. A ladder runs between the two storeys. The action begins from the scaffold, and ends on it; the intermediate action is mainly in the open playing space, where at least two other dramatic *sedes* [mansions]—for *Goods* and *Good Deeds*—are sited, probably directly opposite each other, and some yards in front of the scaffold. The audience will surround the playing-space on three sides.

The Messenger begins, speaking from the front of the *platea:*

> I pray you all give your audience
> And hear this matter with reverence,
> By figure a moral play . . .
> For ye shall hear, how our Heaven King
> Calleth Everyman to a general reckoning:
> Give audience, and hear what he doth say.

He is indicating the upper room of the scaffold, where God now appears:

> I perceive here in my majesty
> How that all creatures be to me unkind
> Living without dread in worldly prosperity:
> Of ghostly sight the people be so blind.

The whole of this speech turns on the repetition of *I perceive . . . I see;* it is God looking out from his high place and judging the sins of the world below. At last he summons Death, who comes up to him from the lower room. The figure of God is of course the traditional image—the white leather coat, and the masked head; the figure of Death is black, masked with a skull. God commands Death to fetch Everyman, and Death replies:

> Lord, I will in the world go run over all . . .

(he is indicating the *platea* and the audience below), and then:

> Lo, yonder I see Everyman walking . . .

(Everyman has entered the *platea,* and now Death goes down to the lower room again, and then emerges to confront Everyman):

> Everyman, stand still; whither art thou going
> Thus gaily?

The pattern, and the immediate dramatic effect, of this action (reinforced by the physical creation of Heaven, the Grave and the World—the upper and lower rooms and the *platea*) is intense and clear. Everyman is confronted by death:

> O Death, thou comest when I had thee least in mind.

As Death convinces him that the summons is inescapable, he looks up to the higher room of the scaffold, where his eyes have not previously been directed; he addresses God, who is seated there, looking down:

> O gracious God, in the high seat celestial,
> Have mercy on me in this most need.
> Shall I have no company from this vale terrestrial
> Of mine acquaintance that way me to lead?

If the play is read, without consideration of the conditions of performance, a speech of this kind (like the previous speeches of God and Death) may appear to be an abstract appeal, with no realizable dramatic relation. It is written, however, for the actual dramatic realization we have described; the physical design corresponds exactly to the design of the verbal pattern. This may be seen throughout the play.

Death now leaves Everyman
>   —And now out of thy sight I will me hie

—and returns to the covered lower room. Everyman is alone in the *platea:*

>   Now have I no manner of company
>   To help me in my journey.

He turns, and looks for support. In turn now he summons aid, and is rejected:

>   . . . Fellowship . . .
>   I see him yonder, certainly;
>   Where be ye now, my friends and kinsmen?
>   My Cousin, will you not with me go?

In turn, these enter and speak with him, in the *platea,* but all go back towards the world, and away from the house of death and salvation. Everyman, again alone, turns to his Goods (the character of *Goods,* encumbered as he describes, is already lying at his place):

>   Where art thou, my Goods and riches?

>   Who calleth me? Everyman? what haste thou hast!
>   I lie here in corners, trussed and piled so high,
>   And in chests I am locked so fast
>   Also sacked in bags, thou mayest see with thine eye,
>   I cannot stir.

There is no one to walk with Everyman here. And the same is true when he turns in the opposite way, and calls on his Good-Deeds:

>   My Good-Deeds, where be you?
>   Here I lie cold in the ground;
>   Thy sins hath me sore bound,
>   That I cannot stir.

It is, I think, very remarkable, this physical, and wholly dramatic, expression of this crisis of the soul. Fellowship and Kindred can walk, but walk away, back towards the world; Goods and Good-Deeds, if for different reasons, cannot move at all, in this necessary journey. But now Knowledge, the sister of Good-Deeds, rises to accompany Everyman; it is knowledge, in these first encounters, that Everyman has gained:

>   Everyman, I will go with thee, and be thy guide,
>   In thy most need to go by thy side.

And they go together in search of Confession, who dwells

> In the house of salvation:
> We shall find him in that place.

They approach the lower room, and the character of Confession emerges from it, standing as it were at the edge of death and of salvation:

> Lo, this is Confession; kneel down and ask mercy.

Everyman kneels, and is given penance. He then prays to his God above—

> O eternal God, O heavenly figure.

Knowledge stands beside him, the means of his redemption. And now Everyman rises, and receives from Knowledge

> the scourge of penance

(this is not a figure, but an actual scourge:

> Everyman . . .
> *Thus* I bequeath you in the hands of our Savior,
> *Thus* may you make your reckoning sure).

The same dramatic process is then repeated, for as Everyman accepts penance, Good-Deeds, who had formerly lain "cold in the ground"

> . . . can walk and go
> . . . delivered of my sickness and woe.

Good-Deeds rises and comes to stand also beside Everyman:

> *Knowledge:* Now is your Good-Deeds whole and sound
> Going upright upon the ground.

Everyman, below the House of Salvation, has now both Knowledge and Good-Deeds at his side. And as Knowledge had given him the scourge of penance, so now Good-Deeds gives him

> a garment of sorrow
> From pain it will you borrow;
> Contrition it is,
> That getteth forgiveness.

He is told to "put on this garment . . . which is wet with your tears," and does so:

> For now have I on true contrition.

In his new condition, he is advised to summon his particular friends—Discretion, Strength, Beauty and Five-wits. He calls them, and they come out across the *platea* and gather around him, to support him in his pilgrimage. He is advised by Knowledge to seek a priest to receive the sacrament, and he goes to do this, while the others wait for his return. (It is probable that Everyman goes at this time to another "fixed point," rather than again to the House of Salvation. He may even go right out of sight of the audience, and then return, for the giving of the sacrament is not represented. And when he returns:

Five-wits: Peace, for yonder I see Everyman come,
     Which hath made true satisfaction.
Good-Deeds: Methinketh it is he indeed.

This is clearly an approach from some distance, and Everyman has certainly been out of sight. The reason against his entering the covered lower room of the House of Salvation becomes apparent in the next scene.)

  When Everyman is back, with all his qualities grouped around, and still wearing the garment of contrition, he enters at last upon his final journey. With the group supporting him, and each setting his hand upon the cross which Everyman now carries, he moves towards the House of Salvation, and approaches the covered lower room in which is Death:

    Alas! I am so faint I may not stand,
    My limbs under me do fold;
    Friends, let us not turn again to this land

(he indicates the whole playing-space and the audience behind him)

    Not for all the world's gold.
    For into this cave must I creep

(he indicates the covered lower room)

    And turn to the earth and there to sleep.

But now, at this last stage of the journey, Beauty leaves him—

    I take my cap in my lap and am gone;

Strength leaves him—

    I will hie me from thee fast;

Discretion leaves him—

    When Strength goeth before
    I follow after evermore;

Five-wits leaves him—

    I will follow the other, for here I thee forsake.

Even Knowledge will finally forsake him—

    But not yet for no manner of danger . . .
    Till I see where ye shall be come.

Only Good-Deeds will go with him all the way:

> All fleeth save Good-Deeds, and that am I . . .
> Fear not, I will speak for thee . . .
> Let us go and never come again.

And Everyman, below the House of Salvation, lifts up his hands to God:

> Into thy hands, Lord, my soul I commend.

With Good-Deeds beside him, he enters the "cave" of Death—the covered lower room—and disappears. Knowledge is left in view, and turns to the audience:

> Now hath he suffered that we all shall endure.
> The Good Deeds shall make all sure.
> Now hath he made ending.
> Methinketh that I hear angels sing
> And make great joy and melody
> Where Everyman's soul received shall be.

The action returns now to the upper room where it began. There is a song of angels, and an angel appears, high on the upper room, looking down into the "cave of Death";

> Come, excellent elect spouse to Jesu:
> Hereabove thou shalt go.

And so Everyman, having passed through Death, comes out at last into the presence of his God, in the upper room of the House of Salvation:

> Unto the which

(adds the angel, as he appears, and speaking out now to the whole audience)

> all ye shall come
> That liveth well before the day of doom.

The climax is reached, and the Doctor ends the play with a committal:

> Unto which place God bring us all thither
> That we may live body and soul together.
> Thereto help the Trinity,
> Amen, say ye, for sainte Charity.

It seems to me, as one follows from the text the detailed performance of this play, that one finds in *Everyman* not only a masterpiece of literature (as which it has been often praised), but a masterpiece of *dramatic* literature. All the elements of drama—speech, movement and design—concentrate into a single pattern. The dramatic imagination of the "abstractions" is such as to make absurd the complaint that the morality play is predramatic, because it uses types rather than individuals. The fact is, surely, that a deeply compelling feeling, at once individual and universal, has been realized in a fully dramatic pattern, where speech, action, and design are one. Examples have already been given, but I would emphasize again the conception of Good-Deeds, at first "lying cold in the ground," and then, after Everyman's confession, able to walk and support him; and, in the matter of design, the compelling beauty of the final movement through the dark "cave" of Death into the revealed glory of salvation. This is physically enacted, and not merely reported; and the same is true of the whole moral pattern, which, as I have tried to show, is not, as drama, in any way abstract, but is wholly and vitally present and actual. The approach to a play like *Everyman* is not, in fact, the examination of a specimen of a primitive dramatic mode; but, rather, the recognition of an absolute dramatic achievement.

ACTING THE PART OF JEDERMANN
An Interview with Will Quadflieg

Will Quadflieg, one of the stars of the German theater, a handsome and vital man, has been playing the title role of Jedermann since 1951. When Quadflieg took over the part, he realized that he was carrying on an important tradition at the Salzburg Festival; Alexander Moissi, who created the role for Reinhardt, had achieved world-wide fame as Everyman, and, after the Second World War, Attila Hörbiger also won acclaim for his performance.

In 1951 Quadflieg was thirty-six years old and a matinee idol; he confesses today that he suffered then from the same weaknesses of character that beset Everyman—an extravagant love of life, and an excessive earthiness, materialism, and superficiality. For that first season, Quadflieg went through five weeks of intensive rehearsal under the direction of Ernst Lothar, but lacking a perspective on the character he was portraying, his performances left a great deal to be desired.

Now that he is ten years older, has suffered many profound and enlightening experiences, has an entirely different outlook on life, has studied the character of Everyman more seriously, and has enacted it more than fifty times, he feels that he has made the role his own. He now comes to Salzburg for only the last week of rehearsals, but the continuing development of his own personality has enabled him to enrich his performance to a greater degree every summer.

"Time passes mercilessly," says Quadflieg, "and it becomes a conscious and poignant experience when the members of the company greet each other each year. Many a colleague who had been playing with us for years has passed away, and now another dresses in his costume and speaks his words. We ourselves, those who go on playing, have changed and developed. It rarely happens in the life of an actor that every year he is able to shape the same role anew with unbroken continuity, and let his own inner and outer maturation flow into the formation of the character. The main point, however, is to find a new approach each time the part is played. My basic concept is that Everyman has been completely seduced by the good things of the world—food, women, clothes, and all sensual pleasures—and is too unmindful of the life of the spirit. That is the impression I try to create as forcefully as I can. Obviously, this idea never occurred to me when I myself resembled Everyman, but as I've grown older and more mature, I've also become more objective and am now able, paradoxically, to portray Everyman's weaknesses not only with greater understanding but with greater abandon and verisimilitude. There is a little chapel not far from the cathedral square where the figure of Christ on the Cross writhes in intense suffering; I go there often to study it because this religious work seems to me to have the same meaning as the play; at any rate, both point the way to Man's redemption."

From a technical point of view, says Quadflieg, performing on an outdoor stage presents special difficulties for the actor. He is not assisted by lighting, scenery, or any of the other productional advantages of an indoor theater. The actor never feels so alone and so completely thrown upon his own resources as when he plays out-of-doors. "You are the loneliest man in the world," says Quadflieg, "because all of your power and skill must come from within."

The first problem is that of controlling the audience's concentration and attention; getting close to the audience is most difficult when the sun is shining and the wind is blowing. The actor's only solution is to develop his powers of projection. Then there is the problem of the language barrier; Jedermann speaks German while at least half the audience has no knowledge of the language. To reach people who do not understand what is being said, the actor must be in command of a rich "vocabulary" of gesture, miming, facial expression, and vocal variety. "The object," Quadflieg believes, "is to find the religious ecstasy in the role, sometimes attained only for seconds, but if it can be found the audience can be reached. In this connection, 'breath' and 'spirit' are very closely related; if the actor has great reserves of breath an impression of 'breadth' of spirit is communicated to the audience. But the task of the actor is more difficult today than it was when *Jedermann* was first performed, because the world is certainly 'colder' and more lacking in faith. It cannot be denied that when Alexander Moissi spoke the Lord's Prayer for the first time the emotional and spiritual conditions were essentially different from those of the present. Now it almost verges on the blasphemous to utter the Lord's Prayer in the presence of a crowd of people that has flocked together from every corner of the globe to 'take the show in' with their cameras instead of with their hearts, so that it is absolutely incumbent upon the actor to make the audience believe that the prayer issues from the distress, the anxiety, the sweat, and the tears of a lost soul. The basic facts and truths of life remain the same, but searching, erring man, enslaved by matter, is, today, more than ever, in need of insight, of self-realization, and of mercy."

Quadflieg is of the opinion that in playing Everyman he is acting in the great tradition not only of those who went before him in this particular role but of all the actors of the Greek and medieval theaters who performed out-of-doors before large groups of people in plays of religious significance. That is the "great world theater." In such a theater modern techniques of acting are useless. The object is to combine the ancient form of acting with the modern world of nerves; instead of psychological introspection, the actor must work for physical projection —instead of cultivating his sensitivity, he must develop his throat, chest, and

(Above) The theater at Epidaurus, Greece, dating from the fourth century B.C. Used today as it was in ancient times, the theater seats about 14,000 people. Performances in antiquity, we are told, ran from sunrise to sunset. *(Right) The Revenge of Medea*, depicted on an early fourth-century B.C. vase from Canosa, Italy, now in Munich. In this version, later than Euripides', the princess' death was reported to the audience by a messenger. Medea escaped in a dragon-drawn chariot that was moved by "the machine." From A. Furtwängler and K. Reichhold, *Griechische Vasenmalerei* (1904-1909).

Three centuries of *Medea.* *(Above left)* An eighteenth-century production. Mlle Clairon played Medea in contemporary dress; Lekain, as Jason, wore the costume *à la Romaine.* *(Above right)* A nineteenth-century English production with Mrs. Siddons. No attempt was made to authenticate scenery or costumes. *(Below)* A twentieth-century German production. The scenery and costumes were theatricalistic and symbolic.

Two American versions of *Medea*. *(Above)* A ballet version, choreographed by Birgit Cullberg for the New York City ballet. The music is by Béla Bartók. The dancers are Violette Verdy, Jacques d'Amboise, and Melissa Hayden. *(Below)* The Robert Whitehead production of Robinson Jeffers' adaptation. Judith Anderson is seated on the palace steps at Gielgud's feet. The entire play was performed in front of this primitive façade.

(*Above*) The medieval pageant-wagon. The engraving was based on contemporary descriptions. The wagons were wheeled into town squares for the performances, and the audience crowded around them. (*Below*) William Poel's production of *Everyman* in 1901. Edith Wynne-Matthison, as Everyman, wore a Flemish costume. Death's symbolic costume was based on the woodcut at right.

Everyman and Death in a wo the frontispiece to John Skot tion of the play (*c.* 1530).

(Above) The Salzburg production of *Everyman*. In this scene Jedermann is entertaining his guests at a banquet only a moment before Death seizes him. The façade of the Cathedral is in the background. *(Below)* The Nederlandse Comedie production of *Elckerlyc* in Delft, Holland. Elckerlyc is shown surrounded by relatives and friends in this rather simple, religious version of *Everyman,* performed in front of the Prinsenhof.

(*Above*) Macbeth and Banquo meeting the "fairies or nymphs" on the heath. From a woodcut illustrating Holinshed's *Chronicles* (1587), the source of Shakespeare's play. (*Below*) The Globe Theater, London, where *Macbeth* had its première. At left is a contemporary engraving of the exterior. At right is a model of the interior, at Hofstra College, Hempstead, New York, as reconstructed by John Cranford Adams and Irwin Smith. Notice the absence of seats in the pit.

W. KILMER—J. C.

Macbeth in the eighteenth and nineteenth centuries. *(Above)* An eighteenth-century production, in an engraving from Nicholas Rowe's 1709 edition of Shakespeare. Garrick, like the actor here, wore small-clothes. *(Above right)* Mrs. Pritchard, Garrick's leading lady, carries the candle in the sleep-walking scene. Mrs. Siddons put the candle down. *(Below)* Charles Kean's 1853 production was noted for historical accuracy of costumes and scenery. The Ghost of Banquo appeared inside the column at left.

Two recent productions of *Macbeth*. *(Above)* The Negro theater unit of the WPA Federal Theater Project performed the play in New York City, in 1936. The witches' scenes were conceived as voodoo rituals. Note the reclining skeleton on the backdrop. *(Below)* The 1955 Stratford-on-Avon production. At left a sketch of Sir Laurence Olivier in the "nightshirt" costume for the porter's scene. At right, Vivien Leigh and Olivier.

belly, his physiological and psychic force and power. Although *Jedermann* is written in rhymed couplets, Quadflieg acts against the lines with rich humor and forceful realism, "because the main job is to seize the audience and take it with you at every moment."

Quadflieg defines acting as "a controlled trance"—a balance between the intellect and the emotions; it is reality governed by form and style. But the word "trance" is misleading if it suggests effortlessness, for the role of Everyman is so taxing that Quadflieg did not want to play it in 1959; he wanted a rest from it for a year, but he finally gave in to the director's entreaties. Here again there is a challenge for the actor, for no matter how tired or drained he feels, his performance must always be fresh and alive even if he is acting "with his blood." "I agreed to do it again," says Quadflieg, "because the Cathedral rises behind and above us like a protecting shield, and the old, grand architecture of the cathedral square—strong with its timeless and incomparable form—surrounds, sustains, and succors us."

THE FIGURE OF DEATH
An Interview with Ernst Deutsch

Ernst Deutsch, an actor on the German-speaking stage for over thirty-five years, who appeared in many of Reinhardt's outstanding productions, has been performing the role of Death in the Salzburg *Jedermann* for more than a decade. Although the role is not a long one, the actor has worked continually on the intricacies of its interpretation and as a result is able to create a powerful and terrifying impression. One of the gestures that he is called upon to make is, Deutsch believes, the most significant in the entire play. That gesture is made at the moment when Death stands face to face with Everyman who is carousing at a banquet and is oblivious of the fact that his last hour is at hand. Everyman speaks scornfully to Death. In reply, Death merely lifts his hand and places it over the heart of Everyman who collapses with an expression of pain and astonishment on his face. It is this gesture, as Deutsch sees it, that contains the quintessence not only of his characterization but also of the central theme of the play.

The part of Death has been called metaphorical and other-worldly and the actor is made up, therefore, in nonrealistic garb. His costume, like the one that William Poel designed for this character, is based on the medieval practice of representing Death as a skeleton. Deutsch's head is completely hidden by a mask that was actually molded from his own features and then painted to show hollow eyes and cheeks and a skull as bald as bone. The actor's body is covered by a tight-fitting black cotton tricot leotard on which are painted the white bones of a skeleton. Over the costume, Deutsch wears a full black cape with a tall, standing collar. Death envelops himself in the cape when he speaks to Everyman.

Death appears in only four scenes in the play. He is seen for the first time when the Lord summons him and orders him to go as a messenger in search of

Everyman. He seems, on this occasion, to rise up out of the earth, as he climbs the stairs behind the platform stage. After the Lord has dismissed him, Death returns the way he came. The "ascending" and "descending" of this figure symbolize his connection with the underworld.

Death's second appearance occurs during the banquet scene. Everyman leaves his seat and strolls off with the Courtesan; Death silently enters and takes Everyman's place at the table. None of the guests is aware of Death's presence; suddenly Everyman turns around, sees Death, and sinks down in a faint. Then Death disappears without having uttered a word. Hofmannsthal obviously borrowed this scene from Shakespeare's *Macbeth,* with Death and Everyman in the roles of Banquo's ghost and the King.

Everyman is sitting at the table, reveling with his companions, when Death enters for the third time. The black-robed figure rises directly behind the chair of Everyman and seems to tower above him (the actor has actually mounted an extra little platform that is invisible to the audience). Everyman asks, "And who's there behind me?" Death replies, "I was sent to thee . . . ," whereupon Everyman begins to laugh in ridicule at the unbidden guest. Death slowly raises his arm to its full length, reaches over Everyman's shoulder, and places his hand upon Everyman's heart. Everyman sinks down but does not die; then a conversation follows between Everyman and Death. Death advises the stricken man to use well the short time remaining to him and to be a good Christian, and then he departs.

Later in the play, at the very moment before Everyman rejects Mammon (his wealth), Death appears for the last time, looks deeply at Everyman, raises his arm in a beckoning gesture—as if to announce that it is time for Everyman to answer the Lord's summons—and then leaves without speaking a word.

From the point of view of the number of lines assigned him, Death has a negligible part in the play; and yet each appearance of this character is so fraught with meaning, and the moment at which his cold hand falls upon Everyman's heart is a symbol of such universal significance, that a chill grips the heart of every spectator and the actor becomes aware of the great importance of his role.

THE DEVIL
An Interview with Ernst Ginsberg

In his long career in the German theater, Ernst Ginsberg has played many devils ranging from the philosophical Mephistopheles to the farcical Titivillus. The Devil in *Everyman* is of the latter type; he is not Evil Incarnate, the great Demon of the World, but a medieval imp full of perverse humor. Ginsberg does not see this particular devil as a fallen angel who requires tragic representation but as a fiend who attempts to storm the citadel of Everyman's soul and fails. In his failure there is cause for laughter, which is not evoked by pure comedy but rather by viciousness and spite.

Ginsberg has worked out stylized movement and gesture; this devil is a great goat with a touch of Pan. The costume consists of medieval horns, tail, fur, claws, and cloven hoof; and the face of the actor is hidden by a mask of make-up which is predominantly green and yellow.

Ginsberg has been playing the Devil in *Jedermann* at Salzburg for four years. When asked if he objected to being concealed completely in an ugly and repulsive costume, this celebrated performer replied that he did not enter the profession of acting in order to exhibit his own private feelings but that his aim was to change his identity with each character he was called upon to portray.

Ginsberg starts to dress for this part a full hour before the performance. He sits at his make-up table in his undershirt and the shaggy trousers of his costume, and stares into the mirror. Then with a small sponge he covers his entire face and neck with green cream; he dips his fingers into yellow cream and outlines the upper and lower lids of his eyes; again with his fingers, he adds a touch of white to the upper lids. He blinks his eyes rapidly so that the cream will set, and one gets the impression that they are not human but are the eyes of a parrot; that is what Ginsberg is trying for.

Using a fine brush and black cream, Ginsberg then increases the size of the nostrils by painting black arches above his own nostrils. The upper edge of the arch is outlined in yellow, a yellow stripe is drawn down the center of the nose from the bridge to the tip, and the tip itself is painted yellow.

The size of the mouth is also increased by the extension of its natural outlines with black cream; then the upper lip is painted black while the lower lip is painted a bright yellow. This gives the mouth a coarse, gross, and sensuous look. With a fine brush, black lines are drawn along the curved creases of the cheeks from nostrils to chin, like parentheses, emphasizing the nose and the mouth and making them stand out from the face. Suddenly the actor's countenance takes on the expression of Pan, sallow and lecherous.

Heavy black eyebrows are painted in with a brush, from the bridge of the nose up to the middle of the forehead, in curving lines which match the lines that curve down around the mouth; the crescent eyebrows are edged above and below with a fine line of yellow in order to highlight them and add further contrast to the face.

The actor is now ready to put on his wig. The hair of the wig is matted and unkempt and its color is a mottled brown and red; there are little bald spots on the scalp, the "flesh" of which is green. Short horns, attached to the wig, rise up pointedly from the ears like Pan's; the horns are pasted to the actor's ears with gum arabic to keep them erect.

Ginsberg next dons a fur jacket, which represents a "hairy body"; this jacket fastens in the back. Then with a sponge and green liquid, the neck and ears are covered and blended in with the facial make-up. Touches of yellow are added to the chin and a faint suggestion of red to the eyes and upper lip. Finishing touches are added to the rest of the makeup—a bit of black here, and green there. The nose becomes beaklike.

An ample cape, flame-colored, is fixed to the actor's shoulders; one edge of the cape has a rubber band that is fastened to the left wrist. Then the actor puts on furry gloves which turn his hands into paws with long claws. The edge of the sleeves of the jacket has loops of rubber tape which go over the middle finger of the hand to hold the cuff and glove together. The lower edge of the coat has shaggy tails of lamb's wool. The furry trousers, which the actor had put on before he started to make up, resemble the lower half of Pan's body—the right foot is furred like the rest of the torso, but the left foot has a large cloven hoof. From the seat of the trousers comes a tail which is almost ten feet long; the actor carries it over his right arm.

Ginsberg's costume and make-up combine to produce a grotesque and terrifying impression; in this pagan, forest-figure there is a defiance of social, sexual, and religious restraint.

THE MUSICAL PLOT
By Einar Nilson

Einar Nilson, a Swedish composer and conductor who was Reinhardt's musical director for more than twenty-five years, created the original score for *Jedermann*. The music first served for an arena-style production, then for a theater with a proscenium arch, and finally for the outdoor presentation at Salzburg, with only minor alterations in each case. Of his association with Reinhardt, Nilson wrote:

"Collaboration with Reinhardt is interesting to the musician, because new perspectives invariably unfold during rehearsals. The proximity of this producer to the essential values of music is an impression that persists and grows. He has drafted music into the service of the theater as no one else had done before him. Sometimes it actually seems that Reinhardt falls back on music whenever the other crafts of the theater prove powerless to gain an effect he desires. . . . Reinhardt frequently likes to place the musicians in costume in full view of the stage, so that these small orchestras become a part of the picture. . . .

"Reinhardt uses music not only as accompaniment, but also for another very important purpose: unification of the production. Music plays during the act intermissions and subdues the rumble of the machinery of the revolving stage. Large orchestras and choruses did not always prove sufficient, and so he installed an organ in the Deutsches Theater.

"In his production book, Reinhardt includes everything essential for the composer and conductor: the atmosphere of the scene, its duration, the quality of the music that appears desirable. Thus he invariably obtains just the music which will be best adapted to his scenic conceptions. . . . Reinhardt's fine feeling for the artistic expression of a period, either sends him back to the old music, or else he asks a composer to write music for him in the spirit of the particular period involved. Examples of the first method may be seen in his use of old French melodies for Molière and for the ballet. . . . The second method was tested in *Everyman*, which had music reminiscent of medieval melodies. . . .

"Here we enter upon a territory where Reinhardt has executed decisive reforms: the wide range of stage sounds and noises. No one before him had any idea of the significance of different sounds as aids to characteristic atmosphere on the stage. These sounds, which Reinhardt heard when he first read the play, are often very hard to reproduce and their materialization encounters technical difficulties. Reinhardt composes them as they rise and fall, mount to a climax and die away, just as you would write a symphony. Either they stand out alone as in *Macbeth*, where the night of the murder is suggested to our minds by a deep rolling sound produced by the organ, intermingled with the ghastly shrieks of the screech-owl. Or else they are combined with other means of expression. Thus the effectiveness of great mass scenes is enhanced by simultaneously striking and holding several deep tones on the organ which have but few vibrations. These sounds, especially when supported by the roll of the low-tuned kettle-drums, produce a prolonged noise resembling thunder, which seems to come directly from the masses on the stage.

"Especially in the Arena, whose vast dimensions demand something to fill them, Reinhardt uses musical sounds to the limit. The performances of . . . *Everyman* . . . are opened by trumpets, the sounding of gongs, and the ringing of bells. Where productions like these are not also accompanied by actual music, their atmosphere is effectively enhanced by sounds and noises from an orchestra with a complete outfit of percussion instruments, trombones, cymbals, triangles, muffled horns, basses and harmonium.

"The Arena, the 'theater of the five thousand,' requires music much more than any other form of the theater. Every aspect of it calls for music. The space itself with its colossal dimensions must never for a moment be left dead and dumb. The character of the scene, cold, immutable, monumental, can find nothing like ever-changing music to create the impression of detail and shading. The specific type of public in the Arena can be reached only by what is clear and of the most general import. How can that effect be attained better than by music? Also, the intrinsic nature of the play in the Arena, always that of a festival, calls for music.

"All forms of music are at home in the Arena: absolute orchestral and vocal music, as well as music which accompanies and interprets the action on the stage, either as rhythmic foundation for the chorus or as stage sounds. As Reinhardt's musical adviser for all his Arena performances, I have had an excellent opportunity to observe to what extent the dramatic and musical atmosphere can be influenced by the latter. It seems to me that Reinhardt has discovered here a source of new possibilities, which may be of great importance for the development and dramatic effect of theater music in the future.

"The principle involved is this: to render the atmosphere of a play not only through word, gesture, line and color, but also through sound, by laying musical stress on the voices of the masses and on sounds emanating from inanimate objects, by tuning them to each other and linking them to an inner harmony. In addition to accentuating through musical means such noises as the squeaking of a door on its hinges, the clatter of hoofs, the clash of arms, the roar of the sea— musical sounds can be used broadly to express the threatening growl of dissatisfied masses, or to intensify an atmosphere of awe, the source of which remains a mystery to the audience. What spectator realizes that the inexplicable, subdued trembling and vibration which he imagines he hears in his own awe-stricken soul while watching an inexorable tragedy, has been imposed on his imagination by the hautboy sounding its F sharp?

"In reality, all of these problems are nothing else than an attempt to intensify and simplify the effectiveness of dramatic expression—more so in the Arena than in the ordinary theater. And that is why every new performance in the Arena brings to the musician new problems and new solutions of problems."

An Interview with Carl Hudez

The present musical director for *Jedermann,* Carl Hudez, during the winter season conducts the orchestra of the Vienna State Opera. Hudez was born in Salzburg and began to play the violin at the age of six; he is a graduate of the Mozarteum. When *Jedermann* was performed in Salzburg for the first time in 1920, Hudez was sixteen years old and played in the violin section of the orchestra under the composer-conductor, Einar Nilson. Nilson was succeeded as conductor by Bernhard Paumgartner who introduced Hudez to Max Reinhardt.

From 1924 to 1938 Hudez served as musical conductor for the Reinhardt Theatre in Vienna, but with the coming of Hitler this theater was closed and Hudez became associated with the Vienna Volksoper. It was about 1930 when Hudez assumed the position of conductor of orchestra and chorus for *Jedermann* in Salzburg. He filled the post until 1938 when Hitler forbade the performance of this "Jewish" play. The production was suspended until 1946; then Helene Thimig, Reinhardt's widow, revived the play and recalled Hudez as musical conductor.

Bernhard Paumgartner created some funeral music that was interpolated into the score, used for a while, and then dropped; Joseph Messner, the organist of the Salzburg Cathedral, composed the music for the dances in the banquet scene, for the organ passages, and for the final chorus, and created the fanfares that are heard at the introduction and conclusion of the words of the Lord; but the major portion of the musical score, says Hudez, is performed as it was originally written by Nilson.

The orchestra is divided into two groups: the first group, which provides the music for the opening and closing of the play, consists of thirteen musicians—ten brasses, two tympani, and the organ; this group is invisible to the audience as it performs in the Cathedral behind the stage. The second group also consists of thirteen musicians—eight woodwinds (two flutes, two oboes, two clarinets, and two bassoons), one viola, two lutes, a little drum, and a triangle. This group, in addition to augmenting the first group for the opening and closing of the play, provides the background music for the Messenger's speech, and appears in costume on stage during the banquet scene, supplying the accompaniment to the songs and dances.

The mixed chorus of thirty voices of the Salzburg Broadcasting Studio performs under the direction of its regular conductor, Ernst Hinreiner; this group is stationed in the Cathedral.

The music is completely integrated with the dialogue and action, sometimes backing up the speeches of the actors and always supplying cues for the movement.

The beginning of the performance is announced by the sounding of four deep chimes which issue from one side of the cathedral square and call the audience to attention; then from the other side of the square five strokes are sounded in a different key and these signify the hour. Six angels appear high up on the parapets of the Cathedral, three on each side facing each other across the great open square. The Angels slowly raise their trumpets, blow a fanfare, and lower the trumpets to their sides; then in a chant they announce the performance.

Woodwinds introduce the Messenger who summarizes the theme of the play; the woodwinds punctuate his exit. Then trumpets and drums are heard and the Chorus singing in dramatic, intense crescendo; suddenly the Voice of the Lord, deep and serious, issues forth from the façade of the Cathedral; the Voice is sustained by the Chorus as of angels chanting. The Lord calls upon Death. To the sound of strange, exotic music produced by xylophones and triangles, the black-clad skeleton enters; his exit is later accompanied by the same music.

The Chorus and the first orchestral group swing into a stirring melody to herald Everyman's entrance; this is actually a repetition of the music used to introduce the Lord, differing only in tempo and volume.

After Everyman's appearance, the play proceeds without music until the banquet scene. The entrances of Fellowship and of Everyman's Mother, which immediately precede this scene, are, however, accompanied by a musical signature played by the second orchestral group; the same musical phrase is used for both characters. After Everyman's Mother departs, the second orchestral group, dressed in medieval costume, comes upon the scene and strikes up gay dance music; this announces the entrance of the Courtesan who hurries in with a crowd of little boys skipping behind her. The Courtesan's speeches are punctuated by music, mainly strings and triangles, and music is heard as the Courtesan crowns Everyman with a floral wreath. Then a chorus of men and girls enters to a gay, lilting tempo, and songs and dances are performed to a variety of melodies. The main dance tempo is that of the Ländler, the forerunner of the waltz, and is not strictly in keeping with the period of the play. As the Guests sit at table, their reveling is interspersed with songs unaccompanied by musical instruments, but when the Thin Cousin rises to entertain the company with a song he accompanies himself on a lute. The part of the Thin Cousin was played by Kurt Sowinetz, an accomplished vocalist, lutanist, and comedian connected with the Theater in the Josefstadt in Vienna. All the Guests sing together and behind their voices is heard the tolling of bells; the sound of the bells is inaudible to everyone except Everyman. He rises in terror. The Guests sing a round-song in his honor, but he pays no attention to it, for suddenly Voices are heard calling Everyman by name from various points in the cathedral square. The Guests, who are oblivious to the Voices, go on with their drinking and love-making. Two bells are sounded with the last Voice; then Fellowship enters.

The play proceeds without music through the scenes involving Death, Fellowship, the Thin and Fat Cousins, Mammon, and Good Deeds. With the entrance of Faith, which is close to the end of the play, organ music of a somber and holy nature is heard; and organ music also serves as a background when Everyman falls to his knees and says the Lord's Prayer. The cathedral bells peal out as Faith confronts the Devil, and Faith's final speech is backed up by organ music. The Chorus of Angels is then heard in rich and beautiful concert, the voices, accompanied by full orchestra, rising to a thrilling crescendo as the play comes to an end.

CHOREOGRAPHY
An Interview with Grete Wiesenthal

The original choreography for *Jedermann* was created by the internationally famous dancer, Harald Kreutzberg, but many alterations and additions were introduced into the work as time went on. In 1951 the dances and stage movement were redesigned by Grete Wiesenthal, and she has been in charge of the choreography since that time. Most of the original dance music has been retained, but it has been augmented by special music for a solo dance and for a group dance, both of which are performed during the banquet scene.

Twelve men and twelve women execute the dances, but only one girl, in the present company, has had professional training as a dancer; the others, who, as guests at the banquet, must sing, speak lines, and take part in the dramatic action as well as dance, are professional actors. Since the performers are primarily actors, they must be specially drilled to move with ease and grace, lightness and humor. Miss Wiesenthal is responsible for their training as well as for that of the twenty-four little page boys who also take part in the choreographic movement of the banquet scene.

It takes ten days of intensive work, rehearsing mornings and afternoons in the great hall known as the Turnsaal, and a week of rehearsals on stage to whip the company into shape. Great patience and special effort are required on the part of the choreographer because of the varied backgrounds of the performers and their lack of basic dance training. It is almost impossible to find a trained dancer who also qualifies as a singer and actor, so every effort is made during the casting period to find actors who have worked in the dance. Miss Wiesenthal tries to have at least one male and one female dancer in the company who has undergone special study, so that she may put these dancers in charge of the group as leaders. During the 1959 season, the only professional dancer in the company was Erika Tron, who had been trained in Miss Wiesenthal's studio in Vienna; the leading male dancer, Horst Fitzthum, was a gifted and spirited performer who had never studied dancing but had a natural talent for it.

All of the dancing occurs in the banquet scene. The basic rhythm of the music is that of the Ländler, an Austrian dance of the early nineteenth century, but for this play the steps devised to accompany the music were adapted from folk dances. If an authentic Ländler were performed, the effect would be too slow, stiff, and formal, but folk dancing, which seems to derive its energy from the earth, has the force, the drive, and the liveliness required for this scene. The dances here are meant to express the joy of life, the pleasures of the flesh, and the ecstasies of this world, which Everyman indulges in to excess and is finally forced to leave.

"The dance," says Miss Wiesenthal, "may play a very insignificant part in a dramatic production, but if the director sees fit to introduce it, it must contribute its full share to the mood, the spirit, and the perfection of the total work."

SCENERY AND COSTUMES
An Interview with Caspar Neher

The set originally conceived for *Jedermann* by Max Reinhardt has been in use at Salzburg without revision since 1920, but the play has been recostumed many times since then. It was Reinhardt's idea to erect a bare, wooden platform directly in front of the baroque façade of the Salzburg Cathedral. The platform is six feet high and fifty feet long, with ramps at each end which the actors use in full view of the audience for their entrances and exits. The stage may also be reached by three flights of stairs directly in front of the platform; a wide flight in the center consists of seven steps, and two narrow flights to the right and left of center have four deep steps each. These stairways, however, are more decorative than useful. The stage itself is divided into two levels: the forward area is ten feet deep and has a trap-door through which Everyman descends to his grave; at the rear of the stage four shallow steps lead to the upper level which is also ten feet deep— the total dimensions of the acting area on the platform are thus fifty feet long by twenty feet deep. Behind the stage, a ramp and two steep sets of stairs lead to the ground and into the Cathedral; this beautiful edifice thus serves as a *skene*, or scene-building. The ground directly in front of the stage, like the medieval *platea*, is used on occasion to represent a street. The entire physical arrangement is extremely flexible and admits of a variety of uses.

Caspar Neher has been associated with the production of *Jedermann* since 1951. He left Reinhardt's stage intact, but he made some alterations in the properties. The long table, for instance, which is on the upper level of the stage during the banquet scene, was originally covered with a white cloth and draped with green garlands, but Neher uses a reddish-brown cloth edged with gold and draped with ivory-colored garlands. The table bears huge baskets of flowers, enormous bowls of fruit, and tall pewter tankards.

Between 1951 and 1955 the play concluded with a startling and impressive scene. The two Gothic arches in the façade of the Cathedral were closed off with curtains until the last scene of the play. When the curtains were opened, the arches were seen to be filled with Angels in striking tableaux. The impression created upon the audience by this sight was breathtaking; but in 1956 the Cathedral was fitted with new front doors and the authorities of the Church, fearing that these expensive portals would be damaged by the trestles needed to sustain the Angels, asked Neher to suggest another idea for the play's finale. He then introduced a procession of nuns, each of whom bore a symbol of the Church—a cross, an open book, the mansions of heaven, and so on.

Neher has not completely redesigned the play's costumes but has supplied new ones as needed; for the summer of 1959, for instance, he created new dresses for the women in the banquet scene and for the nuns who appear at the end of the play. The basic color scheme of the production was a reddish-brown or earth color, *caput mortum*. Max Reinhardt's idea was to play *Jedermann* at sunset so that the costumes would reflect the last rays of the setting sun; then when Everyman goes to his death the shadows of the twilight would give a gray and neutral tone to the white, gray, and ivory costumes of the last scene. Neher will continue to use earth colors since they are brought out best in the russet light of sunset, which invests them with a misty, dusty quality.

The play is opened by six trumpeters who are seen high up on the parapets of the Cathedral; these figures and their instruments appear to be part of the stone façade of the building. They are costumed and made up entirely in stone-gray.

The Messenger, the first actor to appear, is dressed in gray and coral. He wears a tall coral hat decorated with gray plumes, a scalloped doublet, and trouser-legs tucked into his gray boots which are topped by a wide coral cuff. Beige gloves cover his wrists, and his coral cape is edged with a strip of caracul four inches wide.

Death's costume, a white skull and skeleton painted on black tights, was borrowed by Reinhardt from William Poel who adapted it from the medieval representation of this figure.

Everyman, the picture of wealth incarnate, appears all in gold, except for his pleated shirt and cuffs of gleaming white. His richly brocaded overcoat of burnt orange is edged with white ermine, and he carries a golden money-bag.

Fellowship is dressed in gray-green and light mustard color; his false sleeves are long and deeply scalloped; his shoes and silk stockings are gray.

Everyman's Cook wears a green suit, an enormous chef's hat, and a white apron; his Major Domo, a stately man, is dressed in maroon.

The Beggar wears various shades of dull gray but his shoes are brown; his trousers are held up by a thick cord that is knotted at the waist; the cuffs of his sleeves and trousers are ragged; and he wears no socks.

Three soldiers enter leading a Debtor off to prison. The soldiers are uniformed in coral coats and gray trousers and shoes; their silver helmets are flat, shaped like the *petasos*, or coolie hat, and they carry long spears. The Debtor is in a mustard-colored coat and yellow-green trousers. His wife, who follows after, is in a long gray robe and head covering, with a yellow-green shawl; their three children are in gray and white, and all three walk in bare feet.

Everyman's Mother wears a formal black dress and a black headdress with white facing; the gown is double-edged down the front. The overdress is fully pleated and has a short train; the underskirt is also black. The high, stiff cuffs of black velvet are edged with gold. The veil which is part of the head covering falls below the waist in the rear. The old woman wears a wide velvet band at her throat, a large golden cross on her breast, and long golden earrings; she walks with the aid of a cane.

At the banquet there are twenty-four little page boys, all dressed cavalier-style in gray and white with pale coral capes attached at the shoulders; they wear white collars, gloves, and socks, and bows of white ribbon are affixed where trousers and socks meet. Each boy carries a little basket filled with flowers.

The Courtesan is gorgeously and seductively attired in a richly brocaded coral overdress with a laced bodice, and a brocaded and pleated ivory satin underskirt.

The twenty-four men and girls who represent the guests at the banquet are dressed in solid colors—blue, lavender, mustard, green, and rose; the women's gowns have full skirts and puffed sleeves; the hats vary in shape from skull caps to high bonnets. The men's doublets, breeches, and hose are in the same colors as the girls' dresses, extremely attractive but of indeterminate style.

The Thin Cousin wears a suit of bright yellow and tan; while the Fat Cousin has an elaborate yellow-green outfit.

The Musicians who provide the accompaniment at the banquet scene appear in green suits, long brick-colored capes, and medieval hats with high crowns and long visors; while the Serving Men wear coral coats and trousers, pancake hats, and ornamental cloths looped at their shoulders.

Mammon has a gilded skull and face and is entirely costumed in gold: his body is covered with cloth of gold, golden chains hang round his neck; he wears golden gloves and a cape of gold netting; his earrings are tremendous gold coins the size of castanets, and a golden sash encircles his belly. Superimposed on blue-green make-up are golden cheeks and red lips; he stands knee-deep in a trunk full of golden treasures.

Good Deeds appears in a light brown gown with puffed sleeves and a full skirt; her tan bodice has horizontal stripes. Faith wears a white gown with a blue-gray veil that covers her head, shoulders, and arms and falls to the hem of her skirt behind, but just below the waist in front; a white wimple frames her face.

The Elderly Man who accompanies Everyman's Mother at the end of the play wears a coral-colored suit and carries a pewter lantern.

The Devil has a moth-eaten fur suit of mottled black and reddish brown, matted hair and horns on his head, and a billowing flame-colored cloak with a tall stiff collar, long claws on his fingers, furry boots, a long thin tail, and a sickly green facial make-up. His movement is stylized and he capers like an imp from hell.

Everyman makes his last appearance in a long white shroud with full sleeves, and he leans on a wooden crook.

Eight nuns, wearing ivory wimples and gowns with pale gray overgowns, come on in procession carrying symbols of the Church; their clothing is made of monk's cloth, and their faces are covered with pale gray make-up.

For 1960, Caspar Neher provided a new set of costumes for the entire company and redesigned the stage. It is his belief that the platform stage and the clothes described here are more suitable to a production of *Everyman* done in true medieval style than they are to Hofmannsthal's version of the play, which is less religious and less profound than the original; the new scenery and costumes are therefore more in keeping with our own times.

◟◟◟◟ *Everyman*

CHARACTERS

GOD

MESSENGER	KNOWLEDGE
DEATH	CONFESSION
EVERYMAN	BEAUTY
FELLOWSHIP	STRENGTH
KINDRED	DISCRETION
COUSIN	FIVE WITS
GOODS	ANGEL
GOOD DEEDS	DOCTOR

HERE BEGINNETH A TREATISE HOW THE HIGH FATHER OF HEAVEN SENDETH DEATH TO SUMMON EVERY CREATURE TO COME AND GIVE ACCOUNT OF THEIR LIVES IN THIS WORLD, AND IS IN MANNER OF A MORAL PLAY.

(*Enter* MESSENGER *as Prologue.*)

Messenger. I pray you all give your audience,
And hear this matter with reverence,
By figure[1] a moral play—
The *Summoning of Everyman* called it is,   4
That of our lives and ending shows
How transitory we be all day.
This matter is wondrous precious,
But the intent of it is more gracious,[2]
And sweet to bear away.
The story saith: Man, in the beginning   10
Look well, and take good heed to the ending,

Be you never so gay!
Ye think sin in the beginning full sweet,
Which in the end causeth the soul to weep,
When the body lieth in clay.   15
Here shall you see how Fellowship and Jollity,
Both Strength, Pleasure, and Beauty,
Will fade from thee as flower in May;
For ye shall hear how our Heaven King
Calleth Everyman to a general reckoning.   20
Give audience, and hear what he doth say. (*Exit Messenger.*)

(GOD *speaks.*)

God. I perceive, here in my majesty,
How that all creatures be to me unkind,[3]
Living without dread in worldly prosperity;

1. In form.
2. Devout.

3. Ungrateful.

Of ghostly[4] sight the people be so
   blind,   25
Drowned in sin, they know me not
   for their God;
In worldly riches is all their mind,
They fear not my righteousness, the
   sharp rod.
My law that I showed, when I for
   them died,
They forget clean, and shedding of
   my blood red;   30
I hanged between two, it cannot be
   denied;
To get them life I suffered to be
   dead;
I healed their feet, with thorns hurt
   was my head.
I could do no more than I did, truly;
And now I see the people do clean
   forsake me.   35
They use the seven deadly sins dam-
   nable,
As pride, covetise, wrath, and lechery
Now in the world be made com-
   mendable;
And thus they leave of angels the
   heavenly company.
Every man liveth so after his own
   pleasure,   40
And yet of their life they be nothing
   sure.
I see the more that I them forbear
The worse they be from year to year.
All that liveth appaireth[5] fast;
Therefore I will, in all the haste,   45
Have a reckoning of every man's per-
   son;
For, and I leave the people thus alone
In their life and wicked tempests,
Verily they will become much worse
   than beasts;
For now one would by envy another
   up eat;   50

Charity they do all clean forget.
I hoped well that every man
In my glory should make his man-
   sion,
And thereto I had them all elect;
But now I see, like traitors deject,   55
They thank me not for the pleasure
   that I to them meant,
Nor yet for their being that I them
   have lent.
I proffered the people great multitude
   of mercy,
And few there be that asketh it
   heartily.[6]
They be so cumbered with worldly
   riches   60
That needs on them I must do justice,
On every man living without fear.
Where art thou, Death, thou mighty
   messenger?

(*Enter* DEATH.)

Death. Almighty God, I am here at
   your will,
Your commandment to fulfil.   65
God. Go thou to Everyman,
And show him, in my name,
A pilgrimage he must on him take,
Which he in no wise may escape;
And that he bring with him a sure
   reckoning   70
Without delay or any tarrying.

Death. Lord, I will in the world go run
   overall,[7]
And cruelly outsearch both great and
   small;
(GOD *withdraws.*)
Every man will I beset that liveth
   beastly
Out of God's laws, and dreadeth not
   folly.   75
He that loveth riches I will strike with
   my dart,

---

4. Spiritual.
5. Degenerates.
6. Earnestly.
7. Everywhere.

His sight to blind, and from heaven
to depart[8]—
Except that alms be his good friend—
In hell for to dwell, world without
end.   79

(*Enter* EVERYMAN.)

Lo, yonder I see Everyman walking.
Full little he thinketh on my coming;
His mind is on fleshly lusts and his
treasure,
And great pain it shall cause him to
endure
Before the Lord, Heaven King.
Everyman, stand still! Whither art
thou going   85
Thus gaily? Hast thou thy Maker
forgot?

Everyman. Why asketh thou?
Wouldest thou wit[9]?

Death. Yea, sir; I will show you;
In great haste I am sent to thee   90
From God out of his majesty.

Everyman. What, sent to me?

Death. Yea, certainly.
Though thou have forgot him here,
He thinketh on thee in the heavenly
sphere,   95
As, ere we depart, thou shalt know.

Everyman. What desireth God of me?

Death. That shall I show thee;
A reckoning he will needs have
Without any longer respite.   100

Everyman. To give a reckoning longer
leisure I crave;
This blind [10] matter troubleth my
wit.

Death. On thee thou must take a long
journey;
Therefore thy book of count with
thee thou bring,
For turn again thou cannot by no
way.   105

And look thou be sure of thy reckon-
ing,
For before God thou shalt answer,
and show
Thy many bad deeds, and good but
a few;
How thou hast spent thy life, and in
what wise,   109
Before the chief Lord of paradise.
Have ado that we were in that way,[11]
For, wit thou well, thou shalt make
none attorney.

Everyman. Full unready I am such
reckoning to give.
I know thee not. What messenger art
thou?

Death. I am Death, that no man dread-
eth;[12]   115
For every man I rest,[13] and no man
spareth;
For it is God's commandment
That all to me should be obedient.

Everyman. O Death, thou comest when
I had thee least in mind!
In thy power it lieth me to save;   120
Yet of my good [14] will I give thee, if
thou will be kind;
Yea, a thousand pound shalt thou
have,
And defer this matter till another day.

Death. Everyman, it may not be, by no
way.   '   124
I set not by[15] gold, silver, nor riches,
Ne by pope, emperor, king, duke, ne
princes;
For, and I would receive gifts great,
All the world I might get;
But my custom is clean contrary.
I give thee no respite. Come hence,
and not tarry.   130

Everyman. Alas, shall I have no longer
respite?

8. Separate.
9. Know.
10. Obscure.
11. Let's start our journey.

12. Who fears no man.
13. Arrest.
14. Wealth.
15. Care not for.

I may say Death giveth no warning!

To think on thee, it maketh my heart sick,

For all unready is my book of reckoning.

But twelve year and I might have abiding,[16]   135

My counting-book I would make so clear

That my reckoning I should not need to fear.

Wherefore, Death, I pray thee, for God's mercy,

Spare me till I be provided of remedy.

Death. Thee availeth not to cry, weep, and pray;   140

But haste thee lightly that thou were gone that journey,

And prove thy friends if thou can;

For, wit thou well, the tide[17] abideth no man,

And in the world each living creature

For Adam's sin must die of nature.

Everyman. Death, if I should this pilgrimage take,   146

And my reckoning surely make,

Show me, for saint charity,

Should I not come again shortly?

Death. No, Everyman; and thou be once there,   150

Thou mayst never more come here,

Trust me verily.

Everyman. O gracious God in the high seat celestial,

Have mercy on me in this most need!

Shall I have no company from this vale terrestrial   155

Of mine acquaintance, that way me to lead?

Death. Yea, if any be so hardy

That would go with thee and bear thee company.

Hie thee that thou were gone to God's magnificence,

Thy reckoning to give before his presence.   160

What, weenest thou thy life is given thee,

And thy worldly goods also?

Everyman. I had wend [18] so, verily.

Death. Nay, nay; it was but lent thee;

For as soon as thou art go,[19]   165

Another a while shall have it, and then go therefro,

Even as thou hast done.

Everyman, thou art mad! Thou hast thy wits five,

And here on earth will not amend thy life;

For suddenly I do come.   170

Everyman. O wretched caitiff, whither shall I flee,

That I might scape this endless sorrow?

Now, gentle Death, spare me till tomorrow,

That I may amend me

With good advisement.[20]   175

Death. Nay, thereto I will not consent,

Nor no man will I respite;

But to the heart suddenly I shall smite

Without any advisement.

And now out of thy sight I will me hie;   180

See thou make thee ready shortly,

For thou mayst say this is the day

That no man living may scape away.

(*Exit* DEATH.)

Everyman. Alas, I may well weep with sighs deep!   184

Now have I no manner of company

To help me in my journey, and me to keep;[21]

---

16. If I had just twelve more years.
17. Time.
18. Thought.

19. Gone.
20. Reflection.
21. Protect.

And also my writing[22] is full unready.
How shall I do now for to excuse me?
I would to God I had never be get! [23]
To my soul a full great profit it had
    be;   190
For now I fear pains huge and great.
The time passeth. Lord, help, that all
    wrought!
For though I mourn it availeth
    nought.
The day passeth, and is almost ago;[24]
I wot not well what for to do.   195
To whom were I best my complaint
    to make?
What and [25] I to Fellowship thereof
    spake,
And showed him of this sudden
    chance?
For in him is all mine affiance;[26]
We have in the world so many a
    day   200
Be good friends in sport and play.
I see him yonder, certainly.
I trust that he will bear me company;
Therefore to him will I speak to ease
    my sorrow.

(FELLOWSHIP *enters.*)

Well met, good Fellowship, and good
    morrow!   205
Fellowship. Everyman, good morrow,
    by this day!
    Sir, why lookest thou so piteously?
    If any thing be amiss, I pray thee me
    say,
    That I may help to remedy.   209
Everyman. Yea, good Fellowship, yea;
    I am in great jeopardy.
Fellowship. My true friend, show to
    me your mind;
    I will not forsake thee to my life's
    end,

In the way of good company.
Everyman. That was well spoken, and
    lovingly.   215
Fellowship. Sir, I must needs know
    your heaviness;[27]
    I have pity to see you in any distress.
    If any have you wronged, ye shall re-
    venged be,
    Though I on the ground be slain for
    thee,
    Though that I know before that I
    should die.   220
Everyman. Verily, Fellowship, gra-
    mercy.
Fellowship. Tush! by thy thanks I set
    not a straw.
    Show me your grief, and say no more.
Everyman. If my heart should to you
    break,[28]
    And then you to turn your mind from
    me,   225
    And would not me comfort when ye
    hear me speak,
    Then should I ten times sorrier be.
Fellowship. Sir, I say as I will do in-
    deed.
Everyman. Then be you a good friend
    at need;   229
    I have found you true herebefore.
Fellowship. And so ye shall evermore;
    For, in faith, and thou go to hell,
    I will not forsake thee by the way.
Everyman. Ye speak like a good friend;
    I believe you well.
    I shall deserve[29] it, and I may.   235
Fellowship. I speak of no deserving, by
    this day!
    For he that will say, and nothing do,
    Is not worthy with good company to
    go;
    Therefore show me the grief of your
    mind,

---

22. Business ledger.
23. Been born.
24. Gone.
25. If.

26. Trust.
27. Sorrow.
28. Open.
29. Repay.

As to your friend most loving and
kind. 240

Everyman. I shall show you how it is;
Commanded I am to go a journey,
A long way, hard and dangerous,
And give a strait count,[30] without
delay,
Before the high Judge, Adonai.[31] 245
Wherefore, I pray you, bear me com-
pany,
As ye have promised, in this journey.

Fellowship. That is matter indeed.
Promise is duty;
But, and I should take such a voyage
on me,
I know it well, it should be to my
pain; 250
Also it maketh me afeared, certain.
But let us take counsel here as well
as we can,
For your words would fear[32] a strong
man.

Everyman. Why, ye said if I had need
Ye would me never forsake, quick ne
dead, 255
Though it were to hell, truly.

Fellowship. So I said, certainly,
But such pleasures be set aside, the
sooth to say;
And also, if we took such a journey,
When should we come again? 260

Everyman. Nay, never again, till the
day of doom.

Fellowship. In faith, then will not I
come there!
Who hath you these tidings brought?

Everyman. Indeed, Death was with me
here.

Fellowship. Now, by God that all hath
bought,[33] 265
If Death were the messenger,
For no man that is living to-day

I will not go that loath journey—
Not for the father that begat me!

Everyman. Ye promised otherwise,
pardie.[34] 270

Fellowship. I wot well I said so, truly;
And yet if thou wilt eat, and drink,
and make good cheer,
Or haunt to women the lusty com-
pany,[35]
I would not forsake you while the
day is clear,[36]
Trust me verily. 275

Everyman. Yea, thereto ye would be
ready!
To go to mirth, solace, and play,
Your mind will sooner apply,
Than to bear me company in my
long journey.

Fellowship. Now, in good faith, I will
not that way. 280
But and thou will murder, or any
man kill,
In that I will help thee with a good
will.

Everyman. O, that is a simple advice
indeed.
Gentle fellow, help me in my necessity! 284
We have loved long, and now I need;
And now, gentle Fellowship, remember me.

Fellowship. Whether ye have loved me
or no,
By Saint John, I will not with thee
go.

Everyman. Yet, I pray thee, take the
labour, and do so much for me
To bring me forward,[37] for saint
charity, 290
And comfort me till I come without
the town.

30. Strict account.
31. God.
32. Frighten.
33. Redeemed.

34. By God.
35. Or visit lusty women.
36. Until daybreak.
37. Escort me.

Fellowship. Nay, and thou would give me a new gown,
  I will not a foot with thee go;
  But, and thou had tarried, I would not have left thee so.
  And as now God speed thee in thy journey,   295
  For from thee I will depart as fast as I may.
Everyman. Whither away, Fellowship? Will thou forsake me?
Fellowship. Yea, by my fay![38] To God I betake[39] thee.
Everyman. Farewell, good Fellowship; for thee my heart is sore.
  Adieu for ever! I shall see thee no more.   300
Fellowship. In faith, Everyman, farewell now at the ending;
  For you I will remember that parting is mourning.

(*Exit* FELLOWSHIP.)

Everyman. Alack! shall we thus depart[40] indeed—
  Ah, Lady, help!—without any more comfort?
  Lo, Fellowship forsaketh me in my most need.   305
  For help in this world whither shall I resort?
  Fellowship herebefore with me would merry make,
  And now little sorrow for me doth he take.
  It is said, 'In prosperity men friends may find,   309
  Which in adversity be full unkind.'
  Now whither for succour shall I flee,
  Sith[41] that Fellowship hath forsaken me?

To my kinsmen I will, truly,
  Praying them to help me in my necessity;
  I believe that they will do so,   315
  For kind will creep where it may not go.[42]
  I will go say,[43] for yonder I see them.
  Where be ye now, my friends and kinsmen?

(*Enter* KINDRED *and* COUSIN.)

Kindred. Here be we now at your commandment.
  Cousin, I pray you show us your intent   320
  In any wise,[44] and do not spare.
Cousin. Yea, Everyman, and to us declare
  If ye be disposed to go anywhither;
  For, wit you well, we will live and die together.
Kindred. In wealth and woe we will with you hold,   325
  For over his kin a man may be bold.[45]
Everyman. Gramercy, my friends and kinsmen kind.
  Now shall I show you the grief of my mind.
  I was commanded by a messenger,
  That is a high king's chief officer;
  He bade me go a pilgrimage, to my pain,   331
  And I know well I shall never come again;
  Also, I must give a reckoning strait,
  For I have a great enemy[46] that hath me in wait,   334
  Which intendeth me for to hinder.
Kindred. What account is that which ye must render?
  That would I know.

38. Faith.
39. Commend.
40. Part.
41. Since.
42. Blood is thicker than water.

43. Try.
44. Without fail.
45. A man may trust his relatives.
46. The devil.

Everyman. Of all my works I must show
How I have lived and my days spent; 339
Also of ill deeds that I have used[47]
In my time, sith life was me lent;
And of all virtues that I have refused.
Therefore, I pray you, go thither with me
To help to make mine account, for saint charity.

Cousin. What, to go thither? Is that the matter? 345
Nay, Everyman, I had liefer fast bread and water
All this five year and more.

Everyman. Alas, that ever I was bore!
For now shall I never be merry,
If that you forsake me. 350

Kindred. Ah, sir, what ye be a merry man! [48]
Take good heart to you, and make no moan.
But one thing I warn you, by Saint Anne,
As for me, ye shall go alone.

Everyman. My Cousin, will you not with me go? 355

Cousin. No, by our Lady! I have the cramp in my toe.
Trust not to me, for, so God me speed,
I will deceive you in your most need.

Kindred. It availeth not us to tice.[49]
Ye shall have my maid with all my heart; 360
She loveth to go to feasts, there to be nice,[50]
And to dance, and abroad to start;[51]
I will give her leave to help you in that journey,
If that you and she may agree.

47. Done.
48. What a merry man you are!
49. Entice.
50. Wanton.

Everyman. Now show me the very effect[52] of your mind. 365
Will you go with me, or abide behind?

Kindred. Abide behind? Yea, that will I, and I may!
Therefore farewell till another day.

(*Exit* KINDRED.)

Everyman. How should I be merry or glad? 369
For fair promises men to me make,
But when I have most need they me forsake.
I am deceived; that maketh me sad.

Cousin. Cousin Everyman, farewell now,
For verily I will not go with you.
Also of mine own an unready reckoning 375
I have to account; therefore I make tarrying.
Now God keep thee, for now I go.

(*Exit* COUSIN.)

Everyman. Ah, Jesus, is all come hereto?
Lo, fair words maketh fools fain;
They promise, and nothing will do, certain. 380
My kinsmen promised me faithfully
For to abide with me steadfastly,
And now fast away do they flee;
Even so Fellowship promised me.
What friend were best me of to provide? [53] 385
I lose my time here longer to abide.
Yet in my mind a thing there is:
All my life I have loved riches;
If that my Good [54] now help me might, 389
He would make my heart full light.
I will speak to him in this distress—

51. Run wild.
52. Tenor.
53. To provide myself with.
54. Goods.

Where art thou, my Goods and riches?

(Goods *speaks from a corner.*)

Goods. Who calleth me? Everyman? What! hast thou haste?
I lie here in corners, trussed and piled so high,   394
And in chests I am locked so fast,
Also sacked in bags. Thou mayst see with thine eye
I cannot stir; in packs low I lie.
What would ye have? Lightly[55] me say.

Everyman. Come hither, Good, in all the haste thou may,   399
For of counsel I must desire thee.[56]

Goods. Sir, and ye in the world have sorrow or adversity,
That can I help you to remedy shortly.

Everyman. It is another disease[57] that grieveth me;
In this world it is not, I tell thee so.
I am sent for, another way to go,   405
To give a strait count general
Before the highest Jupiter of all;
And all my life I have had joy and pleasure in thee,
Therefore, I pray thee, go with me;
For, peradventure, thou mayst before God Almighty   410
My reckoning help to clean and purify;
For it is said ever among[58]
That money maketh all right that is wrong.

Goods. Nay, Everyman, I sing another song.
I follow no man in such voyages;   415
For, and I went with thee,

55. Quickly.
56. I need your advice.
57. Trouble.
58. It is often said.
59. Obscure.
60. Truly.

Thou shouldst fare much the worse for me;
For because on me thou did set thy mind,
Thy reckoning I have made blotted and blind,[59]
That thine account thou cannot make truly;   420
And that hast thou for the love of me.

Everyman. That would grieve me full sore,
When I should come to that fearful answer.
Up, let us go thither together.

Goods. Nay, not so! I am too brittle, I may not endure;   425
I will follow no man one foot, be ye sure.

Everyman. Alas, I have thee loved, and had great pleasure
All my life-days on good and treasure.

Goods. That is to thy damnation, without leasing,[60]
For my love is contrary to the love everlasting;   430
But if thou had me loved moderately during,[61]
As to the poor to give part of me,
Then shouldst thou not in this dolour be,
Nor in this great sorrow and care.

Everyman. Lo, now was I deceived ere I was ware,[62]   435
And all I may wite misspending of time.[63]

Goods. What, weenest[64] thou that I am thine?

Everyman. I had wend [65] so.

61. During your life.
62. Aware.
63. Because I misused my time.
64. Think.
65. Thought.

Goods. Nay, Everyman, I say no.

As for a while I was lent thee;   440
A season thou hast had me in prosperity.
My condition[66] is man's soul to kill;
If I save one, a thousand I do spill.[67]
Weenest thou that I will follow thee?
Nay, not from this world, verily.   445

Everyman. I had wend otherwise.

Goods. Therefore to thy soul Good is a thief;

For when thou art dead, this is my guise[68]—
Another to deceive in this same wise
As I have done thee, and all to his soul's reprief.[69]   450

Everyman. O false Good, cursed may thou be,

Thou traitor to God, that has deceived me
And caught me in thy snare!

Goods. Marry, thou brought thyself in care,

Whereof I am glad;   455
I must needs laugh, I cannot be sad.

Everyman. Ah, Good, thou hast had long my heartly[70] love;

I gave thee that which should be the Lord's above.
But wilt thou not go with me indeed?
I pray thee truth to say.   460

Goods. No, so God me speed!

Therefore farewell, and have good day.

(*Exit* Goods.)

Everyman. O, to whom shall I make my moan

For to go with me in that heavy journey?
First Fellowship said he would with me gone;[71]   465

His words were very pleasant and gay,
But afterward he left me alone.
Then spake I to my kinsmen, all in despair,
And also they gave me words fair;
They lacked no fair speaking,   470
But all forsook me in the ending.
Then went I to my Goods, that I loved best,
In hope to have comfort, but there had I least;
For my Goods sharply did me tell
That he bringeth many into hell.
Then of myself I was ashamed,   476
And so I am worthy to be blamed;
Thus may I well myself hate.
Of whom shall I now counsel take?
I think that I shall never speed   480
Till that I go to my Good Deed.
But, alas, she is so weak
That she can neither go[72] nor speak;
Yet will I venture[73] on her now.
My Good Deeds, where be you?   485

(Good Deeds *speaks from the ground.*)

Good Deeds. Here I lie, cold in the ground;

Thy sins hath me sore bound,
That I cannot stir.

Everyman. O Good Deeds, I stand in fear!

I must you pray of counsel,   490
For help now should come right well.[74]

Good Deeds. Everyman, I have understanding

That ye be summoned account to make
Before Messias, of Jerusalem King;

66. Nature.
67. Ruin.
68. Practice.
69. Shame.
70. Heartfelt.

71. Go.
72. Walk.
73. Gamble.
74. Help would be welcome.

And you do by me,[75] that journey
with you will I take.   495

Everyman. Therefore I come to you,
my moan to make;

I pray you that ye will go with me.

Good Deeds. I would full fain, but I
cannot stand, verily.

Everyman. Why, is there anything on
you fall? [76]

Good Deeds. Yea, sir, I may thank you
of[77] all;   500

If ye had perfectly cheered [78] me,

Your book of count full ready had be.

(GOOD DEEDS *shows him the Book.*)

Look, the books of your works and
deeds eke! [79]

Behold how they lie under the feet,

To your soul's heaviness.   505

Everyman. Our Lord Jesus help me!

For one letter here I cannot see.

Good Deeds. There is a blind reckoning in time of distress.[80]

Everyman. Good Deeds, I pray you
help me in this need,

Or else I am for ever damned indeed;   510

Therefore help me to make reckoning

Before the Redeemer of all thing,

That King is, and was, and ever shall.

Good Deeds. Everyman, I am sorry of
your fall,

And fain would I help you, and I
were able.   515

Everyman. Good Deeds, your counsel I
pray you give me.

Good Deeds. That shall I do verily;

Though that on my feet I may not
go,

I have a sister that shall with you
also,

Called Knowledge,[81] which shall
with you abide,   520

To help you to make that dreadful
reckoning.

(*Enter* KNOWLEDGE.)

Knowledge. Everyman, I will go with
thee, and be thy guide,

In thy most need to go by thy side.

Everyman. In good condition I am now
in every thing,

And am wholly content with this
good thing,   525

Thanked be God my creator.

Good Deeds. And when she hath
brought you there

Where thou shalt heal thee of thy
smart,[82]

Then go you with your reckoning
and your Good Deeds together,

For to make you joyful at heart   530

Before the blessed Trinity.

Everyman. My Good Deeds, gramercy!

I am well content, certainly,

With your words sweet.

Knowledge. Now go we together lovingly   535

To Confession, that cleansing river.

Everyman. For joy I weep; I would we
were there!

But, I pray you, give me cognition[83]

Where dwelleth that holy man, Confession.

Knowledge. In the house of salvation;[84]

We shall find him in that place,   541

That shall us comfort, by God's grace.

(KNOWLEDGE *takes* EVERYMAN *to*
CONFESSION.)

Lo, this is Confession. Kneel down
and ask mercy,

---

75. If you do as I suggest.
76. Befallen.
77. For.
78. Encouraged.
79. Also.
80. It is hard for a sinful person to recall his
good deeds.
81. Acknowledgment of sins.
82. Pain.
83. Knowledge.
84. In the church.

For he is in good conceit[85] with God Almighty.

Everyman. (*Kneeling.*) O glorious fountain, that all uncleanness doth clarify, 545
Wash from me the spots of vice unclean,
That on me no sin may be seen.
I come with Knowledge for my redemption,
Redempt[86] with heart and full contrition;
For I am commanded a pilgrimage to take, 550
And great accounts before God to make.
Now I pray you, Shrift,[87] mother of salvation,
Help my Good Deeds for my piteous exclamation.[88]

Confession. I know your sorrow well, Everyman.
Because with Knowledge ye come to me, 555
I will you comfort as well as I can,
And a precious jewel I will give thee,
Called penance, voider of adversity;
Therewith shall your body chastised be,
With abstinence and perseverance in God's service. 560
Here shall you receive that scourge of me,

(*Gives* EVERYMAN *a scourge.*)

Which is penance strong that ye must endure,
To remember thy Saviour was scourged for thee
With sharp scourges, and suffered it patiently;

So must thou, ere thou scape that painful pilgrimage. 565
Knowledge, keep him in this voyage,
And by that time Good Deeds will be with thee.
But in any wise be siker[89] of mercy,
For your time draweth fast;[90] and [91] ye will saved be,
Ask God mercy, and he will grant truly. 570
When with the scourge of penance man doth him[92] bind,
The oil of forgiveness then shall he find.

(*Exit* CONFESSION; EVERYMAN *rises.*)

Everyman. Thanked be God for his gracious work!
For now I will my penance begin;
This hath rejoiced and lighted [93] my heart, 575
Though the knots be painful and hard within.[94]

Knowledge. Everyman, look your penance that ye fulfil,
What pain that ever it to you be;
And Knowledge shall give you counsel at will
How your account ye shall make clearly. 580

(EVERYMAN *kneels.*)

Everyman. O eternal God, O heavenly figure,
O way of righteousness, O goodly vision,
Which descended down in a virgin pure
Because he would every man redeem,
Which Adam forfeited by his disobedience; 585

85. Favor.
86. Redeemed.
87. Confession.
88. In answer to my plea.
89. Sure.
90. Draws to an end.
91. If.
92. Himself.
93. Lightened.
94. To my flesh.

O blessed Godhead, elect and high divine,[95]

Forgive my grievous offence;

Here I cry thee mercy in this presence.[96]

O ghostly treasure, O ransomer and redeemer, 589

Of all the world hope and conductor,

Mirror of joy, and founder of mercy,

Which illumineth heaven and earth thereby,[97]

Hear my clamorous complaint, though it late be;

Receive my prayers, of thy benignity;

Though I be a sinner most abominable, 595

Yet let my name be written in Moses' table.[98]

O Mary, pray to the Maker of all thing,

Me for to help at my ending;

And save me from the power of my enemy,[99] 599

For Death assaileth me strongly.

And, Lady, that I may by means of thy prayer

Of your Son's glory to be partner,

By the means of his passion, I it crave;

I beseech you help my soul to save.

(*He rises.*)

Knowledge, give me the scourge of penance; 605

My flesh therewith shall give acquittance.[100]

I will now begin, if God give me grace.

Knowledge. Everyman, God give you time and space! [101]

Thus I bequeath you in the hands of our Saviour;

Now may you make your reckoning sure. 610

Everyman. In the name of the Holy Trinity,

My body sore punished shall be.

Take this, body, for the sin of the flesh!

(*Scourges himself.*)

Also[102] thou delightest to go gay and fresh,

And in the way of damnation thou did me bring, 615

Therefore suffer now strokes and punishing.

Now of penance I will wade the water clear,

To save me from purgatory, that sharp fire.

(GOOD DEEDS *rises from the ground.*)

Good Deeds. I thank God, now I can walk and go,

And am delivered of my sickness and woe. 620

Therefore with Everyman I will go, and not spare;

His good works I will help him to declare.

Knowledge. Now, Everyman, be merry and glad!

Your Good Deeds cometh now; ye may not be sad.

Now is your Good Deeds whole and sound, 625

Going upright upon the ground.

Everyman. My heart is light, and shall be evermore;

Now will I smite faster than I did before.

Good Deeds. Everyman, pilgrim, my special friend,

---

95. Divinity.
96. The presence of these people.
97. Besides.
98. A record of those who have done penance.
99. The devil.
100. Satisfaction.
101. Opportunity.
102. As.

Blessed be thou without end;   630
For thee is preparate[103] the eternal
glory.
Ye have me made whole and sound,
Therefore I will bide by thee in every
stound.[104]

Everyman. Welcome, my Good Deeds;
now I hear thy voice,   634
I weep for very sweetness of love.

Knowledge. Be no more sad, but ever
rejoice;
God seeth thy living in his throne
above.
Put on this garment to thy behoof,[105]
Which is wet with your tears,   639
Or else before God you may it miss,
When ye to your journey's end come
shall.

Everyman. Gentle Knowledge, what do
ye it call?

Knowledge. It is a garment of sorrow;
From pain it will you borrow;[106]
Contrition it is,   645
That getteth forgiveness;
It pleaseth God passing well.[107]

Good Deeds. Everyman, will you wear
it for your heal? [108]

(EVERYMAN *puts on the robe of contrition.*)

Everyman. Now blessed be Jesu, Mary's
Son,   649
For now have I on true contrition.
And let us go now without tarrying;
Good Deeds, have we clear our reck-
oning?

Good Deeds. Yea, indeed, I have it
here.

Everyman. Then I trust we need not
fear;
Now, friends, let us not part in
twain.   655

Knowledge. Nay, Everyman, that will
we not, certain.

Good Deeds. Yet must thou lead with
thee
Three persons of great might.

Everyman. Who should they be?

Good Deeds. Discretion and Strength
they hight,[109]   660
And thy Beauty may not abide behind.

Knowledge. Also ye must call to
mind
Your Five Wits[110] as for your counsellors.

Good Deeds. You must have them ready
at all hours.

Everyman. How shall I get them
hither?   665

Knowledge. You must call them all
together,
And they will hear you incontinent.[111]

Everyman. My friends, come hither
and be present,
Discretion, Strength, my Five Wits,
and Beauty.

(*Enter* BEAUTY, STRENGTH, DISCRE-
TION, *and* FIVE WITS.)

Beauty. Here at your will we be all
ready.   670
What will ye that we should do?

Good Deeds. That ye would with
Everyman go,
And help him in his pilgrimage.
Advise[112] you, will ye with him or not
in that voyage?   674

Strength. We will bring him all
thither,
To his help and comfort, ye may believe me.

Discretion. So will we go with him all
together.

103. Prepared.
104. Trial.
105. Advantage.
106. Release.
107. Exceedingly.

108. Salvation.
109. Are called.
110. Senses.
111. Immediately.
112. Consider.

Everyman. Almighty God, lofed [113] may thou be!

I give thee laud that I have hither brought

Strength, Discretion, Beauty, and Five Wits. Lack I nought;   680

And my Good Deeds, with Knowledge clear,

All be in my company at my will here;

I desire no more to [114] my business.

Strength. And I, Strength, will by you stand in distress,

Though thou would in battle fight on the ground.   685

Five Wits. And though it were through the world round,

We will not depart for sweet ne sour. [115]

Beauty. No more will I unto [116] death's hour,

Whatsoever thereof befall.

Discretion. Everyman, advise you first of all;   690

Go with a good advisement [117] and deliberation.

We all give you virtuous monition [118]

That all shall be well.

Everyman. My friends, harken what I will tell:

I pray God reward you in his heavenly sphere.   695

Now harken, all that be here,

For I will make my testament

Here before you all present:

In alms half my good I will give with my hands twain

In the way of charity, with good intent,   700

And the other half still shall remain

In queth, [119] to be returned there [120] it ought to be. [121]

This I do in despite of the fiend of hell,

To go quit out of his peril [122]

Ever after and this day.   705

Knowledge. Everyman, harken what I say:

Go to priesthood, I you advise,

And receive of him in any wise [123]

The holy sacrament and ointment together.

Then shortly see ye turn again hither;   710

We will all abide you here.

Five Wits. Yea, Everyman, hie you that ye ready were. [124]

There is no emperor, king, duke, ne baron,

That of God hath commission [125]

As hath the least priest in the world being; [126]   715

For of the blessed sacraments pure and benign

He beareth the keys, and thereof hath the cure [127]

For man's redemption—it is ever sure—

Which God for our soul's medicine

Gave us out of his heart with great pine. [128]   720

Here in this transitory life, for thee and me,

The blessed sacraments seven there be:

Baptism, confirmation, with priesthood good,

113. Praised.
114. For.
115. Joy or sorrow.
116. Until.
117. Reflection.
118. Forewarning.
119. Bequest.
120. Where.

121. His body will return to the earth.
122. To get out of his power.
123. Without fail.
124. Hurry and get ready.
125. Authority.
126. Living.
127. Charge.
128. Suffering.

And the sacrament of God's precious
   flesh and blood,
Marriage, the holy extreme unction,
   and penance;   725
These seven be good to have in re-
   membrance,
Gracious sacraments of high divinity.
Everyman. Fain would I receive that
   holy body,[129]
And meekly to my ghostly[130] father I
   will go.
Five Wits. Everyman, that is the best
   that ye can do.   730
God will you to salvation bring,
For priesthood exceedeth all other
   thing;
To us Holy Scripture they do teach,
And converteth man from sin heaven
   to reach;   734
God hath to them more power given
Than to any angel that is in heaven.
With five words he may consecrate,
God's body in flesh and blood to
   make,
And handleth his Maker between his
   hands.
The priest bindeth and unbindeth all
   bands,   740
Both in earth and in heaven.
Thou ministers[131] all the sacraments
   seven;
Though we kissed thy feet, thou were
   worthy;
Thou art surgeon that cureth sin
   deadly;
No remedy we find under God   745
But all only priesthood.[132]
Everyman, God gave priests that
   dignity,
And setteth them in his stead among
   us to be;
Thus be they above angels in degree.

(*Exit* EVERYMAN *to receive the last
rites.*)

Knowledge. If priests be good, it is
   so,[133] surely.   750
But when Jesus hanged on the cross
   with great smart,
There he gave out of his blessed heart
The same sacrament in great tor-
   ment.
He sold them not to us, that Lord
   omnipotent.
Therefore Saint Peter the apostle
   doth say   755
That Jesu's curse hath all they
Which God their Savior do buy or
   sell,
Or they for any money do take or
   tell.[134]
Sinful priests giveth the sinners ex-
   ample bad;
Their children[135] sitteth by other
   men's fires, I have heard;   760
And some haunteth women's com-
   pany
With unclean life, as lusts of lechery.
These be with sin made blind.
Five Wits. I trust to God no such may
   we find;   764
Therefore let us priesthood honor,
And follow their doctrine for our
   souls' succor.
We be their sheep, and they shep-
   herds be
By whom we all be kept in surety.
Peace, for yonder I see Everyman
   come,   769
Which hath made true satisfaction.
Good Deeds. Methink it is he indeed.

(*Re-enter* EVERYMAN.)

Everyman. Now Jesu be your alder
   speed! [136]

---

129. The sacrament.
130. Spiritual.
131. Administer.
132. But for the priesthood.

133. That they are above angels.
134. Pay out.
135. Illegitimate children.
136. Help you all.

I have received the sacrament for my
   redemption,
And then mine extreme unction.
Blessed be all they that counselled
   me to take it!   775
And now, friends, let us go without
   longer respite;
I thank God that ye have tarried so
   long.
Now set each of you on this rood [137]
   your hand,
And shortly follow me.
I go before there I would be; God be
   our guide!   780
Strength. Everyman, we will not from
   you go
Till ye have done this voyage long.
Discretion. I, Discretion, will bide by
   you also.
Knowledge. And though this pilgrimage
   be never so strong,[138]
I will never part you fro.[139]   785
Strength. Everyman, I will be as sure
   by thee[140]
As ever I did by Judas Maccabee.

(*They approach the grave.*)

Everyman. Alas, I am so faint I may
   not stand;
My limbs under me doth fold.
Friends, let us not turn again to this
   land,   790
Not for all the world's gold;
For into this cave must I creep
And turn to earth, and there to sleep.
Beauty. What, into this grave? Alas!
Everyman. Yea, there shall ye consume,
   more and less.[141]   795
Beauty. And what, should I smother
   here?

Everyman. Yea, by my faith, and never
   more appear.
In this world live no more we shall,
But in heaven before the highest
   Lord of all.
Beauty. I cross out[142] all this; adieu, by
   Saint John!   800
I take my cap in my lap,[143] and am
   gone.
Everyman. What, Beauty, whither will
   ye?
Beauty. Peace, I am deaf; I look not
   behind me,
Not and thou wouldest give me all
   the gold in thy chest.   804

(*Exit* BEAUTY.)

Everyman. Alas, whereto may I trust?
Beauty goeth fast away from me;
She promised with me to live and
   die.
Strength. Everyman, I will thee also
   forsake and deny;
Thy game liketh[144] me not at all.
Everyman. Why, then, ye will forsake
   me all?   810
Sweet Strength, tarry a little space.[145]
Strength. Nay, sir, by the rood of grace!
I will hie me from thee fast,
Though thou weep till thy heart to-
   brast.[146]
Everyman. Ye would ever bide by me,
   ye said.   815
Strength. Yea, I have you far enough
   conveyed.
Ye be old enough, I understand,
Your pilgrimage to take on hand;
I repent me that I hither came.
Everyman. Strength, you to displease I
   am to blame;[147]   820

---

137. Cross.
138. Distressing.
139. From you.
140. I will stand by you.
141. Decay, rich and poor alike.
142. Reject.

143. Doff my cap.
144. Pleases.
145. While.
146. Break.
147. You may blame me for displeasing you.

Yet promise is debt, this ye well wot.[148]

Strength. In faith, I care not.
　Thou art but a fool to complain;
　You spend your speech and waste your brain.
　Go thrust thee into the ground!　825

(*Exit* STRENGTH.)

Everyman. I had wend surer I should you have found.
　He that trusteth in his Strength
　She him deceiveth at the length.
　Both Strength and Beauty forsaketh me;
　Yet they promised me fair and lovingly.　830

Discretion. Everyman, I will after Strength be gone;
　As for me, I will leave you alone.

Everyman. Why, Discretion, will ye forsake me?

Discretion. Yea, in faith, I will go from thee,
　For when Strength goeth before　835
　I follow after evermore.

Everyman. Yet, I pray thee, for the love of the Trinity,
　Look in my grave once piteously.

Discretion. Nay, so nigh will I not come;
　Farewell, every one!　840

(*Exit* DISCRETION.)

Everyman. O, all thing faileth, save God alone—
　Beauty, Strength, and Discretion;
　For when Death bloweth his blast,
　They all run from me full fast.

Five Wits. Everyman, my leave now of thee I take;　845
　I will follow the other, for here I thee forsake.

Everyman. Alas, then may I wail and weep,

148. Know.

For I took you for my best friend.

Five Wits. I will no longer thee keep;
　Now farewell, and there an end.　850

(*Exit* FIVE WITS.)

Everyman. O Jesu, help! All hath forsaken me.

Good Deeds. Nay, Everyman; I will bide with thee.
　I will not forsake thee indeed;
　Thou shalt find me a good friend at need.

Everyman. Gramercy, Good Deeds! Now may I true friends see.　855
　They have forsaken me, every one;
　I loved them better than my Good Deeds alone.
　Knowledge, will ye forsake me also?

Knowledge. Yea, Everyman, when ye to Death shall go;　859
　But not yet, for no manner of danger.

Everyman. Gramercy, Knowledge, with all my heart.

Knowledge. Nay, yet I will not from hence depart
　Till I see where ye shall become.[149]

Everyman. Methink, alas, that I must be gone
　To make my reckoning and my debts pay,　865
　For I see my time is nigh spent away.
　Take example, all ye that this do hear or see,
　How they that I loved best do forsake me,
　Except my Good Deeds that bideth truly.

Good Deeds. All earthly things is but vanity.　870
　Beauty, Strength, and Discretion do man forsake,
　Foolish friends, and kinsmen, that fair spake,

149. What shall become of you.

All fleeth save Good Deeds, and that am I.

Everyman. Have mercy on me, God most mighty;
And stand by me, thou mother and maid, holy Mary.   875

Good Deeds. Fear not; I will speak for thee.

Everyman. Here I cry God mercy.

Good Deeds. Short[150] our end, and minish[151] our pain;
Let us go and never come again.

Everyman. Into thy hands, Lord, my soul I commend;   880
Receive it, Lord, that it be not lost.
As thou me boughtest, so me defend,
And save me from the fiend's boast,
That I may appear with that blessed host
That shall be saved at the day of doom.   885

In manus tuas, of mights most[152]
For ever, *commendo spiritum meum.*[153]

(EVERYMAN *and* GOOD DEEDS *descend into the grave.*)

Knowledge. Now hath he suffered that we all shall endure;
The Good Deeds shall make all sure.
Now hath he made ending;   890
Methinketh that I hear angels sing,
And make great joy and melody
Where Everyman's soul received shall be.

(*Exit* KNOWLEDGE; *an* ANGEL *appears.*)

Angel. Come, excellent elect spouse, to Jesu! [154]

Hereabove thou shalt go   895
Because of thy singular virtue.
Now the soul is taken the body fro,
Thy reckoning is crystal-clear.
Now shalt thou into the heavenly sphere,   899
Unto the which all ye shall come
That liveth well before the day of doom.

(*Enter* DOCTOR *as Epilogue.*)

Doctor. This moral men may have in mind.
Ye hearers, take it of worth,[155] old and young,
And forsake Pride, for he deceiveth you in the end;
And remember Beauty, Five Wits, Strength, and Discretion,   905
They all at the last do every man forsake,
Save his Good Deeds there doth he take.
But beware, for and they be small
Before God, he hath no help at all;
None excuse may be there for every man.   910
Alas, how shall he do then?
For after death amends may no man make,
For then mercy and pity doth him forsake.
If his reckoning be not clear when he doth come,
God will say: 'Ite, maledicti, in ignem æternum.' [156]   915
And he that hath his account whole and sound,
High in heaven he shall be crowned;

---

150. Shorten.
151. Diminish.
152. "Into thy hands," most mighty One.
153. "I commit my spirit."

154. The idea that the soul is wedded to God.
155. Value it.
156. "Depart, ye cursed, into everlasting fire."

Unto which place God bring us all
    thither,
That we may live body and soul to-
    gether.

Thereto help the Trinity! 920
Amen, say ye, for saint charity.

THUS ENDETH THIS MORAL PLAY OF
EVERYMAN.

Macbeth

~~~~~~~~~~~~~~~ WILLIAM SHAKESPEARE

INTRODUCTION

William Shakespeare, son of John Shakespeare and Mary Arden, was born on or about April 23, 1564, in Stratford-on-Avon, England. We first hear of his connection with the London theater in 1592 and by 1594 he had become a member of the Lord Chamberlain's Company and shared in the profits as actor and playwright.

It was with this company that he was affiliated for the rest of his life; and for its notable members, headed by Richard Burbage, the finest actor of his day, he wrote at least two plays a year for twenty consecutive years. The actors became the close personal friends of the playwright, and after his death his plays were collected and published in the First Folio (1623) by two of them—Heminges and Condell. The company performed at The Theatre and The Curtain until its new house, The Globe, was opened in 1599. In addition to The Globe, which was situated in the new theater district on the Bankside south of the Thames, the company also bought and refurbished an indoor theater called Blackfriars which was used mainly in the winter. In 1603, ten days after he came to the throne, James I issued an order placing the Chamberlain's Men under his own patronage and bestowing upon them the new title "The King's Men" by which name they were known thereafter. The company was the most successful in London and brought those who shared in its profits great wealth.

In 1611, at the age of forty-seven, Shakespeare retired to Stratford a wealthy man. On April 23, 1616, he died, and was buried in the village church in which he had been baptized. He was survived by his wife and by two daughters, both of whom were married; his son, Hamnet had died in 1596.

It is customary to divide Shakespeare's career as a playwright into four periods. These were once regarded as reflecting his own emotional and intellectual history, but a wider study of the Elizabethan drama has made it clear that changes in the technique, type, and tone of his plays were the results of external conditions rather than inner forces. The first period, extending from 1590 to 1596, is that during which he experimented with a number of kinds of comedy: classical, euphuistic, and romantic. The second period, running from 1596 to 1601, is that of the great history plays. The third period, from 1601 to 1608, is that of the great tragedies and the "bitter" comedies. The final period, 1608 to 1611, is that of the romances; but as late as 1613, after he had apparently retired, he collaborated with John Fletcher in *Henry VIII* and probably in *The Two Noble Kinsmen.*

The uniqueness of Shakespeare's genius is universally admitted; it is so overwhelming, in fact, that some believe that he could not have been the author of the plays ascribed to him in view of his conventional background and uneventful existence. A careful analysis of the plays indicates, however, that his very conventionality is the basis for his continuing appeal. His moral values are the generally accepted ones; his view of life is never sordid; his treatment of women, children, the aged, and unfortunate is sympathetic, and his characteristic viewpoint is distinctly idealistic.

Macbeth was the last of the four great tragedies to be written by Shakespeare when his creative powers were at their height. The play had been preceded by *Hamlet, Othello,* and *King Lear. Macbeth* can be dated with some degree of assurance in 1606. The subject of the play may have been suggested to Shakespeare by an entertainment presented to King James at Oxford in August, 1605, in which three youths dressed as sibyls recited some Latin verses containing the old prophecy that Banquo's descendants should be kings. Since James claimed descent from Banquo, the performance naturally pleased him, though he usually had very little patience with plays of any sort. He did not share Elizabeth's interest in the theater. It is believed that, called upon to provide a play for the entertainment of James and his brother-in-law, King Christian of Denmark, who was visiting England in 1606, Shakespeare was careful to choose a subject that he knew was of interest to the king and made sure, furthermore, not to write at great length. *Macbeth* is the shortest of all Shakespeare's plays except for the *Comedy of Errors;* the text, which we know only from the First Folio, shows many corruptions as if it had been hastily written or carelessly cut.

The source of the material for *Macbeth* was Holinshed's *Chronicles of England, Scotland, and Ireland,* from which Shakespeare had drawn the subjects for his English history plays. From Holinshed came the salient facts about Macbeth and Banquo, the witches on the heath, their prophecies, and the various incidents that follow from them in the play. But according to this account, Macbeth managed to kill King Duncan during a battle, an incident which Shakespeare rejected probably because of its commonplaceness. In another tale in Holinshed, he read of King Duff, who was murdered in his sleep in the castle of Donwald, a subject ambitious for the crown, acting on the instigation of his wife. Shakespeare did not hesitate to depart from historical accuracy by combining these two unrelated stories; by so doing he heightened the interest, the dramatic value, and the impact of his play. All of the action in the scenes involving the witches was original with Shakespeare, as was the dinner scene in which Banquo's ghost returned to confront his murderer. The playwright knew that witches, prophecies, and ghosts would please the king, who was a confirmed believer in the supernatural, and therefore, in the final Witch Scene (IV, 1) he went so far as to introduce Banquo's descendants in a parade of apparitions, with the last spirit carrying "twofold balls and treble scepters," the insignia of King James. But these were merely theatrical trappings, for the story that really interested Shakespeare concerned a man whose unbridled ambitions led him into evil from which, despite his agonies of remorse, he could not escape.

The plot-line of *Macbeth* is extremely simple—the simplest of all the tragedies —for the central figure supplies the main driving power of the action which is straightforward and unswerving from beginning to end. Macbeth and Banquo, two Scottish generals who are on their way home after a victorious battle, cross a deserted heath and there meet three old hags who prophesy that Macbeth shall be the Thane of Cawdor and later on shall be king, while Banquo shall be the father of kings though not one himself. Shortly thereafter a messenger arrives and addresses Macbeth as the Thane of Cawdor, a title just granted him by the king as a reward for his services. The witches' prophecy already seems to be coming true; to hasten its fulfillment, Lady Macbeth urges her husband to murder the king who has come on a visit to their castle. With the assistance of his wife, Macbeth kills Duncan, whose sons flee the country in terror, making it appear as if they had been implicated in the crime. Macbeth is crowned king of Scotland, but he is troubled in his conscience, and also disturbed by the prediction that Banquo's children are to inherit the throne. Fearing that Banquo will take matters into his own hands just as he himself had done, Macbeth arranges for the murder of Banquo and his only son, Fleance. Banquo is killed but Fleance escapes. Macbeth gives a great dinner for the members of the court and is about to take his seat at table when he sees the ghost of Banquo; it is visible to Macbeth alone but his frenzied and incriminating remarks break up the feast. Macbeth then goes to consult the witches about the future and is assured that Banquo's descendants will reign; he is also told to beware Macduff. After his interview with the witches he is greeted with the news that Macduff has fled to England, whereupon he orders the murder of Lady Macduff and her children. Macbeth starts a reign of terror and persecution. Lady Macbeth, who before the murder of Duncan appeared to be stronger than her husband, is now completely overcome by remorse and guilt and, with unsettled mind, dies, probably by her own hand. Macduff leads an army against Macbeth's castle at Dunsinane, the soldiers covering their advance with branches cut from the trees of Birnam wood. Macbeth's nerves are shaken, for the sight recalls two other predictions made by the witches: that he would not be vanquished until Birnam wood came to Dunsinane and that he would not yield to a man born of woman. The castle is attacked and during a hand-to-hand conflict with Macduff, Macbeth learns that his opponent was taken prematurely from his mother's womb. Macbeth realizes that he is doomed, but with great natural courage goes on fighting until he falls.

The play has no subplots and no unnecessary characters; it resembles a Greek tragedy in its stark beauty and its terrifying atmosphere. There are even more specific resemblances: the witches, like the Delphic oracle, announce the hero's fate, but he is powerless to avoid it; the supernatural plays an important part in the lives of the characters; and like Medea, Lady Macbeth, a passionate and faithful wife, does not hesitate to commit crimes for her husband's benefit.

Shakespeare's characterization of Macbeth and Lady Macbeth is superb. As husband and wife these two are well matched, since both are moved by the same passion of ambition; both are haughty and authoritarian; and both, in their egotism, show arrogance toward their inferiors. But they differ from each other in one important respect: Macbeth has a powerful imagination which almost prevents him from killing Duncan, for he seems conscious of what is to follow, and his deep remorse comes as a natural aftermath. Lady Macbeth, on the other hand, suppresses her imagination along with her femininity and sensitivity, and it is not until she sees the shocked faces of the guests at the banquet as her husband betrays himself that the enormity of their crime comes home to her. She faints at the knowledge and from that point on her personality disintegrates rapidly. When we see her for the last time in the sleep-walking scene, we realize how important she has been to the play. The second half of the play is certainly less interesting than the first because of Lady Macbeth's almost total absence from the scene.

The language of the play is unusual for its speed and economy; the condensation of ideas produces many oracular statements and the dialogue bristles with dramatic irony. As he approaches the estate of Macbeth, Duncan remarks, "This castle hath a pleasant seat," but it is there that he meets his death; in urging her husband to kill the king, Lady Macbeth says,

> A little water clears us of this deed:
> How easy is it then,

light words that have a terrible echo in the sleep-walking scene. In 1606, Shakespeare was still experimenting with blank verse so that the meter of the poetry in *Macbeth* looks forward to the freedom he allowed himself in his later plays. The thoughts rush on from line to line—they are not end-stopped—and build in each speech to a climactic effect.

There are two predominant images in the play, darkness and blood. All the scenes but three occur either in the blackness of night or in some dark place. The witches on the heath or in their cave, the murder scenes, the banquet scene, and the sleep-walking scene all take place in thick or subdued light. Three times only during the play does the sun shine: once, at the beginning, most ironically, when Duncan draws near Macbeth's castle of death at Inverness; then in the England scene; and again, at the very end, when Macduff invades Macbeth's castle at Dunsinane and symbolically restores the light to Scotland.

The images involving blood begin at the very opening of the play with the appearance of the bleeding sergeant who, reporting Macbeth's valor in battle, says that his sword "smoked with bloody execution"; then follow the "bloody dagger" that tempts Macbeth to murder, the hands deeply stained in Duncan's blood, the "blood-bolter'd" face of Banquo's ghost, Macbeth's remark that he has waded so deeply in blood that to go back would be no better than to go on, Lady Macbeth's attempt to wash the smell of blood from her hands, the image of Scotland bleeding to death from the wounds inflicted by Macbeth, and, at the close of the play, Macbeth likened by Macduff to a bloody villain and a butcher. And, yet, the final impression left by the play, though harrowing, is not revolting, because of Shakespeare's supreme ability to create characters so human that we are forced to suspend judgment upon actions which arouse deep feelings of pity and terror.

The theme of *Macbeth* might very well be expressed in the words with which Euripides concluded *Medea:* "Those things we count on do not come to pass, while the things we do not dream of are bound to happen." Shakespeare makes it abundantly clear that no man is able to arrange his future or to control his fate; and certainly not the man who meddles with evil and thus willfully exposes himself to the hazards of retaliation and chance. Banquo committed no active wrong, and yet in a sense he had to pay for condoning evil, for he stood silently by, suppressing his knowledge of the witches' predictions while Macbeth took advantage of them and pursued his career of crime. That does not mean that Shakespeare subscribed to the idea of "poetic justice"—punishment for the bad, rewards for the good; Duncan did not deserve to be murdered, nor did Lady Macduff and her children, but that is the unaccountable way in which things happen in this uncertain world. Shakespeare does not deny the existence of free will—Macbeth acts with full consciousness of what he is doing, as does Macduff when he goes off to England for aid—but the results are always in doubt.

About one thing Shakespeare leaves no doubt: Macbeth was a man full of "the milk of human kindness," frank, sociable, and generous, who was tempted to a life of crime by excellent opportunities, the instigations of his wife, and prophetic warnings, and thoughtlessly cast away his loyalty and his virtue. The tragedy lies in the fact that Macbeth "had to pay with his life, for the murder of his principles." And here we have a clue to the profound significance of the witches, who, while they clearly echo emotional drives and deep, unconscious self-knowledge, relate at the same time to the blind, inchoate forces of evil that are at large in the world. Men are thereby seduced, both from within and without, not only to destroy others but to waste their own most precious endowments. Such subtleties, with which the play is rich, help to account for its lasting power and importance.

PRODUCTION IN THE ELIZABETHAN THEATER

The Theater

Before there were any theaters in London, the acting companies gave public performances in the courtyards of such inns as The Bell, The Crosskeys, The Bull, and The Bel Savage. These yards were rectangular or square, surrounded on four sides by the inn but open to the sky. A platform stage was erected at one end of the yard, and the audience entered from the street through an archway at which a money-gatherer was stationed. Galleries, or balconies, ran around the interior of the court, overlooking the yard, and provided excellent locations from which the guests of the inn could watch the plays; these spectators, too, rewarded the players. But the innyards presented certain disadvantages, since the actors were at the mercy of the landlords who demanded a large share of their profits and imposed restrictive rules and regulations upon them, as did the civic authorities who looked upon players as a public menace.

In 1574, Queen Elizabeth, who defended the acted drama against the attacks of the city government, granted a special license to James Burbage and four fellows of the company of the Earl of Leicester to exhibit all kinds of stage plays during the Queen's pleasure in any part of England, "as well for the recreation of her loving subjects as for her own solace and enjoyment." The very next year, however, the mayor and corporation of London formally expelled all players from the city.

Actors had always been at the mercy of the city officials and of the Puritans who complained that public performances attracted great crowds of unruly people, were the breeding-place of infections and plagues, provided a hangout for pickpockets, prostitutes, and other low characters, caused people to waste money on entertainment that should have been spent on more substantial commodities, and, worst of all, were "the sink of all sin" and the enemy "to virtue and religion." None of this was literally true, but in order to escape from these restrictions and reproaches, James Burbage conceived the idea and drew up plans for a building to be devoted solely to the presentation of plays. This theater, the first of its kind in England, would be his own, and so he would be unhampered by the landlords of the inns; and if he selected its site carefully, the City Fathers would have no power over him. He had four locations to choose from; these were the so-called "liberties," the lands taken over from the Catholic church and still held by the Crown free of all city control. He decided to build his playhouse in the Liberty of Holywell, on the edge of Finsbury Fields, a public playground in the north of London to which crowds of people went in a holiday mood seeking pleasure and recreation.

The Theatre, as the playhouse was called, began to go up in April, 1576, and showed clearly that it embodied the best features of the bull- and the bear-baiting rings as well as those of the innyards. Like the bull-ring, it was circular in shape to accommodate large numbers of people and provide excellent sight-lines; like the innyards it had a platform stage and balconies around the interior. In 1577 another playhouse, The Curtain, was built close by The Theatre, and this, too, came under the control of Burbage. Their design served, with improvements, as the model for all the theaters of the period.

When James Burbage died in 1597, his property was left to his sons, Cuthbert and Richard, who two years later formed a company with the actors in the troupe, including William Shakespeare, John Heminges, Augustine Phillips, Thomas Pope, and Will Kempe, for the erection of a new house to replace The Theatre. The old building was torn down and the timber was transported to the south bank of the Thames, which had become the new theater district; there, with the assistance of Peter Street, an expert carpenter and builder, the Burbages built the celebrated Globe Theater.

There have been some rather detailed conjectures about the physical structure of the Globe, but few actual records survive. The house, it is said, was octagonal in shape and open to the sky; it was three stories high and accommodated over two thousand people. The building had two entrances—one in front for the audience; one in the rear for the actors, musicians, and the personnel of the theater. Inside the building, a rectangular platform stage—about 40 feet wide, 25 feet deep, and 6 feet high—projected into the middle of the yard. There were no seats on the ground floor; the audience, called "groundlings," stood in front of and on both sides of the stage. Around and above the yard ran three galleries approached by interior stairs and divided into "rooms" or boxes where the better class of spectators sat on stools. Over a large part of the platform stage there extended a wooden roof, called "the heavens" or "the shadow," which was supported by two pillars that rested on the stage; the roof served partly to protect the actors from bad weather, but primarily to contain the machinery needed to let down such stage properties as thrones or to "fly" actors impersonating fairies or gods. At the rear of the stage there was a deep recess, or alcove, called an "inner stage," that was curtained off and also served as a playing area, mainly for interior scenes. On the right and left at the rear of the platform, there were doors leading into the tiring-house, where the dressing rooms were situated; these doors were used for entrances and exits by the players. In the floors of the platform and of the inner stage there were trapdoors through which actors or properties such as the Witches' cauldron in *Macbeth,* could be made suddenly to appear or disappear. On each of the three stories there was a recess above the inner stage; the recess on the second floor, like the one below it, was curtained off and served as an acting area—for balcony or battlements; the alcove on the third floor was called the Music Room as it was used by the men who supplied the musical accompaniment to the play. Above the "heavens" were little huts and a tower; the huts were used by the sound-effects men and possibly for the storage of costumes and properties; from the tower a flag was unfurled on the days that performances were given in the theater, and in the tower there was a great bell; also from the tower a trumpeter blew three blasts on his horn to announce the beginning of the play. Over the front door of the theater swung a wooden sign showing Hercules carrying the globe on his back, and under him appeared the legend, *Totus mundus agit histrionem* (All the world's a stage).

Admission to the theater was a penny; this entitled the person to stand in the yard. To sit or stand in the galleries, the spectator was required to pay an extra penny or two depending upon the location.

The first Globe playhouse had a thatched roof which proved the theater's undoing. In 1613, at the premiere performance of *Henry VIII,* by Shakespeare and Fletcher, a cannon was fired from one of the huts to signal the entrance of the king at a dramatic moment in the play; some of the sparks or wadding from the cannon lighted on the thatch and in less than an hour the theater was burned to the ground, luckily with no fatalities. One stanza of a popular ballad of the day reports:

> Out run the knights, out run the lords,
> And there was great ado;
> Some lost their hats, and some their swords;
> Then out run Burbage, too.

The following year the New Globe was erected on the old site; it was more beautiful and lavish than the former house, and this time it was roofed with tiles.

Scenery, Lighting, Properties

There was a certain amount of built and painted scenery, flat and three-dimensional pieces, on the Elizabethan stage, as we learn from the *Diary* of Philip Henslowe, one of the important theater-owners of the period; but the scenery was used as it had been in the medieval period, rather than it is in modern times. The modern theater has what is known as a "picture-frame" stage, which is entirely concealed by a front curtain. When the curtain is drawn up, it is as if the wall of a room has been removed, allowing us an intimate view of the goings on inside. The scenery in the modern theater usually represents a definite place at a definite time, a scene-change being a major operation accomplished behind a lowered curtain. The Elizabethan theater, like the medieval, had no front curtain, and the platform stage was unlocalized; that is, it was neutral ground that might represent a public square, a forest, a street, or a seacoast, in rapid succession. This feat was performed by a stagehand who, in full view of the audience, carried on and off such simple set-pieces and properties as a rock, a tree, or a gate. In addition to these significant and movable items, the lines of the play would indicate the locale and the time of day or night at the opening of each scene; it was up to the audience to exercise its imagination and supply the missing details in the décor. On this type of stage, different times and places could succeed each other as rapidly as stagehands and actors came and went.

The inner stage and the chamber above it were curtained off, as has been said, so that it was possible for these areas to be furnished to represent definite places —a bedroom, a prison, or a throne-room. Painted canvas or tapestries were hung in the alcoves to help suggest locale; if a tragedy was being performed, the draperies were black. Very often the inner stage and the platform were combined into a single set; the curtain would open and disclose, for instance, that the inner stage was a throne-room—king and queen would be seated on two large gilded chairs and courtiers stood about. As the scene progressed, the actors would move out of the alcove on to the platform, thus making that area part of the throne-room; in similar manner various other acting areas could be used in combination, thus giving the Elizabethan stage enormous flexibility, variety, and interest.

The Elizabethan play took two and one half to three hours to perform and was presented in the afternoon from three to six in the summer and from two to five in the winter. In this open-air theater, general illumination was provided by natural daylight; the platform always had enough light upon it, and even the alcoves, under the "heavens," were amply lit. But many scenes were supposed to take place at night or in the darkness of caves and cells, and this provided the opportunity for the use of torches, cressets, candles, and lanterns. *Macbeth,* which was called in its entirety "a thing of night," has scene after scene in which special lighting is obligatory: cressets affixed to walls to cast flickering lights on bloody daggers or bloody hands; sad, fluttering candles for the sleep-walking scene; and lurid, miasmic flames for the cauldron of the witches. The fact that all of these things were going on in broad daylight did not disturb the Elizabethan spectator; it was one of the conventions of his theater which he accepted.

The properties in use on the Elizabethan stage served an impressionistic or a symbolic rather than a realistic purpose. Large gilded chairs would signify a throne-room; a fourposter, a bedroom; and a rough-hewn table and some stools, a tavern. The locales changed so quickly that it would have been impossible to "dress a set" in minute detail. There were innumerable hand properties—daggers and swords, fans, handkerchiefs, goblets, musical instruments, and, in the Senecan melodramas, such as *Titus Andronicus,* several heads and hands—but all of these were carried on and off by the actors.

The arras, an imitation tapestry, or "painted cloth," was one type of hanging, but there were various kinds of curtains, all easily removable; and the floors of all the acting areas were covered with rushes, a kind of dried grass, in lieu of carpeting. The rushes were swept out after each performance, and the stage was freshly strewn for the next. Occasionally we hear of matting or rugs being used.

The Actors

Three classes of persons were connected with the theaters: sharers, hirelings, and servants. The "sharers" were the most important actors, who actually made up the "company," and who divided among themselves the money taken in each day at the door; according to their importance, some received whole shares, others half-shares. The "hirelings" were actors of lower rank who did not share in the large profits of the theater but were engaged by the company at a fixed and rather small salary. Many of these were young people who were regarded as apprentices and as possible future sharers, depending upon their development. Musicians were also engaged on a salary basis. The "servants" were employed by the company as prompters, stagehands, property-keepers, money-gatherers, and caretakers of the building.

The actors in the Elizabethan theater were all male; women were not permitted to appear upon the stage. The parts of young women were played by boys, those of old women or of hags, like the witches in *Macbeth,* were played by men. In the days before the theaters were built, a traveling company of players would consist of four or five men and one or two boys; the plays they performed often contained as many as twenty or thirty characters, so that each actor was required to play several parts. This practice of doubling actually remained in force and developed into a high art in Shakespeare's company, which at its peak employed only twelve men and six boys. Yet the cast of *Macbeth* lists twenty-eight characters and requires, in addition, Apparitions, Lords, Gentlemen, Officers, Soldiers, Murderers, Attendants, and Messengers. An analysis of the play will show that only Macbeth and Lady Macbeth remain throughout the action, while the other characters make brief appearances; Malcolm and Macduff, for example, have important scenes at the beginning and the end of the play, but would be free to double at other times.

Each actor in Shakespeare's company, particularly the stars or sharers, had his specialty. Richard Burbage was the leading man; he created the roles of Richard III, Romeo, Hamlet, Othello, Macbeth, and King Lear; Will Kempe, a low comedian, played such parts as Dogberry in *Much Ado about Nothing* and Bottom in *A Midsummer Night's Dream;* his place in the company was later taken by a more subtle and refined comedian, Robert Armin, who acted the First Grave-digger in *Hamlet* and the Fool in *King Lear;* John Heminges specialized in old men: Polonius in *Hamlet* and Brabantio in *Othello;* while Augustine Phillips and Thomas Pope may have played the fickle lovers or the bragging soldiers.

The actors were trained, as in other Elizabethan professions, under an apprenticeship system. A boy would start at the age of ten and be required to pay a sum of money to the master for whom he would work for seven years without receiving a salary; in return he would be given board and lodging and taught his trade thoroughly. The experienced actor would teach the boy in his care to play women's parts and also the type of part in which the older actor specialized so that his apprentice might become his successor. It is believed that the boys were hired in pairs: two who were about ten years of age, two about twelve to fourteen, and two between fifteen and eighteen. The eldest would serve as leading ladies as long as their voices and bodily development allowed, then they would graduate into adult roles, at which point a new pair of ten-year-olds would be taken on. An effort would be made to select a serious, blond, blue-eyed boy along with a boy who was small and dark for comedy; these types are paired in many of Shakespeare's plays. Some of these boys, such as Nathaniel Field and Richard Robinson, went on to become celebrated actors and writers and sharers in the company. Sir Laurence Olivier, in modern times, began his acting career at fifteen by playing Katharine in *The Taming of the Shrew* at Stratford-on-Avon.

In acting the women's parts, the boys played with great simplicity, directness, and restraint; Shakespeare, in fact, underemphasized sex in these roles. In many of the comedies, furthermore, the heroines disguised themselves as boys.

It is more difficult to attempt to describe the acting style of the adults. It could not have been as naturalistic as that of our own day, principally because the dialogue was written in verse. It must to some extent have been stylized and declamatory, although we know from Hamlet's advice to the Players that Shakespeare deplored ranting and bombast and broad, empty gestures. We deduce from Hamlet's speech the following set of rules for the actor: The speeches were to be spoken rapidly but intelligibly; the body movements and gestures were to be natural; the energy and emotions were to be under control at all times; the actor was to identify himself closely not only with the character he was playing but also with the customs and conventions of his day; and, finally, the actor was not to play down to his audience and be satisfied with cheap effects, but was to strive for the approval of the serious and discerning playgoer, rare as he might be.

Costumes

All Elizabethan plays were done, so to speak, in modern dress; that is, the costumes of the actors were the last word in contemporary fashion. The women wore the wide-spreading farthingale made of satin, velvet, taffeta, cloth of gold, silver, or copper, and the ruff of stiff lawn. The person was ornamented with gold and silver jewelry, precious stones, and strings of pearls. The men wore doublet and hose made of rich and contrasting materials, trimmed with lace of gold, silver, or thread; the jacket and cloak were made of silk or velvet; the ruffs, of stiff lawn; the shoes of fine, soft leather; and the outer robes were heavily furred. The actors, like the fops and ladies of the period, were also interested in the high styles of foreign countries and so appeared in German trunks, French hose, Spanish hats, and Italian cloaks confusingly mixed. The satirists of the day ridiculed these fashions, and clowns appeared on the stage in exaggerated parodies of them. In *The Merchant of Venice* (I, 2), Portia remarks of a young English nobleman: "How oddly he is suited! I think he bought his doublet in Italy, his round hose in France, his bonnet in Germany. . . ."

The colors too were dazzling and symbolic. One gown was white, gold, silver, red, and green; another was black, purple, crimson, and white; and there were dresses of such delicate tints as coral pink, silver, and gray. These, among many others, were the colors of the nobility and the courtiers, while servants were limited to dark blue or mustard-colored garments. Green sleeves, which became celebrated in song, were the mark of the courtesan.

In addition to their secular garments, the actors wore elaborate robes of state, impressive ecclesiastical vestments, and the various military and civic uniforms of the day.

Elizabethan stage costumes were undoubtedly magnificent and costly; they represented, in fact, the most expensive item in the production budget. One producer paid a dramatist 8 pounds for a play, then spent 20 pounds on a gown for the leading lady; another garment cost more than the theater took in in a week. But there was obviously a need for this spectacular display to offset the paucity of scenery and to satisfy the demand of the audience for eye-filling splendor and pageantry.

It did not in the least disturb the playgoer that Timon of Athens, Julius Caesar of Rome, and Cleopatra of Egypt all wore Elizabethan costumes. Nor did he appear to be bothered by the fact that ancient and contemporary costumes were worn side by side, a man in medieval armor talking to one in a fashionable doublet, with the occasional intermixture of such foreign items as a Moor's robe, a Turkish turban, or Shylock's "Jewish gaberdine." No attempt was made to achieve complete historical accuracy of costume until the nineteenth century.

A number of fantastic costumes were in use for fairies, devils, and clowns, but these were patterned mainly on traditional representations which had come down from the medieval mystery and miracle plays. The devils wore tails, cloven hoofs, and horns; the clowns were dressed like country yokels or wore the red and yellow motley of the fool; ghosts usually wore sheets, though that of Hamlet's father appeared in full armor; the witches in *Macbeth* wore ugly masks and fright wigs.

The costumes were acquired in various ways and might belong to the company jointly or to the individual actors. Some new garments were bought but these were so expensive as to be almost prohibitive; an effort was therefore made to get hold of secondhand clothing. Many courtiers, either because they were in need or because they did not wish to be seen too frequently in the same outfits, sold their finery to the players. Upon the deaths of some noblemen their expensive clothes were willed to servants or to poor relatives who sold them in turn to the actors. After the death of Mary of Scotland her wardrobe was turned over to Queen Elizabeth who presented these beautiful gowns to actors in lieu of a fee. If a theatrical company failed, its costumes were sold to active competitors. Some theater owners rented their costumes to other companies; and each company had at least one or two tailors in regular employ who busily altered or renovated the costumes on hand.

We may gain some notion of the magnitude of the problem faced in costuming the players when we realize that successful companies produced as many as forty plays in a season.

Music and Dance

The Elizabethan age was a highly musical one; instrumental and vocal music in solo or concert enlivened all public and private occasions. The Elizabethan play was accompanied almost throughout by music that either served an integral dramatic purpose or was merely incidental to the action.

There were four basic types of music used in the plays: military and ceremonial music, songs sung either with or without instrumental accompaniment, incidental instrumental music played as an accompaniment to dancing, action, or speech, and unmotivated background music used to create a special mood or atmosphere. In addition, many sound effects were employed to heighten the aural appeal of the plays by arousing tensions and simulating reality. In A *Midsummer Night's Dream,* the musicians may actually have appeared on the stage, but usually the music emanated from the Music Room on the second gallery above the stage.

The military and ceremonial music was used most frequently in the chronicle history plays, but was also employed in the tragedies. Such directions in the text as "alarums and excursions" called for the blast of trumpets, clash of cymbals, and roll of drums. Charges and retreats required trumpets, as did fanfares or flourishes which announced the entry of royal or noble persons. The hautboy, forerunner of the oboe, was another instrument much used in military scenes.

Many songs found their way into the plays. Shakespeare composed a number of original ones; others were popular songs of the day, or old traditional airs. The clown Feste, in *Twelfth Night,* sings an ancient ballad "Come Away, Death" accompanied by instrumentalists who are on stage. But the old drinking song, "And let me the canikin clink, clink," sung in the tavern scene in *Othello,* was unaccompanied except by the banging of tankards.

From the Music Room came the background, or "still," music, as it was called, which helped to intensify the terrifying atmosphere and eerie mood of the Apparition and Witch scenes in *Macbeth.* A thunderclap is heard as each Apparition appears and his passage across the stage must have been accompanied by strange unearthly sounds; the dance of the witches, too, which was frenzied and frightening, must have been done to music.

Sound effects were closely related to musical effects and were frequently called for in the plays. Thunder, the clashing of metal and clanking of chains, cannon shots and fireworks, the tolling of bells, and winding of hunting horns are only a few of the sounds which the Elizabethan stagehands had to produce.

Dancing, like music, was immensely popular in the social life of the time and played an equally important part in many of the plays. The most popular court dances were the allemande, the courante, the galliard, the lavolta, and the pavan; while the most celebrated country dances were Sellenger's Round and the Hay. Each dance had its own traditional music. Many of the comedies ended with the gayer of these dances, while the more stately dances helped to advance the plots of the serious plays. Shakespeare made use of dances in this dual way—to entertain the audience at his comedies and to heighten the dramatic action in his tragedies. It is at a great formal dance, to which he has come in order to see Rosaline, that Romeo first meets Juliet. And just before the King appears at Cardinal Wolsey's supper-dance, in *Henry VIII*, there is the stage direction, "Drum and trumpet; chambers discharged." As we have noted, at this play's premiere the firing of the cannon caused the Globe Theatre to burn to the ground, but the audience was so enthralled by the music, dancing, and sound effects going on at the moment, that they barely escaped with their lives.

The Audience

The Elizabethan theater was the most democratic institution in an undemocratic age. The audience was socially, economically, and educationally heterogeneous; every class was represented, from cutpurse to courtier.

Many Londoners were indifferent to the theater; others were openly hostile for religious reasons; but those who went attended more or less regularly once a week. It is believed that about 15,000 a week went in 1595, when two companies were operating; 18,000 went in 1601, when four companies were operating; and 21,000 went in 1605, when five companies were operating. By occupation, the largest single group in the audience, about 71 percent, consisted of shopkeepers and craftsmen; the second largest group, about 22 percent, was made up of porters, servants, laborers, with a sprinkling of such miscellaneous characters as prostitutes and pickpockets; the remaining 7 percent was accounted for by members of the nobility, professional men, and the gentry. Men, women, and children attended.

The Elizabethan playhouse accommodated from 2,000 to 2,500 people, but usually played to only half of capacity. On holidays, however, or on days when a special old favorite or a new play was being presented, the house would be jammed; then about one-third of the audience would stand in the yard, while the rest sat or stood in the galleries.

The penny paid as general admission had the buying power equivalent to the price of a movie today, so that the extra pennies charged for the better locations made those seats rather expensive. Only one other place in the theater commanded a higher price: sixpence was charged for a stool on the stage. Young gallants—wealthy playboys—who put on their finest clothes and went to the theater not to see the play but to be seen themselves would occupy these prominent places. The custom of sitting on the stage persisted until the eighteenth century when David Garrick abolished it.

All of the members of the audience put on their best clothes when they went to the theater, but the gallants outdid everyone except perhaps the members of the nobility. The audience was generally relaxed and in a gay mood; people smoked, ate oranges, and nuts during the performance. They cracked the nuts between their teeth and sometimes annoyed the actors and other members of the audience with the sound.

Although the enemies of the theater claimed that audiences were unruly and given to fighting and rioting, unbiased observers of the time speak only of the excellent behavior and rapt attention of the spectators, who laughed, applauded, and wept when their emotions were stirred, hissed or booed when they were displeased, but most of the time listened in interested silence.

The general mingling in the theater of people from all walks of life was a major cause of complaint on the part of public officials and Puritans, who were bent upon maintaining class distinctions and social barriers; but it gave the playwright the unique opportunity of appealing to individuals not as members of a class but simply as men with wide and varied backgrounds and tastes, and in so doing to write great plays of universal significance. This was the Elizabethan audience's contribution to the plays of Shakespeare.

THE PRODUCTION RECORD

Macbeth was especially written to entertain King James I and his guest, King Christian IV of Denmark, at Hampton Court on August 7, 1606. (See *The Royal Play of Macbeth* by Henry N. Paul, Macmillan, N.Y., 1950.) The play was acted at court by Richard Burbage and the King's Men and, a month or so later, was given its first public performance at the Globe Theatre. It was immediately successful and often repeated. At some time between 1610 and 1612, it is believed, the figure of Hecate and three additional witches, who sang and danced, were introduced into the play from Thomas Middleton's work *The Witch*. Since this was in line with the audience's growing taste for spectacle, the play was presented in this manner until the Puritans closed the theaters in 1642.

With the restoration of the drama, Sir William Davenant, who claimed to be Shakespeare's godson, was given authority by the king "to reform and make fit" for the audiences of 1660 the plays of the earlier period. Davenant lost no time in "improving" *Macbeth* by turning it into something like an opera. His version of the play was described as follows: "The Tragedy of Macbeth, alter'd by Sir William Davenant; being drest in all its Finery, as new Cloaths, new Scenes, Machines, as flyings for the Witches; with all the Singing and Dancing in it: The first compos'd by Mr. Lock, the other by Mr. Channell and Mr. Joseph Priest; it being all Excellently perform'd, being in the Nature of an Opera, it Recompenc'd double the Expense; it proves still a lasting play."

Pepys mentions in his *Diary* that he saw *Macbeth* nine times between 1660 and 1669 and liked it better each time, clearly because Davenant kept adding "improvements." Davenant had two favorite hobbies: operatic and scenic splendor, which led particularly to the elaboration of the witch scenes to include songs, dances, and gibberish, which was either borrowed out of old plays or specially written for the occasion; and structural balance in the play in line with neo-classical "rules." This led to the amplification of the role of Lady Macduff so that numerous scenes between her and her husband might be set in contrast to those of Macbeth and his wife. Lady Macduff was terribly virtuous, always cautioning her husband against ambition; in one scene she begs Macduff not to leave his family, but he, resolved to go to England for aid, says of Macbeth:

> He will not injure you, he cannot be
> Possest with such unmanly cruelty.

This is an example of the poetic quality of the material added to the play by Davenant. Yet, poor as it was from a literary point of view and much as it detracted from Shakespeare's work, this material acted so well and was so popular with the public that *Macbeth* was performed in Davenant's version until 1744, when Garrick introduced his own "improvements."

In January, 1744, David Garrick announced that he would produce *Macbeth* "as written by Shakespeare." James Quin, a rival actor, was surprised and shocked; he asked, "What does he mean? Don't I play *Macbeth* as written by Shakespeare?" Garrick removed all of Davenant's ineptly written scenes involving Lady Macduff and her morals, but in his zeal he went so far as to cut Shakespeare's scene of the murder of her children. The drunken porter was also cut out; but the witches with their singing, dancing, and cavorting, were retained, and many additional apparitions were introduced. For Macbeth's death scene, Garrick wrote a speech in which he mentioned "with dying breath, his guilt, delusion, the witches, and those horrid visions of future punishment, which must ever appall and torture the last moments of such accumulated crimes." Garrick was concerned, too, with the costumes in his plays; he mentions the red coats of Macbeth and Banquo, and says that Macbeth's night gown [dressing gown] "ought to be a Red Damask, and not the frippery flower'd one of a Foppington." In accordance with the fashion of the time, all the actors wore wigs, so we are not surprised to learn that Banquo's ghost also appeared in a tie-wig.

Garrick wrote the following remarks as to the manner in which the actor play-ing Macbeth should behave after the murder of Duncan:

> He should at that time, be a moving statue, or indeed a petrified man; his eyes must speak, and his tongue be metaphorically silent; his ears must be sensible of imaginary noises, and deaf to the present and audible voice of his wife; his attitude must be quick and permanent; his voice articulately trembling, and confusedly in-telligible; the murderer should be seen in every limb, and yet every member, at that

instant, should seem separated from his body, and his body from his soul. This is the picture of a complete regicide . . . I hope I shall not be thought minutely circumstantial, if I should advise a real genius to wear cork heels to his shoes, as in this scene he should seem to tread on air, and I promise him he will soon discover the great benefit of this (however seemingly trifling) piece of advice.

In 1773 an attempt was made to introduce historical accuracy into a production of *Macbeth*. Charles Macklin tried for some authenticity in scenery and costumes when he acted the play at Covent Garden. The actors wore Scottish tartans, but the leading lady dressed as she pleased. A contemporary critic, who displays an unusual archeological sense, wrote:

> The Scenes, Decorations and Dresses, were very striking and magnificent, the cannon on Macbeth's castle, however, were a violation of the costume in painting [on the backdrop], as firearms were invented many centuries after the coronation of Malcolm. Lady Macbeth's modern robes by no means accorded with the habits of the other personages, and Mr. Macklin's flowing curls, like the locks of Adonis, were unpardonably out of character.

The reviewer makes no mention of the fact that during the performance the audience broke out in a riot.

The next great innovation in the play was in the acting of Mrs. Sarah Siddons, who first performed the role in 1785 and continued in it for a quarter of a century. Mrs. Siddons depicted Lady Macbeth as an iron woman. From her first scene she showed the decisiveness of the whole character and the daring steadiness of her mind, which could be disturbed by no scruple, intimidated by no danger. When she came on with the letter from Macbeth, in her first entrance, her face, her form, and her deportment gave the impression that she was possessed by a demon. She read the whole letter with the greatest skill and novelty and after an instant of reflection, exclaimed,

> Glamis thou art, and Cawdor—and shalt be
> What thou art promised.

The amazing burst of energy upon the words "shalt be" perfectly electrified the house. In the performance of the sleep-walking scene, Mrs. Siddons differed essentially from every other actress. "The actresses previous to herself," the account continues, "rather glided than walked, and every other action had a feebler character than is exhibited by one awake. Their figure, too, was kept perpendicularly erect, and the eye, though open, studiously avoided motion. . . . Mrs. Siddons seemed to conceive the fancy as having equal power over the whole frame, and all her actions had the wakeful vigor; she laded the water from the imaginary ewer over her hands—bent her body to listen to the sounds presented by her fancy, and hurried to resume the taper where she had left it, that she might with all speed drag her pallid husband to their chamber."

The character of Lady Macbeth seemed to become the exclusive possession of Mrs. Siddons during her lifetime; there was a mystery about it which she alone appeared to have penetrated. Mrs. Siddons also made a strong attempt to reform stage costume; she did away with the hoop skirts, flounces, trains, and enormous headgear which were the order of the day; her costumes were simpler and more in keeping with the characters she portrayed. In the sleep-walking scene in *Macbeth* it was observed: "The quantity of white drapery in which the actress was enveloped had a singular and stimulating effect . . . majestic both in form and motion—it was, however, the majesty of the tomb." Despite all of these genuine innovations, her production still contained Davenant's music, dancing, and spectacle.

Every important English actor of the nineteenth century—John Kemble, Edmund Kean, Charles Kemble, Charles Macready—appeared in an elaborately mounted production of *Macbeth*, but it never occurred to these men to act the play as it had originally been written. That honor belongs to Samuel Phelps, who in 1847 produced the play from the text of the First Folio. It had not been done in this manner for about two hundred years. Not only were all of Davenant's and Garrick's interpolations omitted, but even Macklin's tartans were rejected as not accurate for the early times of Macbeth. Instead Phelps's actors wore "primitive mantles, with their heavy bars and ponderous folds," harmonizing well "with our notions of the early, almost traditional period of the play." Sir Laurence Olivier's production at Stratford-on-Avon in 1955 was conceived in similar fashion.

Charles Kean went further than anyone else in attempting to achieve archeological correctness in the scenery and costumes; he consulted the most important scholars in England, and his program notes read like a doctoral dissertation. The actor knew what the eleventh-century Scotsman wore, what he ate, what weapons he fought with, and how he illuminated his home, but he used Davenant's mutilated version of the play. That mistake was not made by the early actors of the present century—Henry Irving, Forbes-Robertson, and Beerbohm Tree—but *they* failed as Macbeth because they lacked the voice, physical power, stature, or temperament for the role.

The first recorded performance of *Macbeth* in America took place in 1768, when, in its initial season in New York, the American Company, headed by David Douglass and Lewis Hallam, Jr., mounted the play at the John Street Theatre. It was produced many times and in many cities after that. Early in the nineteenth century, Thomas Abthorpe Cooper, the manager of the Park Theatre, New York, and its leading actor, created a sensation with his stirring performance as Macbeth; he took the play on tour to Boston and Philadelphia and won applause wherever he appeared. In his capacity as manager, Cooper brought the great English star, George Frederick Cooke, to America and Cooke's interpretation of the role surpassed even Cooper's. Washington Irving saw Cooke perform in Philadelphia and in a letter to his brother Pierre recorded his impressions:

> I stopped in accidentally at the theater a few evenings since, when he [Cooke] was playing Macbeth; not expecting to receive any pleasure, for you recollect he performed it very indifferently in New York. I entered just at the time he was meditating the murder, and I remained to the end of the play in a state of admiration and delight. The old boy absolutely outdid himself; his dagger scene, his entrance to

Duncan's chamber, and his horror after the commission of the dead, completed a dramatic action that I shall never forget as long as I live; it was sublime. I place the performance of that evening among the higher pieces of acting I have ever witnessed. You know I had before considered Cooper as much superior to him in Macbeth, but on this occasion the character made more impression on me than when played by Cooper, or even Kemble. The more I see of Cooke, the more I admire his style of acting; he is very unequal, from his irregular habits and nervous affections; but when he is in proper mood, there is a truth and, of course, a simplicity in his performance, that throws all rant, stage-trick, and stage-effect completely in the background. Were he to remain here a sufficient time for the public to perceive and dwell upon his merits, and the true character of his playing, he would produce a new taste in acting.

Throughout the nineteenth century the play was performed in many different styles of acting not only by all the important native stars, such as Edwin Forrest, James H. Hackett, and Edwin Booth, but also by such visiting luminaries as Edmund Kean, Charles Mathews, and Junius Brutus Booth. During her final American engagement in 1885, Adelaide Ristori, the "Italian Siddons," played Lady Macbeth to the Macbeth of Edwin Booth. Here was a masterful performance which she later described in detail in her *Memoirs and Artistic Studies*. The following is a brief illustration of her technique. Macbeth has just seen Banquo's ghost; the guests have departed; the unhappy king is alone with his wife. Ristori writes:

> At the end of the act, at the moment of leaving, I make it apparent that I am penetrated with a deep sense of pity for Macbeth who for my sake has become the most miserable of men, and tell him: "You lack the season of all natures, sleep." I take hold of his left hand with my right and place it over my right shoulder, then painfully bending my head in deep reflection and turning toward my husband with a look filled with remorse which is agitating my mind, I drag him toward our chamber in the same manner that one leads an insane person. When reaching the limit of the stage Macbeth, frightened by the tail of his cloak lining trailing at my feet, again shudders suddenly. Then with a quick turn, I pass on the other side of him, and try to master the terror with which I am also seized in spite of myself. Using a little violence I succeed in pushing him behind the wings, while quieting him with affectionate gestures. This mode of acting was not contradictory to the logic and reality of the situation, and always produced a great effect.

It was not until the present century that any serious or concerted effort was made to present Shakespeare's plays exactly as they were written, in conditions approximating to those of their original performance, that is, on a platform stage without scenery. Credit for initiating the return to this mode of production must go to William Poel, who in 1895 founded the Elizabethan Stage Society, and under its auspices put on many of Shakespeare's plays as he conceived that they had been done at the Globe. Poel insisted upon the rapid and clear speaking of the verse, with varied emphasis, and introduced startling stage business so as not to permit the attention of the audience to flag for an instant. He produced *Macbeth* in 1909, with Hubert Carter in the title role and Lillah McCarthy as Lady

Macbeth; the Three Witches were played by the Irish actors William, Frank, and Brigit Fay, whose heavy brogues lent a strange, foreign quality to the proceedings. During the banquet scene, the ghost of Duncan as well as the ghost of Banquo appeared, and Poel showed that there was some warrant for this in the text.

Poel's work met with the opposition of the old-line producers, the objections of the critics, and the indifference of the public; but he left his mark unmistakably upon the more sensitive, intelligent, and enterprising members of his profession. Those who felt his influence and enlarged upon his ideas include Ben Greet, Gordon Craig, Max Reinhardt, Granville-Barker, Tyrone Guthrie, E. Martin Browne, Peter Brook, John Gielgud, and Laurence Olivier.

Two of the most interesting productions of *Macbeth* to be done in America in the present century were notable for the experimental nature of their designs. On February 17, 1921, Arthur Hopkins produced and directed the play at the Apollo Theater, New York, with Lionel Barrymore and Julia Arthur in the leading roles, incidental music by Robert Russell Bennett, and symbolic scenery by Robert Edmond Jones. Jones wrote of his designs:

> These drawings illustrate a tendency to break away from the pictorial conventions of scene-painting made famous by the great European decorators, and to substitute in their place abstract, highly conventionalized arrangements of form and color and light which aim not so much to please the eye as a picture as to give continuous support to the action of the drama. These settings are pure theatric creations, having nothing to do with actual period or place. They may prove to be interesting in their relation to a new form of drama which will deal directly with the realities of vision.

The critics reacted very strongly both for and against this production, but the public was unmoved and it ran for only twenty-eight performances.

Another "designer's version" of the play was put on by George C. Tyler at the Knickerbocker Theatre in New York, November 19, 1928, starring Lyn Harding as Macbeth, Florence Reed as Lady Macbeth, and William Farnum as Banquo. The play was staged by Douglas Ross, who spent some time in Italy consulting with the designer, Gordon Craig. This was Craig's only production in America. From a financial point of view, the play was a failure, since it ran for only sixty four performances; but Craig had been inspired by the scenic principles of the Duke of Saxe-Meiningen as well as by those of the great Adolphe Appia, and helped to pass them on to Robert Edmond Jones, Norman Bel Geddes, and Jo Mielziner.

During 1948 and 1950, Margaret Webster's Travelling Shakespeare Company took two plays—*Hamlet* and *Macbeth*—to high schools, colleges, and universities in various parts of the United States. The problem of the designer was to create scenery that would take up little space and could be packed with speed. Wolfgang Roth solved the problem by using telescoped booms, hanging the front curtain on a wire, the other curtains on aluminum pipes, and painted scenery that rolled up like blinds. Rearranged in different ways the curtains and simple platforms served for both plays. All of the scenery and props were carried in a single truck, while the acting company traveled in a bus.

The most expert and exciting production of *Macbeth* to be presented in English in recent years was that done by Laurence Olivier and Vivien Leigh at the Shakespeare Memorial Theatre, Stratford-on-Avon, in the summer of 1955. The play was directed by Glen Byam Shaw, a Poel disciple, and designed by Roger Furse in colorful and primitive style. Olivier's performance, amply supported by voice and physique, created an overwhelming image of naked force and emphasized, at the same time, the perverse use to which this enormous force was being put. Olivier has prepared a motion picture version of the play, but lack of financial backing is holding up its production.

Macbeth has been translated into many languages and has been acted before enthusiastic theater andiences throughout the world, notably in Germany, where Shakespeare is regarded as highly as he is in his native land. The first German production took place in Biberach in 1771; another was done in Berlin in 1777, and two more followed in Mannheim and Hamburg in 1779. Almost every German theater, large and small, has played it at one time or another, and every important star, male and female, has interpreted the central roles. Eduard Devrient appeared in it in Dresden in 1854; Friedrich Mitterwurzer and Charlotte Wolter in Vienna in 1876; Louise Dumont in Düsseldorf in 1905; and Paul Wegener and Hermine Körner in Max Reinhardt's production in Berlin in 1916 which had expressionistic settings designed by Ernst Stern. Many experimental productions of the play have been mounted in Germany, outstanding among them being Leopold Jessner's fabulous presentation on a flight of stairs in Berlin in 1922, starring Fritz Kortner, and the "symbolic-space" conception done in Frankfurt in 1925.

Macbeth has been filmed several times, by amateurs as well as by professionals; two interesting screen versions were those produced by Reliance and by Republic Pictures. The earlier film was done in 1916 with Sir Herbert Tree and Constance Collier in the title roles; the 1948 version featured Orson Welles, his speech thick with Scottish burrs, and a musical score by Jacques Ibert. A Japanese screen adaptation of *Macbeth, The Throne of Blood (Kumonosu-Jo)*, was produced by the Toho Company in 1957; the story was set in sixteenth-century Japan when the war lords battled each other for supremacy. The role of Lord Washizu (Macbeth) was played by Toshiro Mifune, and Isuzu Yamada enacted the part of Lady Washizu. Akira Kurosawa, Japan's most gifted director, was in charge of the production; although it lacked the greatness of the play, the film had scenes of unusual power; two in particular—the forest moving toward the castle and Washizu meeting his death—have seldom been matched on the screen for beauty or terror. Several television versions of the play have also been done.

The continual revival of *Macbeth* in the legitimate theater is assured, because serious actors will always be challenged and put on their mettle by the play's two leading figures, who are among the most interesting and complex creations in all dramatic literature.

Simon Forman on *Macbeth*

Dr. Simon Forman, the celebrated or, more precisely, the notorious Elizabethan astrologer, left a written record called "The Book of Plays" in which he described performances he had seen of *Richard II, Cymbeline, The Winter's Tale*, and *Macbeth*. It is the only contemporary eyewitness report we have of *Macbeth* and belongs to the year 1610 or 1611, but seems to contain some minor inaccuracies. Although we know that horses were used on the stage in other productions of the time, it appears unlikely that Macbeth and Banquo made their first entrance in this play on horseback. That information comes from Holinshed, as does the expression "three women fairies or nymphs." Forman may have referred to the original source of the play to help piece out his memory. Forman's account does, however, decide a point about which there has been much discussion, namely, whether the Ghost of Banquo really appears or is only imagined by Macbeth. It is quite clear from Forman's vivid description that the Ghost was personally introduced on the stage in the earliest productions, as he was in Davenant's version a century later. It is interesting to note that in Davenant's time Banquo and his Ghost were performed by two different actors, which may have been a practice derived from Shakespeare's day. Since Forman was known to be a quack-doctor, as well as an astrologer, and is said to have caused the deaths of several people with the philters and potions he concocted for them, it is understandable that he should have seen *Macbeth* as a play powerfully portraying the workings of a guilty conscience which would inevitably betray the murderers. He was apparently most impressed by the murderers' bloody hands, by the appearance of Banquo's ghost, and by the sleepwalking scene of Lady Macbeth, which he seems to have set down as an afterthought but could under no circumstances have omitted. The following is Dr. Forman's account of the play:

In Macbeth at the Globe, 1611, the 20 of April, Saturday, there was to be observed, first how Macbeth and Banquo, two noble men of Scotland, riding through a wood, there stood before them three women fairies or nymphs, and saluted Macbeth, saying three times unto him, Hail Macbeth, King of Codon; for thou shalt be a king, but shall beget no kings, etc. Then said Banquo, What, all to Macbeth and nothing to me? Yes, said the nymphs, Hail to thee, Banquo, thou shalt beget kings, yet be no king. And so they departed and came to the court of Scotland, to Duncan, King of Scots, and it was in the days of Edward the Confessor. And Duncan bade them both kindly welcome, and made Macbeth forthwith Prince of Northumberland, and sent him home to his own castle, and appointed Macbeth to provide for him, for he would sup with him the next day at night, and did so. And Macbeth contrived to kill Duncan, and through the persuasion of his wife did that night murder in his own castle, being his guest; and there were many prodigies seen that night and the day before. And when Macbeth had murdered the king, the blood on his hands could not be washed off by any means, nor from his wife's hands, which handled the bloody daggers in hiding them, by which means they became both much amazed and affronted. The murder being known, Duncan's two sons fled, the one to England, the other to Wales, to save themselves. They being fled, they were supposed guilty of the murder of their father, which was nothing so. Then was Macbeth crowned king;

and then he, for fear of Banquo, his old companion, that he should beget kings but be no king himself, he contrived the death of Banquo, and caused him to be murdered on the way as he rode. The next night, being at supper with his noble men whom he had bid to a feast, to the which also Banquo should have come, he began to speak of noble Banquo, and to wish that he were there. And as he thus did, standing up to drink a carouse to him, the ghost of Banquo came and sat down in his chair behind him. And he, turning about to sit down again, saw the ghost of Banquo, which fronted him, so that he fell into a great passion of fear and fury, uttering many words about his murder, by which, when they heard that Banquo was murdered, they suspected Macbeth. Then Macduff fled to England, to the king's son, and so they raised an army, and came into Scotland, and at Dunsinane overthrew Macbeth. In the meantime, while Macduff was in England, Macbeth slew Macduff's wife and children, and after, in the battle, Macduff slew Macbeth. Observe also how Macbeth's queen did rise in the night in her sleep, and walk, and talked and confessed all, and the doctor noted her words.

Mrs. Siddons Speaks of Lady Macbeth

"It was my custom to study my characters at night, when all the domestic cares and business of the day were over. On the night preceding that in which I was to appear in this part for the first time, I shut myself up, as usual, when all the family were retired, and commenced my study of Lady Macbeth. As the character is very short, I thought I should soon accomplish it. Being then only twenty years of age, I believed, as many others do believe, that little more was necessary than to get the words into my head; for the necessity of discrimination, and the development of character, at that time of my life, had scarcely entered into my imagination. But, to proceed. I went on with tolerable composure, in the silence of the night (a night I can never forget), till I came to the assassination scene, when the horrors of the scene rose to a degree that made it impossible for me to get farther. I snatched up my candle, and hurried out of the room, in a paroxysm of terror. My dress was of silk, and the rustling of it, as I ascended the stairs to go to bed, seemed to my panic-struck fancy like the movement of a spectre pursuing me. At last I reached my chamber, where I found my husband fast asleep. I clapt my candlestick down upon the table, without the power of putting the candle out, and threw myself on my bed, without daring to stay even to take off my clothes. At peep of day I rose to resume my task; but so little did I know of my part when I appeared in it, at night, that my shame and confusion cured me of procrastinating my business for the remainder of my life.

"About six years afterwards I was called upon to act the same character in London. By this time I had perceived the difficulty of assuming a personage with whom no one feeling of common general nature was congenial or assistant. One's own heart could prompt one to express, with some degree of truth, the sentiments of a mother, a daughter, a wife, a lover, a sister, &c., but to adopt this character must be an effort of the judgment alone.

"Therefore, it was with the utmost diffidence, nay, terror, that I undertook it, and with the additional fear of Mrs. Pritchard's reputation in it before my eyes. The dreaded first night at length arrived, when, just as I had finished my toilette, and was pondering with fearfulness my first appearance in the grand, fiendish part, comes Mr. Sheridan, knocking at my door, and insisting, in spite of all my entreaties not to be interrupted at this to me tremendous moment, to be admitted. He would not be denied admittance, for he protested he must speak to me on a circumstance which so deeply concerned my own interest, that it was of the most serious nature. Well, after much squabbling, I was compelled to admit him, that I might dismiss him the sooner, and compose myself before the play began. But, what was my distress and astonishment when I found that he wanted me, even at this moment of anxiety and terror, to adopt another mode of acting the sleeping scene. He told me he had heard with greatest surprise and concern that I meant to act it without holding the candle in my hand; and, when I urged the impracticability of washing out that 'damned spot' with the vehemence that was certainly implied by both her own words and by those of her gentlewoman, he insisted, that if I did put the candle out of my hand, it would be thought a presumptuous innovation, as Mrs. Pritchard had always retained it in hers. My mind, however, was made up, and it was then too late to make me alter it; for I was too agitated to adopt another method. My deference to Mr. Sheridan's taste and judgment was, however, so great, that, had he proposed the alteration whilst it was possible for me to change my own plan, I should have yielded to his suggestion; though even then it would have been against my own opinion, and my observation of the accuracy with which somnambulists perform all the acts of waking persons. The scene, of course, was acted as I had myself conceived it, and the innovation, as Mr. Sheridan called it, was received with approbation. Mr. Sheridan himself came to me, after the play, and most ingenuously congratulated me on my obstinacy. When he was gone out of the room I began to undress; and while standing up before my glass, and taking off my mantle, a diverting circumstance occurred to chase away the feelings of this anxious night; for while I was repeating, and endeavoring to call to mind the appropriate tone and action to the following words, 'Here's the smell of blood still!' my dresser innocently exclaimed, 'Dear me, ma'am, how very hysterical you are tonight; I protest and vow, ma'am, it was not blood, but rose-pink and water; for I saw the property-man mix it up, with my own eyes.'"

MAX BEERBOHM REVIEWS *Macbeth*

[*A report of Forbes-Robertson and Mrs. Patrick Campbell in* Macbeth, *which Max Beerbohm reviewed on October 1, 1898. The following are Beerbohm's concluding remarks.*]

Of all Shakespeare's plays, *Macbeth* is, perhaps, the most often enacted. It is the only one that contains two great parts, each of which, susceptible of many interpretations, can be equally well fitted to the temperaments and methods of various mimes. According to Aubrey the play was first acted in 1606, at Hampton Court, in the presence of King James. It is stated that Hal Berridge, the youth who was to have acted the part of Lady Macbeth, "fell sudden sicke of a pleurisie, wherefor Master Shakespeare himself did enacte in his stead." One wishes that Aubrey had given some account of the poet's impersonation. It would be amusing to know Shakespeare's own view of the part—more amusing, however, than valuable, for the actor is the interpreter of the dramatist, and the creative artist is always the least competent interpreter of his own work; besides, as I have said, there can be no final or binding interpretation of so complex a part as Lady Macbeth. Different actresses will always act the part in their different ways, and every way will have its champions among the critics, and every champion will have right on his side. Meanwhile, I find the Macbeth controversy rather tedious. Most critics of the latest production have been talking nonsense about the *Zeitgeist* and about neurotic subtlety and Pre-Raphaelitism and all the rest of it, as though the play had hitherto been acted only in the blood-and-thunder convention of Mrs. Siddons. Mere fallacy! We may be sure that "the gentle poet-philosopher" himself acted in much the same way as Mrs. Patrick Campbell or, for that matter, Miss Ellen Terry. In Pepys' diary, too, there is certain evidence that Mrs. Knipp's famous impersonation was of much the same kind as that which our critics suppose to be a strange phenomenon of 1898. "Thence to the Cockpitt Theatre," writes Pepys in the autumn of 1667, "to witness my dearest Mrs. Knipp in the Tragedie of Macbeth, than which as I did this day say to Mr. Killigrew I do know no play more diverting nor more worthie to the eye. Did secure a prime place in the pitt, whereof I was glad, being neare under my Ladie Dorset and her good husband. The latter did twice salute me with effusion, and I was pleased to note that those around me perceived this. Methought Mrs. Knipp did never play so fine, specially in the matter of the two daggers, yet without brawl or overmuch tragick gesture, the which is most wearisome, as though an actress do care more to affright us than to be approved. She was most comickal and natural when she walks forth sleeping (the which I can testify, for Mrs. Pepys also walks sleeping at some times), and did most ingeniously mimick the manner of women who walk thus." Obviously, then, the critics are wrong in regarding Mrs. Campbell's performance as something peculiar to the spirit of this generation. In the sleep-walking scene, Mrs. Campbell was not "comickal," but she was very "natural," and throughout the play she made her appeal to the sense of beauty and to the intellect rather than to the sense of terror. Mr. Forbes-Robertson acted in a similar way. Both took the line laid down for them by their natural method. I thought that both performances were very beautiful. It does not matter in what method Macbeth and Lady Macbeth be played, so long as they be both played well in the same method. A violent Lady Macbeth and a gentle Macbeth, or *vice versa*, would be a nuisance. Mrs. Campbell and Mr. Forbes-Robertson act in perfect harmony. Mr. Taber is most admirable as Macduff. Indeed, the whole production is a great success. I trust that it will be the latest production of *Macbeth* for many years to come.

LILLAH McCARTHY AS LADY MACBETH

[From June 22 to 26, 1909, Lillah McCarthy and Evelyn Weeden alternated in the role of Lady Macbeth in William Poel's production of the play at the Fulham Grand Theatre, London. Miss McCarthy made a detailed record of Poel's method of work of which the following is an excerpt:]

Make-up. Hair, bright red. Face, pink flush. Eyelids painted light green. Flecks of gold under the eyes. Eyebrows, same color as hair. Mouth very clear, carmine. Neck, white and pale blue. Hands likewise.

The hair or wig was specially handled: the forehead was built up high and broad; the hair was dressed well back from the ears, and swept into towering form from the forehead in front and the neck in back.

Carriage Style. The head was held high, the shoulders up, the spine straight, the legs and feet together. In the movements, there was to be a slight swing from side to side, not up and down.

Costumes. The characters had to wear the correct Elizabethan dress which Poel had copied from models in the art galleries. The wardrobe which he had collected was large and very beautiful as was his collection of stage jewellery.

Rehearsals. William Poel was insistent on the strictest observance of the precise details of rhythm, diction, voice, gesture, carriage, and make-up. He was ruthless in rehearsal. He rehearsed each of us one at a time. We were made to repeat after him our lines until we had got the rhythm and then the right expression of the passion or the tenderness or other essential of the part which the character demanded. While one of us was being rehearsed, the others sat at the back of the room in order to learn how to act.

Poel insisted on the *youth* of Shakespeare's leading characters. They were young boys and girls. Even the "old" parts were by no means aged; Lady Macbeth was thirty-five or so. Youth was exuberant in Shakespeare and old age was only a dim background.

Poel's rehearsing of *Macbeth* was the most tremendous dramatic experience I have ever known. Macbeth, a visionary: no mere murderous plotter. The vision of the deed obsessed him before he perpetrated it and pursued him after the deed was done with fear and apprehension and always his voice echoes chorus-like, haunting and terrible, the voice of a lost soul, itself agonised by the sense of its loss. Lady Macbeth—the realist, devilishly practical. No imagination for her but greed: the greed to govern, too great a greed, so great that it destroys her grasping mind, destroys his also, leaving only the mad and despairing vision of "tomorrow and tomorrow. . . ."

The discipline of William Poel's rehearsals sometimes wore me down. But I emerged from it knowing something. Poel scorned convention and tradition. He gave a brilliant example of his contempt for custom and of his genius when, in the "sleep-walking" scene, he made me, Lady Macbeth, as the scene opens sit at my dressing-table and begin to take off my rings and loosen my hair. The actress, who must presently reach such a dreadful climax of despair, can only rise to it if she begins on the lowest note in the scale of emotions. The tension of apprehension which the silence evokes will, moreover, have pity blended with it; pity for the poor distraught woman doing with hesitating fingers these trivial things of her daily life.

SOME REMARKS ON *Macbeth*
An Interview with Laurence Olivier

Sybil Thorndike once told Olivier, "You must be married to play *Macbeth*." This is not the portrait of a single man; it is not the fissure in the statue, and the statue crumbling. It is a dramatization of the kinship of two bed-fellows, and the actor must be conscious of the other person, his mate, on the stage.

The man in this case has imagination; the woman has none. It is the ability to foresee and to foreknow that at one and the same time provides the bait, and tortures the conscience. The two—husband and wife—pass each other; they do not meet. But as they move closer and then apart, the varying distances of their feeling and understanding are clearly shown. The journey of the plot, therefore, is forever fluctuating; it moves and ceases, flares and fails as does the relationship between Macbeth and Lady Macbeth.

The great moment, early in the play, is the meeting with the Witches. Macbeth's first line, "So foul and fair a day I have not seen," not only echoes the incantation of the Weird Sisters ("Fair is foul, and foul is fair") but is an excellent foreshadowing of the contrasts and conflicts, the tangled emotions that weave their way through the play. In the brilliant scene (I, 7) in which Macbeth is contemplating Duncan's murder, he tries to think "fairly" of his duty to his kinsmen and king but admits that he is "foully" driven to commit the crime by his vaulting ambition. It is a key moment, in which the absolute duplicity of his nature is revealed. Lady Macbeth is completely aware of it and is merely waiting for him to make a slip of the tongue to show that he will comply with her wishes and commit the murder. He gives himself away at last when he utters the lines:

> Bring forth men-children only;
> For thy undaunted mettle should compose
> Nothing but males.

The double pun of "mettle" for metal and "males" for coats of mail springs directly from his overheated imagination which already foresees the battles that are to ensue, and it is only later that he announces, "I am settled. . . ." Lady Macbeth, however, knows that he will do it long before he agrees to; she has known it all along.

The important thing to remember about this ill-starred couple is that they are human beings and not monsters. Lady Macbeth feels that she has a genuine right to the throne because her ancestors occupied it until Duncan's forebears treacherously usurped it; Macbeth, too, has a claim not only because he is first cousin to the king but because he has rendered meritorious service to his country on the field of battle. They have talked these things over at night, as husbands and wives do, and convinced themselves that there is ample justification for the murder. But Lady Macbeth cautions her husband about his guilty look:

> Your face, my thane, is as a book, where men
> May read strange matters.

She urges him to leave "matters" to her:

> . . . you shall put
> This night's great business into my dispatch,
> Which shall to all our nights and days to come
> Give solely sovereign sway, and masterdom.

When the moment comes to do the deed, however, she boggles at it and returns with the excuse:

> Had he [the king] not resembled
> My father as he slept, I had done't.

That is the beginning of the journey through hell for Macbeth and Lady Macbeth; deeper and deeper they wade in a pool of blood, and she goes down before he does.

From the very first moment that he contemplates the murder of the king, Macbeth's piercing imagination makes it clear that he is bound to fail; he is aware

> that we but teach
> Bloody instructions, which being taught, return
> To plague the inventor.

And when failure finally stares him in the face he is forced to capitulate, but not before he cries:

> be these juggling fiends no more believ'd,
> That palter with us in a double sense,
> That keep the word of promise to our ear,
> And break it to our hope.

This is the sort of rationalization that self-deception provides for one.

"Macbeth is the sort of man who makes you feel a little uncomfortable," says Olivier. "I tried to simulate a certain edgier, more resolute voice than I've really got, and to convey an impression of more power than the man sitting before you really suggests." Olivier first played Macbeth, unsuccessfully, at the Old Vic in 1937 but the intervening years have brought him many rich experiences both as a man and as an actor; he says: "You can't possibly play Macbeth without drawing on every single thing you have. You've got to give it everything you've ever done —Hamlet, Richard III, Malvolio, Henry V. There's no hope if you're not repeating yourself, and not making use of what you've learned."

SCENERY AND COSTUMES FOR OLIVIER'S *Macbeth*
An Interview with Roger Furse

Roger Furse, who had played an important part in the design of all of Laurence Olivier's Shakespearean films, was asked to create the scenery and costumes for the Olivier production of *Macbeth* at Stratford-on-Avon. Furse had about six months in which to think his ideas through and work them out in detail, and during that time the basic concept for the production was thoroughly discussed with Glen Byam Shaw, who directed the play, and with Olivier himself. It was decided that the production was to give the impression of power, speed, and fury, and that the heightened tempo of the action would demand quick changes of scenery which could best be accomplished by the use of flat drops and painted effects. It was also felt that the décor should have a barbaric simplicity which Furse conceived of in terms of rough-hewn stone and "pointed" arches which would be unusually fierce and primitive.

Although *Macbeth* was his favorite among the Shakespearean tragedies, Furse had never done the play before and was casting about in his mind for some way to give it a "sharp" look. He had designed the sets for Olivier's film version of *Hamlet* and remembered that during the scene between Hamlet and Polonius, when the young man addressed the older one in a very cutting manner, he had wanted the scenery to have an equally sharp and knifelike effect; so, as Hamlet quits the scene, we see behind him a series of pointed arches which are meant to reinforce the emotional quality of the moment. The idea of pointed arches originally came to Furse in the form of images of the wooden arches used in archaic Norwegian architecture. He had been thinking of the north, its relationship to the Hamlet story, saw the jutting edges of the timber structures in his mind's eye, adapted them for the stone castle at Elsinore, and then for the castle at Dunsinane, even incorporating them into such a detail as the tall pointed backs of the thrones occupied by Macbeth and his queen.

The walls, steps, battlements, and other architectural features, were made of flats, cloth, and board, as already mentioned, painted to simulate the texture of stone. The interior of Macbeth's castle at Inverness was interesting in that it was shown as a two-story structure, with the bedrooms on the upper level and the public rooms on stage level; a flight of stone steps on one side of the stage led up to the door of Duncan's chamber which was visible to the audience, and another flight of steps on the other side of the stage led to the chamber of the Macbeths. This arrangement made it possible for the audience to see Macbeth and Lady Macbeth enter and leave the room of their victim, and also to observe with heightened interest the horrified expressions on the faces of the men who discover the deed. The mechanically operated elevator-platform with which the stage at Stratford is equipped served in this scene as the upper story of the castle; in other scenes it represented the battlements at Inverness and Dunsinane, and supported the Weird Sisters in midair in their first appearance.

The outdoor scenes were distinguished by their contrasting moods. The scene on the heath, at the opening of the play, was backed by a cyclorama; in front of this were some ground rows of mountains and rocks; the elevator-platform was slightly raised, and from it steps led down toward the footlights; on the steps were some stylized stones. The scene was painted and lighted to suggest cloudiness and storm and to establish a threatening and foreboding mood. The scene in England, which represents a clearing in the woods, was done, on the other hand, in delicate greens and blues and, according to Furse, seemed out of keeping with the rest of the production because it comes without preparation and is basically pathetic and sentimental, in contrast to the coldness and brutality of the rest of the play. The back cloth was painted to depict a blue sky and soft, green hills, and in front of this was a thick grove of trees (cut-outs), which were made to look "chunky" and stylized; downstage, there was a section of broken wall on which the actors could sit. The England scene would have been entirely out of place, Furse feels, if the director had not conceived of a brilliant device to tie the scene in which Lady Macduff and her children are murdered to the scene that follows in England in which Macduff learns of the destruction of his family; as the assassin's dagger was driven home, Lady Macduff emitted an ear-piercing scream that did not die out as the murder scene ended but carried over into the opening of the England scene, thus bridging the two.

For the sleep-walking scene, there were three alleys of arches made up of four cut cloths and a backing; the openings cut in the cloths that hung toward the front of the stage were larger than the openings in the cloths at the rear, which produced an effect of perspective in depth; the stage was dimly lighted, but shafts of brighter light fell through the arches, increased the sense of distance, and gave an eerie quality to the scene; the arches at the front were red and shaded down to black at the back; they were not regular or symmetrical but seemed to be edged with blocks of rough-hewn stone upon which the light fell. In this production, Lady Macbeth did not descend from her chamber but, at the opening of the scene, advanced toward the audience from the farthest point upstage, and moved slowly through the series of arches and through the shafts of light, in and out of the shadows, going back at the end of the scene the way she had come.

The final scenes of the play, representing the battlements of Dunsinane, were conceived as a series of levels and steps, and the lighting suggested the reddish hues of blood.

The color scheme for the entire production was humorously known as "Furse's old dried blood"; it was composed mainly of reds and browns, rust-color, black, and green. A year or so after he had done this production, Furse was traveling with Olivier through the highlands of Scotland in search of "locations" for the then contemplated film version of *Macbeth;* it was midwinter and Furse was struck by the colors of the rocks, the dead bracken, dead heather, the lichens and iodine in the streams, which painted the Scottish landscape in the exact shades of red, brown, rust, green, and black that he had used for his stage sets.

Glen Byam Shaw's conception for the treatment of the Weird Sisters was highly original. He decided to present the witches, when they first appear, as if they were flying about in the murky air above the heath. To achieve this effect, the elevator-platform was raised to a great height and the witches were grouped on it, behind a gauze curtain. They made their second appearance on the heath on stage level, again in murky light; the third time they appeared, they were in a deep cave into which Macbeth had to descend in order to consult with them. These witches clearly exerted their supernatural powers in the air, on the earth, and in the dark subterranean regions. The witches' cauldron was placed over a trap-door in the stage and the apparitions came up from below and emerged from the mouth of the cauldron; the voices of the apparitions corresponded to those of Duncan, Banquo, and others with whom they stood in symbolic relationship; other symbols, too, forecasting action to come, emerged from the cauldron, such as the bough of a tree presaging Birnam Wood, and the head of Macbeth on a spear.

Since modern playgoers are cynical concerning the idea of ghosts, Roger Furse is of the opinion that stage apparitions ought to be made to seem as "real" as possible if the intention is to frighten the audience. It was for this reason that he first thought of presenting one of the witches as a ravishingly beautiful girl and rendered her that way in his sketches, but she so closely resembled a Charles Addams creation that he had to discard the idea for fear of causing laughter. In his television production of *Macbeth* in November, 1960, George Schaefer used this very interpretation and was praised for his conception of the apprentice witch.

The treatment of the Weird Sisters met with mixed reactions among the critics but their comments concerning the scenery were generally complimentary; one reviewer called the castle settings "monolithic" and said that the landscapes were "posterlike"; another remarked that the sets were "night-blue and darkly red (the hue of congealed blood)"; a third said, "Furse's settings hold the note of doom, although his Dunsinane battlements remind me of an earthquake-tilted churchyard"; and a fourth noted that the settings gave "the impression of rude and massive halls and storm-wracked wastes in which the gloomy and lurid story unfolded itself with perfect propriety." Two moments, involving the scenery, were thought to be particularly effective. Toward the beginning of the play, Lady Macbeth appeared against the blue, midnight sky up among the arches of Inverness Castle and the stage was filled with poignancy and beauty; and in the final duel, Macduff followed the retreating Macbeth up a winding flight of steps at Dunsinane. There was a last cut-and-thrust with the daggers, and they disappeared. At the next moment, against a sky suddenly clear and serene, Malcolm invited his Earls to see him crowned at Scone, and the beauty of this scene was not marred by the showing of "the usurper's cursed head."

In dressing the actors, it was Roger Furse's idea to design very simple clothes rather than "costumes," nor did he want to emphasize their "Scottishness" but attempted only to hint at it.

"I had no intention," said Furse, "of getting the actors up in vests of shaggy fur, boots in the same style, and double horns on their heads in primitive Scottish fashion. I chose, as a suitable and attractive period, the early Middle Ages—the tenth and eleventh centuries—and studied the scenes depicted in the Winchester Bible in order to adapt the style of clothing shown in the illuminations."

As Macbeth, Laurence Olivier was dressed mainly in browns, reds, and black; for the banquet scene, he wore a scarlet cloak over a dark green tunic, and a heavy, ornate crown. Although Macbeth's clothes—tunics, hose, leggings, and cloaks—resembled those of the other men in style, they were much richer in color and fabric, more highly decorated, and more striking. He also wore heavy golden rings and a massive brooch that held his cloak at the right shoulder. Olivier's make-up was very simple; his hair was soft and wavy and covered his ears, giving his head a slight fullness, but the hair did not reach below the neckline at the back; he had a mustache and a thin beard that outlined his jaw.

As played by Vivien Leigh, Lady Macbeth's glowing beauty helped to explain the influence she exercised over her husband. In her first appearance, the actress wore a gown of dull, mossy green. After the coronation, she was attired in a gown of peacock blue-green that was shiny and seductive; from the waist and shoulders fell panels of cloth decorated with gold; the skirt had a very long train and was embroidered along the edges. Her robes of state included a voluminous red cloak that had gold brooches at each shoulder from which wide gleaming streamers fell to her waist. She wore a red wig, a large crown, and long pendant earrings. Heavy costume jewelry consisting of square or rectangular brooches, bracelets, and rings completed the outfit. For the sleepwalking scene, she appeared in pale night-clothes which were not white but seemed to be so in contrast to the gunmetal dressing-gown that was thrown over her shoulders; the dressing-gown was carefully draped for each performance so that it was crooked and awry and gave her a weird and smoky look. It is interesting to note that during the intensive study that she did in preparation for the part, Vivien Leigh learned that Lady Macbeth's first name was Gruach, or Grace; although Miss Leigh could work no grace into Lady Macbeth's spirit, she was the epitome of grace in all her movements.

Civilian clothes for the men consisted of long-sleeved tunics, skirts, hose, and cross-gartered leggings; a long piece of material was worn over one shoulder like a plaid, and a leather pouch on a belt hung in front, from the waist, to suggest a sporran. The fighting men wore leather armor, hard helmets of papier-mâché to represent leather, and soft leather boots, some of which had rough skin on the outside. Several of the soldiers had belts over one shoulder as well as around the waist, and above this was the plaid, held in place by a large brooch at the left shoulder. No mail or metal armor was used.

After the murder of Duncan, the men awakened from their sleep appeared in long hose made of tightly fitting soft wool, some with plaids slung over their bare shoulders, others in unbelted tunics which gave them a "nightshirty" look. The Messenger who came to warn Lady Macduff was conceived of, for this production, as a shepherd who carried a crook and wore a fleece coat and leggings of a dirty off-white. The Porter, too, was dirty and patchy, his clothes covered with wine and egg stains; he wore a belt to which keys were attached and entered carrying his boots, which he put on during the scene.

The men's make-up did not have a smooth and finished look but was intended to be a bit sweaty; many of the men were sparsely bearded. The fabrics for all the costumes were treated in various ways: The cloth was lightly painted to give a tartan effect; the edges of the skirts were decorated; the leather, papier-mâché, and other materials were sprayed with paint, roughed, bruised, tinted, or toned to suggest the contours of the body. The women's gowns, in particular, were designed to accentuate the physique. They were low-waisted and tight-fitting, and made of soft, clinging materials. In order to achieve a high-bosomed effect, shadows were painted on the gown under the breasts. In several instances, Furse painted the anatomy on the costumes of both men and women; shadows and highlights indicated breasts, ribs, navels, and crotches. The purpose was to emphasize the fact that the clothing was not merely hanging on the body but actually fitted the form.

Roger Furse began work on the production of *Macbeth* with a series of mental images of the sets and costumes that he wanted to use; he made rough sketches of these and took them to the director for approval. Then he drew his ground plans; these are especially complex for productions at Stratford because the use of the elevator-platform is involved and because plays are presented there in repertory, which means that the scenery for several plays must be taken into consideration, in order to avoid hanging and storing conflicts. Some of the scenery may be left in the flies, but most of it has to be taken down to make way for the other productions.

From the ground plans, Furse makes a rough model of the set in order to get the proportions of the elements before proceeding with exact measurements; the main items of scenery are done first so that he will have enough time to work out the snags, and also because building and painting take longer than other jobs. Furse thinks out a palette of colors in his mind and then works out the colors of the costumes as they will be seen against the colors of the scenery; since the costumes must stand out from the scenery, subtleties in harmony and contrast have to be devised.

The job of designing the sets and costumes for *Macbeth* took half a year of intensive work; Furse was occupied the entire time conceiving, executing, and supervising the job from beginning to end. He was not permitted, however, to assume the entire responsibility for the lighting of the production but had to work in consultation with the lighting designer of the Stratford Memorial Theatre.

"A designer has to make financial sacrifices to work at Stratford," says Mr. Furse, "but it is a rewarding experience in other ways. The films certainly pay much better and plans for the filming of *Macbeth* have proceeded to an advanced stage. With Olivier, I worked out the picture scene by scene, even down to the timing of each scene. Every set was planned to fit the locations we selected in Scotland where the film is to be made; the scale and mood of the country are exactly right for the screen. But Scotland is becoming "civilized" so fast—so many telephone poles and TV aerials are going up all over the place—that unless we shoot the film soon the locations we've selected will be useless."

The Tragedy of Macbeth

DRAMATIS PERSONÆ.

DUNCAN, King of Scotland.

MALCOLM,
DONALBAIN, } his sons.

MACBETH,
BANQUO, } Generals of the Scottish Army.

MACDUFF,
LENNOX,
ROSS,
MENTEITH, } Noblemen of Scotland.
ANGUS,
CAITHNESS,

FLEANCE, Son to Banquo.
SIWARD, Earl of Northumberland, General of the English forces.
YOUNG SIWARD, his son.
SEYTON, an Officer attending on Macbeth.
Boy, son to Macduff.
A Sergeant.
A Porter.
An Old Man.
An English Doctor.
A Scottish Doctor.

LADY MACBETH.
LADY MACDUFF.
A Gentlewoman, attending on Lady Macbeth.

Three Witches.
HECATE.
The Ghost of Banquo.
Apparitions.

Lords, Gentlemen, Officers, Soldiers, Murderers, Messengers, Attendants.

SCENE.—SCOTLAND; ENGLAND.

ACT I. SCENE I.
SCOTLAND. AN OPEN PLACE.

(*Thunder and lightning. Enter three* WITCHES.)

1. Witch. When shall we three meet again
In thunder, lightning, or in rain?
2. Witch. When the hurlyburly's done
When the battle's lost and won.

3. Witch. That will be ere the set of sun. 5

1. Witch. Where the place?

2. Witch. Upon the heath.

3. Witch. There to meet with Macbeth.

1. Witch. I come, Graymalkin!

2. Witch. Paddock calls.

3. Witch. Anon!

All. Fair is foul, and foul is fair. 10
Hover through the fog and filthy air.
(*Exeunt.*)

SCENE II. A CAMP NEAR FORRES.

(*Alarum within. Enter* KING DUNCAN,
MALCOLM, DONALBAIN, LENNOX,
with ATTENDANTS, *meeting a bleeding*
SERGEANT.)

King. What bloody man is that? He can report,
As seemeth by his plight, of the revolt
The newest state.[1]

Mal. This is the sergeant
Who like a good and hardy soldier fought
'Gainst my captivity. Hail, brave friend! 5
Say to the King the knowledge of the broil [2]
As thou didst leave it.

Serg. Doubtful it stood,
As two spent swimmers that do cling together
And choke their art. The merciless Macdonwald
(Worthy to be a rebel, for to that 10
The multiplying villanies of nature
Do swarm upon him) from the Western Isles
Of kerns and gallowglasses[3] is supplied;

And Fortune, on his damned [4] quarrel smiling,
Show'd like a rebel's whore. But all's too weak; 15
For brave Macbeth (well he deserves that name),
Disdaining Fortune, with his brandish'd steel,
Which smok'd with bloody execution
(Like valor's minion[5]), carv'd out his passage
Till he fac'd the slave; 20
Which[6] ne'er shook hands nor bade farewell to him
Till he unseam'd him from the nave[7] to th' chaps[8]
And fix'd his head upon our battlements.

King. O valiant cousin! worthy gentleman!

Serg. As whence the sun 'gins his reflection 25
Shipwracking storms and direful thunders break,
So from that spring whence comfort seem'd to come
Discomfort swells. Mark, King of Scotland, mark.
No sooner justice had, with valor arm'd,
Compell'd these skipping kerns to trust their heels 30
But the Norweyan lord, surveying vantage,
With furbish'd arms and new supplies of men,
Began a fresh assault.[9]

King. Dismay'd not this
Our captains, Macbeth and Banquo?

Serg. Yes,

---

1. Latest news.
2. Battle.
3. Irish soldiers.
4. Doomed.
5. Favorite.
6. Macbeth.
7. Navel.
8. Jaws.
9. After the defeat of Macdonwald's men, the Norwegians attacked.

As sparrows eagles, or the hare the
lion.[10]   35

If I say sooth, I must report they
were

As cannons overcharg'd with double
cracks, so they

Doubly redoubled strokes upon the
foe.

Except[11] they meant to bathe in
reeking wounds,

Or memorize[12] another Golgotha,   40
I cannot tell—

But I am faint; my gashes cry for
help.

King. So well thy words become thee
as thy wounds;

They smack of honor both. Go get
him surgeons.

(*Exit* SERGEANT, *attended.*)

(*Enter* Ross.)

Who comes here?

Mal.   The worthy Thane of Ross.   45

Len. What a haste looks through his
eyes! So should he look

That seems to speak things strange.

Ross.   God save the King!

King. Whence cam'st thou, worthy
thane?

Ross.   From Fife, great King,

Where the Norweyan banners flout
the sky

And fan our people cold. Norway
himself,[13]   50

With terrible numbers,

Assisted by that most disloyal traitor

The Thane of Cawdor, began a
dismal conflict,

Till that Bellona's bridegroom, lapp'd
in proof,[14]

Confronted him with self-compari-
sons,[15]   55

Point against point, rebellious arm
'gainst arm,

Curbing his lavish spirit; and to con-
clude,

The victory fell on us.

King.   Great happiness!

Ross.   That now

Sweno, the Norways' king, craves
composition;[16]

Nor would we deign him burial of
his men   60

Till he disbursed, at Saint Colme's
Inch,[17]

Ten thousand dollars to our general
use.

King. No more that Thane of Cawdor
shall deceive

Our bosom interest. Go pronounce
his present death

And with his former title greet Mac-
beth.   65

Ross. I'll see it done.

Dun. What he hath lost noble Macbeth
hath won.

(*Exeunt.*)

SCENE III. A BLASTED HEATH.

(*Thunder. Enter the three* WITCHES.)

1. Witch. Where hast thou been, sister?

2. Witch. Killing swine.

3. Witch. Sister, where thou?

1. Witch. A sailor's wife had chestnuts
in her lap

And munch'd and munch'd and
munch'd. 'Give me,' quoth I.   5

'Aroint[1] thee, witch!' the rump-fed
ronyon[2] cries.

---

10. As sparrows dismay eagles, etc.
11. Whether.
12. Make memorable.
13. The King of Norway.
14. Macbeth in armor.

15. Matched him stroke for stroke.
16. A peace treaty.
17. Island in the Firth of Forth.
1. Begone.
2. Mangy woman.

Her husband's to Aleppo gone, master o' th' Tiger;[3]
But in a sieve I'll thither sail
And, like a rat without a tail,
I'll do, I'll do, and I'll do. 10
2. Witch. I'll give thee a wind.
1. Witch. Th' art kind.
3. Witch. And I another.
1. Witch. I myself have all the other,
And the very ports they blow, 15
All the quarters that they know
I' th' shipman's card.
I will drain him dry as hay.
Sleep shall neither night nor day
Hang upon his penthouse lid. 20
He shall live a man forbid.
Weary sev'nights, nine times nine,
Shall he dwindle, peak, and pine.
Though his bark cannot be lost,
Yet it shall be tempest-tost. 25
Look what I have.
2. Witch. Show me! show me!
1. Witch. Here I have a pilot's thumb,
Wrack'd as homeward he did come.

(*Drum within.*)

3. Witch. A drum, a drum! 30
Macbeth doth come.
All. The Weird Sisters,[4] hand in hand,
Posters of [5] the sea and land,
Thus do go about, about, 34
Thrice to thine, and thrice to mine,
And thrice again, to make up nine.
Peace! The charm's wound up.

(*Enter* MACBETH *and* BANQUO.)

Macb. So foul and fair a day I have not
seen.
Ban. How far is't call'd to Forres? What
are these,
So wither'd, and so wild in their attire, 40

That look not like th' inhabitants o'
th' earth,
And yet are on't? Live you? or are
you aught
That man may question? You seem to
understand me,
By each at once her choppy[6] finger
laying
Upon her skinny lips. You should be
women, 45
And yet your beards forbid me to
interpret
That you are so.
Macb. Speak, if you can. What are you?
1. Witch. All hail, Macbeth! Hail to
thee, Thane of Glamis!
2. Witch. All hail, Macbeth! Hail to
thee, Thane of Cawdor!
3. Witch. All hail, Macbeth, that shalt
be King hereafter! 50
Ban. Good sir, why do you start and
seem to fear
Things that do sound so fair? I' th'
name of truth,
Are ye fantastical, or that indeed
Which outwardly ye show? My noble
partner
You greet with present grace and
great prediction 55
Of noble having and of royal hope,
That he seems rapt withal.[7] To me
you speak not.
If you can look into the seeds of time
And say which grain will grow and
which will not,
Speak then to me, who neither beg
nor fear 60
Your favors nor your hate.
1. Witch. Hail!
2. Witch. Hail!
3. Witch. Hail!

3. Name of a ship.
4. Goddesses of Destiny.
5. Swift travelers over.

6. Chapped.
7. Carried away by it.

1. Witch. Lesser than Macbeth, and
   greater.   65
2. Witch. Not so happy, yet much happier.
3. Witch. Thou shalt get[8] kings, though
   thou be none.
   So all hail, Macbeth and Banquo!
1. Witch. Banquo and Macbeth, all
   hail!
Macb. Stay, you imperfect[9] speakers,
   tell me more!   70
   By Sinel's[10] death I know I am Thane
   of Glamis;
   But how of Cawdor? The Thane of
   Cawdor lives,
   A prosperous gentleman; and to be
   King
   Stands not within the prospect of belief,
   No more than to be Cawdor. Say
   from whence   75
   You owe this strange intelligence, or
   why
   Upon this blasted heath you stop our
   way
   With such prophetic greeting. Speak,
   I charge you.

   (WITCHES *vanish.*)

Ban. The earth hath bubbles, as the
   water has,
   And these are of them. Whither are
   they vanish'd?   80
Macb. Into the air, and what seem'd
   corporal melted
   As breath into the wind. Would they
   had stay'd!
Ban. Were such things here as we do
   speak about?
   Or have we eaten on the insane root[11]
   That takes the reason prisoner?   85

Macb. Your children shall be kings.
Ban.   You shall be King.
Macb. And Thane of Cawdor too. Went
   it not so?
Ban. To th' selfsame tune and words.
   Who's here?

   (*Enter* ROSS *and* ANGUS.)

Ross. The King hath happily receiv'd,
   Macbeth,
   The news of thy success; and when
   he reads   90
   Thy personal venture in the rebels'
   fight,
   His wonders and his praises do contend
   Which should be thine or his. Silenc'd
   with that,
   In viewing o'er the rest o' th' selfsame day,
   He finds thee in the stout Norweyan
   ranks,   95
   Nothing afeard of what thyself didst
   make,
   Strange images[12] of death. As thick
   as hail
   Came post with post,[13] and every one
   did bear
   Thy praises in his kingdom's great
   defense
   And pour'd them down before him.
Ang.   We are sent 100
   To give thee from our royal master
   thanks;
   Only to herald [14] thee into his sight,
   Not pay thee.
Ross. And for an earnest[15] of a greater
   honor,
   He bade me, from him, call thee
   Thane of Cawdor;   105

8. Beget.
9. Puzzling.
10. Macbeth's father.
11. A root supposed to cause insanity.

12. Horrible forms.
13. Messenger after messenger.
14. Conduct.
15. Pledge.

In which addition,[16] hail, most worthy
Thane!
For it is thine.

Ban. What, can the devil speak true?

Macb. The Thane of Cawdor lives. Why
do you dress me
In borrowed robes?

Ang. Who was the Thane lives yet,
But under heavy judgment[17] bears
that life 110
Which he deserves to lose. Whether
he was combin'd
With those of Norway, or did line[18]
the rebel
With hidden help and vantage, or
that with both[19]
He labor'd in his country's wrack, I
know not;
But treasons capital, confess'd and
prov'd, 115
Have overthrown him.

Macb. (*aside*) Glamis, and Thane of
Cawdor!
The greatest is behind.[20]—(*To* ROSS
and ANGUS) Thanks for your pains.
(*Aside to* BANQUO) Do you not hope
your children shall be kings,
When those that gave the Thane of
Cawdor to me
Promis'd no less to them?

Ban. (*aside to* MACBETH) That, trusted
home,[21] 120
Might yet enkindle you unto the
crown,
Besides the Thane of Cawdor. But 'tis
strange!
And oftentimes, to win us to our
harm,
The instruments of darkness tell us
truths, 124
Win us with honest trifles, to be-
tray 's
In deepest consequence.—
Cousins, a word, I pray you.

Macb. (*aside*) Two truths are told,
As happy prologues to the swelling[22]
act
Of the imperial theme.—I thank you,
gentlemen.— 129
(*Aside*) This supernatural soliciting[23]
Cannot be ill; cannot be good. If ill,
Why hath it given me earnest of suc-
cess,
Commencing in a truth? I am Thane
of Cawdor.
If good, why do I yield to that sug-
gestion
Whose horrid image doth unfix my
hair 135
And make my seated [24] heart knock
at my ribs
Against the use of nature? Present
fears
Are less than horrible imaginings.
My thought, whose murder yet is but
fantastical,
Shakes so my single state of man that
function 140
Is smother'd in surmise and nothing
is
But what is not.

Ban. Look how our partner's rapt.

Macb. (*aside*) If chance will have me
King, why, chance may crown me,
Without my stir.[25]

Ban. New honors come upon him,
Like our strange[26] garments, cleave
not to their mold [27] 145
But with the aid of use.

Macb. (*aside*) Come what come may,

16. Title.
17. Sentence.
18. Aid.
19. Macdonwald and the King of Norway.
20. Still to come.
21. If you believe it.

22. Magnificent.
23. Prediction.
24. Firm.
25. Stirring.
26. New.
27. Do not fit.

Time and the hour runs through the roughest day.

Ban. Worthy Macbeth, we stay upon your leisure.

Macb. Give me your favor.[28] My dull brain was wrought
With things forgotten. Kind gentlemen, your pains   150
Are regist'red where every day I turn
The leaf to read them.[29] Let us toward the King.
(*Aside to* BANQUO) Think upon what hath chanc'd; and, at more time,
The interim having weigh'd it,[30] let us speak
Our free hearts each to other.

Ban. (*aside to* MACBETH) Very gladly.

Macb. (*aside to* BANQUO) Till then, enough.—Come, friends.   156

(*Exeunt.*)

SCENE IV. FORRES. THE PALACE.

(*Flourish. Enter* KING DUNCAN, LENNOX, MALCOLM, DONALBAIN, *and* ATTENDANTS.)

King. Is execution done on Cawdor? Are not
Those in commission yet return'd?

Mal.   My liege,
They are not yet come back. But I have spoke
With one that saw him die; who did report
That very frankly he confess'd his treasons,   5
Implor'd your Highness' pardon, and set forth
A deep repentance. Nothing in his life
Became him like the leaving it. He died

As one that had been studied [1] in his death
To throw away the dearest thing he ow'd   10
As 'twere a careless trifle.

King.   There's no art
To find the mind's construction[2] in the face.
He was a gentleman on whom I built
An absolute trust.

(*Enter* MACBETH, BANQUO, *and* ANGUS.)

                              O worthiest cousin,
The sin of my ingratitude even now
Was heavy on me! Thou art so far before   16
That swiftest wing of recompense is slow
To overtake thee. Would thou hadst less deserv'd,
That the proportion both of thanks and payment
Might have been mine! Only I have left to say,   20
More is thy due than more than all can pay.

Macb. The service and the loyalty I owe,
In doing it pays itself. Your Highness' part
Is to receive our duties; and our duties
Are to your throne and state children and servants,   25
Which do but what they should by doing everything
Safe toward your love and honor.

King.   Welcome hither.
I have begun to plant thee and will labor

---

28. Pardon.
29. In my memory.
30. Having considered it meanwhile.

1. As if he had studied the art of dying.
2. Intention.

To make thee full of growing. Noble
  Banquo,
That hast no less deserv'd, nor must
  be known   30
No less to have done so, let me infold
  thee
And hold thee to my heart.
Ban.   There if I grow,
The harvest is your own.
King.   My plenteous joys,
  Wanton in fulness, seek to hide them-
  selves
  In drops of sorrow. Sons, kinsmen,
    thanes,   35
  And you whose places are the near-
    est, know
  We will establish our estate upon
  Our eldest, Malcolm, whom we name
    hereafter
  The Prince of Cumberland; which
    honor must   39
  Not unaccompanied invest him only,
  But signs of nobleness, like stars, shall
    shine
  On all deservers. From hence to In-
    verness,
  And bind us further to you.
Macb. The rest is labor, which is not
  us'd for you!
  I'll be myself the harbinger,[3] and
    make joyful   45
  The hearing of my wife with your
    approach;
  So, humbly take my leave.
King.   My worthy Cawdor!
Macb. (*aside*) The Prince of Cumber-
  land! That is a step
  On which I must fall down, or else
    o'erleap,
  For in my way it lies. Stars, hide your
    fires!   50
  Let not light see my black and deep
    desires.

The eye wink at the hand;[4] yet let
  that be,
Which the eye fears, when it is done,
  to see.

(*Exit.*)

King. True, worthy Banquo: he is full
  so valiant,[5]   54
And in his commendations I am fed;
It is a banquet to me. Let's after him,
Whose care is gone before to bid us
  welcome.
It is a peerless kinsman.

(*Flourish. Exeunt.*)

SCENE V. INVERNESS. MACBETH'S CASTLE.

(*Enter* MACBETH'S WIFE, *alone, with
a letter.*)

Lady. (*reads*) 'They met me in the
day of success; and I have learn'd
by the perfect'st report they have
more in them than mortal knowledge. When I burn'd in desire to
question them further, they made
themselves air, into which they
vanish'd. Whiles I stood rapt in
the wonder of it, came missives
from the King, who all-hail'd me
Thane of Cawdor, by which title,
before, these Weird Sisters saluted
me, and referr'd me to the coming
on of time with "Hail, King that
shalt be!" This have I thought good
to deliver thee, my dearest partner
of greatness, that thou mightst not
lose the dues of rejoicing by being
ignorant of what greatness is
promis'd thee. Lay it to thy heart,
and farewell.'   21

Glamis thou art, and Cawdor, and
  shalt be—

---

3. Messenger.
4. Let the eye not see what the hand does.

5. As valiant as you say he is.

What thou art promis'd. Yet do I fear
thy nature.
It is too full o' th' milk of human
kindness
To catch the nearest way. Thou
wouldst be great;   25
Art not without ambition, but with-
out
The illness[1] should attend it. What
thou wouldst highly,
That wouldst thou holily; wouldst
not play false,
And yet wouldst wrongly win.
Thou'ldst have, great Glamis,
That which cries 'Thus thou must
do,' if thou have it;   30
And that which rather thou dost fear
to do
Than wishest should be undone. Hie
thee hither,
That I may pour my spirits in thine
ear
And chastise with the valor of my
tongue
All that impedes thee from the golden
round [2]   35
Which fate and metaphysical [3] aid
doth seem
To have thee crown'd withal.

(*Enter* MESSENGER.)
                      What is your tidings?
Mess.   The King comes here to-night.
Lady.   Thou'rt mad to say it!
Is not thy master with him? who,
were't so,   39
Would have inform'd for prepara-
tion.
Mess. So please you, it is true. Our
Thane is coming.
One of my fellows had the speed of
him,[4]

Who, almost dead for breath, had
scarcely more
Than would make up his message.
Lady.   Give him tending;
He brings great news.

(*Exit* MESSENGER.)
                   The raven himself is hoarse
That croaks the fatal entrance of
Duncan   46
Under my battlements. Come, you
spirits
That tend on mortal thoughts, unsex
me here,
And fill me, from the crown to the
toe, top-full
Of direst cruelty! Make thick my
blood;   50
Stop up th' access and passage to
remorse,
That no compunctious visitings of
nature[5]
Shake my fell purpose nor keep peace
between
Th' effect and it! Come to my wom-
an's breasts
And take my milk for gall, you mur-
d'ring ministers,   55
Wherever in your sightless[6] sub-
stances
You wait on nature's mischief! [7]
Come, thick night,
And pall [8] thee in the dunnest[9] smoke
of hell,
That my keen knife see not the
wound it makes,
Nor heaven peep through the blanket
of the dark   60
To cry 'Hold, hold!'

(*Enter* MACBETH.)
                   Great Glamis! worthy Cawdor!

---

1. Evil nature.
2. The crown.
3. Supernatural.
4. Outran him.
5. Instinctive feelings of pity.
6. Invisible.
7. Serve evil.
8. Wrap.
9. Blackest.

Greater than both, by the all-hail
    hereafter!

Thy letters have transported me be-
    yond

This ignorant present, and I feel
    now   64

The future in the instant.[10]

Macb.   My dearest love,
Duncan comes here to-night.

Lady.   And when goes hence?

Macb. To-morrow, as he purposes.

Lady.   O, never
Shall sun that morrow see!

Your face, my Thane, is as a book
    where men

May read strange matters. To be-
    guile the time,[11]   70

Look like the time;[12] bear welcome
    in your eye,

Your hand, your tongue; look like the
    innocent flower,

But be the serpent under't. He that's
    coming

Must be provided for; and you shall
    put

This night's great business into my
    dispatch,   75

Which shall to all our nights and
    days to come

Give solely sovereign sway and mas-
    terdom.

Macb. We will speak further.

Lady.   Only look up clear.
To alter favor ever is to fear.[13]

Leave all the rest to me.   80

(*Exeunt.*)

SCENE VI. INVERNESS. BEFORE MACBETH'S
              CASTLE.

(*Hautboys and torches. Enter* KING
DUNCAN, MALCOLM, DONALBAIN,
BANQUO, LENNOX, MACDUFF, ROSS,
ANGUS, *and* ATTENDANTS.)

King. This castle hath a pleasant seat.
    The air

Nimbly and sweetly recommends it-
    self

Unto our gentle senses.

Ban.   This guest of summer,
The temple-haunting martlet,[1] does
    approve

By his lov'd mansionry[2] that the
    heaven's breath   5

Smells wooingly here. No jutty,
    frieze,

Buttress, nor coign of vantage, but
    this bird

Hath made his pendent bed and pro-
    creant cradle.

Where they most breed and haunt,
    I have observ'd

The air is delicate.

(*Enter* LADY MACBETH.)

King. See, see, our honor'd hostess! 10
The love that follows us sometime is
    our trouble,

Which still we thank as love. Herein
    I teach you

How you shall bid God 'ild[3] us for
    your pains

And thank us for your trouble.

Lady.   All our service
In every point twice done, and then
    done double,   15

Were poor and single business to
    contend

Against those honors deep and broad
    wherewith

Your Majesty loads our house. For
    those of old,[4]

---

10. You seem already to be king.
11. To deceive the world.
12. Wear an appropriate expression.
13. To change your facial expression is to
    betray yourself.

1. A small bird.
2. Demonstrates by choosing this place for
    his nest.
3. Reward.
4. Past honors.

And the late[5] dignities heap'd up to
them,   19
We rest your hermits,[6]

King.   Where's the Thane of Cawdor?
We cours'd him at the heels and had
a purpose
To be his purveyor;[7] but he rides
well.
And his great love, sharp as his spur,
hath holp[8] him
To his home before us. Fair and noble
hostess,
We are your guest to-night.

Lady.   Your servants ever 25
Have theirs, themselves, and what
is theirs, in compt,
To make their audit at your High-
ness' pleasure,
Still to return your own.[9]

King.   Give me your hand;
Conduct me to mine host. We love
him highly
And shall continue our graces towards
him.   30
By your leave, hostess.

(*Exeunt.*)

Scene vii. Inverness. Macbeth's
castle.

(*Hautboys. Torches. Enter a* Sewer,[1]
and divers Servants *with dishes and
service, and cross the stage. Then
enter* Macbeth.)

Macb. If it were done when 'tis done,
then 'twere well
It were done quickly. If th' assassination
Could trammel up the consequence,[2]
and catch,

With his surcease,[3] success; that but
this blow
Might be the be-all and the end-all
here,   5
But here, upon this bank and shoal
of time,
We'ld jump[4] the life to come. But in
these cases
We still have judgment here, that we
but teach
Bloody instructions, which, being
taught, return
To plague th' inventor. This even-
handed justice   10
Commends th' ingredients of our
poison'd chalice
To our own lips. He's here in double
trust:
First, as I am his kinsman and his
subject—
Strong both against the deed; then,
as his host,
Who should against his murderer
shut the door,   15
Not bear the knife myself. Besides,
this Duncan
Hath borne his faculties so meek,
hath been
So clear in his great office, that his
virtues
Will plead like angels, trumpet-
tongu'd, against
The deep damnation of his taking-
off;   20
And pity, like a naked new-born
babe,
Striding the blast, or heaven's cheru-
bin, hors'd
Upon the sightless couriers of the air,

5. Recent.
6. Worshipers.
7. Forerunner.
8. Helped.
9. We owe you our duty, and we are ready to
pay it.

1. Butler.
2. Put an end to the matter.
3. Duncan's death.
4. Risk.

Shall blow the horrid deed in every eye,
That tears shall drown the wind. I have no spur 25
To prick the sides of my intent, but only
Vaulting ambition, which o'erleaps itself
And falls on th' other side.

(*Enter* LADY MACBETH.)
How now? What news?

Lady. He has almost supp'd. Why have you left the chamber?

Macb. Hath he ask'd for me?

Lady. Know you not he has? 30

Macb. We will proceed no further in this business.
He hath honor'd me of late, and I have bought
Golden opinions from all sorts of people,
Which would be worn now in their newest gloss,
Not cast aside so soon.

Lady. Was the hope drunk 35
Wherein you dress'd yourself? Hath it slept since?
And wakes it now to look so green and pale
At what it did so freely? From this time
Such I account thy love. Art thou afeard
To be the same in thine own act and valor 40
As thou art in desire? Wouldst thou have that
Which thou esteem'st the ornament of life,
And live a coward in thine own esteem,
Letting 'I dare not' wait upon 'I would,'

Like the poor cat i' th' adage? 5

Macb. Prithee peace! 45
I dare do all that may become a man.
Who dares do more is none.

Lady. What beast was't then
That made you break this enterprise to me?
When you durst do it, then you were a man;
And to be more than what you were, you would 50
Be so much more the man. Nor time nor place
Did then adhere,6 and yet you would make both.
They have made themselves, and that their fitness now
Does unmake you. I have given suck, and I know
How tender 'tis to love the babe that milks me. 55
I would, while it was smiling in my face,
Have pluck'd my nipple from his boneless gums
And dash'd the brains out, had I so sworn as you
Have done to this.

Macb. If we should fail?

Lady. We fail?
But screw your courage to the sticking place, 60
And we'll not fail. When Duncan is asleep
(Whereto the rather shall his day's hard journey
Soundly invite him), his two chamberlains
Will I with wine and wassail 7 so convince
That memory, the warder of the brain, 65
Shall be a fume, and the receipt of reason

5. The cat wanted to eat fish but didn't want to wet her feet.
6. Were then suitable.
7. Punch.

A limbeck[8] only. When in swinish
  sleep
Their drenched natures lie as in a
  death,
What cannot you and I perform upon
Th' unguarded Duncan? what not
  put upon   70
His spongy[9] officers, who shall bear
  the guilt
Of our great quell?[10]

Macb.   Bring forth men-children only;
For thy undaunted mettle should
  compose
Nothing but males. Will it not be
  receiv'd,
When we have mark'd with blood
  those sleepy two   75
Of his own chamber and us'd their
  very daggers,
That they have done't?

Lady.   Who dares receive it other,
As we shall make our griefs and
  clamor roar
Upon his death?

Macb.   I am settled and bend up
Each corporal agent[11] to this terrible
  feat,   80
Away, and mock the time[12] with fair-
  est show;
False face must hide what the false
  heart doth know.

(*Exeunt.*)

Act ii. Scene i. Inverness.
Court of Macbeth's castle.

(*Enter* Banquo, *and* Fleance *with
a torch before him.*)

Ban. How goes the night, boy?
Fle. The moon is down; I have not
  heard the clock.
Ban. And she goes down at twelve.

Fle.   I take't, 'tis later, sir.
Ban. Hold, take my sword. There's
  husbandry in heaven;
Their candles are all out. Take thee
  that too.   5
A heavy summons lies like lead upon
  me,
And yet I would not sleep. Merciful
  powers,
Restrain in me the cursed thoughts
  that nature
Gives way to in repose!

(*Enter* Macbeth, *and a* Servant
with a torch.)

             Give me my sword.
Who's there?   10
Macb. A friend.
Ban. What, sir, not yet at rest? The
  King's abed.
He hath been in unusual pleasure
  and
Sent forth great largess to your of-
  fices.
This diamond he greets your wife
  withal   15
By the name of most kind hostess,
  and shut up
In measureless content.
Macb.   Being unprepar'd,
Our will became the servant to de-
  fect,[1]
Which else should free have wrought.
Ban.   All's well.
I dreamt last night of the three Weird
  Sisters.   20
To you they have show'd some truth.
Macb.   I think not of them.
Yet when we can entreat an hour to
  serve,
We would spend it in some words
  upon that business,

---

8. A still.
9. Drunken.
10. Murder.

11. Bodily faculty.
12. Deceive everyone.
1. We did not entertain the king properly.

If you would grant the time.

Ban. At your kind'st leisure.

Macb. If you shall cleave to my consent, when 'tis,[2] 25
It shall make honor for you.

Ban. So I lose none
In seeking to augment it but still keep
My bosom franchis'd [3] and allegiance clear,
I shall be counsell'd.

Macb. Good repose the while!

Ban. Thanks, sir. The like to you! 30

(*Exeunt* BANQUO *and* FLEANCE.)

Macb. Go bid thy mistress, when my drink is ready,
She strike upon the bell. Get thee to bed.

(*Exit* SERVANT.)

Is this a dagger which I see before me,
The handle toward my hand? Come, let me clutch thee!
I have thee not, and yet I see thee still. 35
Art thou not, fatal vision, sensible
To feeling as to sight? or art thou but
A dagger of the mind, a false creation,
Proceeding from the heat-oppressed brain?
I see thee yet, in form as palpable 40
As this which now I draw.
Thou marshall'st me the way that I was going,
And such an instrument I was to use.
Mine eyes are made the fools o' th' other senses,
Or else worth all the rest. I see thee still; 45

And on thy blade and dudgeon[4] gouts[5] of blood,
Which was not so before. There's no such thing.
It is the bloody business which informs
Thus to mine eyes. Now o'er the one half-world
Nature seems dead, and wicked dreams abuse
The curtain'd sleep. Now witchcraft celebrates
Pale Hecate's offerings; and wither'd murder,
Alarum'd by his sentinel, the wolf,
Whose howl's his watch, thus with his stealthy pace,
With Tarquin's ravishing strides, towards his design 55
Moves like a ghost. Thou sure and firm-set earth,
Hear not my steps which way they walk, for fear
Thy very stones prate of my whereabout
And take the present horror from the time,
Which now suits with it. Whiles I threat, he lives; 60
Words to the heat of deeds too cold breath gives.

(*A bell rings.*)

I go, and it is done. The bell invites me.
Hear it not, Duncan, for it is a knell
That summons thee to heaven, or to hell.

(*Exit.*)

SCENE II. INVERNESS. MACBETH'S CASTLE.

(*Enter* LADY MACBETH.)

2. If you will side with me when the time comes.
3. Free from guilt.

4. Hilt.
5. Big drops.

Lady. That which hath made them drunk hath made me bold;

What hath quench'd them hath given me fire. Hark! Peace!

It was the owl that shriek'd, the fatal bellman

Which gives the stern'st good-night. He is about it.

The doors are open, and the surfeited grooms 5

Do mock their charge with snores. I have drugg'd their possets,[1]

That death and nature do contend about them

Whether they live or die.

Macb. (*Within.*) Who's there? What, ho?

Lady. Alack, I am afraid they have awak'd, 10

And 'tis not done! Th' attempt, and not the deed,

Confounds us. Hark! I laid their daggers ready;

He could not miss 'em. Had he not resembled

My father as he slept, I had done't.

(*Enter* MACBETH.)

My husband!

Macb. I have done the deed. Didst thou not hear a noise? 15

Lady. I heard the owl scream and the crickets cry.

Did you not speak?

Macb. When?

Lady. Now.

Macb. As I descended?

Lady. Ay.

Macb. Hark!

Who lies i' th' second chamber?

Lady. Donalbain. 20

Macb. This is a sorry sight.

(*Looks on his hands.*)

Lady. A foolish thought, to say a sorry sight.

Macb. There's one did laugh in's sleep, and one cried 'Murder!'

That they did wake each other. I stood and heard them.

But they did say their prayers and address'd them 25

Again to sleep.

Lady. There are two lodg'd together.

Macb. One cried 'God bless us!' and 'Amen!' the other,

As[2] they had seen me with these hangman's hands.

List'ning their fear, I could not say 'Amen!'

When they did say 'God bless us!'

Lady. Consider it not so deeply. 30

Macb. But wherefore could not I pronounce 'Amen'?

I had most need of blessing, and 'Amen'

Stuck in my throat.

Lady. These deeds must not be thought After these ways. So, it will make us mad.

Macb. Methought I heard a voice cry 'Sleep no more! 35

Macbeth does murder sleep'—the innocent sleep,

Sleep that knits up the ravell'd sleave of care,

The death of each day's life, sore labor's bath,

Balm of hurt minds, great nature's second course,

Chief nourisher in life's feast.

Lady. What do you mean? 40

Macb. Still it cried 'Sleep no more!' to all the house;

'Glamis hath murder'd sleep, and therefore Cawdor

1. A milk punch.

2. As if.

Shall sleep no more! Macbeth shall sleep no more!'

Lady. Who was it that thus cried? Why, worthy Thane,
You do unbend your noble strength to think 45
So brainsickly of things. Go get some water
And wash this filthy witness from your hand.
Why did you bring these daggers from the place?
They must lie there. Go carry them and smear
The sleepy grooms with blood.

Macb. I'll go no more. 50
I am afraid to think what I have done;
Look on't again I dare not.

Lady. Infirm of purpose!
Give me the daggers. The sleeping and the dead
Are but as pictures. 'Tis the eye of childhood
That fears a painted devil. If he do bleed, 55
I'll gild the faces of the grooms withal,
For it must seem their guilt.

(*Exit. Knocking within.*)

Macb. Whence is that knocking?
How is't with me when every noise appals me?
What hands are here? Ha! they pluck out mine eyes!
Will all great Neptune's ocean wash this blood 60
Clean from my hand? No. This my hand will rather
The multitudinous seas incarnadine,
Making the green one³ red.

(*Enter* LADY MACBETH.)

3. All.
4. Your self-control has deserted you.

Lady. My hands are of your color, but I shame
To wear a heart so white. (*Knock.*)
I hear a knocking 65
At the south entry. Retire we to our chamber.
A little water clears us of this deed.
How easy is it then! Your constancy
Hath left you unattended.⁴ (*Knock.*)
Hark! more knocking.
Get on your nightgown, lest occasion call us 70
And show us to be watchers. Be not lost
So poorly in your thoughts.

Macb. To know my deed, 'twere best not know myself.

(*Knock.*)

Wake Duncan with thy knocking! I would thou couldst!

(*Exeunt.*)

SCENE III. INVERNESS. MACBETH'S CASTLE.

(*Enter a* PORTER. *Knocking within.*)

Porter. Here's a knocking indeed! If a man were porter of hell gate, he should have old turning the key. (*Knock.*) Knock, knock, knock! Who's there, i' th' name of Belzebub? Here's a farmer that hang'd himself on th' expectation of plenty. Come in time! Have napkins enow¹ about you; here you'll sweat for't. (*Knock.*) Knock, knock! Who's there, in th' other devil's name? Faith, here's an equivocator,² that could swear in both the scales against either scale; who committed treason enough for God's sake, yet could not equivocate to heaven.

1. Handkerchiefs enough.
2. Liar.

O, come in, equivocator! (*Knock.*)
Knock, knock, knock! Who's there?
Faith, here's an English tailor come
hither for stealing out of a French
hose. Come in, tailor. Here you
may roast your goose. (*Knock.*)
Knock, knock! Never at quiet!
What are you? But this place is
too cold for hell. I'll devil-porter
it no further. I had thought to have
let in some of all professions that
go the primrose way to th' everlasting bonfire. (*Knock.*) Anon,
anon! (*Opens the gate.*) I pray
you remember the porter.   31

(*Enter* MACDUFF *and* LENNOX.)

Macd. Was it so late, friend, ere you
went to bed,
That you do lie so late?

Port. Faith, sir, we were carousing till
the second cock; and drink, sir, is a
great provoker of three things.   36

Macd. What three things does drink
especially provoke?

Port. Marry, sir, nose-painting, sleep,
and urine. Lechery, sir, it provokes,
and unprovokes: it provokes the
desire, but it takes away the performance. Therefore much drink
may be said to be an equivocator
with lechery: it makes him, and it
mars him; it sets him on, and it
takes him off; it persuades him,
and disheartens him; makes him
stand to, and not stand to; in conclusion, equivocates him in a sleep,
and, giving him the lie, leaves
him.   51

Macd. I believe drink gave thee the lie
last night.

Port. That it did, sir, i' the very throat
on me; but I requited him for his
lie; and, I think, being too strong

for him, though he took up my
legs sometime, yet I made a shift
to cast him.   58

Macd. Is thy master stirring?

(*Enter* MACBETH.)

Our knocking has awak'd him; here
he comes.

Len. Good morrow, noble sir.

Macb.   Good morrow, both.

Macd. Is the King stirring, worthy
Thane?

Macb.   Not yet.   62

Macd. He did command me to call
timely on him;
I have almost slipp'd the hour.

Macb.   I'll bring you to him.

Macd. I know this is a joyful trouble to
you;   65
But yet 'tis one.

Macb. The labor we delight in physics[3]
pain.
This is the door.

Macd.   I'll make so bold to call,
For 'tis my limited service.[4]

(*Exit.*)

Len. Goes the King hence to-day?

Macb.   He does; he did appoint so.

Len. The night has been unruly. Where
we lay,   71
Our chimneys were blown down;
and, as they say,
Lamentings heard i' th' air, strange
screams of death,
And prophesying, with accents terrible,
Of dire combustion[5] and confus'd
events   75
New hatch'd to th' woeful time. The
obscure bird [6]
Clamor'd the livelong night. Some say
the earth
Was feverous and did shake.

3. Cures.
4. Assigned duty.

5. Social upheaval.
6. The owl.

Macb.   'Twas a rough night.
Len. My young remembrance cannot parallel
A fellow to it.   80

(*Enter* MACDUFF.)

Macd. O horror, horror, horror! Tongue nor heart
Cannot conceive nor name thee!
Macb. and Len. What's the matter?
Macd. Confusion now hath made his masterpiece!
Most sacrilegious murder hath broke ope   85
The Lord's anointed temple and stole thence
The life o' th' building!
Macb.   What is't you say? the life?
Len. Mean you his Majesty?
Macd. Approach the chamber, and destroy your sight
With a new Gorgon. Do not bid me speak.   90
See, and then speak yourselves.

(*Exeunt* MACBETH *and* LENNOX.)
       Awake, awake!
Ring the alarum bell. Murder and treason!
Banquo and Donalbain! Malcolm! awake!
Shake off this downy sleep, death's counterfeit,
And look on death itself! Up, up, and see   95
The great doom's image! Malcolm! Banquo!
As from your graves rise up and walk like sprites
To countenance this horror! Ring the bell!

(*Bell rings.*)
(*Enter* LADY MACBETH.)

Lady. What's the business,
That such a hideous trumpet calls to parley   100
The sleepers of the house? Speak, speak!
Macd.   O gentle lady,
'Tis not for you to hear what I can speak!
The repetition in a woman's ear
Would murder as it fell.

(*Enter* BANQUO.)
       O Banquo, Banquo,
Our royal master's murder'd!
Lady.   Woe, alas! 105
What, in our house?
Ban.   Too cruel anywhere.
Dear Duff, I prithee contradict thyself
And say it is not so.

(*Enter* MACBETH, LENNOX, *and* ROSS.)

Macb. Had I but died an hour before this chance,
I had liv'd a blessed time; for from this instant   110
There's nothing serious in mortality;
All is but toys; renown and grace is dead;
The wine of life is drawn, and the mere lees
Is left this vault to brag of.   114

(*Enter* MALCOLM *and* DONALBAIN.)

Don. What is amiss?
Macb.   You are, and do not know't.
The spring, the head, the fountain of your blood
Is stopp'd, the very source of it is stopp'd.
Macd. Your royal father's murder'd.
Mal.   O, by whom?
Len. Those of his chamber, as it seem'd, had done't.
Their hands and faces were all badg'd with blood;   120
So were their daggers, which unwip'd we found
Upon their pillows.

They star'd and were distracted. No man's life
Was to be trusted with them.

Macb. O, yet I do repent me of my fury   125
That I did kill them.

Macd.   Wherefore did you so?

Macb. Who can be wise, amazed, temperate, and furious,
Loyal and neutral, in a moment? No man.
The expedition of my violent love
Outrun the pauser, reason. Here lay Duncan,   130
His silver skin laced with his golden blood,
And his gash'd stabs look'd like a breach in nature
For ruin's wasteful entrance; there, the murderers,
Steep'd in the colors of their trade, their daggers
Unmannerly breech'd [7] with gore. Who could refrain   135
That had a heart to love and in that heart
Courage to make 's love known?

Lady.   Help me hence, ho!

Macd. Look to the lady.

Mal. (*Aside to* DONALBAIN.) Why do we hold our tongues,
That most may claim this argument for ours?   140

Don. (*Aside to* MALCOLM.) What should be spoken here, where our fate,
Hid in an auger hole, may rush and seize us?
Let's away.
Our tears are not yet brew'd.

Mal. (*Aside to* DONALBAIN.) Nor our strong sorrow   145
Upon the foot of motion.

Ban.   Look to the lady.

(LADY MACBETH *is carried out.*)
And when we have our naked frailties hid,
That suffer in exposure, let us meet
And question this most bloody piece of work,
To know it further. Fears and scruples shake us.   150
In the great hand of God I stand, and thence
Against the undivulg'd pretense I fight
Of treasonous malice.

Macd.   And so do I.

All.   So all.

Macb. Let's briefly put on manly readiness
And meet i' th' hall together.

All.   Well contented.   155

(*Exeunt all but* MALCOLM *and* DONALBAIN.)

Mal. What will you do? Let's not consort with them.
To show an unfelt sorrow is an office
Which the false man does easy. I'll to England.

Don. To Ireland I. Our separated fortune
Shall keep us both the safer. Where we are,   160
There's daggers in men's smiles; the near in blood,[8]
The nearer bloody.[9]

Mal. This murderous shaft that's shot
Hath not yet lighted, and our safest way
Is to avoid the aim. Therefore to horse!
And let us not be dainty of leave-taking   165

7. Rudely covered.
8. The more closely related to the King—.
9. The more danger.

But shift[10] away. There's warrant in
   that theft
Which steals itself when there's no
   mercy left.

(*Exeunt.*)

SCENE IV. INVERNESS. OUTSIDE MACBETH'S CASTLE.

(*Enter* ROSS *with an* OLD MAN.)

Old Man. Threescore and ten I can
   remember well;
Within the volume of which time I
   have seen
Hours dreadful and things strange;
   but this sore night
Hath trifled former knowings.
Ross.   Ah, good father,
Thou seest the heavens, as troubled
   with man's act,   5
Threaten his bloody stage.[1] By th'
   clock 'tis day,
And yet dark night strangles the
   traveling lamp.
Is't night's predominance, or the day's
   shame,
That darkness does the face of earth
   entomb
When living light should kiss it?
Old Man.   'Tis unnatural,   10
Even like the deed that's done. On
   Tuesday last
A falcon, tow'ring in her pride of
   place,
Was by a mousing owl hawk'd at and
   kill'd.
Ross. And Duncan's horses (a thing
   most strange and certain),
Beauteous and swift, the minions of
   their race,   15
Turn'd wild in nature, broke their
   stalls, flung out,
Contending 'gainst obedience, as
   they would make

10. Steal.
1. The earth.

War with mankind.
Old Man. 'Tis said they eat each other.
Ross. They did so, to th' amazement of
   mine eyes
That look'd upon't.

(*Enter* MACDUFF.)

Here comes the good Macduff.
How goes the world, sir, now?   21
Macd.   Why, see you not?
Ross. Is't known who did this more
   than bloody deed?
Macd. Those that Macbeth hath slain.
Ross.   Alas, the day!
What good could they pretend?
Macd.   They were suborn'd.[2]
Malcolm and Donalbain, the King's
   two sons,   25
Are stol'n away and fled, which puts
   upon them
Suspicion of the deed.
Ross.   'Gainst nature still!
Thriftless ambition, that wilt ravin
   up[3]
Thine own live's means! Then 'tis
   most like
The sovereignty will fall upon Mac-
   beth.   30
Macd. He is already named, and gone
   to Scone
To be invested.
Ross.   Where is Duncan's body?
Macd. Carried to Colmekill,
The sacred storehouse of his prede-
   cessors
And guardian of their bones.
Ross.   Will you to Scone? 35
Macd. No, cousin, I'll to Fife.
Ross.   Well, I will thither.
Macd. Well, may you see things well
   done there. Adieu!
Lest our old robes sit easier than our
   new!
Ross. Farewell, father.

2. Bribed.
3. Devour.

Old Man. God's benison go with you,
   and with those   40
   That would make good of bad, and
   friends of foes!

(*Exeunt omnes.*)

ACT III. SCENE I. FORRES. THE PALACE.

(*Enter* BANQUO.)

Ban. Thou hast it now—King, Cawdor,
   Glamis, all,
   As the weird women promis'd; and
   I fear
   Thou play'dst most foully for't. Yet it
   was said
   It should not stand in thy posterity,
   But that myself should be the root
   and father   5
   Of many kings. If there come truth
   from them
   (As upon thee, Macbeth, their
   speeches shine),
   Why, by the verities on thee made
   good,
   May they not be my oracles as well
   And set me up in hope? But, hush, no
   more!   10

(*Sennet*[1] *sounded. Enter* MACBETH,
as King; LADY MACBETH, *as Queen;*
LENNOX, ROSS, LORDS, *and* ATTEND-
ANTS.)

Macb. Here's our chief guest.
Lady.   If he had been forgotten,
   It had been as a gap in our great
   feast,
   And all-thing unbecoming.
Macb. To-night we hold a solemn sup-
   per, sir,
   And I'll request your presence.
Ban.   Let your Highness 15
   Command upon me, to the which my
   duties
   Are with a most indissoluble tie
   For ever knit.

Macb.   Ride you this afternoon?
Ban. Ay, my good lord.   20
Macb. We should have else desir'd
   your good advice
   (Which still hath been both grave
   and prosperous)
   In this day's council; but we'll take
   to-morrow.
   Is't far you ride?
Ban. As far, my lord, as will fill up the
   time   25
   'Twixt this and supper. Go not my
   horse the better,
   I must become a borrower of the
   night
   For a dark hour or twain.
Macb.   Fail not our feast.
Ban. My lord, I will not.
Macb. We hear our bloody cousins are
   bestow'd   30
   In England and in Ireland, not con-
   fessing
   Their cruel parricide, filling their
   hearers
   With strange invention. But of that
   to-morrow,
   When therewithal we shall have
   cause of state
   Craving[2] us jointly. Hie you to horse.
   Adieu,   35
   Till you return at night. Goes Fleance
   with you?
Ban. Ay, my good lord. Our time does
   call upon 's.
Macb. I wish your horses swift and sure
   of foot,
   And so I do commend you to their
   backs.
   Farewell.   40

(*Exit* BANQUO.)

   Let every man be master of his time
   Till seven at night. To make society
   The sweeter welcome, we will keep
   ourself

1. Trumpet call.   2. Concerning.

Till supper time alone. While then,
God be with you!

(*Exeunt all but* MACBETH *and a*
SERVANT.)

Sirrah, a word with you. Attend those
men 45
Our pleasure?

Serv. They are, my lord, without the
palace gate.

Macb. Bring them before us.

(*Exit* SERVANT.)

To be thus[3] is nothing,
But to be safely thus. Our fears in
Banquo
Stick deep; and in his royalty of
nature 50
Reigns that which would be fear'd.
'Tis much he dares,
And to that dauntless temper of his
mind
He hath a wisdom that doth guide
his valor
To act in safety. There is none but he
Whose being I do fear; and under
him 55
My Genius is rebuk'd, as it is said
Mark Antony's was by Cæsar. He
chid the sisters
When first they put the name of King
upon me,
And bade them speak to him. Then,
prophet-like,
They hail'd him father to a line of
kings. 60
Upon my head they placed a fruitless
crown
And put a barren sceptre in my gripe,
Thence to be wrench'd with an un-
lineal hand,
No son of mine succeeding. If't be so,
For Banquo's issue have I filed my
mind; 65

For them the gracious Duncan have
I murder'd;
Put rancors in the vessel of my peace
Only for them, and mine eternal
jewel [4]
Given to the common enemy of man[5]
To make them kings, the seed of
Banquo kings! 70
Rather than so, come, Fate, into the
list,
And champion me to th' utterance!
Who's there?

(*Enter* SERVANT *and two* MURDER-
ERS.)

Now go to the door and stay there
till we call.

(*Exit* SERVANT.)

Was it not yesterday we spoke together?

Murderers. It was, so please your Highness.

Macb. Well then, now 75
Have you consider'd of my speeches?
Know
That it was he, in the times past,
which held you
So under fortune, which you thought
had been
Our innocent self. This I made good
to you
In our last conference, pass'd in pro-
bation with you 80
How you were borne in hand, how
cross'd; the instruments;
Who wrought with them; and all
things else that might
To half a soul[6] and to a notion[7]
craz'd
Say 'Thus did Banquo.'

1. Mur. You made it known to us.

Macb. I did so; and went further, which
is now 85

3. King.
4. Immortal soul.
5. The devil.
6. A half-wit.
7. Mind.

Our point of second meeting. Do you
find
Your patience so predominant in your
nature
That you can let this go? Are you so
gospell'd
To pray for this good man and for
his issue,
Whose heavy hand hath bow'd you to
the grave   90
And beggar'd yours for ever?

1. Mur.   We are men, my liege.

Macb. Ay, in the catalogue ye go for
men,
As hounds and greyhounds, mongrels,
spaniels, curs,
Shoughs, water-rugs, and demi-
wolves are clept
All by the name of dogs. The valued
file   95
Distinguishes the swift, the slow, the
subtle,
The housekeeper, the hunter, every
one
According to the gift which bounte-
ous nature
Hath in him closed; whereby he does
receive   99
Particular addition, from the bill
That writes them all alike; and so of
men.
Now, if you have a station in the
file,
Not i' th' worst rank of manhood,
say't;
And I will put that business in your
bosoms
Whose execution takes your enemy
off,   105
Grapples you to the heart and love of
us,
Who wear our health but sickly in his
life,
Which in his death were perfect.

2. Mur.   I am one, my liege,

Whom the vile blows and buffets of
the world
Have so incensed that I am reckless
what   110
I do to spite the world.

1. Mur.   And I another,
So weary with disasters, tugg'd with
fortune,
That I would set my life on any
chance,
To mend it or be rid on't.

Macb.   Both of you
Know Banquo was your enemy.

Murderers.   True, my lord.   115

Macb. So is he mine; and in such
bloody distance
That every minute of his being
thrusts
Against my near'st of life; and though
I could
With barefaced power sweep him
from my sight
And bid my will avouch it, yet I
must not,   120
For certain friends that are both his
and mine,
Whose loves I may not drop, but wail
his fall
Who I myself struck down. And
thence it is
That I to your assistance do make
love,
Masking the business from the com-
mon eye   125
For sundry weighty reasons.

2. Mur.   We shall, my lord,
Perform what you command us.

1. Mur.   Though our lives—

Macb. Your spirits shine through
you.
Within this hour at most
I will advise you where to plant yourselves,
Acquaint you with the perfect spy o'
th' time,   130

The moment on't; for't must be done to-night,

And something from the palace; always thought

That I require a clearness;[8] and with him,

To leave no rubs nor botches in the work,

Fleance his son, that keeps him company,   135

Whose absence is no less material to me

Than is his father's, must embrace the fate

Of that dark hour. Resolve yourselves apart;[9]

I'll come to you anon.

Murderers.   We are resolv'd, my lord.

Macb. I'll call upon you straight. Abide within.   140

(*Exeunt* MURDERERS.)

It is concluded. Banquo, thy soul's flight,

If it find heaven, must find it out to-night.

(*Exit.*)

SCENE II. FORRES. THE PALACE.

(*Enter* LADY MACBETH *and a* SERVANT.)

Lady. Is Banquo gone from court?

Serv. Ay, madam, but returns again to-night.

Lady. Say to the King I would attend his leisure

For a few words.

Serv.   Madam, I will.

(*Exit.*)

Lady.   Naught's had, all's spent,

Where our desire is got without content.   5

'Tis safer to be that which we destroy

Than by destruction dwell in doubtful joy.

(*Enter* MACBETH.)

How now, my lord? Why do you keep alone,

Of sorriest fancies your companions making,

Using those thoughts which should indeed have died   10

With them they think on? Things without all remedy

Should be without regard. What's done is done.

Macb. We have scotch'd the snake, not kill'd it.

She'll close, and be herself, whilst our poor malice

Remains in danger of her former tooth.   15

But let the frame of things disjoint,[1] both the worlds suffer,

Ere we will eat our meal in fear and sleep

In the affliction of these terrible dreams

That shake us nightly. Better be with the dead,

Whom we, to gain our peace, have sent to peace,   20

Than on the torture of the mind to lie

In restless ecstasy. Duncan is in his grave;

After life's fitful fever he sleeps well.

Treason has done his worst. Nor steel nor poison,

Malice domestic, foreign levy, nothing,   25

Can touch him further.

Lady.   Come on.

Gentle my lord, sleek o'er your rugged looks;

8. I must not be suspected.
9. Decide for yourselves.

1. The universe collapse.

Be bright and jovial among your
guests to-night.

Macb. So shall I, love; and so, I pray,
be you.

Let your remembrance apply to
Banquo;   30

Present him eminence both with eye
and tongue—

Unsafe the while, that we

Must lave our honors in these flattering streams

And make our faces vizards to our
hearts,

Disguising what they are.

Lady.   You must leave this. 35

Macb. O, full of scorpions is my mind,
dear wife!

Thou know'st that Banquo, and his
Fleance, lives.

Lady. But in them Nature's copy's not
eterne.

Macb. There's comfort yet! They are
assailable.

Then be thou jocund. Ere the bat
hath flown   40

His cloister'd flight, ere to black
Hecate's summons

The shard-borne beetle with his
drowsy hums

Hath rung night's yawning peal,
there shall be done

A deed of dreadful note.

Lady.   What's to be done?

Macb. Be innocent of the knowledge,
dearest chuck,   45

Till thou applaud the deed. Come,
seeling[2] night,

Scarf up the tender eye of pitiful
day,

And with thy bloody and invisible
hand

Cancel and tear to pieces that great
bond [3]

Which keeps me pale! Light thickens,
and the crow   50

Makes wing to th' rooky wood.

Good things of day begin to droop
and drowse,

Whiles night's black agents to their
preys do rouse.

Thou marvel'st at my words; but
hold thee still:

Things bad begun make strong themselves by ill.   55

So prithee go with me.

(*Exeunt.*)

SCENE III. FORRES. A PARK NEAR THE
PALACE.

(*Enter three* MURDERERS)

1. Mur. But who did bid thee join
with us?

3. Mur.   Macbeth.

2. Mur. He needs not our mistrust,
since he delivers

Our offices, and what we have to do,

To the direction just.

1. Mur.   Then stand with us.

The west yet glimmers with some
streaks of day.   5

Now spurs the lated traveller apace

To gain the timely inn, and near approaches

The subject of our watch.

3. Mur.   Hark! I hear horses.

Ban. (*Within.*) Give us a light there, ho!

2. Mur.   Then 'tis he! The rest

That are within the note of expectation[1]   10

Already are i' th' court.

1. Mur.   His horses go about.

3. Mur. Almost a mile; but he does
usually,

So all men do, from hence to th'
palace gate

---

2. Blinding.
3. Banquo's life.

1. The invited guests.

Make it their walk.

(*Enter* BANQUO, *and* FLEANCE *with a torch.*)

2. Mur. A light, a light!
3. Mur. 'Tis he.
1. Mur. Stand to't. 15
Ban. It will be rain to-night.
1. Mur. Let it come down!

(*They fall upon* BANQUO.)

Ban. O, treachery! Fly, good Fleance, fly, fly, fly!
Thou mayst revenge. O slave!

(*Dies.* FLEANCE *escapes.*)

3. Mur. Who did strike out the light?
1. Mur. Was't not the way?
3. Mur. There's but one down; the son is fled.
2. Mur. We have lost 20
Best half of our affair.
1. Mur. Well, let's away, and say how much is done.

(*Exeunt.*)

SCENE IV. FORRES. HALL IN THE PALACE.

(*Banquet prepared. Enter* MACBETH, LADY MACBETH, ROSS, LENNOX, LORDS, *and* ATTENDANTS.)

Macb. You know your own degrees, sit down. At first
And last the hearty welcome.
Lords. Thanks to your Majesty.
Macb. Ourself will mingle with society
And play the humble host.
Our hostess keeps her state, but in best time 5
We will require her welcome.
Lady. Pronounce it for me, sir, to all our friends,
For my heart speaks they are welcome.

(FIRST MURDERER *appears at the door.*)

1. Respond to.

Macb. See, they encounter[1] thee with their hearts' thanks.
Both sides are even. Here I'll sit i' th' midst. 10
Be large in mirth; anon we'll drink a measure
The table round. (*Goes to the door.*)
There's blood upon thy face.
Mur. 'Tis Banquo's then.
Macb. 'Tis better thee without than he within.
Is he dispatch'd? 15
Mur. My lord, his throat is cut. That I did for him.
Macb. Thou art the best o' th' cut-throats! Yet he's good
That did the like for Fleance. If thou didst it,
Thou art the nonpareil.
Mur. Most royal sir,
Fleance is scap'd. 20
Macb. (*Aside.*) Then comes my fit again. I had else been perfect;
Whole as the marble, founded as the rock,
As broad and general as the casing air.
But now I am cabin'd, cribb'd, con-fin'd, bound in
To saucy doubts and fears.—But Banquo's safe? 25
Mur. Ay, my good lord. Safe in a ditch he bides,
With twenty trenched gashes on his head,
The least a death to nature.
Macb. Thanks for that!
There the grown serpent lies; the worm that's fled
Hath nature that in time will venom breed, 30
No teeth for th' present. Get thee gone. To-morrow
We'll hear ourselves[2] again.

2. Confer with each other.

(*Exit* MURDERER.)

Lady.   My royal lord,
You do not give the cheer. The feast
    is sold
That is not often vouch'd, while 'tis
    a-making,
'Tis given with welcome. To feed
    were best at home.   35
From thence, the sauce to meat is
    ceremony;
Meeting were bare without it.

(*Enter the* GHOST OF BANQUO, *and
sits in* MACBETH'S *place.*)

Macb.   Sweet remembrancer!
Now good digestion wait on appe-
    tite,
And health on both!

Len.   May't please your Highness sit.

Macb. Here had we now our country's
    honor, roof'd,   40
Were the graced person of our Ban-
    quo present;
Who may I rather challenge for un-
    kindness
Than pity for mischance!

Ross.   His absence, sir,
Lays blame upon his promise.
    Please't your Highness
To grace us with your royal com-
    pany.   45

Macb. The table's full.

Len.   Here is a place reserved, sir.

Macb. Where?

Len. Here, my good lord. What is't that
    moves your Highness?

Macb. Which of you have done this?

Lords.   What, my good lord?

Macb. Thou canst not say I did it.
    Never shake   50
    Thy gory locks at me.

Ross. Gentlemen, rise. His Highness is
    not well.

Lady. Sit, worthy friends. My lord is
    often thus,

And hath been from his youth. Pray
    you keep seat.   54
The fit is momentary; upon a thought
He will again be well. If much you
    note him,
You shall offend him and extend his
    passion.
Feed, and regard him not.—Are you
    a man?

Macb. Ay, and a bold one, that dare
    look on that
Which might appal the devil.

Lady.   O proper stuff! 60
This is the very painting of your
    fear.
This is the air-drawn dagger which
    you said
Led you to Duncan. O, these flaws
    and starts
(Impostors to true fear) would well
    become   64
A woman's story at a winter's fire,
Authorized by her grandam. Shame
    itself!
Why do you make such faces? When
    all's done,
You look but on a stool.

Macb. Prithee see there! behold! look!
    lo! How say you?
Why, what care I? If thou canst nod,
    speak too.   70
If charnel houses and our graves
    must send
Those that we bury back, our monu-
    ments
Shall be the maws of kites.

(GHOST *vanishes.*)

Lady. What, quite unmann'd in folly?

Macb. If I stand here, I saw him.

Lady.   Fie, for shame!

Macb. Blood hath been shed ere now,
    i' th' olden time,   75
Ere humane statute purg'd the gentle
    weal;

Ay, and since too, murders have been perform'd
Too terrible for the ear. The time has been
That, when the brains were out, the man would die,
And there an end! But now they rise again,   80
With twenty mortal murders on their crowns,
And push us from our stools. This is more strange
Than such a murder is.

Lady.   My worthy lord,
Your noble friends do lack you.

Macb.   I do forget.
Do not muse at me, my most worthy friends.   85
I have a strange infirmity, which is nothing
To those that know me. Come, love and health to all!
Then I'll sit down. Give me some wine, fill full.
I drink to th' general joy o' th' whole table,
And to our dear friend Banquo, whom we miss.   90
Would he were here! To all, and him, we thirst,
And all to all.

Lords.   Our duties, and the pledge.

(*Re-enter* Ghost.)

Macb. Avaunt, and quit my sight! Let the earth hide thee!
Thy bones are marrowless, thy blood is cold;
Thou hast no speculation in those eyes   95
Which thou dost glare with!

Lady.   Think of this, good peers,
But as a thing of custom. 'Tis no other.

Only it spoils the pleasure of the time.

Macb. What man dare, I dare.
Approach thou like the rugged Russian bear,   100
The arm'd rhinoceros, or th' Hyrcan tiger;
Take any shape but that, and my firm nerves
Shall never tremble. Or be alive again
And dare me to the desert with thy sword.
If trembling I inhabit then, protest me   105
The baby of a girl.[3] Hence, horrible shadow!
Unreal mock'ry, hence!

(Ghost *vanishes.*)
                Why, so! Being gone,
I am a man again. Pray you sit still.

Lady. You have displaced the mirth, broke the good meeting
With most admired disorder.

Macb.   Can such things be, 110
And overcome us like a summer's cloud
Without our special wonder? You make me strange
Even to the disposition that I owe,[4]
When now I think you can behold such sights
And keep the natural ruby of your cheeks   115
When mine is blanch'd with fear.

Ross.   What sights, my lord?

Lady. I pray you speak not. He grows worse and worse;
Question enrages him. At once, good night.
Stand not upon the order of your going,
But go at once.

3. A weakling.

4. Own.

Len.   Good night, and better health
Attend his Majesty!   121
Lady.   A kind good night to all!

(*Exeunt all but* MACBETH *and* LADY
MACBETH.)

Macb. It will have blood, they say;
blood will have blood.

Stones have been known to move
and trees to speak;

Augurs and understood relations
have

By maggot-pies and choughs and
rooks brought forth   125

The secret'st man of blood.[5] What is
the night? [6]

Lady. Almost at odds with morning,
which is which.

Macb. How say'st thou that Macduff
denies his person

At our great bidding?

Lady.   Did you send to him, sir?

Macb. I hear it by the way; but I will
send.   130

There's not a one of them but in his
house

I keep a servant fee'd.[7] I will to-morrow

(And betimes I will) unto the Weird
Sisters.

More shall they speak; for now I am
bent to know

By the worst means the worst. For
mine own good   135

All causes shall give way. I am in
blood

Stepp'd in so far that, should I wade
no more,

Returning were as tedious as go o'er.

Strange things I have in head, that
will to hand,

Which must be acted ere they may
be scann'd.   140

Lady. You lack the season[8] of all natures, sleep.

Macb. Come, we'll to sleep. My strange
and self-abuse[9]

Is the initiate fear that wants hard
use.

We are yet but young in deed.[10]

(*Exeunt.*)

SCENE V. A HEATH.

(*Thunder. Enter the three* WITCHES,
meeting HECATE.)

1. Witch. Why, how now, Hecate? You
look angerly.

Hec. Have I not reason, beldams as you
are,

Saucy and overbold? How did you
dare

To trade and traffic with Macbeth

In riddles and affairs of death;   5

And I, the mistress of your charms,

The close contriver of all harms,

Was never call'd to bear my part

Or show the glory of our art?

And, which is worse, all you have
done   10

Hath been but for a wayward son,

Spiteful and wrathful, who, as others
do,

Loves for his own ends, not for you.

But make amends now. Get you gone

And at the pit of Acheron   15

Meet me i' th' morning. Thither he

Will come to know his destiny.

Your vessels and your spells provide,

Your charms and everything beside.

I am for th' air. This night I'll spend

Unto a dismal and a fatal end.   21

Great business must be wrought ere
noon.

Upon the corner of the moon

5. The least suspected murderer.
6. What time is it?
7. A paid spy.

8. Preservative.
9. Self-deception (seeing ghosts).
10. Novices in crime.

There hangs a vaporous drop pro-
found. 24
I'll catch it ere it come to ground;
And that, distill'd by magic sleights,
Shall raise such artificial sprites
As by the strength of their illusion
Shall draw him on to his confusion.
He shall spurn fate, scorn death, and
bear 30
His hopes 'bove wisdom, grace, and
fear;
And you all know security
Is mortals' chiefest enemy.

(*Music and a song within.* 'Come
away, come away,' &c.)

Hark! I am call'd. My little spirit,
see,
Sits in a foggy cloud and stays for
me. 35

(*Exit.*)

1. Witch. Come, let's make haste. She'll
soon be back again.

(*Exeunt.*)

SCENE VI. FORRES. THE PALACE.

(*Enter* LENNOX *and another* LORD.)

Len. My former speeches have but hit
your thoughts,
Which can interpret farther. Only I
say
Things have been strangely borne.
The gracious Duncan
Was pitied of Macbeth. Marry, he
was dead!
And the right valiant Banquo walk'd
too late; 5
Whom, you may say (if't please you)
Fleance kill'd,
For Fleance fled. Men must not walk
too late.
Who cannot want the thought how
monstrous
It was for Malcolm and for Donalbain

To kill their gracious father? Damned
fact! 10
How it did grieve Macbeth! Did he
not straight,
In pious rage, the two delinquents
tear,
That were the slaves of drink and
thralls of sleep?
Was not that nobly done? Ay, and
wisely too!
For 'twould have anger'd any heart
alive 15
To hear the men deny't. So that I say
He has borne all things well; and I
do think
That, had he Duncan's sons under
his key
(As, an't please heaven, he shall not),
they should find
What 'twere to kill a father. So should
Fleance. 20
But peace! for from broad words,
and 'cause he fail'd
His presence at the tyrant's feasts, I
hear
Macduff lives in disgrace. Sir, can
you tell
Where he bestows himself?

Lord. The son of Duncan,
From whom this tyrant holds the due
of birth, 25
Lives in the English court, and is
received
Of the most pious Edward with such
grace
That the malevolence of fortune
nothing
Takes from his high respect. Thither
Macduff
Is gone to pray the holy King upon
his aid 30
To wake Northumberland and war-
like Siward;
That by the help of these (with Him
above

To ratify the work) we may again
Give to our tables meat, sleep to our
   nights,
Free from our feasts and banquets
   bloody knives,   35
Do faithful homage and receive free
   honors—
All which we pine for now. And this
   report
Hath so exasperate the King that he
Prepares for some attempt of war.
Len.   Sent he to Macduff?
Lord. He did; and with an absolute
   'Sir, not I!'   40
The cloudy messenger turns me his
   back
And hums, as who should say, 'You'll
   rue the time
That clogs me with this answer.'
Len.   And that well might
Advise him to a caution t' hold what
   distance
His wisdom can provide. Some holy
   angel   45
Fly to the court of England and un-
   fold
His message ere he come, that a swift
   blessing
May soon return to this our suffering
   country
Under a hand accursed!
Lord.   I'll send my prayers with him.

(*Exeunt.*)

Act iv. Scene i. A cavern. In the middle, a cauldron boiling.

(*Thunder. Enter the three* Witches.)

1. Witch. Thrice the brinded cat hath
   mew'd.
2. Witch. Thrice and once the hedge-
   pig whin'd.
3. Witch. Harpier cries: 'tis time, 'tis
   time.

1. Witch. Round about the cauldron
   go;
In the poison'd entrails throw.   5
Toad, that under cold stone
Days and nights has thirty-one
Swelt'red venom sleeping got,
Boil thou first i' th' charmed pot.
All. Double, double, toil and trouble;
Fire burn, and cauldron bubble.   11
2. Witch. Fillet of a fenny snake,
In the cauldron boil and bake;
Eye of newt, and toe of frog,
Wool of bat, and tongue of dog,   15
Adder's fork, and blindworm's sting,
Lizard's leg, and howlet's wing;
For a charm of powerful trouble
Like a hell-broth boil and bubble.
All. Double, double, toil and trouble;
Fire burn, and cauldron bubble.   21
3. Witch. Scale of dragon, tooth of
   wolf,
Witch's mummy, maw and gulf
Of the ravin'd salt-sea shark,
Root of hemlock, digg'd i' th' dark;
Liver of blaspheming Jew,   26
Gall of goat, and slips of yew
Sliver'd in the moon's eclipse;
Nose of Turk and Tartar's lips;
Finger of birth-strangled babe   30
Ditch-deliver'd by a drab:
Make the gruel thick and slab.
Add thereto a tiger's chaudron
For th' ingredients of our cauldron.
All. Double, double, toil and trouble;
Fire burn, and cauldron bubble.   36
2. Witch. Cool it with a baboon's blood,
Then the charm is firm and good.

(*Enter* Hecate.)

Hec. O, well done! I commend your
   pains,
And every one shall share i' th' gains.
And now about the cauldron sing   41
Like elves and fairies in a ring,
Enchanting all that you put in.

(*Music and a song,* 'Black spirits,'
&c. *Exit* HECATE.)

2. Witch. By the pricking of my thumbs,
Something wicked this way comes.
  Open locks,   46
  Whoever knocks!

(*Enter* MACBETH.)

Macb. How now, you secret, black, and
  midnight hags?
  What is't you do?

All.   A deed without a name.

Macb. I conjure you by that which you
  profess   50
(Howe'er you come to know it),
  answer me.
Though you untie the winds and let
  them fight
Against the churches; though the
  yesty[1] waves
Confound and swallow navigation
  up;
Though bladed corn be lodged and
  trees blown down;   55
Though castles topple on their
  warders' heads;
Though palaces and pyramids do
  slope
Their heads to their foundations;
  though the treasure
Of nature's germens[2] tumble all together,
Even till destruction sicken—answer
  me   60
To what I ask you.

1. Witch.   Speak.

2. Witch.   Demand.

3. Witch.   We'll answer.

1. Witch. Say, if th' hadst rather hear
  it from our mouths
Or from our masters.

Macb.   Call 'em! Let me see 'em.

1. Witch. Pour in sow's blood, that
  hath eaten

1. Foaming.

Her nine farrow; grease that's
  sweaten   65
From the murderer's gibbet throw
Into the flame.

All.   Come, high or low;
Thyself and office deftly show!

(*Thunder.* FIRST APPARITION, *an
Armed Head.*)

Macb. Tell me, thou unknown power—

1. Witch.   He knows thy thought.
Hear his speech, but say thou
  naught.   70

1. Appar. Macbeth! Macbeth! Macbeth!
  Beware Macduff;
Beware the Thane of Fife. Dismiss
  me. Enough.

(*He descends.*)

Macb. Whate'er thou art, for thy good
  caution thanks!
Thou hast harp'd my fear aright. But
  one word more—

1. Witch. He will not be commanded.
  Here's another,   75
More potent than the first.

(*Thunder.* SECOND APPARITION, *a
Bloody Child.*)

2. Appar. Macbeth! Macbeth! Macbeth!

Macb. Had I three ears, I'ld hear thee.

2. Appar. Be bloody, bold, and resolute;
  laugh to scorn
The power of man, for none of
  woman born   80
Shall harm Macbeth.

(*Descends.*)

Macb. Then live, Macduff. What need
  I fear of thee?
But yet I'll make assurance double
  sure
And take a bond of fate. Thou shalt
  not live!
That I may tell pale-hearted fear it
  lies   85

2. Seeds of all living matter.

And sleep in spite of thunder.

(*Thunder.* THIRD APPARITION, *a Child Crowned, with a tree in his hand.*)

What is this
That rises like the issue of a king
And wears upon his baby-brow the round
And top of sovereignty?

All.   Listen, but speak not to't.

3. Appar. Be lion-mettled, proud, and take no care   90
Who chafes, who frets, or where conspirers are.
Macbeth shall never vanquish'd be until
Great Birnam Wood to high Dunsinane Hill
Shall come against him.

(*Descends.*)

Macb.   That will never be.
Who can impress[3] the forest, bid the tree   95
Unfix his earth-bound root? Sweet bodements,[4] good!
Rebellion's head rise never till the Wood
Of Birnam rise, and our high placed Macbeth
Shall live the lease of nature, pay his breath
To time and mortal custom. Yet my heart   100
Throbs to know one thing. Tell me, if your art
Can tell so much—shall Banquo's issue ever
Reign in this kingdom?

All.   Seek to know no more.

Macb. I will be satisfied. Deny me this,
And an eternal curse fall on you! Let me know.   105
Why sinks that cauldron? and what noise is this?

(*Hautboys.*)

1. Witch. Show!
2. Witch. Show!
3. Witch. Show!
All. Show his eyes, and grieve his heart!   110
Come like shadows, so depart!

(*A show of eight Kings, the last with a glass[5] in his hand; and* BANQUO's GHOST *following.*)

Macb. Thou art too like the spirit of Banquo. Down!
Thy crown does sear mine eyeballs. And thy hair,
Thou other gold-bound brow, is like the first.
A third is like the former. Filthy hags!   115
Why do you show me this? A fourth? Start, eyes!
What, will the line stretch out to th' crack of doom?
Another yet? A seventh? I'll see no more.
And yet the eighth appears, who bears a glass
Which shows me many more; and some I see   120
That twofold balls and treble sceptres carry.
Horrible sight! Now I see 'tis true;
For the blood-bolter'd Banquo smiles upon me
And points at them for his. (*Apparitions vanish.*) What? Is this so?   124

1. Witch. Ay, sir, all this is so. But why
Stands Macbeth thus amazedly?
Come, sisters, cheer we up his sprites
And show the best of our delights.
I'll charm the air to give a sound
While you perform your antic round,
That this great king may kindly say

3. Draft into the army.
4. Prophecies.
5. Mirror.

Our duties did his welcome pay.   132

(*Music. The* WITCHES *dance, and vanish.*)

Macb. Where are they? Gone? Let this pernicious hour

Stand aye accursed in the calendar!
Come in, without there!

(*Enter* LENNOX.)

Len.   What's your Grace's will?   135
Macb. Saw you the Weird Sisters?
Len.   No, my lord.
Macb. Came they not by you?
Len.   No indeed, my lord.
Macb. Infected be the air whereon they ride,

And damn'd all those that trust them!
I did hear

The galloping of horse. Who was't
came by?   140
Len. 'Tis two or three, my lord, that bring you word

Macduff is fled to England.
Macb.   Fled to England?
Len. Ay, my good lord.
Macb. (*Aside.*) Time, thou anticipat'st[6]
my dread exploits.   144

The flighty purpose never is o'ertook
Unless the deed go with it. From this moment

The very firstlings of my heart shall be

The firstlings of my hand. And even now,

To crown my thoughts with acts, be it thought and done!   149

The castle of Macduff I will surprise,
Seize upon Fife, give to the edge o' th' sword

His wife, his babes, and all unfortunate souls

That trace him in his line. No boasting like a fool!

This deed I'll do before this purpose cool.

But no more sights!—Where are these gentlemen?   155

Come, bring me where they are.

(*Exeunt.*)

SCENE II. FIFE. MACDUFF'S CASTLE.

(*Enter* MACDUFF'S WIFE, *her* SON, *and* ROSS.)

Wife. What had he done to make him fly the land?

Ross. You must have patience, madam.
Wife.   He had none.

His flight was madness. When our actions do not,

Our fears do make us traitors.
Ross.   You know not

Whether it was his wisdom or his fear.   5
Wife. Wisdom? To leave his wife, to leave his babes,

His mansion, and his titles, in a place
From whence himself does fly? He loves us not,

He wants the natural touch. For the poor wren,

(The most diminutive of birds) will fight,   10

Her young ones in her nest, against the owl.

All is the fear, and nothing is the love,

As little is the wisdom, where the flight
So runs against all reason.
Ross.   My dearest coz,

I pray you school yourself. But for your husband,   15

He is noble, wise, judicious, and best knows

The fits o' th' season.[1] I dare not

---

5. Forestall.   1. Crises of the time.

speak much further;

But cruel are the times, when we are traitors

And do not know ourselves; when we hold rumor

From what we fear, yet know not what we fear,   20

But float upon a wild and violent sea

Each way and none. I take my leave of you.

Shall not be long but I'll be here again.

Things at the worst will cease, or else climb upward

To what they were before.—My pretty cousin,   25

Blessing upon you!

Wife. Father'd he is, and yet he's fatherless.

Ross. I am so much a fool, should I stay longer,

It would be my disgrace and your discomfort.

I take my leave at once.

(Exit.)

Wife.   Sirrah, your father's dead;   30

And what will you do now? How will you live?

Son. As birds do, mother.

Wife.   What, with worms and flies?

Son. With what I get, I mean; and so do they.

Wife. Poor bird! thou'dst never fear the net nor lime,

The pitfall nor the gin.   35

Son. Why should I, mother? Poor birds they are not set for.

My father is not dead, for all your saying.

Wife. Yes, he is dead. How wilt thou do for a father?

Son. Nay, how will you do for a husband?

Wife. Why, I can buy me twenty at any market.   40

Son. Then you'll buy 'em to sell again.

Wife. Thou speak'st with all thy wit; and yet, i' faith,

With wit enough for thee.

Son. Was my father a traitor, mother?

Wife. Ay, that he was!   45

Son. What is a traitor?

Wife. Why, one that swears, and lies.

Son. And be all traitors that do so?

Wife. Every one that does so is a traitor and must be hanged.   50

Son. And must they all be hanged that swear and lie?

Wife. Every one.

Son. Who must hang them?

Wife. Why, the honest men.   55

Son. Then the liars and swearers are fools; for there are liars and swearers enow to beat the honest men and hang up them.

Wife. Now God help thee, poor monkey!   60

But how wilt thou do for a father?

Son. If he were dead, you'ld weep for him. If you would not, it were a good sign that I should quickly have a new father.   65

Wife. Poor prattler, how thou talk'st!

(Enter a MESSENGER.*)*

Mess. Bless you, fair dame! I am not to you known,

Though in your state of honor I am perfect.

I doubt some danger does approach you nearly.

If you will take a homely[2] man's advice,   70

Be not found here. Hence with your little ones!

To fright you thus methinks I am too savage;

2. Humble.

To do worse to you were fell cruelty,
Which is too nigh your person.
Heaven preserve you! 74
I dare abide no longer.

(*Exit.*)

Wife. Whither should I fly?
I have done no harm. But I remember now
I am in this earthly world, where to do harm
Is often laudable, to do good sometime
Accounted dangerous folly. Why then, alas, 79
Do I put up that womanly defense
To say I have done no harm?—What are these faces?

(*Enter* Murderers.)

Mur. Where is your husband?
Wife. I hope, in no place so unsanctified 83
Where such as thou mayst find him.
Mur. He's a traitor.
Son. Thou liest, thou shag-hair'd villain!
Mur. What, you egg!

(*Stabs him.*)

Young fry of treachery!
Son. He has kill'd me, mother.
Run away, I pray you! 87

(*Dies.*)

(*Exit* Lady Macduff, *crying 'Murder!' and pursued by the* Murderers.)

SCENE iii. ENGLAND.
BEFORE KING EDWARD'S PALACE.

(*Enter* MALCOLM *and* MACDUFF.)

Mal. Let us seek out some desolate shade, and there
Weep our sad bosoms empty.
Macd. Let us rather

Hold fast the mortal sword and, like good men,
Bestride our downfall'n birthdom. Each new morn
New widows howl, new orphans cry, new sorrows 5
Strike heaven on the face, that it resounds
As if it felt with Scotland and yell'd out
Like syllable of dolor.
Mal. What I believe, I'll wail;
What know, believe; and what I can redress,
As I shall find the time to friend, I will. 10
What you have spoke, it may be so perchance.
This tyrant, whose sole name blisters our tongues,
Was once thought honest; you have loved him well;
He hath not touched you yet. I am young; but something
You may deserve of him through me,[1] and wisdom 15
To offer up a weak, poor, innocent lamb
T' appease an angry god.
Macd. I am not treacherous.
Mal. But Macbeth is.
A good and virtuous nature may recoil
In an imperial charge. But I shall crave your pardon. 20
That which you are, my thoughts cannot transpose.
Angels are bright still, though the brightest fell.
Though all things foul would wear the brows of grace,
Yet grace must still look so.
Macd. I have lost my hopes.

1. You may gain something by betraying me.

Mal. Perchance even there where I did
   find my doubts.   25
  Why in that rawness left you wife
   and child,
  Those precious motives, those strong
   knots of love,
  Without leave-taking? I pray you,
  Let not my jealousies be your dis-
   honors,
  But mine own safeties. You may be
   rightly just,   30
  Whatever I shall think.
Macd.   Bleed, bleed, poor country!
  Great tyranny, lay thou thy basis
   sure,
  For goodness dare not check thee!
   Wear thou thy wrongs;
  The title is affeer'd! Fare thee well,
   lord.
  I would not be the villain that thou
   think'st   35
  For the whole space that's in the
   tyrant's grasp
  And the rich East to boot.
Mal.   Be not offended.
  I speak not as in absolute fear of you.
  I think our country sinks beneath the
   yoke,
  It weeps, it bleeds, and each new
   day a gash   40
  Is added to her wounds. I think
   withal
  There would be hands uplifted in my
   right;
  And here from gracious England
   have I offer
  Of goodly thousands. But, for all this,
  When I shall tread upon the tyrant's
   head   45
  Or wear it on my sword, yet my poor
   country
  Shall have more vices than it had
   before,
  More suffer and more sundry ways
   than ever,

  By him that shall succeed.
Macd.   What should he be?
Mal. It is myself I mean; in whom I
   know   50
  All the particulars of vice so grafted
  That, when they shall be open'd,
   black Macbeth
  Will seem as pure as snow, and the
   poor state
  Esteem him as a lamb, being com-
   par'd
  With my confineless harms.
Macd.   Not in the legions 55
  Of horrid hell can come a devil more
   damn'd
  In evils to top Macbeth.
Mal.   I grant him bloody,
  Luxurious, avaricious, false, deceit-
   ful,
  Sudden, malicious, smacking of ev-
   ery sin
  That has a name. But there's no bot-
   tom, none,   60
  In my voluptuousness. Your wives,
   your daughters,
  Your matrons, and your maids could
   not fill up
  The cistern of my lust; and my desire
  All continent impediments would
   o'erbear
  That did oppose my will. Better
   Macbeth   65
  Than such an one to reign.
Macd.   Boundless intemperance
  In nature is a tyranny. It hath been
  Th' untimely emptying of the happy
   throne
  And fall of many kings. But fear not
   yet
  To take upon you what is yours. You
   may   70
  Convey your pleasures in a spacious
   plenty,
  And yet seem cold—the time you may
   so hoodwink.

We have willing dames enough. There cannot be
That vulture in you to devour so many
As will to greatness dedicate themselves, 75
Finding it so inclin'd.

Mal. With this there grows
In my most ill-composed affection such
A stanchless avarice that, were I King,
I should cut off the nobles for their lands,
Desire his jewels, and this other's house, 80
And my more-having would be as a sauce
To make me hunger more, that I should forge
Quarrels unjust against the good and loyal,
Destroying them for wealth.

Macd. This avarice
Sticks deeper, grows with more pernicious root 85
Than summer-seeming lust; and it hath been
The sword of our slain kings. Yet do not fear.
Scotland hath foisons[2] to fill up your will[3]
Of your mere own. All these are portable,
With other graces weigh'd. 90

Mal. But I have none. The king-becoming graces,
As justice, verity, temperance, stableness,
Bounty, perseverance, mercy, lowliness,
Devotion, patience, courage, fortitude, 94
I have no relish of them, but abound

In the division of each several crime,
Acting it many ways. Nay, had I power, I should
Pour the sweet milk of concord into hell,
Uproar the universal peace, confound
All unity on earth.

Macd. O Scotland, Scotland! 100

Mal. If such a one be fit to govern, speak.
I am as I have spoken.

Macd. Fit to govern?
No, not to live. O nation miserable,
With an untitled tyrant bloody-scepter'd,
When shalt thou see thy wholesome days again, 105
Since that the truest issue of thy throne
By his own interdiction stands accurs'd
And does blaspheme his breed? Thy royal father
Was a most sainted king; the queen that bore thee,
Oftener upon her knees than on her feet, 110
Died every day she lived. Fare thee well!
These evils thou repeat'st upon thyself
Have banish'd me from Scotland. O my breast,
Thy hope ends here!

Mal. Macduff, this noble passion,
Child of integrity, hath from my soul 115
Wiped the black scruples, reconciled my thoughts
To thy good truth and honor. Devilish Macbeth
By many of these trains hath sought to win me

---

2. Plenty.

3. Greed.

Into his power; and modest wisdom
plucks me
From over-credulous haste; but God
above   120
Deal between thee and me! for even
now
I put myself to thy direction and
Unspeak mine own detraction, here
abjure
The taints and blames I laid upon
myself   124
For strangers to my nature. I am yet
Unknown to woman, never was for-
sworn,
Scarcely have coveted what was mine
own,
At no time broke my faith, would
not betray
The devil to his fellow, and delight
No less in truth than life. My first
false speaking   130
Was this upon myself. What I am
truly,
Is thine and my poor country's to
command;
Whither indeed, before thy here-
approach,
Old Siward with ten thousand war-
like men   134
Already at a point was setting forth.
Now we'll together; and the chance
of goodness
Be like our warranted quarrel! Why
are you silent?

Macd. Such welcome and unwelcome
things at once
'Tis hard to reconcile.

(*Enter a* Doctor.)

Mal. Well, more anon. Comes the King
forth, I pray you?   140

Doct. Ay, sir. There are a crew of
wretched souls

That stay his cure. Their malady convinces[4]
The great assay of art;[5] but at his
touch,
Such sanctity hath heaven given his
hand,
They presently amend.

Mal.   I thank you, doctor. 145

(*Exit* Doctor.)

Macd. What's the disease he means?

Mal.   'Tis call'd the evil:
A most miraculous work in this good
king,
Which often since my here-remain in
England
I have seen him do. How he solicits
heaven
Himself best knows; but strangely-
visited people,   150
All swol'n and ulcerous, pitiful to the
eye,
The mere despair of surgery, he
cures,
Hanging a golden stamp about their
necks,
Put on with holy prayers; and 'tis
spoken,   154
To the succeeding royalty he leaves
The healing benediction. With this
strange virtue,[6]
He hath a heavenly gift of prophecy,
And sundry blessings hang about his
throne
That speak him full of grace.

(*Enter* Ross.)

Macd.   See who comes here.

Mal. My countryman; but yet I know
him not.   160

Macd. My ever gentle cousin, welcome
hither.

Mal. I know him now. Good God betimes remove

4. Baffles.
5. The greatest efforts of medicine.
6. Power.

The means[7] that makes us strangers!

Ross.   Sir, amen.

Macd. Stands Scotland where it did?

Ross.   Alas, poor country,
Almost afraid to know itself! It cannot   165
Be call'd our mother, but our grave; where nothing,[8]
But who knows nothing, is once seen to smile;
Where sighs and groans, and shrieks that rent the air,
Are made, not mark'd; where violent sorrow seems
A modern ecstasy.[9] The dead man's knell   170
Is there scarce ask'd for who; and good men's lives
Expire before the flowers in their caps,
Dying or ere they sicken.

Macd.   O, relation
Too nice,[10] and yet too true!

Mal.   What's the newest grief?

Ross. That of an hour's age doth hiss the speaker;   175
Each minute teems a new one.

Macd.   How does my wife?

Ross. Why, well.

Macd.   And all my children?

Ross.   Well too.

Macd. The tyrant has not batter'd at their peace?

Ross. No; they were well at peace when I did leave 'em.

Macd. Be not a niggard of your speech. How goes't?   180

Ross. When I came hither to transport the tidings
Which I have heavily borne, there ran a rumor

Of many worthy fellows that were out;
Which was to my belief witness'd the rather
For that I saw the tyrant's power[11] afoot.   185
Now is the time of help. Your eye[12] in Scotland
Would create soldiers, make our women fight
To doff their dire distresses.

Mal.   Be't their comfort
We are coming thither. Gracious England hath
Lent us good Siward and ten thousand men.   190
An older and a better soldier none
That Christendom gives out.

Ross.   Would I could answer
This comfort with the like! But I have words
That would be howl'd out in the desert air,
Where hearing should not latch[13] them.

Macd.   What concern they?   195
The general cause? or is it a fee-grief[14]
Due to some single breast?

Ross.   No mind that's honest
But in it shares some woe, though the main part
Pertains to you alone.

Macd.   If it be mine,
Keep it not from me, quickly let me have it.   200

Ross. Let not your ears despise my tongue for ever,
Which shall possess them with the heaviest sound
That ever yet they heard.

7. Macbeth.
8. No one.
9. An everyday emotion.
10. Narrative too exact.

11. Army.
12. Presence.
13. Catch.
14. Private grief.

Macd.   Humh! I guess at it.

Ross. Your castle is surprised; your wife
    and babes
    Savagely slaughter'd. To relate the
    manner,   205
    Were, on the quarry of these mur-
    der'd deer,
    To add the death of you.

Mal.   Merciful heaven!
    What, man! Ne'er pull your hat upon
    your brows.
    Give sorrow words. The grief that
    does not speak
    Whispers the o'erfraught heart and
    bids it break.   210

Macd. My children too?

Ross.   Wife, children, servants, all
    That could be found.

Macd.   And I must be from thence?
    My wife kill'd too?

Ross.   I have said.

Mal.   Be comforted.
    Let's make us medicines of our great
    revenge
    To cure this deadly grief.   215

Macd. He has no children. All my pretty
    ones?
    Did you say all? O hell-kite! All?
    What, all my pretty chickens and
    their dam
    At one fell swoop?

Mal. Dispute it like a man.

Macd.   I shall do so;   220
    But I must also feel it as a man.
    I cannot but remember such things
    were
    That were most precious to me. Did
    heaven look on
    And would not take their part? Sin-
    ful Macduff,
    They were all struck for thee! Naught
    that I am,   225
    Not for their own demerits, but for
    mine,

    Fell slaughter on their souls. Heaven
    rest them now!

Mal. Be this the whetstone of your
    sword. Let grief
    Convert to anger; blunt not the heart,
    enrage it.

Macd. O, I could play the woman with
    mine eyes   230
    And braggart with my tongue! But,
    gentle heavens,
    Cut short all intermission. Front to
    front
    Bring thou this fiend of Scotland and
    myself.
    Within my sword's length set him. If
    he scape,
    Heaven forgive him too!

Mal.   This tune goes manly.   235
    Come, go we to the King. Our power
    is ready;
    Our lack is nothing but our leave.
    Macbeth
    Is ripe for shaking, and the powers
    above
    Put on their instruments.[15] Receive
    what cheer you may.
    The night is long that never finds the
    day.   240

(*Exeunt.*)

ACT V. SCENE I.
DUNSINANE. MACBETH'S CASTLE.

(*Enter a* DOCTOR OF PHYSIC *and a*
WAITING-GENTLEWOMAN.)

Doct. I have two nights watched with
    you, but can perceive no truth in
    your report. When was it she last
    walked?   4

Gent. Since his Majesty went into the
    field I have seen her rise from her
    bed, throw her nightgown upon
    her, unlock her closet, take forth
    paper, fold it, write upon't, read it,

afterwards seal it, and again return to bed; yet all this while in a most fast sleep. 12

Doct. A great perturbation in nature, to receive at once the benefit of sleep and do the effects of watching! In this slumb'ry agitation, besides her walking and other actual performances, what, at any time, have you heard her say? 19

Gent. That, sir, which I will not report after her.

Doct. You may to me, and 'tis most meet you should.

Gent. Neither to you nor any one, having no witness to confirm my speech. 26

(*Enter* LADY MACBETH, *with a taper.*)

Lo you, here she comes! This is her very guise, and, upon my life, fast asleep! Observe her; stand close.

Doct. How come she by that light? 30

Gent. Why, it stood by her. She has light by her continually. 'Tis her command.

Doct. You see her eyes are open.

Gent. Ay; but their sense is shut. 35

Doct. What is it she does now? Look how she rubs her hands.

Gent. It is an accustomed action with her, to seem thus washing her hands. I have known her continue in this a quarter of an hour. 41

Lady. Yet here's a spot.

Doct. Hark, she speaks! I will set down what comes from her, to satisfy my remembrance the more strongly. 45

Lady. Out, damned spot! out, I say! One; two. Why then 'tis time to do 't. Hell is murky. Fie, my lord, fie! a soldier, and afeard? What need we fear who knows it, when none can call our power to account? Yet who would have thought the old man to have had so much blood in him? 54

Doct. Do you mark that? 54

Lady. The Thane of Fife had a wife. Where is she now? What, will these hands ne'er be clean? No more o' that, my lord, no more o' that! You mar all with this starting. 61

Doct. Go to, go to! You have known what you should not.

Gent. She has spoke what she should not, I am sure of that. Heaven knows what she has known. 66

Lady. Here's the smell of the blood still. All the perfumes of Arabia will not sweeten this little hand. Oh, oh, oh! 70

Doct. What a sigh is there! The heart is sorely charged.

Gent. I would not have such a heart in my bosom for the dignity of the whole body. 75

Doct. Well, well, well.

Gent. Pray God it be, sir.

Doct. This disease is beyond my practice. Yet I have known those which have walked in their sleep who have died holily in their beds. 81

Lady. Wash your hands, put on your nightgown, look not so pale! I tell you yet again, Banquo's buried. He cannot come out on 's grave.

Doct. Even so? 86

Lady. To bed, to bed! There's knocking at the gate. Come, come, come, come, give me your hand! What's done cannot be undone. To bed, to bed, to bed! 91

(*Exit.*)

Doct. Will she go now to bed?

Gent. Directly.

Doct. Foul whisperings are abroad. Un-
  natural deeds   95
  Do breed unnatural troubles. In-
  fected minds
  To their deaf pillows will discharge
  their secrets.
  More needs she the divine than the
  physician.
  God, God forgive us all! Look after
  her;
  Remove from her the means of all
  annoyance,   100
  And still keep eyes upon her. So
  good night.
  My mind she has mated,[1] and
  amazed my sight.
  I think, but dare not speak.
Gent.   Good night, good doctor.

(*Exeunt.*)

SCENE II.
THE COUNTRY NEAR DUNSINANE.

(*Drum and Colors. Enter* MENTEITH,
CAITHNESS, ANGUS, LENNOX, SOL-
DIERS.)

Ment. The English power is near, led
  on by Malcolm,
  His uncle Siward, and the good Mac-
  duff.
  Revenges burn in them; for their
  dear causes
  Would to the bleeding and the grim
  alarm
  Excite the mortified man.
Ang.   Near Birnam Wood 5
  Shall we well meet them; that way
  are they coming.
Caith. Who knows if Donalbain be
  with his brother?
Len. For certain, sir, he is not. I have a
  file

1. Dazed.

Of all the gentry. There is Siward's
son
And many unrough[1] youths that even
now   10
Protest their first of manhood.
Ment.   What does the tyrant?
Caith. Great Dunsinane he strongly
  fortifies.
  Some say he's mad; others, that
  lesser hate him,
  Do call it valiant fury; but for cer-
  tain
  He cannot buckle his distemper'd
  cause   15
  Within the belt of rule.
Ang.   Now does he feel
  His secret murders sticking on his
  hands.
  Now minutely revolts upbraid his
  faith-breach.
  Those he commands move only in
  command,
  Nothing in love. Now does he feel
  his title   20
  Hang loose about him, like a giant's
  robe
  Upon a dwarfish thief.
Ment.   Who then shall blame
  His pester'd senses to recoil and
  start,
  When all that is within him does
  condemn
  Itself for being there?
Caith.   Well, march we on 25
  To give obedience where 'tis truly
  owed.
  Meet we the medicine[2] of the sickly
  weal;[3]
  And with him pour we in our coun-
  try's purge
  Each drop of us.

1. Beardless.
2. Malcolm.
3. Realm.

Len.   Or so much as it needs
To dew the sovereign flower and
 drown the weeds.   30
Make we our march towards Birnam.

(*Exeunt, marching.*)

SCENE III.

DUNSINANE. A ROOM IN THE CASTLE.

(*Enter* MACBETH, DOCTOR, *and* AT-
TENDANTS.)

Macb. Bring me no more reports. Let
 them[1] fly all!
Till Birnam Wood remove to Dun-
 sinane,
I cannot taint with fear. What's the
 boy Malcolm?
Was he not born of woman? The
 spirits that know
All mortal consequences have pro-
 nounced me thus: 5
'Fear not, Macbeth. No man that's
 born of woman
Shall e'er have power upon thee.'
 Then fly, false thanes,
And mingle with the English epi-
 cures.
The mind I sway by and the heart I
 bear
Shall never sag with doubt nor shake
 with fear.   10

(*Enter* SERVANT.)

The devil damn thee black, thou
 cream-faced loon!
Where got'st thou that goose look?
Serv. There is ten thousand—
Macb.   Geese, villain?
Serv.   Soldiers, sir.
Macb. Go prick thy face and over-red [2]
 thy fear,
Thou lily-liver'd boy. What soldiers,
 patch? [3]   15

1. His nobles.
2. Make bloody.
3. Fool.

Death of thy soul! Those linen cheeks
 of thine
Are counsellors to fear. What sol-
 diers, whey-face?
Serv. The English force, so please you.
Macb. Take thy face hence.

(*Exit* SERVANT.)

             Seyton!—I am sick at heart,
When I behold—Seyton, I say!—This
 push   20
Will cheer me ever, or disseat me
 now.
I have lived long enough. My way of
 life
Is fallen into the sere, the yellow
 leaf;
And that which should accompany
 old age,
As honor, love, obedience, troops of
 friends,   25
I must not look to have; but, in their
 stead,
Curses not loud but deep, mouth-
 honor, breath,
Which the poor heart would fain
 deny, and dare not.
Seyton!

(*Enter* SEYTON.)

Sey. What's your gracious pleasure?
Macb.   What news more? 30
Sey. All is confirmed, my lord, which
 was reported.
Macb. I'll fight, till from my bones my
 flesh be hacked.
Give me my armor.
Sey.   'Tis not needed yet.
Macb. I'll put it on.
Send out moe horses,[4] skirr[5] the coun-
 try round;   35
Hang those that talk of fear. Give me
 mine armor.

4. More horsemen.
5. Scurry.

How does your patient, doctor?

Doct.   Not so sick, my lord,
As she is troubled with thick-coming
fancies
That keep her from her rest.

Macb.   Cure her of that!
Canst thou not minister to a mind
diseased,   40
Pluck from the memory a rooted sor-
row,
Raze out the written troubles of the
brain,
And with some sweet oblivious anti-
dote
Cleanse the stuff'd bosom of that
perilous stuff
Which weighs upon the heart?

Doct.   Therein the patient   45
Must minister to himself.

Macb. Throw physic to the dogs, I'll
none of it!—
Come, put mine armor on. Give me
my staff.—
Seyton, send out.—Doctor, the thanes
fly from me.—
Come, sir, dispatch.—If thou couldst,
doctor, cast   50
The water of my land, find her dis-
ease,
And purge it to a sound and pristine
health,
I would applaud thee to the very
echo,
That should applaud again.—Pull't
off, I say.[6]—
What rhubarb, senna, or what pur-
gative drug,   55
Would scour these English hence?
Hear'st thou of them?

Doct. Ay, my good lord. Your royal
preparation
Makes us hear something.

Macb.   Bring it after me![7]

6. A piece of the armor.
7. The piece of armor.

I will not be afraid of death and
bane
Till Birnam Forest come to Dun-
sinane.   60

(*Exeunt all but the* DOCTOR.)

Doct. Were I from Dunsinane away
and clear,
Profit again should hardly draw me
here.

(*Exit.*)

SCENE IV.
COUNTRY NEAR BIRNAM WOOD.

(*Drum and colors. Enter* MALCOLM,
SIWARD, MACDUFF, SIWARD'S SON,
MENTEITH, CAITHNESS, ANGUS, LEN-
NOX, ROSS, *and* SOLDIERS, *marching.*)

Mal. Cousins, I hope the days are near
at hand
That chambers will be safe.

Ment.   We doubt it nothing.

Siw. What wood is this before us?

Ment.   The Wood of Birnam.

Mal. Let every soldier hew him down a
bough
And bear't before him. Thereby shall
we shadow   5
The numbers of our host and make
discovery
Err in report of us.

Soldiers.   It shall be done.

Siw. We learn no other but the confident tyrant
Keeps still in Dunsinane and will endure
Our setting down before't.

Mal.   'Tis his main hope;   10
For where there is advantage to be
given,
Both more and less[1] have given him
the revolt;

1. Men of both high and low rank.

And none serve with him but con-
strained things,
Whose hearts are absent too.
Macd.   Let our just censures
Attend the true event, and put we on
Industrious soldiership.
Siw.   The time approaches 16
That will with due decision make us
know
What we shall say we have, and
what we owe.
Thoughts speculative their unsure
hopes relate,
But certain issue strokes must arbi-
trate;   20
Towards which advance the war.

(*Exeunt, marching.*)

Scene v.
Dunsinane. Within the castle.

(*Enter* Macbeth, Seyton, *and* Soldiers, *with drum and colors.*)

Macb. Hang out our banners on the outward walls.
The cry is still, 'They come!' Our
castle's strength
Will laugh a siege to scorn. Here let
them lie
Till famine and the ague eat them
up.
Were they not forced with those that
should be ours,   5
We might have met them dareful,
beard to beard,
And beat them backward home.

(*A cry within of women.*)
                    What is that noise?
Sey. It is the cry of women, my good
lord.
(*Exit.*)
Macb. I have almost forgot the taste of
fears.

The time has been, my senses would
have cool'd   10
To hear a night-shriek, and my fell
of hair
Would at a dismal treatise rouse and
stir
As life were in't. I have supp'd full
with horrors.
Direness, familiar to my slaughterous
thoughts,
Cannot once start me.

(*Enter* Seyton.)
                    Wherefore was that cry? 15
Sey. The Queen, my lord, is dead.
Macb. She should have died hereafter;
There would have been a time for
such a word.[1]
To-morrow, and to-morrow, and to-
morrow
Creeps in this petty pace from day to
day   20
To the last syllable of recorded time;
And all our yesterdays have lighted
fools
The way to dusty death. Out, out,
brief candle!
Life's but a walking shadow, a poor
player,
That struts and frets his hour upon
the stage   25
And then is heard no more. It is a
tale
Told by an idiot, full of sound and
fury,
Signifying nothing.

(*Enter a* Messenger.)
Thou com'st to use they tongue. Thy
story quickly!
Mess. Gracious my lord,   30
I should report that which I say I
saw,
But know not how to do't.

---

1. Death.

Macb.   Well, say, sir!

Mess. As I did stand my watch upon
  the hill,
  I look'd toward Birnam, and anon
  methought
  The wood began to move.

Macb.   Liar and slave! 35

Mess. Let me endure your wrath if 't be
  not so.
  Within this three mile may you see it
  coming;
  I say, a moving grove.

Macb.   If thou speak'st false,
  Upon the next tree shalt thou hang
  alive,
  Till famine cling thee. If thy speech
  be sooth,   40
  I care not if thou dost for me as
  much.
  I pull in resolution, and begin
  To doubt th' equivocation of the
  fiend,
  That lies like truth. 'Fear not, till
  Birnam Wood
  Do come to Dunsinane!' and now a
  wood   45
  Comes toward Dunsinane. Arm, arm,
  and out!
  If this which he avouches does ap-
  pear,
  There is nor flying hence nor tarrying
  here.
  I 'gin to be aweary of the sun,
  And wish th' estate o' th' world were
  now undone.   50
  Ring the alarum bell! Blow wind,
  come wrack,[2]
  At least we'll die with harness[3] on
  our back!

(*Exeunt.*)

SCENE VI.
DUNSINANE. BEFORE THE CASTLE.

(*Drum and colors. Enter* MALCOLM,

2. Ruin.

SIWARD, MACDUFF, *and their* ARMY,
with boughs.)

Mal. Now near enough. Your leavy
  screens throw down
  And show like those you are. You,
  worthy uncle,
  Shall with my cousin, your right
  noble son,
  Lead our first battle. Worthy Macduff and we
  Shall take upon 's what else remains
  to do,   5
  According to our order.

Siw.   Fare you well.
  Do we but find the tyrant's power
  to-night,
  Let us be beaten if we cannot fight.

Macd. Make all our trumpets speak,
  give them all breath,
  Those clamorous harbingers of blood
  and death.   10

(*Exeunt. Alarums continued.*)

SCENE VII. ANOTHER PART OF THE FIELD.

(*Enter* MACBETH.)

Macb. They have tied me to a stake. I
  cannot fly,
  But bear-like I must fight the course.
  What's he
  That was not born of woman? Such
  a one
  Am I to fear, or none.

(*Enter* YOUNG SIWARD.)

Y. Siw. What is thy name?

Macb.   Thou'lt be afraid to hear it. 5

Y. Siw. No; though thou call'st thyself
  a hotter name
  Than any is in hell.

Macb.   My name's Macbeth.

Y. Siw. The devil himself could not
  pronounce a title

3. Armor.

More hateful to mine ear.

Macb.   No, nor more fearful.

Y. Siw. Thou liest, abhorred tyrant!
With my sword   10
I'll prove the lie thou speak'st.

(*Fight, and* YOUNG SIWARD *slain.*)

Macb.   Thou wast born of woman.
But swords I smile at, weapons laugh
to scorn,
Brandish'd by man that's of a woman
born.

(*Exit.*)
(*Alarums. Enter* MACDUFF.)

Macd. That way the noise is. Tyrant,
show thy face!
If thou be'st slain and with no stroke
of mine,   15
My wife and children's ghosts will
haunt me still.
I cannot strike at wretched kerns,
whose arms
Are hired to bear their staves. Either
thou, Macbeth,
Or else my sword with an unbat-
tered edge
I sheathe again undeeded. There
thou shouldst be.   20
By this great clatter one of greatest
note
Seems bruited.[1] Let me find him,
Fortune!
And more I beg not.

(*Exit. Alarums.*)
(*Enter* MALCOLM *and* SIWARD.)

Siw. This way, my lord. The castle's
gently render'd:[2]
The tyrant's people on both sides do
fight;   25
The noble thanes do bravely in the
war;
The day almost itself professes
yours,

And little is to do.

Mal.   We have met with foes
That strike beside us.

Siw.   Enter, sir, the castle.

(*Exeunt. Alarum.*)

SCENE VIII. ANOTHER PART OF THE FIELD.

(*Enter* MACBETH.)

Macb. Why should I play the Roman
fool and die
On mine own sword? Whiles I see
lives, the gashes
Do better upon them.

(*Enter* MACDUFF.)

Macd.   Turn, hellhound, turn!

Macb. Of all men else I have avoided
thee.
But get thee back! My soul is too
much charged   5
With blood of thine already.

Macd.   I have no words;
My voice is in my sword, thou
bloodier villain
Than terms can give thee out!

(*Fight. Alarum.*)

Macb.   Thou losest labor.
As easy mayst thou the intrenchant
air
With thy keen sword impress as make
me bleed.   10
Let fall thy blade on vulnerable
crests.
I bear a charmed life, which must
not yield
To one of woman born.

Macd.   Despair thy charm!
And let the angel whom thou still
hast served
Tell thee, Macduff was from his
mother's womb   15
Untimely ripp'd.

1. Announced.   2. Tamely surrendered.

Macb. Accursed be that tongue that tells me so,

For it hath cow'd my better part of man!

And be these juggling fiends no more believed,

That palter[1] with us in a double sense,   20

That keep the word of promise to our ear

And break it to our hope! I'll not fight with thee!

Macd. Then yield thee, coward,

And live to be the show and gaze o' th' time!

We'll have thee, as our rarer monsters are,   25

Painted upon a pole, and underwrit 'Here may you see the tyrant.'

Macb.   I will not yield,

To kiss the ground before young Malcolm's feet

And to be baited with the rabble's curse.

Though Birnam Wood be come to Dunsinane,   30

And thou opposed, being of no woman born,

Yet I will try the last. Before my body

I throw my warlike shield. Lay on, Macduff,

And damn'd be him that first cries 'Hold, enough!'

(*Exeunt fighting. Alarums.*)

(*Retreat and flourish. Enter, with drum and colors,* MALCOLM SIWARD, ROSS, THANES, *and* SOLDIERS.)

Mal. I would the friends we miss were safe arrived.   35

Siw. Some must go off; and yet, by these I see,

So great a day as this is cheaply bought.

1. Play false.

Mal. Macduff is missing, and your noble son.

Ross. Your son, my lord, has paid a soldier's debt.   39

He only lived but till he was a man,

The which no sooner had his prowess confirm'd

In the unshrinking station where he fought

But like a man he died.

Siw.   Then he is dead?

Ross. Ay, and brought off the field. Your cause of sorrow

Must not be measured by his worth, for then   45

It hath no end.

Siw.   Had he his hurts before?

Ross. Ay, on the front.

Siw.   Why then, God's soldier be he!

Had I as many sons as I have hairs,

I would not wish them to a fairer death.

And so his knell is knoll'd.[2]

Mal.   He's worth more sorrow,   50

And that I'll spend for him.

Siw.   He's worth no more.

They say he parted well and paid his score,

And so, God be with him! Here comes newer comfort.

(*Enter* MACDUFF, *with* MACBETH'S *head.*)

Macd. Hail, King! for so thou art. Behold where stands

Th' usurper's cursed head. The time is free.   55

I see thee compass'd with thy kingdom's pearl,[3]

That speak my salutation in their minds;

Whose voices I desire aloud with mine—

2. Tolled.
3. Surrounded by your chief supporters.

Hail, King of Scotland!

All. Hail, King of Scotland!

(*Flourish.*)

Mal. We shall not spend a large expense of time 60
Before we reckon with your several
loves[4]
And make us even with you. My
thanes and kinsmen,
Henceforth be earls, the first that
ever Scotland
In such an honor named. What's
more to do
Which would be planted newly with
the time— 65
As calling home our exiled friends
abroad

4. Reward your loyalty.

That fled the snares of watchful tyr-
anny,
Producing forth the cruel ministers
Of this dead butcher and his fiend-
like queen,
Who, as 'tis thought, by self and
violent hands 70
Took off her life—this, and what
needful else
That calls upon us, by the grace of
Grace
We will perform in measure, time,
and place.
So thanks to all at once and to each
one,
Whom we invite to see us crown'd at
Scone. 75

(*Flourish. Exeunt omnes.*)

The Misanthrope

~~~~~~~~~~~~~~~~~~~~~~~~~~~~ MOLIÈRE

INTRODUCTION

Jean-Baptiste Poquelin, better-known as Molière, was born in Paris on January 15, 1622. His father, Jean Poquelin, was an upholsterer and interior decorator, and his mother, Marie Cressé, was the daughter of an upholsterer; both sides of the family were well-to-do. In 1632 Marie died, leaving four children; Jean soon remarried but became a widower again in 1636. This may explain why mothers almost never appear as characters in Molière's plays, for from the age of fourteen he was under the mental and moral influence of his father and grandparents. Jean-Baptiste was educated at the College de Clermont, the best school in Paris, where he distinguished himself both in classics and in philosophy; he completed his education by going to Orleans for a course in law.

His introduction to the theater, and probably his deep love for it, had started long before his school days, however, for his father's shop was situated not very far from two important theatrical sites, the Pont-Neuf and the Rue Mauconseil. At the Pont-Neuf some quack doctors had set up in the street large platform stages upon which comedians acted out plays and farces for the sole purpose of selling patent medicines to the crowds that gathered to watch the free shows. The boy was deeply impressed by the antics of l'Orviétan and Bary, the great comic medicine-men, and stored their tricks and jokes away in his memory for future use. At the corner of the Rue Mauconseil and the Rue Française, even nearer to his father's shop than the Pont-Neuf, stood the Hôtel de Bourgogne, the outstanding theater of the day, where the King's Players put on romantic tragedies and broad farces. The boy was often taken to this theater by his grandfather, Louis de Cressé, who was an ardent playgoer; the tragedies he saw there were second-rate, but the actors of the farces were brilliant and inventive. These actors represented stock characters—The Stingy Father, The Ignorant Doctor, The Bragging Soldier—and performed in the great Italian tradition of improvised comedy, *commedia dell'arte,* making up their lines as they went along; from them, and from the many Italian troupes that later visited Paris, Molière borrowed plot ideas, situations, and actual jests for his own plays.

In 1643, when he was twenty-one, Jean-Baptiste had reached a decision to devote his life to the theater, and for the next thirty years he remained faithful to his profession. He gave up his right to become his father's successor as upholsterer to the King, took possession of a small part of the money that his mother had left him upon her death in 1632, and cast in his lot with the Béjart family.

Jean-Baptiste had fallen in love with Madeleine Béjart, a beautiful, fiery, and gifted girl of twenty-seven who had been an actress for several years, and who, with her brother Joseph and sister Genevieve, now wished to form her own acting company. Madeleine got together about a dozen talented young men and women from well-to-do families and established a dramatic troupe to which she gave the high-sounding name of *L'Illustre Théâtre* (The Illustrious Theater). Jean-Baptiste Poquelin was a member of the original company, which was organized on June 30, 1643; it was shortly after this that he took the surname of Molière, probably to spare his father embarrassment, since actors had no social standing and had even been excommunicated by the church. Though passionately interested in the theater, the members of this newly formed company were unskilled novices for the most part, so that it is no surprise to learn that in the next two years they appeared in three different theaters in various parts of Paris and failed in all of them. These "theaters" were actually indoor tennis courts which had been converted into playhouses by the simple expedient of erecting a platform at one end of the long, narrow room; the audience stood in front of the stage, or sat in the spectators' balcony that ran around three walls and overlooked the playing area. Twice during these early, trying days Molière was arrested for debt and imprisoned, but he was released each time on the bond of a friend. Several of the less hardy members dropped out of the company but the seven who remained, including Molière and the Béjarts, decided to quit Paris and try their luck in the provinces. In 1646 they left the capital and went on a tour of the country that lasted for twelve years.

It was during this period that Molière began to write plays for the company. By the spring of 1658, the playwright's friends were urging him to try his luck once more in Paris. Molière made several trips to the capital, where he managed to get introductions to Cardinal Mazarin and to the King's brother, Philippe, who was known by the title of Monsieur, and who was said to be interested in supporting a dramatic company which would bear his name. The *Illustre Théâtre* left Lyons, acted before Monsieur, and pleased him; then the players were invited to perform for the Court. That was the dream they had had for twelve years while serving their apprenticeship in the provinces.

On the evening of October 24, 1658, Molière acted for the first time before Louis XIV and his courtiers in the Guard Room of the old Louvre Palace on a platform erected at the King's command; the program consisted of Corneille's tragedy *Nicomède,* followed by Molière's farce *The Love-Sick Doctor,* and the whole was brought to a close by a clever speech which Molière addressed to the Court. The evening was a triumph; the King immediately decreed that the company was to be known as the Troupe de Monsieur, and that it was to perform at the Hôtel du Petit Bourbon.

The three most important theaters in Paris at the time were the Hôtel de Bourgogne, the Théâtre du Marais, and the Hôtel du Petit Bourbon, all of which had been developed under the influence of Cardinal Richelieu, who had been intensely interested in every aspect of the theater; he had urged poets to write for the stage, offered pensions to outstanding playwrights and actors, given private performances of new plays in his own home, and in 1641 included in his new palace a magnificent playhouse, later to be known as the Théâtre du Palais Royal. The Petit Bourbon was occupied on Sundays, Tuesdays, and Fridays by an Italian company headed by the celebrated Tiberio Fiorelli whose stage name was Scaramouche; it was in this theater that Molière was granted permission by the King to perform on Mondays, Wednesdays, Thursdays, and Saturdays. The two companies got along admirably and parted friends in July of 1659 when the Italians returned to their own country and left Molière in sole possession of the house.

In November, 1659, Molière opened the season at the Petit Bourbon with an augmented acting company which included the accomplished comic Du Croisy and his wife; the celebrated white-face clown known as Jodolet; and a young actor called La Grange, who became a devoted follower of Molière and the record-keeper for the company. It is from his records that we have learned of the company's casting, performances, payments, and receipts. The first play to be presented at the Petit Bourbon was *Les Précieuses Ridicules* (*The Pretentious Young Ladies*), a comedy in one act which boldly satirized Madame de Rambouillet and her coterie who had set themselves up as the final arbiters of taste and culture in Paris. This was Molière's first attempt at social criticism and proved to be sensationally successful. The King was so pleased that he gave Molière a large gift in cash; but among those whom he had held up to ridicule the playwright made many enemies, and the shrinking receipts of the rival theaters added many more.

In retaliation, these powerful enemies first managed to have Molière's play suspended for fourteen days, then in an effort to drive their adversary out of the city, brought about the complete closing of the Petit Bourbon. Through the good graces of the King, the Théâtre du Palais Royal was turned over to Molière for his own use and was occupied by him for the rest of his life. During the thirteen and a half years that remained to him—a period only slightly longer than that of his twelve-year apprenticeship—Molière worked feverishly, writing, directing, and acting in the thirty-odd plays which have established a reputation that has lasted for three hundred years.

Between 1660 and 1665 French classical comedy assumed a definite form, mainly at the hands of Molière: the masks of the Italians disappeared, characters and situations began to resemble those of contemporary Paris, and plot was developed through the interaction of character rather than through the conduct of intrigues. In *The School for Husbands*, a three-act play in verse, Molière deals with the problems faced by a forty-year-old man who is jealously trying to guard his twenty-year-old wife from the attentions of a younger man. Molière was probably anticipating his own feelings of jealousy, for the play was performed on June 24, 1661, and about eight months later, on February 20, 1662, having just reached the age of forty, the playwright married Armande Béjart, the youngest sister of Madeleine, a beautiful girl of twenty. Armande was a gifted actress, who had been trained for the stage by her sister and by Molière. After her marriage to the dramatist, she took the leading feminine part in each of his plays. For Armande, Molière always wrote parts in which caustic sayings, sharp wit, and a certain amount of coquetry are to be found; the first role of this type is Eliza in *The School for Wives Criticized* and the perfect and final development is Célimène in *The Misanthrope*. Armande bore Molière three children, two of whom died in infancy; the marriage was not a happy one and for several years husband and wife lived apart from each other.

The King recognized Molière's superlative talents and on August 14, 1665, increased the poet's pension and accorded to his acting company the coveted title of "Troupe of the King." In September of the same year, *L'Amour Médecin*, a ballet-play, was written, rehearsed, and acted within a period of five days; it was performed first at Versailles, afterwards in Paris. Molière was obviously working too hard; in December he suffered a serious illness and the Palais Royal had to be closed. It was the beginning of his long struggle against what appears to have been tuberculosis, but he did not let it interfere either with his writing or his acting and, in the last seven years of his life, he produced what are generally considered to be his greatest plays, among them *The Misanthrope*, *The Doctor in Spite of Himself*, *George Dandin*, *Tartuffe* (written in 1664), *The Would-Be Gentleman*, *The Learned Ladies*, and *The Imaginary Invalid*.

On February 25, 1669, Molière's father died, still unreconciled to the fact that his son had chosen to be a dramatist and actor instead of an upholsterer. Not long afterwards, his friends arranged a reconciliation between Molière and Armande, but it was not a happy state of affairs, for Molière knew that his days were numbered. On February 17, 1672, Madeleine Béjart, his oldest and closest friend, died; in August of the same year, Molière lost his young son; and then began his struggle against the intrigues of the composer, Jean Baptiste Lully, who was in charge of music at the court of Louis XIV. The playwright soon realized that he was out of favor with the King; this rejection coupled with his sorrow over the recent deaths of Madeleine Béjart and of his son and his failing health caused Molière to lose heart.

And yet his newest play, his last, which leveled a blast of ridicule against the medical profession, was one of the cleverest and most vigorous of his comedies. In *The Imaginary Invalid*, Molière himself, physically exhausted and wracked with coughing, played the part of the hypochondriac, Argan. On February 17, 1673, the day of the fourth performance of the play and the very day on which Madeleine had died the year before, Molière was so ill that his wife and his protégé, Michel Baron, begged him not to go to the theater, but he would not take their advice. He said, "There are fifty poor workers who have only their daily wage to live on. What will become of them if the performance does not take place?" During the performance he suffered a hemorrhage but played the piece out to the end. That night, in his house in the Rue Richelieu, he died. The local priests would not listen to the confession of an actor, nor would they permit him to be buried in holy ground; it was only after Armande Béjart enlisted the aid of the King that Molière was buried, four nights later, in the Cemetery Saint-Joseph near the Rue Montmartre. The body of the man who had brought laughter and light to the world was borne to its grave under the cover of darkness.

Three months after the death of Molière, in May, 1673, his company gave up the Palais Royal and bought the Théâtre Guénégaud, whereupon the King ordered Molière's players to merge with the company of the Théâtre du Marais. One of the comedians of the Marais, Guérin d'Estriché, married Armande Béjart in 1677. The two outstanding companies in Paris at this time were the Molière-Marais troupe at the Guénégaud and the company at the Hôtel de Bourgogne, but in 1680 the King decided that these companies should join to form one and, in an order countersigned by Colbert, created the Théâtre-Français, which became the national theater of France. Since Molière's plays made up a considerable part of the repertory, and the troupe at the Théâtre-Français had descended in a straight line from the troupe of Molière, this actor-dramatist is considered one of the founders of the great French theatrical institution, the Comédie-Française, which is sometimes known as the House of Molière.

Molière's comedy has remained for the French the most beloved of all their works, not only because it combines gaiety with extreme restraint in the expression of profound feelings, but also because of its social outlook. An individual's eccentricity in conflict with accepted norms provides the basis for most social comedy, and Molière is the undisputed master of this type; no dramatist has ever displayed a keener social consciousness, a sharper wit, more astute common sense, or more Olympian detachment in depicting the foibles of civilized man than he.

Social comedy differs from romantic comedy in that the latter type puts a heavy emphasis upon story and plot, while the former is concerned with the delineation of character and with social criticism. Sentiment is almost entirely lacking in social comedy; there is hardly a word of genuine tenderness between parents and children, or between brothers and sisters, in all of Molière. Even the tenderness of his lovers is always close to laughter. The most sacred relationships and the most serious situations are made to seem absurd, for the writer of social comedy is a reformer at heart who attacks the follies of society by laughing at them. It is a very difficult art, which explains why even a genius of Molière's stature required a lifetime to perfect it. Because his plays recreate the world he lived in—with its social climbers, doctors, lawyers, prudes, peasants, servants, lecherous old men, and amorous young women, all done so naturally, so spontaneously, so ridiculously, and so like our own world—Molière's work has enduring appeal.

Although *The Misanthrope* has universal significance, it is, at the same time, a perfect example of a neoclassical comedy. The French critics of the seventeenth century, having studied the dramatic precepts of Aristotle and Horace, without, however, having fully understood them, insisted that the playwrights of their own day observe the "laws" of the ancients or suffer the critical consequences. The three unbreakable rules, the critics believed, were the three unities: the unity of action, which meant that a good plot could not have more than one main action and that all minor actions had to be related to it; the unity of time, which meant that an action represented on the stage should consume the same amount of time that it would in real life, and that in no case should it exceed one natural day; and the unity of place, which meant that the physical action of the play should be limited to one place with no change of scene whatsoever. To these "classical" rules, the neoclassical critics added several of their own: A complete play, whether tragedy or comedy, was to consist of five acts in alexandrine verse; only four or five persons of elevated station or character were to be shown; and no incident, violent or otherwise, was to occur on the stage but had to be reported. As the "action" seen by the audience consisted entirely of personages engaged in conversation, the characters were to be evaluated by their quickness of wit and soundness of judgment, while the verse was meant to lift the whole play above the plane of reality. It was expected, in addition, that the characters would be drawn true to human nature so that the audience would recognize its own experiences in the passions and decisions depicted; and, finally, that the dialogue and actions would be appropriate for each character according to his age, sex, and condition with strict adherence to the propriety and decorum suited to people of the upper classes.

The three great dramatists of the period, Corneille, Molière, and Racine, wore the straitjacket of these rules with varying degrees of comfort. Racine, though very unhappy with them, seemed least hampered by the limitations imposed upon him; Corneille departed from the rules when it suited his purpose, as in the case of the *Cid,* but by so doing he started a literary war that lasted for years; while Molière pretended to pay no attention whatsoever to the dictates of the critics, maintaining that he listened only to the public and wrote purely to provide pleasure.

A close examination of *The Misanthrope,* however, clearly shows that in form and content the play is a model of neoclassical correctness. It has a single main action—the play opens with Alceste's determination to learn whether Célimène will marry him, and ends when he gets his answer; the dramatic events consume only a few hours in a single day; and the entire action takes place in the second floor drawing-room of Célimène's house in Paris. The play, moreover, is in five acts and was written in alexandrine verse, a line containing six iambic feet (Wilbur's translation, however, has only five iambic feet to the line); there are just six important characters in the play, and all are members of the upper class; no physical action occurs upon the stage, although a duel, a lawsuit, and several other dramatic incidents are discussed; the language is polished and witty; the psychological motivations are realistic and believable; the dialogue is appropriate to each character; and the utmost decorum is observed even when the antagonists are verbally slashing each other to ribbons. The play's content, like its form, appealed to the tastes of the age in the picture it presented of conventional society and the emphasis it placed upon the exercise of reason, although reason here is shown to be a destructive rather than a constructive force.

The sources of *The Misanthrope* are complicated. In about 1661, Molière wrote a tragedy called *Don Garcia of Navarre, or The Jealous Prince;* the play was a

failure. Molière decided to follow it with a comedy on the same theme; the
leading characters in the two plays bore a strong resemblance to each other and
compromising letters served in both to heighten the intrigue. Because of the
similarity of the material, Molière was able to borrow more than one hundred
and fifty lines from the unsuccessful tragedy and to work them, without much
difficulty, into his new comedy. Some of the characters, such as the fops, are
modeled on those in other plays by Molière, particularly the *Impromptu de
Versailles;* and a number of minor details were taken from the works of earlier
writers.

The major portion of the material, however, was based on Molière's own experience and feelings. For more than two years the playwright had been struggling to have his prohibited works, *Tartuffe* and *Don Juan,* produced in Paris, but
at every turn he was thwarted by members of the Court and the Church, by rival
poets, and by adherents to the religious sect called the *devots;* he sharply attacks many of these people in *The Misanthrope.* At the same time, the dramatist
was having marital difficulties which were soon to force him into an open break
with his wife. Molière was inordinately jealous of Armande Béjart, who was
young, beautiful, light-hearted, and inclined, perhaps in all innocence, to be a
flirt. This husband-wife conflict is clearly reflected in the relationship between
Alceste and Célimène.

Molière does not deal in this play with the social order in general but only
with Parisian high society, and not even with every phase of that particular class;
he says very little, for instance, about religious, political, or economic conditions,
or about family relations, and yet he presents a broad canvas upon which are
depicted the many lively interests of this social group: its relation to the Court,
its amusements, its preoccupation with conversation, law suits, dueling, gossip,
portraiture, costume, poetry, and love-making. Add to this the character types
ridiculed by Célimène—the nonstop talker, the man who makes a mystery of
everything, the bore who mixes only with the nobility, the woman whose visits
never end, the critic who likes nothing and works too hard at being clever—and
the sum total is a complete exposé of the superficiality and falsity of society.

The plot of *The Misanthrope* is simplicity itself, as it is largely concerned with
Alceste's love for Célimène and the reasons for his decision not to marry her.
Closely related to this central line are the scenes involving Eliante's and Arsinoé's
love for Alceste, the quarrel with Oronte, and the law-suit. Perhaps more attention
than was absolutely necessary for the structure of the play was devoted to the
scenes between Acaste and Clitandre and between Célimène and Arsinoé, but
the dramatic action concludes with the end of the love affair. There are those
who maintain that the play is plotless, that it is merely an extended conversation
piece, but this is not true. Molière actually displays remarkable skill as a dramatist
in the handling of his materials, since the interest is held and heightened by the
clever arrangement of events. The three most striking scenes: the sonnet, the
verbal portraits, and the women's duel, are distributed among the first three acts,
while the fourth act is devoted to the conflict between Alceste and Célimène, and
the fifth to the cutting of the knot. All of these situations are so adroitly arranged

that there is a definite sense of conflict and climax despite the meagerness of the story. The plot is really incidental, since its function is simply to reveal characters in exemplary situations. Ringing with stage effect, the characters in this play have a social context but no personal history; we are told very little of their past or of their future; they appear, exhibit themselves, and are gone; what is most important are the human traits they reveal in the few moments that they stand before us, their lives arrested and illuminated at a point in time.

Alceste has cast himself in the role of the autocrat and the martyr; he complains of the manners of his contemporaries, their affectations of speech, dress, and behavior; he complains about inferior works of art, about legal procedures, and about the insincerity and infidelity of people in love. He carries his superior notions and ideals to such ridiculous lengths that he succeeds only in defeating himself. Alceste is comic in his lack of a sense of proportion, in the violence of his indignation over small matters, and in the fact that he seems himself to be devoid of a sense of humor; yet, at the same time, his uncompromising honesty wins our admiration, and the intensity of his passion, our sympathy. He has dreamed of an ideal world and follows his aim without regard for his own fortunes or for the feelings of his fellows. He is not a buffoon but neither is he a faultless hero; it is the reality of his character and of his hopes that makes it possible for him to continue to live and to appeal.

Célimène is one of Molière's most brilliant creations; she is beautiful, clever, witty, and cold. She is a widow so that she may entertain freely, but her flirtations lead her into difficulties and make true love impossible for her. She has perfect manners and great tact but is not much troubled by feelings of conscience; she is callous in the manner in which she ridicules her acquaintances, dominates Alceste, and destroys the pretensions of Arsinoé. She has allowed herself to be seduced by society, and consequently she is self-destructive.

Philinte, Alceste's friend, is the intelligent man who is well-adjusted to society. He is not blind to its affectations and faults, but he has learned how to live with them. If he must praise a poor poem, he does so; he knows how to flatter and equivocate, but he retains his personal standards.

Eliante, the most attractive character in the play, is honest and charming. In the expression of her beliefs and in her relationships with others, she is sweet, simple, and sincere. Like Philinte she is warm and direct and knows the meaning of love; these two appear to be the ideal couple.

Arsinoé is a prudish woman who pretends to be high-minded and pure but is actually wicked and hypocritical. After she is defeated by Célimène and rebuffed by Alceste, she displays her stupidity and viciousness by trying to make trouble between them although she can gain nothing by it.

The men in Célimène's entourage—Oronte, Acaste, and Clitandre—are the butts for Alceste's satirical shafts, and at the same time provide a perfect background for his somber figure. The would-be poet and the elegant gallants, who represent the glittering but empty social world of Louis XIV are introduced primarily for the purpose of showing up their mediocrity.

The appeal of *The Misanthrope* lies not only in the skillful arrangement of its incidents, and the richness of its characterization, but in the unusual quality of its verse. In an age of preciosity, when elegant, high-flown, and artificial language was considered the mark of the literary man, Molière's dialogue was notable for its clarity, directness, and force as well as for its heightened realism, its cleverness, and its beauty. Unlike Shakespeare, who was born and bred in the country and whose plays reflect his close observation and love of nature, Molière was by birth and upbringing a city boy, a Parisian, to whom the daffodil, the violet, and the primrose meant nothing. It is safe to say that during the twelve years that he spent wandering through the countryside of France, the only aspect of nature that Molière was aware of was Man. One can almost count on one's fingers the passages in his plays in which he uses nature for the purpose of simile or metaphor, and where he does there is no evidence of direct observation or of deep feeling. Yet his flexible and sonorous verses are alive with vivid images and with subtle, symbolic touches which we find only in the greatest poetry. There is the profound symbolism, for instance, of the veil or the mask to suggest the difference between appearance and reality. Early in the play Philinte informs Alceste that it is not only uncouth but absurd always to speak the naked truth; he says:

> It's often best to veil one's true emotions.
> Wouldn't the social fabric come undone
> If we were wholly frank with everyone?

Later in the play, during the great verbal duel between Célimène and Arsinoé, when these ladies are bent upon unmasking each other, one says:

> if you were more *overtly* good,
> You wouldn't be so much misunderstood; . . .

to which the other replies:

> "What good," they said, "are all these outward shows,
> When everything belies her pious pose?"

Alceste reaches the conclusion that in order to be free to have an honest heart, without masks or veils, one must leave society and live apart from other people.

If *The Misanthrope* has a *theme*, it is extremely difficult to determine exactly what it is. The play has been criticized, by Rousseau among others, on the grounds that Molière has shown the world to be too wicked and that he has permitted the idealist to be defeated while the connivers succeed; actually the reverse is true. Granted that Molière took a dark view of human nature and saw hypocrisy and infidelity on all sides, he was merciless in his castigation of these vices, while he depicted the idealist as a sympathetic figure who has gone woefully astray. We might perhaps come closest to the play's central meaning if we look upon Alceste and Philinte as two aspects of the same character; for we all desire to be individualists and intransigents, like Alceste, while at the same time we are compelled by society to be time-servers and conformists, like Philinte.

Molière always affirmed that "the business of comedy is to represent in a general way all the defects of men, and particularly those of our own age." In

The Misanthrope he produced a play that is not only a perfect example of what he had in mind, but one that has served as a model for countless imitators, none of whom achieved either his deftness or his vitality. The comedy of social criticism, which, to use the playwright's own words, portrays "the manners of the time without aiming at individuals," found its greatest exponent in Molière.

PRODUCTION IN THE NEOCLASSICAL THEATER

The Theater

The social and religious conditions which had created mass audiences for Greek, Roman, and medieval drama had also made outdoor performances feasible, but during the Renaissance both society and the drama became more secular and more commercial and there was a corresponding reduction in the size of the audience and an alteration in the caliber of the people who composed it. The professional neoclassical theater relied for its support mainly upon the king, the members of the nobility, and the upper middle class, and for these people plays were performed indoors.

The earliest indoor theaters were not built specially for dramatic productions but had originally been intended for social gatherings or spectator sports; they had actually been ballrooms or indoor tennis courts which were converted into theaters by the expedient of building a platform at one end of the long, rectangular room. Since the space itself was the wrong shape and the people who renovated it had no principles to guide them (were not aware of the fact, for instance, that the floor of a theater should not be flat but that the seats should rise in tiers), the playhouses of the sixteenth and seventeenth centuries in France were anything but ideal for either playgoers or performers.

An association called the Brotherhood of the Passion (*Confrerie de la Passion*) made up of artisans and tradesmen whose main avocation had been the performance of mystery plays, had a monopoly on dramatic activity in Paris. They had been in existence since the Middle Ages and had presented plays on outdoor platform stages, but in 1548, when public performances of mysteries were forbidden, the members of the Brotherhood took over the town house of the Dukes of Burgundy and turned the grand ballroom into a theater, the Hôtel de Bourgogne. This was the only theater in Paris until a second troupe established itself in 1634, at an indoor tennis court called the *Jeu de paume du Marais*. Indoor tennis had been a very popular sport but interest in it faded; hence the availability of the deserted courts for use as theaters. It was probably the phenomenal success of the companies at the Bourgogne and the Marais that encouraged the Béjart group to attempt to found a third theater in Paris in 1643.

All of the important Parisian theaters of the seventeenth century had the same physical layout as that of the Hôtel de Bourgogne: The auditorium was a long, narrow room at one end of which there was a narrow, shallow stage; the orchestra floor in front of the stage, called the *parterre* or pit, had no seats but accommodated standees only. For the better class of patrons, there were boxes in the two galleries that ran round the sides of the room, and, beneath the galleries, against the walls, were loges or grandstands built up from the floor. The *"loges de face,"* which faced the stage directly from the rear wall of the theater, were the only ones which provided a suitable view of the stage, but were farthest from it. The other seats faced into the house so that the wealthier patrons had a better view of the crowd in the pit than of the action on the stage. Both auditorium and stage were lighted by candles, and the stage had no curtains.

The two theaters in Paris occupied by Molière and his company after 1658 were the Petit Bourbon and the Palais Royal; both were closely connected with the Court, yet, except for the magnificence of the décor, there was very little structural difference between these houses and the others in the city. The Petit Bourbon was a room about 210 feet long by 64 feet wide, with a deep apse at one end where the uncurtained stage was located; there were two galleries, the higher one set back, and the usual loges around the side walls. Forced out of the Petit Bourbon in 1660, Molière was granted the use of the Palais Royal, the theater which had been built for Cardinal Richelieu in 1637. Although the new house was smaller than the old, it was more richly decorated and was furnished with more complete facilities than any other professional theater then existing in Paris. The auditorium was a lofty, rectangular hall, about 70 feet long and 60 wide, with about two dozen chandeliers to provide illumination. The stage stood at one end of the hall behind an ornamented proscenium frame, the first to appear in any French theater, but still there was no curtain. The stage floor had trap doors in it, and machines were concealed behind the proscenium arch; these were used for spectacles in which objects, like chariots and clouds, or people were made to ascend, descend, or fly. Three galleries, divided into compartments, ran along each side of the house; the lowest gallery had rows of gold-decorated boxes for the highest members of society. The loges, which Molière had brought with him from his former theater, were erected at the rear of the hall.

Great advances were made in the structure of the indoor theater in France during the eighteenth century but that was an age of actors; there were no writers then to compare with Corneille, Racine, or Molière whose masterpieces were performed in their own day under rather crude and primitive conditions in makeshift playhouses.

Brief mention should be made of the outdoor theater at Versailles where ballets and interludes were produced for the entertainment of the King and his Court; the stage was set in the midst of the formal gardens with a natural setting for the background, the acting area was carefully delimited, and the seats of the spectators were arranged in a semicircle facing the stage. Courtly outdoor theaters of this type—and there were several of them—were more traditional in construction and more comfortable than the professional theaters in Paris.

Scenery, Lighting, Properties

The scenery used in the French theaters during the sixteenth and seventeenth centuries was an adaptation of the type in vogue on the medieval platform stage. The mystery plays of the Middle Ages, as has been noted, were performed on a long platform on which stood four or five little buildings, called mansions, representing the various locales to be used during the play. This type of scenery was known as "simultaneous setting" and actually gave the spectators a rough synopsis of the plot; the audience saw immediately that at some time during the play there would be a temple scene, a palace scene, and so on. When an actor emerged from the temple, the audience understood that the stage on which he strode represented the temple grounds; if another actor came out of the palace, then the stage represented the street on which the palace was situated. This was called an "unlocalized stage"; it did not represent a definite locale throughout the play, but varied from scene to scene, taking its character from the buildings around it, and from the entrances and exits of the players whose lines helped to establish their whereabouts.

The Hôtel de Bourgogne, with its tiny stage, did not have room enough for the building of mansions, but such clever designers as Laurent Mahelot and Michel Laurent solved that problem by covering the rear wall of the stage with a painted backcloth on which were depicted, side by side, the various locales required. As the plays became more and more romantic, in addition to temples and palaces, they called for woods, seacoasts, grottoes, and arbors, all of which were duly painted on the back curtain. With the aid of the backcloth, the different compartments could represent any of the settings required for tragedy, comedy, tragicomedy, and pastoral. The most important characteristic of these decorations is that they symbolize rather than represent place, and thus have something in common with Elizabethan staging. The actor, having taken a position either in or in front of a given item of décor, moved downstage, and, by convention, the whole stage would become that place. The audience accepted this convention, but as the plays became more complicated and the compartments multiplied, the result was confusing; the audience was often perplexed as to where the action was taking place. Although this type of staging made excessive demands upon the spectators, the simultaneous setting and the unlocalized stage remained in use well into the seventeenth century and returned to play a prominent part in German expressionism in the early years of our own century. But a great curb was put upon the unlocalized stage by the introduction of neoclassical rules.

When the critics began to insist upon the observance of the unities of action, time, and place, the dramatists were constrained to write plays which called for only a single setting, such as a room in a house, a corner of a garden, or a street. The room would be furnished with no more than a single armchair or table; there might be a bench in the garden; while the street scene would need no properties at all. Many of the plays of Racine and Molière can be acted satisfactorily on a bare stage. *The Misanthrope*, for instance, takes place entirely in one room in Célimène's house, and the essential properties consist of a single chair and three or four letters which are read on stage.

As no front curtain was used in the neoclassical theater, the actors left the stage after each scene. They could not be "discovered" in their places at the opening of a scene, nor could they form a tableau at the end. It was not until the eighteenth century, when designers learned how to construct shiftable scenery and how to use a front curtain, that various locales could be shown in succession and scenes could begin or end with a surprise.

The seventeenth-century theater was lighted by hundreds of candles in chandeliers both in the auditorium and on the stage, but the playhouses were dim nevertheless. There was only general illumination on the stage since the lights could not be controlled easily; they could not be focused on particular areas, spotlighted, dimmed or brightened at will. It was considered a great innovation in stage lighting when at a tragic moment in one production many candles were snuffed out suddenly to produce an eerie effect.

Unlike the tragedies and the high comedies which were considered works of neoclassical art, the comedy-ballets, interludes, and pastorals, which were presented at Court and later at the Palais Royal for the entertainment of the King, made use of an enormous amount of built and movable scenery and many complex properties. Under the direction of an Italian designer, Gaspare Vigarani, a special theater called the *Salle des Machines* was erected with a stage 32 feet wide at the proscenium opening and a depth of about 132 feet. There remarkable effects were obtained, the immense size of the stage permitting the building of temples and houses surrounded by bushes, trees, and mountains; and in the sky there were floating clouds on which sat many gods and goddesses. A movable platform, 40 feet wide by 60 feet long, could raise 60 persons into the air, as well as such properties as great horse-drawn chariots. To light this stage brightly, thousands of candles and oil-lamps were required, many of them concealed behind columns and in the side-wings which had now come into use. To achieve atmospheric effects, lamps were fixed behind bottles filled with colored liquid and metal bowls were placed behind the lights to act as reflectors, thus faint rays of red, blue, or green would be cast upon the stage. The excessive heat and the unpleasant odor of the wax candles and the oil, not to mention the great fire hazard, were part of the early efforts to develop an art of stage lighting.

The theaters of the eighteenth and nineteenth centuries whose stages were cluttered with built and painted scenery carried on the efforts of the *Salle des Machines;* while the realistic theater of our own day, with its "one-set show," has more in common with the neoclassical stage which represented a single room with four doors.

The Actors

The three acting companies which dominated the French theater during the seventeenth century, those of the Hôtel de Bourgogne, the Marais, and the Palais Royal, were all organized along similar lines. Although all were subsidized by the King, they were not united as a single professional group. Each company was independent and self-regulated; each elected its own officers, selected its plays, hired its actors, and had full control over its productions. The company usually bought its plays for a flat fee and owned the works outright; sometimes the dramatist was paid each time his play was performed, but he was not given a regular share in the receipts unless he also happened to be an actor in the troupe. It was customary for the members of the company to settle their financial business each day at the end of the performance. After the audience had departed, the actors took off their makeup, put their costumes away, and gathered in the theater. They counted the money that had been taken in at the box-office, subtracted the amount needed for the running expenses of the theater (heating, lighting, cleaning, and so on), and divided the remainder among the actors according to their status in the company. As in the Elizabethan theater, some actors received full shares, others half or quarter shares; a certain number of employees were on a straight salary basis. When an actor was obliged to retire, he was paid a small pension for the rest of his life by the performer who took his place in the company.

Although successful actors earned a great deal of money, their personal expenses were very high. The largest item in their budgets was the maintenance of their wardrobes. They had to provide their own stage costumes, which were extremely lavish and costly, and in addition were obliged to own very elegant personal clothing because of the society in which they moved. The actors were often summoned to give performances at the palaces in Paris and at Versailles, for which they received extra payment and free food and lodging, but they mingled with members of the nobility and had to look their best.

Each of the three troupes had its own acting style and its own stars. The Italian companies which were so popular throughout this period performed at the Hôtel de Bourgogne and preserved the techniques of the *commedia dell'arte*. Their style of acting was broad and impromptu; much of the dialogue was made up on the spot, although the actors had worked out a synopsis of the plot in advance. Broad comedy, farce, and satire were the strong points of these players; many of their jests were obscene and the performances of the women were in questionable taste.

Another style of play, exemplified by the tragicomedies of Alexandre Hardy, was acted by a native company at the Hôtel de Bourgogne. In their troupe there were three performers who were as skillful in serious plays as they were in comedy; known as Lafleur, Flechelles, and Belleville when they undertook serious roles, they achieved greater fame under the comic names of Gros-Guillaume (Fat William), Gaultier-Garguille (Walter Drainpipe), and Turlupin (Atrocious Punster). As comedians, each had an identifying costume and type of makeup: Gros-Guillaume was enormously fat and wore a costume that emphasized the bulge of his stomach; he covered his face with a thick coating of flour and pretended to be bored with love. Gaultier-Garguille dressed in black, had long stringy gray hair, and wore spectacles that had no lenses; he drew laughs with his bitterness, his carping, and his mimicry. Turlupin had a shock of red hair and wore a loose flowing costume of striped material that looked like the suit of a medieval clown; he played the part of a tricky servant who did not hesitate to pick pockets as a sideline.

The great tragic actors—Montdory, Montfleury, Bellerose, and Floridor—appeared both at the Marais and at the Hôtel de Bourgogne. It was the Marais company that first presented the plays of Corneille and Racine and it was there that the "tragic style" of acting was initiated; it was later taken up and developed by the actors at the Hôtel de Bourgogne. Montdory, the earliest of the great tragic actors in France, was a powerful and vigorous performer with a stentorian voice. In 1636, while appearing in the role of Herod, a character noted for his ranting, his vocal and physical exertions brought on an apoplectic fit that paralyzed his tongue and ended his career. His successors were Bellerose and Montfleury; Bellerose was extremely vain and strutted rather than walked on stage, while Montfleury was a mountain of a man about whom it was said, "He is so fat that it takes several days to give him a sound beating." During his performances, Montfleury wore an iron corset. In addition to their other faults, these two performers developed a tragic style of acting that was unnatural and affected; they chanted their lines as if they were singing and stressed the rhymes of the verse to produce a shrill and bombastic effect. They were unmercifully ridiculed by Molière, but persisted in performing in their declamatory style and established it as a tradition that lasted down to the nineteenth century, mainly because it won the approval of audiences. Floridor, another tragic actor at the Hôtel de Bourgogne, was a brilliant performer with a natural style and had the distinction of being the only member of the company about whom Molière never made a disparaging remark. The comedians at the Bourgogne and the Marais—Raymond Poisson, who created the famous character of Crispin, and Jodolet, the white-faced clown who later joined Molière's company—were original, accomplished, and popular performers.

Molière's company which was housed at the Palais Royal, consisted of the most talented, best trained, and most successful actors in Paris. First among them was Molière himself; he played a great variety of parts, from the buffoon Sganarelle to the almost tragic Alceste. Three other extremely versatile men—Brécourt, La Grange, and Du Croisy—also acted leading roles in a broad range of types; while the smaller character parts were taken by La Thorillière and by Louis Béjart. La Thorillière was a tall, well-built man who played both kings and peasants. Béjart acted old women as well as old men because the actresses of the day refused to play elderly parts. In *Le Bourgeois Gentilhomme,* the actor Hubert played both the Music Master and Madame Jourdain. Young Michel Baron, Molière's protégé, was a very valuable member of the company who carried on his teacher's style and techniques and became the greatest naturalistic actor in France during the half century after Molière's death.

The women in the troupe were equally adept and portrayed a wide variety of types, for some of which they became famous. Madeleine Béjart usually acted the clever, quick-thinking maid; Armande played cold, sophisticated heroines, such as Célimène in *The Misanthrope;* Madame Du Parc and Madame Debrie specialized in prudes, coquettes, and ingenues.

Molière was of medium height, attractive, slender, agile and graceful; as an actor he always strove for realistic effects in his own performances, and insisted that the other members of his company perform in the same style. In his one-act play, *The Impromptu of Versailles,* he severely criticized the company at the Hôtel de Bourgogne for their unrealistic and affected methods and manners. He imitated and satirized each one in turn but leveled his heaviest fire against

Montfleury to whom he alludes as "a king who is very fat, and as big as four men. A king, by Jove, well stuffed out. A king of vast circumference, who could fill a throne handsomely." He objects to the way in which Montfleury delivers his lines, saying that he declaims them in a manner that will make the public applaud him, for when he is supposed to be talking in private with a captain of his guards he uses a demoniacal tone merely for the effect it will produce upon the audience. After imitating one of the leading actresses at the Bourgogne, Molière remarks ironically, "See how natural and impassioned this is. Admire the smiling face she maintains in the deepest affliction."

The advice Molière offers to his own players provides us with an excellent clue to his theories of acting. In *The Impromptu of Versailles*, the playwright-director is surrounded by the members of his company and is about to give each one instructions in his part, when Madame Du Parc complains, "I shall act wretchedly. I do not know why you have given me this ceremonious part. . . . There is no one in the world less ceremonious than I." Molière replies:

"True; and that is how you prove yourself to be an excellent actress, by portraying well a character which is opposite to your own. Try then, all of you, to catch the spirit of your parts aright, and to imagine that you are what you represent."

It is quite clear that within the limitations of the dramatic conventions of the theater for which he wrote, such as the strict verse form of the play and the observation of the rules of decorum, Molière was attempting to create a strong impression of reality.

Costumes

French actors of the seventeenth century, like English actors of the same period, appeared on the stage in contemporary dress; no attempt was made to achieve historical accuracy. If the characters were supposed to represent members of the upper classes they wore clothing that was the last word in current fashion; if they represented characters of a lower social order, they wore the dress of the man in the street.

By 1620 the stiff old styles of farthingales and bombasted and padded limbs, stiff ruffles, and tight waists had given way to a new fashion that called for softly curling tresses, full loose skirts, and dainty ribbons and laces. Men's fashions followed closely upon those of women's, and both revealed the endless possibilities of folds and draperies. About 140 yards of silk ribbon were used in a man's costume for loops, flaps, and rosettes, which were arranged all around the waist and the hems of the coats and breeches, on the shoulders, elbows, garters, swordbelt, hat, and shoes, and even in the hair.

After 1660 a new masculine costume gave the figure a firm outline and a slender and distinguished look. It was a tightfitting coat that reached to the knees, worn over a long vest and narrow knee-breeches. The only lace used was as a cravat and as cuffs, while the ribbons were completely eliminated except for a single bow on the right shoulder (even so sober a person as Alceste is identified as "the man with green ribbons"); but the velvet and gold and silver brocades of which the clothing was made were further embellished with silver and gold embroidery. The favorite jewel was the diamond, which was even used for buttons. Men wore silk stockings and high-heeled shoes; their hats were three-cornered with a low crown, and were often not worn on the head but carried under the arm. Women's fashions resembled men's in attempting to make the figure look slimmer and more dignified; women wore tight-waisted gowns, cut low at the neck, with three-quarter sleeves and trains of varying lengths. The materials were rich and ornate; even the high-heeled shoes were made of embroidered silk.

Men began to wear wigs which were curled or waved, the thick hair reaching below the shoulders. At first the wigs were golden-hued; later they were brown or black. Before the women took to wearing wigs, their heads were adorned with a tall cap, called a *fontange*, made of silk ribbons, starched lace and linen, in which they piled their own hair and created an effect similar to that of the wigs of the men. The fashions of this period had all the splendor and dignity for which the court of Louis XIV was noted, and it was from this time that Paris became known as the fashion center of the world.

In addition to their contemporary clothes, as described above, the actors wore two special costumes called *à la Romaine* and *à la Turque*. For the tragedies in which the action took place in Greece or Rome the actors donned a costume that was more or less modeled on genuine Roman style. It consisted of breastplates, a short skirt, a cloak, a plumed helmet, and high cross-gartered boots. Such a costume was extremely expensive as it was made of very fine materials, including real gold and silver. The Turkish costume consisted of long gowns of rich materials with which were worn silk and brocaded robes, a huge feathered turban, and boots of soft leather; this costume signified that the wearer was of Middle Eastern or of Oriental origin. A third type of stage costume was the fantastic or comic get-up worn by affected or simple-minded people, by yokels and clowns. These were often intended as a form of satire.

Since each costume might cost as much as one or two hundred dollars, the actor who was obliged to appear in thirty-five or forty plays during a season might have a wardrobe that represented an investment of about five thousand dollars, even though some of the clothing was bought secondhand, was obtained as gifts from members of the nobility, or was remodeled from season to season. The posthumous inventory of Molière's costumes showed that as Alceste the actor-playwright had worn "breeches and jacket of a gold-colored and gray striped brocade, lined with tabby, ornamented with green ribbons; the waistcoat of gold brocade, silk stockings and garters."

Although the neoclassical stage was virtually bare of scenery and properties, the actors' costumes were sumptuous, colorful, and eye-filling.

Music and Dance

Music and dance were important elements in French drama from its very beginning. The medieval mystery plays featured solo and choral singing, and the later morality plays concluded with gay folk dances. Such practices continued and developed with the complete approval of the public as well as of the Court.

Louis XIII was so fond of the ballet that the late sixteenth century came to be known as "the age of dancing." He subsidized composers, musicians, and dancers and made sure that these artists were employed to provide entertainment for him. Louis XIV surpassed his father in his love of music and the dance and increased both the subsidies and the opportunities for creative and interpretive artists. The King took part himself in many ballets, and his love of music was so great that he gave his chief composer, Jean Baptiste Lully, unheard-of powers and privileges.

Songs and dances which had nothing at all to do with the story were introduced into many of the comedies of the day; and music was played before, during, and after the performances of tragedies. The King was entertained by the *ballet de cour*, a form of production very much like an extravagant vaudeville show or revue, composed of dances, tableaux, songs, music, and poetry which had no relation to one another.

In 1661 Molière was asked to prepare a work which was to be put on as part of a great festival for the amusement of the King. In collaboration with Lully, Molière wrote his first comedy-ballet, *Les Fâcheux* (*The Bores*); this was an enormous innovation in that the songs and dances were integrated with the comedy, and the music not only helped to depict the characters but defined the situations and heightened the mood. In fusing all of these elements, Molière created a form that was to give rise to both comic opera and grand opera in France. Lully learned a great deal about musical drama by working with Molière and the collaboration between the two lasted for ten years, during which time the comedy-ballets created by them became more complex and more brilliant both dramatically and musically.

Each Parisian theater had a group of musicians attached to it, and the actors in the company were proficient vocalists, instrumentalists, and dancers. At the Petit Bourbon and the Palais Royal, the musicians occupied a box adjacent to the stage; while at Versailles an augmented orchestra sat in a pit directly in front of the stage as the musicians do in the modern theater.

The music of the seventeenth century was written mainly for strings. Lully, for instance, was a master of the guitar, the violin, and the clavecin, an early form of the harpsichord; it is significant that his famous orchestra was called "the twenty-four violins of the King," although the group also included such wind instruments as flutes, oboes, and horns.

In the dances of the period, a stock succession of movements was developed until a set rhythmic pattern was established for each; these were the sober allemande, the brisk courante, the slow and stately sarabande, and the lively gigue (jig). The composers of the day also refined and elaborated a number of peasant dances of the French provinces; among them were the *bourrée* (from the Auvergne), the *gavotte* (from the Dauphiné), the *rigaudon* (from Provence), and most important of all, the *minuet* (from Poitou); in addition, certain dances of foreign origin, such as the *anglaise* and the *polonaise,* were introduced at Court and found their way into the plays of the period.

Music and dance were so important in the theater of the seventeenth century that songs and dances were put on between the acts of even such plays as *Tartuffe* and *The Misanthrope*. In the latter play, it should be noted, Alceste speaks of preferring an old song to the tunes written in his day, and at that point in the play, it is believed, Molière sang *The Old Song of King Henry*. In the preface to La Grange's *Register*, it is noted that Michel Baron, who took over the role after Molière's death, had a great success singing the song of *The Misanthrope*, evidently following the example of the author and creator of the character, but the exact song that was sung is unknown.

The Audience

French playgoers, not very numerous during the seventeenth century, consisted of two separate and widely differing groups. The King and the members of the Court circle, together with specially invited guests, comprised the first group. Louis was pleasure-loving and self-indulgent and proved to be an excellent patron of the drama. Acting companies were called upon frequently and were rewarded handsomely when they produced their plays at Versailles or at the various palaces in Paris. Although the royal audiences were highly sophisticated, their tastes ran generally to great musical spectacles and romantic tragedies.

The second group, and the more substantial audience, was made up of the general public which frequented the three theaters in Paris on the regular playing days—Sundays, Tuesdays, and Fridays. A full house at the Palais Royal meant about 1,000 people, but the theater was seldom filled to capacity. Posters were put up around town—red for the Hôtel de Bourgogne, green for Molière's theater —and street criers announced the performances, which were scheduled to begin at 2 P.M., but usually got started a half-hour to a full hour late.

Members of the upper classes, wealthy merchants, professional men, artisans, clerks, soldiers, lackeys, playboys, and prostitutes made up the public audiences. Each occupied the section of the theater suited to his social level or financial condition; members of the upper classes filled the two lower rows of gold-decorated boxes, while people of smaller means went to the upper galleries. The loges at the rear of the parterre were occupied by the well-to-do merchants. The parterre itself, which was the standing-room directly in front of the stage, was filled with the clerks, lackeys, soldiers, and members of the lower orders. Some thirty or forty spectators—mostly young aristocrats who wished to show off— were allowed to sit on the stage; this practice began when an overflow audience filled the theater to see Corneille's *Le Cid*, and continued until the eighteenth century when Voltaire refused to permit spectators to sit on the stage.

The price scale at the Palais Royal was high in comparison with the cost of admission to the theaters in London and other European cities at that time. A chair in the lower boxes or on the stage was three dollars; a seat in the loges was two dollars; the first gallery was one dollar; the second gallery, seventy-five cents; and the parterre was about fifty cents. Prices were always doubled, or multiplied even more, for the premiere of a new play, the revival of a popular old one, or a play that had costly scenery and "machines."

The audience was generally well-behaved, the most unruly groups being the playboys on the stage and the standees. The former often made rude or foolish remarks which annoyed the actors and the other members of the audience, while the standees occasionally became quarrelsome and abusive. This was particularly true when drunken soldiers or the lackeys of great lords thought they had the right to enter the theater without paying; on several occasions they quarreled with and injured the ticket-taker, threatened the actors with bodily harm, broke up the theater, and drove the audience out. But disturbances were rather rare; the audience, which was in a mood for pleasure, usually listened politely to the music played before the performance began as well as during the entr'actes, and bought candy, fruit, and soft drinks from the orange girls who sold these wares.

The general public, with its heterogeneous tastes, provided the greatest stimulus to the playwrights of the day; this was especially true of the crowd in the parterre, which, for all its crudeness, represented the most independent and democratic element in the theater, was most outspoken in its reactions and most appreciative of Molière, when some of his greatest contemporaries were blind to his merits.

THE PRODUCTION RECORD

The first act of The Misanthrope was read in public as early as July, 1664, according to Boileau, the poet, critic, and friend of Molière. The play was probably completed by the end of 1665, but the illness and death of Anne of Austria, mother of Louis XIV, caused the closing of the theaters during January and February, 1666, then Easter intervened, and finally the play was launched on June 4, 1666. The play met with only moderate success at its premiere because of the seriousness of the theme and because of the season of the year: then as now the general public preferred light entertainment and new plays were put on in the winter rather than the summer.

Molière himself played Alceste and his wife played Célimène; so much is known for certain. The rest of the casting is conjectural: Eliante and Arsinoé were acted by Du Parc and Debrie, but it is not known which played which; it is believed that La Grange acted Philinte; Du Croisy, Oronte; Hubert, Acaste; and La Thorillière, Clitandre.

We know that Alceste is the most autobiographical of Molière's characters, but we also know that in this play the dramatist was laughing at himself—at his seriousness, his idealism, and his jealousy. Alceste was meant to be lovable and yet ridiculous, and Molière played him for laughs. Later interpreters of the role, as we shall see, attempted to portray Alceste as a tragic figure.

Armande's interpretation of Célimène created as much of a sensation as did her husband's performance, for the actress was considered the perfect embodiment of the role. Scandalmongers immediately decided that the character was drawn from life. A contemporary wrote: "Armande could not brook contradiction, and pretended that a lover ought to be as submissive as a slave." This view might very easily have grown up as a result of her portrayal of Célimène who is all coquetry, egoism, and wit; the truth of the matter is that we know very little about Armande's real character but there is no doubt about her great acting ability.

Molière kept *The Misanthrope* in his repertory and performed it for the last time on November 8, 1672, three months before his death. In 1668 it was also seen in the repertories of two provincial troupes, that of Villeroy and that of the Dauphin; and, after Molière's death, it was given, in 1677, by the actors of the Hôtel de Bourgogne at Fontainebleau and probably also at Paris. For the performance at Fontainebleau the designer Mahelot in his *Memoirs* states: "Theater is a chamber. Six chairs are needed, three letters, some shoes." The last item was perhaps for the actor DuBois, who liked brocaded shoes. It is interesting to note the simplicity of the stage furnishings.

Between 1680 and 1959, according to the records of the Comèdie-Française, *The Misanthrope* was performed about 1,500 times; it ranks fourth in the frequency of production of Molière's plays.

After the death of Molière the role of Alceste was assumed by the dramatist's protégé, Michel Baron, a vigorous man, with a sonorous, exact, and flexible voice; his diction was excellent and varied; he disliked declamation so much that he broke up the alexandrines with pauses and runs, avoided the rhymes, and achieved great subtlety and interest. All of these techniques he had learned from Molière. In 1691, at the height of his fame, Baron left the stage and during his absence the part of Alceste was played by Dancourt. Thirty years later, Baron returned to the Comèdie-Française, and on June 1, 1720 he again played Alceste, his favorite role. A playgoer who saw him in the part during this period wrote: "He not only put a great deal of nobility and dignity into the role but added a delicate polish and a fund of humanity which made one love *The Misanthrope*. He permitted himself a few brusque moments and some humor but always ennobled them by his tone and by his spirit. Nothing crude, nothing gross was uttered by him. Baron was right in his judgment that it was necessary for the actor to adopt a sophisticated tone. By these sensitive means he sweetened the role instead of pushing it too far and exaggerating it. . . . He never declaimed, he spoke. He acted with great sentiment the scene in the fourth act with Célimène; even in his rages he always kept control and showed the deference which one owes to women even when they don't deserve it. Unlike actors of the present [1776], he never made of the misanthrope a grumbler or a boor." The reference to "actors of the present" was a criticism of Molé, Baron's successor, and whenever the writer says, "Baron played it this way . . . ," he means that Molé acted the role in an entirely different manner. Baron was seventy years old when he returned to the stage but he triumphed as Alceste and captivated audiences to the end of his life. Voltaire, however, criticized *The Misanthrope* as "a work more suitable for sensitive people than for the multitude, and better to be read than to be played." After seeing Baron in the part, Voltaire said, "He never drew a great house, which confirms the opinion one had that this play was more admired than attended."

During the first half of the nineteenth century, the reigning queen of the French stage was Anne-Hippolyte Mars, who began as a rather awkward and plain person, but by dint of hard work and intensive study transformed herself into an actress of unusual beauty and grace. She excelled in the great roles of comedy and was considered incomparable as Célimène in *The Misanthrope*. Her acting technique was magnificent; it was actually a chain of imperceptible tricks that gave the audience enormous pleasure. It is interesting to note that Rachel, an actress of genius who was supreme in tragedy, failed miserably in the part of Célimène while her contemporary, Mlle Mars, on the basis of technical virtuosity, was a scintillating success.

On January 15, 1829, Mlle Mars created a sensation by playing Célimène in a costume of the time of Louis XIV; all her predecessors and contemporaries wore the leg-of-mutton sleeve which was the high style of the day. Yet four years later, in a production of *The Misanthrope* in which Mlle Mars did not appear, the men were dressed in the styles of Louis XV and Louis XVI while the women wore gowns, robes, and accessories featured in the latest fashion journals of 1833.

An outstanding actor during the second half of the nineteenth century was Edmond Geffroy, who performed in a passionate and romantic style. He was one of the first actors to portray Alceste as a serious character. He was interested in the psychology of the man, his personal traits and his morals, as well as in his clothing and his external manners. He gave a powerful and moving rendition of the part that led many later actors, down to modern times, to play it in the same way, although such an interpretation was not intended by Molière. Geffroy tended to emphasize the dark and terrible side of a character, for his acting was severe and rather sad, though he was capable of great energetic movements, with his head thrust forward and his eyes half-closed. Geffroy had a very strong historical sense and tried to achieve accuracy and authenticity in his costumes, but that was the period during which many theater people first attempted to reproduce the past with correctness of detail.

In the present century, *The Misanthrope* has been performed innumerable times in Paris; two years in particular were notable for the number and style of their productions, 1922 and 1947. In the earlier year, Lucien Guitry appeared as Alceste at the Théâtre Edouard VII; he was surrounded by a first-rate company which played, however, in the traditional, dry, and theoretical manner, technically excellent but unexciting. On January 28 of the same year, Jacques Copeau presented his version of the play at his own theater, the Vieux-Colombier; it was a production remarkable in many respects. Copeau not only directed but played the leading role; his Célimène was Valentine Tessier, and his Philinte was Louis Jouvet. Copeau's acting was impulsive and exalted; it had all the drive and force necessary for comedy. A critic wrote: "His first entrance is impetuous and ill-humored, and bluntly opposes to the image of a bookish man that of a distracted 'character' which sets the tone for the entire performance. . . . His fixed almost bewildered eyes, his spasmodic outbursts, his naïve astonishment at men's most natural weaknesses, and his morbid dejection present a complex mixture of emotions that range from burlesque to deep sorrow." The company as a whole, the décor, the costumes, and the wigs were all done in high style and were perfect.

In 1947 four different versions of the play were mounted in four different styles. On the 20th of March at the Théâtre La Bruyère, Pierre Assy played Alceste with all the passion and fury of the nineteenth-century romantic actor Geffroy; on the 31st of the same month, at the Théâtre Antoine, in settings by Pimenoff, Aimé Clariond presented Alceste as a melancholy and tearful soul. On October 8, a new version of the play was put on at the Comédie-Française with Pierre Dux as star and director, Annie Ducaux as Célimène, and settings by Louis Süe. In his review of the play in *Le Figaro*, October 10, 1947, Jean-Jacques Gautier wrote:

> In an architectural décor cleverly contrived by M. Louis Süe, the company of the Comédie-Française now offers us a very interesting production of *The Misanthrope*. Immediately we felt that Pierre Dux would be Alceste, a bull who charges at the red rags of the slightest hypocrisies. His indignation went to his head; a frenzy only slightly controlled was in his movement. Nevertheless, the entire interpretation that he had conceived adhered exactly to the text, and the first act in particular came close to perfection. . . . I return to Alceste, for it was he in his rage of the fourth act; it was he incensed, ready for all outrages, as it was he a moment later, pitiable, sorrowful, overwhelmed by his disgust for himself, but still seeking to discover a reason to be convinced—begging for a word that would enable him to be sure of his faith in Célimène and not be deceived—that was he, that was Alceste. Pierre Dux was Alceste; a severe test, but he passed it.

Four days later Gautier reviewed Jean Marchat's production which had opened at the Théâtre des Mathurins on October 6, 1947. This version was presented in a stylized setting by Jacques Dupont, and Marchat interpreted the play as a comedy with strong farcical overtones. Gautier was not pleased; he wrote:

> The theater-loving Parisian, either before or after seeing *The Misanthrope* at the Comédie-Française, would want to see the one at the Mathurins. As in the former Pierre Dux was Alceste, so in the latter Sophie Desmarets is Célimène. She is that very charming and carefree young woman who amuses herself by flirting without taking into account the seriousness of the wounds she inflicts. Her mockery, her infidelity, her sharp words and cutting looks, her extreme youth: all are there. . . .
>
> But what of Alceste? I criticize him first for inventing stage business, would-be "gags," which are not justified by anything in the text. He is guilty, moreover, of interpolating into the verses such expressions as "Oh, my!" along with murmurs and growls which become veritable interjections. But these interjections are not in Molière. . . . Finally, regarding the total effect of the interpretation, the real Alceste is not a Russian peasant; he is outspoken, not coarse; moody, not savage. But the most serious complaint lies elsewhere: M. Jean Marchat makes it too obvious that he conceives of Alceste as a comic character.
>
> Does Jean Marchat think that he will make us laugh at Alceste by banging his hat on the table again and again? Does he believe that because he enters in the fourth act hopping on one foot that he thereby gladdens our hearts? Finally, does he imagine that his unnatural gestures, which consist above all of pretending to smash the furniture, give us for an instant the feeling of a comical fury directed against Célimène?
>
> I must add that at the very end one does not feel for a single moment the sorrow of Alceste's final mood, of the disheartened Alceste. . . . It should be noted that I appreciate the attempt of M. Jean Marchat: I maintain only that having wished to

present a certain *Misanthrope,* he does not appear to me to have employed the means that he should have in order to achieve his purpose. I am quite willing that you laugh at Alceste, but you must laugh in spite of him!

The Misanthrope has received outstanding productions in almost every country in Europe, and in many other parts of the world. The German-speaking countries lead all the rest, perhaps, for their many State theaters have mounted the plays of Molière continually since the eighteenth century. The most recent version of *The Misanthrope* to be done in German was that presented at the Burgtheater in Vienna in July, 1959, with Ernst Ginsberg as Alceste and Agnes Fink as Célimène, in the décor of Teo Otto.

The Misanthrope has received a number of productions in the United States, but these were more often in French than in English. It was done for the first time in English by the British-born actor-manager Richard Mansfield, who was also the first to produce Bernard Shaw in America; Mansfield's version of *The Misanthrope* became part of the actor's repertory and was performed for the last time at the Grand Opera House, Chicago, in May, 1906. The critic for the *Chicago Record,* May 10, 1906, wrote:

> Mr. Mansfield's revival of *The Misanthrope* is marked by brilliance of investiture, and his embodiment of Alceste is vibrant with pain. Nervous unrest is curiously blended with spiritual fortitude, the utterance of blistering scorn and the gaze of a commanding eye are frequently shadowed by the proofs of inward doubt and self-pity. He moves in his black habiliments against the silver and white background of Célimène's drawing-room, and he is ever the center of a throng of gaily dressed men and women of the period of Louis XIV. The curls of a full dark wig fall about his anxious countenance. His lips are closely compressed even when he speaks, his nostrils usually dilated, as if ever on the scent of villainy and deceit, his eyes heavy with scorn and grief, his movements swift, decisive and so frequent as to betray the nervous and spiritual stress that drives the man ever onward in the search of ideals and of a peace of mind that as constantly elude him. He speaks rapidly, abruptly, and usually in sharp staccato and makes frequent gestures of protest with upraised hands of startling pallor, and when he does this wide lace cuffs fall back upon his black sleeves. The look of pain and uncertainty is seldom absent from his face. He smiles, but it is always the smile of bitterness. . . .
>
> As a study in deep anguish, none the less unbearable because largely imagined, Mr. Mansfield's Alceste is a remarkable achievement, preserving the tone of saturnine humor subtly displayed and, most essential of all, echoing the tribute Alceste won from his easy-going world—"There is something noble and heroic about him." His Alceste rings with the voice of challenge and is rigid with the attitude of defiance. Withal there are tears in the weary, doubting eyes of the soul that was misunderstood yet understood so much.

On November 12, 1956, the play opened at a tiny off-Broadway house called Theatre East and was presented in English in Richard Wilbur's translation, which had first been used at the Poets' Theatre, Cambridge, Massachusetts, on October 25, 1955. Stephen Porter served as producer-director at Theatre East. Ellis Raab gave a well-sustained but rather petulant reading as Alceste, and Jacqueline Brookes was a sparkling Célimène; the members of the supporting cast, which included Arthur Malet, William Ball, Sada Thompson, and Olive Dunbar, were expert and delightful in their highly stylized performances.

While the American production was being acted at Theatre East, with its 125 seats, the Madeleine Renaud-Jean-Louis Barrault Company—brought to America by the impresario S. Hurok—opened at the Winter Garden, whose huge proportions more closely resemble those of Molière's Théâtre du Palais Royal, and there from February 7 to February 9, 1957, the visiting stars, under the direction of M. Barrault, presented the play in French. The identical production had originally been mounted in Paris on November 6, 1954; the sets were by Pierre Delbée, the costumes by Marcel Escoffier; and Barrault's company was the acme of elegance and zest. The American critics were charmed. One wrote: "M. Barrault himself leads the frolic. A man of middle height and early middle years, he is quick of speech and of movement. His misanthrope is a vehement, hot-tempered, nervous fellow." Another said: "A mettlesome performance done in high style. Mlle Renaud is dainty, graceful, scintillating, witty, and full of verve. The acting throughout is limpid, animated, and exquisite." Bert McCord of the New York *Herald Tribune*, took occasion to point out the great contrast between the studied acting of the seventeenth century and the naturalistic style of our own day:

> From his company as a whole, M. Barrault has extracted a classical, highly stylized performance calculated to unnerve the more dedicated disciples of the Actors' Studio. The actors flounce, sweep or stalk majestically on stage; they prance and swirl; the act of sitting down is a ceremonial to be accomplished with the most flamboyant gestures and waving of plumed hats; they bow low in obeisant humility or rise archly to their full height when insulted. It's all delicious fun.

M. Barrault obviously caught both the spirit and the style of this timeless masterpiece.

REPERTORY AND *The Misanthrope*
An Interview with Jean-Louis Barrault

Jean-Louis Barrault began his career as an actor in 1931 and served his apprenticeship under the great Charles Dullin; then he studied mime with Etienne Decroux. In 1937 he still considered himself a very imperfect actor; he was full of theories about acting but felt that he needed very much more actual experience. "It was then that I decided to accept every part offered me without reflection," says Barrault, "and so the following season I leapt at the opportunity given me by Alice Cocéa to play the Misanthrope opposite her. For three months I floundered among Alceste's nine hundred lines, which earned me an excommunication from Decroux and a sharp rebuke from Louis Jouvet. But this kind of cold shower knocked off my corners and my star guided me well."

In 1940 Barrault joined the Comédie Française; but six years later, with a change in the administration, those players who wished to leave the state-owned theater were allowed to do so. On September 1, 1946, the actor, with his wife,

Madeleine Renaud, and several other colleagues—among them Pierre Bertin, Marie-Helene Dasté, Simone Valere, and Jean-Pierre Granval—set out on a new career. The Madeleine Renaud-Jean-Louis Barrault Company was formed, and established itself at the Marigny Theatre, its headquarters until 1956. The Company toured in many countries and continued to grow and develop; its home is now the state-owned Odeon Theatre. It has a troupe of forty-five actors and a repertory of forty plays, and it is Barrault's hope to add six plays each season, always in new productions.

"A company can only be alive if it has a repertory," says Barrault, "and a company can only build up a repertory if it keeps on producing plays one after another and not depending only on those that they have already done well. In order to proceed with these constant changes the company must be able to play, as it were, a number of works at the same time; it must practice a regular, alternating rhythm. With the exception of the Théâtre du Vieux Colombier, that our master Jacques Copeau founded in 1913 and that endured till 1920, there was no example of a private company capable of maintaining this alternating rhythm for more than a short while. To do so was the privilege of the state theaters; the principle was upheld only by virtue of the state subsidy.

"For almost fourteen years we have succeeded in maintaining our rhythm," says Barrault. "The public has become used to it, and we have enjoyed its many advantages. For it is precisely these alternations that have given our work its vitality. If he knows that he will go from a small part today to a big part tomorrow, an actor of high quality is willing to play the small parts, which means that they will be well acted. Playing a number of parts, often entirely different, in a short space of time, the actor grows supple, improves. He does not stiffen, become rusty with routine. And in this jostling of one role against another, the actor's personal, artistic talents become plain; hence it becomes easier to give him the role to which he is best suited. And as they say: 'A play well cast is a play half staged.'

"The constant changes require, no doubt, a large technical staff. This may be costly, but helps to maintain a good team. The scene-shifter, the electrician, the carpenter, all the many tradesmen who collaborate in this fine communal enterprise, are able 'to keep their hands in'; each man's ability is tested and he is made more competent by his varying duties.

"The certainty of seeing a new production at regular intervals has given us a public that is also regular, that follows and supports what we do and enables us to survive in freedom, not at the mercy of the 'passing crowd' that cares only for success. For there is a right that must at times be claimed if you want to chance a bold stroke and contribute your share to the true artistic life of the theater, and that is the 'right to be wrong.' The system of alternation allows us to make mistakes, and our faithful public, ever curious and interested, forgives them. There are numbers of plays that we would never have dared to put on if it were not for the saving grace of alternation.

"We are able, by the same means, to undertake research and, while remaining in constant touch with the classics, to serve the interests of living creative authors.

A study of the classics nourishes the mind and helps it to progress. We are going back to the sources; in our search for the *right tone* we rediscover style; we become fully aware of the intensity, the economy, and the harmony which flow from the exceptional union of good taste and genius. As against this drawing of strength from the classics, we allow ourselves excursions into more or less unknown regions of dramatic art; we are able, as I said, to undertake research. Most writers are ignorant of the full resources of the stage and what can be made of the potentialities of actors. It might be pointed out that the greatest dramatic writers, Shakespeare and Molière, were actors. Our investigations are pursued therefore in a 'clinical' spirit, in the hope that we may, with luck, shed some light on the paths of authorship and, with our special experience, assist young writers in the act of creation. The essential task that we have set before us is to serve present-day authors. We try to be as widely eclectic as possible, however, in our choice of works old and new. In our recent world tour, for example, we presented five plays from various periods: two from the seventeenth century, Lope de Vega's *The Gardener's Dog* and Molière's *Misanthrope;* one from the nineteenth century, Feydeau's *Keep an Eye on Amélie;* and two from the twentieth century, Giraudoux' *Intermezzo* and Claudel's *Christopher Columbus.*

"In our training and practice, although the study of pure diction and the use of words concerns us particularly, we give special attention also to the study of gesture—the most interesting, useful, and deeply poetic performance of pantomime. In fact, we believe that we are developing our art in all its branches in a workmanlike manner, a true spirit of craftsmanship. As for theory, we are inclined to distrust all ready-made ideas and formulas. The stage, like life, is complex and varied; all formulas are good provided they spring from an authentic sensation and, beyond the stirrings of the brain and the senses, reach the heart. That is the reason why, when we give a performance, we are truly rewarded if we feel that our work appeals not only to our own countrymen but reaches a plane of universal humanity; for the theater, like all the arts, is essentially a means of communication, a link between man and man. But drawing its life-blood from a love of mankind, the theater above all is the art of human communion.

"Molière demonstrates this magnificently in his play *The Misanthrope,* in which we see the human side of the dramatist, urging his idealism upon society, although he is finally forced to withdraw in defeat.

"In studying the play for production, I realized that the characters were all of the high social status which would have permitted them to frequent the Court, and I imagined that the play was being given before the King at the Tuileries or at the palace at St. Germain in one of the great rooms. If the play had been presented at Versailles, it would have been done in the gardens out of doors since the palace was still under construction in 1666. I found it very difficult to make up my mind as to where to set the action, in Célimène's *salon* or in a room in the palace. So I asked Pierre Delbée to design two sets—one an elegant upper-class interior, and the other the interior of a magnificent room in a palace; both were built and used during rehearsals and, finally, with the help of the actors, I decided to use the royal apartment. Throughout the production I was trying to remove the middle-class side of the play and to emphasize the regal side and the set helped my conception; if I had been doing *Tartuffe* or *L'Avare*, I would have used the set I rejected in this instance.

"In playing Alceste, I tried for the characteristics of naïveté, credulity, and optimism. I firmly believe that Alceste is an optimistic person because he is sure that he will succeed in changing mankind and, in the beginning of the play, he is also quite certain that he will be able to change Célimène. He fails in both areas, of course, but his naïveté touches the spectator; Alceste must be charming and seductive. If he is played with too much anger and venom, women would not be attracted to him—as they are; but if he is childlike, petulant, and unreasoning women will be irresistibly drawn to him. Philinte is a pessimist because he does not really believe in men; he knows that they are all bears, monkeys, and wolves. Alceste, on the other hand, foolish as the idea may be, actually believes in the perfectibility of man. He reacts with hatred because of his unrequited love; he is, in short, a frustrated idealist.

"Alceste, in my opinion, was not naturally misanthropic, but became a misanthrope through a series of disappointments. He hopes that men will see his point of view but when they take an opposite course he considers them perverse and flies off the handle. Proof of his sensibility is the fact that Alceste boils over suddenly and loses complete control of his temper. Célimène is the perfect foil for him because she is so cool and self-contained. She is very clever, very intelligent, and reacts almost unconsciously; she operates with feminine intuition, but there is a strong strain of irresponsibility in her.

"I think of Alceste, too, as a Chaplinesque character who wrings both laughter and tears from the audience by creating a feeling of pathos. Because of the ambiguity of the emotions aroused, this was the first play by Molière at which the public smiled quietly instead of laughing uproariously, which is one of the reasons why the play was not an immediate success. The public had come to look upon Molière as a *farceur*, but this play was not 'standard' Molière; the audience was therefore confused and disconcerted. In order to correct the impression and to reinstate himself, so to speak, Molière followed *The Misanthrope* immediately with *The Doctor in Spite of Himself*, a broad and brilliant farce in his more usual vein; and the audience felt that the balance had been restored.

"Molière, like Chaplin, must always make the audience laugh, even in the saddest situations. In *The Misanthrope*, therefore, I played everything very broadly —exaggerated grimaces, broad gestures, and so on; even when Alceste was being most naïve and sincere, I tried to make him look ridiculous. My training in pantomime, I believe, helped me tremendously to achieve this mixture of moods."

Barrault's interpretation of Alceste appears to be in line with Molière's original conception of the character. Furthermore, in a recently discovered play by Menander, the *Dyskolos* (*The Misanthrope*), the protagonist, Cnémon, "the hater of Mankind," is also treated humorously by the Greek dramatist; thus the comic treatment of such a serious figure is both ancient and well-founded. The *Dyskolos* was recently produced in Geneva, Switzerland, by actor-director François Simon, who believes that "Menander is closer to our time than Molière is, because modern audiences are better able to understand and appreciate the earthiness of the ancient writer than the formalism of the neoclassical one." Barrault, however, by the depth of his perception and the supreme power of his technique, was able to achieve the combination of these two seemingly disparate elements in his portrayal of Alceste.

Scenery for *The Misanthrope*
An Interview with Pierre Delbée

Jean-Louis Barrault selected Pierre Delbée to design the set for *The Misanthrope* because of Delbée's intensive knowledge of seventeenth- and eighteenth-century décor. Delbée is the head of a celebrated Parisian firm of furniture dealers, which collects genuine antiques and also makes replicas of rare pieces in its own workshops. Barrault and Delbée had long preliminary discussions about the set, and Barrault admitted that he could not make up his mind whether to place the action in the drawing-room in Célimène's house, which would be an elegant, upper-class, seventeenth-century, Parisian interior; or in one of the rooms in the palace where the play was originally presented for the King, and which would represent a royal apartment.

Barrault asked Delbée to make two sketches, which the designer did. Each represented a single formal room, the walls of which were to be depicted on painted canvas. The room in Célimène's house, though done on a smaller scale, was a spacious private *salon,* with a door and two windows in the rear wall, and doors in each of the side walls. The room in the palace was done on a much grander scale, and in false perspective that gave it great height and depth; it had a large central door at the rear and a huge fireplace at one side; openings in the side walls led to other chambers.

Barrault studied the sketches carefully and still could not make up his mind as to which to use, so he had both interiors built and painted, and used them alternately at rehearsals. After a time he asked the actors which décor they preferred, and by a vote they chose the royal apartment, saying that its ornateness and spaciousness gave them more of the feeling of the grandeur of the period, so that they could act with greater freedom and breadth. The drawing-room set was stored away to be used later for another of Molière's plays.

The room in the palace, as designed by Delbée, resembled an old steel engraving; that is, it was painted entirely in black, white, and gray. The starkness of these neutral colors was relieved only by a very narrow border of red and gold near the ceiling. Every inch of wall space was covered with the ornate designs of the aristocratic baroque style; painted on the canvas were cupids in stucco relief, garlands, wreaths, and floral patterns, caryatids perched on fanciful scroll frames, and panels enclosed by columns and pilasters. The fireplace, too, was painted on the canvas.

The furniture was not actually antique although it appeared to be; it was specially designed for the production by Delbée and consisted of straight-backed chairs, armchairs, small stools, and side tables with mirrors above them; the mirrors were painted on the walls. A number of small "props" were on the tables. All of the furnishings were exact reproductions of those in the apartments of Louis XIII and Louis XIV and were made in Delbée's workshops, as were the upholstery fabrics, which suggested rich brocades although actually they were heavy muslin painted red, blue, and gold. The entire décor gave the impression of sumptuousness and formality.

Although the set appeared to be strong and solid, the canvas walls of the room could easily be taken off the pipes from which they were hung and off their frames, and rolled up for traveling. The floor, which represented marble in a black and gray checkerboard pattern, was also painted on canvas and could be rolled up like the walls. The large central door in the rear wall had a removable frame; there were no doors in the left and right walls, only arched openings. Painted backings were seen when the rear doors were opened and outside the openings in the side walls. As Barrault toured with this play in both North and South America, flexibility and ease of handling were major concerns in the basic design of the set, and yet, under lights (Barrault himself did the lighting), the room had great beauty, dignity, and urbanity.

"One of the greatest advantages of the use of neutral background tones in the scenery," said Delbée, "is the fact that it throws the emphasis upon the brilliant and subtle color combinations in the costumes. And yet, strange as it may seem, instead of being ignored, the scenery was singled out for praise by almost every critic who saw the play."

COSTUMES FOR *The Misanthrope*
An Interview with Marcel Escoffier

Marcel Escoffier created the costumes for many of the films of Jean Cocteau, working in close collaboration with Christian Berard who designed the sets. Escoffier won special praise for the costumes he did for *Orphée*, a highly imaginative and fantastic film; and when Cocteau was asked to provide the sketches for the Renaud-Barrault stage production of *Bacchus*, Escoffier was called upon to execute them. When Barrault decided to produce *The Misanthrope*, he offered the job of designing the costumes to Escoffier.

The production plans were worked out very quickly and simply. Delbée's idea to use only black and white as a background for the production gave Escoffier a free hand and made it possible for him to choose any color in the spectrum with the sure knowledge that it would not clash with the scenery. Costume designers usually have a difficult time matching clothing to sets, but this production was a delight to Escoffier, who could give his color sense free rein.

Although he can well afford a large wardrobe, Alceste, who is unpretentious by nature, was given the same costume throughout the play. The other characters, too, were provided with only one costume apiece. Célimène was the single exception; as a foil to Alceste, she was seen in two glorious gowns which provided a striking contrast to the drab colors and simple lines of his suit.

The first gown which Célimène wore was the color of sand or of light caramel and bathed her in a golden aura. It was Louis XIV in style but subtly adapted to the modern taste for *haute couture;* the dress was made of heavy satin, tulle, and organza, and was extremely smart. Escoffier's technique, and one which he has used very often, was to combine several related materials in a single costume. The skirt, for example, of heavy satin, was elaborately embroidered with organza to produce a luxurious and extravagant effect. "I believe in mixing materials," says Escoffier, "in order to emphasize the contrast in textures, to give each material a richness it would not have if it stood alone, and to cause the entire gown to glitter."

Célimène wore a blonde wig in which were fixed soft, curling plumes to match the golden gown, and with this costume she carried a fan made of feathers of bird-of-paradise, arranged like two crossed crescents, which added a note of frivolity. Her satin shoes matched her dress; her jewelry was scintillating; and she wore long white kid gloves.

The second costume in which Célimène appeared was pale blue and off-white, the combination producing a shimmery, watery effect; only white and pale blue lights were used to illuminate the stage. The costume, which was extremely stylized and sophisticated, had an overgown and an underdress. The bodice and the overskirt were a silvery white almost fading into blue and were made of heavy dull satin and faille silk, while the tulle underskirt was a pale and delicate shade of blue. Following the line of the overskirt was a margin, a few inches wide, of blue-white organza placed there to avoid a sharp contrast between the satin and the tulle but to create a soft blending, a sort of smoky fading of the one into the other; the three-quarter sleeves were great puffs of organza.

The ornamentation and accessories that set off the blue gown were masterful creations in themselves. The bodice was elaborately embroidered with beads and pearls, and a beaded bow with half a dozen strands of pendant pearls was affixed to the sleeve below the left shoulder. Rings, earrings, bracelet, and necklace of beads and pearls completed the fantasy.

In Célimène's hair was a diamond brooch in which was set a spray of egrets, according to Escoffier, "like that of a horse in a circus." At times she carried a large handkerchief with a wide border of delicate lace; at other times, a fan of curly plumes from the handle of which hung loops of satin ribbon. She wore long white kid gloves and blue-white satin shoes. From head to toe she sparkled like a blue-white diamond. "She was exciting but cold," says Escoffier, "the quintessence of Célimène!"

Although Escoffier is well aware of the fact that lace was used to excess on the clothing worn in Molière's day, he seldom uses it in his stage designs, even if it means departing from reality, since he does not think that it has much "theatrical" value. No lace was used on either of Célimène's gowns nor on any of the other costumes in this production.

Alceste wore a suit that combined black, gray, and green; a minor concession to fashion were the few loops of dark green ribbon at his right shoulder. The costume was made of wool, with touches of velvet in it; the materials were chosen to characterize a man who was extremely serious, stiff, and formal. The somberness of the costume was relieved only by the white shirt sleeves and cuffs secured with a ribbon at the wrist and by a plain white jabot. No ribbons or buckles enlivened Alceste's black shoes, and there were no decorations or adornments of any kind on his clothing or on his person. He wore a black wig that was uncurled, and to make it even flatter and more unattractive he kept smoothing it down with the palm of his hand.

Arsinoé, the hypocrite, wore a velvet gown of dark red and gray; the overskirt was plum-colored, suggesting subdued passion; while the underskirt was gray to symbolize the woman's false purity. Her hood, shoulder-length cape, long sleeves, and gloves were of royal blue organza; she wore a spray of rubies in her hair and ruby earrings. On her breast was a large, showy cross, but at the same time she had long, sharp, clawlike fingernails—the contrast of the hypocrite.

Philinte is a man of the world who understands the weaknesses of humanity and condones them. His colors were uncomplicated; he wore various shades of brown elegantly put together. His wig was long and curled, in the fashion approved by the Court; it was a chestnut color and matched his costume.

Eliante wore the most charming costume of all; it was light blue and pink, suggested the sweetness and brightness of an innocent young girl, and yet was extremely distinguée. The gown had a "bateau" neckline of stiff organza; on the bodice was a long, triangular bib with a row of buttons which descended from the breast to the waist. Eliante's hair was simply and softly arranged, and except for an oval locket she wore no jewelry; she carried a small handbag of petit-point.

Oronte, the poet, was dressed in flaming red, orange, and green and was meant to suggest a parrot. His enormous wig was reddish-blond and descended to his shoulders in a series of huge corkscrew curls; the wide brim of his large hat was encircled by plumes; and his green gloves were like gauntlets, the stiff cuffs ornamented with fringes. A large muff covered with loops of velvet ribbon was suspended from his neck on a silk cord and hung at his waist; enormous roses bloomed on his shoes; and he wore a great shiny ring on the gloved finger of his right hand.

The two marquises were similarly dressed in that they were both costumed to look like pretentious and ridiculous fools. Since both are exhibitionists and extremely extroverted, they wore shrill, screaming colors. Acaste, who was all in gold, had yards of organza at his wrists and knees, ribbons frothed and floated on his person, and huge rosettes smothered his shoes. Clitandre, in turquoise and blue, was adorned with yards of ribbon done in loops at his throat, shoulders, elbows, wrists, along the edges of his clothes, and on his shoes. Both courtiers had elaborately curled wigs and extravagant hats with enormous plumes. Their ostentatious and flamboyant costumes, all glitter and flutter, dazzled the spectator.

The minor characters, members of the working class, wore simple clothing which did not call attention to itself, since it was unadorned and done in neutral colors.

It is Escoffier's theory that the colors and lines of each costume should indicate clearly the character's psychology as well as his function in the play; if the costume does not fully express the character of its wearer, the designer has failed in his job.

ALCESTE SPEAKS GERMAN
An Interview with Ernst Ginsberg

Talking to Kurt Horwitz, one of the directors of the Schauspielhaus in Zurich, Erich Brock once remarked: "One of these days you ought to produce Molière's *Misanthrope* which is done much too seldom. You have someone in your company for the role of Alceste." He meant Ernst Ginsberg.

Neither the director nor the actor was acquainted with the play; they read it, were fascinated, and decided to do it. "And then wonderful weeks began in the Zurich apartment of Horwitz," says Ginsberg, "where we were surrounded by all the old and new translations of the work accessible to us, and where we composed the German version of the text which we have used in all our productions of the play since then. I still recall—to mention just one example—all the trouble we had at the end of the play where Alceste wants to go into seclusion

> . . . et chercher, sur la terre, un endroit écarté,
> Où d'être homme d'honneur on ait la liberté.

In all the translations we consulted, the words 'man of honor' were too literally expressed by the German *Ehrenmann,* which has the unfortunate connotations of shopkeeper and Philistine. After a great deal of hesitation, we finally dared to translate very freely, 'where one has the freedom to be a *true human being.*' Because that is what the line actually means, and it suits Alceste perfectly."

Ginsberg never tires of praising the play for its complexity and modernity; he is particularly impressed by the manner in which it combines a bold criticism of language and of social conventions with erotic passion and abandonment. The play depicts, as the actor sees it, the defenseless exposure of the naïve man of good will as well as the bitter frustration of the so-called "ultra-modern" woman. "And what a gripping self-portrait of Molière it is," says Ginsberg, "with his genuine feeling for the original and the popular, his contempt for empty estheticism and overblown talk about art, and his manly consideration for a woman which almost ruins him—one knows how much of his heart's blood the poet has poured into the Alceste-Célimène relationship—and all of this is formulated and placed within the framework of the old-fashioned, strict, yet masterfully perfected, rhymed alexandrines.

"Great as the play is, it is not a tragedy and not a comedy; it is pure tragicomedy, the first genuine tragicomedy I have ever come upon in my entire career as an actor. This *genre* fills me with delight, particularly as it is handled by Molière, since it has resulted in a full-blooded character who contains for me the truest and most exhaustive delineation of human life. Tragicomedy is without doubt the most "human" form of the drama, surpassed only, perhaps, by the Christian miracle play; at least, that's the way it seems to me."

Ginsberg has appeared in about six productions of *The Misanthrope*. His first attempt in Zurich, 1943, he admits, only half succeeded. He was much too impressed by the serious aspects of Alceste and modeled the character on Hamlet. This was a mistake, he realized, as the concept was too tragic and too one-sided; Alceste is a many-faceted figure but the difficulty lies in finding the exact balance between the tragic and the comic.

Ginsberg kept working on the role, and in the second production, in Basel, he played Alceste more naïvely and childishly, emphasizing the love story; in addition, he depicted Alceste as a great and powerful spirit with a warm and helpless heart, and came closer to the solution of the problem. Teo Otto's setting and Agnes Fink in the role of Célimène helped enormously; the second production became the basis for all later ones, down to the most recent which he did in Vienna in July, 1959.

"But to go back," said Ginsberg, "we produced the play for a third time, in Munich—it was our first appearance in Germany in sixteen years—and finally we achieved complete success. The premiere was a brilliant triumph for both the play and the production and won, simultaneously, a seat on the Board of Directors of the Bavarian State Theatre for Horwitz and the acclaim of the Munich public for me. We presented the play on German television, and then we went back to Zurich where, in our fourth production of this increasingly popular work, we were finally able to interpret *The Misanthrope* as we had originally conceived it. For me, in the guise of Alceste, the meeting with Molière determined my artistic future.

"The most subtle internal relationship between an actor and the character he portrays cannot be explained verbally and yet the actor must identify himself with and react sympathetically to the fictional creation. The actor, who keeps analyzing his part and working on it, will find that each time he plays it he will be able to merge the contradictory aspects of the character more successfully; that is especially true of a figure as complex as Alceste. His behavior towards Célimène, for instance, shows a remarkable vacillation from the sharpest aggressiveness to the most passive submission; and the struggle and indecision go on throughout the play. Again, although his criticism of his friend Philinte is often caustic and bitter, it is always well-meant; for Philinte represents the average man, who is no better than he ought to be, and whom Alceste probably envies but cannot bring himself to emulate. The misanthrope, who is obsessed by truth, paradoxically loses all his composure and consistency in the face of the glistening deception of Célimène, who surpasses him only in wit.

"Up to the time I attempted this role, I had, I must confess, only a shamefully superficial conception of Molière as a playwright. I thought that he had merely raised the *commedia dell'arte*, with great virtuosity no doubt, to the highest point of its development. I did not have the slightest suspicion of how closely and how completely Molière approaches that other great actor-poet, Shakespeare, in background and in the profundity of his depiction of humanity, or of what unique and exciting discoveries await the actor there in the world of Molière. No other play-wright, it seems to me, has been able to cause the actor to weep and the audience to laugh simultaneously. As I became more actively occupied with the phenom-enon of Molière, I began to understand how the sorrows of a deeply passionate man had been daringly transformed into a light and airy work of art, and how really bravely this man, who had been exposed to hellish tortures, had defended his heart, yes, his very existence, with the shining weapons of the spirit. I knew, too, that I had reached the high point of my artistic love and veneration, and Alceste became my favorite role."

The Misanthrope

DONE INTO ENGLISH VERSE BY RICHARD WILBUR

CHARACTERS

ALCESTE, in love with Célimène
PHILINTE, Alceste's friend
ORONTE, in love with Célimène
CÉLIMÈNE, Alceste's beloved
ELIANTE, Célimène's cousin
ARSINOÉ, a friend of Célimène's

ACASTE ⎫
           ⎬marquesses
CLITANDRE ⎭

BASQUE, Célimène's servant
A GUARD of the Marshalsea
DUBOIS, Alceste's valet

The scene throughout is in Célimène's house at Paris.

ACT ONE. SCENE ONE

PHILINTE, ALCESTE

Philinte. Now, what's got into you?
Alceste (*Seated*)   Kindly leave me alone.
Philinte. Come, come, what is it? This lugubrious tone . . .
Alceste. Leave me, I said; you spoil my solitude.
Philinte. Oh, listen to me, now, and don't be rude.

Alceste. I choose to be rude, Sir, and to be hard of hearing.   5
Philinte. These ugly moods of yours are not endearing;
Friends though we are, I really must insist . . .
Alceste (*Abruptly rising*) Friends? Friends, you say? Well, cross me off your list.
I've been your friend till now, as you well know;
But after what I saw a moment ago

I tell you flatly that our ways must
part.   11
I wish no place in a dishonest heart.
Philinte. Why, what have I done, Al-
ceste? Is this quite just?
Alceste. My God, you ought to die of
self-disgust.
I call your conduct inexcusable, Sir,
And every man of honor will con-
cur.   16
I see you almost hug a man to death,
Exclaim for joy until you're out of
breath,
And supplement these loving demon-
strations
With endless offers, vows, and pro-
testations;   20
Then when I ask you "Who was
that?", I find
That you can barely bring his name
to mind!
Once the man's back is turned, you
cease to love him,
And speak with absolute indifference
of him!
By God, I say it's base and scandal-
ous   25
To falsify the heart's affections thus;
If I caught myself behaving in such
a way,
I'd hang myself for shame, without
delay.
Philinte. It hardly seems a hanging
matter to me;
I hope that you will take it gra-
ciously   30
If I extend myself a slight reprieve,
And live a little longer, by your
leave.
Alceste. How dare you joke about a
crime so grave?
Philinte. What crime? How else are
people to behave?
Alceste. I'd have them be sincere, and
never part   35

With any word that isn't from the
heart.
Philinte. When someone greets us with
a show of pleasure,
It's but polite to give him equal
measure,
Return his love the best that we
know how,
And trade him offer for offer, vow
for vow.   40
Alceste. No, no, this formula you'd
have me follow,
However fashionable, is false and
hollow,
And I despise the frenzied opera-
tions
Of all these barterers of protesta-
tions,
These lavishers of meaningless em-
braces,   45
These utterers of obliging common-
places,
Who court and flatter everyone on
earth
And praise the fool no less than the
man of worth.
Should you rejoice that someone
fondles you,
Offers his love and service, swears to
be true,   50
And fills your ears with praises of
your name,
When to the first damned fop he'll
say the same?
No, no: no self-respecting heart
would dream
Of prizing so promiscuous an esteem;
However high the praise, there's
nothing worse   55
Than sharing honors with the uni-
verse.
Esteem is founded on comparison:
To honor all men is to honor none.
Since you embrace this indiscrimi-
nate vice,

Your friendship comes at far too
cheap a price;   60
I spurn the easy tribute of a heart
Which will not set the worthy man
apart:
I choose, Sir, to be chosen; and in
fine,
The friend of mankind is no friend of
mine.
Philinte. But in polite society, custom
decrees   65
That we show certain outward cour-
tesies. . . .
Alceste. Ah, no! we should condemn
with all our force
Such false and artificial intercourse.
Let men behave like men; let them
display
Their inmost hearts in everything
they say;   70
Let the heart speak, and let our senti-
ments
Not mask themselves in silly compli-
ments.
Philinte. In certain cases it would be
uncouth
And most absurd to speak the naked
truth;
With all respect for your exalted no-
tions,   75
It's often best to veil one's true emo-
tions.
Wouldn't the social fabric come un-
done
If we were wholly frank with everyone?
Suppose you met with someone you
couldn't bear;
Would you inform him of it then and
there?   80
Alceste. Yes.
Philinte.   Then you'd tell old Emilie
it's pathetic
The way she daubs her features with
cosmetic

And plays the gay coquette at sixty-
four?
Alceste. I would.
Philinte. And you'd call Dorilas a
bore,
And tell him every ear at court is
lame   85
From hearing him brag about his
noble name?
Alceste. Precisely.
Philinte.   Ah, you're joking.
Alceste.   *Au contraire:*
In this regard there's none I'd choose
to spare.
All are corrupt; there's nothing to be
seen
In court or town but aggravates my
spleen.   90
I fall into deep gloom and melan-
choly
When I survey the scene of human
folly,
Finding on every hand base flattery,
Injustice, fraud, self-interest, treach-
ery. . . .
Ah, it's too much; mankind has
grown so base,   95
I mean to break with the whole
human race.
Philinte. This philosophic rage is a bit
extreme;
You've no idea how comical you
seem;
Indeed, we're like those brothers in
the play
Called *School for Husbands,* one of
whom was prey . . .   100
Alceste. Enough now! None of your
stupid similes.
Philinte. Then let's have no more ti-
rades, if you please.
The world won't change, whatever
you say or do;
And since plain speaking means so
much to you,

I'll tell you plainly that by being
frank 105
You've earned the reputation of a
crank,
And that you're thought ridiculous
when you rage
And rant against the manners of the
age.
Alceste. So much the better; just what
I wish to hear.
No news could be more grateful to
my ear. 110
All men are so detestable in my eyes,
I should be sorry if they thought me
wise.
Philinte. Your hatred's very sweeping,
is it not?
Alceste. Quite right: I hate the whole
degraded lot.
Philinte. Must all poor human creatures
be embraced, 115
Without distinction, by your vast dis-
taste?
Even in these bad times, there are
surely a few . . .
Alceste. No, I include all men in one
dim view:
Some men I hate for being rogues;
the others
I hate because they treat the rogues
like brothers, 120
And, lacking a virtuous scorn for
what is vile,
Receive the villain with a com-
plaisant smile.
Notice how tolerant people choose to
be
Toward that bold rascal who's at law
with me.
His social polish can't conceal his
nature; 125
One sees at once that he's a treacherous creature;
No one could possibly be taken in

By those soft speeches and that
sugary grin.
The whole world knows the shady
means by which
The low-brow's grown so powerful
and rich, 130
And risen to a rank so bright and high
That virtue can but blush, and merit
sigh.
Whenever his name comes up in con-
versation,
None will defend his wretched repu-
tation;
Call him knave, liar, scoundrel, and
all the rest, 135
Each head will nod, and no one will
protest.
And yet his smirk is seen in every
house,
He's greeted everywhere with smiles
and bows,
And when there's any honor that can
be got
By pulling strings, he'll get it, like as
not. 140
My God! It chills my heart to see the
ways
Men come to terms with evil nowadays;
Sometimes, I swear, I'm moved to
flee and find
Some desert land unfouled by hu-
mankind.
Philinte. Come, let's forget the follies
of the times 145
And pardon mankind for its petty
crimes;
Let's have an end of rantings and of
railings,
And show some leniency toward human failings.
This world requires a pliant rectitude;
Too stern a virtue makes one stiff and
rude; 150

Good sense views all extremes with detestation,
And bids us to be noble in moderation.
The rigid virtues of the ancient days
Are not for us; they jar with all our ways   154
And ask of us too lofty a perfection.
Wise men accept their times without objection,
And there's no greater folly, if you ask me,
Than trying to reform society.
Like you, I see each day a hundred and one
Unhandsome deeds that might be better done,   160
But still, for all the faults that meet my view,
I'm never known to storm and rave like you.
I take men as they are, or let them be,
And teach my soul to bear their frailty;
And whether in court or town, whatever the scene,   165
My phlegm's as philosophic as your spleen.

Alceste. This phlegm which you so eloquently commend,
Does nothing ever rile it up, my friend?
Suppose some man you trust should treacherously
Conspire to rob you of your property,   170
And do his best to wreck your reputation?
Wouldn't you feel a certain indignation?

Philinte. Why, no. These faults of which you so complain
Are part of human nature, I maintain,   174
And it's no more a matter for disgust
That men are knavish, selfish and unjust,
Than that the vulture dines upon the dead,
And wolves are furious, and apes ill-bred.

Alceste. Shall I see myself betrayed, robbed, torn to bits,
And not . . . Oh, let's be still and rest our wits.   180
Enough of reasoning, now. I've had my fill.

Philinte. Indeed, you would do well, Sir, to be still.
Rage less at your opponent, and give some thought
To how you'll win this lawsuit that he's brought.

Alceste. I assure you I'll do nothing of the sort.   185

Philinte. Then who will plead your case before the court?

Alceste. Reason and right and justice will plead for me.

Philinte. Oh, Lord. What judges do you plan to see?

Alceste. Why, none. The justice of my cause is clear.

Philinte. Of course, man; but there's politics to fear. . . .   190

Alceste. No, I refuse to lift a hand. That's flat.
I'm either right, or wrong.

Philinte.   Don't count on that.

Alceste. No, I'll do nothing.

Philinte.   Your enemy's influence
Is great, you know . . .

Alceste.   That makes no difference.

Philinte. It will; you'll see.

Alceste.   Must honor bow to guile?
If so, I shall be proud to lose the trial.   196

Philinte. Oh, really . . .

Alceste.   I'll discover by this case

Whether or not men are sufficiently
base
And impudent and villainous and
perverse   199
To do me wrong before the universe.
Philinte. What a man!
Alceste.   Oh, I could wish, whatever
the cost,
Just for the beauty of it, that my trial
were lost.
Philinte. If people heard you talking so,
Alceste,
They'd split their sides. Your name
would be a jest.
Alceste. So much the worse for jesters.
Philinte.   May I enquire   205
Whether this rectitude you so ad-
mire,
And these hard virtues you're en-
amored of
Are qualities of the lady whom you
love?
It much surprises me that you, who
seem
To view mankind with furious dis-
esteem,   210
Have yet found something to enchant
your eyes
Amidst a species which you so de-
spise.
And what is more amazing, I'm
afraid,
Is the most curious choice your heart
has made.   214
The honest Eliante is fond of you,
Arsinoé, the prude, admires you too;
And yet your spirit's been perversely
led
To choose the flighty Célimène in-
stead,
Whose brittle malice and coquettish
ways   219
So typify the manners of our days.
How is it that the traits you most
abhor

Are bearable in this lady you adore?
Are you so blind with love that you
can't find them?
Or do you contrive, in her case, not
to mind them?
Alceste. My love for that young widow's
not the kind   225
That can't perceive defects; no, I'm
not blind.
I see her faults, despite my ardent
love,
And all I see I fervently reprove.
And yet I'm weak; for all her falsity,
That woman knows the art of pleas-
ing me,   230
And though I never cease com-
plaining of her,
I swear I cannot manage not to love
her.
Her charm outweighs her faults; I
can but aim
To cleanse her spirit in my love's
pure flame.
Philinte. That's no small task; I wish
you all success.   235
You think then that she loves you?
Alceste.   Heavens, yes!
I wouldn't love her did she not love
me.
Philinte. Well, if her taste for you is
plain to see,
Why do these rivals cause you such
despair?
Alceste. True love, Sir, is possessive,
and cannot bear   240
To share with all the world. I'm here
today
To tell her she must send that mob
away.
Philinte. If I were you, and had your
choice to make,
Eliante, her cousin, would be the one
I'd take;
That honest heart, which cares for
you alone,   245

Would harmonize far better with your own.

Alceste. True, true: each day my reason tells me so;

But reason doesn't rule in love, you know.

Philinte. I fear some bitter sorrow is in store;

This love . . .   250

SCENE TWO

ORONTE, ALCESTE, PHILINTE

Oronte (*To* ALCESTE) The servants told me at the door

That Eliante and Célimène were out,

But when I heard, dear Sir, that you were about,

I came to say, without exaggeration,

That I hold you in the vastest admiration,   5

And that it's always been my dearest desire

To be the friend of one I so admire.

I hope to see my love of merit requited,

And you and I in friendship's bond united.

I'm sure you won't refuse—if I may be frank—   10

A friend of my devotedness—and rank.

(*During this speech of* ORONTE'S, ALCESTE *is abstracted, and seems unaware that he is being spoken to. He only breaks off his reverie when* ORONTE *says:*)

It was for you, if you please, that my words were intended.

Alceste. For me, Sir?

Oronte. Yes, for you. You're not offended?

Alceste. By no means. But this much surprises me. . . .

The honor comes most unexpectedly. . . .

Oronte. My high regard should not astonish you;

The whole world feels the same. It is your due.

Alceste. Sir . . .

Oronte. Why, in all the State there isn't one

Can match your merits; they shine, Sir, like the sun.

Alceste. Sir . . .

Oronte. You are higher in my estimation   20

Than all that's most illustrious in the nation.

Alceste. Sir . . .

Oronte. If I lie, may heaven strike me dead!

To show you that I mean what I have said,

Permit me, Sir, to embrace you most sincerely,

And swear that I will prize our friendship dearly.   25

Give me your hand. And now, Sir, if you choose,

We'll make our vows.

Alceste.   Sir . . .

Oronte.   What! You refuse?

Alceste. Sir, it's a very great honor you extend:

But friendship is a sacred thing, my friend;   29

It would be profanation to bestow

The name of friend on one you hardly know.

All parts are better played when well-rehearsed;

Let's put off friendship, and get acquainted first.

We may discover it would be unwise

To try to make our natures harmonize.   35

Oronte. By heaven! You're sagacious to the core;
This speech has made me admire you even more.
Let time, then, bring us closer day by day;
Meanwhile, I shall be yours in every way.
If, for example, there should be anything   40
You wish at court, I'll mention it to the King.
I have his ear, of course; it's quite well known
That I am much in favor with the throne.
In short, I am your servant. And now, dear friend,
Since you have such fine judgment, I intend   45
To please you, if I can, with a small sonnet
I wrote not long ago. Please comment on it,
And tell me whether I ought to publish it.
Alceste. You must excuse me, Sir; I'm hardly fit
To judge such matters.
Oronte.   Why not?
Alceste.   I am, I fear,   50
Inclined to be unfashionably sincere.
Oronte. Just what I ask; I'd take no satisfaction
In anything but your sincere reaction.
I beg you not to dream of being kind.
Alceste. Since you desire it, Sir, I'll speak my mind.   55
Oronte. Sonnet. It's a sonnet. . . .
     Hope . . . The poem's addressed
To a lady who wakened hopes within my breast.
Hope . . . this is not the pompous sort of thing,

Just modest little verses, with a tender ring.
Alceste. Well, we shall see.
Oronte.   Hope . . . I'm anxious to hear   60
Whether the style seems properly smooth and clear,
And whether the choice of words is good or bad.
Alceste. We'll see, we'll see.
Oronte.   Perhaps I ought to add
That it took me only a quarter-hour to write it.
Alceste. The time's irrelevant, Sir: kindly recite it.   65
Oronte (*Reading*) *Hope comforts us awhile, t'is true,*
   Lulling our cares with careless laughter,
   And yet such joy is full of rue,
   My Phyllis, if nothing follows after.
Philinte. I'm charmed by this already; the style's delightful.   70
Alceste (*Sotto voce, to* PHILINTE) How can you say that? Why, the thing is frightful.
Oronte. Your fair face smiled on me awhile,
   But was it kindness so to enchant me?
   'Twould have been fairer not to smile,
   If hope was all you meant to grant me.   75
Philinte. What a clever thought! How handsomely you phrase it!
Alceste (*Sotto voce, to* PHILINTE) You know the thing is trash. How dare you praise it?
Oronte. If it's to be my passion's fate
   Thus everlastingly to wait,
   Then death will come to set me free: 80
   For death is fairer than the fair;
   Phyllis, to hope is to despair

When one must hope eternally.

Philinte. The close is exquisite—full of feeling and grace.

Alceste (*Sotto voce, aside*) Oh, blast the close; you'd better close your face   85
Before you send your lying soul to hell.

Philinte. I can't remember a poem I've liked so well.

Alceste (*Sotto voce, aside*) Good Lord!

Oronte (*To* PHILINTE)   I fear you're flattering me a bit.

Philinte. Oh, no!

Alceste (*Sotto voce, aside*)   What else d'you call it, you hypocrite?

Oronte (*To* ALCESTE) But you, Sir, keep your promise now: don't shrink   90
From telling me sincerely what you think.

Alceste. Sir, these are delicate matters; we all desire
To be told that we've the true poetic fire.
But once, to one whose name I shall not mention,
I said, regarding some verse of his invention,   95
That gentlemen should rigorously control
That itch to write which often afflicts the soul;
That one should curb the heady inclination
To publicize one's little avocation;
And that in showing off one's works of art   100
One often plays a very clownish part.

Oronte. Are you suggesting in a devious way
That I ought not . . .

Alceste.   Oh, that I do not say.
Further, I told him that no fault is worse

Than that of writing frigid, lifeless verse,   105
And that the merest whisper of such a shame
Suffices to destroy a man's good name.

Oronte. D'you mean to say my sonnet's dull and trite?

Alceste. I don't say that. But I went on to cite
Numerous cases of once-respected men   110
Who came to grief by taking up the pen.

Oronte. And am I like them? Do I write so poorly?

Alceste. I don't say that. But I told this person, "Surely
You're under no necessity to compose;
Why you should wish to publish, heaven knows.   115
There's no excuse for printing tedious rot
Unless one writes for bread, as you do not.
Resist temptation, then, I beg of you;
Conceal your pastimes from the public view;
And don't give up, on any provocation,   120
Your present high and courtly reputation,
To purchase at a greedy printer's shop
The name of silly author and scribbling fop."
These were the points I tried to make him see.

Oronte. I sense that they are also aimed at me;   125
But now—about my sonnet—I'd like to be told . . .

Alceste. Frankly, that sonnet should be pigeonholed.

You've chosen the worst models to imitate.
The style's unnatural. Let me illustrate:

For example, *Your fair face smiled on me awhile,* 130
Followed by, *'Twould have been fairer not to smile!*
Or this: *such joy is full of rue;*
Or this: *For death is fairer than the fair;*
Or, *Phyllis, to hope is to despair*
      When one must hope
            eternally! 135

This artificial style, that's all the fashion,
Has neither taste, nor honesty, nor passion;
It's nothing but a sort of wordy play,
And nature never spoke in such a way.
What, in this shallow age, is not debased? 140
Our fathers, though less refined, had better taste;
I'd barter all that men admire today
For one old love-song I shall try to say:

If the King had given me for my own
Paris, his citadel, 145
And I for that must leave alone
Her whom I love so well,
I'd say then to the Crown,
Take back your glittering town;
My darling is more fair, I swear, 150
My darling is more fair.

The rhyme's not rich, the style is rough and old,
But don't you see that it's the purest gold
Beside the tinsel nonsense now preferred,

And that there's passion in its every word? 155

If the King had given me for my own
Paris, his citadel,
And I for that must leave alone
Her whom I love so well,
I'd say then to the Crown, 160
Take back your glittering town;
My darling is more fair, I swear,
My darling is more fair.

There speaks a loving heart. (*To* PHILINTE) You're laughing, eh?
Laugh on, my precious wit. Whatever you say, 165
I hold that song's worth all the bibelots
That people hail today with ah's and oh's.
Oronte. And I maintain my sonnet's very good.
Alceste. It's not at all surprising that you should.
You have your reasons; permit me to have mine 170
For thinking that you cannot write a line.
Oronte. Others have praised my sonnet to the skies.
Alceste. I lack their art of telling pleasant lies.
Oronte. You seem to think you've got no end of wit.
Alceste. To praise your verse, I'd need still more of it. 175
Oronte. I'm not in need of your approval, Sir.
Alceste. That's good; you couldn't have it if you were.
Oronte. Come now, I'll lend you the subject of my sonnet;
I'd like to see you try to improve upon it.
Alceste. I might, by chance, write something just as shoddy; 180

But then I wouldn't show it to everybody.

Oronte. You're most opinionated and
conceited.

Alceste. Go find your flatterers, and be
better treated.

Oronte. Look here, my little fellow,
pray watch your tone.

Alceste. My great big fellow, you'd better watch your own.　185

Philinte (*Stepping between them*) Oh,
please, please, gentlemen! This will
never do.

Oronte. The fault is mine, and I leave
the field to you.
I am your servant, Sir, in every
way.

Alceste. And I, Sir, am your most abject
valet.

Scene Three

PHILINTE, ALCESTE

Philinte. Well, as you see, sincerity in
excess
Can get you into a very pretty
mess;
Oronte was hungry for appreciation. . . .

Alceste. Don't speak to me.

Philinte.　　　　　　　What?

Alceste.　　　　No more conversation.

Philinte. Really, now . . .

Alceste.　　　　Leave me alone.

Philinte.　　　　If I . . .

Alceste.　　　　　Out of my sight!

Philinte. But what . . .　　　　6

Alceste.　　　I won't listen.

Philinte.　　　　　　But . . .

Alceste.　　　　　　Silence!

Philinte.　　Now, is it polite . . .

Alceste. By heaven, I've had enough.
Don't follow me.

Philinte. Ah, you're just joking. I'll keep
you company.

Act Two. Scene One.

ALCESTE, CÉLIMÈNE

Alceste. Shall I speak plainly, Madam?
I confess
Your conduct gives me infinite dis-
tress,
And my resentment's grown too hot
to smother.
Soon, I foresee, we'll break with one
another.
If I said otherwise, I should deceive
you;　　　　5
Sooner or later, I shall be forced to
leave you,
And if I swore that we shall never
part,
I should misread the omens of my
heart.

Célimène. You kindly saw me home, it
would appear,　　　　9
So as to pour invectives in my ear.

Alceste. I've no desire to quarrel. But I
deplore
Your inability to shut the door
On all these suitors who beset you
so.
There's what annoys me, if you care
to know.

Célimène. Is it my fault that all these
men pursue me?　　　　15
Am I to blame if they're attracted to
me?
And when they gently beg an audience,
Ought I to take a stick and drive
them hence?

Alceste. Madam, there's no necessity
for a stick;
A less responsive heart would do the
trick.　　　　20
Of your attractiveness I don't complain;
But those your charms attract, you
then detain

By a most melting and receptive
manner,
And so enlist their hearts beneath
your banner.
It's the agreeable hopes which you
excite   25
That keep these lovers round you
day and night;
Were they less liberally smiled upon,
That sighing troop would very soon
be gone.
But tell me, Madam, why it is that
lately
This man Clitandre interests you so
greatly?   30
Because of what high merits do you
deem
Him worthy of the honor of your
esteem?
Is it that your admiring glances
linger
On the splendidly long nail of his
little finger?
Or do you share the general deep
respect   35
For the blond wig he chooses to af-
fect?
Are you in love with his embroidered
hose?
Do you adore his ribbons and his
bows?
Or is it that this paragon bewitches
Your tasteful eye with his vast German
breeches?   40
Perhaps his giggle, or his falsetto
voice,
Makes him the latest gallant of your
choice?
Célimène. You're much mistaken to
resent him so.
Why I put up with him you surely
know: 44
My lawsuit's very shortly to be tried,
And I must have his influence on my
side.

Alceste. Then lose your lawsuit,
Madam, or let it drop;
Don't torture me by humoring such a
fop.
Célimène. You're jealous of the whole
world, Sir.
Alceste.   That's true,
Since the whole world is well-re-
ceived by you.   50
Célimène. That my good nature is so
unconfined
Should serve to pacify your jealous
mind;
Were I to smile on one, and scorn
the rest,
Then you might have some cause to
be distressed.
Alceste. Well, if I mustn't be jealous,
tell me, then,   55
Just how I'm better treated than
other men.
Célimène. You know you have my love.
Will that not do?
Alceste. What proof have I that what
you say is true?
Célimène. I would expect, Sir, that my
having said it
Might give the statement a sufficient
credit.   60
Alceste. But how can I be sure that you
don't tell
The selfsame thing to other men as
well?
Célimène. What a gallant speech! How
flattering to me!
What a sweet creature you make me
out to be!
Well then, to save you from the pangs
of doubt,   65
All that I've said I hereby cancel out;
Now, none but yourself shall make a
monkey of you:
Are you content?
Alceste.   Why, why am I doomed to
love you?

I swear that I shall bless the blissful
   hour
When this poor heart's no longer in
   your power!   70
I make no secret of it: I've done my
   best
To exorcise this passion from my
   breast;
But thus far all in vain; it will not
   go;
It's for my sins that I must love you
   so.
Célimène. Your love for me is match-
   less, Sir; that's clear.   75
Alceste. Indeed, in all the world it has
   no peer;
Words can't describe the nature of
   my passion,
And no man ever loved in such a
   fashion.
Célimène. Yes, it's a brand-new fashion,
   I agree:
You show your love by castigating
   me,   80
And all your speeches are enraged
   and rude.
I've never been so furiously wooed.
Alceste. Yet you could calm that fury,
   if you chose.
Come, shall we bring our quarrels to
   a close?
Let's speak with open hearts, then,
   and begin . . .   85

Scene Two

CÉLIMÈNE, ALCESTE, BASQUE

Célimène. What is it?
Basque.   Acaste is here.
Célimène.   Well, send him in.

Scene Three

CÉLIMÈNE, ALCESTE

Alceste. What! Shall we never be alone
   at all?
You're always ready to receive a call,

And you can't bear, for ten ticks of
   the clock,
Not to keep open house for all who
   knock.
Célimène. I couldn't refuse him: he'd
   be most put out.   5
Alceste. Surely that's not worth worry-
   ing about.
Célimène. Acaste would never forgive
   me if he guessed
That I consider him a dreadful pest.
Alceste. If he's a pest, why bother with
   him then?
Célimène. Heavens! One can't antag-
   onize such men;   10
Why, they're the chartered gossips of
   the court,
And have a say in things of every
   sort.
One must receive them, and be full
   of charm;
They're no great help, but they can
   do you harm,
And though your influence be ever
   so great,   15
They're hardly the best people to
   alienate.
Alceste. I see, dear lady, that you could
   make a case
For putting up with the whole human race;
These friendships that you calculate
   so nicely . . .

Scene Four

ALCESTE, CÉLIMÈNE, BASQUE

Basque. Madam, Clitandre is here as
   well.
Alceste.   Precisely.
Célimène. Where are you going?
Alceste.   Elsewhere.
Célimène.   Stay.
Alceste.   No, no.
Célimène. Stay, Sir.

Alceste.   I can't.
Célimène.   I wish it.
Alceste.   No, I must go.
  I beg you, Madam, not to press the
    matter;
  You know I have no taste for idle
    chatter.   5
Célimène. Stay: I command you.
Alceste.   No, I cannot stay.
Célimène. Very well; you have my
    leave to go away.

Scene Five

ELIANTE, PHILINTE, ACASTE, CLITANDRE,
    ALCESTE, CÉLIMÈNE, BASQUE

Eliante (*To* Célimène) The Mar-
    quesses have kindly come to call.
  Were they announced?
Célimène.   Yes. Basque, bring chairs
    for all.

(Basque *provides the chairs, and
exits.*)
(*To* Alceste)

  You haven't gone?
Alceste.   No; and I shan't depart
  Till you decide who's foremost in
    your heart.
Célimène. Oh, hush.
Alceste.   It's time to choose; take
    them, or me.   5
Célimène. You're mad.
Alceste.   I'm not, as you shall shortly
    see.
Célimène. Oh?
Alceste.   You'll decide.
Célimène.   You're joking now,
    dear friend.
Alceste. No, no; you'll choose; my pa-
    tience is at an end.
Clitandre. Madam, I come from court,
    where poor Cléonte
  Behaved like a perfect fool, as is his
    wont.   10

Has he no friend to counsel him, I
    wonder,
  And teach him less unerringly to
    blunder?
Célimène. It's true, the man's a most
    accomplished dunce;
  His gauche behavior strikes the eye
    at once;
  And every time one sees him, on my
    word,   15
  His manner's grown a trifle more ab-
    surd.
Acaste. Speaking of dunces, I've just
    now conversed
  With old Damon, who's one of the
    very worst;
  I stood a lifetime in the broiling sun
  Before his dreary monologue was
    done.   20
Célimène. Oh, he's a wondrous talker,
    and has the power
  To tell you nothing hour after hour:
  If, by mistake, he ever came to the
    point,
  The shock would put his jawbone
    out of joint.
Eliante (*To* Philinte) The conversa-
    tion takes its usual turn,   25
  And all our dear friends' ears will
    shortly burn.
Clitandre. Timante's a character,
    Madam.
Célimène.   Isn't he, though?
  A man of mystery from top to toe,
  Who moves about in a romantic mist
  On secret missions which do not
    exist.   30
  His talk is full of eyebrows and
    grimaces;
  How tired one gets of his momentous
    faces;
  He's always whispering something
    confidential
  Which turns out to be quite inconse-
    quential;

Nothing's too slight for him to mys-
tify;   35
He even whispers when he says
"good-by."

Acaste. Tell us about Géralde.

Célimène.   That tiresome ass.
He mixes only with the titled class,
And fawns on dukes and princes, and
is bored
With anyone who's not at least a
lord.   40
The man's obsessed with rank, and
his discourses
Are all of hounds and carriages and
horses;
He uses Christian names with all the
great,
And the word Milord, with him, is
out of date.

Clitandre. He's very taken with Bélise,
I hear.   45

Célimène. She is the dreariest company,
poor dear.
Whenever she comes to call, I grope
about
To find some topic which will draw
her out,
But, owing to her dry and faint re-
plies,
The conversation wilts, and droops,
and dies.   50
In vain one hopes to animate her face
By mentioning the ultimate common-
place;
But sun or shower, even hail or frost
Are matters she can instantly exhaust.
Meanwhile her visit, painful though
it is,   55
Drags on and on through mute
eternities,
And though you ask the time, and
yawn, and yawn,
She sits there like a stone and won't
be gone.

Acaste. Now for Adraste.

Célimène.   Oh, that conceited elf
Has a gigantic passion for himself;
He rails against the court, and cannot
bear it   61
That none will recognize his hidden
merit;
All honors given to others give of-
fense
To his imaginary excellence.

Clitandre. What about young Cléon?
His house, they say,   65
Is full of the best society, night and
day.

Célimène. His cook has made him
popular, not he:
It's Cléon's table that people come to
see.

Eliante. He gives a splendid dinner,
you must admit.

Célimène. But must he serve himself
along with it?   70
For my taste, he's a most insipid
dish
Whose presence sours the wine and
spoils the fish.

Philinte. Damis, his uncle, is admired
no end.
What's your opinion, Madam?

Célimène.   Why, he's my friend.

Philinte. He seems a decent fellow, and
rather clever.   75

Célimène. He works too hard at clever-
ness, however.
I hate to see him sweat and struggle
so
To fill his conversation with bons
mots.
Since he's decided to become a wit
His taste's so pure that nothing
pleases it;   80
He scolds at all the latest books and
plays,
Thinking that wit must never stoop
to praise,
That finding fault's a sign of intellect,

That all appreciation is abject,
And that by damning everything in
sight   85
One shows oneself in a distinguished
light.
He's scornful even of our conversations:
Their trivial nature sorely tries his
patience;
He folds his arms, and stands above
the battle,
And listens sadly to our childish prat-
tle.   90
Acaste. Wonderful, Madam! You've hit
him off precisely.
Clitandre. No one can sketch a character so nicely.
Alceste. How bravely, Sirs, you cut and
thrust at all
These absent fools, till one by one
they fall:
But let one come in sight, and you'll
at once   95
Embrace the man you lately called a
dunce,
Telling him in a tone sincere and
fervent
How proud you are to be his humble
servant.
Clitandre. Why pick on us? Madame's
been speaking, Sir,
And you should quarrel, if you must,
with her.   100
Alceste. No, no, by God, the fault is
yours, because
You lead her on with laughter and
applause,
And make her think that she's the
more delightful
The more her talk is scandalous and
spiteful.
Oh, she would stoop to malice far,
far less   105
If no such claque approved her
cleverness.

It's flatterers like you whose foolish
praise
Nourishes all the vices of these days.
Philinte. But why protest when some-
one ridicules
Those you'd condemn, yourself, as
knaves or fools?   110
Célimène. Why, Sir? Because he loves
to make a fuss.
You don't expect him to agree with
us,
When there's an opportunity to ex-
press
His heaven-sent spirit of contrari-
ness?
What other people think, he can't
abide;   115
Whatever they say, he's on the other
side;
He lives in deadly terror of agreeing;
'Twould make him seem an ordinary
being.
Indeed, he's so in love with contradic-
tion,
He'll turn against his most profound
conviction   120
And with a furious eloquence de-
plore it,
If only someone else is speaking for
it.
Alceste. Go on, dear lady, mock me as
you please;
You have your audience in ecstasies.
Philinte. But what she says is true: you
have a way   125
Of bridling at whatever people say;
Whether they praise or blame, your
angry spirit
Is equally unsatisfied to hear it.
Alceste. Men, Sir, are always wrong,
and that's the reason
That righteous anger's never out of
season;   130
All that I hear in all their conversa-
tion

Is flattering praise or reckless con-
        demnation.
Célimène. But . . .
Alceste.   No, no, Madam, I am
        forced to state
That you have pleasures which I
        deprecate,
And that these others, here, are much
        to blame   135
For nourishing the faults which are
        your shame.
Clitandre. I shan't defend myself, Sir;
        but I vow
I'd thought this lady faultless until
        now.
Acaste. I see her charms and graces,
        which are many;
But as for faults, I've never noticed
        any.   140
Alceste. I see them, Sir; and rather than
        ignore them,
I strenuously criticize her for them.
The more one loves, the more one
        should object
To every blemish, every least defect.
Were I this lady, I would soon get
        rid   145
Of lovers who approved of all I
        did,
And by their slack indulgence and
        applause
Endorsed my follies and excused my
        flaws.
Célimène. If all hearts beat according
        to your measure,
The dawn of love would be the end
        of pleasure;   150
And love would find its perfect con-
        summation
In ecstasies of rage and reprobation.
Eliante. Love, as a rule, affects men
        otherwise,
And lovers rarely love to criticize.
They see their lady as a charming
        blur,   155

And find all things commendable in
        her.
If she has any blemish, fault, or
        shame,
They will redeem it by a pleasing
        name.
The pale-faced lady's lily-white, per-
        force;
The swarthy one's a sweet brunette,
        of course;   160
The spindly lady has a slender grace;
The fat one has a most majestic pace;
The plain one, with her dress in dis-
        array,
They classify as *beauté négligée;*
The hulking one's a goddess in their
        eyes,   165
The dwarf, a concentrate of Para-
        dise;
The haughty lady has a noble mind;
The mean one's witty, and the dull
        one's kind;
The chatterbox has liveliness and
        verve,   169
The mute one has a virtuous reserve.
So lovers manage, in their passion's
        cause,
To love their ladies even for their
        flaws.
Alceste. But I still say . . .
Célimène.   I think it would be nice
To stroll around the gallery once or
        twice.
What! You're not going, Sirs?
Clitandre and Acaste.   No, Madam,
        no.   175
Alceste. You seem to be in terror lest
        they go.
Do what you will, Sirs; leave, or
        linger on,
But I shan't go till after you are gone.
Acaste. I'm free to linger, unless I
        should perceive
Madame is tired, and wishes me to
        leave.   180

Clitandre. And as for me, I needn't go
   today
Until the hour of the King's *coucher.*
Célimène (*To* ALCESTE) You're joking,
   surely?
Alceste.   Not in the least; we'll see
   Whether you'd rather part with
   them, or me.

SCENE SIX

ALCESTE, CÉLIMÈNE, ELIANTE, ACASTE,
   PHILINTE, CLITANDRE, BASQUE

Basque (*To* ALCESTE) Sir, there's a
   fellow here who bids me state
That he must see you, and that it
   can't wait.
Alceste. Tell him that I have no such
   pressing affairs.
Basque. It's a long tailcoat that this
   fellow wears,
With gold all over.
Célimène (*To* ALCESTE)   You'd best
   go down and see.   5
Or—have him enter.

SCENE SEVEN

ALCESTE, CÉLIMÈNE, ELIANTE, ACASTE,
PHILINTE, CLITANDRE, A GUARD of the
   Marshalsea

Alceste (*Confronting the* GUARD) Well,
   what do you want with me?
   Come in, Sir.
Guard.   I've a word, Sir, for your ear.
Alceste. Speak it aloud, Sir; I shall
   strive to hear.
Guard. The Marshals have instructed
   me to say
You must report to them without
   delay.   5
Alceste. Who? Me, Sir?
Guard.   Yes, Sir; you.
Alceste.   But what do they want?
Philinte (*To* ALCESTE) To scotch your
   silly quarrel with Oronte.

Célimène (*To* PHILINTE) What quar-
   rel?
Philinte. Oronte and he have fallen out
   Over some verse he spoke his mind
   about;
The Marshals wish to arbitrate the
   matter.   10
Alceste. Never shall I equivocate or
   flatter!
Philinte. You'd best obey their sum-
   mons; come, let's go.
Alceste. How can they mend our quar-
   rel, I'd like to know?
Am I to make a cowardly retraction,
And praise those jingles to his satis-
   faction?   15
I'll not recant; I've judged that son-
   net rightly.
It's bad.
Philinte.   But you might say so more
   politely. . . .
Alceste. I'll not back down; his verses
   make me sick.
Philinte. If only you could be more
   politic!   19
But come, let's go.
Alceste.   I'll go, but I won't unsay
A single word.
Philinte.   Well, let's be on our way.
Alceste. Till I am ordered by my lord
   the King
To praise that poem, I shall say the
   thing
Is scandalous, by God, and that the
   poet
Ought to be hanged for having the
   nerve to show it.   25

(*To* CLITANDRE *and* ACASTE, *who are
laughing*)

By heaven, Sirs, I really didn't know
That I was being humorous.
Célimène.   Go, Sir, go;
Settle your business.

Alceste.　I shall, and when I'm through,

I shall return to settle things with you

ACT THREE. SCENE ONE.

CLITANDRE, ACASTE

Clitandre. Dear Marquess, how contented you appear;

All things delight you, nothing mars your cheer.

Can you, in perfect honesty, declare

That you've a right to be so debonair?

Acaste. By Jove, when I survey myself, I find　　　　　5

No cause whatever for distress of mind.

I'm young and rich; I can in modesty

Lay claim to an exalted pedigree;

And owing to my name and my condition

I shall not want for honors and position.　　　　　10

Then as to courage, that most precious trait,

I seem to have it, as was proved of late

Upon the field of honor, where my bearing,

They say, was very cool and rather daring.

I've wit, of course; and taste in such perfection　　　　　15

That I can judge without the least reflection,

And at the theater, which is my delight,

Can make or break a play on opening night,

And lead the crowd in hisses or bravos,

And generally be known as one who knows.　　　　　20

I'm clever, handsome, gracefully polite;

My waist is small, my teeth are strong and white;

As for my dress, the world's astonished eyes

Assure me that I bear away the prize.

I find myself in favor everywhere,

Honored by men, and worshiped by the fair;　　　　　26

And since these things are so, it seems to me

I'm justified in my complacency.

Clitandre. Well, if so many ladies hold you dear,

Why do you press a hopeless courtship here?　　　　　30

Acaste. Hopeless, you say? I'm not the sort of fool

That likes his ladies difficult and cool.

Men who are awkward, shy, and peasantish

May pine for heartless beauties, if they wish,

Grovel before them, bear their cruelties,　　　　　35

Woo them with tears and sighs and bended knees,

And hope by dogged faithfulness to gain

What their poor merits never could obtain.

For men like me, however, it makes no sense

To love on trust, and foot the whole expense.　　　　　40

Whatever any lady's merits be,

I think, thank God, that I'm as choice as she;

That if my heart is kind enough to burn

For her, she owes me something in return;　　　　　44

And that in any proper love affair
The partners must invest an equal
  share.
Clitandre. You think, then, that our
  hostess favors you?
Acaste. I've reason to believe that that
  is true.
Clitandre. How did you come to such
  a mad conclusion?
You're blind, dear fellow. This is
  sheer delusion.   50
Acaste. All right, then: I'm deluded
  and I'm blind.
Clitandre. Whatever put the notion in
  your mind?
Acaste. Delusion.
Clitandre.   What persuades you that
  you're right?
Acaste. I'm blind.
Clitandre.   But have you any proofs
  to cite?
Acaste. I tell you I'm deluded.
Clitandre.   Have you, then, 55
  Received some secret pledge from
  Célimène?
Acaste. Oh, no: she scorns me.
Clitandre.   Tell me the truth, I beg.
Acaste. She just can't bear me.
Clitandre.   Ah, don't pull my leg.
  Tell me what hope she's given you, I
  pray.
Acaste. I'm hopeless, and it's you who
  win the day.   60
She hates me thoroughly, and I'm so
  vexed
I mean to hang myself on Tuesday
  next.
Clitandre. Dear Marquess, let us have
  an armistice
And make a treaty. What do you say
  to this?
If ever one of us can plainly prove 65
That Célimène encourages his love,
The other must abandon hope, and
  yield,

And leave him in possession of the
  field.
Acaste. Now, there's a bargain that appeals to me;
With all my heart, dear Marquess, I
  agree   70
But hush.

Scene Two

CÉLIMÈNE, ACASTE, CLITANDRE

Célimène. Still here?
Clitandre.   T'was love that stayed
  our feet.
Célimène. I think I heard a carriage
  in the street.
  Whose is it? D'you know?

Scene Three

CÉLIMÈNE, ACASTE, CLITANDRE, BASQUE

Basque.   Arsinoé is here,
  Madame.
Célimène.   Arsinoé, you say? Oh,
  dear.
Basque. Eliante is entertaining her be-
  low.
Célimène. What brings the creature
  here, I'd like to know?
Acaste. They say she's dreadfully prud-
  ish, but in fact   5
I think her piety   . .
Célimène.   It's all an act.
At heart she's worldly, and her poor
  success
In snaring men explains her prudish-
  ness.
It breaks her heart to see the beaux
  and gallants
Engrossed by other women's charms
  and talents,   10
And so she's always in a jealous rage
Against the faulty standards of the
  age.
She lets the world believe that she's
  a prude
To justify her loveless solitude,

And strives to put a brand of moral
    shame   15
On all the graces that she cannot
    claim.
But still she'd love a lover; and
    Alceste
Appears to be the one she'd love the
    best.
His visits here are poison to her
    pride;
She seems to think I've lured him
    from her side;   20
And everywhere, at court or in the
    town,
The spiteful, envious woman runs me
    down.
In short, she's just as stupid as can
    be,
Vicious and arrogant in the last de-
    gree,
And . . .   25

SCENE FOUR

ARSINOÉ, CÉLIMÈNE, CLITANDRE, ACASTE

Célimène. Ah! What happy chance has
    brought you here?
I've thought about you ever so much,
    my dear.
Arsinoé. I've come to tell you some-
    thing you should know.
Célimène. How good of you to think of
    doing so!

(CLITANDRE *and* ACASTE *go out,
laughing.*)

SCENE FIVE

ARSINOÉ, CÉLIMÈNE

Arsinoé. It's just as well those gentle-
    men didn't tarry.
Célimène. Shall we sit down?
Arsinoé.   That won't be necessary.
Madam, the flame of friendship
    ought to burn

Brightest in matters of the most con-
    cern,
And as there's nothing which con-
    cerns us more   5
Than honor, I have hastened to your
    door
To bring you, as your friend, some
    information
About the status of your reputation.
I visited, last night, some virtuous
    folk,
And, quite by chance, it was of you
    they spoke;   10
There was, I fear, no tendency to
    praise
Your light behavior and your dash-
    ing ways.
The quantity of gentlemen you see
And your by now notorious coquetry
Were both so vehemently criticized
By everyone, that I was much sur-
    prised.   16
Of course, I needn't tell you where I
    stood;
I came to your defense as best I
    could,
Assured them you were harmless,
    and declared
Your soul was absolutely unimpaired.
But there are some things, you must
    realize,   21
One can't excuse, however hard one
    tries,
And I was forced at last into con-
    ceding
That your behavior, Madam, is mis-
    leading,
That it makes a bad impression, giv-
    ing rise   25
To ugly gossip and obscene surmise,
And that if you were more *overtly*
    good,
You wouldn't be so much misunder-
    stood.

Not that I think you've been unchaste
—no! no!
The saints preserve me from a
thought so low!   30
But mere good conscience never did
suffice:
One must avoid the outward show of
vice.
Madam, you're too intelligent, I'm
sure,
To think my motives anything but
pure
In offering you this counsel—which
I do   35
Out of a zealous interest in you.
Célimène. Madam, I haven't taken you
amiss;
I'm very much obliged to you for
this;
And I'll at once discharge the obliga-
tion
By telling you about *your* reputa-
tion.   40
You've been so friendly as to let me
know
What certain people say of me, and
so
I mean to follow your benign ex-
ample
By offering you a somewhat similar
sample.   44
The other day, I went to an affair
And found some most distinguished
people there
Discussing piety, both false and true.
The conversation soon came round to
you.
Alas! Your prudery and bustling
zeal
Appeared to have a very slight ap-
peal.   50
Your affectation of a grave demeanor,
Your endless talk of virtue and of
honor,

The aptitude of your suspicious mind
For finding sin where there is none
to find,
Your towering self-esteem, that pity-
ing face   55
With which you contemplate the hu-
man race,
Your sermonizings and your sharp
aspersions
On people's pure and innocent diver-
sions—
All these were mentioned, Madam,
and, in fact,
Were roundly and concertedly at-
tacked.   60
"What good," they said, "are all these
outward shows,
When everything belies her pious
pose?
She prays incessantly; but then, they
say,
She beats her maids and cheats them
of their pay;
She shows her zeal in every holy
place,   65
But still she's vain enough to paint
her face;
She holds that naked statues are immoral,
But with a naked *man* she'd have no
quarrel."
Of course, I said to everybody there
That they were being viciously un-
fair;   70
But still they were disposed to criti-
cize you,
And all agreed that someone should
advise you
To leave the morals of the world
alone,
And worry rather more about your
own.
They felt that one's self-knowledge
should be great   75

Before one thinks of setting others
straight;
That one should learn the art of living well
Before one threatens other men with
hell,
And that the Church is best
equipped, no doubt,
To guide our souls and root our vices
out.   80
Madam, you're too intelligent, I'm
sure,
To think my motives anything but
pure
In offering you this counsel—which I
do
Out of a zealous interest in you.

Arsinoé. I dared not hope for gratitude,
but I   85
Did not expect so acid a reply;
I judge, since you've been so extremely tart,
That my good counsel pierced you to
the heart.

Célimène. Far from it, Madam. Indeed,
it seems to me
We ought to trade advice more frequently.   90
One's vision of oneself is so defec-
tive
That it would be an excellent cor-
rective.
If you are willing, Madam, let's arrange
Shortly to have another frank exchange
In which we'll tell each other, *entre
nous,*   95
What you've heard tell of me, and I
of you.

Arsinoé. Oh, people never censure you,
my dear;
It's me they criticize. Or so I hear.

Célimène. Madam, I think we either
blame or praise

According to our taste and length of
days.   100
There is a time of life for coquetry,
And there's a season, too, for prudery.
When all one's charms are gone, it is,
I'm sure,
Good strategy to be devout and
pure:
It makes one seem a little less for-
saken.   105
Some day, perhaps, I'll take the road
you've taken:
Time brings all things. But I have
time aplenty,
And see no cause to be a prude at
twenty.

Arsinoé. You give your age in such a
gloating tone
That one would think I was an an-
cient crone;   110
We're not so far apart, in sober truth,
That you can mock me with a boast
of youth!
Madam, you baffle me, I wish I knew
What moves you to provoke me as
you do.

Célimène. For my part, Madam, I
should like to know   115
Why you abuse me everywhere you
go.
Is it my fault, dear lady, that your
hand
Is not, alas, in very great demand?
If men admire me, if they pay me
court   119
And daily make me offers of the sort
You'd dearly love to have them make
to you,
How can I help it? What would you
have me do?
If what you want is lovers, please feel
free
To take as many as you can from me.

Arsinoé. Oh, come. D'you think the
world is losing sleep   125

Over that flock of lovers which you keep,
Or that we find it difficult to guess
What price you pay for their devotedness?
Surely you don't expect us to suppose
Mere merit could attract so many beaux?   130
It's not your virtue that they're dazzled by;
Nor is it virtuous love for which they sigh.
You're fooling no one, Madam; the world's not blind;
There's many a lady heaven has designed
To call men's noblest, tenderest feelings out,   135
Who has no lovers dogging her about;
From which it's plain that lovers nowadays
Must be acquired in bold and shameless ways,
And only pay one court for such reward   139
As modesty and virtue can't afford.
Then don't be quite so puffed up, if you please,
About your tawdry little victories;
Try, if you can, to be a shade less vain,
And treat the world with somewhat less disdain.   144
If one were envious of your amours,
One soon could have a following like yours;
Lovers are no great trouble to collect
If one prefers them to one's self-respect.

Célimène. Collect them then, my dear; I'd love to see
You demonstrate that charming theory;   150
Who knows, you might . . .

Arsinoé.   Now, Madam, that will do;
It's time to end this trying interview.
My coach is late in coming to your door,
Or I'd have taken leave of you before.

Célimène. Oh, please don't feel that you must rush away;   155
I'd be delighted, Madam, if you'd stay.
However, lest my conversation bore you,
Let me provide some better company for you;
This gentleman, who comes most apropos,
Will please you more than I could do, I know.   160

SCENE SIX

ALCESTE, CÉLIMÈNE, ARSINOÉ

Célimène. Alceste, I have a little note to write
Which simply must go out before tonight;
Please entertain *Madame;* I'm sure that she
Will overlook my incivility.

SCENE SEVEN

ALCESTE, ARSINOÉ

Arsinoé. Well, Sir, our hostess graciously contrives
For us to chat until my coach arrives;
And I shall be forever in her debt
For granting me this little tête-à-tête.
We women very rightly give our hearts   5
To men of noble character and parts,
And your especial merits, dear Alceste,
Have roused the deepest sympathy in my breast.

Oh, how I wish they had sufficient
  sense
At court, to recognize your excel-
  lence!   10
They wrong you greatly, Sir. How it
  must hurt you
Never to be rewarded for your vir-
  tue!
Alceste. Why, Madam, what cause have
  I to feel aggrieved?
What great and brilliant thing have
  I achieved?
What service have I rendered to the
  King   15
That I should look to him for any-
  thing?
Arsinoé. Not everyone who's honored
  by the State
Has done great services. A man must
  wait
Till time and fortune offer him the
  chance.   19
Your merit, Sir, is obvious at a glance,
And . . .
Alceste.   Ah, forget my merit; I'm
  not neglected.
The court, I think, can hardly be
  expected
To mine men's souls for merit, and
  unearth
Our hidden virtues and our secret
  worth.
Arsinoé. *Some* virtues, though, are far
  too bright to hide;   25
Yours are acknowledged, Sir, on
  every side.
Indeed, I've heard you warmly
  praised of late
By persons of considerable weight.
Alceste. This fawning age has praise
  for everyone,
And all distinctions, Madam, are un-
  done.   30
All things have equal honor nowadays,

And no one should be gratified by
  praise.
To be admired, one only need exist,
And every lackey's on the honors
  list.
Arsinoé. I only wish, Sir, that you had
  your eye   35
On some position at court, however
  high;
You'd only have to hint at such a
  notion
For me to set the proper wheels in
  motion;
I've certain friendships I'd be glad to
  use
To get you any office you might
  choose.   40
Alceste. Madam, I fear that any such
  ambition
Is wholly foreign to my disposition.
The soul God gave me isn't of the
  sort
That prospers in the weather of a
  court.
It's all too obvious that I don't pos-
  sess   45
The virtues necessary for success.
My one great talent is for speaking
  plain;
I've never learned to flatter or to
  feign;
And anyone so stupidly sincere   49
Had best not seek a courtier's career.
Outside the court, I know, one must
  dispense
With honors, privilege, and influ-
  ence;
But still one gains the right, forego-
  ing these,
Not to be tortured by the wish to
  please.
One needn't live in dread of snubs
  and slights,   55
Nor praise the verse that every idiot
  writes,

Nor humor silly Marquesses, nor be-
stow
Politic sighs on Madam So-and-So.
Arsinoé. Forget the court, then; let the
matter rest.
But I've another cause to be dis-
tressed   60
About your present situation, Sir.
It's to your love affair that I refer.
She whom you love, and who pre-
tends to love you,
Is, I regret to say, unworthy of you.
Alceste. Why, Madam! Can you seri-
ously intend   65
To make so grave a charge against
your friend?
Arsinoé. Alas, I must. I've stood aside
too long
And let that lady do you grievous
wrong;
But now my debt to conscience shall
be paid:
I tell you that your love has been be-
trayed.   70
Alceste. I thank you, Madam; you're
extremely kind.
Such words are soothing to a lover's
mind.
Arsinoé. Yes, though she *is* my friend,
I say again
You're very much too good for
Célimène.
She's wantonly misled you from the
start.   75
Alceste. You may be right; who knows
another's heart?
But ask yourself if it's the part of
charity
To shake my soul with doubts of her
sincerity.
Arsinoé. Well, if you'd rather be a dupe
than doubt her,
That's your affair. I'll say no more
about her.   80

Alceste. Madam, you know that doubt
and vague suspicion
Are painful to a man in my position;
It's most unkind to worry me this
way
Unless you've some real proof of
what you say.
Arsinoé. Sir, say no more: all doubt
shall be removed,   85
And all that I've been saying shall be
proved.
You've only to escort me home, and
there
We'll look into the heart of this affair.
I've ocular evidence which will persuade you
Beyond a doubt, that Célimène's betrayed you.   90
Then, if you're saddened by that
revelation,
Perhaps I can provide some consolation.

ACT FOUR. SCENE ONE.

ELIANTE, PHILINTE

Philinte. Madam, he acted like a stubborn child;
I thought they never would be reconciled;
In vain we reasoned, threatened, and
appealed;
He stood his ground and simply
would not yield.
The Marshals, I feel sure, have never
heard   5
An argument so splendidly absurd.
"No, gentlemen," said he, "I'll not
retract.
His verse is bad: extremely bad, in
fact.
Surely it does the man no harm to
know it.
Does it disgrace him, not to be a
poet?   10

A gentleman may be respected still,
Whether he writes a sonnet well or
ill.
That I dislike his verse should not of-
fend him;
In all that touches honor, I commend
him;
He's noble, brave, and virtuous—but
I fear   15
He can't in truth be called a son-
neteer.
I'll gladly praise his wardrobe; I'll
endorse
His dancing, or the way he sits a
horse;
But, gentlemen, I cannot praise his
rhyme.   19
In fact, it ought to be a capital crime
For anyone so sadly unendowed
To write a sonnet, and read the thing
aloud."
At length he fell into a gentler mood
And, striking a concessive attitude,
He paid Oronte the following cour-
tesies: 25
"Sir, I regret that I'm so hard to
please,
And I'm profoundly sorry that your
lyric
Failed to provoke me to a panegyric."
After these curious words, the two
embraced,
And then the hearing was adjourned
—in haste.   30
Eliante. His conduct has been very
singular lately;
Still, I confess that I respect him
greatly.
The honesty in which he takes such
pride
Has—to my mind—its noble, heroic
side.
In this false age, such candor seems
outrageous;   35

But I could wish that it were more
contagious.
Philinte. What most intrigues me in our
friend Alceste
Is the grand passion that rages in his
breast.
The sullen humors he's compounded
of
Should not, I think, dispose his heart
to love;   40
But since they do, it puzzles me still
more
That he should choose your cousin to
adore.
Eliante. It does, indeed, belie the
theory
That love is born of gentle sympathy,
And that the tender passion must be
based   45
On sweet accords of temper and of
taste.
Philinte. Does she return his love, do
you suppose?
Eliante. Ah, that's a difficult question,
Sir. Who knows?
How can we judge the truth of her
devotion?
Her heart's a stranger to its own emo-
tion.   50
Sometimes it thinks it loves, when no
love's there;
At other times it loves quite unaware.
Philinte. I rather think Alceste is in for
more
Distress and sorrow than he's bar-
gained for;
Were he of my mind, Madam, his
affection   55
Would turn in quite a different direc-
tion,
And we would see him more respon-
sive to
The kind regard which he receives
from you.

Eliante. Sir, I believe in frankness, and
   I'm inclined,
   In matters of the heart, to speak my
     mind.   60
   I don't oppose his love for her; in-
     deed,
   I hope with all my heart that he'll
     succeed,
   And were it in my power, I'd rejoice
   In giving him the lady of his choice.
   But if, as happens frequently enough
   In love affairs, he meets with a re-
     buff—   66
   If Célimène should grant some rival's
     suit—
   I'd gladly play the role of substitute;
   Nor would his tender speeches please
     me less
   Because they'd once been made with-
     out success.   70
Philinte. Well, Madam, as for me, I
   don't oppose
   Your hopes in this affair; and heaven
     knows
   That in my conversations with the
     man
   I plead your cause as often as I can.
   But if those two should marry, and
     so remove   75
   All chance that he will offer you his
     love,
   Then I'll declare my own, and hope
     to see
   Your gracious favor pass from him to
     me.
   In short, should you be cheated of
     Alceste,   79
   I'd be most happy to be second best.
Eliante. Philinte, you're teasing.
Philinte.   Ah, Madam, never fear;
   No words of mine were ever so
     sincere,
   And I shall live in fretful expectation
   Till I can make a fuller declaration.

SCENE TWO

ALCESTE, ELIANTE, PHILINTE

Alceste. Avenge me, Madam! I must
   have satisfaction,
   Or this great wrong will drive me to
     distraction!
Eliante. Why, what's the matter?
   What's upset you so?
Alceste. Madam, I've had a mortal,
   mortal blow.
   If Chaos repossessed the universe,   5
   I swear I'd not be shaken any worse.
   I'm ruined. . . . I can say no more.
   . . . My soul . . .
Eliante. Do try, Sir, to regain your self-
   control.
Alceste. Just heaven! Why were so
   much beauty and grace
   Bestowed on one so vicious and so
     base?   10
Eliante. Once more, Sir, tell us. . . .
Alceste.   My world has gone to
   wrack;
   I'm—I'm betrayed; she's stabbed me
     in the back:
   Yes, Célimène (who would have
     thought it of her?)
   Is false to me, and has another lover.
Eliante. Are you quite certain? Can
   you prove these things?   15
Philinte. Lovers are prey to wild im-
   aginings
   And jealous fancies. No doubt there's
     some mistake. . . .
Alceste. Mind your own business, Sir,
   for heaven's sake.

(*To* ELIANTE)

   Madam, I have the proof that you
     demand
   Here in my pocket, penned by her
     own hand.   20
   Yes, all the shameful evidence one
     could want

Lies in this letter written to Oronte—
Oronte! whom I felt sure she couldn't
love,
And hardly bothered to be jealous of.
Philinte. Still, in a letter, appearances
may deceive;   25
This may not be so bad as you be-
lieve.
Alceste. Once more I beg you, Sir, to
let me be;
Tend to your own affairs; leave mine
to me.
Eliante. Compose yourself; this anguish
that you feel . . .
Alceste. Is something, Madam, you
alone can heal.   30
My outraged heart, beside itself with
grief,
Appeals to you for comfort and re-
lief,
Avenge me on your cousin, whose
unjust
And faithless nature has deceived my
trust;
Avenge a crime your pure soul must
detest.   35
Eliante. But how, Sir?
Alceste.   Madam, this heart within
my breast
Is yours; pray take it; redeem my
heart from her,
And so avenge me on my torturer.
Let her be punished by the fond
emotion,
The ardent love, the bottomless de-
votion,   40
The faithful worship which this
heart of mine
Will offer up to yours as to a
shrine.
Eliante. You have my sympathy, Sir, in
all you suffer;
Nor do I scorn the noble heart you
offer;   44
But I suspect you'll soon be mollified,

And this desire for vengeance will
subside.
When some beloved hand has done
us wrong
We thirst for retribution—but not for
long;
However dark the deed that she's
committed,
A lovely culprit's very soon acquit-
ted.   50
Nothing's so stormy as an injured
lover,
And yet no storm so quickly passes
over.
Alceste. No, Madam, no—this is no
lovers' spat;
I'll not forgive her; it's gone too far
for that;
My mind's made up; I'll kill myself
before   55
I waste my hopes upon her any more.
Ah, here she is. My wrath intensifies.
I shall confront her with her tricks
and lies,
And crush her utterly, and bring you
then   59
A heart no longer slave to Célimène.

Scene Three

CÉLIMÈNE, ALCESTE

Alceste (*Aside*) Sweet heaven, help
me to control my passion.
Célimène. (*Aside*) Oh, Lord. (*To* AL-
CESTE) Why stand there staring in
that fashion?
And what d'you mean by those dramatic sighs,
And that malignant glitter in your
eyes?
Alceste. I mean that sins which cause
the blood to freeze   5
Look innocent beside your treacheries;
That nothing Hell's or Heaven's
wrath could do

Ever produced so bad a thing as you.
Célimène. Your compliments were always sweet and pretty.
Alceste. Madam, it's not the moment to be witty. 10
No, blush and hang your head; you've ample reason,
Since I've the fullest evidence of your treason.
Ah, this is what my sad heart prophesied;
Now all my anxious fears are verified;
My dark suspicion and my gloomy doubt 15
Divined the truth, and now the truth is out.
For all your trickery, I was not deceived;
It was my bitter stars that I believed.
But don't imagine that you'll go scot-free; 19
You shan't misuse me with impunity.
I know that love's irrational and blind;
I know the heart's not subject to the mind,
And can't be reasoned into beating faster;
I know each soul is free to choose its master;
Therefore had you but spoken from the heart, 25
Rejecting my attentions from the start,
I'd have no grievance, or at any rate
I could complain of nothing but my fate.
Ah, but so falsely to encourage me—
That was a treason and a treachery
For which you cannot suffer too severely, 31
And you shall pay for that behavior dearly.
Yes, now I have no pity, not a shred;

My temper's out of hand; I've lost my head;
Shocked by the knowledge of your double-dealings, 35
My reason can't restrain my savage feelings;
A righteous wrath deprives me of my senses,
And I won't answer for the consequences.
Célimène. What does this outburst mean? Will you please explain?
Have you, by any chance, gone quite insane? 40
Alceste. Yes, yes, I went insane the day I fell
A victim to your black and fatal spell,
Thinking to meet with some sincerity
Among the treacherous charms that beckoned me.
Célimène. Pooh. Of what treachery can you complain? 45
Alceste. How sly you are, how cleverly you feign!
But you'll not victimize me any more.
Look: here's a document you've seen before.
This evidence, which I acquired today,
Leaves you, I think, without a thing to say. 50
Célimène. Is this what sent you into such a fit?
Alceste. You should be blushing at the sight of it.
Célimène. Ought I to blush? I truly don't see why.
Alceste. Ah, now you're being bold as well as sly;
Since there's no signature, perhaps you'll claim . . . 55
Célimène. I wrote it, whether or not it bears my name.

Alceste. And you can view with equa-
nimity
This proof of your disloyalty to me!

Célimène. Oh, don't be so outrageous
and extreme.

Alceste. You take this matter lightly, it
would seem.   60
Was it no wrong to me, no shame to
to you,
That you should send Oronte this
billet-doux?

Célimène. Oronte! Who said it was for
him?

Alceste.   Why, those
Who brought me this example of
your prose.
But what's the difference? If you
wrote the letter   65
To someone else, it pleases me no
better.
My grievance and your guilt remain
the same.

Célimène. But need you rage, and need
I blush for shame,
If this was written to a *woman*
friend?

Alceste. Ah! Most ingenious. I'm im-
pressed no end;   70
And after that incredible evasion
Your guilt is clear. I need no more
persuasion.
How dare you try so clumsy a decep-
tion?
D'you think I'm wholly wanting in
perception?
Come, come, let's see how brazenly
you'll try   75
To bolster up so palpable a lie:
Kindly construe this ardent closing
section
As nothing more than sisterly affec-
tion!
Here, let me read it. Tell me, if you
dare to,
That this is for a woman . . .

Célimène.   I don't care to. 80
What right have you to badger and
berate me,
And so highhandedly interrogate
me?

Alceste. Now, don't be angry; all I ask
of you
Is that you justify a phrase or
two . . .

Célimène. No, I shall not. I utterly
refuse,   85
And you may take those phrases as
you choose.

Alceste. Just show me how this letter
could be meant
For a woman's eyes, and I shall be
content.

Célimène. No, no, it's for Oronte;
you're perfectly right.
I welcome his attentions with de-
light,   90
I prize his character and his intellect,
And everything is just as you suspect.
Come, do your worst now; give your
rage free rein;
But kindly cease to bicker and com-
plain.

Alceste (*Aside*) Good God! Could anything be more inhuman?   95
Was ever a heart so mangled by a
woman?
When I complain of how she has betrayed me,
She bridles, and commences to upbraid me!
She tries my tortured patience to the
limit;
She won't deny her guilt; she glories
in it!   100
And yet my heart's too faint and
cowardly
To break these chains of passion, and
be free,
To scorn her as it should, and rise
above

This unrewarded, mad, and bitter love.

(*To* CÉLIMÈNE)

Ah, traitress, in how confident a
 fashion   105
You take advantage of my helpless
 passion,
And use my weakness for your faithless charms
To make me once again throw down
 my arms!
But do at least deny this black trans-
 gression;
Take back that mocking and perverse confession;   110
Defend this letter and your innocence,
And I, poor fool, will aid in your
 defense.
Pretend, pretend, that you are just
 and true,
And I shall make myself believe in
 you.
Célimène. Oh, stop it. Don't be such a
 jealous dunce,   115
Or I shall leave off loving you at
 once.
Just why should I *pretend?* What
 could impel me
To stoop so low as that? And kindly
 tell me
Why, if I loved another, I shouldn't
 merely
Inform you of it, simply and sin-
 cerely!   120
I've told you where you stand, and
 that admission
Should altogether clear me of suspicion;
After so generous a guarantee,
What right have you to harbor
 doubts of me?
Since women are (from natural
 reticence)   125

Reluctant to declare their sentiments,
And since the honor of our sex
 requires
That we conceal our amorous desires,
Ought any man for whom such laws
 are broken
To question what the oracle has
 spoken?   130
Should he not rather feel an obliga-
 tion
To trust that most obliging declara-
 tion?
Enough, now. Your suspicions quite
 disgust me;
Why should I love a man who doesn't
 trust me?   134
I cannot understand why I continue,
Fool that I am, to take an interest in
 you.
I ought to choose a man less prone to
 doubt,
And give you something to be vexed
 about.
Alceste. Ah, what a poor enchanted
 fool I am;
These gentle words, no doubt, were
 all a sham;   140
But destiny requires me to entrust
My happiness to you, and so I must.
I'll love you to the bitter end, and see
How false and treacherous you dare
 to be.
Célimène. No, you don't really love me
 as you ought.   145
Alceste. I love you more than can be
 said or thought;
Indeed, I wish you were in such
 distress
That I might show my deep devoted-
 ness.
Yes, I could wish that you were
 wretchedly poor,
Unloved, uncherished, utterly ob-
 scure;   150

That fate had set you down upon the earth
Without possessions, rank, or gentle birth;
Then, by the offer of my heart, I might
Repair the great injustice of your plight;
I'd raise you from the dust, and proudly prove   155
The purity and vastness of my love.

Célimène. This is a strange benevolence indeed!
God grant that I may never be in need. . . .
Ah, here's Monsieur Dubois, in quaint disguise.

SCENE FOUR

CÉLIMÈNE, ALCESTE, DUBOIS

Alceste. Well, why this costume? Why those frightened eyes?
What ails you?

Dubois.   Well, Sir, things are most mysterious.

Alceste. What do you mean?

Dubois.   I fear they're very serious.

Alceste. What?

Dubois.   Shall I speak more loudly?

Alceste.   Yes; speak out.

Dubois. Isn't there someone here, Sir?

Alceste.   Speak, you lout!   5
Stop wasting time.

Dubois.   Sir, we must slip away.

Alceste. How's that?

Dubois.   We must decamp without delay.

Alceste. Explain yourself.

Dubois.   I tell you we must fly.

Alceste. What for?

Dubois.   We mustn't pause to say good-by.

Alceste. Now what d'you mean by all of this, you clown?   10

Dubois. I mean, Sir, that we've got to leave this town.

Alceste. I'll tear you limb from limb and joint from joint
If you don't come more quickly to the point.

Dubois. Well, Sir, today a man in a black suit,
Who wore a black and ugly scowl to boot,   15
Left us a document scrawled in such a hand
As even Satan couldn't understand.
It bears upon your lawsuit, I don't doubt;
But all hell's devils couldn't make it out.

Alceste. Well, well, go on. What then? I fail to see   20
How this event obliges us to flee.

Dubois. Well, Sir: an hour later, hardly more,
A gentleman who's often called before
Came looking for you in an anxious way.
Not finding you, he asked me to convey   25
(Knowing I could be trusted with the same)
The following message. . . . Now, what *was* his name?

Alceste. Forget his name, you idiot. What did he say?

Dubois. Well, it was one of your friends, Sir, anyway.
He warned you to begone, and he suggested   30
That if you stay, you may well be arrested.

Alceste. What? Nothing more specific? Think, man, think!

Dubois. No, Sir. He had me bring him pen and ink,

And dashed you off a letter which,
I'm sure,
Will render things distinctly less ob-
scure.   35
Alceste. Well—let me have it!
Célimène.   What *is* this all about?
Alceste. God knows; but I have hopes
of finding out.
How long am I to wait, you blitherer?
Dubois (*After a protracted search for
the letter*) I must have left it on
your table, Sir.
Alceste. I ought to . . .
Célimène.   No, no, keep your self-
control;   40
Go find out what's behind his rig-
marole.
Alceste. It seems that fate, no matter
what I do,
Has sworn that I may not converse
with you;
But, Madam, pray permit your faith-
ful lover
To try once more before the day is
over.   45

ACT FIVE. SCENE ONE.

ALCESTE, PHILINTE

Alceste. No, it's too much. My mind's
made up, I tell you.
Philinte. Why should this blow, however hard, compel you . . .
Alceste. No, no, don't waste your breath
in argument;
Nothing you say will alter my intent;
This age is vile, and I've made up my
mind   5
To have no further commerce with
mankind.
Did not truth, honor, decency, and
the laws
Oppose my enemy and approve my
cause?

My claims were justified in all men's
sight;   9
I put my trust in equity and right;
Yet, to my horror and the world's dis-
grace,
Justice is mocked, and I have lost my
case!
A scoundrel whose dishonesty is
notorious
Emerges from another lie victorious!
Honor and right condone his brazen
fraud,   15
While rectitude and decency ap-
plaud!
Before his smirking face, the truth
stands charmed,
And virtue conquered, and the law
disarmed!
His crime is sanctioned by a court
decree!
And not content with what he's done
to me,   20
The dog now seeks to ruin me by
stating
That I composed a book now circu-
lating,
A book so wholly criminal and vi-
cious
That even to speak its title is sedi-
tious!
Meanwhile Oronte, my rival, lends
his credit   25
To the same libelous tale, and helps
to spread it!
Oronte! a man of honor and of rank,
With whom I've been entirely fair
and frank;
Who sought me out and forced me,
willy-nilly,
To judge some verse I found ex-
tremely silly;   30
And who, because I properly refused
To flatter him, or see the truth
abused,

Abets my enemy in a rotten slander!
There's the reward of honesty and
   candor!
The man will hate me to the end of
   time   35
For failing to commend his wretched
   rhyme!
And not this man alone, but all hu-
   manity
Do what they do from interest and
   vanity;
They prate of honor, truth, and
   righteousness,
But lie, betray, and swindle nonethe-
   less.   40
Come then: man's villainy is too
   much to bear;
Let's leave this jungle and this jackal's
   lair.
Yes! treacherous and savage race of
   men,
You shall not look upon my face
   again.
Philinte. Oh, don't rush into exile pre-
   maturely;   45
Things aren't as dreadful as you
   make them, surely.
It's rather obvious, since you're still
   at large,
That people don't believe your enemy's charge.
Indeed, his tale's so patently untrue
That it may do more harm to him
   than you.   50
Alceste. Nothing could do that scoundrel any harm:
His frank corruption is his greatest
   charm,
And, far from hurting him, a further
   shame
Would only serve to magnify his
   name.
Philinte. In any case, his bald prevari-
   cation   55

Has done no injury to your reputa-
   tion,
And you may feel secure in that
   regard.
As for your lawsuit, it should not be
   hard
To have the case reopened, and con-
   test   59
This judgment . . .
Alceste.   No, no, let the verdict rest.
Whatever cruel penalty it may
   bring,
I wouldn't have it changed for any-
   thing.
It shows the times' injustice with
   such clarity
That I shall pass it down to our
   posterity
As a great proof and signal demon-
   stration   65
Of the black wickedness of this gen-
   eration.
It may cost twenty thousand francs;
   but I
Shall pay their twenty thousand, and
   gain thereby
The right to storm and rage at hu-
   man evil,
And send the race of mankind to the
   devil.   70
Philinte. Listen to me. . . .
Alceste.   Why? What can you pos-
   sibly say?
Don't argue, Sir; your labor's thrown
   away.
Do you propose to offer lame ex-
   cuses
For men's behavior and the times'
   abuses?
Philinte. No, all you say I'll readily
   concede: 75
This is a low, conniving age indeed;
Nothing but trickery prospers now-
   adays,

And people ought to mend their
shabby ways.
Yes, man's a beastly creature; but
must we then
Abandon the society of men?   80
Here in the world, each human
frailty
Provides occasion for philosophy,
And that is virtue's noblest exercise;
If honesty shone forth from all men's
eyes,
If every heart were frank and kind
and just,   85
What could our virtues do but gather
dust
(Since their employment is to help
us bear
The villainies of men without de-
spair)?
A heart well-armed with virtue can
endure. . . .

Alceste. Sir, you're a matchless rea-
soner, to be sure;   90
Your words are fine and full of co-
gency;
But don't waste time and eloquence
on me.
My reason bids me go, for my own
good.
My tongue won't lie and flatter as it
should;
God knows what frankness it might
next commit,   95
And what I'd suffer on account of it.
Pray let me wait for Célimène's return
In peace and quiet. I shall shortly
learn,
By her response to what I have in
view,
Whether her love for me is feigned
or true.   100

Philinte. Till then, let's visit Eliante upstairs.

Alceste. No, I am too weighed down
with somber cares.
Go to her, do; and leave me with my
gloom
Here in the darkened corner of this
room.

Philinte. Why, that's no sort of company, my friend;   105
I'll see if Eliante will not descend.

SCENE TWO

CÉLIMÈNE, ORONTE, ALCESTE

Oronte. Yes, Madam, if you wish me to
remain
Your true and ardent lover, you must
deign
To give me some more positive assurance.
All this suspense is quite beyond
endurance.
If your heart shares the sweet desires of mine,   5
Show me as much by some convincing sign;
And here's the sign I urgently suggest:
That you no longer tolerate Alceste,
But sacrifice him to my love, and
sever
All your relations with the man forever.   10

Célimène. Why do you suddenly dislike him so?
You praised him to the skies not long
ago.

Oronte. Madam, that's not the point.
I'm here to find
Which way your tender feelings are
inclined.
Choose, if you please, between Al-
ceste and me,   15
And I shall stay or go accordingly.

Alceste (Emerging from the corner)

Yes, Madam, choose; this gentleman's demand
Is wholly just, and I support his
stand.
I too am true and ardent; I too am
here
To ask you that you make your feel-
ings clear.   20
No more delays, now; no equivoca-
tion;
The time has come to make your
declaration.

Oronte. Sir, I've no wish in any way to
be
An obstacle to your felicity.

Alceste. Sir, I've no wish to share her
heart with you;   25
That may sound jealous, but at least
it's true.

Oronte. If, weighing us, she leans in
your direction . . .

Alceste. If she regards you with the
least affection . . .

Oronte. I swear I'll yield her to you
there and then.

Alceste. I swear I'll never see her face
again.   30

Oronte. Now, Madam, tell us what
we've come to hear.

Alceste. Madam, speak openly and
have no fear.

Oronte. Just say which one is to remain
your lover.

Alceste. Just name one name, and it
will all be over.

Oronte. What! Is it possible that you're
undecided?   35

Alceste. What! Can your feelings possibly be divided?

Célimène. Enough: this inquisition's
gone too far:
How utterly unreasonable you are!
Not that I couldn't make the choice
with ease;

My heart has no conflicting sympa-
thies;   40
I know full well which one of you I
favor,
And you'd not see me hesitate or
waver.
But how can you expect me to reveal
So cruelly and bluntly what I feel?
I think it altogether too unpleasant
To choose between two men when
both are present;   46
One's heart has means more subtle
and more kind
Of letting its affections be divined,
Nor need one be uncharitably plain
To let a lover know he loves in vain.

Oronte. No, no, speak plainly; I for one
can stand it.   51
I beg you to be frank.

Alceste.   And I demand it.
The simple truth is what I wish to
know,
And there's no need for softening the
blow.
You've made an art of pleasing everyone,   55
But now your days of coquetry are
done:
You have no choice now, Madam,
but to choose,
For I'll know what to think if you
refuse;
I'll take your silence for a clear admission
That I'm entitled to my worst suspicion.   60

Oronte. I thank you for this ultimatum,
Sir,
And I may say I heartily concur.

Célimène. Really, this foolishness is
very wearing:
Must you be so unjust and overbear-
ing?
Haven't I told you why I must
demur?   65

Ah, here's Eliante; I'll put the case to her.

SCENE THREE

ELIANTE, PHILINTE, CÉLIMÈNE, ORONTE, ALCESTE

Célimène. Cousin, I'm being persecuted here
By these two persons, who, it would appear,
Will not be satisfied till I confess
Which one I love the more, and which the less,
And tell the latter to his face that he   5
Is henceforth banished from my company.
Tell me, has ever such a thing been done?
Eliante. You'd best not turn to me; I'm not the one
To back you in a matter of this kind:
I'm all for those who frankly speak their mind.   10
Oronte. Madam, you'll search in vain for a defender.
Alceste. You're beaten, Madam, and may as well surrender.
Oronte. Speak, speak, you must; and end this awful strain.
Alceste. Or don't, and your position will be plain.
Oronte. A single word will close this painful scene.   15
Alceste. But if you're silent, I'll know what you mean.

SCENE FOUR

ARSINOÉ, CÉLIMÈNE, ELIANTE,
ALCESTE, PHILINTE,
ACASTE, CLITANDRE, ORONTE

Acaste (*To* CÉLIMÈNE) Madam, with all due deference, we two
Have come to pick a little bone with you.

Clitandre (*To* ORONTE *and* ALCESTE)
I'm glad you're present, Sirs; as you'll soon learn,
Our business here is also your concern.
Arsinoé (*To* CÉLIMÈNE) Madam, I visit you so soon again   5
Only because of these two gentlemen,
Who came to me indignant and aggrieved
About a crime too base to be believed.
Knowing your virtue, having such confidence in it,
I couldn't think you guilty for a minute,   10
In spite of all their telling evidence;
And, rising above our little difference,
I've hastened here in friendship's name to see
You clear yourself of this great calumny.
Acaste. Yes, Madam, let us see with what composure   15
You'll manage to respond to this disclosure.
You lately sent Clitandre this tender note.
Clitandre. And this one, for Acaste, you also wrote.
Acaste (*To* ORONTE *and* ALCESTE)
You'll recognize this writing, Sirs, I think;   19
The lady is so free with pen and ink
That you must know it all too well, I fear.
But listen: this is something you should hear.

"How absurd you are to condemn my lightheartedness in society, and to accuse me of being happiest in the company of others. Nothing could be more unjust; and if you do not come to me instantly and beg pardon for saying such a thing, I shall never forgive you as long as I live. Our big bumbling friend the Viscount . . ."

What a shame that he's not here. 32

"Our big bumbling friend the Viscount, whose name stands first in your complaint, is hardly a man to my taste; and ever since the day I watched him spend three-quarters of an hour spitting into a well, so as to make circles in the water, I have been unable to think highly of him. As for the little Marquess . . ." 41

In all modesty, gentlemen, that is I.

"As for the little Marquess, who sat squeezing my hand for such a long while yesterday, I find him in all respects the most trifling creature alive; and the only things of value about him are his cape and his sword. As for the man with the green ribbons . . ." 50

(*To* ALCESTE)
It's your turn now, Sir.

"As for the man with the green ribbons, he amuses me now and then with his bluntness and his bearish ill-humor; but there are many times indeed when I think him the greatest bore in the world. And as for the sonneteer . . ." 58

(*To* ORONTE)
Here's your helping.

"And as for the sonneteer, who has taken it into his head to be witty, and insists on being an author in the teeth of opinion, I simply cannot be bothered to listen to him, and his prose wearies me quite as much as his poetry. Be assured that I am not always so well-entertained as you suppose; that I long for your company, more than I dare to say, at all these entertainments to which people drag me; and that the presence of those one loves is the true and perfect seasoning to all one's pleasures." 74

Clitandre. And now for me.

"Clitandre, whom you mention, and who so pesters me with his saccharine speeches, is the last man on earth for whom I could feel any affection. He is quite mad to suppose that I love him, and so are you, to doubt that you are loved. Do come to your senses; exchange your suppositions for his; and visit me as often as possible, to help me bear the annoyance of his unwelcome attentions." 87

It's a sweet character that these letters show,
And what to call it, Madam, you well know.
Enough. We're off to make the world acquainted 90
With this sublime self-portrait that you've painted.
Acaste. Madam, I'll make you no farewell oration;
No, you're not worthy of my indignation.
Far choicer hearts than yours, as you'll discover,
Would like this little Marquess for a lover. 95

SCENE FIVE

CÉLIMÈNE, ELIANTE, ARSINOÉ, ALCESTE, ORONTE, PHILINTE

Oronte. So! After all those loving letters you wrote,

You turn on me like this, and cut my
   throat!
And your dissembling, faithless heart,
   I find,
Has pledged itself by turns to all
   mankind!
How blind I've been! But now I
   clearly see; 5
I thank you, Madam, for enlight-
   ening me.
My heart is mine once more, and I'm
   content;
The loss of it shall be your punish-
   ment.

(*To* ALCESTE)

Sir, she is yours; I'll seek no more to
   stand
Between your wishes and this lady's
   hand. 10

SCENE SIX

CÉLIMÈNE, ELIANTE, ARSINOÉ, ALCESTE,
PHILINTE

Arsinoé (*To* CÉLIMÈNE) Madam, I'm
   forced to speak. I'm far too stirred
To keep my counsel, after what I've
   heard.
I'm shocked and staggered by your
   want of morals.
It's not my way to mix in others'
   quarrels;
But really, when this fine and noble
   spirit, 5
This man of honor and surpassing
   merit,
Laid down the offering of his heart
   before you,
How *could* you . . .
Alceste.   Madam, permit me, I im-
   plore you,
To represent myself in this debate.
Don't bother, please, to be my ad-
   vocate. 10
My heart, in any case, could not af-
   ford

To give your services their due re-
   ward;
And if I chose, for consolation's
   sake,
Some other lady, t'would not be you
   I'd take.
Arsinoé. What makes you think you
   could, Sir? And how dare you 15
Imply that I've been trying to en-
   snare you?
If you can for a moment entertain
Such flattering fancies, you're ex-
   tremely vain.
I'm not so interested as you suppose
In Célimène's discarded gigolos. 20
Get rid of that absurd illusion, do.
Women like me are not for such as
   you.
Stay with this creature, to whom
   you're so attached;
I've never seen two people better
   matched.

SCENE SEVEN

CÉLIMÈNE, ELIANTE, ALCESTE, PHILINTE

Alceste (*To* CÉLIMÈNE) Well, I've been
   still throughout this exposé,
Till everyone but me has said his say.
Come, have I shown sufficient self-
   restraint?
And may I now . . .
Célimène.   Yes, make your just com-
   plaint.
Reproach me freely, call me what
   you will; 5
You've every right to say I've used
   you ill.
I've wronged you, I confess it; and
   in my shame
I'll make no effort to escape the
   blame.
The anger of those others I could
   despise;
My guilt toward you I sadly recog-
   nize. 10

Your wrath is wholly justified, I fear;
I know how culpable I must appear,
I know all things bespeak my treach-
   ery,
And that, in short, you've grounds for
   hating me.
Do so; I give you leave.
Alceste.   Ah, traitress—how, 15
How should I cease to love you, even
   now?
Though mind and will were pas-
   sionately bent
On hating you, my heart would not
   consent.

(*To* Eliante *and* Philinte)

Be witness to my madness, both of
   you;   19
See what infatuation drives one to;
But wait; my folly's only just begun,
And I shall prove to you before I'm
   done
How strange the human heart is, and
   how far
From rational we sorry creatures are.

(*To* Célimène)

Woman, I'm willing to forget your
   shame,   25
And clothe your treacheries in a
   sweeter name;
I'll call them youthful errors, instead
   of crimes,
And lay the blame on these cor-
   rupting times.
My one condition is that you agree
To share my chosen fate, and fly
   with me   30
To that wild, trackless, solitary place
In which I shall forget the human
   race.
Only by such a course can you atone
For those atrocious letters; by that
   alone
Can you remove my present horror of
   you,   35

And make it possible for me to love
   you.
Célimène. What! I renounce the world
   at my young age,
And die of boredom in some her-
   mitage?
Alceste. Ah, if you really loved me as
   you ought,
You wouldn't give the world a mo-
   ment's thought;   40
Must you have me, and all the world
   beside?
Célimène. Alas, at twenty one is ter-
   rified
Of solitude. I fear I lack the force
And depth of soul to take so stern a
   course.
But if my hand in marriage will con-
   tent you,   45
Why, there's a plan which I might
   well consent to,
And . . .
Alceste.   No, I detest you now. I
   could excuse
Everything else, but since you thus
   refuse
To love me wholly, as a wife should
   do,
And see the world in me, as I in
   you,   50
Go! I reject your hand, and disen-
   thrall
My heart from your enchantments,
   once for all.

Scene Eight

ELIANTE, ALCESTE, PHILINTE

Alceste (*To* Eliante) Madam, your
   virtuous beauty has no peer;
Of all this world, you only are sincere;
I've long esteemed you highly, as you
   know;
Permit me ever to esteem you so,

And if I do not now request your
hand,   5
Forgive me, Madam, and try to un-
derstand.
I feel unworthy of it; I sense that fate
Does not intend me for the married
state,
That I should do you wrong by offer-
ing you
My shattered heart's unhappy resi-
due,   10
And that in short . . .

Eliante.   Your argument's well
taken:
Nor need you fear that I shall feel
forsaken.
Were I to offer him this hand of
mine,
Your friend Philinte, I think, would
not decline.

Philinte. Ah, Madam, that's my heart's
most cherished goal,   15
For which I'd gladly give my life and
soul.

Alceste (*To* ELIANTE *and* PHILINTE)
May you be true to all you now.
profess,
And so deserve unending happiness.
Meanwhile, betrayed and wronged
in everything,
I'll flee this bitter world where vice
is king,   20
And seek some spot unpeopled and
apart
Where I'll be free to have an honest
heart.

Philinte. Come, Madam, let's do everything we can
To change the mind of this unhappy
man.

A Streetcar Named Desire

TENNESSEE WILLIAMS

INTRODUCTION

Thomas Lanier Williams was born on March 26, 1911, in the rectory of the Episcopal church in Columbus, Mississippi. His mother, Edwina, was the daughter of the Reverend Walter E. Dakin; his father, Cornelius Coffin Williams, a descendant of Tennessee pioneers, was a loud and energetic man who worked as a traveling salesman for the International Shoe Company and was often absent from home. The boy spent the first eight years of his life with his mother and sister Rose, who was two years his senior, in the rather sheltered and literary atmosphere of his maternal grandparents' home. He suffered from a number of childhood illnesses and was very much pampered; he became a hypochondriac, extremely delicate and sensitive; he did not take part in the ordinary boys' activities, but read a great deal, played games with his sister, and had a rich imaginative life.

Just before the end of World War I, the family moved to St. Louis. The sensitive boy regarded this as a tragic event, for he found it almost impossible to adjust himself to life in the midwestern city. He hated the Eugene Field School where the boys made fun of him and beat him because he was small and weak for his age, and had a Southern accent. He hated the succession of small and dingy apartments in which the family was forced to live mainly because of his father's niggardliness. In one such apartment, to make his sister's dark little room livable, the boy helped her to paint the walls and furniture white and to install her collection of glass animals, "making a place of white and crystal in the midst of squalor." This collection of tiny glass creatures years later provided the material and title for Williams's first successful play.

The birth of a brother, named Walter Dakin for his grandfather, did not particularly please the boy, and the illness of his mother, who was stricken with influenza which weakened her lungs and brought on a slight case of tuberculosis, frightened him; these occurrences fostered feelings of anxiety and insecurity in Williams. "At the age of fourteen," he says, "I discovered writing as an escape from a world of reality in which I felt acutely uncomfortable. It immediately became my place of retreat, my cave, my refuge. From what? From being called a sissy by the neighborhood kids, and Miss Nancy by my father, because I would rather read books . . . than play marbles and baseball and other normal kid games."

While he had lived with his grandparents, he had never been aware of any privation, but in St. Louis it was forcibly impressed upon his mind that there were two distinct social classes—the rich and the poor. He had only to walk to that part of the city where there were many magnificent homes surrounded by beautiful gardens and then return to his own jungle of grimy tenements to have this inequality forced upon his consciousness and to arouse his resentment. "It produced a shock and a rebellion," says Williams, "that has grown into an inherent part of my work. It was the beginning of the social-consciousness which I think has marked most of my writing."

Reaching college age at the time of the depression, Williams continued to face unsettled and unsettling conditions which disrupted his formal education. He entered the University of Missouri in 1931 and quit in 1933 to go to work for the shoe company that employed his father. Although he was temperamentally unsuited to the job, he kept it for two years until he suffered a nervous breakdown. Upon his recovery, he was more of a hypochondriac than ever, but he had decided that he was going to be a writer and that he would finish his education. He attended Washington University from 1936 to 1937 and finally put himself through the University of Iowa, which granted him a B. A. degree in 1938. Whether he was attending school or not, he continued to write poems, essays, short stories, and plays; at the time of his graduation he had two full-length plays and innumerable one-acters to his credit.

After receiving his degree, Williams left St. Louis for New Orleans, arriving there at the end of the summer of 1938, a proper young man called Thomas Lanier, neatly dressed in a conservative suit, white shirt, tie, and polished shoes; when he left the French Quarter, at the beginning of the summer of 1939, he was the complete bohemian in sport shirt and sandals, carrying a typewriter, phonograph, a volume of Hart Crane's poetry, and the name of Tennessee.

It was in New Orleans that Williams discovered that all his material as a writer would henceforth be cut from the fabric of his own life. In the French Quarter he waited on table for little more than room and board, and wrote in his spare time; he read a great deal, too, his favorite writers being Hart Crane, D. H. Lawrence, Anton Chekhov, and Rainer Maria Rilke. One day he learned that the Group Theater in New York was holding a contest for writers of full-length plays, but he sent in his one-act pieces—four plays collectively titled *American Blues*. He was awarded a prize of one hundred dollars and came to the attention of Audrey Wood, who shortly afterward became his agent and has represented him ever since.

Williams's first recognition came in 1940 when, through the efforts of Miss Wood, he received a Rockefeller grant for playwriting and completed the script of *Battle of Angels,* which was produced by the Theater Guild under the direction of Margaret Webster, with Miriam Hopkins in the leading role. The play opened in Boston on December 30, 1940, and closed during its tryout there; it was banned by that city's Watch and Ward Society. "I never heard of an audience getting so infuriated," said Williams, and added by way of explanation, "The thing is, you can't mix up sex and religion, as I did in *Battle of Angels*." His total income from this play was two hundred dollars.

The Rockefeller grant was renewed; then the Institute of Arts and Letters awarded him a thousand dollars, and Williams set out on a roving writing career. He traveled all over the country working as a bellhop, elevator operator, waiter, teletype clerk, reciter of verses in a Greenwich Village nightclub, and usher in a Broadway movie-house. "I lived carefully," says Williams, "and whenever I'd saved enough to go some place else, I'd get a bus ticket and go." Gradually he became known in theatrical circles as his plays were presented by Little Theater and community groups in different parts of the country. Suddenly Miss Wood summoned him to New York, and then shipped him off to Hollywood to write screen plays for Metro-Goldwyn-Mayer under a contract that called for a salary of $250 a week, but he lasted on the job only six months. During that time he wrote an original screen play, *The Gentleman Caller*, which did not interest the studio. He proceeded to turn the script into a stage play called *The Glass Menagerie*. When his contract expired, he left Hollywood.

The Glass Menagerie opened in Chicago on December 26, 1944, to critical acclaim but an indifferent public. The critics refused to let the play die, and before long people were flocking to see it; it ran for three months and then moved to the Playhouse in New York on March 31, 1945. The play was co-directed by Margo Jones and Eddie Dowling, and the cast of four consisted of Laurette Taylor, Julie Haydon, Eddie Dowling, and Anthony Ross. The play won the Drama Critics' Circle Award as the best American work produced in New York during the season 1944-45, and chalked up a run of 563 performances, closing in early August, 1946. Two road companies, one with the original cast, toured with the play in the fall of 1946. "I was snatched out of virtual oblivion," said Williams, "and thrust into sudden prominence."

You Touched Me!, a play based on a story by D. H. Lawrence, was written by Williams in collaboration with Donald Windham; it had been produced at the Cleveland Playhouse and the Pasadena Playhouse before opening in New York on September 25, 1946, but it failed to catch on.

A year later, on December 3, 1947, Williams won enormous acclaim and the Pulitzer Prize for *A Streetcar Named Desire*, a play that made its author a figure of international as well as national importance in the theater.

Summer and Smoke, which followed on October 6, 1948, had proved highly successful when staged by Margo Jones in her arena theater in Dallas; transferred to the proscenium stage of the Music Box Theater in New York the play failed despite an excellent production. When it was done in 1952 at the Circle-in-the-Square, an arena theater in Greenwich Village, it not only attracted enthusiastic audiences but brought stardom to Geraldine Page and plaudits to its director José Quintero.

To prove that he was capable of dealing with subjects other than neurotic Southern women, Williams wrote *The Rose Tattoo*, whose heroine is the living embodiment of elemental sexuality. The play opened at the Martin Beck Theater,

New York, on February 3, 1951, and enjoyed a moderate success, but it received a much warmer reception in Europe.

The dramatist's next work was a theatricalist and symbolist drama; the play, called *Camino Real,* which dealt with the dreams and defeat of modern man, failed on Broadway in 1953 but was revived off-Broadway in 1960.

On March 27, 1955, three days after the opening of *Cat on a Hot Tin Roof,* Williams's father died in Knoxville, Tennessee, at the age of 77. Although the playwright had not been on good terms with him for many years, he attended his father's funeral. Williams, Sr. had served as the model for the father in *The Glass Menagerie* and also for Big Daddy in *Cat on a Hot Tin Roof.*

Cat on a Hot Tin Roof, presented at the Morosco Theater, New York, on March 24, 1955, won for its author his second Pulitzer Prize. Despite the unpleasantness of its subject matter (homosexuality and cancer), the play was a resounding success and led to Williams' exploitation of ever more perverse and violent themes.

Orpheus Descending (1958), a revision of Williams's earlier play, *Battle of Angels,* ends with a lynching; *Suddenly Last Summer,* the more important of two one-act plays presented under the title of *Garden District* (1959), concerns itself with homosexuality and cannibalism; and *Sweet Bird of Youth* (1959) deals with castration both symbolically and actually.

Concerning his tendency to deal with lurid material in an exacerbated manner, Williams said not long ago: "All my life I have been haunted by the obsession that to desire a thing or to love a thing intensely is to place yourself in a vulnerable position, to be a possible, if not a probable, loser of what you most want. . . . Having always to contend with this adversary of fear, which was sometimes terror, gave me a certain tendency toward an atmosphere of hysteria and violence in my writing, an atmosphere that has existed in it since the beginning. What surprises me is the degree to which both critics and audience have accepted this barrage of violence." More recently he announced: "I'm through with what have been called my 'black' plays. Maybe analysis has helped me to get them out of my system. . . . Bestiality still exists, but I don't want to write about it any more. . . . From now on I want to be concerned with the kinder aspects of life."

Williams is working on several "brighter" plays at the present time. *Period of Adjustment* opened on Broadway in the fall of 1960; *A Night of the Iguana,* which was done as a one-act play in the summer of 1959 at the Festival of Two Worlds in Spoleto, Italy, was developed into a full-length play; another script, *The Milk Train Does Not Stop Here Any More,* is in rough draft; and an untitled work, originally intended for Maureen Stapleton and the late Diana Barrymore, is in an unfinished state.

Tennessee Williams has written screen adaptations of several of his plays, has turned out an original film scenario, poems, short stories, a novel and the libretto for an opera. Williams has had an unmistakable influence on the American theater. His personal, poetic expression and his free and unrestrained treatment of "untouchable" themes have broadened the horizons of playgoers as well as of other playwrights. Besides personally helping to bring into the theater such excellent writers as William Inge and Carson McCullers, Williams has played a part in creating a renewed interest in the work of Eugene O'Neill (who had been neglected in the late '30s and '40s); and has also prepared American audiences to accept and appreciate the works of such nonnaturalistic and avant-garde writers as Giraudoux, Anouilh, Beckett, Ionesco, and Genet. That Williams takes his playwriting seriously (his aim is: Not to deceive and not to bore) and that he continues to work with unabated imagination and energy augurs well for American drama.

In New Orleans, Williams lived near a main thoroughfare called Royal. Up and down this avenue, running on the same track, were two streetcars, one named Desire, the other Cemetery. As he watched the cars go back and forth, Williams was impressed by the symbolic significance of these names and their bearing upon life everywhere. They gave him the title for the story of Blanche DuBois, a sensitive woman driven beyond the brink of sanity by her brutish brother-in-law. The playwright has said that the theme of this play is "The apes shall inherit the earth." It is thus quite obvious that Williams regards most men as savages and that his sympathies lie with the fine-grained individual who is lacerated by the coarseness of life. A *Streetcar Named Desire* may thus be read as an allegorical representation of the author's view of the world he lives in.

Of all his plays, Williams believes, this is the only one whose success was fully deserved. "It has an epic quality that the others don't have, and it said everything I had to say." Most critics agree that this is Williams's best piece of work, without being aware of his own private reasons for cherishing it; when he wrote it he was sure it was going to be his last play; he expected to die immediately. And so he felt it was, and still feels it is, his swan song.

The plot of the play is rich in suggestions and overtones and moves forward through eleven scenes at a furious pace. At the beginning there is the suggestion of tragedy hovering over the action but as the work develops it slowly veers toward melodrama and culminates in the insanity of the protagonist, which is a questionable solution. Interweaving humor and pathos as it does, the story has the richness and variety of a good novel.

The characterization is strong and interesting. Blanche and Stanley are full-length portraits; one a study in abnormal, the other in normal, psychology. Despite his social consciousness, Williams is much more concerned with the psychological than with the sociological situations of his characters. Without passing moral judgments on them, Williams is ruthless in his exposure of the people in the play. His use of symbolism helps immeasurably to make them vivid; Blanche's horror of unshaded light bulbs expresses her inability to face reality, as Stanley's devotion to poker games and undershirts announces his virility. Stella is commonplace and finds complete gratification in marriage; the other characters are small, mean, frustrated, and violent. It is an exciting and colorful gallery.

Williams's dialogue not only characterizes carefully but always carries the action forward; his language has an aura of poetry and a certainty based on a kind of interior syntax. Blanche speaks in complex and periodic sentences which are full of imagery; Stanley's explosive and staccato speeches also contain imagery but on a coarser level. The speech of the other characters is colloquial, slipshod, and typical. Humor and poetry raise Williams's dialogue to levels much above the journalese written by the average realistic and naturalistic playwright.

Discounting the author's own statement, the theme of the play is the break-up of a social order and its effect on the women, bearers of life, who survive. Stella is able to renew the cycle of life because she joins forces with a man who represents fresh and virile stock; while Blanche is the symbol and the victim of the old order which faces decay and death.

The play is an example of "poetic naturalism"; the speeches have the rhythms and images of ordinary life, subtly combined and contrasted with a verselike elegance of phrase. It has the surprising effect of seeming more real, more life-like than the clipped banalities of the more prosaic realists. The title of the play, itself, may seem like fantasy or symbolism but it has a rational explanation, as has been noted.

The production of the play was an excellent example of the element of "spectacle"—lighting, music, unusual stage effects, such as the backdrop which becomes transparent and shows the street beyond the house wall, street cries, church bells, the thousand sounds of activity which heighten the sense of palpitating urban life, of brutal intimacies, and close-packed, crowded living; all these were called for by the playwright and brilliantly supplied by the director, designer, and technicians.

PRODUCTION IN THE MODERN THEATER

It is necessary to understand the change in man's thinking from the seventeenth century to our own in order to see how the drama has reflected it step by step. The religious fervor which had given the drama its initial impetus in the medieval period and had sustained it through its flowering in the Renaissance began to die out in the latter part of the seventeenth century. Men were turning away from faith and relying instead upon the mind for guidance in worldly affairs. Reason and logic were valued above everything else, and men began to believe that all human difficulties could be alleviated, if not completely eliminated, by the proper use of the intellect. The Age of Reason began in high spirits and the greatest optimism, as did the theater in the Restoration. The plays of the period were divided between cynical, witty, and immoral comedies of manners, and a long succession of bombastic and false heroic tragedies.

The Deists of the eighteenth century tried to reduce even religion to an intellectual formula, and men started to put their minds to work on social and economic problems and to take a special interest in the downtrodden, the exploited, and the poverty-stricken. This ushered in a procession of sentimental comedies and middle-class tragedies; these plays were highly moral, superficial, and didactic. Almost as an antidote to them there suddenly appeared a great number of revivals, and adaptations, parodies and burlesques—all filled with music, song, and dance; theatergoers, apparently, were more interested in lively and spectacular entertainments than in uplifting dramas. Through the efforts of the pantheists and transcendentalists of the first half of the nineteenth century, orthodox religious feeling was dissipated still further, giving way to a romantic and idealistic program for ethical and moral behavior and universal love. This brought on a rash of windy "poetic" works steeped in sentimentality and romanticism.

Toward the end of the century men were making gigantic strides in industry and economics, social reforms and scientific discoveries; and the ideas of Darwin, Marx, and Freud were beginning to make themselves felt. Darwin taught that man is related to the animals; Marx, that "thinking" animals can arrange society to suit their needs; and Freud, that the nervous mechanisms of these animals can be repaired if they break down during the process of living. Realism reflected this thinking in the theater; the Duke of Saxe-Meiningen tried to create the illusion of reality in the visual aspects of his productions and the dramatists of the period were striving for the same effect in their plays. The works of Ibsen and Shaw mirror modern man thinking; social, scientific, philosophical, and even religious questions provided the themes for their dramas.

By the twentieth century, man's outlook had become mechanistic, materialistic, cynical, and skeptical. After a depression and two world wars, optimism had completely evaporated. The increasing tension, violence, and nausea in the individual and the world are mirrored in the plays of Eugene O'Neill and Tennessee Williams, and the utter despair of life in an atomic age is depicted in its most revolting aspects in the avant-garde dramas of Eugene Ionesco (where men turn into rhinoceroses), of Jean Genet (where the world is seen as a brothel in which men live fantasy lives), and of Samuel Beckett (where we all end up in garbage cans).

In desperation men are beginning to concede, though reluctantly, that they cannot live by reason alone. A random playwright here and there—T. S. Eliot, Graham Greene, Christopher Fry—has tried to start a religious revival, but faith cannot be imposed from above; it must flower in the hearts of the people. Since this is an eclectic age and there is no single conventional form in which a modern play must be cast, even our most accomplished playwrights have produced works imitative of those of earlier traditions. O'Neill's *Mourning Becomes Electra* looks back to a Greek model; Eliot's *Murder in the Cathedral*, to a medieval one; Anderson's *Elizabeth and Essex*, in form, subject-matter, and title, to the English Renaissance; S. N. Behrman's *Amphitryon 38* to French neoclassical style; and Lillian Hellman's *The Little Foxes*, to Ibsen. Thus in a single season on Broadway, we may harvest, if we wish, the fruits of western drama.

The Theater

The theater, which began in the open air, was at first partly and then completely covered over; and from a place of occasional festival its character was gradually transformed until it became a place of regular entertainment. By a process of evolution the stage gradually receded from its original position in the midst of the playhouse to its present position behind a proscenium frame.

The style of playhouse we are accustomed to had its origin in the Italian Renaissance. The theater is built of brick, the front covered with stone or plaster; the playhouse faces the street and its entryway is often decorated with sculptured figures, tall columns, and an overhanging marquee. The stage door is at the back of the house at the end of a long dim passageway, and leads into a maze of iron steps, unadorned brick walls, and a welter of stage scenery and machinery; the contrast between the warmth and gaiety of the front of the house and the cold and businesslike grimness backstage dramatizes the contrast between illusion and reality.

The auditorium of the traditional indoor theater that has persisted from the seventeenth century to the present is roughly in the shape of a horseshoe. Its balconies are raised one above the other in order to accommodate the greatest possible number of spectators. In the seventeenth and eighteenth centuries, playhouses had as many as six tiers of balconies; in the nineteenth century, the number was reduced to three; while modern theater architects incline to the installation of just one balcony. But the auditorium has become wider and deeper and the single balcony extends further forward toward the stage. Private boxes are a vestige of the days when the balconies were completely divided up into little cubicles for the special use of the royal family, the members of the nobility, and the upper classes; the common people were huddled into the orchestra. The growth of democracy has tended to remove the social differences between the members of the audience, and the absence of private boxes in modern playhouses is a clear indication of this trend.

The stage is the area behind the proscenium frame but only one-half or two-thirds of it at most is ever visible to the spectator; the audience merely sees an area enclosed by draperies or by painted or built scenery, as if a three-walled room had been set down in the center of the stage. The rest of the space, behind the set, is filled with scenery, properties, and lighting equipment. The stage floor has trap doors in it, and many modern playhouses are equipped with revolving stages. In height the stage extends to the roof of the theater, and scenery not in use may be lifted by means of a counterweight system and hung in the area above and behind the proscenium arch. The actors' dressing-rooms are ranged along corridors on various levels backstage. Most of the professional theaters in use today were built in the nineteenth century or earlier, and few have adequate space for workshops and wardrobes, storage or rehearsal rooms.

The newest trend in theater-building is the erection of playhouses specially designed for central staging. In this type of theater the acting area may be of any shape and either completely or only partially surrounded by the seats of the spectators; but the house is small, usually seating under 300. Among the advantages of theater-in-the-round are the intimate relationship it establishes between performer and audience, its economy of operation, and its ease of management. It has been most effectively handled by college and community groups, and by semiprofessional and off-Broadway companies.

The Actors

Women made their first appearance on the English stage in the plays of the Restoration, and immediately achieved great fame and some notoriety. Nell Gwynn, a clever comedienne, became the mistress of Charles II.

Although playwriting was at a low ebb, there was no dearth of great perform-ances during the eighteenth and nineteenth centuries. The tastes of the day made the actor a ranter, a puppet, a declaimer, or a model of fashion, but he always approached his work with great seriousness and even attempted to develop theories and techniques which would advance his personal skill as well as the art in general. It was in the eighteenth century that the great controversy arose, which continues to the present time, as to whether actors should themselves feel the emotions they portray or simply by the use of various external devices be able to arouse the emotions of the spectators. In his celebrated pamphlet, *The Paradox of Acting*, Denis Diderot spoke out strongly against acting based on genuine emotion, and concluded his argument with the following words:

> They say an actor is all the better for being excited, for being angry. I deny it. He is best when he imitates anger. Actors impress the public not when they are furious, but when they play fury well. In tribunals, in assemblies, everywhere where a man wishes to make himself master of others' minds, he feigns now anger, now fear, now pity, now love, to bring others into these diverse states of feeling. What passion itself fails to do, passion well imitated accomplishes.

The opposite view was expressed by Charles Macklin, the English actor, who was an exponent of "naturalism" long before the term was in use. Macklin wrote:

> It is the duty of an actor always to know the passion and the humor of each character so correctly, so intimately, and (if you will allow me the expression) to feel it so enthusiastically, as to be able to define and describe it as a philosopher; to give its operations on the looks, tones, and gestures of general nature, as it is ranked in classes of character; and to mold all this knowledge, mental and corporeal, to the characteristic that the poet has given to a particular character. . . . He [the actor] must suit his looks, tones, gestures, and manners to the character: the suiting the character to the powers of the actor, is imposture.

Such theoretical discussions had little effect in actual practice, however, for even during the greater part of the nineteenth century, "romantic" acting con-tinued to be exaggerated and artificial. Actors ranted and raved; the plays of the period were for the most part "cloak and dagger" dramas which provided actors with excellent opportunities to use vocal gymnastics and flamboyant gestures. Even Rachel in the restrained plays of Racine, and Edmund Kean in Shake-spearean roles were noted for acting that went beyond passion to violence. It was Coleridge who said, "To see Kean was to read Shakespeare by flashes of lightning."

The widespread interest in the late nineteenth century in sociology and psy-chology led actors to a study of human emotions, motivations, and relationships and the effect of the environment on character and personality, and produced naturalistic acting as we know it. It was seen first in the handling of the crowd scenes in the plays put on by George II, the Duke of Saxe-Meiningen, the first of the great modern stage directors. In the Duke's productions, the people in the crowds seemed to have stepped in off the street, so lifelike were their actions and reactions; but whether this could be considered *acting* is questionable, since the director dictated every gesture and inflection of the group. These actors behaved like intelligent puppets. Stanislavsky, seeing the Duke's company when it toured in Russia, was so impressed that he at once began to work for the same sort of ensemble effects; but instead of manipulating his actors like a puppeteer (a procedure he tried at first but later gave up), Stanislavsky developed a method of acting by which the actor, drawing upon his own psyche, was able to achieve emotional identification with the character he was portraying.

The Stanislavsky method, which aims at preparing a performer to create dramatic characterizations of great realism and psychological truth, requires the actor to do special exercises and improvisations in order to stimulate sense and affective memories and to achieve relaxation and concentration. It aims first at arousing in the actor those emotions he felt in the past in specific situations which can be grafted on to the scene and character he is at present portraying. The actor must work for absolute relaxation while on stage, be totally unaware of the existence of the audience, and concentrate deeply in order to attain complete identification—intellectual, emotional, and spiritual—with the character he is embodying, while there is a free flow of psychic energy from his unconscious. The system is not cut-and-dried, but plastic and variable, since each actor must draw upon his own psychological and emotional equipment. As Lee Strasberg, a celebrated teacher of the "method," explains it: "It does not give the actor rules, but tools." At present there are many variations of the Stanislavsky method in use, and no modern actor or teacher of acting ignores it completely, though some question its value. In combination with the photographic accuracy of costumes and settings, and many refinements in makeup and stage lighting, "internal" acting has produced the most realistic theatrical representation the stage has ever known. In America, this style of acting has superseded every other; at the present time, we cannot match the beautiful stylization of period acting which the British achieve nor the extraordinary mime and movement of the French. Acting is a plastic and evolving art. The present realistic phase is as much of a convention as were the masks and robes of Greece. It is impossible to predict what the acting of the future will be like, for as the aims and ideals of a culture change so do its art forms.

The actor in America today is not entirely free from the stigma of his profession, which still retains an aura of bohemianism and irresponsibility. But acting, as an occupation, seems so colorful and exciting that it attracts many young people who are under the impression that great and immediate financial rewards are to be gained in this field. Nothing could be further from the truth; according to the statistics of Actors' Equity Association, the trade union of the profession, the great majority of its members are totally unemployed in the theater; those who do get more or less regular work earn rather small annual salaries; while the comparatively few who achieve great fame earn the large salaries we read about.

Stage employment has actually decreased sharply in recent years; many actors have turned to motion pictures, radio, and television in search of jobs. Recently, too, there has grown up in the entertainment world a cult of "personality" which requires a performer to possess highly individualistic talents or unusual physical characteristics, which are exploited in the manner of a commercial commodity. Still, no actor may hope to reach the highest levels of his art unless that art is founded on sound discipline and fostered by unswerving dedication.

Direction

The theatrical director first made his appearance less than one hundred years ago. Before that time, the task of coordinating the various elements of a production was in the hands of the playwright, the star, or the stage manager. There was no actual need for a director in the Greek, medieval, Elizabethan, or Neoclassical theaters for in each of them dramatic presentations had more or less fixed and traditional forms which audiences expected and the acting companies supplied.

The plays of the Greek dramatists were the central ritual of a public festival, and the writers, like officiating priests, concerned themselves with the mounting as well as with the writing of the scripts. Aeschylus, for instance, designed costumes and scenery and trained the chorus and dancers. In the medieval theater, ordained priests of the Catholic faith, acted in and designed the plays they had helped to compose. The theaters of Shakespeare and Molière expressed the social rather than the religious concepts of their societies, in which the actors and audiences were unified by collective values and conventions that permeated the culture from the monarch to the masses. Here, too, we find that the staging of plays was performed by the playwrights themselves.

During the next two centuries, however, the dramatist went into eclipse and all communal traditions disappeared. Then the actor became the dominant figure in the theater, and began to assume the responsibility for the style, tone, and management of the productional aspects of the plays in which he appeared. David Garrick concerned himself with scenery and costumes; John Philip Kemble, William Charles Macready, and Samuel Phelps paid increasing attention to the total integration of their productions, including the careful rehearsal of extras. Charles Kean went further than any other actor in insisting upon the archeological correctness of sets and costumes, and the planned movements of stage crowds as well as of featured players in all his productions. These actor-producers were assisted by a staff of stage managers and technical experts, including scholars and historians.

The man who surpassed all his predecessors in integrating the theatrical arts and who deserves the honor of being called the first stage director is George II, Duke of Saxe-Meiningen (1866-1914). He designed and directed every detail that went into his astounding productions; while his wife, who had been an actress, and his stage manager Ludwig Chronegk worked under his orders. In an attempt to create a realistic stage picture, the Duke demanded historical accuracy in his sets and costumes, and expert ensemble acting which was arrived at after weeks and even months of intensive rehearsals. From the very first rehearsal the actors used the actual sets, costumes, and properties designed for the play. As Lee Simonson has said, the Duke's work revealed "the necessity for a commanding director who could visualize an entire performance and give it unity as an interpretation by complete control of every moment of it; the interpretive value of the smallest details of lighting, costuming, makeup, stage setting; the immense discipline and the degree of organization needed before the performance was capable of expressing the 'soul of the play.'"

Between 1874 and 1890 the Duke's company traveled throughout Europe and gave about twenty-six hundred performances in such cities as London, Berlin, Brussels, Stockholm, Basel, and Moscow. These productions created a sensation wherever they were seen and started a chain reaction of imitation and innovation. Antoine in Paris, Brahm in Berlin, and Stanislavsky in Moscow became the greatest naturalistic directors in the European theater. Stanislavsky began by behaving like a drill sergeant, giving his actors every inflection, every movement and gesture, all worked out in advance and set down in detailed production notes. It took him about twenty-five years to realize that his technique produced only an external realism. By throwing away his production notes, planning nothing in advance but working plastically with his actors step by step through a play, he was finally able to achieve an inner, or psychological realism of greater validity.

As society has become more eclectic, materialistic, and cynical, two types of plays have come to dominate the stages of the world: the didactic and the spectacular. The former consists of "the slice of life," the case history, or the social problem set upon the stage; the latter ranges from the classical revival to the latest musical comedy. Modern directors have mounted these two basic types of plays in an enormous variety of productional styles; most practitioners have now departed from photographic realism and scientific naturalism and have introduced elements of symbolism, expressionism, impressionism, constructivism, and other forms of theatricalism. The outstanding directors in the newer styles have been Max Reinhardt, Vsevolod Meyerhold, Jacques Copeau, Bertolt Brecht, Tyrone Guthrie, Peter Brook, and Elia Kazan. In our fragmented age, each of these men has stamped his productions with the special imprint of his own personality and predilections; and directors will go on working in this individualistic manner until plays once again mirror the "form and pressure" of a cohesive culture, an eventuality not likely to occur within the foreseeable future.

Scenery, Properties, and Lighting

Scenery in the modern sense of the word began to be used only after the withdrawal of the stage behind the proscenium; that is to say, in the time of the later Renaissance in Europe generally, and of the Restoration in England. When the stage was presented to view within the frame of the proscenium arch, it was natural that the stage picture should be embellished accordingly. The stage was divided from the auditorium by a front curtain behind which was an elaborate scene calculated to move the audience to delight and surprise. The stage designs of Burnacini and of the Bibbiena family still fill us with wonder at their complexity and grandeur and continue to exert an influence on modern designers. To heighten the pictorial quality of the scene and to preserve the illusion of reality within the picture frame, David Garrick in England and Voltaire in France drove the spectators from the stage.

The stage picture changed its character as it reflected contemporary taste in art and architecture and as it capitulated to theatrical expediency. During the seventeenth and eighteenth centuries, scenery consisted mainly of a backdrop (a painted cloth that hung at the rear of the stage) and sidewings (painted canvas flats ranging in parallel rows on each side of the stage from the footlights to the backdrop). The flats represented buildings or trees rendered in perspective which continued in painting on the back-cloth and disappeared on the distant horizon. To make scene-shifting easier, painted flats and cloths gradually replaced all solidly built scenery, though scene-painters themselves admitted that a painted representation could never achieve the realism of an architectural column or cornice. The interior of a castle, nevertheless, was painted in detail complete with paneled walls, mullioned windows, stags' antlers, and coats of arms, while the interiors of humbler homes showed rough plaster walls, bare tables, rickety chairs, and pots and pans around the hearth. Actual stage furnishings were extremely meager. The stage itself during the eighteenth and nineteenth centuries became shallower and forced the actor to stand closer to the painted drops, which showed up the false perspective and destroyed all illusion of reality.

The cult of realism brought with it a revolution in stage settings. The box-set, a room with the "fourth wall" removed, became the standard interior, and persists to the present time. At first the walls of the room were constructed of painted canvas with openings for practical doors and windows; gradually the walls were built of sturdier materials and the stage was furnished in elaborate detail with rugs, pictures, curtains, plants, and bric-a-brac.

Two leaders in the revolt against naturalistic settings were Gordon Craig and Adolphe Appia; neither was a man of the theater; both were influential theoreticians who objected to papier-mâché buildings, painted canvas, and cluttered stages, and advocated instead almost bare stages with stylized and impressionistic scenery and the creative use of lights and shadows. Their theories were brought to fruition by such men as Robert Edmond Jones, Norman Bel Geddes, Lee Simonson, Jo Mielziner, and Teo Otto. As Sheldon Cheney remarks, "Today the setting is flat, perspectiveless, simplified almost to bareness; surface reality no longer is pictured, but only faintly suggested, the 'atmosphere' is caught in color and light. Progress today seems all in the direction of space stages and honestly architectural stages. Painting on the stage seems to have gone into almost complete eclipse." The newer styles in scene design include Expressionism, in which the forms are sculptural and symbolic; Constructivism, in which they are architectural and skeletal; and Theatricalism, in which they are antirealistic, symbolic, and fantastic.

The invention of electric lighting provided the modern scene designer with one of his most important tools. Lighting presented a problem in the seventeenth-century theater because candles, even when used in enormous quantities, did not furnish sufficient illumination and could not be properly controlled. There was a decided improvement when candles were replaced by oil lamps, and a further advance with the introduction of gas. By the end of the nineteenth century a dimmer-switchboard was in use; this instrument controlled the level of light by regulating the flow of gas. It was not until the installation of electricity, however, that stage lighting could develop into a full-fledged art.

The principles of stage lighting were actually worked out by Adolphe Appia, but his theories have been put into practice by modern lighting experts and scene designers. Lighting may be used in two ways: for general illumination, flooding the stage with an even radiance; and for focused or spot lighting, picking out and emphasizing certain areas or people. By the use of colored gelatins and various levels and intensities of light, the designer is able to add mood and atmosphere to the setting, and to achieve great plasticity and the most subtle emotional effects.

Stage lighting is controlled from a switchboard which can keep a constant intensity, or range it up or down to a brilliant glare or faintly perceptible glow. Banks of "dimmers," adjustable lenses on individual flood or spot lamps, and an enormous array of border, strip, foot, and portable units make stage lighting so flexible and so expressive that changes in the level of the illumination may go unnoticed by the spectator and yet intensify his emotional reactions to the performance. The concept of space has also been altered by modern stage lighting; an actor stepping out of a "hot" spot into semidarkness just a few feet away appears to have moved farther than one who goes clear across the stage in bright and even light.

A light-plot is a very important part of every modern production; scene by scene throughout the play, it is a visual comment on the action. It is a part of the stage manager's prompt-book, and the work plan for the stage electrician. There are special light rehearsals, and for a complicated production several days may be consumed while the scene designer, who usually handles the lighting, sets the instruments and the readings. The latest electronic switchboard permits the presetting of hundreds of light cues in the most complicated combinations.

In addition to enforcing the three-dimensional quality of the modern stage, electric lighting has made the use of projected scenery feasible. Enlarged images may be thrown upon a screen or screens, and these serve, in place of either painted or built scenery, as the background against which the actor performs. Slide projections and motion-picture films have been widely used in theatricalist productions.

Costumes

Throughout the eighteenth century and well into the nineteenth there was a unity of style in theatrical costuming that had carried over from the entertainments of Louis XIV. All stage heroes—in Europe and America—wore a variation of the Roman military tunic which consisted of a breastplate, short skirt, helmet surmounted by plumes, and high, cross-gartered boots. A shield or spear often completed the costume. If the character was supposed to be an Oriental or exotic in any way, he wore a turban with plumes and a long robe. The costumes of the women resembled the high style of their own day; no matter how theatrical they were made to appear, they always contained a suggestion of the laced corsage, the puffed sleeve, the hoop skirt.

David Garrick created a furor when he abolished the Roman costume and adopted contemporary male attire for Romeo and Hamlet; he played Macbeth in the scarlet of the King's livery. During the greater part of the nineteenth century, the "costume play" contained an unbelievably weird assortment of styles. It was not until individual actors such as Samuel Phelps and Charles Kean strove for historical correctness in their productions that stage costume improved.

In the twentieth century there have been three main types of costume: historical, contemporary, and theatricalist.

Designers of historical costumes strive for authenticity of silhouette, texture, and color. Before embarking on a project, the designer will study the records and pictures of the period in which he is interested in order to reproduce the clothing with a high degree of reality. The stage costume will not be identical to the real one; it will merely appear to be so. It may be necessary to make minor modifications in the structure of the clothing to enable the actor to move with greater ease or to speed the change from one costume to another; and certain materials, such as satin brocades, may be too expensive to buy or too difficult to handle, but the clever designer is able to treat a cheaper and lighter fabric in such a way as to create a luxurious impression. Properties and makeup are also designed with an eye for archeological accuracy.

Contemporary clothing is designed to create a realistic effect, but stage costumes are usually done more broadly than those ordinarily worn at home. This is necessary so that they will be visible from the stage; to achieve the desired effect the lines of the costume are exaggerated and certain elements are emphasized. Colors are frequently modified and cover larger areas; and fabrics are specially selected for ease of handling and to facilitate the movement of the actor. Modern clothes may heighten the actor's characterization, as in the case of Stanley Kowalski's torn shirt and Blanche DuBois's fluffy dresses, or intensify the mood and tone of the entire play, the effect created by the homespun clothing in Desire Under the Elms and by Claire Zachanassian's magnificent wardrobe, befitting the "richest woman in the world," in The Visit.

A rather recent development in stage costuming is the practice of calling in a famous fashion designer, not ordinarily connected with the theater, to provide the dresses for the wealthy heroine of the play. Mainbocher, Schiaparelli, Valentina, Castillo, and Dior are some of the couturiers whose gowns have been seen on Broadway stages.

Theatricalist costumes are the stylized or fantastic creations used in non-naturalistic plays. In Rostand's Chanticleer, for example, the characters are dressed to resemble barnyard animals. Roger Furse combined historical and theatricalist costumes in his production of Macbeth; the Scotsmen were attired in clothing patterned on that actually worn in the period, while the witches were dressed in fantastic creations. Many expressionist, constructivist, and theatricalist plays use highly stylized costumes for the purpose of symbolism and allegory.

Music and Dance

The forerunners of musical comedy—ballet, opera, operetta, burletta, and pantomime—as well as modern musical plays and revues, have always depended upon music and dance. But from the seventeenth century to the early twentieth, music and dance also played an important, though impertinent, part in serious drama and even in tragedy. All theatrical productions were looked upon merely as "entertainments" and "shows," and those plays were considered most successful into which elaborate song and dance interludes were injected no matter how inappropriate they might be.

Davenant virtually turned *Macbeth* into an opera whose lavishness increased from season to season (see p. 129); and a Restoration tragedy, *The Empress of Morocco* (1673), was actually a pastiche of rhymed speeches, songs, and dances. In 1747 Charles Macklin—the first actor to conceive of Shylock as a serious, almost tragic figure—appeared in a production of *The Merchant of Venice* that had in the midst of it a spectacular dancing interlude performed by the ballet stars of the day. About one hundred years later, Charles Kean, who was noted for the historical accuracy of his Shakespearean productions, appeared in a performance of *Hamlet*, about which a contemporary paper said: "The house was filled in every part long before the rising of the curtain—all present being anxious to catch a glimpse of the 'greatest actor of the day.' The discussion as to his merits or demerits, during the performance of the overture, was such as to drown all the beauty of the music, which was performed on this occasion for the sole amusement of the gentlemen of the orchestra."

Toward the middle of the nineteenth century, Richard Wagner tried to integrate meaning, movement, and music in what he called "music drama," but the result was opera. The realists succeeded, however, in eliminating extraneous songs and dances from serious plays; they retained only those that were appropriate to the action or the characters.

The music and dance in use in serious modern drama are mainly of two types: Integrated and incidental. Integrated songs and dances are those called for by the playwright because they are relevant to the dramatic action, help to delineate character, or heighten the mood or atmosphere of the play. Examples are the Varsouviana, a song associated with the past in the mind of Blanche, in *Streetcar;* and the music played by the blind eunuchs for Claire's personal satisfaction in *The Visit.*

Incidental music may or may not be called for by the dramatist but it is specially composed to accompany the action and is intended to enhance the emotional impact of the play. Edvard Grieg's score for *Peer Gynt* and Alex North's for *Death of a Salesman* are examples of this type of musical accompaniment.

Irrelevant music is still occasionally heard in many theaters where it serves as an overture to the play and as "entertainment" during intermissions; its use, fortunately, appears to be declining.

Nonnaturalistic drama leans much more heavily upon music and dance than does drama that attempts to create the illusion of reality. The Epic theater of Bertolt Brecht, the Expressionism of Ernst Toller, and the Theatricalism of the Habima make extensive use of choreographic movement that resembles dance, chanted speech that approaches song, and specially composed musical scores. These newer styles of production have had a noticeable influence on modern musical comedies and revues, which often contain allegorical and symbolic elements expressed in abstract movement and atonal music.

The Audience

The playgoer always determines the type and quality of the plays that are written and produced for him, and this is especially true in the commercial theater. Audiences represent, in little, the tastes, aims, and interests of the entire society; they are a microcosm of the culture.

When the Puritans closed the theaters in England in 1642, they brought to an end the great mass audiences of the Renaissance. The playgoers of the Restoration (1660) were members of a very special class. At first the main support for the theater came from the Court and its entourage; this in part explains the sophisticated wit and immorality in the plays of the period.

During the eighteenth and nineteenth centuries, the middle classes began to flock to the theater and brought with them their more moral and conventional tastes, as well as their materialistic interests. The plays they applauded were bourgeois tragedies and melodramas full of pathos and platitudes. By the middle of the nineteenth century, audiences were ready for a closer and less sentimental look at the world, and realism began to make its appearance on the stage; the average playgoer's increasing interest in sociology and psychology was maintained into the twentieth century, and naturalism, expressionism, and symbolism followed in regular order. Writers were allowed ever greater freedom to explore sexual themes and sordid situations, and many plays were frankly polemical and reformatory. Dramatized case histories of abnormal people vied with spectacular musical comedies for the attention of materialistic, cynical, and generally bored audiences.

The program called *Playbill* which is distributed free of charge in all commercial theaters in New York City has, during the past twenty years, sponsored numerous market surveys in an effort to determine the exact composition of the Broadway audience, its frequency of attendance, and other pertinent facts concerning it. The following are some of its conclusions: About a million and a quarter people (natives and out-of-towners combined) attend the theaters in New York over nine and one-half million times during the year. Seventy percent of these people are over thirty years old; and women make up slightly more than half the number. The three largest occupational groups are housewives, professionals and semiprofessionals, and major and minor executives in large business concerns. Seventy-eight percent of the audience earn over five thousand dollars a year, and a very large percentage are home and car owners, and have traveled widely both in this country and abroad. For their seats at musical comedies these people pay from $2.30 to $9.40, and at straight plays from $2.30 to $7.50.

A relatively small number of people in each audience wear dinner jackets and evening gowns to the theater, but the average playgoer appears in informal attire. John Chapman, the drama critic, has complained bitterly in his columns because audiences turn up at the theater in "drab business suits" instead of "dressing" for the occasion, but despite the high price of tickets and the difficulty of obtaining them, theatergoing is no longer considered an "event."

The behavior of the Broadway playgoer is reserved and subdued. There are few outbursts of enthusiasm and fewer of resentment; no riots have occurred because of artistic principles or personal partisanships in over a century. If displeased, audiences are inclined to be contemptuous rather than indignant. A very bad play will send them into fits of laughter; a very dull one will send them home.

Because of the theater shortage, plays which are not immediate hits disappear quickly from the scene. This creates an abnormally heavy demand for tickets to current plays. Immediately upon the announcement of a play that seems likely to be a success, though the opening date is months in the future, people send checks to the producers' offices with orders for seats. On the day after the opening of a play that has received good notices, long lines form at the box-office; tickets are bought three to six months in advance of the actual performance. Theatergoers also buy tickets at set fees above the box-office price from legal brokers, at high premiums through charitable organizations, and at exorbitant prices from speculators. There are preview clubs, play-of-the-month clubs, and other ticket-supplying organizations. Out-of-towners have all of these devices and several others at their disposal; they may buy tickets to plays through travel agencies as part of a "tour" of New York, or book passage on a show-train or show-plane which makes a special excursion from some distant city to Broadway, providing dinner, a play, and transportation in a neat little package.

In addition to Broadway audiences there are, in America, at least six other categories of playgoers for semiprofessional and amateur theaters: audiences who attend the many little theaters off-Broadway; "road" audiences in the eighteen or twenty cities throughout the nation where commercial theater is presented more or less regularly during the year; audiences for summer and winter stock companies; community theater audiences; college and university theater audiences, a growing and discriminating brotherhood; and finally, a very special and important group, juvenile audiences—the audience of the future.

THE PRODUCTION RECORD

A *Streetcar Named Desire* opened on Broadway on December 3, 1947, and closed on December 17, 1949, achieving a run of 855 performances. Only 18 other nonmusical plays have had longer runs in the history of the New York stage.

The play won three important theater awards—the Pulitzer Prize, the New York Drama Critics' Circle Award, and the Donaldson Award—as the best work of the season 1947-48; and grossed approximately $2,900,000, with the motion picture rights going for about $300,000.

Jessica Tandy and Marlon Brando left the cast before the play had concluded its Broadway run. They were replaced by Uta Hagen and Anthony Quinn, who stayed with the play until it closed in New York, then headed the company that went on a long national tour, which included Boston, Philadelphia, Chicago, and many other cities, and returned for a final two-week engagement at the New York City Center from May 23 to June 11, 1950.

A production directed by Laurence Olivier, starring Vivien Leigh and Bonar Colleano, opened in October, 1949, at the Aldwych Theater, London. In November, 1949, a French adaptation by Jean Cocteau, with sets by Christian Berard, was put on in Paris with Arletty and Yves Vincent in the leading roles.

In May, 1950, the acting company of the celebrated Schlosspark Theater in East Berlin gave a series of guest performances of *Streetcar* at the Comedy Playhouse, under the direction of Berthold Viertel. The critics wrote the following about Marianne Hoppe as Blanche and Peter Mosbacher as Stanley: "Marianne Hoppe offered a performance in tone, gesture, and movements that was in the best tradition of the Berlin theater. With a great variety of expression and dramatic intensity, she mastered the brutal as well as the delicate aspects of her role. She rendered the smooth transitions as well as the abrupt ones, and from scene to scene she made the compulsive elements in her physical, psychic, and spiritual disintegration so depressingly clear that the final onset of insanity actually came as a relief."—(From *The Daily Mirror*). "Peter Mosbacher, as Kowalski, is an unbridled and vital animal that defends its mate (Stella) and its position as a male, with tooth and claw, and just like a healthy animal he bites the sick one (Blanche) and drives it away. It is not sadism that causes Stanley to perpetrate his unspeakable cruelties but the rude healthiness that loathes the sick."—(From *The Telegraph*).

For the next half dozen years, the play was produced repeatedly in summer stock, community, semiprofessional, and professional theaters, not only in the United States and in Canada, but throughout the world. Some of the well-known actors who appeared in the play at one time or another include Judith Evelyn, Richard Kiley, and Kim Stanley.

In March, 1955, the play was put on, partly under Tennessee Williams's own supervision, by Originals Only, an off-Broadway group whose theater was situated in a cellar on Seventh Avenue South in New York. Seen in the leading role was a Russian actress, Maria Britneva, who according to Williams, gave the only "perfect" performance of Blanche DuBois.

The last professional production of the play opened in New York on February 15, 1956, for a limited engagement, again at the City Center, with a company headed by Tallulah Bankhead.

A *Streetcar Named Desire* was also successfully adapted into other theatrical forms. The film, produced in Hollywood by Warner Brothers and directed by

Kazan, was released in 1951 with the original cast intact, except for Jessica Tandy, whose role was assumed by Vivien Leigh. The film received three awards from the New York Film Critics' Circle, and three Academy Awards.

As a ballet, A *Streetcar Named Desire* was choreographed by Valerie Bettis to the musical score which Alex North had written for the film. This music is available on a long-playing record. Peter Larkin provided the sets, and the leading roles were danced by Mia Slavenska and Frederic Franklin. The ballet opened at the Century Theater, New York, on December 8, 1952, for what was planned as a very brief run, but the acclaim of critics and audiences kept it going for several months. The attraction broke records for ballet by taking in over $19,000 a week.

On October 30, 1955, as a regular part of its Sunday evening program on WCBS-TV, *Omnibus* presented Scene Six from A *Streetcar Named Desire* with Jessica Tandy as Blanche, and Hume Cronyn at Mitch.

The film version of *Streetcar* had been one of the greatest money-making motion pictures of all time, having grossed $4,250,000 by 1952; in 1958 the picture was reissued for showings around the country and during the next two years earned an additional one million dollars.

The World I Live In
Tennessee Williams Interviews Himself *

Question. Can we talk frankly?
Answer. There's no other way we can talk.
Q. Perhaps you know that when your first successful play, *The Glass Menagerie*, was revived early this season, a majority of the reviewers felt that it was still the best play you have written, although it is now twelve years old?
A. Yes, I read all my play notices and criticisms, even those that say that I write for money and that my primary appeal is to brutal and ugly instincts.
Q. Where there is so much smoke—!
A. A fire smokes the most when you start pouring water on it.
Q. But surely you'll admit that there's been a disturbing note of harshness and coldness and violence and anger in your more recent works?
A. I think, without planning to do so, I have followed the developing tension and anger and violence of the world and time that I live in through my own steadily increasing tension as a writer and person.
Q. Then you admit that this "developing tension," as you call it, is a reflection of a condition in yourself?
A. Yes.
Q. A morbid condition?
A. Yes.
Q. Perhaps verging on the psychotic?
A. I guess my work has always been a kind of psychotherapy for me.

* *The Observer*, London, April 7, 1957. Reprinted by permission.

Q. But how can you expect audiences to be impressed by plays and other writings that are created as a release for the tensions of a possible or incipient madman?

A. It releases their own.

Q. Their own what?

A. Increasing tensions, verging on the psychotic.

Q. You think the world's going mad?

A. Going? I'd say nearly gone! As the Gipsy said in *Camino Real,* the world is a funny paper read backwards. And that way it isn't so funny.

Q. How far do you think you can go with this tortured view of the world?

A. As far as the world can go in its tortured condition, maybe that far, but no further.

Q. You don't expect audiences and critics to go along with you, do you?

A. No.

Q. Then why do you push and pull them that way?

A. I go that way. I don't push or pull anyone with me.

Q. Yes, but you hope to continue to have people listen to you, don't you?

A. Naturally I hope to.

Q. Even if you throw them off by the violence and horror of your works?

A. Haven't you noticed that people are dropping all around you, like moths out of season, as the result of the present plague of violence and horror in this world and time that we live in?

Q. But you're an entertainer, with artistic pretensions, and people are not entertained any more by cats on hot tin roofs and Baby Dolls and passengers on crazy streetcars!

A. Then let them go to the musicals and the comedies. I'm not going to change my ways. It's hard enough for me to write what I want to write without me trying to write what you say they want me to write which I don't want to write.

Q. Do you have any positive message, in your opinion?

A. Indeed I do think that I do.

Q. Such as what?

A. The crying, almost screaming, need of a great worldwide human effort to know ourselves and each other a great deal better, well enough to concede that no man has a monopoly on right or virtue any more than any man has a corner on duplicity and evil and so forth. If people, and races and nations, would start with that self-manifest truth, then I think that the world could sidestep the sort of corruption which I have involuntarily chosen as the basic, allegorical theme of my plays as a whole.

Q. You sound as if you felt quite detached and superior to this process of corruption in society.

A. I have never written about any kind of vice which I can't observe in myself.

Q. But you accuse society, as a whole, of succumbing to a deliberate mendacity, and you appear to find yourself separate from it as a writer.

A. As a writer, yes, but not as a person.

Q. Do you think this is a peculiar virtue of yours as a writer?

A. I'm not sentimental about writers. But I'm inclined to think that most writers, and most other artists, too, are primarily motivated in their desperate vocation by a desire to find and to separate truth from the complex of lies and evasions they live in, and I think that this impulse is what makes their work not so much a profession as a vocation, a true "calling."

Q. Why don't you write about nice people? Haven't you ever known any nice people in your life?

A. My theory about nice people is so simple that I am embarrassed to say it.

Q. Please say it!

A. Well, I've never met one that I couldn't love if I completely knew him and understood him, and in my work I have at least tried to arrive at knowledge and understanding.

I don't believe in "original sin." I don't believe in "guilt." I don't believe in villains or heroes—only in right or wrong ways that individuals have taken, not by choice but by necessity or by certain still-uncomprehended influences in themselves, their circumstances and their antecedents.

This is so simple I'm ashamed to say it, but I'm sure it's true. In fact, I would bet my life on it! And that's why I don't understand why our propaganda machines are always trying to teach us, to persuade us, to hate and fear other people on the same little world that we live in.

Why don't we meet these people and get to know them as I try to meet and know people in my plays? This sounds terribly vain and egotistical.

I don't want to end on such a note. Then what shall I say? That I know that I am a minor artist who has happened to write one or two major works? I can't even say which they are. It doesn't matter. I have said my say. I may still say it again, or I may shut up now. It doesn't depend on you, it depends entirely on me, and the operation of chance or Providence in my life.

(*The interview ends.*)

THE DIRECTOR'S NOTEBOOK
By Elia Kazan

The richness of the characterizations in both the stage and screen versions of *A Streetcar Named Desire* is the result of Elia Kazan's careful, detailed, and penetrating analysis of the central figures in the drama. Kazan, who had been an actor with the Group Theater before embarking on his brilliant career as a director, makes use of the Stanislavsky system of isolating the "spine" (the basic motivation) of each character. In his personal notebook, dated August, 1947, Kazan recorded his thoughts and feelings concerning his "work in progress." The following are some of his notes:

A *thought*—directing finally consists of turning Psychology into Behavior.

Theme—this is a message from the dark interior. This little twisted, pathetic, confused bit of light and culture puts out a cry. It is snuffed out by the crude forces of violence, insensibility and vulgarity which exists in our South—and this cry is the play.

Style—one reason a "style," a stylized production is necessary is that a subjective factor—Blanche's memories, inner life, emotions, are a real factor. We cannot really understand her behavior unless we see the effect of her past on her present behavior.

This play is a poetic tragedy. We are shown the final dissolution of a person of worth, who once had great potential, and who, even as she goes down, has worth exceeding that of the "healthy," coarse-grained figures who kill her.

Blanche is a social type, an emblem of a dying civilization, making its last curlicued and romantic exit. All her behavior patterns are those of the dying civilization she represents. In other words her behavior is *social*. Therefore find social modes! This is the source of the play's stylization and the production's style and color. Likewise Stanley's behavior is *social* too. It is the basic animal cynicism of today. "Get what's coming to you! Don't waste a day! Eat, drink, get yours!" This is the basis of his stylization, of the choice of his props. All props should be stylized: they should have a color, shape and weight that spell: style.

An effort to put poetic names on scenes to edge me into stylizations and physicalizations. Try to keep each scene in terms of Blanche.

1. Blanche comes to the last stop at the end of the line.
2. Blanche tries to make a place for herself.
3. Blanche breaks them apart, but when they come together, Blanche is more alone than ever!
4. Blanche, more desperate because more excluded, tries the direct attack and makes the enemy who will finish her.
5. Blanche finds that she is being tracked down for the kill. She must work fast.
6. Blanche suddenly finds, suddenly makes for herself, the only possible, perfect man for her.
7. Blanche comes out of the happy bathroom to find that her own doom has caught up with her.
8. Blanche fights her last fight. Breaks down. Even Stella deserts her.
9. Blanche's last desperate effort to save herself by telling the whole truth. *The truth dooms her.*
10. Blanche escapes out of this world. She is brought back by Stanley and destroyed.
11. Blanche is disposed of.

The style—the real deep style—consists of one thing only: to find behavior that's truly social, significantly typical, at each moment. It's not so much what Blanche has done—it's how she does it—with such style, grace, manners, old-world trappings and effects, props, tricks, swirls, etc., that they seem anything but vulgar.

And for the other characters, too, you face the same problem. To find the Don Quixote character for them. *This is a poetic tragedy, not a realistic or a naturalistic one. So you must find a Don Quixote scheme of things for each.*

Stylized acting and direction is to realistic acting and direction as poetry is to prose. The acting must be styled, not in the obvious sense. (Say nothing about it to the producer and actors.) But you will fail unless you find this kind of poetic realization for the behavior of these people.

BLANCHE
"Blanche is Desperate"

"This is the End of the Line of the Streetcar Named Desire"

Spine—find Protection: the tradition of the old South says that it must be through another person.

Her problem has to do with her tradition. Her notion of what a woman should be. She is stuck with this "ideal." It is her. It is her ego. Unless she lives by it, she cannot live; in fact her whole life has been for nothing. Even the Allan Grey incident as she now tells it and believes it to have been, is a necessary piece of romanticism. Essentially, in outline, she tells what happened, but it also serves the demands of her notion of herself, to make her *special* and different, out of the tradition of the romantic ladies of the past: Swinburne, Wm. Morris, Pre-Raphaelites, etc. This way it serves as an excuse for a great deal of her behavior.

Because this image of herself cannot be accomplished in reality, certainly not in the South of our day and time, it is her effort and practice to *accomplish it in fantasy.* Everything that she does in *reality* too is colored by this necessity, this compulsion to be *special.* So, in fact, *reality becomes fantasy too.* She makes it so!

The variety essential to the play, and to Blanche's playing and to Jessica Tandy's achieving the role demands that she be a "heavy" at the beginning. For instance: contemplate the inner character contradiction: bossy yet helpless, domineering yet shaky, etc. The audience at the beginning should see her bad effect on Stella, want Stanley to tell her off. He does. He exposes her and then gradually, as they see how genuinely in pain, how actually desperate she is, how warm, tender and loving she can be (the Mitch story) how freighted with need she is—then they begin to go with her. They begin to realize that they are sitting in at the death of something extraordinary . . . colorful, varied, passionate, lost, witty, imaginative, of her own integrity . . . and then they feel the tragedy. In the playing too there can be a growing sincerity and directness.

The thing about the "tradition" in the nineteenth century was that *it worked then.* It made a woman feel important, with her own secure positions and functions, her own special worth. It also made a woman at that time *one with her society.* But *today* the tradition is an anachronism which simply does not function. *It does not work.* So while Blanche must believe it because it makes her special, because it makes her sticking by Belle Reve an act of heroism, rather than an absurd romanticism, still *it does not work.* It makes Blanche feel *alone, outside of her society.* Left out, insecure, shaky. The airs the "tradition" demands isolate her further, and every once in a while, her resistance weakened by drink, she breaks down and seeks human warmth and contact where she can find it, not on her terms, on theirs: the merchant, the traveling salesman and the others . . . Since she cannot integrate these episodes, she rejects them, begins to forget them, begins to live in fantasy, begins to rationalize and explain them to herself thus:

"I never was hard or self-sufficient enough . . ." As if you had to apologize for needing human contact! Also n.b. above—the word: protection. That is what she, as a woman in the tradition, so desperately needs. That's what she comes to Stella for, Stella and her husband. Not finding it from them she tries to get it from Mitch. *Protection*. A haven, a *harbor*. She is a refugee, punch drunk, and on the ropes, making her last stand, trying to keep up a gallant front, because she is a proud person. But really if Stella doesn't provide her haven, *where is she to go*. She's a misfit, a liar, her "airs" alienate people, she must act superior to them which alienates them further. She doesn't know how to work. So she can't make a living. She's really helpless. She needs someone to help her. Protection. She's a last dying relic of the last century now adrift in our unfriendly day. From time to time, for reasons of simple human loneliness and need she goes to pieces, smashes her tradition . . . then goes back to it. This conflict has developed into a terrible crisis. All she wants is a haven: "I want to rest! I want to breathe quietly again . . . just think! If it happens! I can leave here and have a home of my own . . ."

If this is a romantic tragedy, what is its inevitability and what is the tragic flaw? In the Aristotelian sense, the flaw is the need to be superior, special (or *her* need for protection and what it means to her), the "tradition." This creates an apartness so intense, a loneliness so gnawing that only a complete breakdown, a refusal, as it were, to contemplate what she's doing, a *binge* as it were, a destruction of all her standards, a desperate violent ride on the Streetcar Named Desire can break through the walls of her tradition. The tragic flaw creates the circumstances, inevitably, that destroy her. More later.

Try to find an entirely different character, a self-dramatized and self-romanticized character for Blanche to play in each scene. She is playing 11 different people. This will give it a kind of changeable and shimmering surface it should have. And all these 11 self-dramatized and romantic characters should be out of the romantic tradition of the pre-bellum South, etc. Example: Sc. 2 Gay Miss Devil-may-care.

There is another, simpler, and equally terrible contradiction in her own nature. She won't face her physical or sensual side. She calls it "brutal desire." She thinks she sins when she gives into it . . . yet she does give in to it, out of loneliness . . . but by calling it "brutal desire," she is able to separate it from her "real self," her "cultured," refined self. Her tradition makes no allowance, allows no space for this very real part of herself. So she is constantly in conflict, not at ease, sinning. *She's still looking for something that doesn't exist today, a gentleman*, who will . . . marry her, protect her, defend and maintain her honor, etc. She wants an old-fashioned wedding dressed in white . . . and still she does things out of "brutal desire" that make this impossible. *All this too is tradition*.

She has worth too—she is better than Stella. She says: "There has been some kind of progress . . . Such things as art—as poetry and music—such kinds of new light have come into the world . . . in some kinds of people some kinds of tenderer feelings have had some little beginning that we've got to make *grow!* And cling to, and hold as our flag! In this dark march toward whatever it is we're approaching . . . don't . . . don't hang back with the brutes!" And though the direct psychological motivation for this is jealousy and personal frustration, still she, alone and abandoned in the crude society of New Orleans back streets, is the *only voice of light*. It is flickering and, in the course of the play, goes out. But it is valuable because it is unique.

Blanche is a butterfly in a jungle looking for just a little momentary protection, doomed to a sudden, early violent death. The more I work on Blanche, incidentally, the less insane she seems. She is caught in a fatal inner contradiction, but in another society, she *would* work. In Stanley's society, no!

This is like a classic tragedy. Blanche is Medea or someone pursued by the Harpies, the Harpies being *her own nature*. Her inner sickness pursues her like *doom* and makes it impossible for her to attain the one thing she needs, the only thing she needs: a safe harbor.

An effort to phrase Blanche's spine: to find *protection,* to find something to hold onto, some strength in whose protection she can live, like a sucker shark or a parasite. The tradition of *woman* (or all women) can only live through the strength of someone else. Blanche is entirely dependent. Finally the doctor!

Blanche is an outdated creature, approaching extinction . . . like the dinosaur. She is about to be pushed off the edge of the earth. On the other hand she is a heightened version, an artistic intensification of all women. That is what makes the play universal. Blanche's special relation to all women is that she is at the critical point where *the one thing above all else that she is dependent on: her attraction for men, is beginning to go.* Blanche is like all women, dependent on a man, looking for one to hang onto; only *more so!*

So beyond being deeply desperate, Blanche is in a hurry. She'll be pushed off the earth soon. She carries her doom in her character. Also, her past is chasing her, catching up with her. Is it any wonder that she tries to attract each and every man she meets. She'll even take that protected feeling, that needed feeling, that superior feeling, for a moment. Because, at least for a moment, that anxiety, the hurt and the pain will be quenched. . . . Desire is the opposite of Death. For a moment the anxiety is still, for a moment the complete desire and concentration of a man is on her. He clings to you. He may say I love you. All else is anxiety, loneliness and being adrift.

Compelled by her nature (she must be special, superior) she makes it impossible with Stanley and Stella. She acts in a way that succeeds in being destructive. But the last bit of luck is with her. She finds the only man on earth whom she suits, a man who is looking for a dominant woman. For an instant she is happy. But her past catches up with her. Stanley, whom she's antagonized by her destructiveness aimed at his home, but especially by her need to be superior, uses her past, which he digs up, to destroy her. Finally she takes refuge in fantasy. She must have protection, closeness, love, safe harbor. The only place she can obtain them any longer is in her own mind. She "goes crazy."

Blanche is a stylized character, she should be played, should be dressed, should move like a stylized figure. What is the physicalization of an aristocratic woman pregnant with her own doom? . . . Behaving by a tradition that dooms her in this civilization, in this "culture"? All her behavior patterns are *old-fashioned, pure tradition.* All as if jellied in rote—

Why does the "blues" music fit the play? The Blues is an expression of the loneliness and rejection, the exclusion and isolation of the Negro and their (opposite) longing for love and connection. Blanche too is "looking for a home," abandoned, friendless. "I don't know where I'm going, but I'm going." Thus the Blue piano catches the soul of Blanche, the miserable unusual human side of the girl which is beneath her frenetic duplicity, her trickery, lies, etc. It tells, it emotionally reminds you what all the fireworks are caused by.

Blanche—Physically. Must at all times give a single impression: her social mask is: *the High-Bred Genteel Lady in Distress.* Her past, her destiny, her falling from grace is just a surprise . . . then a tragic contradiction. But the mask never breaks down.

The only way to understand any character is through yourself. Everyone is much more alike than they willingly admit. Even as frantic and fantastic a creature as Blanche is created by things you have felt and known, *if you'll dig for them and be honest about what you see.*

STELLA

One reason Stella submits to Stanley's solution at the end, is perfectly ready to, is that she has an unconscious hostility toward Blanche. Blanche is so patronizing, demanding and superior toward her . . . makes her so useless, old-fashioned and helpless . . . everything that Stanley has got her out of. Stanley has made a woman out of her. Blanche immediately returns her to the subjugation of childhood, younger-sisterness.

Stella would have been Blanche except for Stanley. She now knows what, how much Stanley means to her health. So . . . no matter what Stanley does . . . she must cling to him, as she does to life itself. To return to Blanche would be to return to the subjugation of the tradition.

The play is a triangle. Stella is the Apex. Unconsciously, Stella wants Blanche to go to Mitch because that will take Blanche off Stella.

And there is a Terrific Conflict between Blanche and Stella, especially in Stella's feelings. Blanche in effect in. Sc. 1 *Resubjugates* Stella. Stella loves her, hates her, fears her, pities her, is really through with her. Finally rejects her for Stanley.

All this of course Stella is aware of only unconsciously. It becomes a matter of conscious choice only in Sc. 11 . . . the climax of the play as it is the climax of the triangle story.

Stella is a refined girl who has found a kind of salvation or realization, *but at a terrific price.* She keeps her eyes closed, even stays in bed as much as possible so that she won't realize, won't *feel the pain* of this terrific price. She walks around as if narcotized, as if sleepy, as if in a daze. She is waiting for night. She's waiting for the dark where Stanley makes her feel *only him* and she has no reminder of the price she is paying. She wants no intrusion from the other world. She is drugged, trapped. She's in a sensual stupor. She shuts out all challenge all day long. She loafs, does her hair, her nails, fixes a dress, doesn't eat much, but prepares Stanley's dinner and waits for Stanley. She hopes for no other meaning from life. . . . Her entire attention is to make herself pretty and attractive for Stanley, kill time till night. In a way she is actually narcotized all day. She is buried alive in her flesh. She's half asleep. She is glazed across her eyes. She doesn't seem to see much. She laughs incessantly like a child tickled and stops abruptly as the stimuli, the tickling, stops and returns to the same condition, a pleasantly drugged child. Give her all kinds of narcotized business.

She has a paradise—a serenely limited paradise when Blanche enters—but Blanche makes her consider Stanley, judge Stanley and find him wanting, for the first time. But it is too late. In the end she returns to Stanley.

Stella is doomed too. She has sold herself out for a temporary solution. She's given up all hope, everything, just to live for Stanley's pleasures. So she is dependent on Stanley's least whim. But this can last only as long as Stanley wants her. And *secondly* and *chiefly*—Stella herself cannot live narcotized forever. There is more to her. She begins to feel . . . unfilled—not recognized . . . and besides she's deeper, needs more variety. Her only hope is her children, and, like so many women, she will begin to live more and more for her children.

She tries to conceal from herself her true needs. . . . But her real needs, for tenderness, for the several aspects of living, for realization in terms of herself— not only in terms of Stanley, *still live . . . she can't kill them* by ignoring them. Blanche, despite apparent failure, makes her realize certain things about Stanley. She hugs Stanley in Sc. 4 out of desperation, and out of a need to silence her doubts . . . but Blanche has succeeded in calling Stella's attention to her own "sell-out" . . . she never sees Stanley the same again—or their relationship.

Stella, at the beginning of the play won't face a *hostility* (concealed from herself and unrecognized) toward Stanley. She is *so* dependent on him, so compulsively compliant. She is giving up so much of herself, quieting so many voices of protest. She is Stanley's slave. She has sold out most of her life. Latent in Stella is rebellion. Blanche arouses it.

Stella is plain out of her head about Stanley. She has to keep herself from constantly touching him. She can hardly keep her hands off him. She is setting little traps all the time to conquer his act of indifference. . . . She embarrasses him (though he is secretly proud) by following him places. They have a game where he tries to shake her all the time and she pursues him, etc. . . . At the end of the play, her life is entirely different. It will never be the same with Stanley again.

Note from Tennessee Williams on the fourth day of rehearsal: "Gadge—I am a bit concerned over Stella in Scene One. It seems to me that she has too much vivacity, at times she is bouncing around in a way that suggests a co-ed on a benzedrine kick. I know it is impossible to be literal about the description 'narcotized tranquility' but I do think there is an important value in suggesting it, in contrast to Blanche's rather feverish excitability. Blanche is the quick, light one. Stella is relatively slow and almost indolent. Blanche mentions her 'Chinese philosophy'—the way she sits with her little hands folded like a cherub in a choir, etc. I think her natural passivity is one of the things that makes her acceptance of Stanley acceptable. She naturally 'gives in,' accepts, lets things slide, she does not make much of an effort."

STANLEY

The hedonist, objects, props, etc. Sucks on a cigar all day. Fruit, food, etc. He's got it all figured out, what fits, what doesn't. The pleasure scheme. He has all the confidence of resurgent flesh.

Also with a kind of naïveté . . . even slowness . . . he means no harm. He wants to knock no one down. He only doesn't want to be taken advantage of. His code is simple and simple-minded. He is adjusted *now* . . . later, as his sexual powers die, so will he; the trouble will come later, the "problems."

But what is the chink in his armor now, the contradiction? Why does Blanche get so completely under his skin? Why does he want to bring Blanche and, before her, Stella *down to his level?* It's as if he said: "I know I haven't got much, but no one has more and no one's going to have more." It's the hoodlum aristocrat. He's deeply dissatisfied, deeply hopeless, deeply cynical . . . the physical immediate pleasures, if they come in a steady enough stream quiet this *as long as no one gets more* . . . then his bitterness comes forth and he tears down the pretender. But Blanche he can't seem to do anything with. . . .

One of the important things for Stanley is that Blanche *would wreck his home.* Blanche is dangerous. She is destructive. She would soon have him and Stella fighting. He's got things the way he wants them around there and he does *not* want them upset by a phony, corrupt, sick, destructive woman. *This makes Stanley right!* Are we going into the era of Stanley? He may be practical and right . . . but what the hell does it leave us? Make this a removed objective characterization for Marlon Brando.

Choose Marlon's objects . . . the things he loves and prizes: all sensuous and sensual—the shirt, the cigar, the beer (how it's poured and nursed, etc.).

The one thing that Stanley can't bear is someone who thinks that he or she is better than he. His only way of explaining himself—he thinks he stinks—is that everyone else stinks. This is symbolic. True of our National State of Cynicism. No values. . . . There is nothing to command his loyalty. Stanley rapes Blanche because he has tried and tried to keep her down to his level. This way is the last. For a moment he succeeds. And then, in Scene 11, he has failed!

Stanley has got things his way. He fits into his environment. The culture and the civilization, even the neighborhood, etc., etc., the food, the drink, etc., are all his way. And he's got a great girl, with just enough hidden neuroticism for him— yet not enough to even threaten a real fight. Also their history is right: he conquered her. Their relationship is right: she waits up for him. Finally God and Nature gave him a fine sensory apparatus . . . he enjoys! The main thing the actor has to do in the early scenes is make the physical environment of Stanley, the *props* come to life.

Stanley is deeply indifferent. When he first meets Blanche he doesn't really seem to care if she stays or not. Stanley is interested in his own pleasures. He is completely self-absorbed to the point of fascination.

To physicalize this: he has a most annoying way of being preoccupied—or of busying himself with something else while people are talking with him, at him it becomes. Example, first couple of pages Scene 2, 11. Stanley thinks Stella is very badly brought up. She can't do any of the ordinary things—he had a girl before this that could really cook, but she drank an awful lot. Also she, Stella, has a lot of airs, most of which he's knocked out of her by now, but which still crop up. Emphasize Stanley's love for Stella. It is rough, embarrassed and he rather truculently *won't show it*. But it is there. He's proud of her. When he's not on guard and looking at her his eyes suddenly shine. He is grateful too, proud, satisfied. But he'd never show it, demonstrate it.

Stanley is supremely indifferent to everything except his own pleasure and comfort. He is marvelously selfish, a miracle of sensuous self-centeredness. He builds a hedonist life, and fights to the death to defend it—but finally it is *not* enough to hold Stella AND this philosophy is not successful even for him— because every once in a while the silenced, frustrated part of Stanley breaks loose in unexpected and unpredictable ways and we suddenly see, as in a burst of lightning, his real frustrated self. Usually this frustration is worked off by eating a lot, drinking a lot, gambling a lot. . . . He's going to get very fat later. He's desperately trying to drug his senses . . . overwhelming them with a constant round of sensation so that he will feel nothing else.

In Stanley sex goes under a disguise. Nothing is more erotic and arousing to him than "airs" . . . she thinks she's better than me . . . I'll show her . . . Sex equals domination . . . anything that challenges him—like calling him "common" arouses him. . . .

In the case of Brando, the question of enjoyment is particularly important. Stanley feeds himself. His world is hedonist. But what does he enjoy. . . . Conquest is poker, food . . . sweat. *Exercise*. But Enjoy! As a character Stanley is most interesting in his "contradictions," his "soft" moments, his sudden pathetic little-tough-boy tenderness toward Stella. Scene 3 he cries like a baby. Somewhere in Scene 8 he almost makes it up with Blanche. In Scene 10 he *does* try to make it up with her—and except for her doing the one thing that most arouses him . . . he might have.

MITCH

He wants the perfection his mother gave him . . . everything is approving, protective, *perfect for him*. Naturally no girl, today, no sensible, decent girl will give him this. But the tradition will.

Like Stella, Mitch hides from his own problem through mother-love.

Mitch is the end product of a matriarchy . . . his mother has robbed him of all daring, initiative, self-reliance. He does not face his own needs.

Mitch is Blanche's ideal in a comic form, 150 years late. He is big, tough, burly, has a rough southern voice and a manner of a homespun, coarse, awkward, overgrown boy, with a heart of mush. He's like that character (who cries easy) in

Sing Out Sweet Land. He is a little embarrassed by his strength in front of women. He is straight out of Mack Sennett comedy—but Malden has to create the reality of it, the truth behind that corny image. Against his blundering strength there is shown off the fragility and fragrance of a girl. Her delicacy. "Lennie" in *Mice and Men.*

Mitch, too, is most interesting in his basic contradictions. He doesn't want to be Mother's Boy. . . . He just can't help it. He does love his Mother, but is a little embarrassed at how much. Blanche makes a man out of him, makes him important and grown-up. His Mother—he dimly realizes—keeps him eternally adolescent, forever dependent. . . . The reason he's so clumsy with women is that he's so full of violent desire for them.

BLANCHE DUBOIS
An Interview with Jessica Tandy

In 1946, Jessica Tandy appeared under the direction of Hume Cronyn at the Actors' Lab in Hollywood in a production of Tennessee Williams's one-act *Portrait of a Madonna.* The central figure in this short play, the frustrated Miss Lucretia Collins, resembles Blanche DuBois in some ways, but whereas Miss Collins has never had the courage to face reality and has retreated from life consistently since her youth, Blanche has battled most courageously and met life time and again head on until she, too, finds it necessary to retreat into a kindlier world of dreams. Miss Tandy's performance in *Portrait of a Madonna* was highly praised. While visiting New York, shortly after this production, Mr. Cronyn was given the opportunity to read Tennessee Williams's new play, *A Streetcar Named Desire,* and when he was asked by Audrey Wood, "Who do you think could play Blanche?" he replied without hesitation, "Jessica Tandy." Several months passed, and in June, 1947, Miss Tandy got a call from Elia Kazan, who had heard glowing reports of her acting in *Portrait.* After a couple of reading sessions, the director seemed satisfied; then Miss Tandy read for Irene Mayer Selznick, the producer, and was given a contract.

"When an actress reads a play in which she is to appear," says Miss Tandy, "she may be moved to laughter or tears by the character she is to portray, but then she is reacting as the audience would. While she is actually performing the role, however, she must only think and act subjectively. She must identify herself with her role, and not merely pass judgment on it; and the approach to a classic is basically the same as to a new role. It is true that before attempting Ophelia, I read a great many accounts of other productions, but once I started studying the part for myself, I had to treat it as a new part and approach it as though it had never been played before. This is apt sometimes to get you into trouble with people who have seen someone else's performance and liked their interpretation better. I certainly do *not* believe in innovation for the sake of being different oı shocking. One must try to play the character that the author wrote however long ago he wrote it."

As far as Blanche is concerned, says Miss Tandy, "She is not really a destructive person; she is destroyed." Her unfortunate marital experience was one of the strongest factors in the disintegration of her personality; ever after that she was searching for the chance to relive that experience, to "change the ending," to give the understanding that she had denied her husband—through ignorance and innocence, of course—to be able to take back, "You disgust me."

On her first appearance in the play, it is plain to see that Blanche is at the end of the line; this is the symbolism of the title, the streetcar has reached its terminus, desire can go no further. Having lived through one shattering experience after another, Blanche has begun to create a world of pretense. She takes one look at her sister's home and is almost overcome by the ghastliness of the place; but having nowhere else to go she attempts to transform this refuge into something "dainty" and exotic.

Miss Tandy has enormous admiration for Blanche, although a number of people who saw the play did not share her opinion. Audiences were quite ready to censure, and even damn, Blanche for being a dipsomaniac and a nymphomaniac. "But these words are merely labels," says Miss Tandy, "and are unimportant, unless you look at the significance behind them. Blanche was using liquor to deaden her pain and to create an illusion of pleasure; she wanted to live, and she was trying desperately to find a solution to her problem, a way out. Some people did not take the trouble to understand Blanche's sensitivity, or the sacrifices she had made in staying on at Belle Reve. It is easy to overlook the fact that Blanche had accepted the responsibilities and burdens of nursing her parents and relatives through their last illnesses and deaths—how bravely she must have managed to swallow her distaste for the unpleasant details of caring for the sick—how she must have worried and fretted about debts and mortgages, and then inevitably lost her home at the end of it; while Stella, feeling no obligation, had left home, found a husband, and indulged herself in his love."

It is quite possible that in her choice of Stanley as a mate, Stella was rebelling against the decadence of Belle Reve; his virility was preferable to death. But Blanche, too, was sorely in need of love and protection, which led to her promiscuity, and finally made her look upon Mitch as her only salvation.

American audiences find it very hard to have compassion for a person like Blanche, Miss Tandy feels, perhaps because of our Puritan background; but audiences have no trouble in understanding Stanley's point of view. Stanley's complaint, in fact, seems quite legitimate; his apartment is very small, his sister-in-law is a nuisance and a troublemaker, so he cannot be blamed for wanting to get her out. It is a mistake, however, to think that Stanley is solely responsible for Blanche's insanity. At her very first entrance she shows unmistakable signs of mental instability. When Blanche irritates or baits him, Stanley naturally strikes back in self-defense; it is true that he is unnecessarily cruel but the extent of his brutality is the measure of his insecurity and ignorance. Miss Tandy was reminded that Williams once said that the theme of his play was, "The apes shall inherit the earth!" The actress objected strenuously, saying that for all his coarseness, Stanley is no ape. He not only expresses himself very well but often is extremely witty, and he is clearly very much in love with his wife. There are certain aspects of his characterization, however, that do seem inconsistent. It is mentioned early in the play that Stanley is a traveling salesman, which would lead one to think that he might dress with a certain amount of conservatism and care; the torn undershirt, therefore, was not strictly in character, but was meant to enforce the image of his virility. As a traveling man, moreover, Stanley might be expected to be absent from home at some time during the play, but he never is. Blanche's characterization is much more consistent; and her fate, in an ironic way, brings the fulfillment of her desires: she has always wanted to be looked after, and finally shelter and care are provided for her—in an institution.

Miss Tandy has enormous admiration for the directorial ability of Elia Kazan. He made her feel as if she were contributing importantly to the play and did the same for each member of the cast; the group worked as a smooth-running ensemble. Kazan gets to know each actor personally and manages to extract the best possible performance from each one. He is aware of the actor's strengths and weaknesses and never indulges in "pussy-footing" or nonsense, as he is very serious about his work and expects everyone associated with him to be as dedicated as he is. Though he "blocks" the movement of the play very carefully, he gives no specific gestures or line-readings. He welcomes an actor's suggestions if they are right for the situation and character; with Kazan's approval Miss Tandy made many contributions to the portrayal of the role of Blanche. To give the play fluidity and speed, Kazan originally planned to have the actors go from scene to scene without lowering the curtain; but stage managers and actors having to move about in the dark led to confusion and slowed the play. The curtain was therefore lowered between scenes and the changes went faster.

Although Miss Tandy had appeared in many plays before she was seen in *Streetcar* and has starred in many since, the Williams work remains her favorite, mainly because the role of Blanche is so "richly satisfying." She likes the part so much that she hopes some day to play it again, but next time she wants to do some things differently. Specifically, Miss Tandy always hated her first entrance; she was seen behind the rear wall (scrim) where a sailor approached her and asked directions, but this encounter, the actress feels, gave the audience the wrong notion because it suggested a pick-up and labeled her "whore" from the beginning. This bit of action, incidentally, is not in the script but was a "director's touch." Next time Miss Tandy would like to enter "straight" and take the time to react in her own fashion to the neighborhood in which her sister lives. Another fault with the play's opening, so far as the characterization of Blanche is concerned, was the "hopped up" tempo. Stanley yells, "Meat," and tosses a bloody package at Stella, then they both rush out noisily to the bowling alley; at this point Blanche enters and, after her meeting with the sailor and a neighbor, goes like a whirlwind for a shot of whiskey. The actress felt that she needed more time to take in her surroundings and to communicate her feelings of bewilderment and shock to the audience. Miss Tandy had an impulse to slow down at various points in the play but could not; the problem of tempo was caused by the extreme length of the script which would permit no letup in the speed of the acting.

"To master the Southern speech pattern, and I'm not sure that I did," says Miss Tandy, "I spent as much time as possible before rehearsals with an honest-to-goodness Southerner, trying to absorb the rudiments of the accent. During the three and a half weeks of rehearsals, I spent a lot of time at fittings with the costume designer, Lucinda Ballard, and was able to listen to her speech and to ask her to correct anything which struck her ear as false. There was a particular difficulty for me in achieving the impression of a Southerner. One of the first rules of voice production is to be careful to sound the final consonants of words, and one of the first rules of Southern speech, as far as I could hear, was to elide as many syllables as possible. Furthermore, it is perhaps a cliché, but certainly a widely held opinion, that Southerners speak very slowly, an impossibility in a play of this depth of feeling and passion."

When asked how she felt about playing the same part for two years, Miss Tandy replied: "To be happy an actor must act. Ideally, he would function best in an economy that favored repertory, where he could constantly refresh himself by playing a variety of roles. As things are presently constituted, he considers himself extremely lucky to find himself in a hit. Yet, it is in the nature of acting that the longer one plays a role, the more difficult it becomes. To keep his performance from becoming mechanical he has to bring more and more creative energy to it. If strong incentives are not ever-present, the day inevitably arrives when it is an effort to drag one's self to the theater. I have no special formula or bending exercise for reducing the ennui. Every actor has to solve the problem in his own way. I would be a liar if I denied that Blanche sometimes got on my nerves as well as on Marlon Brando's, but I owe the dear girl a lot." Miss Tandy, as a matter of fact, received the Antoinette Perry Award as the best actress of the season for her portrayal of Blanche.

Many people went to see the play because of its reputation for sensationalism and violence; some did not even understand exactly what was going on. One woman wondered, "What was wrong with Blanche's young husband?" But no one could have left the theater, Miss Tandy believes, without having been moved by the beauty, compassion, and sensitivity of Tennessee Williams's play.

BLANCHE DUBOIS ON STAGE AND SCREEN
An Interview with Vivien Leigh

After a short tryout at the Opera House in Manchester, England, A Streetcar Named Desire opened at the Aldwych Theater, London, on October 12, 1949, under the direction of Laurence Olivier, with Vivien Leigh as Blanche DuBois. Long lines formed at the box-office a full day before the play actually opened, and the demand for tickets was enormous throughout the play's run. The London critics agreed that Vivien Leigh's performance was superb, overwhelming, and the chief reason for the play's success, but they damned the play itself, as a grubby picture of a worthless woman, with every adjective in the thesaurus. They called it vicious, brutal, repellent, sordid, revolting, and an actual move was started in Parliament to ban the play as obscene and immoral.

Miss Leigh explains the negative reaction of the critics as the result of shock induced by a play that was "stronger" and more violent than any they had ever seen before; the violence, in fact, blinded the reviewers to the play's all-pervading poetry, truth, and tenderness. The general public, Miss Leigh feels, had heard of Williams's great reputation in America and wanted to see the work of this celebrated writer; it is true that because of its controversial and sensational nature the play attracted some people for the wrong reasons, and a good deal of unnecessary mud was flung at Blanche by people who had failed to comprehend her character.

Miss Leigh had a copy of the script of *Streetcar* for a year before she actually appeared in the play. She kept reading and rereading it in an effort to understand Blanche and her problems. She had never played a character of this sort before and had to get inside her skin before she could make her real and believable. She finally saw Blanche as a pitiful soul who was the unfortunate victim of loneliness. There was no evidence, either in the author's dialogue or in Laurence Olivier's production, to suggest that Blanche had at any time commercialized her charms. Had that been so, she would have had more than sixty-five cents in her purse when she arrived. She owned some paltry finery and a rhinestone tiara, but far from being ill-gotten gains, they were trumperies that her sister recognized as having belonged to Blanche in their more prosperous past, when they had a family place of their own. Rather than being an evil character, Blanche was simply a sensitive young girl, who, at the age of sixteen, faced the horrifying disillusionment of having married a handsome degenerate. After his suicide on their honeymoon, she endured a heart-searing loneliness which led her, when she could endure solitude no longer, to accept the favors of strangers. There was never any question of taking money, and when her savings as a schoolmistress were spent and her health had deteriorated, she sought the hospitality of her sister and brother-in-law.

There is no doubt that when we first meet Blanche we find that her delicacy has been overlaid by a veneer of harshness, for life has proved to be too much for her; she has been hurt and coarsened by the world. In seeking refuge in her sister's home, it is as if she were attempting to return to Belle Reve, her beautiful dream, but there is one jarring note—Stanley. He is capable of turning the dream into a nightmare. Fearing this, Blanche would like to get him out of the picture, and tries to break up her sister's marriage. By a process of rationalization she decides that Stanley is too crude for Stella and that Stella is cheapening herself by remaining with her husband; the aggressiveness which Blanche displays is not a show of real strength but a desperate attempt to protect her dream.

Some of these ideas were suggested to Miss Leigh by Williams himself, with whom she discussed the play during the summer of 1949. The author explained how he had traced the journeys of his two leading characters: Blanche passes

Molière's theaters. *(Above)* The Petit Bourbon, assigned to Molière by Louis XIV. Note the loges and galleries around the sides, the apselike stage, and the absence of proscenium and curtain. *(Below)* Ousted from the Petit Bourbon by the intrigue of his enemies, Molière was granted the use of the Palais Royal, the theater built for Richelieu with proscenium, curtain, and elaborate backstage machinery.

The Misanthrope: three styles. *(Above left)* La Thorillière as Philinte and Molière (seated) as Alceste, both in contemporary costumes, as shown in an engraving from the 1684 Amsterdam edition of the play. Note the sparseness of furnishings. *(Above right)* A modern-dress version with Célimène (Madeleine Delavaivre) flanked by Acaste (Jacques Ciron) and Clitandre (Etienne Aubray). *(Below)* The Barrault production, with Madeleine Renaud (seated) as Célimène. Barrault stands in the background.

A *Streetcar Named Desire* in three countries. *(Above)* Vivien Leigh as Blanche and Marlon Brando as Stanley in the American film version, directed by Elia Kazan and produced by Warner Brothers. *(Below left)* Yves Vincent as Stanley and Arletty as Blanche in the French stage version, adapted by Jean Cocteau, with sets designed by Christian Berard. *(Below right)* Marcello Mastroianni as Mitch and Rossella Falk as Stella in the Italian stage version, directed by Luchino Visconti.

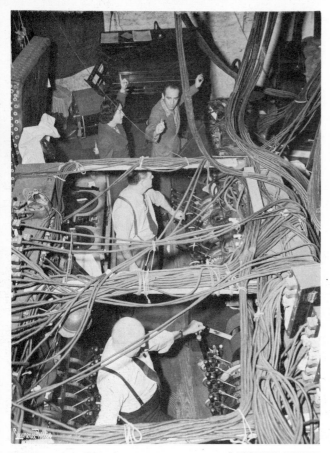

American productions of *A Streetcar Named Desire*. Technicians at work backstage creating the lighting, music, and sound effects at the Harris Theater in Chicago. *(Below)* The original New York production. Jo Mielziner's set provided acting areas on several levels and also interior and exterior scenes which could be used simultaneously. Complex lighting effects helped to control the audience's mood. Stella and Stanley, played by Kim Hunter and Marlon Brando, are embracing at the left of the picture below, while Blanche (Jessica Tandy) is being led away.

LAWRENCE–PHILLIP

The Vienna Burgtheater before 1945 *(top)* and in 1956 *(middle)*. Before it was damaged in a bombing, the theater was a typical nineteenth-century house with five tiers of boxes and heavy rococo décor. It was rebuilt and remodeled in accordance with modern concepts of functionalism; and partitions between the boxes were altered to permit the audience to mingle more freely. *(Below)* The German production of *Streetcar*, at the Stadttheater, Regensburg. The style was theatricalistic, resembling Mielziner's (see photo opposite).

The Visit in Europe. *(Above left)* Therese Giehse and Gustav Knuth in the original sceneryless production. The man holding the branches represents a tree. *(Above right)* Friedrich Duerrenmatt (wearing glasses), author of the play, and Teo Otto, scene designer, conferring during rehearsals. *(Below)* The Norwegian production in Oslo. This shot of the final scene shows Claire Zachanassian, played by Lillebil Ibsen, leaving Güllen in her sedan chair.

The restaurant scene from the American production of *The Visit*. *(Above)* Alfred Lunt, as Schill, pleading for his life at the feet of the inflexible Lynn Fontanne, as Claire. John Wyse and Eric Porter look on. Miss Fontanne's gown, by Castillo, was a stunning apricot-colored velvet. *(Below)* A full-stage view showing the wires from which the restaurant front was hung and the partially constructed decorative element above the door. These are theatricalist techniques.

Two scenes from the German production of *The Visit (Der Besuch der alten Dame)* at the State Theater, Muenster, Germany. *(Above)* The restaurant scene. Note the beer and water glasses, and compare the shabby appearance of the table and guests with the lavishness of the American production. *(Below)* The death scene, after which Claire hands her check to the townspeople.

from delicacy to decadence, and her brother-in-law from simplicity to brutality. When she comes to stay under his roof in New Orleans, their paths cross and tragedy is inevitable. Williams felt that their story was an eloquent plea for tolerance and understanding. Stella believes that people should tolerate each other's habits, and thus manages to make a success of life with her primitive young Polish husband; while Stanley, lacking his wife's tolerance, sees only evil in Blanche and intentionally wrecks her chance of marriage to his friend Mitch, thus denying her the last hope of settling down with a man who could have given her the kindness and understanding for which she yearned. It is true that Blanche goes out of her way to irritate Stanley and he is determined to be rid of her, but he practices a piece of deliberate cruelty when he presents her, on her birthday, with a bus ticket back to Laurel, the town from which she has fled. It is too much for Blanche, and from that moment her delicate and unstable mental makeup begins to crack under the strain.

Her careful analysis of the character and personality of Blanche made it possible for Miss Leigh to fit herself into the picture of this particular human being, but the next problem was that of putting the picture into actual practice by making the character come alive on the stage. What did Blanche look like? She was a faded blonde; Miss Leigh, who is a natural brunette, had to dye her hair to achieve this effect. She is tired, worn, frightened; makeup provided the pallor of the complexion, sunken cheeks, and dark welts under the eyes, but the mask of gaiety and bravado that Blanche habitually wore resulted from the subtle facial expressions of the actress. What sort of voice did Blanche have? Soft and low, gentle and refined, until she is driven into a corner and in her terror and self-defense turns shrill. Miss Leigh had made a careful study of the American "southern accent" for the role of Scarlett O'Hara which she played in the film *Gone With the Wind* so that it was not difficult for her to reproduce it in Blanche's speech. Much more difficult than Blanche's accent was the variety of tone, pitch, and timbre required for the shifting moods and emotions of the various scenes. The use of the hands, tilt of the head, line of the body, and movement of the feet all had to be worked out to complete the visual image of the character.

"When I agreed to create the part in London," said Miss Leigh, "I purposely avoided seeing Jessica Tandy in the Broadway production though I have long admired her work. In my opinion it would have been a mistake to see another actress playing Blanche before I had worked out my own interpretation. It would have made it impossible to tackle the part from an unbiased standpoint, as impressions of the other performance would have subconsciously remained in my mind and the character would have become blurred, even before I started a serious study of the lines."

The actress was immediately aware, however, of the difficulty and complexity of the role. "When I first read the play," says Miss Leigh, "I told Tennessee Williams that in Blanche he had written an 'actor-killer' part. I have never tackled so physically exhausting a role. Apart from its abnormal length, it is written on a highly emotional level, with constant and rapid switching from one scene to another." The part was so taxing that after playing it on the stage for two months

Miss Leigh was forced to request that the number of performances be reduced from eight a week to seven in order to give her an opportunity to rest. The ability to sustain emotion at a high pitch is almost intuitive, but it is a drain nevertheless upon the stamina and psyche of the performer. The achievement of complete control comes, in the final analysis, with the development of acting techniques learned through long experience on the stage. It is only by playing innumerable types of characters under the most varied conditions that the performer can be aware at every moment of the other actors, of the audience, and of his own moods and physical reactions and thus have absolute command of the timing of gesture, body movement, and speech—the tools with which he projects and arouses emotion. "It would have been easier," says Miss Leigh, "to play so lengthy and demanding a role as part of a repertory season, with two or three other works in active presentation at the same time. Then the actress playing Blanche would only be called upon to perform the part about three times a week instead of the usual eight expected by a West End management putting on a play for a run. During the Old Vic season when I played Lady Teazle in *The School for Scandal*, Antigone, and Lady Anne in *Richard III* all in the same week, I developed a lasting sense of exhilaration through performing such varied parts in ever-changing succession."

Miss Leigh's interpretation of the character of Blanche was basically the same on the London stage and in the Hollywood film, but the directors' viewpoints differed in certain minor respects. Laurence Olivier saw Blanche as a soft and gentle creature who yearned desperately to love and be loved; her many humorous lines were delivered in a lightly sarcastic or ironic vein. Elia Kazan, on the other hand, conceived of Blanche as a harsher and more frenetic person whose humorous thrusts were bitter and acerb, whose tongue was the weapon of a frustrated woman. Vivien Leigh's film performance was a remarkable achievement in that it represented a coalescence of these two concepts; underneath the surface hardness of Blanche one could clearly detect the frightened, ill, and pathetic creature fighting for peace, security, and a place in society. Miss Leigh, quite understandably, was unable to explain how she managed to project this complex characterization; the art of acting is so closely related to the mysteries of the human personality that the more profound the effort the more carefully are its well-springs hidden from the performer himself.

When a play is transferred from the stage to the screen, the concept of a character may remain unchanged but the manner in which it is performed is different. "If one has acted a part on the stage," says Miss Leigh, "it becomes very much easier to do it on the screen. Blanche was the first part I played in both mediums. I did not have to act as broadly for the cameras as I did for theater audiences because the cameras and microphones magnify the facial expressions and the voice. The stage actor must always remember to 'project,' while projection from the screen is done mechanically. Studio acting tends, therefore, to be smaller in scale, tempered down, more economical, and more internal, although the end result, as flashed upon the screen, often gives the impression that it has been done on a larger scale than a stage performance."

A play presents its story straight through from beginning to end with its climaxes in logical sequence, which helps the actor to control and build the emotional pitch of his performance; but the scenes and sequences of a film are not always shot in consecutive order. This makes it very difficult for the actor who first creates a new character on the screen; but the actor who has previously played the part on the stage is able to dissect the scenes and remember what pitch the emotion had reached at each particular point.

Perhaps the greatest difference between acting for the films and acting on stage is the presence of the audience. In the theater, the participation of the audience is very important to the actor especially in the playing of comedy; the audience's silence is equally important during the playing of tragedy, for by the very quality of the silence an actor is able to judge of the effect he is producing. The absence of audience reactions during the making of a film places a distinct handicap upon the performer, and is particularly missed by actors with stage experience.

Almost everyone who saw the film version of *Streetcar*, including Tennessee Williams, thought that it was superior to any of the stage productions of the play that had been done. Miss Leigh is of the opinion that the play was of a deeply psychological nature and that the camera, in bringing the characters so close to the audience, was able to highlight nuances in the expressions of their faces and to reveal subtleties of feeling that were lost in their passage over the footlights; it was possible, too, for the director to focus the camera—and thus the audience's attention—upon movements or objects that could easily be overlooked in the theater although they might be particularly significant in the establishment of character relationships. The scene, for example, in which Mitch tears the paper lantern off the light bulb and turns the glaring light directly into Blanche's face provides a highly exciting moment in the theater as Blanche gasps, cries out, and turns her head aside; but in the film, as the light falls upon Blanche, we are immediately shown an enormously large image (technically known as a "tight close-up") of her face. The camera has not only taken us closer to the action but has given us a penetrating glimpse into this woman's feelings. The film, moreover, had greater scope than the stage productions because the camera was able to leave the confines of the house and, in so doing, supplied a larger setting for the action and suggested the social milieu in which the story took place. Even in the scene in which Blanche speaks of her husband's homosexuality there was a gain, Miss Leigh feels, for as Williams rewrote it for the films he did it so cleverly that not only was the suggestion left intact but the dire effect that the experience had had upon Blanche was clarified and heightened.

Williams, on one occasion, as mentioned above, spoke of *Streetcar* as a plea for tolerance, and at another time said that the theme of the play was that brutality triumphs over sensitivity. Miss Leigh does not see this as a contradiction because, as she explains it, the "brutality" exists in the present while the "plea" is for the future. "Tennessee Williams," says Miss Leigh, "is a very sensitive writer who has a deep insight into contemporary life; that is the reason why *Streetcar* was such a timely play, and Blanche such a perfect embodiment of the anxiety of our age."

DESIGNING AND LIGHTING *Streetcar*
An Interview with Jo Mielziner

Jo Mielziner read the script of *A Streetcar Named Desire* several times before formulating his ideas for the play's setting. The reading process is an important one because during it Mielziner's feelings are stirred and his imagination is kindled concerning the people in the play, their motivations, and their physical surroundings, the palpable world in which they live and move, and which it is his job to create.

The sketches which he prepared for the approval of the playwright and the director indicated that Mielziner's primary idea was to show the exterior as well as the interior of the house in which Stanley and Stella live and where all the action of the play takes place. The interior represented a crowded apartment consisting of a living room, bedroom, bathroom, and entryway; just outside the entryway was a flight of spiral steps leading to the upper floor of the house. The rear walls of this apartment were to be translucent so that when they were lighted from behind the audience would see as well as hear the Mexican woman peddling her flowers, the lovers walking down the street arm in arm, and the street brawl —the so-called "ballet"—in all its violent details. Behind the translucency, there was to be a double set of backdrops painted to represent the street and the railroad tracks beyond it; by a special lighting setup, the audience would be able to see past the interior of the apartment to the street outside, and past that to the railroad. The object of this arrangement was to establish the environment in which the action took place and to create a suitable background mood for it; the set made very clear that these people lived on the wrong side of the tracks.

Mielziner called the style of his design "selective realism," and the sketches met with the approval of both Williams and Kazan; but because of the liberal use of scrims, Kazan wanted to be sure that the scenery would not tremble or flap as a result of all the violent physical action that was to take place both in front of and behind the rear wall of the apartment. Mielziner solved this problem by having the walls braced by elements cut out of metal instead of the heavy lumber he would ordinarily have used. The spiral staircase, too, was made of a combination of metal and wood for lightness and strength, and the wrought iron work of the balcony railings, which gave the impression of New Orleans architecture, was constructed in the same way. This sort of set required two or three times the amount of lighting equipment used for the ordinary production.

"To create a mood on the stage," says Mielziner, "requires a careful combination of painting and lighting. The designer should do his own lighting. One person, in fact, should be responsible for all the visual elements of a production." It is the primary responsibility of the director, however, to carry out the playwright's conception and to find the best people for each department. "I could not have designed *Streetcar* without laying out the lighting scheme at the same time." The effects of lighting and painting must work together. In his studio, Mielziner has a darkroom in which he checks all colors under various lights; no color sketches or pieces of material go out of his workroom without being tested and checked, so that he knows in advance exactly what they will look like on the stage.

Certain scenes in the play required special lighting effects. Blanche's "memory" scene, for example, was played in a blue spot in order to suggest coolness and distance; to remove the scene from reality, the warm tones were omitted from the lights. The blue was deep and rich, however, because the play is very colorful and vivid; there is nothing pallid about it in characterization or action and it could not therefore be pallid in the lighting. In other scenes, Blanche moved about the stage in a follow-spot; this gave her emphasis and also a certain luminosity that had symbolic value.

The street brawl, or "ballet" scene, was particularly difficult to light; special batteries of spots had to be mounted at strategic points so that the translucency of the rear wall would not be lost and all the off-stage action could be clearly seen.

During the scene in which Stanley rapes Blanche, the usual source of light was altered. The stage is usually lighted from the front, but this scene was "back-lighted" (that is, the light came from behind the actors so that they were seen in partial silhouette) in order to soften the shock and reduce the effect of violence; the lighting thus both revealed and concealed form and action alternately, and in so doing decreased the brutality and heightened the artistry of the scene.

The subtlety and variation displayed in this production required a great deal of extra technical effort and expense; extra manpower was needed to handle the unusual amount of special electrical equipment, as well as extra time in which to rehearse and prepare the production.

Alva Johnston, writing in *The New Yorker,* made the following comments:

> In recent years, Mielziner has been increasingly interested in the power of scenery to transmit psychological suggestion. The typical Mielziner setting is intended primarily not as an eye-filling spectacle but as an array of clues, hints, symptoms, innuendoes, keys to personality. One of the "house-lovely" magazines not long ago asked Mielziner to write an article treating stage design as a branch of interior decoration. He was outraged. The enormity of the suggestion caused him to burst into a heated monologue. He pointed out to the editor that the mission of scene design is to give the inside information, the lowdown, on the characters on the stage, while interior decoration tells nothing about its customers except that they have money enough to hire an interior decorator. . . . He told the editor that interior decoration is static and unrevealing, whereas stage scenery must sometimes run amuck in order to allow the audience to peer into the emotional centers of a character. . . . In *A Streetcar Named Desire* Mielziner took a door that was a first-class item of interior decoration in its original state and worked on it long and painstakingly to make it both a document of family history and a character analysis of the people in the play. The door had been rather ornate, like the family, but had become seedy, like the family. Heavily smudged with handprints, it testified that the lady of the house had lost interest in appearances. Scuffed by heel marks and slightly askew from rough handling, it testified that the man of the house had the tempera-

ment of a kicker and a slammer. The old door is supposed to diagnose the family. . . .*

Mielziner had the great advantage, when doing *Streetcar*, of having a playwright and a director who understood the endless time and effort required to achieve the proper effects. A designer must have the support of his coworkers. Once a production gets under way, a designer cannot redesign as a writer can rewrite or a director redirect. Unless the error is absolutely major or triflingly minor, nothing can be done about it. The designer starts his work very early in the production schedule, and once it goes into the building shops, he is committed. A designer should have, ideally, two or three months before the play goes into rehearsal, whereas the time he is actually allowed varies from three weeks to three months. Mielziner had six to eight weeks in which to design *Streetcar* before rehearsals began.

If a play requires many rewrites but the designer's work is "frozen" and his original set must stand, he is under a severe handicap. If the designer and the director do not work in the same style, it can be dangerous and sometimes fatal to the play. Style is undoubtedly the most difficult element of a production to establish at the beginning and to maintain throughout, but that is mainly the director's job. A designer may have a strong sense of style (which is a very valuable thing), but because a play is a collaborative effort the designer's work depends for its ultimate success on the coordinated elements of the entire production.

Here's News! "Streetcar" Has a Ballet
New York Herald Tribune, *November 7, 1948*

It would be a shock to a visitor backstage at the Barrymore, where "A Streetcar Named Desire" is playing, to hear the stage manager call: "On stage for the ballet!" While this hypothetical visitor scurries out front to consult the houseboards to make sure he is in the right theater, the reader will be let in on a little secret. "Streetcar" is not a musical and the ballet is not a ballet. And thereby hangs a well-known tale.

There was a moment during the rehearsals of "Streetcar" when Tennessee Williams, its author, thought his own sanity was deserting him when he observed Elia Kazan carefully staging a scene, ostensibly from his play, which he never remembered having written.

Up there, on the bare stage, he saw members of the cast enacting, mainly in pantomime, a scene of violence. Off to the side was another small group of actors with their fingers in their mouths, making unintelligible noises.

As near as he could determine the sense of the scene, one of the actresses had just rolled a drunk for his wallet and was making off with it. The drunk staggered after her but was stopped by a male accomplice who felled him with a right to

* By permission; © 1948 The New Yorker Magazine, Inc.

the jaw. The drunk was left on the floor moaning while the pair returned to the bar from which they had emerged. This was followed by a pandemonium of shouts, police whistles and sirens.

It began to dawn on Tennessee Williams that this was something that he had parenthetically indicated in his script as an off-stage accompaniment to one of the scenes in the play, part of which would be visible through the transparent back wall of the scene. Here, however, Kazan was giving it as careful staging as any of the other scenes.

Theatergoers who have seen "Streetcar" will be hard pressed to define the scene so elaborately staged. While it is going on their attention is fixed on Jessica Tandy, whose frantic efforts to escape the clutches of Marlon Brando are hindered by the noises she hears on the outside.

There are eleven scenes in "Streetcar," each of which is referred to backstage by their number. Since the pantomime is part of scene ten, a way had to be found to differentiate it. Robert Downing, the stage manager, tagged it "the ballet," and Elia Kazan is the choreographer.

BACKSTAGE AT "Streetcar" PROVIDES OWN DRAMA, TOO
Chicago Sun-Times, *January 16, 1949*

That STREETCAR NAMED DESIRE runs on electricity! Every night at the Harris [Theater, Chicago], where Uta Hagen, Anthony Quinn, Mary Welch and Russell Hardie play out the Tennessee Williams melodrama, there is another performance going on backstage, a long and ticklishly difficult one run by Karl Nielsen, Phil Peltz, Dearon Darnay, and Bea Chilson. They sit and move in a black cave, the cave of an octopus family.

From half a dozen big instrument boards the heavy dark cables wind up into the flies and out into the set. And the above-mentioned, respectively the stage manager, the chief electrician and the two assistant stage managers, pull the levers for light and shade and provide the sound effects.

Jo Mielziner, who designed the "Streetcar" set, is the most experimental of stage craftsmen in the lighting department. Ask Eddie Dowling about the hundreds of hours of Mielziner experimentation on "The Glass Menagerie" in advance of opening night. The emphasis on lighting in "Streetcar" calls for more electrical equipment than you will find backstage at a big musical. The average piece requires one, or at the most, two switchboards. Mielziner installed seven, three big ones and four small pre-set boards. The average dramatic play has from 2 to 10 light cues, a musical perhaps 40 or 50. "Streetcar" has 68. To provide all this illumination the show carries equipment consisting of 168 units and 20,000 feet of cable. On the road one baggage car is needed for the electrical gadgets alone.

The best stage lighting induces a change of mood in the audience but is characteristically done so gradually that the mechanics can't be noticed. For instance, when the pathological heroine and her gentleman friend come home to the dingy apartment in New Orleans, they are drenched in blue moonlight as they pause on the front stoop. Inside the living room the light changes to amber, then to blue again as they pass toward the bedroom. When Uta Hagen lights a candle the area slowly floods with white. Backstage, electrician Peltz is operating four separate dimmers with his hands and a fifth with his knees.

Music is an integral part of the proceedings and is provided by a novachord and a small jazz band. The "Varsouviana" is heard every time Blanche speaks of her long-dead young husband. The band pipes up with low-down New Orleans blues, echoes of bars and night clubs in the French Quarter. Bea Chilson guides the four musicians with hand signals on cue and also signals an assistant electrician when she wants sound effects, the whistle of the Louisville and Nashville fast freight or the crash of thunder. There is even an understudy, Virginia Baker, who can make a noise like a tomcat and does . . . every night and matinees.

A carefully rehearsed backstage bit is called "The Ballet." This occurs toward the end of the play in Uta Hagen's impressive mad scene. The audience is barely conscious of figures running back and forth behind the scrim and the piercing laughter of a woman. This movement behind the main set parallels the hysterical break-up of the principal character and adds mightily to the force of the scene. It is interesting to note that most of this stage business was carefully indicated by the playwright.

Coordinating all these effects of light and sound is the production's stage manager, Karl Nielsen, a kind of backstage Toscanini. He sits off-stage right from the beginning to the end of every performance, cuing his assistants (the principals in the orchestra of sound and light). They in turn set off signals for the various technicians and back-stage bit players.

THE PLAYBILL

ꙮ *A Streetcar Named Desire*

A play in eleven scenes by Tennessee Williams. Presented by Irene M. Selznick at the Barrymore Theater, New York, December 3, 1947.

CAST OF CHARACTERS

NEGRO WOMAN	GEE GEE JAMES
EUNICE HUBBELL	PEG HILLIAS
STANLEY KOWALSKI	MARLON BRANDO
STELLA KOWALSKI	KIM HUNTER
BLANCHE DUBOIS	JESSICA TANDY
STEVE HUBBELL	RUDY BOND
HAROLD MITCHELL (MITCH)	KARL MALDEN
PABLO GONZALES	NICK DENNIS
A YOUNG COLLECTOR	VITO CHRISTI

MEXICAN WOMAN	EDNA THOMAS
NURSE	ANN DERE
DOCTOR	RICHARD GARRICK

Spring, summer, and early fall in New Orleans. There are intermissions after Scene Four and Scene Six.

Staged by Elia Kazan, settings and lighting by Jo Mielziner, costumes by Lucinda Ballard, musical direction by Lehman Engel.

SCENE ONE

The exterior of a two-story corner building on a street in New Orleans which is named Elysian Fields and runs between the L & N tracks and the river. The section is poor but, unlike corresponding sections in other American cities, it has a raffish charm. The houses are mostly white frame, weathered grey, with rickety outside stairs and galleries and quaintly ornamented gables. This building contains two flats, upstairs and down. Faded white stairs ascend to the entrances of both.

It is first dark of an evening early in May. The sky that shows around the dim white building is a peculiarly tender blue, almost a turquoise, which invests the scene with a kind of lyricism and gracefully attenuates the atmosphere of decay. You can almost feel the warm breath of the brown river beyond the river warehouses with their faint redolences of bananas and coffee. A corresponding air is evoked by the music of Negro entertainers at a barroom around the corner. In this part of New Orleans you are practically always just around the corner, or a few doors down the street, from a tinny piano being played with the infatuated fluency of brown fingers. This "Blue Piano" expresses the spirit of the life which goes on here.

Two women, one white and one colored, are taking the air on the steps of the building. The white woman is EUNICE, who occupies the upstairs flat; the colored woman a neighbor, for New Orleans is a cosmopolitan city where there is a relatively warm and easy intermingling of races in the old part of town.

Above the music of the "Blue Piano" the voices of people on the street can be heard overlapping.

(Two men come around the corner, STANLEY KOWALSKI and MITCH. They are about twenty-eight or thirty years old, roughly dressed in blue denim work clothes. STANLEY carries his bowling jacket and a red-stained package from a butcher's. They stop at the foot of the steps.)

Stanley *(Bellowing).* Hey, there! Stella, Baby!

(STELLA comes out on the first floor landing, a gentle young woman, about twenty-five, and of a background obviously quite different from her husband's.)

Stella (*Mildly*). Don't holler at me like that. Hi, Mitch.

Stanley. Catch!

Stella. What?

Stanley. Meat!

(*He heaves the package at her. She cries out in protest but manages to catch it; then she laughs breathlessly. Her husband and his companion have already started back around the corner.*)

Stella (*Calling after him*). Stanley! Where are you going?

Stanley. Bowling!

Stella. Can I come watch?

Stanley. Come on. (*He goes out.*)

Stella. Be over soon. (*To the white woman*) Hello, Eunice. How are you?

Eunice. I'm all right. Tell Steve to get him a poor boy's sandwich 'cause nothing's left here.

(*They all laugh; the NEGRO WOMAN does not stop. STELLA goes out.*)

Negro Woman. What was that package he th'ew at 'er? (*She rises from steps, laughing louder.*)

Eunice. You hush, now!

Negro Woman. Catch *what*!

(*She continues to laugh. BLANCHE comes around the corner, carrying a valise. She looks at a slip of paper, then at the building, then again at the slip and again at the building. Her expression is one of shocked disbelief. Her appearance is incongruous to this setting. She is daintily dressed in a white suit with a fluffy bodice, necklace and earrings of pearl, white gloves and hat, looking as if she were arriving at a summer tea or cocktail party in the garden district. She is about five years older than STELLA. Her delicate beauty must avoid a strong light. There is something about her uncertain manner, as well as her white clothes, that suggests a moth.*)

Eunice (*Finally*). What's the matter, honey? Are you lost?

Blanche (*With faintly hysterical humor*). They told me to take a streetcar named Desire, and then transfer to one called Cemeteries and ride six blocks and get off at—Elysian Fields!

Eunice. That's where you are now.

Blanche. At Elysian Fields?

Eunice. This here is Elysian Fields.

Blanche. They mustn't have—understood—what number I wanted.

Eunice. What number you lookin' for?

(BLANCHE *wearily refers to the slip of paper.*)

Blanche. Six thirty-two.

Eunice. You don't have to look no further.

Blanche (*Uncomprehendingly*). I'm looking for my sister, Stella DuBois. I mean—Mrs. Stanley Kowalski.

Eunice. That's the party.—You just did miss her, though.

Blanche. This—can this be—her home?

Eunice. She's got the downstairs here and I got the up.

Blanche. Oh. She's—out?

Eunice. You noticed that bowling alley around the corner?

Blanche. I'm—not sure I did.

Eunice. Well, that's where she's at, watchin' her husband bowl. (*There is a pause*) You want to leave your suitcase here an' go find her?

Blanche. No.

Negro Woman. I'll go tell her you come.

Blanche. Thanks.

Negro Woman. You welcome. (*She goes out.*)

Eunice. She wasn't expecting you?

Blanche. No. No, not tonight.

Eunice. Well, why don't you just go in and make yourself at home till they get back.

Blanche. How could I—do that?

Eunice. We own this place so I can let you in.

(*She gets up and opens the downstairs door. A light goes on behind the blind, turning it light blue.* BLANCHE *slowly follows her into the downstairs flat. The surrounding areas dim out as the interior is lighted.*)

(*Two rooms can be seen, not too clearly defined. The one first entered is primarily a kitchen but contains a folding bed to be used by* BLANCHE. *The room beyond this is a bedroom. Off this room is a narrow door to a bathroom.*)

Eunice (*Defensively, noticing* BLANCHE'S *look*). It's sort of messed up right now but when it's clean it's real sweet.

Blanche. Is it?

Eunice. Uh-huh, I think so. So you're Stella's sister?

Blanche. Yes. (*Wanting to get rid of her*) Thanks for letting me in.

Eunice. Por nada, as the Mexicans say, *por nada!* Stella spoke of you.

Blanche. Yes?

Eunice. I think she said you taught school.

Blanche. Yes.

Eunice. And you're from Mississippi, huh?

Blanche. Yes.

Eunice. She showed me a picture of your home-place, the plantation.

Blanche. Belle Reve?

Eunice. A great big place with white columns.

Blanche. Yes . . .

Eunice. A place like that must be awful hard to keep up.

Blanche. If you will excuse me. I'm just about to drop.

Eunice. Sure, honey. Why don't you set down?

Blanche. What I meant was I'd like to be left alone.

Eunice. Aw. I'll make myself scarce, in that case.

Blanche. I didn't mean to be rude, but—

Eunice. I'll drop by the bowling alley an' hustle her up. (*She goes out the door.*)

(BLANCHE *sits in a chair very stiffly with her shoulders slightly hunched and her legs pressed close together and her hands tightly clutching her purse as if she were quite cold. After a while the blind look goes out of her eyes and she begins to look slowly around. A cat screeches. She catches her breath with a startled gesture. Suddenly she notices something in a half opened closet. She springs up and crosses to it, and removes a whiskey bottle. She pours a half tumbler of whiskey and tosses it down. She carefully replaces the bottle and washes out the tumbler at the sink. Then she resumes her seat in front of the table.*)

Blanche (*Faintly to herself.*) I've got to keep hold of myself!

(STELLA *comes quickly around the corner of the building and runs to the door of the downstairs flat.*)

Stella (*Calling out joyfully*). Blanche!

(*For a moment they stare at each*

other. Then BLANCHE *springs up and runs to her with a wild cry.*)

Blanche. Stella, oh, Stella! Stella! Stella for Star!

(*She begins to speak with feverish vivacity as if she feared for either of them to stop and think. They catch each other in a spasmodic embrace.*)

Blanche. Now, then, let me look at you. But don't you look at me, Stella, no, no, no, not till later, not till I've bathed and rested! And turn that over-light off! Turn that off! I won't be looked at in this merciless glare! (STELLA *laughs and complies*) Come back here now! Oh, my baby! Stella! Stella for Star! (*She embraces her again*) I thought you would never come back to this horrible place! What am I saying? I didn't mean to say that. I meant to be nice about it and say—Oh, what a convenient location and such—Ha-a-ha! Precious lamb! You haven't said a *word* to me.

Stella. You haven't given me a chance to, honey! (*She laughs, but her glance at* BLANCHE *is a little anxious.*)

Blanche. Well, now you talk. Open your pretty mouth and talk while I look around for some liquor! I know you must have some liquor on the place! Where could it be, I wonder? Oh, I spy, I spy!

(*She rushes to the closet and removes the bottle; she is shaking all over and panting for breath as she tries to laugh. The bottle nearly slips from her grasp.*)

Stella (*Noticing*). Blanche, you sit down and let me pour the drinks. I don't know what we've got to mix with. Maybe a coke's in the icebox. Look'n see, honey, while I'm—

Blanche. No coke, honey, not with my nerves tonight! Where—where—where is—?

Stella. Stanley? Bowling! He loves it. They're having a—found some soda! —tournament . . .

Blanche. Just water, baby, to chase it! Now don't get worried, your sister hasn't turned into a drunkard, she's just all shaken up and hot and tired and dirty! You sit down, now, and explain this place to me! What are you doing in a place like this?

Stella. Now, Blanche—

Blanche. Oh, I'm not going to be hypocritical, I'm going to be honestly critical about it! Never, never, never in my worst dreams could I picture— Only Poe! Only Mr. Edgar Allan Poe! —could do it justice. Out there I suppose is the ghoul-haunted woodland of Weir! (*She laughs.*)

Stella. No, honey, those are the L & N tracks

Blanche. No, now seriously, putting joking aside. Why didn't you tell me, why didn't you write me, honey, why didn't you let me know?

Stella (*Carefully, pouring herself a drink*). Tell you what, Blanche?

Blanche. Why, that you had to live in these conditions!

Stella. Aren't you being a little intense about it? It's not that bad at all! New Orleans isn't like other cities.

Blanche. This has got nothing to do with New Orleans. You might as well say—forgive me, blessed baby! (*She suddenly stops short*) The subject is closed!

Stella (*A little drily*). Thanks.

(*During the pause,* BLANCHE *stares at her. She smiles at* BLANCHE.)

Blanche (*Looking down at her glass, which shakes in her hand*). You're all I've got in the world, and you're not glad to see me!

Stella (*Sincerely*). Why, Blanche, you know that's not true.

Blanche. No?—I'd forgotten how quiet you were.

Stella. You never did give me a chance to say much, Blanche. So I just got in the habit of being quiet around you.

Blanche (*Vaguely*). A good habit to get into . . . (*Then, abruptly*) You haven't asked me how I happened to get away from the school before the spring term ended.

Stella. Well, I thought you'd volunteer that information—if you wanted to tell me.

Blanche. You thought I'd been fired?

Stella. No, I—thought you might have —resigned . . .

Blanche. I was so exhausted by all I'd been through my—nerves broke. (*Nervously tamping cigarette*) I was on the verge of—lunacy, almost! So Mr. Graves—Mr. Graves is the high school superintendent—he suggested I take a leave of absence. I couldn't put all of those details into the wire . . . (*She drinks quickly*) Oh, this buzzes right through me and feels so good!

Stella. Won't you have another?

Blanche. No, one's my limit.

Stella. Sure?

Blanche. You haven't said a word about my appearance.

Stella. You look just fine.

Blanche. God love you for a liar! Daylight never exposed so total a ruin! But you—you've put on some weight, yes, you're just as plump as a little partridge! And it's so becoming to you!

Stella. Now, Blanche—

Blanche. Yes, it is, it is or I wouldn't say it! You just have to watch around the hips a little. Stand up.

Stella. Not now.

Blanche. You hear me? I said stand up! (STELLA *complies reluctantly*) You messy child, you, you've spilt something on the pretty white lace collar! About your hair—you ought to have it cut in a feather bob with your dainty features. Stella, you have a maid, don't you?

Stella. No. With only two rooms it's—

Blanche. What? *Two* rooms, did you say?

Stella. This one and—(*She is embarrassed.*)

Blanche. The other one? (*She laughs sharply. There is an embarrassed silence.*)

Blanche. I am going to take just one little tiny nip more, sort of to put the stopper on, so to speak. . . . Then put the bottle away so I won't be tempted. (*She rises*) I want you to look at *my* figure! (*She turns around*) You know I haven't put on one ounce in ten years, Stella? I weigh what I weighed the summer you left Belle Reve. The summer Dad died and you left us . . .

Stella (*A little wearily*). It's just incredible, Blanche, how well you're looking.

Blanche. (*They both laugh uncomfortably*) But, Stella, there's only two rooms. I don't see where you're going to put me!

Stella. We're going to put you in here.

Blanche. What kind of bed's this—one of those collapsible things?

(*She sits on it.*)

Stella. Does it feel all right?

Blanche (*Dubiously*). Wonderful,

honey. I don't like a bed that gives much. But there's no door between the two rooms, and Stanley—will it be decent?

Stella. Stanley is Polish, you know.

Blanche. Oh, yes. They're something like Irish, aren't they?

Stella. Well—

Blanche. Only not so—highbrow? (*They both laugh again in the same way*) I brought some nice clothes to meet all your lovely friends in.

Stella. I'm afraid you won't think they are lovely.

Blanche. What are they like?

Stella. They're Stanley's friends.

Blanche. Polacks?

Stella. They're a mixed lot, Blanche.

Blanche. Heterogeneous—types?

Stella. Oh, yes. Yes, types is right!

Blanche. Well—anyhow—I brought nice clothes and I'll wear them. I guess you're hoping I'll say I'll put up at a hotel, but I'm not going to put up at a hotel. I want to be *near* you, got to be *with* somebody, I *can't* be *alone!* Because—as you must have noticed—I'm—*not* very *well* . . . (*Her voice drops and her look is frightened.*)

Stella. You seem a little bit nervous or overwrought or something.

Blanche. Will Stanley like me, or will I be just a visiting in-law, Stella? I couldn't stand that.

Stella. You'll get along fine together, if you'll just try not to—well—compare him with men that we went out with at home.

Blanche. Is he so—different?

Stella. Yes. A different species.

Blanche. In what way; what's he like?

Stella. Oh, you can't describe someone you're in love with! Here's a picture of him! (*She hands a photograph to* Blanche.)

Blanche. An officer?

Stella. A Master Sergeant in the Engineers' Corps. Those are decorations!

Blanche. He had those on when you met him?

Stella. I assure you I wasn't just blinded by all the brass.

Blanche. That's not what I—

Stella. But of course there were things to adjust myself to later on.

Blanche. Such as his civilian background! (Stella *laughs uncertainly*) How did he take it when you said I was coming?

Stella. Oh, Stanley doesn't know yet.

Blanche (*Frightened*). You—haven't told him?

Stella. He's on the road a good deal.

Blanche. Oh. Travels?

Stella. Yes.

Blanche. Good. I mean—isn't it?

Stella (*Half to herself*). I can hardly stand it when he is away for a night . . .

Blanche. Why, Stella!

Stella. When he's away for a week I nearly go wild!

Blanche. Gracious!

Stella. And when he comes back I cry on his lap like a baby . . . (*She smiles to herself.*)

Blanche. I guess that is what is meant by being in love . . . (Stella *looks up with a radiant smile.*) Stella—

Stella. What?

Blanche (*In an uneasy rush*). I haven't asked you the things you probably thought I was going to ask. And so I'll expect you to be understanding about what *I* have to tell *you.*

Stella. What, Blanche? (*Her face turns anxious.*)

Blanche. Well, Stella—you're going to reproach me, I know that you're bound to reproach me—but before you do—take into consideration—you left! I stayed and struggled! You came to New Orleans and looked out for yourself! *I* stayed at *Belle Reve* and tried to hold it together! I'm not meaning this in any reproachful way, but *all* the burden descended on *my* shoulders.

Stella. The best I could do was make my own living, Blanche. (BLANCHE *begins to shake again with intensity.*)

Blanche. I know, I know. But you are the one that abandoned Belle Reve, not I! I stayed and fought for it, bled for it, almost died for it!

Stella. Stop this hysterical outburst and tell me what's happened? What do you mean fought and bled? What kind of—

Blanche. I knew you would, Stella. I knew you would take this attitude about it!

Stella. About—what?—please!

Blanche (*Slowly*). The loss—the loss . . .

Stella. Belle Reve? Lost, is it? No!

Blanche. Yes, Stella.

(*They stare at each other across the yellow-checked linoleum of the table.* BLANCHE *slowly nods her head and* STELLA *looks slowly down at her hands folded on the table. The music of the "blue piano" grows louder.* BLANCHE *touches her handkerchief to her forehead.*)

Stella. But how did it go? What happened?

Blanche (*Springing up*). You're a fine one to ask me how it went!

Stella. Blanche!

Blanche. You're a fine one to sit there *accusing me* of it!

Stella. Blanche!

Blanche. I, I, *I* took the blows in my face and my body! All of those deaths! The long parade to the graveyard! Father, mother! Margaret, that dreadful way! So big with it, it couldn't be put in a coffin! But had to be burned like rubbish! You just came home in time for the funerals, Stella. And funerals are pretty compared to deaths. Funerals are quiet, but deaths—not always. Sometimes their breathing is hoarse, and sometimes it rattles, and sometimes they even cry out to you, "Don't let me go!" Even the old, sometimes, say, "Don't let me go." As if you were able to stop them! But funerals are quiet, with pretty flowers. And, oh, what gorgeous boxes they pack them away in! Unless you were there at the bed when they cried out, "Hold me!" you'd never suspect there was the struggle for breath and bleeding. You didn't dream, but I saw! *Saw! Saw!* And now you sit there telling me with your eyes that I let the place go! How in hell do you think all that sickness and dying was paid for? Death is expensive, Miss Stella! And old Cousin Jessie's right after Margaret's, hers! Why, the Grim Reaper had put up his tent on our doorstep! . . . Stella. Belle Reve was his headquarters! Honey—that's how it slipped through my fingers! Which of them left us a fortune? Which of them left a cent of insurance even? Only poor Jessie—one hundred to pay for her coffin. That was all, Stella! And I with my pitiful salary at the school. Yes, accuse me! Sit there and stare at me, thinking I let the place go! *I* let the place go? Where were *you!* In bed with your— Polack!

Stella (*Springing*). Blanche! You be still! That's enough! (*She starts out.*)

Blanche. Where are you going?

Stella. I'm going into the bathroom to wash my face.

Blanche. Oh, Stella, Stella, you're crying!

Stella. Does that surprise you?

Blanche. Forgive me—I didn't mean to—

(*The sound of men's voices is heard. STELLA goes into the bathroom, closing the door behind her. When the men appear, and BLANCHE realizes it must be STANLEY returning, she moves uncertainly from the bathroom door to the dressing table, looking apprehensively towards the front door. STANLEY enters, followed by STEVE and MITCH. STANLEY pauses near his door, STEVE by the foot of the spiral stair, and MITCH is slightly above and to the right of them, about to go out. As the men enter, we hear some of the following dialogue.*)

Stanley. Is that how he got it?

Steve. Sure that's how he got it. He hit the old weather-bird for 300 bucks on a six-number-ticket.

Mitch. Don't tell him those things; he'll believe it.

(*MITCH starts out.*)

Stanley (*Restraining Mitch*). Hey, Mitch—come back here.

(*BLANCHE, at the sound of voices, retires in the bedroom. She picks up STANLEY's photo from dressing table, looks at it, puts it down. When STANLEY enters the apartment, she darts*

and hides behind the screen at the head of bed.)

Steve (*To STANLEY and MITCH*). Hey, are we playin' poker tomorrow?

Stanley. Sure—at Mitch's.

Mitch (*Hearing this, returns quickly to the stair rail*). No—not at my place. My mother's still sick!

Stanley. Okay, at my place . . . (*MITCH starts out again*) But you bring the beer!

(*MITCH pretends not to hear,—calls out "Goodnight all," and goes out, singing. EUNICE's voice is heard, above*)

Eunice. Break it up down there! I made the spaghetti dish and ate it myself.

Steve (*Going upstairs*). I told you and phoned you we was playing. (*To the men*) Jax beer!

Eunice. You never phoned me once.

Steve. I told you at breakfast—and phoned you at lunch . . .

Eunice. Well, never mind about that. You just get yourself home here once in a while.

Steve. You want it in the papers?

(*More laughter and shouts of parting come from the men. STANLEY throws the screen door of the kitchen open and comes in. He is of medium height, about five feet eight or nine, and strongly, compactly built. Animal joy in his being is implicit in all his movements and attitudes. Since earliest manhood the center of his life has been pleasure with women, the giving and taking of it, not with weak indulgence, dependently, but with the power and pride of a richly feathered male bird among hens. Branching out from this complete and satisfying center are all the auxiliary channels of his life, such as his heartiness with men, his appreciation of rough humor, his love of good drink and food and games, his car, his radio, everything that is his, that bears his emblem of the gaudy seed-bearer. He sizes women up at a glance, with sexual classifications, crude images flashing into his mind and determining the way he smiles at them.)*

Blanche (*Drawing involuntarily back from his stare*). You must be Stanley. I'm Blanche.

Stanley. Stella's sister?

Blanche. Yes.

Stanley. H'lo. Where's the little woman?

Blanche. In the bathroom.

Stanley. Oh. Didn't know you were coming in town.

Blanche. I—uh—

Stanley. Where you from, Blanche?

Blanche. Why, I—live in Laurel.

(*He has crossed to the closet and removed the whiskey bottle.*)

Stanley. In Laurel, huh? Oh, yeah. Yeah, in Laurel, that's right. Not in my territory. Liquor goes fast in hot weather.

(*He holds the bottle to the light to observe its depletion.*)

Have a shot?

Blanche. No, I—rarely touch it.

Stanley. Some people rarely touch it, but it touches them often.

Blanche (*Faintly*). Ha-ha.

Stanley. My clothes're stickin' to me. Do you mind if I make myself comfortable? (*He starts to remove his shirt.*)

Blanche. Please, please do.

Stanley. Be comfortable is my motto.

Blanche. It's mine, too. It's hard to stay looking fresh. I haven't washed or even powdered my face and—here you are!

Stanley. You know you can catch cold sitting around in damp things, especially when you been exercising hard like bowling is. You're a teacher, aren't you?

Blanche. Yes.

Stanley. What do you teach, Blanche?

Blanche. English.

Stanley. I never was a very good English student. How long you here for, Blanche?

Blanche. I—don't know yet.

Stanley. You going to shack up here?

Blanche. I thought I would if it's not inconvenient for you all.

Stanley. Good.

Blanche. Traveling wears me out.

Stanley. Well, take it easy.

(*A cat screeches near the window.* BLANCHE *springs up.*)

Blanche. What's that?

Stanley. Cats . . . Hey, Stella!

Stella (*Faintly, from the bathroom*). Yes, Stanley.

Stanley. Haven't fallen in, have you? (*He grins at* BLANCHE. *She tries unsuccessfully to smile back. There is a silence*) I'm afraid I'll strike you as being the unrefined type. Stella's spoke of you a good deal. You were married once, weren't you?

(*The music of the polka rises up, faint in the distance.*)

Blanche. Yes. When I was quite young.

Stanley. What happened?

Blanche. The boy—the boy died. (*She sinks back down*) I'm afraid I'm—going to be sick!

(*Her head falls on her arms.*)

Scene Two

It is six o'clock the following evening. Blanche *is bathing.*
Stella *is completing her toilette.* Blanche's *dress, a flowered
print, is laid out on* Stella's *bed.*

Stanley *enters the kitchen from outside, leaving the door open
on the perpetual "blue piano" around the corner.*

Stanley. What's all this monkey doings?

Stella. Oh, Stan! (*She jumps up and
kisses him which he accepts with
lordly composure*) I'm taking Blanche
to Galatoire's for supper and then to
a show, because it's your poker night.

Stanley. How about my supper, huh?
I'm not going to no Galatoire's for
supper!

Stella. I put you a cold plate on ice.

Stanley. Well, isn't that just dandy!

Stella. I'm going to try to keep Blanche
out till the party breaks up because
I don't know how she would take it.
So we'll go to one of the little places
in the Quarter afterwards and you'd
better give me some money.

Stanley. Where is she?

Stella. She's soaking in a hot tub to
quiet her nerves. She's terribly upset.

Stanley. Over what?

Stella. She's been through such an
ordeal.

Stanley. Yeah?

Stella. Stan, we've—lost Belle Reve!

Stanley. The place in the country?

Stella. Yes.

Stanley. How?

Stella (*Vaguely*). Oh, it had to be—
sacrificed or something. (*There is a
pause while Stanley considers. Stella
is changing into her dress*) When she
comes in be sure to say something
nice about her appearance. And, oh!
Don't mention the baby. I haven't
said anything yet, I'm waiting until
she gets in a quieter condition.

Stanley (*Ominously*). So?

Stella. And try to understand her and
be nice to her, Stan.

Blanche (*Singing in the bathroom*).
"From the land of the sky blue water,
They brought a captive maid!"

Stella. She wasn't expecting to find us
in such a small place. You see I'd
tried to gloss things over a little in
my letters.

Stanley. So?

Stella. And admire her dress and tell
her she's looking wonderful. That's
important with Blanche. Her little
weakness!

Stanley. Yeah. I get the idea. Now let's
skip back a little to where you said
the country place was disposed of.

Stella. Oh!—yes . . .

Stanley. How about that? Let's have a
few more details on that subjeck.

Stella. It's best not to talk much about
it until she's calmed down.

Stanley. So that's the deal, huh? Sister
Blanche cannot be annoyed with
business details right now!

Stella. You saw how she was last night.

Stanley. Uh-hum, I saw how she was.
Now let's have a gander at the bill of
sale.

Stella. I haven't seen any.

Stanley. She didn't show you no papers,
no deed of sale or nothing like that,
huh?

Stella. It seems like it wasn't sold.

Stanley. Well what in hell was it then,
give away? To charity?

Stella. Shhh! She'll hear you.

Stanley. I don't care if she hears me. Let's see the papers!

Stella. There weren't any papers, she didn't show any papers, I don't care about papers.

Stanley. Have you ever heard of the Napoleonic code?

Stella. No, Stanley, I haven't heard of the Napoleonic code and if I have, I don't see what it—

Stanley. Let me enlighten you on a point or two, baby.

Stella. Yes?

Stanley. In the state of Louisiana we have the Napoleonic code according to which what belongs to the wife belongs to the husband and vice versa. For instance if I had a piece of property, or you had a piece of property—

Stella. My head is swimming!

Stanley. All right. I'll wait till she gets through soaking in a hot tub and then I'll inquire if *she* is acquainted with the Napoleonic code. It looks to me like you have been swindled, baby, and when you're swindled under the Napoleonic code I'm swindled *too.* And I don't like to be *swindled.*

Stella. There's plenty of time to ask her questions later but if you do now she'll go to pieces again. I don't understand what happened to Belle Reve but you don't know how ridiculous you are being when you suggest that my sister or I or anyone of our family could have perpetrated a swindle on anyone else.

Stanley. Then where's the money if the place was sold?

Stella. Not sold—*lost, lost!*

(*He stalks into bedroom, and she follows him.*)

Stanley!

(*He pulls open the wardrobe trunk standing in middle of room and jerks out an armful of dresses.*)

Stanley. Open your eyes to this stuff! You think she got them out of a teacher's pay?

Stella. Hush!

Stanley. Look at these feathers and furs that she come here to preen herself in! What's this here? A solid-gold dress, I believe! And this one! What is these here? Fox-pieces! (*He blows on them*) Genuine fox fur-pieces, a half a mile long! Where are your fox-pieces, Stella? Bushy snow-white ones, no less! Where are your white fox-pieces?

Stella. Those are inexpensive summer furs that Blanche has had a long time.

Stanley. I got an acquaintance who deals in this sort of merchandise. I'll have him in here to appraise it. I'm willing to bet you there's thousands of dollars invested in this stuff here!

Stella. Don't be such an idiot, Stanley!

(*He hurls the furs to the daybed. Then he jerks open small drawer in the trunk and pulls up a fist-full of costume jewelry.*)

Stanley. And what have we here? The treasure chest of a pirate!

Stella. Oh, Stanley!

Stanley. Pearls! Ropes of them! What is this sister of yours, a deepsea diver? Bracelets of solid gold, too! Where are your pearls and gold bracelets?

Stella. Shhh! Be still, Stanley!

Stanley. And diamonds! A crown for an empress!

Stella. A rhinestone tiara she wore to a costume ball.

Stanley. What's rhinestone?

Stella. Next door to glass.

Stanley. Are you kidding? I have an acquaintance that works in a jewelry store. I'll have him in here to make an appraisal of this. Here's your plantation, or what was left of it, here!

Stella. You have no idea how stupid and horrid you're being! Now close that trunk before she comes out of the bathroom!

(*He kicks the trunk partly closed and sits on the kitchen table.*)

Stanley. The Kowalskis and the DuBois have different notions.

Stella (*Angrily*). Indeed they have, thank heavens!—*I'm* going outside. (*She snatches up her white hat and gloves and crosses to the outside door*) You come out with me while Blanche is getting dressed.

Stanley. Since when do you give me orders?

Stella. Are you going to stay here and insult her?

Stanley. You're damn tootin' I'm going to stay here.

(STELLA *goes out to the porch.* BLANCHE *comes out of the bathroom in a red satin robe.*)

Blanche (*Airily*). Hello, Stanley! Here I am, all freshly bathed and scented, and feeling like a brand new human being!

(*He lights a cigarette.*)

Stanley. That's good.

Blanche (*Drawing the curtains at the windows*). Excuse me while I slip on my pretty new dress!

Stanley. Go right ahead, Blanche.

(*She closes the drapes between the rooms.*)

Blanche. I understand there's to be a little card party to which we ladies are cordially *not* invited!

Stanley (*Ominously*). Yeah?

(BLANCHE *throws off her robe and slips into the flowered print dress.*)

Blanche. Where's Stella?

Stanley. Out on the porch.

Blanche. I'm going to ask a favor of you in a moment.

Stanley. What could that be, I wonder?

Blanche. Some buttons in back! You may enter!

(*He crosses through drapes with a smoldering look.*)

How do I look?

Stanley. You look all right.

Blanche. Many thanks! Now the buttons!

Stanley. I can't do nothing with them.

Blanche. You men with your big clumsy fingers. May I have a drag on your cig?

Stanley. Have one for yourself.

Blanche. Why, thanks! . . . It looks like my trunk has exploded.

Stanley. Me an' Stella were helping you unpack.

Blanche. Well, you certainly did a fast and thorough job of it!

Stanley. It looks like you raided some stylish shops in Paris.

Blanche. Ha-ha! Yes—clothes are my passion!

Stanley. What does it cost for a string of fur-pieces like that?

Blanche. Why, those were a tribute from an admirer of mine!

Stanley. He must have had a lot of—admiration!

Blanche. Oh, in my youth I excited some admiration. But look at me now! (*She smiles at him radiantly*) Would you think it possible that I was once considered to be—attractive?

Stanley. Your looks are okay.

Blanche. I was fishing for a compliment, Stanley.

Stanley. I don't go in for that stuff.

Blanche. What—stuff?

Stanley. Compliments to women about their looks. I never met a woman that didn't know if she was good-looking or not without being told, and some of them give themselves credit for more than they've got. I once went out with a doll who said to me, "I am the glamorous type, I am the glamorous type!" I said, "So what?"

Blanche. And what did she say then?

Stanley. She didn't say nothing. That shut her up like a clam.

Blanche. Did it end the romance?

Stanley. It ended the conversation—that was all. Some men are took in by this Hollywood glamor stuff and some men are not.

Blanche. I'm sure you belong in the second category.

Stanley. That's right.

Blanche. I cannot imagine any witch of a woman casting a spell over you.

Stanley. That's—right.

Blanche. You're simple, straightforward and honest, a little bit on the primitive side I should think. To interest you a woman would have to— (*She pauses with an indefinite gesture.*)

Stanley (*Slowly*). Lay . . . her cards on the table.

Blanche (*Smiling*). Well, I never cared for wishy-washy people. That was why, when you walked in here last night, I said to myself—"My sister has married a man!"—Of course that was all that I could tell about you.

Stanley (*Booming*). Now let's cut the re-bop!

Blanche (*Pressing hands to her ears*). Ouuuuu!

Stella (*Calling from the steps*). Stanley! You come out here and let Blanche finish dressing!

Blanche. I'm through dressing, honey.

Stella. Well, you come out, then.

Stanley. Your sister and I are having a little talk.

Blanche (*Lightly*). Honey, do me a favor. Run to the drug-store and get me a lemon-coke with plenty of chipped ice in it!—Will you do that for me, Sweetie?

Stella (*Uncertainly*). Yes. (*She goes around the corner of the building.*)

Blanche. The poor little thing was out there listening to us, and I have an idea she doesn't understand you as well as I do. . . . All right; now, Mr. Kowalski, let us proceed without any more double-talk. I'm ready to answer all questions. I've nothing to hide. What is it?

Stanley. There is such a thing in this State of Louisiana as the Napoleonic code, according to which whatever belongs to my wife is also mine—and vice versa.

Blanche. My, but you have an impressive judicial air!

(*She sprays herself with her atomizer; then playfully sprays him with it. He seizes the atomizer and slams it down on the dresser. She throws back her head and laughs.*)

Stanley. If I didn't know that you was my wife's sister I'd get ideas about you!

Blanche. Such as what!

Stanley. Don't play so dumb. You know what!

Blanche (*She puts the atomizer on the table*). All right. Cards on the table. That suits me. (*She turns to Stanley.*) I know I fib a good deal. After all, a woman's charm is fifty per cent illusion, but when a thing is important I tell the truth, and this is the truth: I haven't cheated my sister or you or anyone else as long as I have lived.

Stanley. Where's the papers? In the trunk?

Blanche. Everything that I own is in that trunk.

(STANLEY *crosses to the trunk, shoves it roughly open and begins to open compartments.*)

Blanche. What in the name of heaven are you thinking of! What's in the back of that little boy's mind of yours? That I am absconding with something, attempting some kind of treachery on my sister?—Let me do that! It will be faster and simpler . . . (*She crosses to the trunk and takes out a box*) I keep my papers mostly in this tin box. (*She opens it.*)

Stanley. What's them underneath? (*He indicates another sheaf of papers.*)

Blanche. These are love-letters, yellowing with antiquity, all from one boy. (*He snatches them up. She speaks fiercely*) Give those back to me!

Stanley. I'll have a look at them first!

Blanche. The touch of your hands insults them!

Stanley. Don't pull that stuff!

(*He rips off the ribbon and starts to examine them.* BLANCHE *snatches them from him, and they cascade to the floor.*)

Blanche. Now that you've touched them I'll burn them!

Stanley (*Staring, baffled*). What in hell are they?

Blanche (*On the floor gathering them up*). Poems a dead boy wrote. I hurt him the way that you would like to hurt me, but you can't! I'm not young and vulnerable any more. But my young husband was and I— never mind about that! Just give them back to me!

Stanley. What do you mean by saying you'll have to burn them?

Blanche. I'm sorry, I must have lost my head for a moment. Everyone has something he won't let others touch because of their—intimate nature . . .

(*She now seems faint with exhaustion and she sits down with the strong box and puts on a pair of glasses and goes methodically through a large stack of papers.*)

Ambler & Ambler. Hmmmmm. . . . Crabtree. . . . More Ambler & Ambler.

Stanley. What is Ambler & Ambler?

Blanche. A firm that made loans on the place.

Stanley. Then it *was* lost on a mortgage?

Blanche (*Touching her forehead*). That must've been what happened.

Stanley. I don't want no ifs, ands or buts! What's all the rest of them papers?

(*She hands him the entire box. He carries it to the table and starts to examine the papers.*)

Blanche (*Picking up a large envelope containing more papers*). There are thousands of papers, stretching back over hundreds of years, affecting Belle Reve as, piece by piece, our improvident grandfathers and father and uncles and brothers exchanged the land for their epic fornications—to put it plainly! (*She removes her glasses with an exhausted laugh*) The four-letter word deprived us of our plantation, till finally all that was left—and Stella can verify that!—was the house itself and about twenty acres of ground, including a graveyard, to which now all but Stella and I have retreated. (*She pours the contents of the envelope on the table*) Here all of them are, all papers! I hereby endow you with them! Take them, peruse them—commit them to memory, even! I think it's wonderfully fitting that Belle Reve should finally be this bunch of old papers in your big, capable hands! . . . I wonder if Stella's come back with my lemon-coke . . . (*She leans back and closes her eyes.*)

Stanley. I have a lawyer acquaintance who will study these out.

Blanche. Present them to him with a box of aspirin tablets.

Stanley (*Becoming somewhat sheepish*). You see, under the Napoleonic code—a man has to take an interest in his wife's affairs—especially now that she's going to have a baby.

(BLANCHE *opens her eyes. The "blue piano" sounds louder.*)

Blanche. Stella? Stella going to have a baby? (*Dreamily*) I didn't know she was going to have a baby!

(*She gets up and crosses to the out-side door.* STELLA *appears around the corner with a carton from the drugstore.*)

(STANLEY *goes into the bedroom with the envelope and the box.*

(*The inner rooms fade to darkness and the outside wall of the house is visible.* BLANCHE *meets* STELLA *at the foot of the steps to the sidewalk.*)

Blanche. Stella, Stella for star! How lovely to have a baby! It's all right. Everything's all right.

Stella. I'm sorry he did that to you.

Blanche. Oh, I guess he's just not the type that goes for jasmine perfume, but maybe he's what we need to mix with our blood now that we've lost Belle Reve. We thrashed it out. I feel a bit shaky, but I think I handled it nicely, I laughed and treated it all as a joke. (STEVE *and* PABLO *appear, carrying a case of beer.*) I called him a little boy and laughed and flirted. Yes, I was flirting with your husband! (*As the men approach*) The guests are gathering for the poker party.

(*The two men pass between them, and enter the house.*)

Which way do we go now, Stella—this way?

Stella. No, this way. (*She leads* BLANCHE *away.*)

Blanche (*Laughing*). The blind are leading the blind!

(*A tamale* VENDOR *is heard calling.*)

Vendor's Voice. Red-hot!

SCENE THREE

THE POKER NIGHT
There is a picture of Van Gogh's of a billiard-parlor at night.

The kitchen now suggests that sort of lurid nocturnal brilliance, the raw colors of childhood's spectrum. Over the yellow linoleum of the kitchen table hangs an electric bulb with a vivid green glass shade. The poker players—STANLEY, STEVE, MITCH and PABLO—wear colored shirts, solid blues, a purple, a red-and-white check, a light green, and they are men at the peak of their physical manhood, as coarse and direct and powerful as the primary colors. There are vivid slices of watermelon on the table, whiskey bottles and glasses. The bedroom is relatively dim with only the light that spills between the portieres and through the wide window on the street.

For a moment, there is absorbed silence as a hand is dealt.

Steve. Anything wild this deal?

Pablo. One-eyed jacks are wild.

Steve. Give me two cards.

Pablo. You, Mitch?

Mitch. I'm out.

Pablo. One.

Mitch. Anyone want a shot?

Stanley. Yeah. Me.

Pablo. Why don't somebody go to the Chinaman's and bring back a load of chop suey?

Stanley. When I'm losing you want to eat! Ante up! Openers? Openers! Get y'r ass off the table, Mitch. Nothing belongs on a poker table but cards, chips and whiskey.

(He lurches up and tosses some watermelon rinds to the floor.)

Mitch. Kind of on your high horse, ain't you?

Stanley. How many?

Steve. Give me three.

Stanley. One.

Mitch. I'm out again. I oughta go home pretty soon.

Stanley. Shut up.

Mitch. I gotta sick mother. She don't go to sleep until I come in at night.

Stanley. They why don't you stay home with her?

Mitch. She says to go out, so I go, but I don't enjoy it. All the while I keep wondering how she is.

Stanley. Aw, for the sake of Jesus, go home, then!

Pablo. What've you got?

Steve. Spade flush.

Mitch. You all are married. But I'll be alone when she goes.—I'm going to the bathroom.

Stanley. Hurry back and we'll fix you a sugar-tit.

Mitch. Aw, go rut. *(He crosses through the bedroom into the bathroom.)*

Steve *(Dealing a hand).* Seven card stud. *(Telling his joke as he deals)* This ole farmer is out in back of his house sittin' down th'owing corn to the chickens when all at once he hears a loud cackle and this young hen comes lickety split around the side of the house with the rooster right behind her and gaining on her fast.

Stanley *(Impatient with the story).* Deal!

Steve. But when the rooster catches sight of the farmer th'owing the corn he puts on the brakes and lets the hen get away and starts pecking corn. And the old farmer says, "Lord God, I hopes I never gits *that* hongry!"

(STEVE and PABLO laugh. The sisters appear around the corner of the building.)

Stella. The game is still going on.

Blanche. How do I look?

Stella. Lovely, Blanche.

Blanche. I feel so hot and frazzled. Wait till I powder before you open the door. Do I look done in?

Stella. Why no. You are as fresh as a daisy.

Blanche. One that's been picked a few days.

(STELLA *opens the door and they enter.*)

Stella. Well, well, well. I see you boys are still at it!

Stanley. Where you been?

Stella. Blanche and I took in a show. Blanche, this is Mr. Gonzales and Mr. Hubbell.

Blanche. Please don't get up.

Stanley. Nobody's going to get up, so don't be worried.

Stella. How much longer is this game going to continue?

Stanley. Till we get ready to quit.

Blanche. Poker is so fascinating. Could I kibitz?

Stanley. You could not. Why don't you women go up and sit with Eunice?

Stella. Because it is nearly two-thirty. (BLANCHE *crosses into the bedroom and partially closes the portieres*) Couldn't you call it quits after one more hand?

(*A chair scrapes.* STANLEY *gives a loud whack of his hand on her thigh.*)

Stella (*Sharply*). That's not fun, Stanley.

(*The men laugh.* STELLA *goes into the bedroom.*)

Stella. It makes me so mad when he does that in front of people.

Blanche. I think I will bathe.

Stella. Again?

Blanche. My nerves are in knots. Is the bathroom occupied?

Stella. I don't know.

(BLANCHE *knocks.* MITCH *opens the door and comes out, still wiping his hands on a towel.*)

Blanche. Oh!—good evening.

Mitch. Hello. (*He stares at her.*)

Stella. Blanche, this is Harold Mitchell. My sister, Blanche DuBois.

Mitch (*With awkward courtesy*). How do you do, Miss DuBois.

Stella. How is your mother now, Mitch?

Mitch. About the same, thanks. She appreciated your sending over that custard.—Excuse me, please.

(*He crosses slowly back into the kitchen, glancing back at* BLANCHE *and coughing a little shyly. He realizes he still has the towel in his hands and with an embarrassed laugh hands it to* STELLA. BLANCHE *looks after him with a certain interest.*)

Blanche. That one seems—superior to the others.

Stella. Yes, he is.

Blanche. I thought he had a sort of sensitive look.

Stella. His mother is sick.

Blanche. Is he married?

Stella. No.

Blanche. Is he a wolf?

Stella. Why, Blanche! (BLANCHE *laughs.*) I don't think he would be.

Blanche. What does—what does he do?

(*She is unbuttoning her blouse.*)

Stella. He's on the precision bench in the spare parts department. At the plant Stanley travels for.

Blanche. Is that something much?

Stella. No. Stanley's the only one of his crowd that's likely to get anywhere.

Blanche. What makes you think Stanley will?

Stella. Look at him.

Blanche. I've looked at him.

Stella. Then you should know.

Blanche. I'm sorry, but I haven't noticed the stamp of genius even on Stanley's forehead.

(*She takes off the blouse and stands in her pink silk brassiere and white skirt in the light through the portieres. The game has continued in undertones.*)

Stella. It isn't on his forehead and it isn't genius.

Blanche. Oh. Well, what is it, and where? I would like to know.

Stella. It's a drive that he has. You're standing in the light, Blanche!

Blanche. Oh, am I!

(*She moves out of the yellow streak of light.* STELLA *has removed her dress and put on a light blue satin kimono.*)

Stella (*With girlish laughter*). You ought to see their wives.

Blanche (*Laughingly*). I can imagine. Big, beefy things, I suppose.

Stella. You know that one upstairs? (*More laughter*) One time (*Laughing*) the plaster—(*Laughing*) cracked—

Stanley. You hens cut out that conversation in there!

Stella. You can't hear us.

Stanley. Well, you can hear me and I said to hush up!

Stella. This is my house and I'll talk as much as I want to!

Blanche. Stella, don't start a row.

Stella. He's half drunk!—I'll be out in a minute.

(*She goes into the bathroom.* BLANCHE *rises and crosses leisurely to a small white radio and turns it on.*)

Stanley. Awright, Mitch, you in?

Mitch. What? Oh!—No, I'm out!

(BLANCHE *moves back into the streak of light. She raises her arms and stretches, as she moves indolently back to the chair.*)

(*Rhumba music comes over the radio.* MITCH *rises at the table.*)

Stanley. Who turned that on in there?

Blanche. I did. Do you mind?

Stanley. Turn it off!

Steve. Aw, let the girls have their music.

Pablo. Sure, that's good, leave it on!

Steve. Sounds like Xavier Cugat!

(STANLEY *jumps up and, crossing to the radio, turns it off. He stops short at the sight of* BLANCHE *in the chair. She returns his look without flinching. Then he sits again at the poker table.*)

(*Two of the men have started arguing hotly.*)

Steve. I didn't hear you name it.

Pablo. Didn't I name it, Mitch?

Mitch. I wasn't listenin'.

Pablo. What were you doing, then?

Stanley. He was looking through them drapes. (*He jumps up and jerks roughly at curtains to close them*) Now deal the hand over again and let's play cards or quit. Some people get ants when they win.

(MITCH *rises as* STANLEY *returns to his seat.*)

Stanley (*Yelling*). Sit down!

Mitch. I'm going to the "head." Deal me out.

Pablo. Sure he's got ants now. Seven five-dollar bills in his pants pocket folded up tight as spitballs.

Steve. Tomorrow you'll see him at the cashier's window getting them changed into quarters.

Stanley. And when he goes home he'll deposit them one by one in a piggy bank his mother give him for Christmas. (*Dealing*) This game is Spit in the Ocean.

(MITCH *laughs uncomfortably and continues through the portieres. He stops just inside.*)

Blanche (*Softly*). Hello! The Little Boys' Room is busy right now.

Mitch. We've—been drinking beer.

Blanche. I hate beer.

Mitch. It's—a hot weather drink.

Blanche. Oh, I don't think so; it always makes me warmer. Have you got any cigs? (*She has slipped on the dark red satin wrapper.*)

Mitch. Sure.

Blanche. What kind are they?

Mitch. Luckies.

Blanche. Oh, good. What a pretty case. Silver?

Mitch. Yes. Yes; read the inscription.

Blanche. Oh, is there an inscription? I can't make it out. (*He strikes a match and moves closer*) Oh! (*Reading with feigned difficulty*):

"And if God choose,
I shall but love thee better—after—
death!"

Why, that's from my favorite sonnet by Mrs. Browning!

Mitch. You know it?

Blanche. Certainly I do!

Mitch. There's a story connected with that inscription.

Blanche. It sounds like a romance.

Mitch. A pretty sad one.

Blanche. Oh?

Mitch. The girl's dead now.

Blanche (*In a tone of deep sympathy*). Oh!

Mitch. She knew she was dying when she give me this. A very strange girl, very sweet—very!

Blanche. She must have been fond of you. Sick people have such deep, sincere attachments.

Mitch. That's right, they certainly do.

Blanche. Sorrow makes for sincerity, I think.

Mitch. It sure brings it out in people.

Blanche. The little there is belongs to people who have experienced some sorrow.

Mitch. I believe you are right about that.

Blanche. I'm positive that I am. Show me a person who hasn't known any sorrow and I'll show you a shuperficial—Listen to me! My tongue is a little—thick! You boys are responsible for it. The show let out at eleven and we couldn't come home on account of the poker game so we had to go somewhere and drink. I'm not accustomed to having more than one drink. Two is the limit—and *three!* (*She laughs*) Tonight I had three.

Stanley. Mitch!

Mitch. Deal me out. I'm talking to Miss—

Blanche. DuBois.

Mitch. Miss DuBois?

Blanche. It's a French name. It means woods and Blanche means white, so the two together mean white woods. Like an orchard in spring! You can remember it by that.

Mitch. You're French?

Blanche. We are French by extraction.

Our first American ancestors were French Huguenots.

Mitch. You are Stella's sister, are you not?

Blanche. Yes, Stella is my precious little sister. I call her little in spite of the fact she's somewhat older than I. Just slightly. Less than a year. Will you do something for me?

Mitch. Sure. What?

Blanche. I bought this adorable little colored paper lantern at a Chinese shop on Bourbon. Put it over the light bulb! Will you, please?

Mitch. Be glad to.

Blanche. I can't stand a naked light bulb, any more than I can a rude remark or a vulgar action.

Mitch (*Adjusting the lantern*). I guess we strike you as being a pretty rough bunch.

Blanche. I'm very adaptable—to circumstances.

Mitch. Well, that's a good thing to be. You are visiting Stanley and Stella?

Blanche. Stella hasn't been so well lately, and I came down to help her for a while. She's very run down.

Mitch. You're not—?

Blanche. Married? No, no. I'm an old maid schoolteacher!

Mitch. You may teach school but you're certainly not an old maid.

Blanche. Thank you, sir! I appreciate your gallantry!

Mitch. So you are in the teaching profession?

Blanche. Yes. Ah, yes . . .

Mitch. Grade school or high school or—

Stanley (*Bellowing*). *Mitch!*

Mitch. Coming!

Blanche. Gracious, what lung-power! . . . I teach high school. In Laurel.

Mitch. What do you teach? What subject?

Blanche. Guess!

Mitch. I bet you teach art or music (BLANCHE *laughs delicately*) Of course I could be wrong. You might teach arithmetic.

Blanche. Never arithmetic, sir, never arithmetic! (*With a laugh*) I don't even know my multiplication tables! No, I have the misfortune of being an English instructor. I attempt to instill a bunch of bobby-soxers and drug-store Romeos with reverence for Hawthorne and Whitman and Poe!

Mitch. I guess that some of them are more interested in other things.

Blanche. How very right you are! Their literary heritage is not what most of them treasure above all else! But they're sweet things! And in the spring, it's touching to notice them making their first discovery of love! As if nobody had ever known it before!

(*The bathroom door opens and* STELLA *comes out.* BLANCHE *continues talking to* MITCH.)

Oh! Have you finished? Wait—I'll turn on the radio.

(*She turns the knobs on the radio and it begins to play "Wien, Wien, nur du allein."* BLANCHE *waltzes to the music with romantic gestures.* MITCH *is delighted and moves in awkward imitation like a dancing bear.*

(STANLEY *stalks fiercely through the portieres into the bedroom. He crosses to the small white radio and snatches it off the table. With a shouted oath, he tosses the instrument out the window.*)

Stella. Drunk—drunk—animal thing, you! (*She rushes through to the poker table*) All of you—please go home! If any of you have one spark of decency in you—

Blanche (*Wildly*). Stella, watch out, he's—

(STANLEY *charges after* STELLA.)

Men (*Feebly*). Take it easy, Stanley. Easy, fellow.—Let's all—

Stella. You lay your hands on me and I'll—

(*She backs out of sight. He advances and disappears. There is the sound of a blow. STELLA cries out. BLANCHE screams and runs into the kitchen. The men rush forward and there is grappling and cursing. Something is overturned with a crash.*)

Blanche (*Shrilly*). My sister is going to have a baby!

Mitch. This is terrible.

Blanche. Lunacy, absolute lunacy!

Mitch. Get him in here, men.

(STANLEY *is forced, pinioned by the two men, into the bedroom. He nearly throws them off. Then all at once he subsides and is limp in their grasp.*

(*They speak quietly and lovingly to him and he leans his face on one of their shoulders.*)

Stella (*In a high, unnatural voice, out of sight*). I want to go away, I want to go away!

Mitch. Poker shouldn't be played in a house with women.

(BLANCHE *rushes into the bedroom.*)

Blanche. I want my sister's clothes! We'll go to that woman's upstairs!

Mitch. Where is the clothes?

Blanche (*Opening the closet*). I've got them! (*She rushes through to* STELLA) Stella, Stella, precious! Dear, dear little sister, don't be afraid!

(*With her arms around* STELLA, BLANCHE *guides her to the outside door and upstairs.*)

Stanley (*Dully*). What's the matter; what's happened?

Mitch. You just blew your top, Stan.

Pablo. He's okay, now.

Steve. Sure, my boy's okay!

Mitch. Put him on the bed and get a wet towel.

Pablo. I think coffee would do him a world of good, now.

Stanley (*Thickly*). I want water.

Mitch. Put him under the shower!

(*The men talk quietly as they lead him to the bathroom.*)

Stanley. Let the rut go of me, you sons of bitches!

(*Sounds of blows are heard. The water goes on full tilt.*)

Steve. Let's get quick out of here!

(*They rush to the poker table and sweep up their winnings on their way out.*)

Mitch (*Sadly but firmly*). Poker should not be played in a house with women.

(*The door closes on them and the place is still. The Negro entertainers in the bar around the corner play "Paper Doll" slow and blue. After a moment* STANLEY *comes out of the bathroom dripping water and still in his clinging wet polka dot drawers.*)

Stanley. Stella! (*There is a pause*) My baby doll's left me!

(*He breaks into sobs. Then he goes to the phone and dials, still shuddering with sobs.*)

Eunice? I want my baby! (*He waits a moment; then he hangs up and dials again*) Eunice! I'll keep on ringin' until I talk with my baby!

(*An indistinguishable shrill voice is heard. He hurls phone to floor. Dissonant brass and piano sounds as the rooms dim out to darkness and the outer walls appear in the night light. The "blue piano" plays for a brief interval.*)

(*Finally,* STANLEY *stumbles half-dressed out to the porch and down the wooden steps to the pavement before the building. There he throws back his head like a baying hound and bellows his wife's name: "Stella! Stella, sweetheart! Stella!"*)

Stanley. Stell-*lahhhhh!*

Eunice (*Calling down from the door of her upper apartment*). Quit that howling out there an' go back to bed!

Stanley. I want my baby down here. Stella, Stella!

Eunice. She ain't comin' down so you quit! Or you'll git th' law on you!

Stanley. Stella!

Eunice. You can't beat on a woman an' then call 'er back! She won't come! And her goin' t' have a baby! . . . You stinker! You whelp of a Polack, you! I hope they do haul you in and turn the fire hose on you, same as the last time!

Stanley (*Humbly*). Eunice, I want my girl to come down with me!

Eunice. Hah! (*She slams her door.*)

Stanley (*With heaven-splitting violence*). STELL-LAHHHHH!

(*The low-tone clarinet moans. The door upstairs opens again.* STELLA slips down the rickety stairs in her robe. Her eyes are glistening with tears and her hair loose about her throat and shoulders. They stare at each other. Then they come together with low, animal moans. He falls to his knees on the steps and presses his face to her belly, curving a little with maternity. Her eyes go blind with tenderness as she catches his head and raises him level with her. He snatches the screen door open and lifts her off her feet and bears her into the dark flat.*)

(BLANCHE *comes out on the upper landing in her robe and slips fearfully down the steps.*)

Blanche. Where is my little sister? Stella? Stella?

(*She stops before the dark entrance of her sister's flat. Then catches her breath as if struck. She rushes down to the walk before the house. She looks right and left as if for a sanctuary.*)

(*The music fades away.* MITCH *appears from around the corner.*)

Mitch. Miss DuBois?

Blanche. Oh!

Mitch. All quiet on the Potomac now?

Blanche. She ran downstairs and went back in there with him.

Mitch. Sure she did.

Blanche. I'm terrified!

Mitch. Ho-ho! There's nothing to be scared of. They're crazy about each other.

Blanche. I'm not used to such—

Mitch. Naw, it's a shame this had to happen when you just got here. But don't take it serious.

Blanche. Violence! Is so—

Mitch. Set down on the steps and have a cigarette with me.

Blanche. I'm not properly dressed.

Mitch. That don't make no difference in the Quarter.

Blanche. Such a pretty silver case.

Mitch. I showed you the inscription, didn't I?

Blanche. Yes. (*During the pause, she looks up at the sky*) There's so much —so much confusion in the world . . . (*He coughs diffidently*) Thank you for being so kind! I need kindness now.

SCENE FOUR

It is early the following morning. There is a confusion of street cries like a choral chant.

STELLA *is lying down in the bedroom. Her face is serene in the early morning sunlight. One hand rests on her belly, rounding slightly with new maternity. From the other dangles a book of colored comics. Her eyes and lips have that almost narcotized tranquility that is in the faces of Eastern idols.*

The table is sloppy with remains of breakfast and the debris of the preceding night, and STANLEY'S *gaudy pyjamas lie across the threshold of the bathroom. The outside door is slightly ajar on a sky of summer brilliance.*

BLANCHE *appears at this door. She has spent a sleepless night and her appearance entirely contrasts with* STELLA'S. *She presses her knuckles nervously to her lips as she looks through the door, before entering.*

Blanche. Stella?

Stella (*Stirring lazily*). Hmmh?

(BLANCHE *utters a moaning cry and runs into the bedroom, throwing herself down beside Stella in a rush of hysterical tenderness.*)

Blanche. Baby, my baby sister!

Stella (*Drawing away from her*). Blanche, what is the matter with you?

(BLANCHE *straightens up slowly and stands beside the bed looking down at her sister with knuckles pressed to her lips.*)

Blanche. He's left?

Stella. Stan? Yes.

Blanche. Will he be back?

Stella. He's gone to get the car greased. Why?

Blanche. Why! I've been half crazy, Stella! When I found out you'd been insane enough to come back in here after what happened—I started to rush in after you!

Stella. I'm glad you didn't.

Blanche. What were you thinking of? (STELLA *makes an indefinite gesture*) Answer me! What? What?

Stella. Please, Blanche! Sit down and stop yelling.

Blanche. All right, Stella. I will repeat the question quietly now. How could you come back in this place last night? Why, you must have slept with him!

(STELLA *gets up in a calm and leisurely way.*)

Stella. Blanche, I'd forgotten how excitable you are. You're making much too much fuss about this.

Blanche. Am I?

Stella. Yes, you are, Blanche. I know how it must have seemed to you and I'm awful sorry it had to happen, but it wasn't anything as serious as you seem to take it. In the first place, when men are drinking and playing poker anything can happen. It's always a powder-keg. He didn't know what he was doing. . . . He was as good as a lamb when I came back and he's really very, very ashamed of himself.

Blanche. And that—that makes it all right?

Stella. No, it isn't all right for anybody to make such a terrible row, but—people do sometimes. Stanley's always smashed things. Why, on our wedding night—soon as we came in here—he snatched off one of my slippers and rushed about the place smashing the light-bulbs with it.

Blanche. He did—*what?*

Stella. He smashed all the light-bulbs with the heel of my slipper!

(*She laughs.*)

Blanche. And you—you *let* him? Didn't *run*, didn't *scream?*

Stella. I was—sort of—thrilled by it. (*She waits for a moment*) Eunice and you had breakfast?

Blanche. Do you suppose I wanted any breakfast?

Stella. There's some coffee left on the stove.

Blanche. You're so—matter of fact about it, Stella.

Stella. What other can I be? He's taken the radio to get it fixed. It didn't land on the pavement so only one tube was smashed.

Blanche. And you are standing there smiling!

Stella. What do you want me to do?

Blanche. Pull yourself together and face the facts.

Stella. What are they, in your opinion?

Blanche. In my opinion? You're married to a madman!

Stella. No!

Blanche. Yes, you are, your fix is worse than mine is! Only you're not being sensible about it. I'm going to *do* something. Get hold of myself and make myself a new life!

Stella. Yes?

Blanche. But you've given in. And that isn't right, you're not old! You can get out.

Stella (*Slowly and emphatically*). I'm not in anything I want to get out of.

Blanche (*Incredulously*). What—Stella?

Stella. I said I am not in anything that I have a desire to get out of. Look at the mess in this room! And those empty bottles! They went through two cases last night! He promised this morning that he was going to quit having these poker parties, but you know how long such a promise is going to keep. Oh, well, it's his pleasure, like mine is movies and bridge. People have got to tolerate each other's habits, I guess.

Blanche. I don't understand you. (STELLA *turns toward her*) I don't understand your indifference. Is this a Chinese philosophy you've—cultivated?

Stella. Is what—what?

Blanche. This—shuffling about and mumbling—'One tube smashed—beer-bottles—mess in the kitchen.'—as if nothing out of the ordinary has happened! (STELLA *laughs uncer-*

*tainly and picking up the broom,
twirls it in her hands.*)

Blanche. Are you deliberately shaking that thing in my face?

Stella. No.

Blanche. Stop it. Let go of that broom. I won't have you cleaning up for him!

Stella. Then who's going to do it? Are you?

Blanche. I? I!

Stella. No, I didn't think so.

Blanche. Oh, let me think, if only my mind would function! We've got to get hold of some money, that's the way out!

Stella. I guess that money is always nice to get hold of.

Blanche. Listen to me. I have an idea of some kind. (*Shakily she twists a cigarette into her holder*) Do you remember Shep Huntleigh? (STELLA *shakes her head*) Of course you remember Shep Huntleigh. I went out with him at college and wore his pin for a while. Well—

Stella. Well?

Blanche. I ran into him last winter. You know I went to Miami during the Christmas holidays?

Stella. No.

Blanche. Well, I did. I took the trip as an investment, thinking I'd meet someone with a million dollars.

Stella. Did you?

Blanche. Yes. I ran into Shep Huntleigh—I ran into him on Biscayne Boulevard, on Christmas Eve, about dusk . . . getting into his car—Cadillac convertible; must have been a block long!

Stella. I should think it would have been—inconvenient in traffic!

Blanche. You've heard of oil-wells?

Stella. Yes—remotely.

Blanche. He has them, all over Texas. Texas is literally spouting gold in his pockets.

Stella. My, my.

Blanche. Y'know how indifferent I am to money. I think of money in terms of what it does for you. But he could do it, he could certainly do it!

Stella. Do what, Blanche?

Blanche. Why—set us up in a—shop!

Stella. What kind of a shop?

Blanche. Oh, a—shop of some kind! He could do it with half what his wife throws away at the races.

Stella. He's married?

Blanche. Honey, would I be here if the man weren't married? (STELLA *laughs a little.* BLANCHE *suddenly springs up and crosses to phone. She speaks shrilly*) How do I get Western Union?—Operator! Western Union!

Stella. That's a dial phone, honey.

Blanche. I can't dial, I'm too—

Stella. Just dial O.

Blanche. O?

Stella. Yes, "O" for Operator! (BLANCHE *considers a moment; then she puts the phone down.*)

Blanche. Give me a pencil. Where is a slip of paper? I've got to write it down first—the message, I mean . . .

(*She goes to the dressing table, and grabs up a sheet of Kleenex and an eyebrow pencil for writing equipment.*)

Let me see now . . . (*She bites the pencil*) 'Darling Shep. Sister and I in desperate situation.'

Stella. I beg your pardon!

Blanche. 'Sister and I in desperate situation. Will explain details later. Would you be interested in—?' (*She bites the pencil again*) 'Would you be —interested—in . . .' (*She smashes* *the pencil on the table and springs up*) You never get anywhere with direct appeals!

Stella (*With a laugh*). Don't be so ridiculous, darling!

Blanche. But I'll think of something, I've *got* to think of—*some*thing! Don't, don't laugh at me, Stella! Please, please don't—I—I want you to look at the contents of my purse! Here's what's in it! (*She snatches her purse open*) Sixty-five measly cents in coin of the realm!

Stella (*Crossing to bureau*). Stanley doesn't give me a regular allowance, he likes to pay bills himself, but— this morning he gave me ten dollars to smooth things over. You take five of it, Blanche, and I'll keep the rest.

Blanche. Oh, no. No, Stella.

Stella (*Insisting*). I know how it helps your morale just having a little pocket-money on you.

Blanche. No, thank you—I'll take to the streets!

Stella. Talk sense! How did you happen to get so low on funds?

Blanche. Money just goes—it goes places. (*She rubs her forehead*) Sometime today I've got to get hold of a bromo!

Stella. I'll fix you one now.

Blanche. Not yet—I've got to keep thinking!

Stella. I wish you'd just let things go, at least for a—while . . .

Blanche. Stella, I can't live with him! You can, he's your husband. But how could I stay here with him, after last night, with just those curtains between us?

Stella. Blanche, you saw him at his worst last night.

Blanche. On the contrary, I saw him at his best! What such a man has to offer is animal force and he gave a wonderful exhibition of that! But the only way to live with such a man is to—go to bed with him! And that's your job—not mine!

Stella. After you've rested a little, you'll see it's going to work out. You don't have to worry about anything while you're here. I mean—expenses . . .

Blanche. I have to plan for us both, to get us both—out!

Stella. You take it for granted that I am in something that I want to get out of.

Blanche. I take it for granted that you still have sufficient memory of Belle Reve to find this place and these poker players impossible to live with.

Stella. Well, you're taking entirely too much for granted.

Blanche. I can't believe you're in earnest.

Stella. No?

Blanche. I understand how it happened —a little. You saw him in uniform, an officer, not here but—

Stella. I'm not sure it would have made any difference where I saw him.

Blanche. Now don't say it was one of those mysterious electric things between people! If you do I'll laugh in your face.

Stella. I am not going to say anything more at all about it!

Blanche. All right, then, don't!

Stella. But there are things that happen between a man and a woman in the dark—that sort of make everything else seem—unimportant. (*Pause.*)

Blanche. What you are talking about is brutal desire—just—Desire!—the name of that rattle-trap street-car that bangs through the Quarter, up one old narrow street and down another . . .

Stella. Haven't you ever ridden on that street-car?

Blanche. It brought me here.—Where I'm not wanted and where I'm ashamed to be . . .

Stella. Then don't you think your superior attitude is a bit out of place?

Blanche. I am not being or feeling at all superior, Stella. Believe me I'm not! It's just this. This is how I look at it. A man like that is someone to go out with—once—twice—three times when the devil is in you. But live with? Have a child by?

Stella. I have told you I love him.

Blanche. Then I *tremble* for you! I just —*tremble* for you. . . .

Stella. I can't help your trembling if you insist on trembling!

(*There is a pause.*)

Blanche. May I—speak—*plainly?*

Stella. Yes, do. Go ahead. As plainly as you want to.

(*Outside, a train approaches. They are silent till the noise subsides. They are both in the bedroom.*

(*Under cover of the train's noise* STANLEY *enters from outside. He stands unseen by the women, holding some packages in his arms, and overhears their following conversation. He wears an undershirt and grease-stained seersucker pants.*)

Blanche. Well—if you'll forgive me— he's *common!*

Stella. Why, yes, I suppose he is.

Blanche. Suppose! You can't have forgotten that much of our bringing up, Stella, that you just *suppose* that any part of a gentleman's in his nature! *Not one particle, no!* Oh, if he was just—*ordinary!* Just *plain*—but good and wholesome, but—*no.* There's something downright—*bestial*— about him! You're hating me saying this, aren't you?

Stella (*Coldly*). Go on and say it all, Blanche.

Blanche. He acts like an animal, has an animal's habits! Eats like one, moves like one, talks like one! There's even something—sub-human—something not quite to the stage of humanity yet! Yes, something—ape-like about him, like one of those pictures I've seen in—anthropological studies! Thousands and thousands of years have passed him right by, and there he is—Stanley Kowalski—survivor of the stone age! Bearing the raw meat home from the kill in the jungle! And you—*you* here—*waiting* for him! Maybe he'll strike you or maybe grunt and kiss you! That is, if kisses have been discovered yet! Night falls and the other apes gather! There in the front of the cave, all grunting like him, and swilling and gnawing and hulking! His poker night!—you call it—this party of apes! Somebody growls—some creature snatches at something—the fight is on! *God!* Maybe we are a long way from being made in God's image, but Stella—my sister—there has been *some* progress since then! Such things as art—as poetry and music—such kinds of new light have come into the world since then! In some kinds of people some tenderer feelings have had some little beginning! That we have got to make *grow!* And *cling* to, and hold as our flag! In this dark march toward whatever it is we're approaching. . . . *Don't—don't hang back with the brutes!*

(*Another train passes outside.* STANLEY *hesitates, licking his lips. Then suddenly he turns stealthily about and withdraws through front door. The women are still unaware of his presence. When the train has passed he calls through the closed front door.)*

Stanley. Hey! Hey, Stella!

Stella (*Who has listened gravely to* BLANCHE). Stanley!

Blanche. Stell, I—

(*But* STELLA *has gone to the front door.* STANLEY *enters casually with his packages.)*

Stanley. Hiyuh, Stella. Blanche back?

Stella. Yes, she's back.

Stanley. Hiyuh, Blanche. (*He grins at her.)*

Stella. You must've got under the car.

Stanley. Them darn mechanics at Fritz's don't know their ass fr'm—*Hey!*

(STELLA *has embraced him with both arms, fiercely, and full in the view of* BLANCHE. *He laughs and clasps her head to him. Over her head he grins through the curtains at* BLANCHE.

(*As the lights fade away, with a lingering brightness on their embrace, the music of the "blue piano" and trumpet and drums is heard.)*

SCENE FIVE

BLANCHE *is seated in the bedroom fanning herself with a palm leaf as she reads over a just completed letter. Suddenly she bursts into a peal of laughter.* STELLA *is dressing in the bedroom.*

Stella. What are you laughing at, honey?

Blanche. Myself, myself, for being such a liar! I'm writing a letter to Shep. (*She picks up the letter*) "Darling Shep. I am spending the summer on the wing, making flying visits here and there. And who knows, perhaps I shall take a sudden notion to *swoop* down on *Dallas!* How would you feel about that? Ha-ha! (*She laughs nervously and brightly, touching her throat as if actually talking to Shep*) Forewarned is forearmed, as they say!"—How does that sound?

Stella. Uh-huh . . .

Blanche (*Going on nervously*). "Most of my sister's friends go north in the summer but some have homes on the Gulf and there has been a continued round of entertainments, teas, cocktails, and luncheons—"

(*A disturbance is heard upstairs at the Hubbell's apartment*)

Stella. Eunice seems to be having some trouble with Steve.

(EUNICE's *voice shouts in terrible wrath.)*

Eunice. I heard about you and that blonde!

Steve. That's a damn lie!

Eunice. You ain't pulling the wool over my eyes! I wouldn't mind if you'd stay down at the Four Deuces, but you always going up.

Steve. Who ever seen me up?

Eunice. I seen you chasing her 'round the balcony—I'm gonna call the vice squad!

Steve. Don't you throw that at me!

Eunice (*Shrieking*). You hit me! I'm gonna call the police!

(*A clatter of aluminum striking a*

wall is heard, followed by a man's angry roar, shouts and overturned furniture. There is a crash; then a relative hush.)

Blanche (*Brightly*). Did he *kill* her?

(EUNICE *appears on the steps in daemonic disorder.*)

Stella. No! She's coming downstairs.

Eunice. Call the police. I'm going to call the police! (*She rushes around the corner.*)

(*They laugh lightly.* STANLEY *comes around the corner in his green and scarlet silk bowling shirt. He trots up the steps and bangs into the kitchen.* BLANCHE *registers his entrance with nervous gestures.*)

Stanley. What's a matter with Eun-uss?

Stella. She and Steve had a row. Has she got the police?

Stanley. Naw. She's gettin' a drink.

Stella. That's much more practical!

(STEVE *comes down nursing a bruise on his forehead and looks in the door.*)

Steve. She here?

Stanley. Naw, naw. At the Four Deuces.

Steve. That rutting hunk! (*He looks around the corner a bit timidly, then turns with affected boldness and runs after her.*)

Blanche. I must jot that down in my notebook. Ha-ha! I'm compiling a notebook of quaint little words and phrases I've picked up here.

Stanley. You won't pick up nothing here you ain't heard before.

Blanche. Can I count on that?

Stanley. You can count on it up to five hundred.

Blanche. That's a mighty high number.

(*He jerks open the bureau drawer, slams it shut and throws shoes in a corner. At each noise* BLANCHE *winces slightly. Finally she speaks*)
What sign were you born under?

Stanley (*While he is dressing*). Sign?

Blanche. Astrological sign. I bet you were born under Aries. Aries people are forceful and dynamic. They dote on noise! They love to bang things around! You must have had lots of banging around in the army and now that you're out, you make up for it by treating inanimate objects with such a fury!

(STELLA *has been going in and out of closet during this scene. Now she pops her head out of the closet.*)

Stella. Stanley was born just five minutes after Christmas.

Blanche. Capricorn—the Goat!

Stanley. What sign were *you* born under?

Blanche. Oh, my birthday's next month, the fifteenth of September; that's under Virgo.

Stanley. What's Virgo?

Blanche. Virgo is the Virgin.

Stanley (*Contemptuously*). Hah! (*He advances a little as he knots his tie*) Say, do you happen to know somebody named Shaw?

(*Her face expresses a faint shock. She reaches for the cologne bottle and dampens her handkerchief as she answers carefully.*)

Blanche. Why, everybody knows somebody named Shaw!

Stanley. Well, this somebody named Shaw is under the impression he met you in Laurel, but I figure he must have got you mixed up with some other party because this other party is someone he met at a hotel called the Flamingo.

(BLANCHE *laughs breathlessly as she touches the cologne-dampened handkerchief to her temples.*)

Blanche. I'm afraid he does have me mixed up with this "other party." The Hotel Flamingo is not the sort of establishment I would dare to be seen in!

Stanley. You know of it?

Blanche. Yes, I've seen it and smelled it.

Stanley. You must've got pretty close if you could smell it.

Blanche. The odor of cheap perfume is penetrating.

Stanley. That stuff you use is expensive?

Blanche. Twenty-five dollars an ounce! I'm nearly out. That's just a hint if you want to remember my birthday!

(*She speaks lightly but her voice has a note of fear.*)

Stanley. Shaw must've got you mixed up. He goes in and out of Laurel all the time so he can check on it and clear up any mistake.

(*He turns away and crosses to the portieres.* BLANCHE *closes her eyes as if faint. Her hand trembles as she lifts the handkerchief again to her forehead.*

(STEVE *and* EUNICE *come around corner.* STEVE'S *arm is around* EUNICE'S *shoulder and she is sobbing luxuriously and he is cooing lovewords. There is a murmur of thunder as they go slowly upstairs in a tight embrace.*)

Stanley (*To Stella*). I'll wait for you at the Four Deuces!

Stella. Hey! Don't I rate one kiss?

Stanley. Not in front of your sister.

(*He goes out.* BLANCHE *rises from her chair. She seems faint; looks about her with an expression of almost panic.*)

Blanche. Stella! What have you heard about me?

Stella. Huh?

Blanche. What have people been telling you about me?

Stella. Telling?

Blanche. You haven't heard any—unkind—gossip about me?

Stella. Why, no, Blanche, of course not!

Blanche. Honey, there was—a good deal of talk in Laurel.

Stella. About *you*, Blanche?

Blanche. I wasn't so good the last two years or so, after Belle Reve had started to slip through my fingers.

Stella. All of us do things we—

Blanche. I never was hard or self-sufficient enough. When people are soft —soft people have got to shimmer and glow—they've got to put on soft colors, the colors of butterfly wings, and put a—paper lantern over the light. . . . It isn't enough to be soft. You've got to be soft *and attractive*. And I—I'm fading now! I don't know how much longer I can turn the trick.

(*The afternoon has faded to dusk.* STELLA *goes into the bedroom and turns on the light under the paper lantern. She holds a bottled soft drink in her hand.*)

Blanche. Have you been listening to me?

Stella. I don't listen to you when you are being morbid! (*She advances with the bottled coke.*)

Blanche (*With abrupt change to*

gaiety). Is that coke for me?

Stella. Not for anyone else!

Blanche. Why, you precious thing, you! Is it just coke?

Stella (*Turning*). You mean you want a shot in it!

Blanche. Well, honey, a shot never does a coke any harm! Let me! You mustn't wait on me!

Stella. I like to wait on you, Blanche. It makes it seem more like home. (*She goes into the kitchen, finds a glass and pours a shot of whiskey into it.*)

Blanche. I have to admit I love to be waited on . . .

(*She rushes into the bedroom.* STELLA *goes to her with the glass.* BLANCHE *suddenly clutches* STELLA's *free hand with a moaning sound and presses the hand to her lips.* STELLA *is embarrassed by her show of emotion.* BLANCHE *speaks in a choked voice.*) You're—you're—so *good* to me! And I—

Stella. Blanche.

Blanche. I know, I won't! You hate me to talk sentimental! But honey, *believe* I feel things more than I *tell* you! I *won't* stay long! I won't, I *promise* I—

Stella. Blanche!

Blanche (*Hysterically*). I won't, I promise, *I'll* go! Go *soon!* I will *really!* I *won't* hang around until he —throws me out . . .

Stella. Now will you stop talking foolish?

Blanche. Yes, honey. Watch how you pour—that fizzy stuff foams over!

(BLANCHE *laughs shrilly and grabs the glass, but her hand shakes so it almost slips from her grasp.* STELLA *pours the coke into the glass. It foams over and spills.* BLANCHE *gives a piercing cry.*)

Stella (*Shocked by the cry*). Heavens!

Blanche. Right on my pretty white skirt!

Stella. Oh . . . Use my hanky. Blot gently.

Blanche (*Slowly recovering*). I know —gently—gently . . .

Stella. Did it stain?

Blanche. Not a bit. Ha-ha! Isn't that lucky? (*She sits down shaking, taking a grateful drink. She holds the glass in both hands and continues to laugh a little.*)

Stella. Why did you scream like that?

Blanche. I don't know why I screamed! (*Continuing nervously*) Mitch— Mitch is coming at seven. I guess I am just feeling nervous about our relations. (*She begins to talk rapidly and breathlessly*) He hasn't gotten a thing but a goodnight kiss, that's all I have given him, Stella. I want his respect. And men don't want anything they get too easy. But on the other hand men lose interest quickly. Especially when the girl is over— thirty. They think a girl over thirty ought to—the vulgar term is—"put out." . . . And I—I'm not "putting out." Of course he—he doesn't know —I mean I haven't informed him—of my real age!

Stella. Why are you sensitive about your age?

Blanche. Because of hard knocks my vanity's been given. What I mean is —he thinks I'm sort of—prim and proper, you know! (*She laughs out sharply*) I want to *deceive* him enough to make him—want me . . .

Stella. Blanche, do you want *him*?

Blanche. I want to *rest!* I want to breathe quietly again! Yes—I *want*

Mitch . . . *very badly!* Just think! If it happens! I can leave here and not be anyone's problem . . .

(STANLEY *comes around the corner with a drink under his belt.*)

Stanley (*Bawling*). Hey, Steve! Hey, Eunice! Hey, Stella!

(*There are joyous calls from above. Trumpet and drums are heard from around the corner.*)

Stella (*Kissing* BLANCHE *impulsively*). It *will* happen!

Blanche (*Doubtfully*). It will?

Stella. It *will!* (*She goes across into the kitchen, looking back at* BLANCHE.) It will, honey, *it will.* . . . But don't take another drink! (*Her voice catches as she goes out the door to meet her husband.*

(BLANCHE *sinks faintly back in her chair with her drink.* EUNICE *shrieks with laughter and runs down the steps.* STEVE *bounds after her with goat-like screeches and chases her around corner.* STANLEY *and* STELLA *twine arms as they follow, laughing.*)

(*Dusk settles deeper. The music from the Four Deuces is slow and blue.*)

Blanche. Ah, me, ah, me, ah, me . . .

(*Her eyes fall shut and the palm leaf fan drops from her fingers. She slaps her hand on the chair arm a couple of times. There is a little glimmer of lightning about the building.*)

(*A* YOUNG MAN *comes along the street and rings the bell.*)

Blanche. Come in.

(*The* YOUNG MAN *appears through the portieres. She regards him with interest.*)

Blanche. Well, well! What can I do for you?

Young Man. I'm collecting for *The Evening Star.*

Blanche. I didn't know that stars took up collections.

Young Man. It's the paper.

Blanche. I know. I was joking—feebly! Will you—have a drink?

Young Man. No, ma'am. No, thank you. I can't drink on the job.

Blanche. Oh, well, now, let's see. . . . No, I don't have a dime! I'm not the lady of the house. I'm her sister from Mississippi. I'm one of those poor relations you've heard about.

Young Man. That's all right. I'll drop by later. (*He starts to go out. She approaches a little.*)

Blanche. Hey! (*He turns back shyly. She puts a cigarette in a long holder*) Could you give me a light? (*She crosses toward him. They meet at the door between the two rooms.*)

Young Man. Sure. (*He takes out a lighter*) This doesn't always work.

Blanche. It's temperamental? (*It flares*) Ah!—thank you. (*He starts away again*) Hey! (*He turns again, still more uncertainly. She goes close to him*) Uh—what time is it?

Young Man. Fifteen of seven, ma'am.

Blanche. So late? Don't you just love these long rainy afternoons in New Orleans when an hour isn't just an hour—but a little piece of eternity dropped into your hands—and who knows what to do with it? (*She touches his shoulders.*) You—uh— didn't get wet in the rain?

Young Man. No, ma'am. I stepped inside.

Blanche. In a drug store? And had a soda?

Young Man. Uh-huh.

Blanche. Chocolate?

Young Man. No, ma'am. Cherry.

Blanche (*Laughing*). Cherry!

Young Man. A cherry soda.

Blanche. You make my mouth water. (*She touches his cheek lightly, and smiles. Then she goes to the trunk.*)

Young Man. Well, I'd better be going—

Blanche (*Stopping him*). Young man!

(*He turns. She takes a large, gossamer scarf from the trunk and drapes it about her shoulders.*)

(*In the ensuing pause, the "blue piano" is heard. It continues through the rest of this scene and the opening of the next. The* YOUNG MAN *clears his throat and looks yearningly at the door.*)

Young man! Young, young, young man! Has anyone ever told you that you look like a young Prince out of the Arabian Nights?

(*The* YOUNG MAN *laughs uncomfortably and stands like a bashful kid.* BLANCHE *speaks softly to him.*)

Well, you do, honey lamb! Come here. I want to kiss you, just once, softly and sweetly on your mouth!

(*Without waiting for him to accept, she crosses quickly to him and presses her lips to his.*)

Now run along, now, quickly! It would be nice to keep you, but I've got to be good—and keep my hands off children.

(*He stares at her a moment. She opens the door for him and blows a kiss at him as he goes down the steps with a dazed look. She stands there a little dreamily after he has disappeared. Then* MITCH *appears around the corner with a bunch of roses.*)

Blanche (*Gaily*). Look who's coming! My Rosenkavalier! Bow to me first . . . now present them! *Ahhh—Merciiii!*

(*She looks at him over them, coquettishly pressing them to her lips. He beams at her selfconsciously.*)

SCENE SIX

It is about two A.M. *on the same evening. The outer wall of the building is visible.* BLANCHE *and* MITCH *come in. The utter exhaustion which only a neurasthenic personality can know is evident in* BLANCHE'S *voice and manner.* MITCH *is stolid but depressed. They have probably been out to the amusement park on Lake Pontchartrain, for* MITCH *is bearing, upside down, a plaster statuette of Mae West, the sort of prize won at shooting-galleries and carnival games of chance.*

Blanche (*Stopping lifelessly at the steps*). Well—

(MITCH *laughs uneasily.*)

Well . . .

Mitch. I guess it must be pretty late— and you're tired.

Blanche. Even the hot tamale man has deserted the street, and he hangs on till the end. (MITCH *laughs uneasily again*) How will you get home?

Mitch. I'll walk over to Bourbon and catch an owl-car.

Blanche (*Laughing grimly*). Is that street-car named Desire still grinding along the tracks at this hour?

Mitch (*Heavily*). I'm afraid you haven't gotten much fun out of this evening, Blanche.

Blanche. I spoiled it for *you.*

Mitch. No, you didn't, but I felt all the time that I wasn't giving you much—entertainment.

Blanche. I simply couldn't rise to the occasion. That was all. I don't think I've ever tried so hard to be gay and made such a dismal mess of it. I get ten points for trying!—I *did* try.

Mitch. Why did you try if you didn't feel like it, Blanche?

Blanche. I was just obeying the law of nature.

Mitch. Which law is that?

Blanche. The one that says the lady must entertain the gentleman—or no dice! See if you can locate my door-key in this purse. When I'm so tired my fingers are all thumbs!

Mitch (*Rooting in her purse*). This it?

Blanche. No, honey, that's the key to my trunk which I must soon be packing.

Mitch. You mean you are leaving here soon?

Blanche. I've outstayed my welcome.

Mitch. This it?

(*The music fades away.*)

Blanche. Eureka! Honey, you open the door while I take a last look at the sky. (*She leans on the porch rail. He opens the door and stands awkwardly behind her.*) I'm looking for the Pleiades, the Seven Sisters, but these girls are not out tonight. Oh, yes they are, there they are! God bless them! All in a bunch going home from their little bridge party. . . . Y'get the door open? Good boy! I guess you—want to go now . . .

(*He shuffles and coughs a little.*)

Mitch. Can I—uh—kiss you—good-night?

Blanche. Why do you always ask me if you may?

Mitch. I don't know whether you want me to or not.

Blanche. Why should you be so doubt-ful?

Mitch. That night when we parked by the lake and I kissed you, you—

Blanche. Honey, it wasn't the kiss I objected to. I liked the kiss very much. It was the other little—famil-iarity—that I—felt obliged to—dis-courage. . . . I didn't resent it! Not a bit in the world! In fact, I was somewhat flattered that you—desired me! But, honey, you know as well as I do that a single girl, a girl alone in the world, has got to keep a firm hold on her emotions or she'll be lost!

Mitch (*Solemnly*). Lost?

Blanche. I guess you are used to girls that like to be lost. The kind that get lost immediately, on the first date!

Mitch. I like you to be exactly the way that you are, because in all my—ex-perience—I have never known any-one like you.

(BLANCHE *looks at him gravely; then she bursts into laughter and then claps a hand to her mouth.*)

Mitch. Are you laughing at me?

Blanche. No, honey. The lord and lady of the house have not yet returned, so come in. We'll have a night-cap. Let's leave the lights off. Shall we?

Mitch. You just—do what you want to.

(BLANCHE *precedes him into the kitchen. The outer wall of the build-ing disappears and the interiors of the two rooms can be dimly seen.*)

Blanche (*Remaining in the first room*). The other room's more comfortable

—go on in. This crashing around in the dark is my search for some liquor.

Mitch. You want a drink?

Blanche. I want *you* to have a drink! You have been so anxious and solemn all evening, and so have I; we have both been anxious and solemn and now for these few last remaining moments of our lives together—I want to create—*joie de vivre!* I'm lighting a candle.

Mitch. That's good.

Blanche. We are going to be very Bohemian. We are going to pretend that we are sitting in a little artists' cafe on the Left Bank in Paris! (*She lights a candle stub and puts it in a bottle.*) *Je suis la Dame aux Camellias! Vous êtes—Armand!* Understand French?

Mitch. (*Heavily*). Naw. Naw, I—

Blanche. Voulez-vous coucher avec moi ce soir? Vous ne comprenez pas? Ah, quelle dommage!—I mean it's a damned good thing. . . . I've found some liquor! Just enough for two shots without any dividends, honey . . .

Mitch (*Heavily*). That's—good.

(*She enters the bedroom with the drinks and the candle.*)

Blanche. Sit down! Why don't you take off your coat and loosen your collar?

Mitch. I better leave it on.

Blanche. No. I want you to be comfortable.

Mitch. I am ashamed of the way I perspire. My shirt is sticking to me.

Blanche. Perspiration is healthy. If people didn't perspire they would die in five minutes. (*She takes his coat from him*) This is a nice coat. What kind of material is it?

Mitch. They call that stuff alpaca.

Blanche. Oh. Alpaca.

Mitch. It's very light weight alpaca.

Blanche. Oh. Light weight alpaca.

Mitch. I don't like to wear a wash-coat even in summer because I sweat through it.

Blanche. Oh.

Mitch. And it don't look neat on me. A man with a heavy build has got to be careful of what he puts on him so he don't look too clumsy.

Blanche. You are not too heavy.

Mitch. You don't think I am?

Blanche. You are not the delicate type. You have a massive bone-structure and a very imposing physique.

Mitch. Thank you. Last Christmas I was given a membership to the New Orleans Athletic Club.

Blanche. Oh, good.

Mitch. It was the finest present I ever was given. I work out there with the weights and I swim and I keep myself fit. When I started there, I was getting soft in the belly but now my belly is hard. It is so hard now that a man can punch me in the belly and it don't hurt me. Punch me! Go on! See?

(*She pokes lightly at him.*)

Blanche. Gracious. (*Her hand touches her chest.*)

Mitch. Guess how much I weigh, Blanche?

Blanche. Oh, I'd say in the vicinity of —one hundred and eighty?

Mitch. Guess again.

Blanche. Not that much?

Mitch. No. More.

Blanche. Well, you're a tall man and you can carry a good deal of weight without looking awkward.

Mitch. I weigh two hundred and seven pounds and I'm six feet one and one

half inches tall in my bare feet—
without shoes on. And that is what I
weigh stripped.

Blanche. Oh, my goodness, me! It's
awe-inspiring.

Mitch (*Embarrassed*). My weight is
not a very interesting subject to talk
about.

(*He hesitates for a moment*) What's
yours?

Blanche. My weight?

Mitch. Yes.

Blanche. Guess!

Mitch. Let me lift you.

Blanche. Samson! Go on, lift me. (*He
comes behind her and puts his hands
on her waist and raises her lightly off
the ground*) Well?

Mitch. You are light as a feather.

Blanche. Ha-ha! (*He lowers her but
keeps his hands on her waist. Blanche
speaks with an affectation of demure-
ness*) You may release me now.

Mitch. Huh?

Blanche (*Gaily*). I said unhand me, sir.
(*He fumblingly embraces her. Her
voice sounds gently reproving*) Now,
Mitch. Just because Stanley and
Stella aren't at home is no reason
why you shouldn't behave like a
gentleman.

Mitch. Just give me a slap whenever I
step out of bounds.

Blanche. That won't be necessary.
You're a natural gentleman, one of
the very few that are left in the
world. I don't want you to think that
I am severe and old maid school-
teacherish or anything like that. It's
just—well—

Mitch. Huh?

Blanche. I guess it is just that I have—
old-fashioned ideals! (*She rolls her
eyes, knowing he cannot see her
face.* MITCH *goes to the front door.*

*There is a considerable silence be-
tween them.* BLANCHE *sighs and*
MITCH *coughs selfconsciously.*)

Mitch (*Finally*). Where's Stanley and
Stella tonight?

Blanche. They have gone out. With
Mr. and Mrs. Hubbell upstairs.

Mitch. Where did they go?

Blanche. I think they were planning to
go to a midnight prevue at Loew's
State.

Mitch. We should all go out together
some night.

Blanche. No. That wouldn't be a good
plan.

Mitch. Why not?

Blanche. You are an old friend of
Stanley's?

Mitch. We was together in the Two-
forty-first.

Blanche. I guess he talks to you
frankly?

Mitch. Sure.

Blanche. Has he talked to you about
me?

Mitch. Oh—not very much.

Blanche. The way you say that, I suspect that he has.

Mitch. No, he hasn't said much.

Blanche. But what he *has* said. What
would you say his attitude toward
me was?

Mitch. Why do you want to ask that?

Blanche. Well—

Mitch. Don't you get along with him?

Blanche. What do you think?

Mitch. I don't think he understands
you.

Blanche. That is putting it mildly. If
it weren't for Stella about to have
a baby, I wouldn't be able to endure
things here.

Mitch. He isn't—nice to you?

Blanche. He is insufferably rude. Goes
out of his way to offend me.

Mitch. In what way, Blanche?

Blanche. Why, in every conceivable way.

Mitch. I'm surprised to hear that.

Blanche. Are you?

Mitch. Well, I—don't see how anybody could be rude to you.

Blanche. It's really a pretty frightful situation. You see, there's no privacy here. There's just these portieres between the two rooms at night. He stalks through the rooms in his underwear at night. And I have to ask him to close the bathroom door. That sort of commonness isn't necessary. You probably wonder why I don't move out. Well, I'll tell you frankly. A teacher's salary is barely sufficient for her living-expenses. I didn't save a penny last year and so I had to come here for the summer. That's why I have to put up with my sister's husband. And he has to put up with me, apparently so much against his wishes. . . . Surely he must have told you how much he hates me!

Mitch. I don't think he hates you.

Blanche. He hates me. Or why would he insult me? The first time I laid eyes on him I thought to myself, that man is my executioner! That man will destroy me, unless—

Mitch. Blanche—

Blanche. Yes, honey?

Mitch. Can I ask you a question?

Blanche. Yes. What?

Mitch. How old are you?

(*She makes a nervous gesture.*)

Blanche. Why do you want to know?

Mitch. I talked to my mother about you and she said, "How old is Blanche?" And I wasn't able to tell her. (*There is another pause.*)

Blanche. You talked to your mother about me?

Mitch. Yes.

Blanche. Why?

Mitch. I told my mother how nice you were, and I liked you.

Blanche. Were you sincere about that?

Mitch. You know I was.

Blanche. Why did your mother want to know my age?

Mitch. Mother is sick.

Blanche. I'm sorry to hear it. Badly?

Mitch. She won't live long. Maybe just a few months.

Blanche. Oh.

Mitch. She worries because I'm not settled.

Blanche. Oh.

Mitch. She wants me to be settled down before she—(*His voice is hoarse and he clears his throat twice, shuffling nervously around with his hands in and out of his pockets.*)

Blanche. You love her very much, don't you?

Mitch. Yes.

Blanche. I think you have a great capacity for devotion. You will be lonely when she passes on, won't you? (*MITCH clears his throat and nods.*) I understand what that is.

Mitch. To be lonely?

Blanche. I loved someone, too, and the person I loved I lost.

Mitch. Dead? (*She crosses to the window and sits on the sill, looking out. She pours herself another drink.*) A man?

Blanche. He was a boy, just a boy, when I was a very young girl. When I was sixteen, I made the discovery —love. All at once and much, much too completely. It was like you suddenly turned a blinding light on something that had always been half in shadow, that's how it struck the world for me. But I was unlucky.

Deluded. There was something different about the boy, a nervousness, a softness and tenderness which wasn't like a man's, although he wasn't the least bit effeminate looking—still—that thing was there. . . . He came to me for help. I didn't know that. I didn't find out anything till after our marriage when we'd run away and come back and all I knew was I'd failed him in some mysterious way and wasn't able to give the help he needed but couldn't speak of! He was in the quicksands and clutching at me—but I wasn't holding him out, I was slipping in with him! I didn't know that. I didn't know anything except I loved him unendurably but without being able to help him or help myself. Then I found out. In the worst of all possible ways. By coming suddenly into a room that I thought was empty—which wasn't empty, but had two people in it . . . the boy I had married and an older man who had been his friend for years. . . .

(*A locomotive is heard approaching outside. She claps her hands to her ears and crouches over. The headlight of the locomotive glares into the room as it thunders past. As the noise recedes she straightens slowly and continues speaking.*)

Afterwards we pretended that nothing had been discovered. Yes, the three of us drove out to Moon Lake Casino, very drunk and laughing all the way.

(*Polka music sounds, in a minor key faint with distance.*)

We danced the Varsouviana! Suddenly in the middle of the dance the boy I had married broke away from me and ran out of the casino. A few moments later—a shot!

(*The Polka stops abruptly.*

(BLANCHE *rises stiffly. Then, the Polka resumes in a major key.*)

I ran out—all did!—all ran and gathered about the terrible thing at the edge of the lake! I couldn't get near for the crowding. Then somebody caught my arm. "Don't go any closer! Come back! You don't want to see!" See? See what! Then I heard voices say—Allan! Allan! The Grey boy! He'd stuck the revolver into his mouth, and fired—so that the back of his head had been—blown away!

(*She sways and covers her face.*)

It was because—on the dance-floor —unable to stop myself—I'd suddenly said—"I saw! I know! You disgust me . . ." And then the searchlight which had been turned on the world was turned off again and never for one moment since has there been any light that's stronger than this—kitchen—candle . . .

(MITCH *gets up awkwardly and moves toward her a little. The Polka music increases.* MITCH *stands beside her.*)

Mitch (*Drawing her slowly into his arms*). You need somebody. And I need somebody, too. Could it be— you and me, Blanche?

(*She stares at him vacantly for a moment. Then with a soft cry huddles in his embrace. She makes a sobbing effort to speak but the words won't come. He kisses her forehead and her eyes and finally her lips. The Polka tune fades out. Her breath is drawn and released in long, grateful sobs.)*

Blanche. Sometimes—there's God—so quickly!

SCENE SEVEN

It is late afternoon in mid-September.

The portieres are open and a table is set for a birthday supper, with cake and flowers.

STELLA *is completing the decorations as* STANLEY *comes in.*

Stanley. What's all this stuff for?

Stella. Honey, it's Blanche's birthday.

Stanley. She here?

Stella. In the bathroom.

Stanley (*Mimicking*). "Washing out some things"?

Stella. I reckon so.

Stanley. How long she been in there?

Stella. All afternoon.

Stanley (*Mimicking*). "Soaking in a hot tub"?

Stella. Yes.

Stanley. Temperature 100 on the nose, and she soaks herself in a hot tub.

Stella. She says it cools her off for the evening.

Stanley. And you run out an' get her cokes, I suppose? And serve 'em to Her Majesty in the tub? (STELLA *shrugs*) Set down here a minute.

Stella. Stanley, I've got things to do.

Stanley. Set down! I've got th' dope on your big sister, Stella.

Stella. Stanley, stop picking on Blanche.

Stanley. That girl calls *me* common!

Stella. Lately you been doing all you can think of to rub her the wrong way, Stanley, and Blanche is sensitive and you've got to realize that Blanche and I grew up under very different circumstances than you did.

Stanley. So I been told. And told and told and told! You know she's been feeding us a pack of lies here?

Stella. No, I don't, and—

Stanley. Well, she has, however. But now the cat's out of the bag! I found out some things!

Stella. What—things?

Stanley. Things I already suspected. But now I got proof from the most reliable sources—which I have checked on!

(BLANCHE *is singing in the bathroom a saccharine popular ballad which is used contrapuntally with* STANLEY's *speech.*)

Stella (*To* STANLEY). Lower your voice!

Stanley. Some canary-bird, huh!

Stella. Now please tell me quietly what you think you've found out about my sister.

Stanley. Lie Number One: All this squeamishness she puts on! You should just know the line she's been feeding to Mitch. He thought she had never been more than kissed by a fellow! But Sister Blanche is no lily! Ha-ha! Some lily she is!

Stella. What have you heard and who from?

Stanley. Our supply-man down at the plant has been going through Laurel for years and he knows all about her and everybody else in the town of Laurel knows all about her. She is as famous in Laurel as if she was the President of the United States, only she is not respected by any party! This supply-man stops at a hotel called the Flamingo.

Blanche (*Singing blithely*).

"Say, it's only a paper moon, Sailing over a cardboard sea
—But it wouldn't be make-believe If you believed in me!"

Stella. What about the—Flamingo?

Stanley. She stayed there, too.

Stella. My sister lived at Belle Reve.

Stanley. This is after the home-place had slipped through her lily-white fingers! She moved to the Flamingo! A second-class hotel which has the advantage of not interfering in the private social life of the personalities there! The Flamingo is used to all kinds of goings-on. But even the management of the Flamingo was impressed by Dame Blanche! In fact they was so impressed by Dame Blanche that they requested her to turn in her room-key—for permanently! This happened a couple of weeks before she showed here.

Blanche (*Singing*).

"It's a Barnum and Bailey world, Just as phony as it can be—
But it wouldn't be make-believe If you believed in me!"

Stella. What—contemptible—lies!

Stanley. Sure, I can see how you would be upset by this. She pulled the wool over your eyes as much as Mitch's!

Stella. It's pure invention! There's not a word of truth in it and if I were a man and this creature had dared to invent such things in my presence—

Blanche (*Singing*).

"Without your love,
It's a honky-tonk parade!
Without your love,
It's a melody played In a penny arcade . . ."

Stanley. Honey, I told you I thoroughly checked on these stories! Now wait till I finished. The trouble with Dame Blanche was that she couldn't put on her act any more in Laurel! They got wised up after two or three dates with her and then they quit, and she goes on to another, the same old line, same old act, same old hooey! But the town was too small for this to go on forever! And as time went by she became a town character. Regarded as not just different but downright loco—nuts.

(Stella *draws back.*)

And for the last year or two she has been washed up like poison. That's why she's here this summer, visiting royalty, putting on all this act—because she's practically told by the mayor to get out of town! Yes, did you know there was an army camp near Laurel and your sister's was one of the places called "Out-of-Bounds?"

Blanche. "It's only a paper moon, Just as phony as it can be—
But it wouldn't be make-believe If you believed in me!"

Stanley. Well, so much for her being such a refined and particular type of girl. Which brings us to Lie Number Two.

Stella. I don't want to hear any more!

Stanley. She's not going back to teach school! In fact I am willing to bet you that she never had no idea of returning to Laurel! She didn't resign temporarily from the high school because of her nerves! No, siree, Bob! She didn't. They kicked her out of that high school before the spring term ended—and I hate to tell you the reason that step was taken! A seventeen-year-old boy—she'd gotten mixed up with!

Blanche. "It's a Barnum and Bailey world, Just as phony as it can be—"

(*In the bathroom the water goes on loud; little breathless cries and peals of laughter are heard as if a child were frolicking in the tub.*)

Stella. This is making me—sick!

Stanley. The boy's dad learned about it and got in touch with the high school superintendent. Boy, oh, boy, I'd like to have been in that office when Dame Blanche was called on the carpet! I'd like to have seen her trying to squirm out of that one! But they had her on the hook good and proper that time and she knew that the jig was all up! They told her she better move on to some fresh territory. Yep, it was practickly a town ordinance passed against her!

(*The bathroom door is opened and* BLANCHE *thrusts her head out, holding a towel about her hair.*)

Blanche. Stella!

Stella (*Faintly*). Yes, Blanche?

Blanche. Give me another bath-towel to dry my hair with. I've just washed it.

Stella. Yes, Blanche. (*She crosses in a dazed way from the kitchen to the bathroom door with a towel.*)

Blanche. What's the matter, honey?

Stella. Matter? Why?

Blanche. You have such a strange expression on your face!

Stella. Oh—(*She tries to laugh*) I guess I'm a little tired!

Blanche. Why don't you bathe, too, soon as I get out?

Stanley (*Calling from the kitchen*). How soon is that going to be?

Blanche. Not so terribly long! Possess your soul in patience!

Stanley. It's not my soul, it's my kidneys I'm worried about!

(BLANCHE *slams the door.* STANLEY *laughs harshly.* STELLA *comes slowly back into the kitchen.*)

Stanley. Well, what do you think of it?

Stella. I don't believe all of those stories and I think your supply-man was mean and rotten to tell them. It's possible that some of the things he said are partly true. There are things about my sister I don't approve of—things that caused sorrow at home. She was always—flighty!

Stanley. Flighty!

Stella. But when she was young, very young, she married a boy who wrote poetry. . . . He was extremely good-looking. I think Blanche didn't just love him but worshipped the ground he walked on! Adored him and thought him almost too fine to be human! But then she found out—

Stanley. What?

Stella. This beautiful and talented young man was a degenerate. Didn't your supply-man give you that information?

Stanley. All we discussed was recent history. That must have been a pretty long time ago.

Stella. Yes, it was—a pretty long time ago . . .

(STANLEY *comes up and takes her by the shoulders rather gently. She gently withdraws from him. Automatically she starts sticking little pink candles in the birthday cake.*)

Stanley. How many candles you putting in that cake?

Stella. I'll stop at twenty-five.

Stanley. Is company expected?

Stella. We asked Mitch to come over for cake and ice-cream.

(STANLEY *looks a little uncomfortable. He lights a cigarette from the one he has just finished.*)

Stanley. I wouldn't be expecting Mitch over tonight.

(STELLA *pauses in her occupation with candles and looks slowly around at* STANLEY.)

Stella. Why?

Stanley. Mitch is a buddy of mine. We were in the same outfit together— Two-forty-first Engineers. We work in the same plant and now on the same bowling team. You think I could face him if—

Stella. Stanley Kowalski, did you—did you repeat what that—?

Stanley. You're goddam right I told him! I'd have that on my conscience the rest of my life if I knew all that stuff and let my best friend get caught!

Stella. Is Mitch through with her?

Stanley. Wouldn't you be if—?

Stella. I said, *Is Mitch through with her?*

(BLANCHE'S *voice is lifted again, serenely as a bell. She sings "But it wouldn't be make-believe if you believed in me.")*

Stanley. No, I don't think he's necessarily through with her—just wised up!

Stella. Stanley, she thought Mitch was —going to—going to marry her. I was hoping so, too.

Stanley. Well, he's not going to marry her. Maybe he *was,* but he's not going to jump in a tank with a school of sharks—now! (*He rises*) Blanche! Oh, Blanche! Can I please get in my bathroom? (*There is a pause.*)

Blanche. Yes, indeed, sir! Can you wait one second while I dry?

Stanley. Having waited one hour I guess one second ought to pass in a hurry.

Stella. And she hasn't got her job? Well, what will she do!

Stanley. She's not stayin' here after Tuesday. You know that, don't you? Just to make sure I bought her ticket myself. A bus-ticket!

Stella. In the first place, Blanche wouldn't go on a bus.

Stanley. She'll go on a bus and like it.

Stella. No, she won't, no, she won't, Stanley!

Stanley. She'll go! Period. P.S. She'll go *Tuesday!*

Stella (*Slowly*). What'll—she—do? What on earth will she—*do!*

Stanley. Her future is mapped out for her.

Stella. What do you mean?

(BLANCHE *sings.*)

Stanley. Hey, canary bird! Toots! Get *OUT* of the *BATHROOM!*

(*The bathroom door flies open and* BLANCHE *emerges with a gay peal of laughter, but as* STANLEY *crosses past her, a frightened look appears on her face, almost a look of panic. He doesn't look at her but slams the bathroom door shut as he goes in.*)

Blanche (*Snatching up a hair-brush*). Oh, I feel so good after my long, hot bath, I feel so good and cool and— rested!

Stella (*Sadly and doubtfully from the kitchen*). Do you, Blanche?

Blanche (*Brushing her hair vigorously*). Yes, I do, so refreshed! (*She tinkles her highball glass.*) A hot bath and a long, cold drink always give me a brand new outlook on life! (*She looks through the portieres at* STELLA, *standing between them, and slowly stops brushing*) Something has happened!—What is it?

Stella (*Turning away quickly*). Why, nothing has happened, Blanche.

Blanche. You're lying! Something has!

(*She stares fearfully at* STELLA, *who pretends to be busy at the table. The distant piano goes into a hectic breakdown.*)

SCENE EIGHT

Three-quarters of an hour later.

The view through the big windows is fading gradually into a still-golden dusk. A torch of sunlight blazes on the side of a big water-tank or oil-drum across the empty lot toward the business district which is now pierced by pin-points of lighted windows or windows reflecting the sunset.

The three people are completing a dismal birthday supper. STAN-LEY *looks sullen.* STELLA *is embarrassed and sad.*

BLANCHE *has a tight, artificial smile on her drawn face. There is a fourth place at the table which is left vacant.*

Blanche (*Suddenly*). Stanley, tell us a joke, tell us a funny story to make us all laugh. I don't know what's the matter, we're all so solemn. Is it because I've been stood up by my beau?

(STELLA *laughs feebly.*)

It's the first time in my entire experience with men, and I've had a good deal of all sorts, that I've actually been stood up by anybody! Ha-ha! I don't know how to take it. . . . Tell us a funny little story, Stanley! Something to help us out.

Stanley. I didn't think you liked my stories, Blanche.

Blanche. I like them when they're amusing but not indecent.

Stanley. I don't know any refined enough for your taste.

Blanche. Then let me tell one.

Stella. Yes, you tell one, Blanche. You used to know lots of good stories.

(*The music fades.*)

Blanche. Let me see, now. . . . I must run through my repertoire! Oh, yes —I love parrot stories! Do you all like parrot stories? Well, this one's about the old maid and the parrot. This old maid, she had a parrot that cursed a blue streak and knew more vulgar expressions than Mr. Kowalski!

Stanley. Huh.

Blanche. And the only way to hush the parrot up was to put the cover back on its cage so it would think it was night and go back to sleep. Well, one morning the old maid had just uncovered the parrot for the day— when who should she see coming up the front walk but the preacher! Well, she rushed back to the parrot and slipped the cover back on the cage and then she let in the preacher. And the parrot was perfectly still, just as quiet as a mouse, but just as she was asking the preacher how much sugar he wanted in his coffee—the parrot broke the silence with a loud—(*She whistles*)

—and said—"God *damn,* but that was a short day!"

(*She throws back her head and laughs.* STELLA *also makes an ineffectual effort to seem amused.* STANLEY *pays no attention to the story but reaches way over the table to spear his fork into the remaining chop which he eats with his fingers.*)

Blanche. Apparently Mr. Kowalski was not amused.

Stella. Mr. Kowalski is too busy making a pig of himself to think of anything else!

Stanley. That's right, baby.

Stella. Your face and your fingers are disgustingly greasy. Go and wash up and then help me clear the table.

(*He hurls a plate to the floor.*)

Stanley. That's how I'll clear the table! (*He seizes her arm*) Don't ever talk that way to me! "Pig—Polack—disgusting—vulgar—greasy!"—them kind of words have been on your tongue and your sister's too much around here! What do you two think you are? A pair of queens? Remember what Huey Long said—"Every Man is a King!" And I am the king around here, so don't forget it! (*He hurls a cup and saucer to the floor*) My place is cleared! You want me to clear your places?

(STELLA *begins to cry weakly.* STANLEY *stalks out on the porch and lights a cigarette.*

(*The Negro entertainers around the corner are heard.*)

Blanche. What happened while I was bathing? What did he tell you, Stella?

Stella. Nothing, nothing, nothing!

Blanche. I think he told you something about Mitch and me! You know why Mitch didn't come but you won't tell me! (STELLA *shakes her head helplessly*) I'm going to call him!

Stella. I wouldn't call him, Blanche.

Blanche. I am, I'm going to call him on the phone.

Stella (*Miserably*). I wish you wouldn't.

Blanche. I intend to be given some explanation from someone!

(*She rushes to the phone in the bedroom.* STELLA *goes out on the porch and stares reproachfully at her husband. He grunts and turns away from her.*)

Stella. I hope you're pleased with your doings. I never had so much trouble swallowing food in my life, looking at that girl's face and the empty chair! (*She cries quietly.*)

Blanche (*At the phone*). Hello. Mr. Mitchell, please. . . . Oh. . . . I would like to leave a number if I may. Magnolia 9047. And say it's important to call. . . . Yes, very important. . . . Thank you.

(*She remains by the phone with a lost, frightened look.*)

(STANLEY *turns slowly back toward his wife and takes her clumsily in his arms.*)

Stanley. Stell, it's gonna be all right after she goes and after you've had the baby. It's gonna be all right again between you and me the way that it was. You remember that way that it was? Them nights we had together? God, honey, it's gonna be sweet when we can make noise in the night the way that we used to and get the colored lights going with nobody's sister behind the curtains to hear us!

(*Their upstairs neighbors are heard*

in bellowing laughter at something. STANLEY *chuckles.*)

Steve an' Eunice . . .

Stella. Come on back in. (*She returns to the kitchen and starts lighting the candles on the white cake.*) Blanche?

Blanche. Yes. (*She returns from the bedroom to the table in the kitchen.*) Oh, those pretty, pretty little candles! Oh, don't burn them, Stella.

Stella. I certainly will.

(STANLEY *comes back in.*)

Blanche. You ought to save them for baby's birthdays. Oh, I hope candles are going to glow in his life and I hope that his eyes are going to be like candles, like two blue candles lighted in a white cake!

Stanley (*Sitting down*). What poetry!

Blanche (*She pauses reflectively for a moment*). I shouldn't have called him.

Stella. There's lots of things could have happened.

Blanche. There's no excuse for it, Stella. I don't have to put up with insults. I won't be taken for granted.

Stanley. Goddamn, it's hot in here with the steam from the bathroom.

Blanche. I've said I was sorry three times. (*The piano fades out.*) I take hot baths for my nerves. Hydrotherapy, they call it. You healthy Polack, without a nerve in your body, of course you don't know what anxiety feels like!

Stanley. I am not a Polack. People from Poland are Poles, not Polacks. But what I am is a one hundred percent American, born and raised in the greatest country on earth and proud as hell of it, so don't ever call me a Polack.

(*The phone rings.* BLANCHE *rises expectantly.*)

Blanche. Oh, that's for me, I'm sure.

Stanley. I'm not sure. Keep your seat. (*He crosses leisurely to phone.*) H'lo. Aw, yeh, hello, Mac.

(*He leans against wall, staring insultingly in at* BLANCHE. *She sinks back in her chair with a frightened look.* STELLA *leans over and touches her shoulder.*)

Blanche. Oh, keep your hands off me, Stella. What is the matter with you? Why do you look at me with that pitying look?

Stanley (*Bawling*). QUIET IN THERE!—We've got a noisy woman on the place. Go on, Mac. At Riley's? No, I don't wanta bowl at Riley's. I had a little trouble with Riley last week. I'm the team-captain, ain't I? All right, then, we're not gonna bowl at Riley's, we're gonna bowl at the West Side or the Gala! All right, Mac. See you!

(*He hangs up and returns to the table.* BLANCHE *fiercely controls herself, drinking quickly from her tumbler of water. He doesn't look at her but reaches in a pocket. Then he speaks slowly and with false amiability.*)

Sister Blanche, I've got a little birthday remembrance for you.

Blanche. Oh, have you, Stanley? I wasn't expecting any, I—I don't know why Stella wants to observe my birthday! I'd much rather forget it—when you—reach twenty-seven! Well—age is a subject that you'd prefer to—ignore!

Stanley. Twenty-seven?

Blanche (*Quickly*). What is it? Is it for me?

(He is holding a little envelope toward her.)

Stanley. Yes, I hope you like it!

Blanche. Why, why—Why, it's a—

Stanley. Ticket! Back to Laurel! On the Greyhound! Tuesday!

(The Varsouviana music steals in softly and continues playing. STELLA rises abruptly and turns her back. BLANCHE tries to smile. Then she tries to laugh. Then she gives both up and springs from the table and runs into the next room. She clutches her throat and then runs into the bathroom. Coughing, gagging sounds are heard.)

Well!

Stella. You didn't need to do that.

Stanley. Don't forget all that I took off her.

Stella. You needn't have been so cruel to someone alone as she is.

Stanley. Delicate piece she is.

Stella. She is. She was. You didn't know Blanche as a girl. Nobody, nobody, was tender and trusting as she was. But people like you abused her, and forced her to change.

(He crosses into the bedroom, ripping off his shirt, and changes into a brilliant silk bowling shirt. She follows him.)

Do you think you're going bowling now?

Stanley. Sure.

Stella. You're not going bowling. *(She catches hold of his shirt)* Why did you do this to her?

Stanley. I done nothing to no one. Let go of my shirt. You've torn it.

Stella. I want to know why. Tell me why.

Stanley. When we first met, me and you, you thought I was common. How right you was, baby. I was common as dirt. You showed me the snapshot of the place with the columns. I pulled you down off them columns and how you loved it, having them colored lights going! And wasn't we happy together, wasn't it all okay till she showed here?

(STELLA makes a slight movement. Her look goes suddenly inward as if some interior voice had called her name. She begins a slow, shuffling progress from the bedroom to the kitchen, leaning and resting on the back of the chair and then on the edge of a table with a blind look and listening expression. STANLEY, finishing with his shirt, is unaware of her reaction.)

And wasn't we happy together? Wasn't it all okay? Till she showed here. Hoity-toity, describing me as an ape. *(He suddenly notices the change in STELLA)* Hey, what is it, Stell?

(He crosses to her.)

Stella *(Quietly)*. Take me to the hospital.

(He is with her now, supporting her with his arm, murmuring indistinguishably as they go outside.)

SCENE NINE

A while later that evening. BLANCHE is seated in a tense hunched position in a bedroom chair that she has re-covered with diagonal green and white stripes. She has on her scarlet satin robe. On the table beside chair is a bottle of liquor and a glass. The rapid, feverish polka tune, the "Varsouviana," is heard. The music is in her mind; she is drinking to escape it and the sense of disaster closing in on her, and she seems to whisper the words of the song. An electric fan is turning back and forth across her.

MITCH *comes around the corner in work clothes: blue denim shirt and pants. He is unshaven. He climbs the steps to the door and rings.* BLANCHE *is startled.*

Blanche. Who is it, please?
Mitch (*Hoarsely*). Me. Mitch.

(*The polka tune stops.*)

Blanche. Mitch!—Just a minute.

(*She rushes about frantically, hiding the bottle in a closet, crouching at the mirror and dabbing her face with cologne and powder. She is so excited that her breath is audible as she dashes about. At last she rushes to the door in the kitchen and lets him in.*)

Mitch!—Y'know, I really shouldn't let you in after the treatment I have received from you this evening! So utterly uncavalier! But hello, beautiful!

(*She offers him her lips. He ignores it and pushes past her into the flat. She looks fearfully after him as he stalks into the bedroom.*)

My, my, what a cold shoulder! And such uncouth apparel! Why, you haven't even shaved! The unforgivable insult to a lady! But I forgive you. I forgive you because it's such a relief to see you. You've stopped that polka tune that I had caught in my head. Have you ever had anything caught in your head? No, of course you haven't, you dumb angelpuss, you'd never get anything awful caught in your head!

(*He stares at her while she follows him as she talks. It is obvious that*

he has had a few drinks on the way over.)

Mitch. Do we have to have that fan on?
Blanche. No!
Mitch. I don't like fans.
Blanche. Then let's turn it off, honey. I'm not partial to them!

(*She presses the switch and the fan nods slowly off. She clears her throat uneasily as* MITCH *plumps himself down on the bed in the bedroom and lights a cigarette.*)

I don't know what there is to drink. I—haven't investigated.
Mitch. I don't want Stan's liquor.
Blanche. It isn't Stan's. Everything here isn't Stan's. Some things on the premises are actually mine! How is your mother? Isn't your mother well?
Mitch. Why?
Blanche. Something's the matter tonight, but never mind. I won't crossexamine the witness. I'll just—(*She touches her forehead vaguely. The polka tune starts up again.*)—pretend I don't notice anything different about you! That—music again . . .
Mitch. What music?
Blanche. The "Varsouviana!" The polka tune they were playing when Allan—Wait!

(*A distant revolver shot is heard.* BLANCHE *seems relieved.*)

There now, the shot! It always stops after that.

(*The polka music dies out again.*) Yes, now it's stopped.

Mitch. Are you boxed out of your mind?

Blanche. I'll go and see what I can find in the way of—(*She crosses into the closet, pretending to search for the bottle.*) Oh, by the way, excuse me for not being dressed. But I'd practically given you up! Had you forgotten your invitation to supper?

Mitch. I wasn't going to see you any more.

Blanche. Wait a minute. I can't hear what you're saying and you talk so little that when you do say something, I don't want to miss a single syllable of it. . . . What am I looking around here for? Oh, yes—liquor! We've had so much excitement around here this evening that I *am* boxed out of my mind! (*She pretends suddenly to find the bottle. He draws his foot up on the bed and stares at her contemptuously.*) Here's something. Southern Comfort! What is that, I wonder?

Mitch. If you don't know, it must belong to Stan.

Blanche. Take your foot off the bed. It has a light cover on it. Of course you boys don't notice things like that. I've done so much with this place since I've been here.

Mitch. I bet you have.

Blanche. You saw it before I came. Well, look at it now! This room is almost—dainty! I want to keep it that way. I wonder if this stuff ought to be mixed with something? Ummm, it's sweet, so sweet! It's terribly, terribly sweet! Why, it's a *liqueur,* I believe! Yes, that's what it *is,* a liqueur! (MITCH *grunts.*) I'm afraid you won't like it, but try it, and maybe you will.

Mitch. I told you already I don't want none of his liquor and I mean it. You ought to lay off his liquor. He says you been lapping it up all summer like a wild-cat!

Blanche. What a fantastic statement! Fantastic of him to say it, fantastic of you to repeat it! I won't descend to the level of such cheap accusations to answer them, even!

Mitch. Huh.

Blanche. What's in your mind? I see something in your eyes!

Mitch (*Getting up*). It's dark in here.

Blanche. I like it dark. The dark is comforting to me.

Mitch. I don't think I ever seen you in the light. (BLANCHE *laughs breathlessly*) That's a fact!

Blanche. Is it?

Mitch. I've never seen you in the afternoon.

Blanche. Whose fault is that?

Mitch. You never want to go out in the afternoon.

Blanche. Why, Mitch, you're at the plant in the afternoon!

Mitch. Not Sunday afternoon. I've asked you to go out with me sometimes on Sundays but you always make an excuse. You never want to go out till after six and then it's always some place that's not lighted much.

Blanche. There is some obscure meaning in this but I fail to catch it.

Mitch. What it means is I've never had a real good look at you, Blanche. Let's turn the light on here.

Blanche (*Fearfully*). Light? Which light? What for?

Mitch. This one with the paper thing

on it. (*He tears the paper lantern off the light bulb. She utters a frightened gasp.*)

Blanche. What did you do that for?

Mitch. So I can take a look at you good and plain!

Blanche. Of course you don't really mean to be insulting!

Mitch. No, just realistic.

Blanche. I don't want realism. I want magic! (MITCH *laughs*) Yes, yes, magic! I try to give that to people. I misrepresent things to them. I don't tell truth, I tell what *ought* to be truth. And if that is sinful, then let me be damned for it!—*Don't turn the light on!*

(MITCH *crosses to the switch. He turns the light on and stares at her. She cries out and covers her face. He turns the light off again.*)

Mitch (*Slowly and bitterly*). I don't mind you being older than what I thought. But all the rest of it—Christ! That pitch about your ideals being so old-fashioned and all the malarkey that you've dished out all summer. Oh, I knew you weren't sixteen any more. But I was a fool enough to believe you was straight.

Blanche. Who told you I wasn't— 'straight'? My loving brother-in-law. And you believed him.

Mitch. I called him a liar at first. And then I checked on the story. First I asked our supply-man who travels through Laurel. And then I talked directly over long-distance to this merchant.

Blanche. Who is this merchant?

Mitch. Kiefaber.

Blanche. The merchant Kiefaber of Laurel! I know the man. He whistled at me. I put him in his place. So now for revenge he makes up stories about me.

Mitch. Three people, Kiefaber, Stanley and Shaw, swore to them!

Blanche. Rub-a-dub-dub, three men in a tub! And such a filthy tub!

Mitch. Didn't you stay at a hotel called The Flamingo?

Blanche. Flamingo? No! Tarantula was the name of it! I stayed at a hotel called The Tarantula Arms!

Mitch (*Stupidly*). Tarantula?

Blanche. Yes, a big spider! That's where I brought my victims. (*She pours herself another drink*) Yes, I had many intimacies with strangers. After the death of Allan—intimacies with strangers was all I seemed able to fill my empty heart with. . . . I think it was panic, just panic, that drove me from one to another, hunting for some protection—here and there, in the most—unlikely places—even, at last, in a seventeen-year-old boy but—somebody wrote the superintendent about it—"This woman is morally unfit for her position!"

(*She throws back her head with convulsive, sobbing laughter. Then she repeats the statement, gasps, and drinks.*)

True? Yes, I suppose—unfit somehow—anyway. . . . So I came here. There was nowhere else I could go. I was played out. You know what played out is? My youth was suddenly gone up the water-spout, and —I met you. You said you needed somebody. Well, I needed somebody, too. I thanked God for you, because you seemed to be gentle—a cleft in the rock of the world that I could hide in! But I guess I was asking, hoping—too much! Kiefaber, Stanley and Shaw have tied an old tin can to the tail of the kite.

(*There is a pause.* MITCH *stares at her dumbly.*)

Mitch. You lied to me, Blanche.

Blanche. Don't say I lied to you.

Mitch. Lies, lies, inside and out, all lies.

Blanche. Never inside, I didn't lie in my heart . . .

(*A* Vendor *comes around the corner. She is a blind Mexican woman in a dark shawl, carrying bunches of those gaudy tin flowers that lower class Mexicans display at funerals and other festive occasions. She is calling barely audibly. Her figure is only faintly visible outside the building.*)

Mexican Woman. Flores. Flores. Flores para los muertos. Flores. Flores.

Blanche. What? Oh! Somebody outside . . . (*She goes to the door, opens it and stares at the* MEXICAN WOMAN.)

Mexican Woman (*She is at the door and offers* BLANCHE *some of her flowers*). Flores? Flores para los muertos?

Blanche (*Frightened*). No, no! Not now! Not now!

(*She darts back into the apartment, slamming the door.*)

Mexican Woman (*She turns away and starts to move down the street*). Flores para los muertos.

(*The polka tune fades in.*)

Blanche (*As if to herself*). Crumble and fade and—regrets—recriminations . . . 'If you'd done this, it wouldn't've cost me that!'

Mexican Woman. Corones para los muertos. Corones . . .

Blanche. Legacies! Huh . . . And other things such as bloodstained pillow-slips—'Her linen needs changing'—'Yes Mother. But couldn't we get a colored girl to do it?' No, we couldn't of course. Everything gone but the—

Mexican Woman. Flores.

Blanche. Death—I used to sit here and she used to sit over there and death was as close as you are. . . . We didn't dare even admit we had ever heard of it!

Mexican Woman. Flores para los muertos, flores—flores . . .

Blanche. The opposite is desire. So do you wonder? How could you possibly wonder! Not far from Belle Reve, before we had lost Belle Reve, was a camp where they trained young soldiers. On Saturday nights they would go in town to get drunk—

Mexican Woman (*Softly*). Corones . . .

Blanche.—and on the way back they would stagger onto my lawn and call —'Blanche! Blanche!'—The deaf old lady remaining suspecting nothing. But sometimes I slipped outside to answer their calls. . . . Later the paddy-wagon would gather them up like daisies . . . the long way home . . .

(*The* MEXICAN WOMAN *turns slowly and drifts back off with her soft mournful cries.* BLANCHE *goes to the dresser and leans forward on it. After a moment,* MITCH *rises and follows her purposefully. The polka music fades away. He places his hands on her waist and tries to turn her about.*)

Blanche. What do you want?

Mitch (*Fumbling to embrace her*). What I been missing all summer.

Blanche. Then marry me, Mitch!

Mitch. I don't think I want to marry you any more.

Blanche. No?

Mitch (*Dropping his hands from her waist*). You're not clean enough to bring in the house with my mother.

Blanche. Go away, then. (*He stares at her*) Get out of here quick before I start screaming fire! (*Her throat is tightening with hysteria*) Get out of here quick before I start screaming fire. (*He still remains staring. She suddenly rushes to the big window with its pale blue square of the soft summer light and cries wildly.*)

Fire! Fire! Fire!

(*With a startled gasp,* Mitch *turns and goes out the outer door, clatters awkwardly down the steps and around the corner of the building.* Blanche *staggers back from the window and falls to her knees. The distant piano is slow and blue.*)

SCENE TEN

It is a few hours later that night.

Blanche *has been drinking fairly steadily since* Mitch *left.*

She has dragged her wardrobe trunk into the center of the bedroom. It hangs open with flowery dresses thrown across it. As the drinking and packing went on, a mood of hysterical exhilaration came into her and she has decked herself out in a somewhat soiled and crumpled white satin evening gown and a pair of scuffed silver slippers with brilliants set in their heels.

Now she is placing the rhinestone tiara on her head before the mirror of the dressing-table and murmuring excitedly as if to a group of spectral admirers.

Blanche. How about taking a swim, a moonlight swim at the old rock-quarry? If anyone's sober enough to drive a car! Ha-ha! Best way in the world to stop your head buzzing! Only you've got to be careful to dive where the deep pool is—if you hit a rock you don't come up till tomorrow . . .

(*Tremblingly she lifts the hand mirror for a closer inspection. She catches her breath and slams the mirror face down with such violence that the glass cracks. She moans a little and attempts to rise.*)

(Stanley *appears around the corner of the building. He still has on the vivid green silk bowling shirt. As he rounds the corner the honky-tonk music is heard. It continues softly throughout the scene.*)

(*He enters the kitchen, slamming the door. As he peers in at* Blanche, *he gives a low whistle. He has had a few drinks on the way and has brought some quart beer bottles home with him.*)

Blanche. How is my sister?

Stanley. She is doing okay.

Blanche. And how is the baby?

Stanley (*Grinning amiably*). The baby won't come before morning so they told me to go home and get a little shut-eye.

Blanche. Does that mean we are to be alone in here?

Stanley. Yep. Just me and you, Blanche. Unless you got somebody hid under the bed. What've you got on those fine feathers for?

Blanche. Oh, that's right. You left before my wire came.

Stanley. You got a wire?

Blanche. I received a telegram from an old admirer of mine.

Stanley. Anything good?

Blanche. I think so. An invitation.

Stanley. What to? A fireman's ball?

Blanche (*Throwing back her head*). A cruise of the Caribbean on a yacht!

Stanley. Well, well. What do you know?

Blanche. I have never been so surprised in my life.

Stanley. I guess not.

Blanche. It came like a bolt from the blue!

Stanley. Who did you say it was from?

Blanche. An old beau of mine.

Stanley. The one that give you the white fox-pieces?

Blanche. Mr. Shep Huntleigh. I wore his ATO pin my last year at college. I hadn't seen him again until last Christmas. I ran into him on Biscayne Boulevard. Then—just now—this wire—inviting me on a cruise of the Caribbean! The problem is clothes. I tore into my trunk to see what I have that's suitable for the tropics!

Stanley. And come up with that—gorgeous—diamond—tiara?

Blanche. This old relic? Ha-ha! It's only rhinestones.

Stanley. Gosh. I thought it was Tiffany diamonds. (*He unbuttons his shirt.*)

Blanche. Well, anyhow, I shall be entertained in style.

Stanley. Uh-huh. It goes to show, you never know what is coming.

Blanche. Just when I thought my luck had begun to fail me—

Stanley. Into the picture pops this Miami millionaire.

Blanche. This man is not from Miami. This man is from Dallas.

Stanley. This man is from Dallas?

Blanche. Yes, this man is from Dallas where gold spouts out of the ground!

Stanley. Well, just so he's from somewhere! (*He starts removing his shirt.*)

Blanche. Close the curtains before you undress any further.

Stanley (*Amiably*). This is all I'm going to undress right now. (*He rips the sack off a quart beer-bottle*) Seen a bottle-opener?

(*She moves slowly toward the dresser, where she stands with her hands knotted together.*)

I used to have a cousin who could open a beer-bottle with his teeth. (*Pounding the bottle cap on the corner of table*) That was his only accomplishment, all he could do—he was just a human bottle-opener. And then one time, at a wedding party, he broke his front teeth off! After that he was so ashamed of himself he used t' sneak out of the house when company came . . .

(*The bottle cap pops off and a geyser of foam shoots up. STANLEY laughs happily, holding up the bottle over his head.*) Ha-ha! Rain from heaven! (*He extends the bottle toward her*) Shall we bury the hatchet and make it a loving-cup? Huh?

Blanche. No, thank you.

Stanley. Well, it's a red letter night for us both. You having an oil-millionaire and me having a baby.

(*He goes to the bureau in the bedroom and crouches to remove something from the bottom drawer.*)

Blanche (*Drawing back*). What are you doing in here?

Stanley. Here's something I always break out on special occasions like this. The silk pyjamas I wore on my wedding night!

Blanche. Oh.

Stanley. When the telephone rings and they say, "You've got a son!" I'll tear this off and wave it like a flag! (*He shakes out a brilliant pyjama coat*) I guess we are both entitled to put on the dog. (*He goes back to the kitchen with the coat over his arm.*)

Blanche. When I think of how divine it is going to be to have such a thing as privacy once more—I could weep with joy!

Stanley. This millionaire from Dallas is not going to interfere with your privacy any?

Blanche. It won't be the sort of thing you have in mind. This man is a gentleman and he respects me. (*Improvising feverishly*) What he wants is my companionship. Having great wealth sometimes makes people lonely! A cultivated woman, a woman of intelligence and breeding, can enrich a man's life—immeasurably! I have those things to offer, and this doesn't take them away. Physical beauty is passing. A transitory possession. But beauty of the mind and richness of the spirit and tenderness of the heart—and I have all of those things—aren't taken away, but grow! Increase with the years! How strange that I should be called a destitute woman! When I have all of these treasures locked in my heart. (*A choked sob comes from her*) I think of myself as a very, very rich woman! But I have been foolish—casting my pearls before swine!

Stanley. Swine, huh?

Blanche. Yes, swine! Swine! And I'm thinking not only of you but of your friend, Mr. Mitchell. He came to see me tonight. He dared to come here in his work-clothes! And to repeat slander to me, vicious stories that he had gotten from you! I gave him his walking papers . . .

Stanley. You did, huh?

Blanche. But then he came back. He returned with a box of roses to beg my forgiveness! He implored my forgiveness. But some things are not forgivable. Deliberate cruelty is not forgivable. It is the one unforgivable thing in my opinion and it is the one thing of which I have never, never been guilty. And so I told him, I said to him, "Thank you," but it was foolish of me to think that we could ever adapt ourselves to each other. Our ways of life are too different. Our attitudes and our backgrounds are incompatible. We have to be realistic about such things. So farewell, my friend! And let there be no hard feelings . . .

Stanley. Was this before or after the telegram came from the Texas oil millionaire?

Blanche. What telegram? No! No, after! As a matter of fact, the wire came just as—

Stanley. As a matter of fact there wasn't no wire at all!

Blanche. Oh, oh!

Stanley. There isn't no millionaire! And

Mitch didn't come back with roses 'cause I know where he is—

Blanche. Oh!

Stanley. There isn't a goddam thing but imagination!

Blanche. Oh!

Stanley. And lies and conceit and tricks!

Blanche. Oh!

Stanley. And look at yourself! Take a look at yourself in that wornout Mardi Gras outfit, rented for fifty cents from some ragpicker! And with the crazy crown on! What queen do you think you are?

Blanche. Oh—God . . .

Stanley. I've been on to you from the start! Not once did you pull any wool over this boy's eyes! You come in here and sprinkle the place with powder and spray perfume and cover the light-bulb with a paper lantern, and lo and behold the place has turned into Egypt and you are the Queen of the Nile! Sitting on your throne and swilling down my liquor! I say—*Ha!* —*Ha!* Do you hear me? *Ha—ha— ha!* (*He walks into the bedroom.*)

Blanche. Don't come in here!

(*Lurid reflections appear on the walls around* BLANCHE. *The shadows are of a grotesque and menacing form. She catches her breath, crosses to the phone and jiggles the hook.* STANLEY *goes into the bathroom and closes the door.*)

Operator, operator! Give me long-distance, please. . . . I want to get in touch with Mr. Shep Huntleigh of Dallas. He's so well-known he doesn't require any address. Just ask anybody who—Wait!!—No, I couldn't find it right now. . . . Please understand, I—No! No, wait! . . . One moment! Someone is— Nothing! Hold on, please!

(*She sets the phone down and crosses warily into the kitchen. The night is filled with inhuman voices like cries in a jungle.*

(*The shadows and lurid reflections move sinuously as flames along the wall spaces.*

(*Through the back wall of the rooms, which have become transparent, can be seen the sidewalk. A prostitute has rolled a drunkard. He pursues her along the walk, overtakes her and there is a struggle. A policeman's whistle breaks it up. The figures disappear.*

(*Some moments later the* NEGRO WOMAN *appears around the corner with a sequined bag which the prostitute had dropped on the walk. She is rooting excitedly through it.*

(BLANCHE *presses her knuckles to her lips and returns slowly to the phone. She speaks in a hoarse whisper.*)

Blanche. Operator! Operator! Never mind long-distance. Get Western Union. There isn't time to be—Western—Western Union!

(*She waits anxiously.*)

Western Union? Yes! I—want to— Take down this message! "In desperate, desperate circumstances! Help me! Caught in a trap. Caught in—" Oh!

(*The bathroom door is thrown open and* STANLEY *comes out in the brilliant silk pyjamas. He grins at her as he knots the tasseled sash about his waist. She gasps and backs away from the phone. He stares at her for a count of ten. Then a clicking becomes audible from the telephone, steady and rasping.*)

Stanley. You left th' phone off th' hook.

(*He crosses to it deliberately and sets it back on the hook. After he has replaced it, he stares at her again, his mouth slowly curving into a grin, as he weaves between Blanche and the outer door.*)

(*The barely audible "blue piano" begins to drum up louder. The sound of it turns into the roar of an approaching locomotive.* BLANCHE *crouches, pressing her fists to her ears until it has gone by.*)

Blanche (*Finally straightening*). Let me—let me get by you!

Stanley. Get by me? Sure. Go ahead. (*He moves back a pace in the doorway.*)

Blanche. You—you stand over there! (*She indicates a further position.*)

Stanley (*Grinning*). You got plenty of room to walk by me now.

Blanche. Not with you there! But I've got to get out somehow!

Stanley. You think I'll interfere with you? Ha-ha!

(*The "blue piano" goes softly. She turns confusedly and makes a faint gesture. The inhuman jungle voices rise up. He takes a step toward her, biting his tongue which protrudes between his lips.*)

Stanley (*Softly*). Come to think of it— maybe you wouldn't be bad to—interfere with . . .

(BLANCHE *moves backward through the door into the bedroom.*)

Blanche. Stay back! Don't you come toward me another step or I'll—

Stanley. What?

Blanche. Some awful thing will happen! It will!

Stanley. What are you putting on now?

(*They are now both inside the bedroom.*)

Blanche. I warn you, don't, I'm in danger!

(*He takes another step. She smashes a bottle on the table and faces him, clutching the broken top.*)

Stanley. What did you do that for?

Blanche. So I could twist the broken end in your face!

Stanley. I bet you would do that!

Blanche. I would! I will if you—

Stanley. Oh! So you want some rough-house! All right, let's have some rough-house!

(*He springs toward her, overturning the table. She cries out and strikes at him with the bottle top but he catches her wrist.*)

Tiger—tiger! Drop the bottle-top! Drop it! We've had this date with each other from the beginning!

(*She moans. The bottle-top falls. She sinks to her knees. He picks up her inert figure and carries her to the bed. The hot trumpet and drums from the Four Deuces sound loudly.*)

SCENE ELEVEN

It is some weeks later. STELLA *is packing* BLANCHE's *things. Sound of water can be heard running in the bathroom.*

*The portieres are partly open on the poker players—*STANLEY, STEVE, MITCH *and* PABLO—*who sit around the table in the kitchen. The atmosphere of the kitchen is now the same raw, lurid one of the disastrous poker night.*

The building is framed by the sky of turquoise. STELLA *has been crying as she arranges the flowery dresses in the open trunk.*

EUNICE *comes down the steps from her flat above and enters the kitchen. There is an outburst from the poker table.*

Stanley. Drew to an inside straight and made it, by God.

Pablo. *Maldita sea tu suerte!*

Stanley. Put it in English, greaseball.

Pablo. I am cursing your rutting luck.

Stanley (*Prodigiously elated*). You know what luck is? Luck is believing you're lucky. Take at Salerno. I believed I was lucky. I figured that 4 out of 5 would not come through but I would . . . and I did. I put that down as a rule. To hold front position in this rat-race you've got to believe you are lucky.

Mitch. You . . . you . . . you . . . Brag. . . . brag . . . bull . . . bull.

(STELLA *goes into the bedroom and starts folding a dress.*)

Stanley. What's the matter with him?

Eunice (*Walking past the table*). I always did say that men are callous things with no feelings, but this does beat anything. Making pigs of yourselves. (*She comes through the portieres into the bedroom.*)

Stanley. What's the matter with her?

Stella. How is my baby?

Eunice. Sleeping like a little angel. Brought you some grapes. (*She puts them on a stool and lowers her voice.*) Blanche?

Stella. Bathing.

Eunice. How is she?

Stella. She wouldn't eat anything but asked for a drink.

Eunice. What did you tell her?

Stella. I—just told her that—we'd made arrangements for her to rest in the country. She's got it mixed in her mind with Shep Huntleigh.

(BLANCHE *opens the bathroom door slightly.*)

Blanche. Stella.

Stella. Yes, Blanche?

Blanche. If anyone calls while I'm bathing take the number and tell them I'll call right back.

Stella. Yes.

Blanche. That cool yellow silk—the bouclé. See if it's crushed. If it's not too crushed I'll wear it and on the lapel that silver and turquoise pin in the shape of a seahorse. You will find them in the heart-shaped box I keep my accessories in. And Stella . . . Try and locate a bunch of artificial violets in that box, too, to pin with the seahorse on the lapel of the jacket.

(*She closes the door.* STELLA *turns to* EUNICE.)

Stella. I don't know if I did the right thing.

Eunice. What else could you do?

Stella. I couldn't believe her story and go on living with Stanley.

Eunice. Don't ever believe it. Life has got to go on. No matter what happens, you've got to keep on going.

(*The bathroom door opens a little.*)

Blanche (*Looking out*). Is the coast clear?

Stella. Yes, Blanche. (*To* EUNICE) Tell her how well she's looking.

Blanche. Please close the curtains before I come out.

Stella. They're closed.

Stanley.—How many for you?

Pablo.—Two.

Steve.—Three.

(BLANCHE *appears in the amber light of the door. She has a tragic radiance in her red satin robe following the sculptural lines of her body. The "Varsouviana" rises audibly as* BLANCHE *enters the bedroom.*)

Blanche (*With faintly hysterical vivacity*). I have just washed my hair.

Stella. Did you?

Blanche. I'm not sure I got the soap out.

Eunice. Such fine hair!

Blanche (*Accepting the compliment*). It's a problem. Didn't I get a call?

Stella. Who from, Blanche?

Blanche. Shep Huntleigh . . .

Stella. Why, not yet, honey!

Blanche. How strange! I—

(*At the sound of* BLANCHE'S *voice* MITCH'S *arm supporting his cards has sagged and his gaze is dissolved into space.* STANLEY *slaps him on the shoulder.*)

Stanley. Hey, Mitch, come to!

(*The sound of this new voice shocks* BLANCHE. *She makes a shocked gesture, forming his name with her lips.* STELLA *nods and looks quickly away.* BLANCHE *stands quite still for some moments—the silverbacked mirror in her hand and a look of sorrowful perplexity as though all human experience shows on her face.* BLANCHE *finally speaks but with sudden hysteria.*)

Blanche. What's going on here?

(*She turns from* STELLA *to* EUNICE *and back to* STELLA. *Her rising voice penetrates the concentration of the game.* MITCH *ducks his head lower but* STANLEY *shoves back his chair as if about to rise.* STEVE *places a restraining hand on his arm.*)

Blanche (*Continuing*). What's happened here? I want an explanation of what's happened here.

Stella (*Agonizingly*). Hush! Hush!

Eunice. Hush! Hush! Honey.

Stella. Please, Blanche.

Blanche. Why are you looking at me like that? Is something wrong with me?

Eunice. You look wonderful, Blanche. Don't she look wonderful?

Stella. Yes.

Eunice. I understand you are going on a trip.

Stella. Yes, Blanche *is*. She's going on a vacation.

Eunice. I'm green with envy.

Blanche. Help me, help me get dressed!

Stella (*Handing her dress*). Is this what you—

Blanche. Yes, it will do! I'm anxious to get out of here—this place is a trap!

Eunice. What a pretty blue jacket.

Stella. It's lilac colored.

Blanche. You're both mistaken. It's Della Robbia blue. The blue of the robe in the old Madonna pictures. Are these grapes washed?

(*She fingers the bunch of grapes which* EUNICE *had brought in.*)

Eunice. Huh?

Blanche. Washed, I said. Are they washed?

Eunice. They're from the French Market.

Blanche. That doesn't mean they've been washed. (*The cathedral bells chime*) Those cathedral bells— they're the only clean thing in the Quarter. Well, I'm going now. I'm ready to go.

Eunice (*Whispering*). She's going to walk out before they get here.

Stella. Wait, Blanche.

Blanche. I don't want to pass in front of those men.

Eunice. Then wait'll the game breaks up.

Stella. Sit down and . . .

(BLANCHE *turns weakly, hesitantly about. She lets them push her into a chair.*)

Blanche. I can smell the sea air. The rest of my time I'm going to spend on the sea. And when I die, I'm going to die on the sea. You know what I shall die of? (*She plucks a grape*) I shall die of eating an unwashed grape one day out on the ocean. I will die—with my hand in the hand of some nice-looking ship's doctor, a very young one with a small blond mustache and a big silver watch. "Poor lady," they'll say, "the quinine did her no good. That unwashed grape has transported her soul to heaven." (*The cathedral chimes are heard*) And I'll be buried at sea sewn up in a clean white sack and dropped overboard—at noon—in the blaze of summer—and into an ocean as blue as (*Chimes again*) my first lover's eyes!

(A DOCTOR *and a* MATRON *have appeared around the corner of the building and climbed the steps to the porch. The gravity of their profession is exaggerated—the unmistakable aura of the state institution with*

its cynical detachment. The DOCTOR *rings the doorbell. The murmur of the game is interrupted.*)

Eunice (*Whispering to* STELLA). That must be them.

(STELLA *presses her fists to her lips.*)

Blanche (*Rising slowly*). What is it?

Eunice (*Affectedly casual*). Excuse me while I see who's at the door.

Stella. Yes.

(EUNICE *goes into the kitchen.*)

Blanche (*Tensely*). I wonder if it's for me.

(A *whispered colloquy takes place at the door.*)

Eunice (*Returning, brightly*). Someone is calling for Blanche.

Blanche. It *is* for me, then! (*She looks fearfully from one to the other and then to the portieres. The "Varsouviana" faintly plays*) Is it the gentleman I was expecting from Dallas?

Eunice. I think it is, Blanche.

Blanche. I'm not quite ready.

Stella. Ask him to wait outside.

Blanche. I . . .

(EUNICE *goes back to the portieres. Drums sound very softly.*)

Stella. Everything packed?

Blanche. My silver toilet articles are still out.

Stella. Ah!

Eunice (*Returning*). They're waiting in front of the house.

Blanche. They! Who's "they"?

Eunice. There's a lady with him.

Blanche. I cannot imagine who this "lady" could be! How is she dressed?

Eunice. Just—just a sort of a—plain-tailored outfit.

Blanche. Possibly she's—(*Her voice dies out nervously.*)

Stella. Shall we go, Blanche?

Blanche. Must we go through that room?

Stella. I will go with you.

Blanche. How do I look?

Stella. Lovely.

Eunice (*Echoing*). Lovely.

(BLANCHE *moves fearfully to the portieres.* EUNICE *draws them open for her.* BLANCHE *goes into the kitchen.*)

Blanche (*To the men*). Please don't get up. I'm only passing through.

(*She crosses quickly to outside door.* STELLA *and* EUNICE *follow. The poker players stand awkwardly at the table—all except* MITCH, *who remains seated, looking down at the table.* BLANCHE *steps out on a small porch at the side of the door. She stops short and catches her breath.*)

Doctor. How do you do?

Blanche. You are not the gentleman I was expecting. (*She suddenly gasps and starts back up the steps. She stops by* STELLA, *who stands just outside the door, and speaks in a frightening whisper*) That man isn't Shep Huntleigh.

(*The "Varsouviana" is playing distantly.*

(STELLA *stares back at* BLANCHE. EUNICE *is holding* STELLA'S *arm. There is a moment of silence—no sound but that of* STANLEY *steadily shuffling the cards.*

(BLANCHE *catches her breath again and slips back into the flat with a peculiar smile, her eyes wide and brilliant. As soon as her sister goes past her,* STELLA *closes her eyes and clenches her hands.* EUNICE *throws her arms comfortingly about her. Then she starts up to her flat.*

BLANCHE *stops just inside the door.* MITCH *keeps staring down at his hands on the table, but the other men look at her curiously. At last she starts around the table toward the bedroom. As she does,* STANLEY *suddenly pushes back his chair and rises as if to block her way. The* MATRON *follows her into the flat.*)

Stanley. Did you forget something?

Blanche (*Shrilly*). Yes! Yes, I forgot something!

(*She rushes past him into the bedroom. Lurid reflections appear on the walls in odd, sinuous shapes. The "Varsouviana" is filtered into a weird distortion, accompanied by the cries and noises of the jungle.* BLANCHE *seizes the back of a chair as if to defend herself.*)

Stanley (*Sotto voce*). Doc, you better go in.

Doctor (*Sotto voce, motioning to the* MATRON). Nurse, bring her out.

(*The* MATRON *advances on one side,* STANLEY *on the other. Divested of all the softer properties of womanhood, the* MATRON *is a peculiarly sinister figure in her severe dress. Her voice is bold and toneless as a firebell.*)

Matron. Hello, Blanche.

(*The greeting is echoed and re-echoed by other mysterious voices behind the walls, as if reverberated through a canyon of rock.*)

Stanley. She says that she forgot something.

(*The echo sounds in threatening whispers.*)

Matron. That's all right.

Stanley. What did you forget, Blanche?

Blanche. I—I—

Matron. It don't matter. We can pick it up later.

Stanley. Sure. We can send it along with the trunk.

Blanche (Retreating in panic). I don't know you—I don't know you. I want to be—left alone—please!

Matron. Now, Blanche!

Echoes (Rising and falling). Now, Blanche—now, Blanche—now, Blanche!

Stanley. You left nothing here but spilt talcum and old empty perfume bottles—unless it's the paper lantern you want to take with you. You want the lantern?

(He crosses to dressing table and seizes the paper lantern, tearing it off the light bulb, and extends it toward her. She cries out as if the lantern was herself. The MATRON *steps boldly toward her. She screams and tries to break past the* MATRON. *All the men spring to their feet.* STELLA *runs out to the porch, with* EUNICE *following to comfort her, simultaneously with the confused voices of the men in the kitchen.* STELLA *rushes into* EUNICE'S *embrace on the porch.)*

Stella. Oh, my God, Eunice help me! Don't let them do that to her, don't let them hurt her! Oh, God, oh, please God, don't hurt her! What are they doing to her? What are they doing?

(She tries to break from EUNICE'S *arms.)*

Eunice. No, honey, no, no, honey. Stay here. Don't go back in there. Stay with me and don't look.

Stella. What have I done to my sister? Oh, God, what have I done to my sister?

Eunice. You done the right thing, the only thing you could do. She couldn't stay here; there wasn't no other place for her to go.

(While STELLA *and* EUNICE *are speaking on the porch the voices of the men in the kitchen overlap them.* MITCH *has started toward the bedroom.* STANLEY *crosses to block him.* STANLEY *pushes him aside.* MITCH *lunges and strikes at* STANLEY. STANLEY *pushes* MITCH *back.* MITCH *collapses at the table, sobbing.)*

(During the preceding scenes, the MATRON *catches hold of* BLANCHE'S *arm and prevents her flight.* BLANCHE *turns wildly and scratches at the* MATRON. *The heavy woman pinions her arms.* BLANCHE *cries out hoarsely and slips to her knees.)*

Matron. These fingernails have to be trimmed. *(The* DOCTOR *comes into the room and she looks at him.)* Jacket, Doctor?

Doctor. Not unless necessary.

(He takes off his hat and now he becomes personalized. The unhuman quality goes. His voice is gentle and reassuring as he crosses to BLANCHE *and crouches in front of her. As he speaks her name, her terror subsides a little. The lurid reflections fade from the walls, the inhuman cries and noises die out and her own hoarse crying is calmed.)*

Doctor. Miss DuBois.

(She turns her face to him and stares at him with desperate pleading. He smiles; then he speaks to the MATRON.)*

It won't be necessary.

Blanche (*Faintly*). Ask her to let go of me.

Doctor (*To the* MATRON). Let go.

(*The* MATRON *releases her.* BLANCHE *extends her hands toward the* DOCTOR. *He draws her up gently and supports her with his arm and leads her through the portieres.*)

Blanche (*Holding tight to his arm*). Whoever you are—I have always depended on the kindness of strangers.

(*The poker players stand back as* BLANCHE *and the* DOCTOR *cross the kitchen to the front door. She allows him to lead her as if she were blind. As they go out on the porch,* STELLA *cries out her sister's name from where she is crouched a few steps up on the stairs.*)

Stella. Blanche! Blanche! Blanche!

(BLANCHE *walks on without turning, followed by the* DOCTOR *and the* MATRON. *They go around the corner of the building.*)

(EUNICE *descends to* STELLA *and places the child in her arms. It is wrapped in a pale blue blanket.* STELLA *accepts the child, sobbingly.* EUNICE *continues downstairs and enters the kitchen where the men, except for* STANLEY, *are returning silently to their places about the table.* STANLEY *has gone out on the porch and stands at the foot of the steps looking at* STELLA).

Stanley (*A bit uncertainly*). Stella?

(*She sobs with inhuman abandon. There is something luxurious in her complete surrender to crying now that her sister is gone.*)

Stanley (*Voluptuously, soothingly*). Now, honey. Now, love. Now, now, love. (*He kneels beside her and his fingers find the opening of her blouse*) Now, now, love. Now, love. . . .

(*The luxurious sobbing, the sensual murmur fade away under the swelling music of the "blue piano" and the muted trumpet.*)

Steve. This game is seven-card stud.

CURTAIN

The Visit

FRIEDRICH DUERRENMATT

INTRODUCTION

Friedrich Duerrenmatt was born on January 5, 1921, in Konolfingen, in the canton of Bern, Switzerland, the son of Reinhold and Hulda (Zimmermann) Duerrenmatt; his father was a Lutheran minister and his grandfather, Ulrich Duerrenmatt, was a well-known satirist and political poet. The boy's thinking was shaped by a fusion of the two strains: moral rectitude and social criticism intermixed and cemented with his own special brand of wit and irony. "My grandfather was once sent to prison for ten days because of a poem he wrote," says Duerrenmatt. "I haven't been honored in that way yet. Maybe it's my fault, or maybe the world has gone so far to the dogs that it doesn't even feel insulted any more if it's criticized most severely."

As a boy, Duerrenmatt, like the young Ibsen, wanted to be a painter; he was especially interested in the dramatic moments of history and drew many bloody battle scenes. He still owns the notebook containing his drawings of the Battle of the Nibelungen. At the age of twelve, he entered a drawing competition with a picture called "Swiss Battle," and won a watch—his first prize. At thirteen the boy moved with his family to the city of Bern, where he was enrolled in the free high school. From there he went to the University of Bern and took courses in literature, theology, philosophy, and science. He first became interested in the theater in Bern and attended the operettas there regularly. He spent one semester at the University of Zurich, going to lectures in philosophy and art, when suddenly his interest in painting waned and he had a fervent desire to write. He withdrew from the University without taking a degree, and his painting became merely a hobby. "The things we like best are not always the things we do best," says Duerrenmatt. "For me writing is far more difficult than painting."

He completed his military service and began to read seriously; among his favorite authors were the expressionist poet Georg Heym, Kierkegaard, Aristophanes, and Thornton Wilder. He tried his hand at playwriting at this time; while on an excursion to Wallis, in the fall of 1943, he completed *Comedy*, a lyrical and apocalyptic work. At twenty-two he was already leveling serious criticisms against society, for in a preface to this play he said, in part, "The State, Religion, and Art are only related to themselves, they are not related to each other; they are abstract, immersed in technicalities, the symbols of unreality." The play remained unpublished and unproduced.

Duerrenmatt's first play to reach the stage was written during 1945 and 1946 and was called *Es steht geschrieben* (*It Is Decreed*); the author describes it as "a wild story of German Anabaptists during the Reformation." It had its premiere at the Schauspielhaus in Zurich on April 19, 1947, and created a mild furor because of its unorthodox religious sentiments; after the excitement died down, it won a prize for the playwright.

In 1947 Duerrenmatt married the actress Lotti Geissler and moved to Basel. Then followed several difficult years for the playwright; in order to earn money, he turned to the writing of short stories, mystery novels, and radio plays. Friends helped out with loans and even total strangers made small donations. He continued to write for the theater, however; two plays, *The Blind Man* and *Romulus the Great*, were produced at the Stadttheater, Basel, in 1948 and 1949 respectively, but they caused no great stir.

What Duerrenmatt calls his "breakthrough" came in 1952 with the production of his comedy *Die Ehe des Herrn Mississippi* (*The Marriage of Mr. Mississippi*), which was directed by Hans Schweikart at the Munich Chamber Theater. Boos and hisses greeted the play, but the applauders won out. This work established Duerrenmatt as one of the most gifted of contemporary European dramatists; his style, with its peculiar mixture of the serious and the grotesque, was recognized as a unique and distinguishing feature of his work. An unusual setting was required for this play; as the action progressed, a splendidly furnished middle-class interior was to disintegrate slowly into a veritable slum in order to reflect visually the course of events and the degeneration of the characters. Under the title *Fools Are Passing Through*, this play was given in English at the Jan Hus House, an off-Broadway theater in New York, for a brief run starting on April 2, 1958.

Two other plays were produced at the Munich Chamber Theater: *Nocturnal Conversation with a Scorned Man,* a one-acter, opened on July 25, 1952; and *Ein Engel kommt nach Babylon* (*An Angel Comes to Babylon*), a comedy in three acts, had its premiere on December 22, 1953.

To accommodate a growing family—there were now three children, Peter, Barbara, and Ruth—Duerrenmatt moved into larger living quarters, a house in Neuchâtel, high up on the mountainside overlooking the lake. He prefers to live at some distance from Bern, Basel, and Zurich because friends and relatives disturb a writer's routine. He takes no part in community life and is known to his neighbors only through the articles about him which appear in the newspapers from time to time. It was in Neuchâtel that Duerrenmatt wrote his "tragic comedy" *Der Besuch der alten Dame* (*The Old Lady's Visit*) and his even more bitter satire *Frank V.*

Der Besuch der alten Dame had its premiere at the Zurich Schauspielhaus in 1956, and was an immediate success. This play brought international fame to its author. When *The Visit* (its title shortened from the original) opened in New York, the critics agreed almost to a man that the play was a brilliant theatrical work, but they, and many playgoers as well, took note of the author's cynicism and wondered about his central meaning. "People should accept my fancies and ignore the deeper meanings," says Duerrenmatt. "Claire Zachanassian symbolizes neither Justice, nor the Marshall Plan, nor the Apocalypse; she is just what she is supposed to be—the richest woman in the world. With her fortune she is in a position to behave like the heroine of a Greek tragedy, arbitrarily, dreadfully, like Medea."

The dramatist's next play, *Frank V—Oper einer Privatbank* (*Frank the Fifth— Opera about a Private Bank*), probably his most furious attack upon society to date, opened at the Zurich Schauspielhaus on March 20, 1959, with Therese Giehse and Maria Becker, that theater's foremost actresses, in leading roles. The play presents a ruthless picture of the hopelessly racket-ridden business world from which there can be no escape, depicted in the manner of a gangster comic. Duerrenmatt indulged in as much exaggeration as possible, but enlisted the cooperation of composer Paul Burkhard to set this horror comic to the kind of music that would tone down his overstatement so that it might seem "like the heartless flippancy of a limerick engraved on a tombstone." Not as yet translated into English, *Frank V* has been produced by several theaters in Germany.

With an increasingly heavy writing schedule, Duerrenmatt seldom takes time out to travel, but in April, 1959, he went to New York to receive the Drama Critics' Circle Award for *The Visit*, and in July of the same year, he went to Mannheim, Germany, where in a public ceremony he was awarded the renowned Schiller Prize of ten thousand German marks (about $2500). His play, *The Visit*, had been performed seventeen times to great acclaim in the repertory of the Mannheim National Theater during the 1958-1959 season. The dramatist occasionally attends performances of his plays in various cities in Germany, but he spends most of his time at his writing table and for relaxation either paints or plays with his children, his dogs, and his cats.

His method of work is unusual and exhausting; he rewrites and re-edits his plays endlessly—revising them completely after almost every production—probably because of the experimental nature of his work. "His plays, though realistic on the surface, transcend reality in many ways," according to critic, H. F. Garten. "But this surrealism is far removed from the symbolism of neoromantic drama or the abstractions of expressionism. It has the oppressive quality of a dream in which every detail stands out with glaring clarity while the whole remains unfathomable and obscure. The characters are frighteningly real, though often distorted into caricature. The fundamental mood is one of profound pessimism, reflecting the fear and insecurity of our present world. But against this background there is a sense of the grotesque, a readiness to laugh, which turns tragedy as if by magic into comedy." In a long critical essay called *Problems of the Theater* (1955), Duerrenmatt argued that the time for writing tragedies has passed. Tragedy, he contended, presupposes a well-ordered cosmos with established standards of guilt and retribution. Our disintegrating world, however, in which we live "like Gulliver amongst the giants," powerless to resist the course of events bigger than ourselves, calls for comedy—a comedy born not of despair, but of courage.

Duerrenmatt, personally, is a tall, heavy-set man, who weighs over 225 pounds;

he is witty and genial and much given to smoking long black cigars. When he smiles, the twinkle in his blue eyes and the dimples in his face belie his probing intellect and his horrendous view of life. This man has said, "The world, for me, stands as something monstrous, an enigma of calamity that has to be accepted but to which there must be no surrender." Later, he added: "Long ago I learned from my grandfather that writing can be a form of fighting!"

Duerrenmatt's interests of his university days—theology, philosophy, science, literature, and art—have carried over into his work as a novelist and playwright, and are nowhere more manifest than in *The Visit*.

Although he is the son of a minister of the Protestant faith, he does not feel obligated to any religious dogma; he satirizes orthodox beliefs as well as men of the cloth. In *The Visit*, the Pastor is shown to be as weak a vessel and as corrupt a man as the Policeman. Despite an avowed belief in the existence of God, Duerrenmatt sees the world as empty and meaningless; only great material wealth and worldly power, he feels, can give certain individuals the semblance of divinity. Claire Zachanassian, who controls such a large share of the world's goods, moves, according to the playwright, "outside of the human order; she has become fixed and immutable, incapable of growth, unless it be to turn into stone, to become an idol." Only self-discipline, love, and mercy, says Duerrenmatt, can assure the salvation of man.

Duerrenmatt's philosophy shows the strong influence of the existentialism of Kierkegaard; in this hollow, hopeless world, a man's character is his fate. Man is free to choose his path but once the first step is taken everything that follows is inevitable. Claire Zachanassian points this out to Anton Schill. Schill is even given a second chance: offered a gun with which to destroy himself, he prefers to let the town punish him for his guilt. This choice signifies the distinction between cowardice and courage.

The branch of science that interests Duerrenmatt above all others is psychology. His stories and plays deal extensively with the minds and motivations of his characters; most of his dramatic situations depend for their effectiveness upon the psychological tensions inherent in them. The second act of *The Visit* provides an excellent example of the manner in which the playwright has explored the psychology of fear in all its nuances. A brilliant psychological touch occurs at the railroad station where Schill is confronted by the natives of Güllen; not a threatening word is uttered and yet he behaves like a man possessed, betrayed by his own fear.

A man's relationship to his God, to other men, and to himself are like the interwoven threads of a tapestry which cannot be separated out; as an impartial, almost Olympian, observer of life, Duerrenmatt has noted this and has said:

"I was able to see that there were Germans who took no part in the atrocities, but who nonetheless felt guilty. True justice is tied to conscience and, as such, it too is capable of guilt. In *The Visit*, the villagers desperately want money, which they consider their just due. Accordingly, they seek to buy justice for themselves by killing the guilty man among them. The fact that the man, Anton Schill, is guilty of a crime provides their justification, but this, of course, is not justice. Schill's justice is a personal matter between himself and God. Because of his guilt, however, the whole community is in danger. This is the central problem of the play. The theater for me is a totality like the world and has many facets. The playwright's job is to show these facets no matter how depressing they may be, for they do exist and are real."

Duerrenmatt has given a great deal of serious thought to the ways in which other literature differs from drama and has arrived at workable conclusions for himself. When he writes a story or novel he sets the action in Switzerland and describes the locale with absolute literalness, but when he writes a play he creates a world of his own and counts on active collaboration from the theatergoer. "Güllen, as presented on the stage, does not exist," says the playwright, "except in the imagination of the audience. Just as it is impossible to have theater without spectators, so it is senseless to treat a play as if it were a kind of ode. A piece written for the theater becomes living theater when it is played, when it can be seen, heard, felt, and thus experienced immediately. This immediacy is one of the most essential aspects of the theater; a play is an event, is something that happens. In the theater everything must be transformed into the visible and sensible, and must seem to be happening at the present moment."

Dialogue, of course, is the life-blood of the drama; but it must be brief and of a very special kind. In describing dramatic dialogue, Duerrenmatt has given a clear and concise summary of the art of playwriting. He has said:

"The human being of the drama is, after all, a talking individual, and speech is his limitation. The action only serves to force this human being on the stage to talk in a certain way. The action is the crucible in which the human being is melted into words. This, of course, means that I, as the playwright, have to get the people in my drama into situations which force them to speak. If I merely show two people sitting together and drinking coffee while they talk about the weather, politics, or the latest fashions, then I provide neither a dramatic situation nor dramatic dialogue, no matter how clever their talk. Some other ingredient must be added to their conversation, something to cause wounds, conflicts, double meanings. If the audience knows that there is some poison in one of the coffee cups, or perhaps even in both, so that the conversation is really one between two poisoners, then an innocuous tête-à-tête over a coffee table is transformed by this technical device into a dramatic situation, out of which dramatic dialogue can develop. The tension in the situation creates dialogue which causes conflict and produces new situations and dialogue, and so on throughout the play."

But the art of drama is also the dramatist's total view of life as expressed in an individual style. Duerrenmatt's uncommon imagination and biting wit lend themselves naturally to nonrealistic treatment. In his plays, as in many of his paintings, there is a conscious mixture of styles; The Visit, for instance, is predominantly realistic with a strong intermingling of symbolism and expressionism. It is Duerrenmatt's wish to avoid literal statement and a photographic representation of life; he attempts by the use of theatricalist techniques to intensify the spectator's interest and excitement and to achieve a degree of universality.

Although symbolism is the tool of the poet rather than of the playwright, Duerrenmatt often uses it to heighten the mood and mystery of his work. One eloquent symbol in *The Visit* is the panther, which, in representing Schill, not only expresses the destructive power of the young seducer but also prefigures his eventual fate. A more important element in the author's style was supplied by expressionism, which is the escape from literal reality into broader forms that embrace allegory, symbolism, fantasy, or any other expression of the dramatist's free-roving mind. From expressionism Duerrenmatt has taken the short scenes, terse dialogue, unnamed characters, "space" staging, stylized acting, interpolated songs, and sinister poetic atmosphere which are to be found in all plays of this genre from August Strindberg's to Thornton Wilder's. Having Claire Zachanassian sit on the balcony of The Golden Apostle while life goes on in the town below her as if within her purview is an expressionistic device; and the same is true of the terrifying panther hunt with armed men stalking across the stage from opposite directions like automata with highly stylized movements.

It has been noted by almost all critics that Duerrenmatt takes special delight in the grotesque; many of his characters and situations are absurd, exaggerated, or bizarre. Maurice Valency felt that it was necessary to alter or omit the most fantastic aspects of *The Visit* to suit the tastes of English-speaking audiences. Duerrenmatt gave the semblance of an explanation for the presence of the grotesque in his plays when he said:

"Man expresses his need by crying and his freedom by laughing. Our task today is to demonstrate freedom. The tyrants of this planet are not moved by the works of poets. They yawn at a poet's lamentations. For them heroic epics are silly fairy tales and religious poetry puts them to sleep. Tyrants fear only one thing: a writer's mockery. For this reason, then, parody has crept into all literary genres, into the novel, into lyric poetry, into drama. Much of painting, even of music, has been invaded by parody, and the grotesque has followed, often well-camouflaged, on the heels of parody: all of a sudden the grotesque is there."

Duerrenmatt's concern with the effect of his plays upon "tyrants" marks him as a moralist, and *The Visit* becomes thereby an elaborate exemplum.

The plot of *The Visit* is basically uncomplicated and relatively unadorned; it has the simplicity and directness characteristic of classical drama. There are no involved subplots, and the numerous and varied incidents are all completely integrated into the main line of the action. The story unfolds in a small and impoverished provincial town "somewhere in Europe," to which an old woman returns after an absence of many years. Now fabulously wealthy, she has come back to get revenge on the man who had seduced her many years before. Gradually and relentlessly she buys up the entire town, corrupting even the most respected citizens, until they accede to her wishes and cold-bloodedly execute her former lover. Her mission accomplished, she leaves the town.

The characterization, except for that of Anton Schill, is one-dimensional. The townspeople are not individually explored in depth, and even Claire Zachanassian has a singleness of purpose that does not permit us to see very deeply into her character. We are presented, in her case, with a wealth of biographical details which help us to understand the facets of her personality rather than those of her psyche. Schill, on the other hand, is brilliantly depicted as step by step he makes the lacerating journey to his Gethsemane. He begins as a poor, insignificant shopkeeper, an unsuspecting victim, guilty, of course, but certain that life itself has canceled the debt. He is the image of the simple, thoughtless man upon whom it slowly dawns, through fear, horror, and personal suffering, that justice is being meted out and that he will have to pay for his guilt. It is in this recognition and in the acceptance of his fate that he becomes great in his death, if he was not great in his life; by his insight and resignation he achieves, as it were, a certain monumentality.

The play's dialogue is sharp, mordant, contemporary; it crackles with wit and irony. It not only presents the characters in clear outline, but carries the action forward at breakneck pace. Its subtlety includes a hint, beyond the artlessness of the various speeches, of the author's cynical comment on what is being said.

The theme of *The Visit* is difficult to pinpoint; some critics have seen it as the mercilessness of revenge, others as the ravaging force of greed, and still others as the brutalizing effect of grinding poverty; it is all of these things and, like life, much more, including the dire results of frustrated love, the ruthless drive for power, the fruitless search for justice, and the importance of human dignity. Concerning didacticism in art, Duerrenmatt has said:

"When you write a play you don't do it to teach a lesson or prove a point or build a philosophy, because you can never force art to prove anything. The fault of most critics is that they think a play, or a novel, must be based on a thesis. I don't work that way. I write something, and then there may or may not be a thesis in it."

The element of spectacle plays a much more important part in *The Visit* than it does in most modern plays. Probably because of his visualmindedness as well as his special training in art, Duerrenmatt integrates scenery and action in such a way as to make each serve his dramatic purpose more effectively. When we first see the town of Güllen, for instance, it is drab, ramshackle, and wretched; with the arrival of Claire Zachanassian, the natives begin to paint and refurbish the buildings, tend their gardens, buy typewriters, television sets, and new church bells; when the town's benefactor is finally ready to depart, her generosity is clearly visible in the bright and beautiful buildings and other civic improvements that fill the stage. Güllen (the name is a variation of the word Gülle, Swiss dialect for excrement) is resurrected, in an unobstrusive but constant crescendo, from the shabbiest poverty and neglect to the most sparkling opulence—worthy, indeed, of a happier ending.

THE PRODUCTION RECORD

Friedrich Duerrenmatt's *Der Besuch der alten Dame* (*The Visit*) was performed for the first time at the Zurich Schauspielhaus on January 29, 1956. The press said the play was "full of original ideas, uncommon imagination, and a new type of wit," and hailed the work of the director, Oskar Wälterlin, of the scene designer, Teo Otto, and of the stars, Therese Giehse and Gustav Knuth. Almost immediately after its premiere, the play was performed in half a dozen cities in Switzerland, Austria, and Germany.

The critical acclaim accorded the play in the various German-speaking countries led to a number of foreign translations. A French version, *La Visite de la Vieille Dame*, was produced in Paris at the Marigny Theater; the play was adapted by Jean-Pierre Porret, directed by Jean-Pierre Grenier, designed by Jacques Noël, and acted by Mme Sylvie and Olivier Hussenot. The play received excellent notices and ran from March 1 to May 15, 1957.

Maurice Valency's English version of the play, called at first *Time and Again* and later renamed *The Visit*, opened in Brighton, England, on December 24, 1957. It then went on a tour of the English provinces and also was seen in Scotland and Ireland, but it was not taken to London. The explanation offered for this was that British critics and audiences were so shocked by the harshness and horror of the play that the producers hesitated to take it to London, in spite of the fact that Valency's adaptation had subdued much of "the macabre gallows-humor of the original" and had heightened the romantic elements.

In a pre-Broadway tour it was seen in Boston and New Haven. All important newspapers in New York have "stringers," or scouts, who attend the out-of-town tryouts of every play prior to its Broadway opening and phone or wire in a report of the proceedings. In April, 1958, the "stringer" in New Haven, Connecticut, sent the following dispatch to the drama desk of a New York paper:

> Swiss playwright Friedrich Duerrenmatt's unusual play, "The Visit," opened its six-day run at the Shubert Theater last night with the Lunts in command. It produced a violent reaction among the audience.
>
> Most theatergoers and critics praised it. Others said they disliked it intensely. But even the dislikers admitted that this strange and curious drama about how a psychotic woman wreaks a terrible revenge on the seducer of her girlhood has a compelling fascination.
>
> Alfred Lunt and Lynn Fontanne give thoroughly effective performances as the now-respectable storekeeper who once started a girl on the road to prostitution and the much-married victim who comes back to her native European town to bribe the townsfolk into killing him.
>
> As performed here in its pre-Broadway run, "The Visit" is smoothly executed. The acting is excellent, the staging and lighting weirdly effective. It is now in a finished stage of production and sure to provoke controversy in New York. The Shubert audience called the Lunts back for numerous curtain calls but argued violently on the merits of the play on their way out of the theater. It is not a play one easily forgets.

The play opened at the Lunt-Fontanne Theater on Broadway on May 5, 1958, and after a run of nine weeks, suspended for the summer. It reopened on August 20 at the Morosco Theater and remained there until November 29, 1958. *The Visit* received the Drama Critics' Circle Award as the best foreign play on Broadway for the season 1958-1959.

After an interval of ten months, the Lunts, under the joint sponsorship of the American Theater Society and the Council of the Living Theater, took *The Visit* on a tour of the United States and Canada that included seventeen cities and lasted from September, 1959, to March, 1960. The engagement concluded with two weeks at the City Center in New York (March 8 to March 20) where the attraction played to completely sold out houses. The New York critics were more enthusiastic about the play on this occasion than they had been at its premiere two years before. Lewis Funke, of the New York *Times*, wrote in part: "To see Friedrich Duerrenmatt's *The Visit* again is to understand why it has lingered so powerfully in memory. It happens to be one of the more trenchant and mordant plays of our time. . . . *The Visit* reminds us what a temple the theater actually can be."

From a financial point of view, too, *The Visit* was phenomenally successful in America; in fifty-four weeks of interrupted playing time from the start of its pre-Broadway tryout in April, 1958, to the closing of its post-Broadway tour in March, 1960, the play grossed over two million dollars and broke the box-office records for straight dramatic plays at the Biltmore Theater, Los Angeles; the National Theater, Washington; the Forrest Theater, Philadelphia; and the City Center, New York.

During the fourth season of the International Theater Festival which opened in Paris on March 15, 1960, Peter Brook mounted a new production of *La Visite de la Vieille Dame;* and on June 23, 1960, the Lunts had the honor of opening a new theater in London, The Royalty, where they appeared in *The Visit* for an engagement, scheduled for eight weeks, that actually stretched out to twenty.

At last report, the play has been translated into more than fifteen languages and has been produced in over twenty-five countries, including Japan and Israel.

CONCEIVING *The Visit*
An Interview with Friedrich Duerrenmatt

Duerrenmatt first thought of writing *The Visit* in the form of a short novel. Originally, there was no Claire Zachanassian in the story. The central figure was a man who returned to his home town after he had made a great fortune. He offered a huge sum of money to the townspeople if they would kill an old enemy of his, the rival who had won his boyhood sweetheart away from him. The townspeople objected and, feeling offended, evolved a plan to thwart the millionaire. It was midwinter, deep snows were on the ground; they were felling trees in the forest and managed to arrange to kill the "visitor" by having him struck by a falling tree.

Duerrenmatt was not satisfied with the idea. It seemed to him that the story would be more interesting if a woman were more prominently involved in it. He mulled over the idea for a long time and finally decided to have a wealthy woman return to her native town for the purpose of revenge. The models Duerrenmatt kept in mind while creating the background and character of Claire were the reputations and careers of the internationally famous millionaires Zacharoff, Onassis, and Gulbenkian, and from their names he concocted his heroine's— Zacha-nass-ian. Her money gave Claire the status and power that royal birth had given to Medea and to the other heroines of classical tragedy.

As he began to envision the action centered in a single locale, Duerrenmatt thought of it more and more in theatrical terms and decided that it would be more effective as a play than as a novel. It is his opinion that, on the stage, *place* is more important than character, and that it is the function of the dramatist to create a world that is palpable and entire. In this play the conflict takes a triangular form—the man, the woman, and the people of Güllen are pitted against each other—and the Town must therefore have the force and concreteness of each of the other protagonists.

Contrary to the belief of the critics, Duerrenmatt did not start his play with a theme, and he never does, since he is convinced that although a problem may be inherent in a play it should not be the primary element. The problem should emerge as a "by-product" created by the interrelationship of the characters and the situations. If a play has real depth and value, moreover, it usually concerns itself with more than one problem; it suggests all sorts of problems—a whole "spindle" of them. In Duerrenmatt's imagination, the play actually started with the town. It must be shown to be very poor. How? The men of the town are unemployed and have nothing better to do than to sit around the railroad station and watch the trains go by. The railroad station itself is rundown, shabby, neglected. What are the men waiting for? A rich and charitable woman who will come and help them out of their distress. But if she is so rich, why does she come by train? She ought to arrive in her own chauffeur-driven limousine. But she has been in many accidents and no longer travels by plane or by motor car. She has lost a hand and a leg, but these mutilations do not immobilize her. She has a will of steel and is unswerving in the pursuit of her goal; her powerful aggressiveness contains an element of the superhuman.

Claire Zachanassian turns up in Güllen with a coffin prepared for her former lover, who, in her youth, she called her "black panther"; she also travels with a black panther which she keeps as a pet; and to complete the collection of grotesqueries, she has, in the original version of the play, a wooden leg. It was pointed out to Duerrenmatt that these three identical circumstances resemble actual details in the life of Sarah Bernhardt. Bernhardt owned a rosewood coffin with which she traveled and in which she often slept; she kept a pet panther; and at the age of seventy-one, she underwent an operation for the amputation of her leg, but this did not deter her from appearing on the stage and in films. Duerrenmatt declared that he was completely unaware of these facts in the life of Bernhardt, and that his choice of them was purely coincidental, but he could not vouch for the part that his unconscious had played in the process. "To make his characters interesting and theatrical," said the playwright, "the writer thinks of many things, but these things must be unified and consistent; they must be true for the character. It is for that reason that a play is much more complicated and demanding than a novel; on the stage the personalities of the characters should have a startling and grotesque quality."

It is Duerrenmatt's opinion that a play is not entirely written by the playwright; the director and the actors make important contributions to both characterization and plot. Alfred Lunt, for example, wanted a more pointed climax than had originally been written for the railroad scene at the end of the second act, so a brand-new character was introduced at this point, one whom the playwright had never thought of during the process of composition: the man who stopped for a pail of water and casually offered Anton a lift in his truck; he added greatly to both plot and characterization. Duerrenmatt has no objection to making changes, whether minor or drastic ones, if they will serve the good of the play; he feels that professional directors and actors, if they are genuine artists, know instinctively what makes good theater. He has tremendous respect for both Peter Brook and Alfred Lunt as creative technicians; before the English version of his play was done, the dramatist talked the script through scene by scene with Peter Brook and made many changes in accordance with Brook's views. And yet Duerrenmatt does not feel that there is only one way to mount a play; the text is merely a plan for a production, it is the unfulfilled "possibility" of a theatrical presentation. He liked the forest scene, for instance, when it was done in Zurich with men representing trees expressionistically, and he liked it just as well when it was done by the Lunts on an absolutely bare stage. Each actor creates a role differently and an author is often amazed to see things he never dreamed of emerge from his work; but he is not always pleased, he may quite often be disappointed or dismayed.

To Duerrenmatt, Anton Schill is the more important of the two central figures in the play, since he starts out as a small and insignificant human being and develops as the action progresses into a person with a strong and courageous character. The playwright feels that Lunt did a brilliant job in showing this development. Claire Zachanassian, on the other hand, remains unchanged throughout, but Fontanne played the part with such a strong undercurrent of wit and humor that she gave it enormous variety.

The original version of *The Visit* was thought to be too fantastic and grotesque to suit the tastes of American audiences, so the most extreme examples of these elements were removed from the play by the director and the adaptor. But Duerrenmatt says, "I do not understand why Broadway is so realistic and naturalistic when the greatest figures in American literature and American films were masters of fantasy and the grotesque." To prove his point, the playwright named Mark Twain—(a strong resemblance has been noted between the Twain story "The Man Who Corrupted Hadleyburg" and *The Visit*). In his enthusiasm for Mark Twain, the playwright compared him to Aristophanes and Swift in the manner in which he satirized politics and democracy. "Mark Twain's stories are written in every conceivable style, including surrealism," says Duerrenmatt. "If modern literature can do it, why can't the stage?" Duerrenmatt also mentioned Poe, Hawthorne, Melville, and Faulkner, whom he admires tremendously, and also Chaplin, whose best work was a magnificent tissue of odd, whimsical, and startling conceits. It is only in the theater, apparently, that English-speaking audiences seem to be afraid of nonrealistic work, but Duerrenmatt would like to be influential in introducing a freer use of the imagination to British and American stages; European audiences accept his work unaltered.

Duerrenmatt also remarked about other differences between European and American theatrical conditions which affect the playwright. When *The Visit* and his later play, *Frank V*, were done in Zurich, the critics had some harsh things to say about them, but they also offered many constructive suggestions. Duerrenmatt pondered the reviewers' advice, then changed, rewrote, and improved the scripts, which were subsequently mounted in many cities in Switzerland, Germany, and Austria. He saw many productions of these plays and continued to make changes over a long period of time. The same system proved to be of invaluable aid to Ionesco and Beckett, who came out of the little theaters of Paris and looked upon each production as an opportunity to make further improvements; a failure in Europe is not considered a calamity. But the American theater is so highly financed that Broadway cannot afford to take a chance on the serious, young, experimental writer and will only produce the young writer's work if it happens to fall into a fairly conventional mold. Broadway is more daring, but still full of trepidation, if the "odd-ball" play happens to come from the pen of an internationally famous writer. On the American stage, said Duerrenmatt, we see pictures of the South and of the Bronx, but we don't see America; that is because the realistic style has a tendency to emphasize the local rather than the universal, or world, view.

Duerrenmatt insists that he will continue to be antinaturalistic, will put anything into his plays that occurs to him because all things are possible on the stage. In *The Visit*, for instance, it delighted him to think that Claire Zachanassian was so rich that she could do her shopping all over the world: She got her sedan-chair from the Louvre and then bought two gangsters in America to serve as chair-bearers.

The Visit UNDERGOES A SEA CHANGE
An Interview with Maurice Valency

Everyone knows that translators are traitors, and no one knows it better than does Maurice Valency whose English versions of the plays of Jean Giraudoux and Friedrich Duerrenmatt have been praised and applauded in both England and America. There is no such thing in the theater as simple translation, says Valency. If a play is to come alive in a foreign environment it must be adapted; that is, it must be rethought and rephrased. In order to interpret the original author it is necessary first to determine as well as we can his essential meaning, and to underline ideas where needed. To achieve a translation that is a faithful reproduction of the original is extremely difficult, since it is absolutely necessary for the adaptor to inject some of his own creativity and vitality if the translation is to have any life at all. Translation is a worthwhile task, though the translator is seldom thanked for his pains.

In 1955 Valency's agent received a manuscript copy of a play written in German and called *Der Besuch der alten Dame;* it had been forwarded from Germany by a literary agent who had received the play from the agent of Friedrich Duerrenmatt. Accompanying the script was a note suggesting that this play would probably interest Valency. It did very much, and Valency agreed to undertake the job of adaptation if a clause were inserted in the contract to the effect that he could make any changes in the play he thought necessary; he was given *carte blanche.*

Valency went to work. He discovered that the doctrine of *The Visit* had nothing to do with any current political ideology. The theme is medieval and Christian—*radix malorum cupiditas:* love of money is the root of all evil. It is a doctrine immovably rooted in our culture—it is, perhaps, the basic conflict of our age—a stereotype as self-evident and inescapable as fate among the Greeks. Duerrenmatt calls his play a "tragic comedy," but Valency found that the propulsive force of the action was neither external destiny nor an inner feeling of guilt. The implacable necessity which drives the action to its conclusion is economic, a force which we understand better than the Greeks and which in our theater may be said to take the place of Greek fate. But it has certain inconveniences as a basis for tragedy, for in coming to terms with money we do not necessarily achieve purification. In the world of things, where possession is the only virtue, Claire Zachanassian is monstrously "virtuous," but the soul of man is bigger than the world, and in this thought lies the didactic force of the play.

Valency points out, furthermore, that in defining the pleasurable effect of tragedy, Aristotle says that the monstrous does not give pleasure but that pity and terror are felt when a person inflicts pain upon someone he loves. The problem in adapting *The Visit* was to keep the audience from looking upon Claire as a monster and to emphasize the fact that, perverted as her passion may have become, she never ceased to love Anton Schill. Duerrenmatt's penchant for the grotesque made Claire a horrible creature, but Valency's reworking of the story rather stressed the love and the pain that Claire endured and inflicted.

Valency believes that the play proceeds according to a very clear plan: The antagonists are Schill and the Town, and over all broods a woman—like an Eros-possessed divinity—with very strong erotic and romantic motives. The design is a triangle; at the apex is Claire Zachanassian, in one of the lover angles is Schill, in the other, the Town. There is a reciprocal movement of the antagonists, the man and the city, but in the course of this action the lady remains fixed and invariable; the city grows daily more evil; the man grows progressively purer and better, until in his despair he attains the possible height of moral goodness. So the outlines of tragedy in the Christian sense also are rounded out. But the passion of this protagonist has no sequel in heaven, and on earth the outcome of justice is seen to be a greater injustice still.

Valency completed the English version of the play in August, 1956, and in July, 1957, he met with Duerrenmatt and with Peter Brook, the play's director, in Paris. During conferences there, many alterations were made in the adaptation with the assistance of the author; the over-all concept of the play and production was discussed with the director and with Alfred Lunt who was present at one of the meetings; and the script received final approval. The play opened with the Lunts in the leading roles on Christmas Eve, 1957, in Brighton, England. The adaptor was not able to attend rehearsals but Duerrenmatt was present at some, and Valency approved by mail of a number of slight changes requested by the director.

The changes from the German which the adaptor made in the script are so numerous and in some cases so subtle that it is impossible to discuss all of them here. It should be noted, for instance, that many of the speeches, though identical in content, are much briefer in English than they are in the original, the ideas having been compressed and crystallized, and often rearranged so that the significant point is not buried in the text but is placed at the very end of the speech. The following are the major alterations from the German and Valency's reasons for making them:

The original title of the play is *The Old Lady's Visit*, which to American ears is both awkward and sentimental. In England it was called *Time and Again,* but the British reviewers complained that the title had no significance, and after a certain amount of insistence from this side of the Atlantic, it was christened *The Visit.*

There were 35 people in the original cast, but only 32 appear in the English version; in the general streamlining of the script, two of Claire's former husbands (Numbers 8 and 9) and Fraulein Luise, the town prostitute, were eliminated. These characters were not essential to the story line and confused rather than clarified the dramatic values. Another reason for their elimination was economy; three salaries were saved, which is always an important consideration in the commercial theater.

The names of almost all the male characters were changed in the adaptation. In the original, Anton Schill is known as Alfred Ill; with Alfred Lunt playing the part, the first name would obviously have to be altered, as would the surname, Ill, because of its unpleasant or humorous connotations in our language. The members of Claire Zachanassian's retinue—the ex-judge, the two gangsters, and the two blind men—bear in German the strange names of Boby, Toby, Roby, Koby, and Loby. This is a form of expressionism that would undoubtedly have more appeal for Europeans than for Americans, especially as it is meant to satirize American mass culture; it also springs from the Swiss notion of assembly-line gangster-life in the United States; and, in addition, the names have a humorous intent, since all of these characters behave in comic-strip fashion. In the English version, they are known as Bobby, Max, Mike, and so on.

A number of changes were made in the play for the specific purpose of heightening the erotic element. Duerrenmatt tells us that Claire's seduction took place about forty-five years ago, thus when the original play opens Claire is a woman of sixty-three. Valency reduced the lapse of time, so that she would be under fifty; Claire Zachanassian, moreover, is depicted as a much less grotesque figure in the adaptation than she is in the original. Duerrenmatt likens her to the

Greek Fate Clotho, the goddess of destiny who spins the thread of life; feeling that this allusion would have little meaning for an American audience and seeking a more vivid image, Valency refers to her as a fury with black wings. In the original, Claire is made to have suffered severe physical disfigurement as a result of a series of accidents and so she appears with a wooden leg and an ivory hand; in the English version, these grotesque and unpleasant elements are to some extent eliminated. The various accidents are mentioned but Claire's physical attractiveness is emphasized for the express purpose of intensifying the love story.

Duerrenmatt's play is a mixture of many styles, but this is a practice in European dramaturgy which foreign audiences do not seem to object to; American audiences, on the other hand, are apt to find such techniques confusing. Along with its basic naturalism, Valency and Brook wished to retain some of the play's expressionism and lyricism but the more extreme examples of these genres had to be cut. In the original, for instance, four men take up positions on the stage to represent the trees in the forest where Claire and Anton meet on two occasions, once in the first act and once in the third; these men perform pantomimic gestures, sway in the breeze, and chant, "We are beech trees, we are dark green firs." Valency wished to preserve this manner of presentation, but Hugh Beaumont, the English producer, and Peter Brook felt that these scenes were not in keeping with the style they wanted to create, and after consultation, they cut them. Also cut, because it violated the style, was a scene in the second act in which an artist tries to sell Mrs. Schill a portrait of her husband; in a quarrel with the schoolteacher, the artist breaks the canvas over the teacher's head. This low comedy byplay was considered too farcical and "cabaretish" to be retained. Another scene that was thought to be out of key with the general style of the production, and for still another reason, came at the very end of the play when a choral group sums up the theme and moral of the drama in Euripidean fashion. This lent a classical note to the work but was stylistically inconsistent with the rest of the play, and it was felt that without preparation it would be a hazardous thing to use.

The greatest number of cuts and changes were made in the second act. The act consists mainly of scenes which alternate between Claire sitting on the balcony of The Golden Apostle—waiting, while Anton frantically pursues his fate on the stage below her. In the original there are many more scenes and many more shifts between them than there are in the adaptation. This heightens the contrapuntal effect of the action and throws more light on Claire's past life and present power, but it also breaks the continuity of the story and at times becomes slightly confusing. In the English version, the balcony scenes were condensed and the balcony itself was drawn upstage into a dim area so as not to prove distracting during Schill's scenes; these cuts and changes were made during the rehearsal period, with Duerrenmatt's collaboration.

The second act of the original script contains two ideological concepts that are very strongly presented: First, international society is shown to be unified and to rule the world; and second, the common man confronting local institutions for help invariably has the door slammed in his face. These concepts are less sharply delineated in the adaptation and might very easily escape the notice of the average playgoer; but what the adaptation lacks in topical allusions and specific ideologies it more than makes up in universality. It presents a horrifying picture of man's weakness and corruptibility as well as of his driving desire for revenge, and it is not limited to any particular time or place.

An important change was made at the very end of the second act. Just before the curtain falls, in the original version, Anton Schill says, "I'm lost," and he decides to return to his home resigned to his fate; in the English version, however, when Schill is offered a lift by the truck driver, he declines it, and says, "I'm staying," and the stage directions inform us that he has acquired a "strange new dignity." This effect was arrived at during the play's long tour in England and after a great deal of experimentation. Valency points out that if Schill is allowed to express utter defeat at the end of the second act, Act Three becomes anti-climactic, whereas Schill's determination to stay on at that point leads the audience to expect further conflict.

Act Three was highly streamlined by the adaptor in order to hasten the story to its conclusion. Duerrenmatt introduces a couple of newspaper reporters who give their own sentimental and soap-opera version as to why Claire has returned to her native town and has so handsomely endowed it; they believe that her "charity" was motivated by nostalgia and love. All of this material was cut, as were many of the reporters' speeches during the murder scene later in the act. Thus a great deal of irony, satire, and farce was sacrificed because of the need for acceleration at the end of the play, for the adaptor and the director had agreed that it was imperative to rush the final, dreadful events of the action to a speedy culmination.

In only one respect is the adaptation more brutal and grotesque than the original play, and that is in the treatment of Anton Schill in his relationship to his family. In the German version, the father joins his son, his wife, and his daughter for a jaunt in the boy's car, and there is a long idyllic scene during which they drive through and admire the local countryside. In the English version, the boy refuses to give his father a ride, and the other members of the family show themselves to be equally self-centered and callous. Because of its pastoral and romantic qualities, the "motor trip" would provide, one might think, an excellent contrast to the more somber moments of the play, but it was found during rehearsals that the scene did not "work" on stage and so it was cut; it was also omitted from some of the German productions of the play.

Valency's treatment of the play's symbolism differs somewhat from the original. Claire's panther is mentioned more frequently in the German version; at the end of the play, for example, when Schill lies dead, Claire says, "He is again what he was, a long time ago, the black panther. Cover him up." There is no mention of the panther at this point in the adaptation; Claire simply says, "Cover his face." The presence of the panther in the English version is actually a compromise, since Valency wanted it to be cut out altogether. There was still another significant alteration in this scene: in the original, Claire herself hands over her check to the burgomaster when the job is done; in the adaptation, the check is tendered by Bobby, the ex-judge. The reason for the change, Valency explains, is that Claire is above such sordid details; because of her enormous, almost supernatural power, she requires a certain degree of remoteness. When Claire leaves Güllen for the last time, she is, in the original, carried off in her sedan-chair and Schill's coffin follows her out; in the adaptation, the coffin is borne out first and Claire walks after it mourning. This alteration serves three purposes at once: it reinforces the idea of the love story, it heightens the pathos, and it gives the star an important exit.

The very last moments of the play posed a problem for the adaptor; in the German version, a Euripidean chorus of townspeople brings the curtain down with a philosophical and lyrical ode in prose-poetry but, as has already been mentioned, that chorus was eliminated. During rehearsals in England, and on the road in the United States, four different endings were tried out. The difficulty arose from the fact that at the end of this play the audience does not wish to applaud immediately; it has been deeply stirred by significant ideas and emotionally moved by profound and shocking behavior. There must be a period of silence during which the audience can regain its equilibrium and adjust to reality before it can express its appreciation. The first ending tried was to have the townspeople cheer as Claire went off with her retinue; this confused the emotional mood. As an alternative to the cheering, the town's brass band started to play as Claire left, but this was even more discrepant. As a third attempt, the bells of the town which were heard softly ringing during the scene were brought up to a deafening pitch at the very end, but this solution like the others failed. It was finally realized that what was wanted was silence, so that as the train bearing Claire and Company away from Güllen pulls out of the station, the townsfolk line up along the tracks and in silence follow the train's departure with their eyes until the sounds of engine and wheels have completely faded away. This ending has a double value: practically, it permits the audience to achieve a readjustment to reality, and artistically, it provides a balance for the opening of the play which depicts the train's arrival.

To illustrate the difference between translation and adaptation, Valency offers as an example a single exchange of speeches from the play. Anton and Claire meet in the woods for the last time; he knows that he is soon to die. She says tenderly, "I shall take you in your coffin to Capri. You will have your tomb in the park of my villa, where I can see you from my bedroom window. White marble and onyx in a grove of green cypress. With a beautiful view of the Mediterranean." This is very close to literal translation, but Schill's reply is the work of the adaptor. His response, in the original, is, "I know it only from pictures." In Valency's version, Anton makes a comment that is both pathetic and bitterly ironic; he says, "I've always wanted to see it." Clever as this line is, it is no longer spoken on the stage, because once in England when Alfred Lunt uttered it, a false laugh in the audience broke the mood of the scene, and it was henceforth considered a hazardous line.

"If you don't feel that you can improve the play a little," says Valency, "don't adapt it!" Without at least some impulse of inventiveness to put soul into the adaptation, an adaptor is likely to vitiate the force of his original in the process of translation. The special problem confronting the adaptor in handling *The Visit* was to transform the grotesque into the beautiful, the poignant into art, and a somewhat cynical, bitter comedy into a modern tragedy.

THE ACTOR ATTACKS HIS PART
*Morton Eustis Interviews Lynn Fontanne and Alfred Lunt**

The Lunts approach the problem of acting in a manner all their own. From years of working together, they have developed a technique in which each actor complements the other to an extraordinary degree. The play selected, the Lunts do not waste much time analyzing it from a literary viewpoint nor ponder long upon nuances of character and interpretation. They visualize a drama instantly as theater—a stage, settings, props, costumes, musicians in the pit. When they study a script, they do so with the perception of the actor, director, designer, and producer rolled into one. Only *after* they have already begun to act out their parts do they concentrate on subtleties of impersonation, on definitions of character.

The Lunts rarely plan out a scene in advance. Their first move is to learn the lines mechanically, by rote, to get them out of the way. Then, in the privacy of their home, where they do most of their work, they improvise their scenes together and "see what happens." They throw themselves into the extracurricular rehearsals with even more gusto than they exhibit in their playing. Acting the same scene over and over, they discard what is bad, keep what is good, then "polish, polish, polish." There is nothing objective about their method. At the same time it is not a casual, undisciplined charade; it is based on a serious understanding of, and respect for, their craft. They enjoy themselves enormously in their improvisations. But they are always careful, to the point of exactitude, to work within the script. And always they are guided by the reactions of an imaginary audience, composed of stern, uncompromising critics, most exacting among them Mr. Lunt and Miss Fontanne. From a dramatic instinct, sharpened, heightened, tempered and chastened by years of acting experience—in a collaboration at once mystical and practical, real and theatrical—emerged order and discipline.

The Lunts find it very difficult to analyze their method of attack. Mr. Lunt dismisses all the preliminaries with: "Miss Fontanne and I do a lot of work at home together. But I can't describe what it is. We've done it so long, it's become almost instinctive." Both are extremely loath to talk about technique, personally or impersonally. If talk they must, however, they are adamant on one point. They must take the stage individually. "Mr. Lunt's opinions about technique, his reactions to the theater, are often quite different from mine," says Miss Fontanne. "Just because we work together is no reason we should be classed as a team." "What Miss Fontanne does on the stage," choruses Mr. Lunt in the adjacent dressing room, "what she thinks about acting, is a personal equation. I wouldn't

* By permission; © 1936 by Theatre Arts Magazine.

dream of intruding on that side of her life. You must talk to each of us alone."

Lynn Fontanne

The first essential of acting technique, Lynn Fontanne believes, is voice con-trol—"knowing how to pitch and throw your voice so as to fill a theater." This is the one histrionic facility which Miss Fontanne is willing to admit may be classed as "technique, pure and simple"—one requiring long and arduous training. All the rest are amalgams of many qualities.

Timing, for instance, so vital a factor in acting, especially in the projection of comic dialogue, is "purely a matter of ear—something instinctive, which the actor either has or has not got." The actor's timing must be adjusted to other actors and to an audience. "Perhaps that may be technique, though even it is largely ear training." But the moment timing becomes methodical, deliberate and overstudied—simply an exercise in technique—the actor becomes like a clock ticking. "And precision is bad. *It is far better for the actor to be a little off beat, to jangle!*"

Set movements and gestures, symbolizing the tragic or the comic, are absolutely meaningless, in Miss Fontanne's judgment. The actor supplies the movement, the gesture, the carriage, out of his sense of character, his natural instinct of rhythm and mobility. For a long time, Miss Fontanne was convinced that she never used her hands on stage, except for obvious movements called for by the action. Alexander Woollcott, to whom—"rashly"—she confided this belief, laughed her out of that fond assurance. But, to this day, she insists, she is rarely conscious of what she is doing with her hands. Instinctively, she will raise her arm or move her body as she speaks a line—"just as you do in real life"—but she never, in *preparing* her part, maps out a mechanical line of movement.

Technique, likewise, cannot teach an actor how to know, before he has finished speaking a line, that the expected laugh, the gasp of horror, the ripple of merri-ment, will not be forthcoming on a particular evening. "That is a telepathic quality, born with the actor—an essential sixth sense that every fine actor must possess." The actor, perhaps, may learn by technical device how to carry on the next line, or piece of stage business, without a pause, so that the audience is unaware of its delinquency that evening. "But that, too, is something more than technique . . . Call it *acting!*"

Miss Fontanne used to read a play primarily with an eye to her own role. Her first reaction was: "There's a *part* I should like to play." Lately, she has shifted her point of attack. The play itself now engages her first attention: consideration of her own role is a secondary step. The instant Miss Fontanne reads a play, a visual picture of the person springs to her mind. She does not attempt, however, to probe her character until she has worked on the part as an actress. Acting out the part with Mr. Lunt, improvising details of character—walk, gesture, carriage, tone of voice—she begins, "slowly, to get into the character of the person." And without analytical reason—"I try not to use my intellect at this stage at all"—a conception gradually, "mysteriously," emerges.

"Suddenly, on the stage or in the dressing room, walking in the park or motoring to the theater, you discover something about the character you never knew even existed. In a flash, you derive a new slant on an action, a motive. You see that you are wrong in one scene; the woman could never use that tone of voice. No sooner is that place rectified than another horrible gap appears. This refining process continues all during the run of the play. The impersonation is *never* complete, though it is truer on the last night of the run—if you are a real actor—than at any other time."

It is impossible on the face of it, for an actor to disassociate himself completely from his own self. "You remain the same size and you have the same vocal cords. But, if you are a good actor, you should not be bound by your physical presence." Creating the part as Miss Fontanne does—working inward from without—the problem of adapting her own self to the role is "something that seems to do itself." Playing too many one-color parts, an actor is apt to imagine that he cannot play any other type of role. After acting a string of comedy parts, Miss Fontanne began to feel that way herself. Then she realized that "acting is a bastard art, if it is an art at all. The author creates the character. The actor's only job is to *go ahead and play the part*. With a well-trained voice and the proper use of make-up, an actor should be able to compass any role. And the less he *reasons* about the complexities of impersonation, the better."

Although Miss Fontanne does not rationalize movement when she is building a part, she follows the same general routine at each public performance. Lighting cues, if nothing else, would force an actor to adhere to a more or less rigid pattern. Too many unexpected movements, also, would throw the other actors into confusion and destroy the play's flow of action. "Too much movement, at any time, by the way, is bad. The eye is so much quicker than the ear that movement tends to destroy words." None the less, she says, "you do change the part very much during a play's run. Little things, here and there, are added or left out. If a certain scene doesn't jell—and there always is a scene that doesn't—you try to go to the bottom of what you've got and find out what is wrong. In other words, you don't fritter a part away, playing it mechanically."

This is where the "dangerous subject" of emotion enters the scene—how much, how little, emotion the actor actually feels. Although—"emphatically"—Miss Fontanne does not live the part or lose herself in the role, she plays emotional scenes with a much surer touch if she, herself, is "highly emotional" while playing them. "When my senses—or perhaps it's just my nerves—are keyed to a high pitch, I find I have a sharper ear, a much quicker response, to anything going on in the audience. I have, too, an uncanny awareness of the rightness or wrongness of my performance." This quality of emotion is "probably a form of self-hypnosis." She does not actually feel the emotion, but she hypnotizes herself into thinking that she does—"always being perfectly aware of what is going on, of how I am playing the part." This hypnosis, however, cannot always be turned on and off at will, "which is probably why my performances vary so distressingly. Sometimes, you know, they are so bad I should like to advance to the footlights and urge the audience to get their money back. At other times, well, I feel they have not paid enough."

People often ask Miss Fontanne: "Why is acting in a play so tiring? You work only a few hours eight times a week." The usual answer to this question is that acting is a nervous job, and physically tiring from the strain of using tremendous breath control. Miss Fontanne believes there is still another reason why a big role is so exhausting. "Being the focus of thousands of eyes produces an hypnotic magnetism which makes the actor physically stronger than he is himself, so that when the eyes are withdrawn and the current is switched off he feels like a pricked balloon."

"The bad parts are the most difficult. The best you can hope to do with a bad part is to make it human, to fill in gaps." Once Miss Fontanne had a very bad part to play—a costume role. She did not know how to play it. "I went to the Metropolitan [Museum of Art] and saw all the Peter Lylys. I copied one person exactly, down to the jewelry. My make-up and my appearance were so startling that the part made quite an impression. But that was only trickery. In some respects, however, the parts that do one the most good as an actor are the bad parts. If a good actor plays a lot of bad parts he can become endlessly resourceful so that when, at last, he plays a good one, *something happens!* And then he never wants to play *another bad part!"*

Alfred Lunt

If Alfred Lunt has any fixed idea about the actor's place in the theater's sun, it is this: "The actor is not a creative, but an interpretive artist. His one and *only* job is to work *within the play*, to translate the ideas of the author. The play itself is what counts." Mr. Lunt entertains quite violent opinions about the actor—star or bit player—who tries to "hog center stage," who puts himself on a loftier plane than his fellow-actors and the author's script—"not that I know any such actors today." The important thing is for everyone in the show to make good.

It is not surprising to discover that Mr. Lunt, holding these views, always reads a play first to see whether it is a good play, only secondly to determine whether or not it is a good play for him and Miss Fontanne—or him alone—to act in. The wide range in which Mr. Lunt's parts have fallen indicates great variety and flexibility of interpretation in the actor. Mr. Lunt professes to be ignorant of the actual method by which he creates a part, differentiates one characterization from another. Like Miss Fontanne, he believes that is something that does itself. He is sure, however, that he always attempts to make each role something new and noncharacteristic of himself. He has little respect for the actor who simply projects his own personality, charming or otherwise.

Rehearsals to Mr. Lunt are even more fascinating than actual performances. He never tires of standing on a bare, ill-lighted stage, watching others perform, acting himself. His improvisations with Miss Fontanne are elixir to his actor's soul. He never relies on the director to shape his concept of a part. "If you know your job and work for the play and not for yourself, you don't need a director to develop the part for you." The director must work to perfect every detail in the show, to pull together all the loose strings. For that matter, so must each member of the cast.

How Mr. Lunt achieves his effects is a question he cannot—or will not—elucidate. Technique, he admits, is part of an actor's equipment. "But no actor can define what his own technique is, or tell how he uses it." He is extremely scornful of theories and rules. "No good actor is bound by any rules. It's absurd to say there are any set formulas for acting comedy or tragedy—one set of gestures the actor pulls out of the hat when he is a clown, another when he is a tragic figure. *What* you do and *how* you do it depends entirely on the play and the part you portray. You *play* serious and comic scenes differently. Of course. The timing is quite different, the whole interpretation—just as it is in life. But that depends on character more than technique. Often you do the best you can and then something happens you hadn't expected at all. Something you hadn't thought out at all brings down the house. *You can't be sure of anything.*"

Mr. Lunt's description of his playing, once rehearsals are done, is this: "I try to relax into the part and play it as nearly the same way as I can each night. But when I say relax, I *don't* mean get slovenly. Every performance, whether in New York or Squedunk, is as important as the opening night. You've got to be on your toes all the time." Stage business, as a rule, is set in rehearsal and the actor goes through the same routine every night. In certain types of comedy, however, business may vary considerably with each performance . . . "but obviously ad libbing or changing business would be *outrageous* in anything but a very special type of comedy. . . . Still, in every play, you are consciously studying your part, adding new shades of meaning, building it all the time. *And you know what you are doing every second you are on stage.*"

You cannot cut and piece a performance on the stage as you can in the films. "That's why an actor can never let himself be overcome by emotion. If he started to cry during a scene, there wouldn't be any play." Emotion can play a big part in acting. "Sometimes a role can tear you to pieces. But it must always be *controlled emotion,* which is what makes it all the worse."

Mr. Lunt refuses to place on the record the names of his favorite roles, the easiest, the hardest, or the most rewarding. (He dislikes putting anything at all on the record about his acting.) All his roles were hard. They all taught him something. He liked them all. In general, the comedy roles were the "toughest" assignments. "Anyone who says comedy isn't harder to act than tragedy doesn't know what he's talking about. Timing in comedy is so much more difficult. Waiting for the laughs. Not waiting for them when they don't come, which is even more important. And no emotional undercurrent to sustain the interest." The chief reason Mr. Lunt hates to expound on his technique is that, despite all his experience, he is "never overburdened with confidence at any time."

He acts "because it's fun—more fun than anything else I know." He loves to dress up, just as a child does. If rehearsals are his greatest joy, long runs are never tiresome to him. He is always learning new things about the part, playing to new audiences. He is never bored in the theater. He never has been bored.

Concerning the production of *The Visit*, Alfred Lunt had the following to say to the author of this book:

"The late Theresa Helburn of the Theatre Guild sent us *The Visit* in April, 1957. We thought it an extraordinary, a fascinating play; original, superb 'theater,' and important, but we turned it down as we needed a long rest and wished, for that reason, to make no commitments. But we urged Miss Helburn to buy it and by all means to put it on as quickly as possible. Two weeks later Roger Stevens telephoned us, said he had bought the play, and wanted us to do it. Again we declined for the same reason. We went to England in June, where the producer, Hugh Beaumont, offered us the play and this time we agreed, since rehearsals could not begin for five months—because of Peter Brook's busy schedule—and five months was exactly the length of the vacation we wanted.

"Miss Fontanne thought, moreover, that the script needed straightening out; she felt that there was something wrong with the translation since it had been done from German into French and then into English. Peter Brook, too, had many reservations about the script. Brook, Valency, and Duerrenmatt met in Paris and the reworking of the play began, to the delight of all.

"In rehearsal, we put ourselves in Peter Brook's hands entirely, and tried to do everything he asked. Although I myself have done a great deal of directing, that makes no difference in my relationship with a director. In fact, we both like being directed. We thought we worked slowly but it was Brook's opinion that we worked with 'lightning speed.' Actors, you see, are not the best judges of how they operate or even of what they do best, any more than an author or, say, a cook is. You may like to do certain parts better than others, because they come easier, just as authors may like to write novels rather than plays or cooks may prefer to prepare a ragout rather than a soufflé but that doesn't mean that the customers will like it better. Playing a part is like baking bread [according to Mr. Lunt, who is an expert cook]; the best cooks know when the dough has reached the right consistency, no cookbook can teach that. You can't teach timing, and you can't teach a person to be amusing. A young actor I knew who was supposed to get laughs never got them. I asked him, 'Are you afraid of criticism? Do you dislike being laughed at?' He said, 'That's the one thing that terrifies me.' He was afraid to get laughs even for the character he was playing.

"In studying a part, the first thing we do is learn our lines, which is agony, and we always perform within the pattern of the play. We try to act with truth, hoping the author and the audience will find our characters *real*, without trace of what some people call 'technique.' Around the 200th performance, we find we are getting nearer to our 'people.' We played *There Shall Be No Night* and *O Mistress Mine* sixteen hundred times and still found much to do. Movements and gestures must be in character, not like *us*. I built Anton Schill on a man in Genesee Depot, in looks, in clothes, in gestures. Miss Fontanne had many 'Claires' in mind, one in particular. You'd be surprised if you dig into the past what you will find—not always pleasant. We've never played roles like Anton and Claire before. Has anyone? They are not sympathetic parts. They are not really 'star' parts; this is an ensemble play from the actors' point of view, but they are fascinating roles to play, difficult as they are short.

"Many people find *The Visit* uncomfortable to watch and hear, repellent, unbearable. One lady in Cleveland wrote, 'Dear Mr. and Mrs. Lunt: I saw your play. It was well acted, as is always the case with you. But it made me quite ill and I am going straight to bed.' 'Why do you do it?' they ask us. We do it because of its terrible truth, its seriousness of purpose, its universality. These people make Claire the villain. She is not! I say, 'It is the townspeople who are the villains. You!' They say, 'No, it's not so; we are innately good, underneath.' That's an awful rationalization.

"On our cross-country tour, *The Visit* was given a remarkable reception. It may sound vain of me to say so, but when we played in Salt Lake City they stood up and cheered. If we could have stood one-night stands, we could have stayed out for years and years with this play. We were brought up in a theater where touring was part of your job. If you had a success in New York, you naturally took it out. The road is still very much alive and hungry for plays but the cost of touring—transportation, actors' salaries and so on—makes it prohibitive for a big production."

After thirty-six years of acting as a team, the longest in recent stage history, the Lunts were asked if they have any plans for retiring. "How can we retire," said Mr. Lunt. "We find the theater fascinating. We'll keep on as long as we have our health and strength."

"Just let us have one flop," said Miss Fontanne, "and the audiences will retire us."

DIRECTING *The Visit*
An Interview with Peter Brook

"Everyone may not like this play," says Peter Brook, "because it shows so vividly that people will do absolutely anything for money. It has a simple, direct story but it takes a certain amount of sophistication on the part of the audience to appreciate its cynicism." He feels that the play is written in epic and fabulous terms. It is interesting to note that the productions of the play done in Germany and France differ vastly from those done in England and America because of the different cultural and theatrical traditions in each country.

The German tradition places a particularly heavy emphasis on grim and grotesque comedy, ironic humor, and caricature; and these elements are easily identifiable in Duerrenmatt's play. The French tradition tends toward fantasy as *jeu d'esprit*, harlequinade, and eccentricity for stylistic enjoyment.

Brook's interpretation of the play differed from both the German and the French in that he was not trying for a detached alienation from the audience but wanted to tell the story in heightened human terms. He wanted the audience to feel that Claire Zachanassian and Anton Schill were two comprehensible human beings whose actions were real and motivated, and he could only achieve this effect by dramatizing their human traits.

The continental actresses who had undertaken the part invariably stressed Claire's grossness, coarseness, and physical disfigurement. Brook felt, however, that to portray Claire as a dazzling, impersonal beauty would be more vivid and effective and would cast a mythical aura about her, while Anton was to be presented with the utmost realism, since he was utterly a creature of the terrestrial plane. It worked out as planned; Lynn Fontanne had the cool impersonality of a goddess, while Alfred Lunt was torn by the conflicts in the common man.

In the strong feelings he has against the purely "theatrical" approach, Brook is anti-Brechtian; he believes that the interest of the audience is, and should be, caught by the imagination, and that the stimulation of the imagination is one of the great social and artistic functions performed by the theater. Teo Otto's scenery was exciting because it built up feeling by impressionistic means and demanded the creative cooperation of the audience. The Lunts, too, alone on a bare stage, just sitting on a bench, had a deeper and more intimate relationship than they would have had if they had been surrounded by a clutter of scenery.

Brook tried to bring out the subtle mood of each scene and so he minimized the broadly stylized and exaggerated elements in the original script. Out and out expressionism, he felt, would have had very little meaning for Anglo-Saxon audiences.

Peter Brook came to direct *The Visit* by a series of international arrangements. He was working on *Cat on a Hot Tin Roof* at the Théâtre Antoine in Paris, when he learned that a play called *The Visit* by a new Swiss dramatist was being presented at the Théâtre Marigny. He stopped in to see it, was impressed enough to read it in French, and then learned that Maurice Valency had done a version in English. Shortly afterwards, in London, Brook had a discussion with Roger Stevens, who owned the American production rights to the play, and both agreed that if the play were to be done, the Lunts would have to do it; but Stevens had already offered the play to them and they had turned it down. Later, while Brook was on tour in Belgrade, with his production of *Titus Andronicus*, Hugh Beaumont informed him that the Lunts had agreed to do the play. Brook returned from Belgrade, Valency came on from New York, and Duerrenmatt from Switzerland, and the three men met in Paris. There they worked on the script together, retranslating and rewriting. Alfred Lunt turned up at one of these meetings and immediately began to talk about his costumes; he said that Lynn Fontanne, too, had begun to think of her gowns and had decided that she wanted Castillo, whose studio is in Paris, to design them. Brook was delighted, since it is his feeling that the better the actor the more thought he gives to his stage-clothes.

Brook then went to Switzerland with Duerrenmatt to continue work on the play. The dramatist suggested that Teo Otto, who had provided the scenery for the original production, be engaged for the English version. Brook was disconcerted; he had always begun a play with his own pictorial "vibration"—a visual solution which came to him in the form of a definite image; *Titus Andronicus*, for example, evoked a barbaric décor in which architectural columns served as trees. It was for that reason that he had reservations about Otto; he did not think that he could work with someone else's designs. He began to brood about the problem. One day he noticed four sketches for stage settings which had been framed and hung on the walls in Duerrenmatt's home, and he became terribly excited by them. When he learned that they were the work of Teo Otto, Brook immediately agreed that this artist was the man to design *The Visit*.

Working with Otto was a pleasure, Brook discovered, because, being more highly creative than imaginative, Otto was extremely amenable to suggestions. When Brook proposed that certain of the details in his designs be altered, Otto promptly consented. It was not necessary, Brook felt, to have men masquerade as trees; the Lunts and a simple wooden bench were sufficient to transform a bare stage into a forest. Brook believes that all forms of theater are related to specific social and cultural conditions, and that one change in a production determines many others. In the last scene of the play as it was done in Switzerland a gilded, rococo proscenium, with a scarlet front-curtain, was dropped in from the "flies," and the murder of Anton Schill took place behind the curtain; this scene provided a great contrast to the style of the rest of the production, but its intention was to give an unreal and "theatrical" quality to the brutal act. Hugh Beaumont objected to the set because, although it suggested the stage of a local municipal theater which is a familiar sight to all European playgoers, it would mean nothing to English and American audiences. It occurred to Brook that a Gothic hall with hanging lamps in a dark and somber mood would be more appropriate for the scene, and that is the set that Otto provided, with such skill that many critics singled it out for special praise.

Rehearsals of *The Visit* were held at the Lyric Theater in the West End, London. At the first rehearsal, Brook usually delivers a long talk so that the actors will have some idea about the play, the sets, and the costumes. Then the actors read the script aloud; Brook never reads to the actors because he considers it boring. In France it is regarded as revolutionary to allow the actors to read, but Brook observes the practice even in that country. He believes that reading serves no purpose but a social one for the first meeting, since it is a way of breaking the ice for the members of the company who are to work together.

"My method of directing is like painting a picture in oils," says Brook. "First I make a large free sketch, then I put in more and more details, but I keep changing and adding throughout the rehearsal period. I give the actors rough positions but each day I make changes until exactly the right places are found. Old-school actors want the very thing that should be most insulting to them, that is, to be told what to do, when to do it, and where to do it." An actor often asks a direct question but instead of replying Brook works with him in rehearsals and it is sometimes three weeks later that the question will be answered. The director considers this sort of cooperative creation the only way that he can work. It results in choreographic patterns without endless planning in advance. Brook makes very few notes and preserves nothing on paper. Even the crowd scenes are worked out slowly and experimentally to get richness and complexity. In Duerrenmatt's original script, the townsmen echo every line that Lunt speaks at the railroad station. This did not seem to play properly and Brook wanted to change it; he tried many variations until it finally occurred to him to have all the men suddenly speak in chorus at one point, then have one speak alone, and at another time allow them all to remain silent, and this gave him the variety and effect that he wanted.

"If you plan too precisely in advance," says Brook, "you get parental, possessive, and proprietary; if you don't plan, you don't mind scrapping what you've done. The danger in the latter technique, however, is that in continually revising you sometimes scrap something that is excellent and ought to be retained. The Lunts were able to hold me down. They would say, 'You've done something good, let's save it.' Lynn has great stability; Alfred is mercurial. In Stratford, we introduced a completely new version of the play with much less text and more action; Lynn went on trembling, but came off convinced that the new version was better than the old."

In the original play, the schoolteacher is depicted as a weak man who suddenly comes to the forefront of those who denounce Schill at the public trial. Duerrenmatt did not hesitate to exaggerate or to use unmotivated reversals of character, but Brook thought that it would be more effective to show the teacher breaking down slowly rather than changing suddenly. Brook tried several approaches; in England, the teacher's final speech was a total denunciation, but in New York it was the expression of a man without moral courage who finally did not dare to act upon his convictions. Duerrenmatt had also put a heavy layer of farce and "cabaret" humor over his serious play, and these had to be removed along with many grotesque elements. The author, for instance, had conceived of Claire as a spitting, biting, ugly, and hard old witch, but that did not accord with either the director's or the American actress's conception. Lynn Fontanne played her twenty percent witch, eighty percent other qualities: success in life, attractive to men, and so on. "Lynn thinks Claire is mad," says Brook, "so in order to give her some 'balance' she added the attributes of tenderness, grace, and style." It was Duerrenmatt's idea that the part of the pastor ought to be played by a physically heavy man who had a worldly heartiness; Brook adopted the suggestion and a big, genial man created the role in England, but it did not work. "In New York," says Brook, "I used William Hansen, who is short and slight, quiet and serious, and whose performance was remarkable for its understanding."

The most difficult act to direct, Brook found, was Act II. Act I was sheer story-telling; and Act III simply had to be trimmed so that it would move more quickly and more starkly to its conclusion. In Act II, however, Schill starts out by being self-satisfied and ends up by being submissive and it is necessary to show this slow and subtle development; but many of the scenes in this act are repetitious and all are in the same tone and are predictable. There were, in addition, too many scenes on the balcony of the hotel that added nothing to the play. What was to be done? Maurice Valency wrote a big scene for the Lunts in order to bring the principals on, but the scene was finally discarded. Another scene was added in which Claire visited a tailor and ordered her funeral clothes; the scene ended with a monologue specially written by Duerrenmatt. That too was dropped. The problem was solved mainly by judicious cutting. The scene in which Claire stands on the balcony and confronts Anton as he levels a gun at her was an inspiration; somehow Lynn Fontanne was impelled to point her finger at Alfred Lunt at the very moment that he was pointing the gun at her. This simultaneous action is followed by Claire's long speech during which Anton is called upon to react in silence. Lunt found this particularly exciting because he enjoys communicating ideas in pantomime. Brooks Atkinson has called Alfred Lunt "the master of wordless eloquence."

"Directing Lunt is a revelation," says Brook. "You can't imagine the countless tiny details that Alfred puts into a performance. This may sound like finicky acting but these painstaking details make up an enormous conception. It is like one of Seurat's pointillist paintings. Each little dot is not art, but the whole is magnificent. Alfred and Lynn start by getting a broad outline of what they're going to do and then they fill in the details. It's absolutely like somebody making a mosaic. They work endlessly from one detail to the next—fine, fine points—one after another. They're deep and flexible people and they have lightning speed and great artistic glory."

Peter Brook called on his stage manager, Mary Lynn, to help select English actors for the New York production because he did not want two different speech patterns in the same play, but when he heard the entire cast speaking in English accents he felt that it was wrong and suggested that they all adopt a slightly American accent.

"It is important for every aspiring stage director to possess several special attributes," says Peter Brook; "prominent among them are imagination, patience, and the ability to deal with seemingly infinite details."

Stage Managing *The Visit*
An Interview with Mary Lynn

The job of the stage manager is the most complex of all those connected with a theatrical presentation. It entails intensive and detailed work before and during the production. Functioning primarily as a coordinator, the stage manager must see that the various elements of the production are properly organized and integrated; he works closely, therefore, with the artists—author, actors, director; with the technicians—property, electrical, and carpentry departments; and with the producer's office—accounting, legal, and publicity divisions.

Mary Lynn, one of the few women to hold the position of professional stage manager, has had a varied career in the theater. She began as a dancer in the celebrated revues of André Charlot and remained with his company for two and a half years. She then joined Ivor Novello, the star and producer of elaborate operettas, and for four years at the Drury Lane Theater served as ballet mistress and organizer of the road companies of the plays that were sent on tour. In about 1939, Miss Lynn became connected with the H. M. Tennent producing organization, one of the most important in London, in the dual capacities of ballet mistress and second assistant stage manager. She rose to the position of first assistant stage manager, a post she also held for John Gielgud's productions of *Macbeth, Love for Love,* and *Hamlet.* For the last five years, she has not only been a full-fledged stage manager but a company manager as well, which means that she concerns herself with the business end of the production.

"Long before the opening of the play," says Miss Lynn, "the stage manager sends out calls for the audition of actors, takes charge of the readings, and books the halls for the rehearsals." On the first day of rehearsal, she arranges the chairs in a semicircle on the stage for the actors and sets up a table and chair facing them for the director. She introduces the actors to each other and holds a copy of the script as they read through the play. She attends all readings and rehearsals and makes a note of everything needed for the production; this includes all line changes, positions and movements of actors, light and sound cues, and any other special notes given by the director. At the end of each rehearsal, she finds out from the director which actors he will want to see the following day and when and where they will meet.

In England, a small model of the set is made for every production and the ground plan is painted to scale on a cloth which is put on the stage floor during rehearsals for the guidance of the actors; it is the stage manager's duty to attend to both the model and the cloth.

Because *The Visit* was played on a practically bare stage, the properties were not only numerous but were extremely important; Miss Lynn had a complete list of the properties needed for the play and checked them at every rehearsal and performance. During the rehearsals in England, every property was used from the very first day, since benches, ladders, and streamers, as well as many other items, had to be handled with extreme precision. In this play, the actors themselves brought on and removed the various properties and pieces of furniture needed for each scene. That meant that the movement of the actors had to be organized; but "since actors are notoriously careless," says Miss Lynn, "they had to be drilled like soldiers so that they would enter and exit precisely on cue." Because of the union rules in New York, actors are not permitted to handle actual props during the rehearsal period; Miss Lynn conceived the idea of making rehearsal props out of newspaper and cardboard. Many products used on the stage, including foods and beverages, are supplied by the manufacturer in exchange for program credit, but most properties are rented or bought; large and expensive items which can serve for many productions are even bought on the installment plan. It is the job of the stage manager to secure the needed properties in good time.

When the director is absent, the stage manager is in charge of rehearsals, and it is always his special job to rehearse the understudies. Miss Lynn takes this task seriously and makes sure that the understudies are letter perfect before opening night. On two occasions involving productions with which she was connected, the stars were absent during the very first week but the understudies stepped in without any difficulty.

The final week of rehearsal is the most difficult one for the stage manager for then he must prepare all the "plots"—the costume, property, lighting, sound, and music cues. The complete script of the play including all of these cues must be ready at this time. And it is then that the stage manager works most closely with the property master and the chief carpenter.

The Visit had about fifty-six light cues and forty-eight sound cues. "All stage managers should know something about music, should have a sense of rhythm and timing," Miss Lynn believes, "because all plays contain many sound cues, and it may even be necessary to raise or lower the curtain on a certain bar of music." For the English production, the sounds were supplied by records and a panatrope machine, but in New York the sound was put on tape. Peter Brook wanted the growling panther to sound authentic, and Miss Lynn tried several experiments. She is able to make a snarling sound and she put this noise on record; then she enlisted the two Siamese cats owned by the New York stage manager, Fritz de Wilde, when she noticed that these animals made a rumbling growl when they were hungry. The two sounds—Miss Lynn's snarl and the cats' growl—recorded together gave the impression of an angry jungle beast. Then Miss Lynn went to the Boston Zoo and recorded the growling of a real panther; both tapes were played for Peter Brook who, without knowing the source of either, selected the one featuring Miss Lynn and the two cats, and that was used for the play.

The original opening of the play in Brighton, England, fell on a Tuesday night Dress rehearsals were held on the previous Saturday night and all day Sunday to perfect the lighting. Two dress rehearsals were held on Monday and one on Tuesday. In addition to her regular dressing room, Lynn Fontanne had a portable dressing room just off-stage in the wings, where she made several quick changes. The stage manager allots dressing rooms to the members of the cast and sees that the house staff keeps them clean. The theater in Dublin did not have adequate dressing room space so Alfred Lunt was forced to use a little closet which did not even have a sink in it.

During the run of the play, the stage manager is in complete charge of the show. Since he has the final responsibility for the smooth running of the performance, he must check every item involved, from the personal props of the stars to the furniture markings on the stage. He makes sure that everything is shipshape before he takes up his post at the switchboard. One evening Lynn Fontanne sat beside Mary Lynn at the switchboard, watching the stage manager marshal her forces before the curtain went up, and said, "I wouldn't have your job for anything." "Miss Fontanne," says Miss Lynn, "was always completely relaxed and ready to go on. She has a superstition which she calls her Green Umbrella. When she has fixed on the right thing to do, she says she has "found her green umbrella."

Since the stage manager works more closely with the director than with anyone else connected with the production, Mary Lynn had ample opportunity to observe closely the methods of Peter Brook and to develop a great admiration for him. According to Miss Lynn, Brook is especially adept at casting a play. He never selects an actor primarily on the basis of "type" or looks, but on the affinity of the actor's character for the role.

On the first day of rehearsal, the company got together in the morning and began to read the play; they sat around a table and Brook interrupted the reading to talk about the theme of the work, the town in which the action takes place, and what the people are like. After a break for lunch, the reading continued until the play was completed. On the second day the actors were on their feet; Brook does not believe in long discussion sessions. He starts at the beginning of the script and blocks it out, scene by scene, straight through to the end. He is very soft-spoken, and uses his hands a great deal while he speaks to give the actors the mood and meaning of each scene; he often communicates more clearly with his hands than he does with words. Although he adopts many suggestions made by the actors, producers, or writer, he knows what he wants and will not budge an inch when he feels that he is right. Many evening rehearsals were held in the ballet room under the stage at the Drury Lane Theater. After Brook had roughly blocked out the play from beginning to end, he broke it down into individual scenes and worked separately with the actors involved. The rehearsals went on for a month before the opening, but after the opening Brook kept changing and perfecting the play; then he went away for a fortnight and came back to take a fresh look at it.

Because his style of directing is basically improvisational, Brook continues to make changes as new thoughts and insights strike him. This often drives the actors mad but they go along with him because they realize that the changes are usually for the better. In the English production, the small set-pieces of scenery were backed by a velvet drop and there were three returns (drops serving as wings) on each side of the stage. All of these curtains were covered with multicolored paint in bright colors such as orange and green; when Brook arrived in America he had an inspiration concerning the curtains. In Boston, where the play was trying out before its New York opening, Brook suddenly decided to have the curtains sprayed with a thin coating of black paint so that all the colors would be toned down and muted which not only gave them a sad, old, and poverty-stricken look but also made the brilliant costumes of Lynn Fontanne stand out against them in striking contrast. In the same way Brook thought spontaneously of individualizing the properties and costumes of the men who sat around the railroad station in Güllen; one was to be smoking an old German pipe, another was to wear worn and raveling mittens, and so on.

Seven members of the English cast went with the Lunts to America where innumerable alterations were made in both the play and the characterizations. In the English version, for instance, Peter Woodthorpe, who is only in his twenties, was made up as an old man for the role of the Schoolteacher; he shaved off part of his own hair, donned a gray wig, and behaved in a patriarchal manner. Brook had one of his flashes of intuition and when the play went into rehearsal in New York, Woodthorpe emerged as a young, energetic, and passionate figure, whose confrontation of Claire Zachanassian and stubbornness in resisting the arguments of the other townspeople were perfect expressions of the intransigence of youth, and took audiences by storm.

After the New York cast had been selected, Brook worked with the company for a week in the little theater atop the New Amsterdam in Forty-second Street. There were about twenty-seven new people involved and Brook continued his practice of reworking and reshaping the play both in structure and in dialogue as he went along. A scene in which the Schill family went for a drive originally followed a family scene in the grocery store; the automobile was created by simply turning the shop counter around and pulling out two drawers, which served as the front seats of the car. These were occupied by the son and the daughter, while Anton and his wife stood behind them. Brook then decided to do away with the car scene so the grocery counter was removed along with the shelves; the family went off-stage to where the car was parked and Anton was left to walk into the forest alone; a few lines of dialogue were cut and the scenes flowed smoothly together.

Even the Lunts made constant changes in their roles always seeking improvements. Lynn Fontanne's scenes involving the panther were tried in many ways; in one of them the blind men were beaten; in another, when it was announced that the animal had been killed, Miss Fontanne cried like a panther; and in still another, she stated proudly that the panther had originally been ferocious, had killed more than two hundred men, but she had tamed him and slept with him. All of these "bits," which were tried out at one time or another, were eventually omitted.

The scene at the railroad station, during which Anton Schill attempts to run away, had fewer men threatening him as it was played in England and yet the effect was quite terrifying; in New York, more actors were added but their threats were psychological rather than physical and Alfred Lunt consequently reacted differently; he added the retching and vomiting which he had not done in England. In the strangling scene, as performed in England, however, he not only thrashed his feet about but also made unearthly gurgling sounds in his throat; while in America, he used only the beating of the feet. To express his fear of death Lunt uttered the words, "Oh, God . . . oh, God!" with great depth and fervency, and once told Miss Lynn that he remembered hearing his mother utter those words in just that way as she lay dying.

During the play's first week of tryout in Brighton, England, at the Saturday matinee, while Lunt was gurgling and kicking his feet as he was being strangled, an elderly woman sitting in the orchestra made a gurgling noise in her throat and people sitting near her thought she was snoring; when the house emptied out at the end of the play, the woman continued to sit in her seat and it was found that she was dead. The manager of the Theater Royal knew the woman, as she had attended the Saturday matinee regularly for many years, and during the intermission of The Visit she had gone up to him and told him how much she was enjoying the play; it was his unpleasant duty to notify her relatives and then have a coffin brought round to the front of the house so that her body could be removed to a chapel. In the very same week, Miss Lynn recalled, a man in the audience had suffered a heart attack during the performance. These occurrences had a demoralizing effect upon some of the members of the company; the assistant stage manager almost had a nervous breakdown because of the "wickedness" of the play, and a female member of the cast announced, "This is an evil play; it will never get to London." It seemed for a time as if that prediction would come true, for after its tour of the provinces, *The Visit* went to New York.

SCENERY FOR *The Visit*
An Interview with Teo Otto

As chief designer for the Schauspielhaus in Zurich, Teo Otto has provided the scenery for all of Duerrenmatt's plays, and from the very beginning has had the greatest respect for the playwright not only as an artist but as an exceptionally skillful technician. Otto had many discussions with Duerrenmatt concerning the treatment of the sets for *The Visit* while the play was still in the process of being written. These preliminary talks were of considerable importance to the designer, as they enabled him to create the locale and mood of the play in accordance with the author's basic concept. During the discussions, Otto made innumerable sketches; he likes to sketch while the author or director is talking so that he can get an immediate reaction to his ideas. If he is told, "No, not this . . . That's more like it!" he can proceed with greater assurance.

When Duerrenmatt had completed the play he turned a copy over to Otto who read it very carefully four or five times. The designer made a new set of sketches and then met with the author and the director (Oskar Wälterlin, who mounted the original production at the Schauspielhaus); during the talk that followed, Otto continued to revise his work. It is interesting to note that Teo Otto performs as a designer in the identical way that Peter Brook does as a director: neither has any fixed ideas about a production, nor any hesitation about altering his work completely or in part, and both are able to improvise with the greatest freedom and speed. About seven different sets are required for *The Visit*. When Otto arrived at his final sketches, he prepared them in gouache, pencil, crayon, and tempera, the mediums in which he generally works.'

At the Schauspielhaus, the sets are built in the theater's own workshop, and Otto supervises the construction and the painting. If a set contains elements that are particularly difficult, complex, or tricky, Otto himself builds and paints them as he is an expert craftsman and technician. He has also built and "touched up" scenery of his own design for productions done outside the Schauspielhaus.

The Visit required special rehearsals for the handling of the scenery and the lighting. Otto himself lighted the play with the help of a technical assistant and the advice and approval of the director. But even after the opening of the play, changes that were felt to be necessary were made in both sets and lights; this is almost never done in America because of prohibitive costs. The scenery for the Berlin production was identical to that used in Zurich, but for the Munich production the designer made a number of minor alterations in accordance with the director in that city. Otto also advised the director of the Habima Theater, Tel Aviv, Israel, where a production of *The Visit* was done in the fall of 1959.

When the play was bought for production in England and America, Peter Brook entered the picture as the director and brought with him many definite ideas for revising the scenery. Brook wanted the sets to be the essence of simplicity; he thought that the changes in the town, showing its rise from abject poverty to comparative wealth, ought to be depicted more gradually. He insisted upon the removal of most of the fantastic, grotesque, and symbolic elements from the scenery; the men who represented trees were eliminated, as were the counter and chairs which symbolized the family automobile. The evolution of the automobile was interesting; at first a real automobile was used on stage, then a counter that swung around so that its drawers could be used as seats replaced the actual car, after that four chairs were tried in place of the counter, and finally all actual properties were eliminated and the car was said to be off-stage.

A major change was made in the strangling scene at the end of the play; originally, in the meeting-hall in which this scene takes place, there was a little theater proscenium with a red curtain draped in it; this type of proscenium is an imitation of those used in the local municipal theaters on the Continent. Brook felt that since the theaters and meeting-halls in England and America had no such ornate prosceniums, the locale would not be recognized, so Teo Otto submitted sketches of several other possible settings for this scene. Brook thought at first that it would be interesting to set the action in a tent; then he asked for a meeting-hall in Gothic style, with three double hanging lamps which would produce a dim and melancholy effect. The lamps were to give the impression that they were illuminated by gas, and were to be pulled down from the ceiling to be lighted.

As the play was done in Zurich, the final scene showed Güllen entirely reconstructed (with Zachanassian's tainted money, of course), but Brook objected to the fact that there were too many structures on the stage and that they appeared to be too new. He asked that the town be shown instead in the process of being rebuilt, and so there was red scaffolding visible. Otto agreed that this was a much more poetic conception than the one originally used. He also preferred the way the opening scene was done in the English and American version; it was superior to the original, he thought, because it better expressed the basic idea of the play. In the Swiss version of the play, the railroad station was painted white and was decorated with many travel posters, but in the English version the curtain rose on buildings that were old and dilapidated, and no posters were in sight since the people could not afford to go anywhere.

Teo Otto is of the opinion that *The Visit* should not be presented in the most extreme form of expressionism or surrealism, but that the style most suitable for the play is symbolic realism. As an example of what he meant, he described the way in which he created the hotel in Güllen: a signboard reading "The Golden Apostle" was suspended over a set-piece, executed with the most realistic detail, showing a French window with a little balcony in front of it, about five or six feet above stage level; sign and set-piece, nothing more, evoked the entire hotel.

"Millions of dollars are being spent on the building of new theaters," says Teo Otto, "in which unheard-of sums of money are invested in mechanical and electrical equipment to lift, turn, and push tons of scenery and to flood the stage with cascades of light; but the financiers, architects, and engineers are overlooking the most important elements in the theater—the actors, the audience, and the play itself. The modern play requires concentration, intimacy, and subtlety; the actor's few square feet of body surface are lost on a gigantic stage, and the audience feels alienated in a huge auditorium.

"The scenic designer, who must do the practical job of creating the world— and sometimes heaven and hell—in which the drama takes place, knows that, except when he is mounting a big and empty musical spectacle, he must make every effort to reduce the size of the stage in order to bring the actor closer to the area of the audience; otherwise, the artistic climax—which is the response of audience to actor—is impossible. It is for that reason that serious plays are usually more effective when produced in little theaters, and that arena staging has become so popular in recent times.

"The bare boards of a stage have an overwhelming fascination in themselves and that is where the actors carry out their constantly changing process of gestures and movements which are the basis of theatrical art; the inexhaustible geometry of the scenic backgrounds is merely accessory to the creation of an artistic experience. I am thinking of the bench on an empty stage in New York on which Alfred Lunt and Lynn Fontanne, in *The Visit*, played the overwhelming love scene in the forest, and solely by their acting created the forest, the foliage, the deer, and the bird calls. That is scene design at its best."

Of the innumerable productions that Teo Otto has designed in his thirty years in the professional theater, two are his special favorites: Brecht's *Mother Courage* and Duerrenmatt's *The Visit;* the reason for his preference is that when he had completed his work on these plays he felt that he could not improve upon what he had done in any way.

COSTUMES FOR LYNN FONTANNE
An Interview with Antonio del Castillo

Antonio Canovas del Castillo, of the house of Lanvin-Castillo, Paris, created Lynn Fontanne's costumes for *The Visit*. Because of his experience as the designer for some of the wealthiest women in international society, Castillo was especially suited to do the costumes for Claire Zachnassian, "the richest woman in the world." The play impressed the designer as being "modern Shake-speare . . . bloody," but he thought it would be "great fun to do" because it allowed him imaginative scope with "its capes, its veils, and even a wedding dress."

After reading the script, Castillo invited Alfred Lunt, Lynn Fontanne, and Peter Brook tŏ dinner at his flat in Paris, and during the evening the play was discussed in minute detail. It was decided that Lynn Fontanne was to have six gowns: a traveling costume for her first entrance, an evening gown for the restaurant scene at the end of Act I, a hostess gown for the balcony scenes in the second act, a wedding gown for the barn scene, a peasant dress for the forest scene in the third act, and widow's weeds for her final scene and exit. One particular accessory, which, in addition to being decorative, was symbolic of Claire's wealth and power, was to be worn throughout the play regardless of the costume; that was an elaborate pearl necklace, its design suggested to Castillo by a famous old piece of jewelry which had formerly belonged to the Queen of France.

Peter Brook suggested that it would be interesting if the peasant dress for the third act were done in genuine Hungarian style, full of gold thread and decorative embroidery. Castillo objected; the "peasant" costumes he has been making for rich women for years are always the last word in simplicity. This was the keynote adopted by Castillo as the basis for all of Miss Fontanne's clothes; the designer started by asking himself, "What sort of clothes would a woman as rich as Claire Zachanassian order if she were going on such a trip?" Castillo then made preliminary sketches of the gowns; it is interesting to note that in all of these original drawings the skirts are so long that the hems touch the floor. The designer explained that he was attempting to conceal the wooden leg that this character had in the original version of the play, but after Peter Brook changed his conception of Claire and decided that she was to be as attractive as possible, all mention of the wooden leg was removed from the script and the gowns were altered to various lengths. The peasant dress was shortest, the dresses for arrival and departure were of street length, the evening, hostess, and wedding gowns were long.

Castillo draped materials in various colors and textures on Miss Fontanne before a final selection was made. The actress's measurements were taken, and the first patterns were turned out in muslin. Miss Fontanne had only two fittings; then the gowns were made in the final fabrics. The designer and his assistants went to London twice to complete the fittings and to attend early rehearsals of the play. Castillo was particularly concerned about a difficult change from street dress to evening gown in the first act; he was convinced, however, that the gowns worked very well. And he came away speaking in glowing terms of the actress. "She is wonderful to work with," said Castillo, "very easygoing and extremely clever, but most important of all, she carries herself magnificently, with tremendous awareness, and has a sense of real elegance." Castillo added, "One reason why Miss Fontanne's clothes look so effective on stage is that she takes such good care of them; she wears and handles them with tenderness, and she even wraps her gloves in cellophane between performances."

When creating costumes for a play, Castillo always works very closely with the scene designer; *The Visit* provided an unusual experience as he did not see the scenery until long after the play's opening. In their preliminary talks, Brook described the sets in detail, but the principle that guided Castillo in his designs was that Miss Fontanne had to be seen in contrast to everyone else on stage at all times. Throughout, the natives of Güllen were plainly dressed while Claire appeared in rich attire; they were drab and she was bright. In the last act, however, the contrast was reversed when all the townspeople turned out in gay clothing, their Sunday best, and Claire Zachanassian moved among them in funereal black.

Although it did not take Castillo very long either to create or to complete the costumes, the quality of the materials and the workmanship brought their cost to between six hundred and one thousand dollars apiece.

For her first appearance in the play, Miss Fontanne was dressed in a single shade of red. With a red woolen dress and cape, she wore a red felt cloche hat, a long red chiffon scarf, red shoes, and carried a red umbrella. Her red hair was streaked with white and her make-up was extremely pale. The panels affixed to the shoulders of the dress appeared to be "wings" but were described by Castillo as "three large petals." The actress carried no handbag with this outfit, since a woman of Claire's wealth and position would be presumed to travel with attendants who paid the bills, carried the keys, and so on. Claire did carry a cane, not because of any obvious infirmity but rather as a symbol of authority.

Because of the demands of the action of the play, Miss Fontanne had to change from the red dress into her most elaborate evening costume for the restaurant scene in just twenty-two seconds. This change was made in the portable dressing room just off-stage in the wings, and in darkness. The red hat had a large button at the back which a dresser could undo in a second; the hat then opened out like a belt and came off easily without disturbing the actress's hairdo. The red dress was zipped off; Miss Fontanne stepped into the gown, put her hands through the armholes, the gown was zipped up the back—and the change was made. The long gown was of apricot velvet with matching apricot gloves. The dress appeared to be extremely complicated because the entire bodice was embroidered in pearls and rubies, and pendants of pearls fell from the shoulder straps, but these jewels were actually attached to the gown and though they gave an extremely elaborate effect they did not require separate handling; the basic idea behind the design was ease of management for the quick change. With this costume Miss Fontanne wore dangling earrings of rubies and pearls.

The yellow hostess gown worn in the balcony scenes in the second act, was, from the point of view of materials and workmanship, the most intricate and expensive of the six dresses created by Castillo. It was made of cloth of silver and gold and of brocaded satin of a very unusual pattern. Miss Fontanne hesitated to approve it because of the price, but Peter Brook thought it was worth it because of the effect it would create. When Alfred Lunt saw the gown, he said jokingly to Castillo: "What have you done to me? If she is dressed so beautifully during that scene, no one will look at or listen to *me*."

The wedding gown was of white satin moiré, brocaded with water lilies to make the fabric heavier and richer. The veil, topped by a coronet of white flowers and pearls, was fastened under the chin and formed a free floating panel behind, and billows of veiling were draped carefully around the actress before each performance. A macabre note in this scene was that the bride smoked a cigar and sent up clouds of smoke that mingled with and seemed to augment the veiling. She wore, of course, the ubiquitous pearl necklace. As Miss Fontanne sat in the sedan-chair, waiting for the curtain to go up and the performance to begin, other members of the company would stand around and talk to her, always at a distance so as not to disarrange her gown.

The colors in the peasant dress were mainly brown, black, and white, and were meant to be slightly reminiscent of those worn by the peasants in Castillo's native Spain; but the designer made sure that the dress would give the impression of wealth rather than of poverty by combining several rich materials: brown wool, black velvet, and a blouse of white organza. Black vertical stripes in the bodice enhanced Miss Fontanne's slim, young look. At first it was thought that for this scene the actress should wear her hair loose or in braids over her shoulders, but that seemed too coy; instead, the hair was swept up from her ears in a very attractive arrangement. Castillo pointed out that the red wig worn by Miss Fontanne in this production was specially made for her in London; it was a beautiful creation whose three-part construction assured that it would fit perfectly, and its luxuriant hair could be dressed like one's own.

The black dress worn in the final scenes was done in a heavy silk known as widow's crepe; the ensemble was completed by black shoes and a black circular hat. The hat was covered by a black veil that fell to the waist in front and below the skirt in back. "Miss Fontanne thought the hat so becoming," said Castillo, "that she ordered one for her personal use in private life for street wear." The identical pattern was used for the red dress at the beginning and the black dress at the end of the play, except that the cape was omitted from the latter.

"The gowns were made in Paris and sent to Brighton, England, for the opening," said Castillo, "but I could not attend the opening, unfortunately, because I was ill at the time. Several months later, I went to New York and saw the play for the first time in a rehearsal hall on the roof of the New Amsterdam Theater. The company went through the action without scenery or adequate lighting, but I felt that the costumes were what I had planned. Later, when I saw the play in its own theater under proper conditions, I was satisfied that the costumes were right."

After the New York opening, *Vogue* Magazine published photographs of Miss Fontanne's costumes, and Castillo's creations caused a great stir in the world of high fashion.

CREATING THE ROLE OF CLAIRE
An Interview with Therese Giehse

Therese Giehse, one of the stars of the Zurich Schauspielhaus and Friedrich Duerrenmatt's favorite actress, feels that Claire Zachanassian—a role she was the first to create—is one of the most important characters in modern dramatic literature. She is great because, her evil growing out of her love, she is inexplicably complex; in this sense, she is a genuine Medea-figure. Everything she does —buying and selling, changing and molding the world and its people—stems from her frustrated and perverted love. Like a fallen angel, Claire tries to debase other people and drag the whole world down into her own private hell.

Miss Giehse felt that the best way to communicate the basic meaning of the play was to avoid all naturalistic effects, even in costume and make-up. In the opening scene, the actress entered in a flaming wig, a little black hat, and a black silk dress of very modern design; she wore eight long strings of pearls and a great deal of costume jewelry. Although the black dress was entirely inappropriate for the forest scenes, it served as the basic costume throughout the play and became a symbol of the woman's social status and inherent evil. For the balcony scenes, the actress wore a morning gown of black and white silk and lace, the black reminding the audience of the basic dress and the white foreshadowing the wedding gown to come. The wedding gown was made of silk, lace, and tulle, the pure whiteness and design of which suggested absolute virginity. For the final scenes, the actress reverted to the original black dress and its accessories.

Miss Giehse believes that Claire Zachanassian must be so made up as to suggest at once to the audience that here is an old woman who is trying desperately to be young; if she cannot recapture her youth, she will create the illusion of it with the aid of cosmetic art. "Make-up," said Miss Giehse, "must never be a mask that completely conceals the actor's own face; it must so be applied that it always remains plastic and transparent. The actor's face must be free to take on or to drop years, and to reflect feelings and emotions in their most subtle variations."

Claire Zachanassian should be played as if she were ice cold, but under her frigid façade there must be all the possibilities of human temperament, including flaming passion; it is as if she were a demon on a leash. Claire should also be played as *nouveau riche,* with a slight affectation and coarseness (the result of her sordid experiences) showing through her "refinement." This should be done delicately, however, not crudely, merely suggesting that her refinement was achieved by hard work.

Another example of a subtle reaction that Miss Giehse considered extremely important and tried to express occurred when Claire returned to Güllen and saw Anton for the first time in many years. Although this wronged woman had been harboring hate for her former lover for a lifetime, she was shocked when she set eyes on the harmless old man she had come back to destroy and for a moment she weakened—but it was only for a moment. This "shock" was felt by the actress, if not overtly expressed, but she hoped that it would communicate itself to the audience.

Originally, at the end of the play, when Anton lay dead at her feet, Claire knelt beside him and addressed him. Later, after his coffin had been carried out, Claire, seated in her sedan chair, was brought down to the very front of the stage. She turned to the audience and spoke six or eight lines of verse which summed up the meaning of the play and were related to the final chorus. The verses opened with the line, "Not with love but with hate I came here," and ended with, "Not with hate but with love I am here." These lines were intended to give the play both a political and psychological significance and, written in a very formal style, also added an antique flavor. The verses were spoken in Munich, but not in Zurich; then they were cut out altogether, and do not appear in the published version.

Miss Giehse declares that she has very strong ideas about the characters she portrays and is usually quite stubborn in upholding her point of view, but during this production she worked very closely with the author and the director (Oskar Wälterlin) and achieved a perfect accord. The role of Claire was discussed and developed step by step and the completely realized character was the result of ensemble thinking and perfect harmony.

"The most uninteresting sort of character for an actress to portray," said Miss Giehse, "is one who is completely good or completely bad. Much greater skill is required to create a complex figure who, like a real human being, combines both good and evil impulses in strange and unpredictable constellations." Miss Giehse admits that she enjoys playing characters who are predominantly evil "because in real life we must always be so proper and correct that it is a relief to be allowed to give vent to some of our darker instincts on stage." It is not hard for an actor to identify himself with an evil character, or with a saintly one, for that matter, because in all of us there is the "possibility" of performing the most extreme sorts of action, whether demonic or angelic. Miss Giehse used the word "possibility" very often and seemed to be echoing Duerrenmatt, who over and over again speaks of "möglichkeit"—the unforeseen and unknown potentialities in human character and human relationships—which amounts to a kind of fatalism.

Apropos of "black" and "white" characters, Miss Giehse mentioned "black" and "white" situations in what she called "political plays." These didactic works are poor, she believes, because they resemble nothing in the real world; they merely express a kind of "wish fulfillment" on the part of their authors. The actress excluded Friedrich Duerrenmatt from the category of writers of problem plays because his work, though pessimistic, is probing and profound; like the great dramatic writers of the past, he is a contemplative man whose dramatic creations throw a penetrating light on human nature and human affairs.

CLAIRE ZACHANASSIAN IN NORWAY
An Interview with Lillebil Ibsen

Lillebil Ibsen, one of Norway's leading actresses, appeared in the role of Claire Zachanassian at the Oslo National Theater during the season 1957-58. The director of the theater, Knut Hergel, was in charge of the production; the Norwegian translation was the work of Carl Fredrick Engelstad; and Claire's costumes were conceived by Mrs. Ibsen with the assistance of Lita Prahl.

The costumes, according to Mrs. Ibsen, were a great aid to characterization, and were meant, therefore, to express the strange mixture of the real, the fabulous, and the grotesque in the figure of Claire. The basic costume was an unusual black silk gown in modern design; its extremely long and full train was draped in many different ways and gave enormous variety to the dress.

For the opening scene, Mrs. Ibsen used the train of the dress as a cape, and over her arm she carried a chinchilla wrap. She wore heavy golden chains at her throat; and her make-up was grotesque: a flamboyant red wig, deep green eyeshadow, white cheeks, an enlarged nose and a hard, red mouth.

In the restaurant scene, the black dress seemed to be an entirely new costume as the train was used as a head covering and was also arranged in folds reminiscent of Greek drapery. Mrs. Ibsen was decked out, in addition, in glowing pearls, gleaming diamonds, and glittering brilliants, in the manner of an Oriental goddess or, as she put it, "a bejeweled Buddha."

The costume for the balcony scenes carried out the eastern motif to an even greater extent. Claire wore a brocaded morning coat of cloth of gold over light green trousers; the wide sleeves of the coat were lined with silk of a lighter shade of green; heavy strands of pearls, diamonds, and chains of gold were braided into thick cables which circled her throat and wrist.

In the barn scene, Claire was seated in a gilded sedan-chair lined with brilliant red velvet that provided a striking contrast to her low-cut wedding dress of heavy white silk with white silk flowers edging the decolletage. Claire's bosom was covered with tulle over which there were massive necklaces and brooches of brilliants. The wedding veil was held on the head by a small coronet, and a very full veil covered the skirt. Claire's "paralyzed" arm was covered from wrist to elbow with glittering bracelets, and huge solitaire diamonds concealed her "ivory" fingers.

For the second forest scene, and for the final scenes of the play, the black dress was worn but variety was obtained by the careful redraping of the train.

In consultation with the director, Mrs. Ibsen worked out her own interpretation of the role of Claire Zachanassian, a part she found both demanding and exciting because of the ambivalence of the character; here was a woman who was clever, resourceful, and capable of love, yet frustrated, revengeful, and destructive. It would not have mattered whether Claire had achieved great position and wealth or had remained obscure, Mrs. Ibsen feels, if she could only have found happiness, but without happiness, nothing could fill the emptiness of her life.

Despite her incalculable fortune, continual globe-trotting, and nine husbands, Claire remained unfulfilled.

"I'm sure that in every evil or unhappy person there must be a streak of good that will show up at some time or other," said Mrs. Ibsen. "That's why I tried to play Claire for all the sympathy I could get, and yet you can't think of Claire as living entirely on the human plane. There is something larger than life-size about her that puts her in the realm of the Fates and the deities." Mrs. Ibsen used every technical means at her command, therefore, to create the impression that Claire was a semilegendary or quasi-mythical figure.

At the Oslo National Theater, the play was presented exactly as written by Duerrenmatt, complete with all its formal and fanciful elements. The opening and closing choruses were retained, as were the men who represented trees in the forest, and the motoring scene in which two chairs and a large wheel symbolized the automobile. The motoring scene, incidentally, though omitted from almost every other production of the play, was well received by the Norwegian audience. A single actor portrayed Husbands Seven, Eight, and Nine, which proved to be very amusing. To suggest that she was wearing artificial limbs, Mrs. Ibsen kept her right hand and right leg completely stiff throughout the play, as if they were paralyzed. The stiffness of her limbs helped the actress to develop her characterization, because it kept in the forefront of her mind the life Claire had lived, the trials she had endured, and the hostility she felt towards the world; it not only dictated her movements but motivated her coarseness and bitterness.

The thinking members of the audience considered the play one of the masterpieces of the modern theater, but the general public found it too serious and too morbid. Despite the fact that the play did not prove to be a popular success, Lillebil Ibsen received many expressions of praise for her performance, in the form of reviews, letters, and personal comments.

PUBLICIZING *The Visit*
An Interview with Barry Hyams

Barry Hyams has spent over twenty-five years in the theater as press agent for some of the most important productions to reach Broadway. He has publicized ballet and opera attractions as well as the drama and says that the press agent's basic job is "selling the show to the public." He has three main avenues of approach for bringing his play to the notice of the potential theatergoer: media publicity, advertising, and promotion and exploitation.

Newspapers, magazines, television, and radio comprise the media to which the press agent sends news items, feature stories, and photographs, and with which he arranges interviews for the personalities connected with the play. Editors and program directors are willing to make space and time in their media available free of charge because of the reader's and listener's appetite for human interest and news stories concerning the theater.

Advertising differs from publicity in that, although the same media are used, the space and time are paid for; "ads" range in size from the half-inch single-column notice in the local newspaper to the monster billboard on the public highway and include one-minute spots on radio or television, window cards, three-sheet posters, and the display materials seen in such public places as railroad and subway stations, airport terminals, and trains.

The field of promotion and exploitation is so complex that it almost defies description; it includes but is not limited to circulation by mail, preparation of heralds, flyers, and leaflets of many sorts, window display tie-ups with department stores and individual shops, advertising tie-ups with the manufacturers of various products, and preparation of the signs and photographs displayed in theater lobbies and elsewhere.

A press agent's "campaign" is a plan whereby the various channels—publicity, advertising, promotion—are combined in the best way to sell a particular play; campaigns differ, of course, from production to production, depending upon the nature of the play, the stature of the author, stars, director, and upon many other significant factors. "But there are really only two basic ways to run a campaign," says Barry Hyams, "and these accomplish the same purpose, although they start from opposite directions. According to one plan, a detailed announcement is sent to the press far in advance of the opening of the production; then day by day the various aspects of the story are developed in more elaborate form. This approach, going from the general to the particular, as it were, was used to announce the arrival of the Sadler's Wells Ballet on its first visit to America; the initial release acquainted the American public with the history, techniques, traditions, and aims of the English company; then followed news and features of its personnel, while the repertory schedule was withheld until the public had been warmed with anticipation and had become eager to purchase tickets. The second, and more 'classic,' approach works from the particular to the general; the idea is to start the campaign with a small announcement and to increase the size and importance of the releases as time goes on, allowing the information to take root and flourish. The ideal campaign, whichever system is adopted, is based on good material astutely used."

The publicity campaign for *The Visit* emerged as a perfect example of the "classic" type; the event evolved and "built" like a well-constructed drama in three acts with a clearly defined beginning, middle, and end. The strongest elements in the "plot" were the refurbishing and renaming of an old theater, the return of the Lunts in a serious play, and a brand new playwright; among the important "sub-plots" were a brilliant director, and a fabulous set of costumes for the feminine star.

In May, 1957, an announcement was sent to the newspapers concerning the purchase of the Globe Theater on Broadway by Robert W. Dowling, Roger L. Stevens, and Robert Whitehead, the directors of the Producers' Theater. The Globe had been built in 1910 for legitimate drama but had been serving since 1931 as a movie-house; it was the intention of its new owners to restore the old playhouse to its original glory by transmuting it into a model of ease and beauty and initiating its reclamation with a dramatic offering of distinction.

Instantly the drama reporters and gossip columnists let loose a succession of conjectures as to who the first tenant of the new Globe would be. Meanwhile, work had begun on the theater and the plans and progress of its transformation were detailed regularly to the press; the completion date was predicted for March 1, 1958. In February, the Producers' Theater released the news that the Lunts would open the Globe in *The Visit*.

It was a freezing Sunday morning when the members of the press were invited to a conference in the drafty unfinished cellar of the theater where they huddled in a makeshift cubicle in front of electric heaters, while technicians hurried to set up a two-way radio hookup to Dublin. At eleven o'clock, the three executives of the Producers' Theater, in the presence of the reporters, took turns speaking with the Lunts in Ireland where they were then performing *The Visit*, and announced that the new playhouse on West 46th Street, directly opposite the Helen Hayes Theater, would thereafter be known as the Lunt-Fontanne.

The naming of the new theater for the stars who were to open the house with their latest play provided an exciting climax to the first act of the publicity campaign. The Lunts are the most celebrated pair in the American Theater, and their uninterrupted joint career of the preceding three decades, representing the quintessence of acting art, has always made excellent copy. Now every nugget of information, every anecdote dealing with the couple was mined and immediately minted into journalistic currency. Their public and private lives, beginning professionally in 1905 and maritally in 1922, were reviewed in text and photos. Among the data that most fascinated the chroniclers of the coming event was that *The Visit* would provide the Lunts' twenty-eighth joint appearance in New York, and would be the first serious drama they had acted since Robert E. Sherwood's *There Shall Be No Night*. To spice the occasion, the *New York Times* reported that *The Visit* might well be the Lunts' farewell.

When the date of the theater opening was moved ahead to April 14th, wagers were made as to whether the event would take place on schedule. One look at the heaps of unfinished masonry, acres of unlaid carpet, miles of wiring awaiting installation, and the odds rose. Postponement was inevitable, and a bulletin was issued designating Monday, May 5th, as the definite opening day.

The press fed on the features of the theater's design and made copy of everything from the fact that the audience in the mezzanine and balcony would enjoy smoking privileges, to the novelty of the tickets being colored red, white, and blue for easier identification of seat locations.

Simultaneously with this publicity program, its practical goal, the sale of seats, was proceeding with the aid and stimulation of advertising. *The Visit* played a pre-Broadway engagement in Boston in mid-April and was greeted with cheers. Several days later a demure advertisement was inserted in New York's papers simply quoting a statement made by the drama critic of the *Boston Traveler*: "The Lunts are superb! If they really mean it—that *The Visit* is their last play— they couldn't take their final curtain in a greater glory." A few days later this was repeated along with excerpts from the other Boston reviews. As the New York opening approached, further advertising of a more formal character began to appear. It stressed the names of the stars, of the new theater, of the play, and made a point of the fact that the engagement was limited to nine weeks.

The race to finish the theater on time was a neck-and-neck affair until the very end of April. The Lunts and a group of supporting players arrived on the 27th and the following day in the *New York Times* Meyer Berger described the sounds of "hammers pounding, sprayers hissing and vacuum cleaners droning," attesting to the management's doggedness to meet the deadline.

On the Friday before the official opening of the theater, a dedication ceremony was held in the mezzanine foyer. The splendors of the design and décor were unveiled before the press and a crowd of glamorous guests. The Lunt-Fontanne Theater was christened. Helen Hayes, the "neighbor from across the street," presented the couple with a "housewarming" gift, after which they were photographed under the marquee bearing their names.

At this point, the publicity which had been launched shortly after the theater campaign had got well under way, began to make itself felt. Just prior to the premiere, in addition to articles such as the *World-Telegram and Sun* published in its weekend magazine under the headline: "All That Glitters Is Gold, Blue, and Lunt-Fontanne," the newspapers treated in detail the serious values inherent in the play, the new playwright, and the style of the production. For this, the stage designs of Teo Otto, the costumes Castillo fashioned for Miss Fontanne, the return of director Peter Brook, and the introduction of a new young Swiss playwright, all provided fertile fields for feature writers on the art, fashion, and drama pages. Duerrenmatt, obscure in New York until then, became capital. Maurice Valency wrote an article on the playwright for *Theatre Arts Magazine,* as well as a briefer piece that was featured on the first page of the drama section of the Sunday *Times;* and shortly afterward, the *Times* printed an interview with the dramatist under the by-line of their foreign correspondent Joseph Morgenstern. Thus, the weekend prior to opening night was the climax of the second act of the publicity campaign.

The third act of the campaign began with the first performance of *The Visit* and the public opening of the Lunt-Fontanne Theater. It was a brilliant occasion; a superb play was magnificently acted. The final curtain was the signal for an ovation from Broadway celebrities and luminaries of the business, political, and industrial worlds. Following the performance, a grand fete was held in the ballroom of the Hotel Astor in honor of Alfred Lunt and Lynn Fontanne, and the next morning pictures of the event made most of the newspapers, while laudatory reviews and "word-of-mouth" started long lines at the box office. The succeeding weeks' strategy was more akin to a mopping-up action. The national magazines moved in to complete their photo and text assignments. Wire services, local and out-of-town correspondents were scheduled for interviews, all sorts of promotional tie-ups were arranged, and before long the nine weeks had passed and the job was done.

The entire engagement was sold out and the demand for tickets was so insistent and widespread that the Lunts returned after a holiday for fourteen additional weeks on Broadway, terminating on November 29th. They then set out on a national tour lasting until March, 1960, followed it with a two-week run in New York, and a production in London. The question whether *The Visit* was their farewell play was never answered during the entire campaign, and recently there have been rumors that the Lunts are thinking of appearing in a musical version of *The Madwoman of Chaillot*.

THE PLAYBILL

The Visit ADAPTED BY MAURICE VALENCY

The Visit was first presented by the Producers' Theater at the Lunt-Fontanne Theater, New York City, on May 5, 1958, with the following cast:

HOFBAUER (FIRST MAN)	KENNETH THORNETT
HELMESBERGER (SECOND)	DAVID CLARKE
WECHSLER (THIRD)	MILTON SELZER
VOGEL (FOURTH)	HARRISON DOWD
PAINTER	CLARENCE NORDSTROM
STATION MASTER	JOSEPH LEBERMAN
BURGOMASTER	ERIC PORTER
TEACHER	PETER WOODTHORPE
PASTOR	WILLIAM HANSEN
ANTON SCHILL	ALFRED LUNT
CLAIRE ZACHANASSIAN	LYNN FONTANNE
CONDUCTOR	JONATHAN ANDERSON
PEDRO CABRAL	MYLES EASON
BOBBY	JOHN WYSE
POLICEMAN	JOHN RANDOLPH
FIRST GRANDCHILD	LESLEY HUNT
SECOND GRANDCHILD	LOIS MCKIM
MIKE	STANLEY ERICKSON
MAX	WILLIAM THOURLBY
FIRST BLIND MAN	VINCENT GARDENIA
SECOND BLIND MAN	ALFRED HOFFMAN
ATHLETE	JAMES MacAARON
FRAU BURGOMASTER	FRIEDA ALTMAN
FRAU SCHILL	DAPHNE NEWTON
DAUGHTER	MARLA ADAMS
SON	KEN WALKEN

DOCTOR NÜSSLIN	HOWARD FISCHER
FRAU BLOCK (FIRST WOMAN)	GERTRUDE KINNELL
TRUCK DRIVER	JOHN KANE
REPORTER	EDWARD MOOR
TOWNSMAN	ROBERT DONLEY
TOWNSMAN	KENT MONTROY

Directed by Peter Brook, designed by Teo Otto, supervision and lighting by Paul Morrison, Miss Fontanne's clothes by Castillo, incidental music arranged by James Stevens.

PROGRAM CREDITS

Miss Fontanne's dresses executed by Lanvin-Castillo of Paris. Shoes for Miss Fontanne by Delman. Miss Fontanne's gloves by Wear-Right. Stockings by Phoenix Hosiery. Lighting by Duwico. Sound Equipment by Masque Sound Company. Television set courtesy of General Electric. Lightweight baggage by Daisy Products. Hats by John B. Stetson Co. Luggage by Lee Fordin Co. Cosmetics by Diedre.

ACT ONE

A railway-crossing bell starts ringing. Then is heard the distant sound of a locomotive whistle. The curtain rises.

The scene represents, in the simplest possible manner, a little town somewhere in Central Europe. The time is the present. The town is shabby and ruined, as if the plague had passed there. Its name, Güllen, is inscribed on the shabby signboard which adorns the façade of the railway station. This edifice is summarily indicated by a length of rusty iron paling, a platform parallel to the proscenium, beyond which one imagines the rails to be, and a baggage truck standing by a wall on which a torn timetable, marked "Fahrplan," is affixed by three nails. In the station wall is a door with a sign: "Eintritt Verboten." This leads to the STATION MASTER's office.

Left of the station is a little house of gray stucco, formerly whitewashed. It has a tile roof, badly in need of repair. Some shreds of travel posters still adhere to the windowless walls. A shingle hanging over the entrance, left, reads: "Männer." On the other side the shingle reads: "Damen." Along the wall of the little house there is a wooden bench, backless, on which four men are lounging cheerlessly, shabbily dressed, with cracked shoes. A fifth man is busied with paintpot and brush. He is kneeling on the ground, painting a strip of canvas with the words: "Welcome, Clara."

The warning signal rings uninterruptedly. The sound of the approaching train comes closer and closer. The STATION MASTER issues from his office, advances to the center of the platform and salutes.

The train is heard thundering past in a direction parallel to the footlights, and is lost in the distance. The men on the bench follow its passing with a slow movement of their heads, from left to right.

First Man. The "Emperor." Hamburg-Naples.

Second Man. Then comes the "Diplomat."

Third Man. Then the "Banker."

Fourth Man. And at eleven twenty-seven the "Flying Dutchman." Venice-Stockholm.

First Man. Our only pleasure—watching trains.

(*The station bell rings again. The* STATION MASTER *comes out of his office and salutes another train. The men follow its course, right to left*)

Fourth Man. Once upon a time the "Emperor" and the "Flying Dutchman" used to stop here in Güllen. So did the "Diplomat," the "Banker" and the "Silver Comet."

Second Man. Now it's only the local from Kaffigen and the twelve-forty from Kalberstadt.

Third Man. The fact is, we're ruined.

First Man. What with the Wagonworks shut down . . .

Second Man. The Foundry finished . . .

Fourth Man. The Golden Eagle Pencil Factory all washed up . . .

First Man. It's life on the dole.

Second Man. Did you say life?

Third Man. We're rotting.

First Man. Starving.

Second Man. Crumbling.

Fourth Man. The whole damn town.

(*The station bell rings*)

Third Man. Once we were a center of industry.

Painter. A cradle of culture.

Fourth Man. One of the best little towns in the country.

First Man. In the world.

Second Man. Here Goethe slept.

Fourth Man. Brahms composed a quartet.

Third Man. Here Berthold Schwarz invented gunpowder.

Painter. And I once got first prize at the Dresden Exhibition of Contemporary Art. What am I doing now? Painting signs.

(*The station bell rings. The* STATION MASTER *comes out. He throws away a cigarette butt. The men scramble for it*)

First Man. Well, anyway, Madame Zachanassian will help us.

Fourth Man. If she comes . . .

Third Man. If she comes.

Second Man. Last week she was in France. She gave them a hospital.

First Man. In Rome she founded a free public nursery.

Third Man. In Leuthenau, a bird sanctuary.

Painter. They say she got Picasso to design her car.

First Man. Where does she get all that money?

Second Man. An oil company, a shipping line, three banks and five railways—

Fourth Man. And the biggest string of geisha houses in Japan.

(*From the direction of the town come the* BURGOMASTER, *the* PASTOR, *the* TEACHER *and* ANTON SCHILL. *The* BURGOMASTER, *the* TEACHER *and* SCHILL *are men in their fifties. The* PASTOR *is ten years younger. All four are dressed shabbily and are sad-*

looking. The BURGOMASTER *looks official.* SCHILL *is tall and handsome, but graying and worn; nevertheless a man of considerable charm and presence. He walks directly to the little house and disappears into it*)

Painter. Any news, Burgomaster? Is she coming?

All. Yes, is she coming?

Burgomaster. She's coming. The telegram has been confirmed. Our distinguished guest will arrive on the twelve-forty from Kalberstadt. Everyone must be ready.

Teacher. The mixed choir is ready. So is the children's chorus.

Burgomaster. And the church bell, Pastor?

Pastor. The church bell will ring. As soon as the new bell ropes are fitted. The man is working on them now.

Burgomaster. The town band will be drawn up in the market place and the Athletic Association will form a human pyramid in her honor—the top man will hold the wreath with her initials. Then lunch at the Golden Apostle. I shall say a few words.

Teacher. Of course.

Burgomaster. I had thought of illuminating the town hall and the cathedral, but we can't afford the lamps.

Painter. Burgomaster—what do you think of this?

(*He shows the banner*)

Burgomaster (*Calls*). Schill! Schill!
Teacher. Schill!

(SCHILL *comes out of the little house*)

Schill. Yes, right away. Right away.

Burgomaster. This is more in your line. What do you think of this?

Schill (*Looks at the sign*). No, no, no. That certainly won't do, Burgomaster. It's much too intimate. It shouldn't read: "Welcome, Clara." It should read: "Welcome, Madame . . ."

Teacher. Zachanassian.

Burgomaster. Zachanassian.

Schill. Zachanassian.

Painter. But she's Clara to us.

First Man. Clara Wäscher.

Second Man. Born here.

Third Man. Her father was a carpenter. He built this.

(*All turn and stare at the little house*)

Schill. All the same . . .

Painter. If I . . .

Burgomaster. No, no, no. He's right. You'll have to change it.

Painter. Oh, well, I'll tell you what I'll do. I'll leave this and I'll put "Welcome, Madame Zachanassian" on the other side. Then if things go well, we can always turn it around.

Burgomaster. Good idea. (*To* SCHILL) Yes?

Schill. Well, anyway, it's safer. Everything depends on the first impression.

(*The train bell is heard. Two clangs. The* PAINTER *turns the banner over and goes to work*)

First Man. Hear that? The "Flying Dutchman" has just passed through Leuthenau.

Fourth Man. Eleven twenty.

Burgomaster. Gentlemen, you know that the millionairess is our only hope.

Pastor. Under God.

Burgomaster. Under God. Naturally. Schill, we depend entirely on you.

Schill. Yes, I know. You keep telling me.

Burgomaster. After all, you're the only one who really knew her.

Schill. Yes, I knew her.

Pastor. You were really quite close to one another, I hear, in those days.

Schill. Close? Yes, we were close, there's no denying it. We were in love. I was young—good-looking, so they said—and Clara—you know, I can still see her in the great barn coming toward me—like a light out of the darkness. And in the Konradsweil Forest she'd come running to meet me—barefooted—her beautiful red hair streaming behind her. Like a witch. I was in love with her, all right. But you know how it is when you're twenty.

Pastor. What happened?

Schill (*Shrugs*). Life came between us.

Burgomaster. You must give me some points about her for my speech.

(*He takes out his notebook*)

Schill. I think I can help you there.

Teacher. Well, I've gone through the school records. And the young lady's marks were, I'm afraid to say, absolutely dreadful. Even in deportment. The only subject in which she was even remotely passable was natural history.

Burgomaster. Good in natural history. That's fine. Give me a pencil.

(*He makes a note*)

Schill. She was an outdoor girl. Wild. Once, I remember, they arrested a tramp, and she threw stones at the policeman. She hated injustice passionately.

Burgomaster. Strong sense of justice. Excellent.

Schill. And generous . . .

All. Generous?

Schill. Generous to a fault. Whatever little she had, she shared—so good-hearted. I remember once she stole a bag of potatoes to give to a poor widow.

Burgomaster (*Writing in notebook*). Wonderful generosity—

Teacher. Generosity.

Burgomaster. That, gentlemen, is something I must not fail to make a point of.

Schill. And such a sense of humor. I remember once when the oldest man in town fell and broke his leg, she said, "Oh, dear, now they'll have to shoot him."

Burgomaster. Well, I've got enough. The rest, my friend, is up to you.

(*He puts the notebook away*)

Schill. Yes, I know, but it's not so easy. After all, to part a woman like that from her millions—

Burgomaster. Exactly. Millions. We have to think in big terms here.

Teacher. If she's thinking of buying us off with a nursery school—

All. Nursery school!

Pastor. Don't accept.

Teacher. Hold out.

Schill. I'm not so sure that I can do it. You know, she may have forgotten me completely.

Burgomaster (*He exchanges a look with the* TEACHER *and the* PASTOR). Schill, for many years you have been our most popular citizen. The most respected and the best loved.

Schill. Why, thank you . . .

Burgomaster. And therefore I must tell you—last week I sounded out the political opposition, and they agreed. In the spring you will be elected to succeed me as Burgomaster. By unanimous vote.

(*The others clap their hands in approval*)

Schill. But, my dear Burgomaster—!

Burgomaster. It's true.

Teacher. I'm a witness. I was at the meeting.

Schill. This is—naturally, I'm terribly flattered— It's a completely unexpected honor.

Burgomaster. You deserve it.

Schill. Burgomaster! Well, well—! (*Briskly*) Gentlemen, to business. The first chance I get, of course, I shall discuss our miserable position with Clara.

Teacher. But tactfully, tactfully—

Schill. What do you take me for? We must feel our way. Everything must be correct. Psychologically correct. For example, here at the railway station, a single blunder, one false note, could be disastrous.

Burgomaster. He's absolutely right. The first impression colors all the rest. Madame Zachanassian sets foot on her native soil for the first time in many years. She sees our love and she sees our misery. She remembers her youth, her friends. The tears well up into her eyes. Her childhood companions throng about her. I will naturally not present myself like this, but in my black coat with my top hat. Next to me, my wife. Before me, my two grandchildren all in white, with roses. My God, if it only comes off as I see it! If only it comes off. (*The station bell begins ringing*) Oh, my God! Quick! We must get dressed.

First Man. It's not her train. It's only the "Flying Dutchman."

Pastor (*Calmly*). We have still two hours before she arrives.

Schill. For God's sake, don't let's lose our heads. We still have a full two hours.

Burgomaster. Who's losing their heads?

(*To* Second *and* Fourth Man) When her train comes, you two, Helmesberger and Vogel, will hold up the banner with "Welcome Madame Zachanassian." The rest will applaud.

Third Man. Bravo!

(*He applauds*)

Burgomaster. But, please, one thing—no wild cheering like last year with the government relief committee. It made no impression at all and we still haven't received any loan. What we need here is a feeling of genuine sincerity. That's how we greet with full hearts our beloved sister who has been away from us so long. Be sincerely moved, my friends, that's the secret; be sincere. Remember you're not dealing with a child. Next a few brief words from me. Then the church bell will start pealing—

Pastor. If he can fix the ropes in time.

(*The station bell rings*)

Burgomaster.—Then the mixed choir moves in. And then—

Teacher. We'll form a line down here.

Burgomaster. Then the rest of us will form in two lines leading from the station—

(*He is interrupted by the thunder of the approaching train. The men crane their heads to see it pass. The* Station Master *advances to the platform and salutes. There is a sudden shriek of air brakes. The train screams to a stop. The four men jump up in consternation*)

Painter. But the "Flying Dutchman" never stops!

First Man. It's stopping.

Second Man. In Güllen!

Third Man. In the poorest—

First Man. The dreariest—

Second Man. The lousiest—

Fourth Man. The most God-forsaken hole between Venice and Stockholm.

Station Master. It cannot stop!

(*The train noises stop. There is only the panting of the engine*)

Painter. It's stopped!

(*The* STATION MASTER *runs out*)

Offstage Voices. What's happened? Is there an accident?

(*A hubbub of offstage voices, as if the passengers on the invisible train were alighting*)

Claire (*Offstage*). Is this Güllen?

Conductor (*Offstage*). Here, here, what's going on?

Claire (*Offstage*). Who the hell are you?

Conductor (*Offstage*). But you pulled the emergency cord, madame!

Claire (*Offstage*). I always pull the emergency cord.

Station Master (*Offstage*). I must ask you what's going on here.

Claire (*Offstage*). And who the hell are you?

Station Master (*Offstage*). I'm the Station Master, madame, and I must ask you—

Claire (*Enters*). No!

(*From the right* CLAIRE ZACHANASSIAN *appears. She is an extraordinary woman. She is in her fifties, red-haired, remarkably dressed, with a face as impassive as that of an ancient idol, beautiful still, and with a singular grace of movement and manner. She is simple and unaffected, yet she has the haughtiness of a world power. The entire effect is striking to the point of the unbelievable. Behind her comes her fiancé,* PEDRO CABRAL, *tall, young, very handsome,*

and completely equipped for fishing, with creel and net, and with a rod case in his hand. An excited CONDUCTOR *follows*)

Conductor. But, madame, I must insist! You have stopped "The Flying Dutchman." I must have an explanation.

Claire. Nonsense. Pedro.

Pedro. Yes, my love?

Claire. This is Güllen. Nothing has changed. I recognize it all. There's the forest of Konradsweil. There's a brook in it full of trout, where you can fish. And there's the roof of the great barn. Ha! God! What a miserable blot on the map.

(*She crosses the stage and goes off with* PEDRO)

Schill. My God! Clara!

Teacher. Claire Zachanassian!

All. Claire Zachanassian!

Burgomaster. And the town band? The town band! Where is it?

Teacher. The mixed choir! The mixed choir!

Pastor. The church bell! The church bell!

Burgomaster (*To the* FIRST MAN). Quick! My dress coat. My top hat. My grandchildren. Run! Run! (FIRST MAN *runs off. The* BURGOMASTER *shouts after him*) And don't forget my wife!

(*General panic. The* THIRD MAN *and* FOURTH MAN *hold up the banner, on which only part of the name has been painted: "Welcome Mad—"* CLAIRE *and* PEDRO *re-enter, right*)

Conductor (*Mastering himself with an effort*). Madame. The train is waiting. The entire international railway schedule has been disrupted. I await your explanation.

Claire. You're a very foolish man. I wish to visit this town. Did you expect me to jump off a moving train?

Conductor (*Stupefied*). You stopped the "Flying Dutchman" because you wished to visit the town?

Claire. Naturally.

Conductor (*Inarticulate*). Madame!

Station Master. Madame, if you wished to visit the town, the twelve forty from Kalberstadt was entirely at your service. Arrival in Güllen, one seventeen.

Claire. The local that stops at Loken, Beisenbach and Leuthenau? Do you expect me to waste three-quarters of an hour chugging dismally through this wilderness?

Conductor. Madame, you shall pay for this!

Claire. Bobby, give him a thousand marks.

(BOBBY, *her butler, a man in his seventies, wearing dark glasses, opens his wallet. The townspeople gasp*)

Conductor (*Taking the money in amazement*). But, madame!

Claire. And three thousand for the Railway Widows' Relief Fund.

Conductor (*With the money in his hands*). But we have no such fund, madame.

Claire. Now you have.

(*The* BURGOMASTER *pushes his way forward*)

Burgomaster (*He whispers to the* CONDUCTOR *and* TEACHER). The lady is Madame Claire Zachanassian!

Conductor. Claire Zachanassian? Oh, my God! But that's naturally quite different. Needless to say, we would have stopped the train if we'd had the slightest idea. (*He hands the money back to* BOBBY) Here, please. I couldn't dream of it. Four thousand. My God!

Claire. Keep it. Don't fuss.

Conductor. Would you like the train to wait, madame, while you visit the town? The administration will be delighted. The cathedral porch. The town hall—

Claire. You may take the train away. I don't need it any more.

Station Master. All aboard!

(*He puts his whistle to his lips.* PEDRO *stops him*)

Pedro. But the press, my angel. They don't know anything about this. They're still in the dining car.

Claire. Let them stay there. I don't want the press in Güllen at the moment. Later they will come by themselves. (*To* STATION MASTER) And now what are you waiting for?

Station Master. All aboard!

(*The* STATION MASTER *blows a long blast on his whistle. The train leaves. Meanwhile, the* FIRST MAN *has brought the* BURGOMASTER'S *dress coat and top hat. The* BURGOMASTER *puts on the coat, then advances slowly and solemnly*)

Conductor. I trust madame will not speak of this to the administration. It was a pure misunderstanding.

(*He salutes and runs for the train as it starts moving*)

Burgomaster (*Bows*). Gracious lady, as Burgomaster of the town of Güllen, I have the honor—

(*The rest of the speech is lost in the roar of the departing train. He continues speaking and gesturing, and at last bows amid applause as the train noises end*)

Claire. Thank you, Mr. Burgomaster.

(*She glances at the beaming faces, and lastly at* SCHILL, *whom she does not recognize. She turns upstage*)

Schill. Clara!

Claire (*Turns and stares*). Anton?

Schill. Yes. It's good that you've come back.

Claire. Yes. I've waited for this moment. All my life. Ever since I left Güllen.

Schill (*A little embarrassed*). That is very kind of you to say, Clara.

Claire. And have you thought about me?

Schill. Naturally. Always. You know that.

Claire. Those were happy times we spent together.

Schill. Unforgettable.

(*He smiles reassuringly at the* BURGO-MASTER)

Claire. Call me by the name you used to call me.

Schill (*Whispers*). My kitten.

Claire. What?

Schill (*Louder*). My kitten.

Claire. And what else?

Schill. Little witch.

Claire. I used to call you my black panther. You're gray now, and soft.

Schill. But you are still the same, little witch.

Claire. I am the same? (*She laughs*) Oh, no, my black panther, I am not at all the same.

Schill (*Gallantly*). In my eyes you are. I see no difference.

Claire. Would you like to meet my fiancé? Pedro Cabral. He owns an enormous plantation in Brazil.

Schill. A pleasure.

Claire. We're to be married soon.

Schill. Congratulations.

Claire. He will be my eighth husband. (PEDRO *stands by himself downstage, right*) Pedro, come here and show your face. Come along, darling—come here! Don't sulk. Say hello.

Pedro. Hello.

Claire. A man of few words! Isn't he charming? A diplomat. He's interested only in fishing. Isn't he handsome, in his Latin way? You'd swear he was a Brazilian. But he's not—he's a Greek. His father was a White Russian. We were betrothed by a Bulgarian priest. We plan to be married in a few days here in the cathedral.

Burgomaster. Here in the cathedral? What an honor for us!

Claire. No. It was my dream, when I was seventeen, to be married in Güllen cathedral. The dreams of youth are sacred, don't you think so, Anton?

Schill. Yes, of course.

Claire. Yes, of course. I think so, too. Now I would like to look at the town. (*The mixed choir arrives, breathless, wearing ordinary clothes with green sashes*) What's all this? Go away. (*She laughs*) Ha! Ha! Ha!

Teacher. Dear lady—(*He steps forward, having put on a sash also*) Dear lady, as Rector of the high school and a devotee of that noble muse, Music, I take pleasure in presenting the Güllen mixed choir.

Claire. How do you do?

Teacher. Who will sing for you an ancient folk song of the region, with specially amended words—if you will deign to listen.

Claire. Very well. Fire away.

(*The* TEACHER *blows a pitch pipe. The mixed choir begins to sing the ancient folk song with the amended words. Just then the station bell starts ringing. The song is drowned in the roar of the passing express. The* STATION MASTER *salutes. When the train has passed, there is applause*)

Burgomaster. The church bell! The church bell! Where's the church bell?

(*The* PASTOR *shrugs helplessly*)

Claire. Thank you, Professor. They sang beautifully. The little blond bass—no, not that one—the one with the big Adam's apple—was most impressive. (*The* TEACHER *bows. The* POLICEMAN *pushes his way professionally through the mixed choir and comes to attention in front of* CLAIRE ZACHANASSIAN) Now, who are you?

Policeman (*Clicks heels*). Police Chief Schultz. At your service.

Claire (*She looks him up and down*) I have no need of you at the moment. But I think there will be work for you by and by. Tell me, do you know how to close an eye from time to time?

Policeman. How else could I get along in my profession?

Claire. You might practice closing both.

Schill (*Laughs*). What a sense of humor, eh?

Burgomaster (*Puts on the top hat*) Permit me to present my grandchildren, gracious lady. Hermine and Adolphine. There's only my wife still to come.

(*He wipes the perspiration from his brow, and replaces the hat. The little girls present the roses with elaborate curtsies*)

Claire. Thank you, my dears. Congrat-ulations, Burgomaster. Extraordinary children.

(*She plants the roses in* PEDRO's *arms. The* BURGOMASTER *secretly passes his top hat to the* PASTOR, *who puts it on*)

Burgomaster. Our pastor, madame.

(*The* PASTOR *takes off the hat and bows*)

Claire. Ah. The pastor. How do you do? Do you give consolation to the dying?

Pastor (*A bit puzzled*). That is part of my ministry, yes.

Claire. And to those who are condemned to death?

Pastor. Capital punishment has been abolished in this country, madame.

Claire. I see. Well, it could be restored, I suppose.

(*The* PASTOR *hands back the hat. He shrugs his shoulders in confusion*)

Schill (*Laughs*). What an original sense of humor!

(*All laugh, a little blankly*)

Claire. Well, I can't sit here all day— I should like to see the town.

(*The* BURGOMASTER *offers his arm*)

Burgomaster. May I have the honor, gracious lady?

Claire. Thank you, but these legs are not what they were. This one was broken in five places.

Schill (*Full of concern*). My kitten!

Claire. When my airplane bumped into a mountain in Afghanistan. All the others were killed. Even the pilot. But as you see, I survived. I don't fly any more.

Schill. But you're as strong as ever now.

Claire. Stronger.

Burgomaster. Never fear, gracious lady. The town doctor has a car.

Claire. I never ride in motors.

Burgomaster. You never ride in motors?

Claire. Not since my Ferrari crashed in Hong Kong.

Schill. But how do you travel, then, little witch? On a broom?

Claire. Mike—Max! (*She claps her hands. Two huge bodyguards come in, left, carrying a sedan chair. She sits in it*) I travel this way—a bit antiquated, of course. But perfectly safe. Ha! Ha! Aren't they magnificent? Mike and Max. I bought them in America. They were in jail, condemned to the chair. I had them pardoned. Now they're condemned to my chair. I paid fifty thousand dollars apiece for them. You couldn't get them now for twice the sum. The sedan chair comes from the Louvre. I fancied it so much that the President of France gave it to me. The French are so impulsive, don't you think so, Anton? Go!

(*MIKE and MAX start to carry her off*)

Burgomaster. You wish to visit the cathedral? And the old town hall?

Claire. No. The great barn. And the forest of Konradsweil. I wish to go with Anton and visit our old haunts once again.

The Pastor. Very touching.

Claire (*To the butler*) Will you send my luggage and the coffin to the Golden Apostle?

Burgomaster. The coffin?

Claire. Yes. I brought one with me. Go!

Teacher. Hip-hip—

All. Hurrah! Hip-hip, hurrah! Hurrah!

(*They bear her off in the direction of the town. The* TOWNSPEOPLE *burst into cheers. The church bell rings*)

Burgomaster. Ah, thank God—the bell at last.

(*The* POLICEMAN *is about to follow the others, when the two* BLIND MEN *appear. They are not young, yet they seem childish—a strange effect. Though they are of different height and features, they are dressed exactly alike, and so create the effect of being twins. They walk slowly, feeling their way. Their voices, when they speak, are curiously high and flutelike, and they have a curious trick of repetition of phrases*)

First Blind Man. We're in—

Both Blind Men. Güllen.

First Blind Man. We breathe—

Second Blind Man. We breathe—

Both Blind Men. We breathe the air, the air of Güllen.

Policeman (*Startled*). Who are you?

First Blind Man. We belong to the lady.

Second Blind Man. We belong to the lady. She calls us—

First Blind Man. Kobby.

Second Blind Man. And Lobby.

Policeman. Madame Zachanassian is staying at the Golden Apostle.

First Blind Man. We're blind.

Second Blind Man. We're blind.

Policeman. Blind? Come along with me, then. I'll take you there.

First Blind Man. Thank you, Mr. Policeman.

Second Blind Man. Thanks very much.

Policeman. Hey! How do you know I'm a policeman, if you're blind?

Both Blind Men. By your voice. By your voice.

First Blind Man. All policemen sound the same.

Policeman. You've had a lot to do with the police, have you, little men?

First Blind Man. Men he calls us!

Both Blind Men. Men!

Policeman. What are you then?

Both Blind Men. You'll see. You'll see.

(*The* POLICEMAN *claps his hands suddenly. The* BLIND MEN *turn sharply toward the sound. The* POLICEMAN *is convinced they are blind*)

Policeman. What's your trade?

Both Blind Men. We have no trade.

Second Blind Man. We play music.

First Blind Man. We sing.

Second Blind Man. We amuse the lady.

First Blind Man. We look after the beast.

Second Blind Man. We feed it.

First Blind Man. We stroke it.

Second Blind Man. We take it for walks.

Policeman. What beast?

Both Blind Men. You'll see—you'll see.

Second Blind Man. We give it raw meat.

First Blind Man. And she gives us chicken and wine.

Second Blind Man. Every day—

Both Blind Men. Every day.

Policeman. Rich people have strange tastes.

Both Blind Men. Strange tastes— strange tastes. (*The* POLICEMAN *puts on his helmet*)

Policeman. Come along, I'll take you to the lady.

(*The two* BLIND MEN *turn and walk off*)

Both Blind Men. We know the way— we know the way.

(*The station and the little house*

vanish. A sign representing the Golden Apostle descends. The scene dissolves into the interior of the inn. The Golden Apostle is seen to be in the last stages of decay. The walls are cracked and moldering, and the plaster is falling from the ancient lath. A table represents the café of the inn. The BURGOMASTER *and the* TEACHER *sit at this table, drinking a glass together. A procession of* TOWNSPEOPLE, *carrying many pieces of luggage, passes. Then comes a coffin, and, last, a large box covered with a canvas. They cross the stage from right to left*)

Burgomaster. Trunks. Suitcases. Boxes. (*He looks up apprehensively at the ceiling*) The floor will never bear the weight. (*As the large covered box is carried in, he peers under the canvas, then draws back*) Good God!

Teacher. Why, what's in it?

Burgomaster. A live panther. (*They laugh. The* BURGOMASTER *lifts his glass solemnly*) Your health, Professor. Let's hope she puts the Foundry back on its feet.

Teacher (*Lifts his glass*). And the Wagonworks.

Burgomaster. And the Golden Eagle Pencil Factory. Once that starts moving, everything else will go. *Prosit.*

(*They touch glasses and drink*)

Teacher. What does she need a panther for?

Burgomaster. Don't ask me. The whole thing is too much for me. The Pastor had to go home and lie down.

Teacher (*Sets down his glass*). If you want to know the truth, she frightens me.

Burgomaster (*Nods gravely*). She's a strange one.

Teacher. You understand, Burgomaster, a man who for twenty-two years has been correcting the Latin compositions of the students of Güllen is not unaccustomed to surprises. I have seen things to make one's hair stand on end. But when this woman suddenly appeared on the platform, a shudder tore through me. It was as though out of the clear sky all at once a fury descended upon us, beating its black wings—

(*The* POLICEMAN *comes in. He mops his face*)

Policeman. Ah! Now the old place is livening up a bit!

Burgomaster. Ah, Schultz, come and join us.

Policeman. Thank you. (*He calls*) Beer!

Burgomaster. Well, what's the news from the front?

Policeman. I'm just back from Schiller's barn. My God! What a scene! She had us all tiptoeing around in the straw as if we were in church. Nobody dared to speak above a whisper. And the way she carried on! I was so embarrassed I let them go to the forest by themselves.

Burgomaster. Does the fiancé go with them?

Policeman. With his fishing rod and his landing net. In full marching order. (*He calls again*) Beer!

Burgomaster. That will be her seventh husband.

Teacher. Her eighth.

Burgomaster. But what does she expect to find in the Konradsweil forest?

Policeman. The same thing she expected to find in the old barn, I suppose. The—the—

Teacher. The ashes of her youthful love.

Policeman. Exactly.

Teacher. It's poetry.

Policeman. Poetry.

Teacher. Sheer poetry! It makes one think of Shakespeare, of Wagner. Of Romeo and Juliet.

(*The* SECOND MAN *comes in as a waiter. The* POLICEMAN *is served his beer*)

Burgomaster. Yes, you're right. (*Solemnly*) Gentlemen, I would like to propose a toast. To our great and good friend, Anton Schill, who is even now working on our behalf.

Policeman. Yes! He's really working.

Burgomaster. Gentlemen, to the best-loved citizen of this town. My successor, Anton Schill!

(*They raise their glasses. At this point an unearthly scream is heard. It is the black panther howling offstage. The sign of the Golden Apostle rises out of sight. The lights go down. The inn vanishes. Only the wooden bench, on which the four men were lounging in the opening scene, is left on the stage, downstage right. The procession comes on upstage. The two bodyguards carry in* CLAIRE'S *sedan chair. Next to it walks* SCHILL. PEDRO *walks behind, with his fishing rod. Last come the two* BLIND MEN *and the butler.* CLAIRE *alights*)

Claire. Stop! Take my chair off somewhere else. I'm tired of looking at you. (*The bodyguards and the sedan chair go off*) Pedro darling, your brook is just a little further along down that path. Listen. You can hear it from here. Bobby, take him and show him where it is.

Both Blind Men. We'll show him the way—we'll show him the way.

(*They go off, left.* PEDRO *follows.* BOBBY *walks off, right*)

Claire. Look, Anton. Our tree. There's the heart you carved in the bark long ago.

Schill. Yes. It's still there.

Claire. How it has grown! The trunk is black and wrinkled. Why, its limbs are twice what they were. Some of them have died.

Schill. It's aged. But it's there.

Claire. Like everything else. (*She crosses, examining other trees*) Oh, how tall they are. How long it is since I walked here, barefoot over the pine needles and the damp leaves! Look, Anton. A fawn.

Schill. Yes, a fawn. It's the season.

Claire. I thought everything would be changed. But it's all just as we left it. This is the seat we sat on years ago. Under these branches you kissed me. And over there under the hawthorn, where the moss is soft and green, we would lie in each other's arms. It is all as it used to be. Only we have changed.

Schill. Not so much, little witch. I remember the first night we spent together, you ran away and I chased you till I was quite breathless—

Claire. Yes.

Schill. Then I was angry and I was going home, when suddenly I heard you call and I looked up, and there you were sitting in a tree, laughing down at me.

Claire. No. It was in the great barn. I was in the hayloft.

Schill. Were you?

Claire. Yes. What else do you remember?

Schill. I remember the morning we went swimming by the waterfall, and afterwards we were lying together on the big rock in the sun, when suddenly we heard footsteps and we just had time to snatch up our clothes and run behind the bushes when the old pastor appeared and scolded you for not being in school.

Claire. No. It was the schoolmaster who found us. It was Sunday and I was supposed to be in church.

Schill. Really?

Claire. Yes. Tell me more.

Schill. I remember the time your father beat you, and you showed me the cuts on your back, and I swore I'd kill him. And the next day I dropped a tile from a roof top and split his head open.

Claire. You missed him.

Schill. No!

Claire. You hit old Mr. Reiner.

Schill. Did I?

Claire. Yes. I was seventeen. And you were not yet twenty. You were so handsome. You were the best-looking boy in town.

(*The two* BLIND MEN *begin playing mandolin music offstage, very softly*)

Schill. And you were the prettiest girl.

Claire. We were made for each other.

Schill. So we were.

Claire. But you married Mathilde Blumhard and her store, and I married old Zachanassian and his oil wells. He found me in a whorehouse in Hamburg. It was my hair that entangled him, the old golden beetle.

Schill. Clara!

Claire (*She claps her hands*). Bobby! A cigar.

(BOBBY *appears with a leather case.*

He selects a cigar, puts it in a holder, lights it, and presents it to CLAIRE)

Schill. My kitten smokes cigars!

Claire. Yes. I adore them. Would you care for one?

Schill. Yes, please. I've never smoked one of those.

Claire. It's a taste I acquired from old Zachanassian. Among other things. He was a real connoisseur.

Schill. We used to sit on this bench once, you and I, and smoke cigarettes. Do you remember?

Claire. Yes. I remember.

Schill. The cigarettes I bought from Mathilde.

Claire. No. She gave them to you for nothing.

Schill. Clara—don't be angry with me for marrying Mathilde.

Claire. She had money.

Schill. But what a lucky thing for you that I did!

Claire. Oh?

Schill. You were so young, so beautiful. You deserved a far better fate than to settle in this wretched town without any future.

Claire. Yes?

Schill. If you had stayed in Güllen and married me, your life would have been wasted, like mine.

Claire. Oh?

Schill. Look at me. A wretched shopkeeper in a bankrupt town!

Claire. But you have your family.

Schill. My family! Never for a moment do they let me forget my failure, my poverty.

Claire. Mathilde has not made you happy?

Schill (*Shrugs*). What does it matter?

Claire. And the children?

Schill (*Shakes his head*). They're so completely materialistic. You know,

they have no interest whatever in higher things.

Claire. How sad for you.

(*A moment's pause, during which only the faint tinkling of the music is heard*)

Schill. Yes. You know, since you went away my life has passed by like a stupid dream. I've hardly once been out of this town. A trip to a lake years ago. It rained all the time. And once five days in Berlin. That's all.

Claire. The world is much the same everywhere.

Schill. At least you've seen it.

Claire. Yes. I've seen it.

Schill. You've lived in it.

Claire. I've lived in it. The world and I have been on very intimate terms.

Schill. Now that you've come back, perhaps things will changes.

Claire. Naturally. I certainly won't leave my native town in this condition.

Schill. It will take millions to put us on our feet again.

Claire. I have millions.

Schill. One, two, three.

Claire. Why not?

Schill. You mean—you will help us?

Claire. Yes.

(*A woodpecker is heard in the distance*)

Schill. I knew it—I knew it. I told them you were generous. I told them you were good. Oh, my kitten, my kitten.

(*He takes her hand. She turns her head away and listens*)

Claire. Listen! A woodpecker.

Schill. It's all just the way it was in the days when we were young and full of courage. The sun high above the pines. White clouds, piling up on one another. And the cry of the cuckoo in the distance. And the wind rustling the leaves, like the sound of surf on a beach. Just as it was years ago. If only we could roll back time and be together always.

Claire. Is that your wish?

Schill. Yes. You left me, but you never left my heart. (*He raises her hand to his lips*) The same soft little hand.

Claire. No, not quite the same. It was crushed in the plane accident. But they mended it. They mend everything nowadays.

Schill. Crushed? You wouldn't know it. See, another fawn.

Claire. The old wood is alive with memories.

(PEDRO *appears, right, with a fish in his hand*)

Pedro. See what I've caught, darling. See? A pike. Over two kilos.

(*The* BLIND MEN *appear onstage*)

Both Blind Men (*Clapping their hands*). A pike! A pike! Hurrah! Hurrah!

(*As the* BLIND MEN *clap their hands,* CLAIRE *and* SCHILL *exit, and the scene dissolves. The clapping of hands is taken up on all sides. The* TOWNSPEOPLE *wheel in the walls of the café. A brass band strikes up a march tune. The door of the Golden Apostle descends. The* TOWNSPEOPLE *bring in tables and set them with ragged tablecloths, cracked china and glassware. There is a table in the center, upstage, flanked by two tables perpendicular to it, right and left. The* PASTOR *and the* BURGO-MASTER *come in.* SCHILL *enters. Other* TOWNSPEOPLE *filter in, left and right. One, the* ATHLETE, *is in gym-*

nastic costume. The applause continues)

Burgomaster. She's coming! (CLAIRE *enters upstage, center, followed by* BOBBY) The applause is meant for you, gracious lady.

Claire. The band deserves it more than I. They blow from the heart. And the human pyramid was beautiful. You, show me your muscles. (*The* ATHLETE *kneels before her*) Superb. Wonderful arms, powerful hands. Have you ever strangled a man with them?

Athlete. Strangled?

Claire. Yes. It's perfectly simple. A little pressure in the proper place, and the rest goes by itself. As in politics.

(*The* BURGOMASTER's *wife comes up, simpering*)

Burgomaster (*Presents her*). Permit me to present my wife, Madame Zachanassian.

Claire. Annette Dummermuth. The head of our class.

Burgomaster. (*He presents another sour-looking woman*) Frau Schill.

Claire. Mathilde Blumhard. I remember the way you used to follow Anton with your eyes, from behind the shop door. You've grown a little thin and dry, my poor Mathilde.

Schill. My daughter, Ottilie.

Claire. Your daughter . . .

Schill. My son, Karl.

Claire. Your son. Two of them!

(*The town* DOCTOR *comes in, right. He is a man of fifty, strong and stocky, with bristly black hair, a mustache, and a saber cut on his cheek. He is wearing an old cutaway*)

Doctor. Well, well, my old Mercedes

got me here in time after all!

Burgomaster. Dr. Nüsslin, the town physician. Madame Zachanassian.

Doctor. Deeply honored, madame.

(*He kisses her hand.* CLAIRE *studies him*)

Claire. It is you who signs the death certificates?

Doctor. Death certificates?

Claire. When someone dies.

Doctor. Why certainly. That is one of my duties.

Claire. And when the heart dies, what do you put down? Heart failure?

Schill (*Laughing*). What a golden sense of humor!

Doctor. Bit grim, wouldn't you say?

Schill (*Whispers*). Not at all, not at all. She's promised us a million.

Burgomaster (*Turns his head*). What?

Schill. A million!

All (*Whisper*). A million!

(CLAIRE *turns toward them*)

Claire. Burgomaster.

Burgomaster. Yes?

Claire. I'm hungry. (*The girls and the waiter fill glasses and bring food. There is a general stir. All take their places at the tables*) Are you going to make a speech?

(*The* BURGOMASTER *bows.* CLAIRE *sits next to the* BURGOMASTER. *The* BURGOMASTER *rises, tapping his knife on his glass. He is radiant with good will. All applaud*)

Burgomaster. Gracious lady and friends. Gracious lady, it is now many years since you first left your native town of Güllen, which was founded by the Elector Hasso and which nestles in the green slope between the forest of Konradsweil and the beautiful valley of Pückenried.

Much has taken place in this time, much that is evil.

Teacher. That's true.

Burgomaster. The world is not what it was; it has become harsh and bitter, and we too have had our share of harshness and bitterness. But in all this time, dear lady, we have never forgotten our little Clara. (*Applause*) Many years ago you brightened the town with your pretty face as a child, and now once again you brighten it with your presence. (*Polite applause*) We haven't forgotten you, and we haven't forgotten your family. Your mother, beautiful and robust even in her old age—(*He looks for his notes on the table*)—although unfortunately taken from us in the bloom of her youth by an infirmity of the lungs. Your respected father, Siegfried Wäscher, the builder, an example of whose work next to our railway station is often visited—(SCHILL *covers his face*)—that is to say, admired—a lasting monument of local design and local workmanship. And you, gracious lady, whom we remember as a golden-haired—(*He looks at her*)—little red-headed sprite romping about our peaceful streets—on your way to school—which of us does not treasure your memory? (*He pokes nervously at his notebook*) We well remember your scholarly attainments—

Teacher. Yes.

Burgomaster. Natural history . . . Extraordinary sense of justice . . . And, above all, your supreme generosity. (*Great applause*) We shall never forget how you once spent the whole of your little savings to buy a sack of potatoes for a poor starving widow who was in need of food. Gracious lady, ladies and gentlemen, today, our little Clara has become the world-famous Claire Zachanassian who has founded hospitals, soup kitchens, charitable institutes, art projects, libraries, nurseries and schools, and now that she has at last once more returned to the town of her birth, sadly fallen as it is, I say in the name of all her loving friends who have sorely missed her: Long live our Clara!

All. Long live our Clara!

(*Cheers. Music. Fanfare. Applause.* CLAIRE *rises*)

Claire. Mr. Burgomaster. Fellow townsmen. I am greatly moved by the nature of your welcome and the disinterested joy which you have manifested on the occasion of my visit to my native town. I was not quite the child the Burgomaster described in his gracious address . . .

Burgomaster. Too modest, madame.

Claire. In school I was beaten—

Teacher. Not by me.

Claire. And the sack of potatoes which I presented to Widow Boll, I stole with the help of Anton Schill, not to save the old trull from starvation, but so that for once I might sleep with Anton in a real bed instead of under the trees of the forest. (*The* TOWNS-PEOPLE *look grave, embarrassed*) Nevertheless, I shall try to deserve your good opinion. In memory of the seventeen years I spent among you, I am prepared to hand over as a gift to the town of Güllen the sum of one billion marks. Five hundred million to the town, and five hundred million to be divided per capita among the citizens.

(*There is a moment of dead silence*)

Burgomaster. A billion marks?

Claire. On one condition.

(*Suddenly a movement of uncontrollable joy breaks out. People jump on chairs, dance about, yell excitedly. The* ATHLETE *turns handsprings in front of the speaker's table*)

Schill. Oh, Clara, you astonishing, incredible, magnificent woman! What a heart! What a gesture! Oh—my little witch!

(*He kisses her hand*)

Burgomaster (*Holds up his arms for order*). Quiet! Quiet, please! On one condition, the gracious lady said. Now, madame, may we know what that condition is?

Claire. I will tell you. In exchange for my billion marks, I want justice.

(*Silence*)

Burgomaster. Justice, madame?

Claire. I wish to buy justice.

Burgomaster. But justice cannot be bought, madame.

Claire. Everything can be bought.

Burgomaster. I don't understand at all.

Claire. Bobby, step forward.

(*The butler goes to the center of the stage. He takes off his dark glasses and turns his face with a solemn air*)

Bobby. Does anyone here present recognize me?

Frau Schill. Hofer! Hofer!

All. Who? What's that?

Teacher. Not Chief Magistrate Hofer?

Bobby. Exactly. Chief Magistrate Hofer. When Madame Zachanassian was a girl, I was presiding judge at the criminal court of Güllen. I served there until twenty-five years ago, when Madame Zachanassian offered me the opportunity of entering her service as butler. I accepted. You may consider it a strange employment for a member of the magistracy, but the salary—

(CLAIRE *bangs the mallet on the table*)

Claire. Come to the point.

Bobby. You have heard Madame Zachanassian's offer. She will give you a billion marks—when you have undone the injustice that she suffered at your hands here in Güllen as a girl.

(*All murmur*)

Burgomaster. Injustice at our hands? Impossible!

Bobby. Anton Schill . . .

Schill. Yes?

Bobby. Kindly stand.

(SCHILL *rises. He smiles, as if puzzled. He shrugs*)

Schill. Yes?

Bobby. In those days, a bastardy case was tried before me. Madame Claire Zachanassian, at that time called Clara Wäscher, charged you with being the father of her illegitimate child. (*Silence*) You denied the charge. And produced two witnesses in your support.

Schill. That's ancient history. An absurd business. We were children. Who remembers?

Claire. Where are the blind men?

Both Blind Men. Here we are. Here we are.

(MIKE *and* MAX *push them forward*)

Bobby. You recognize these men, Anton Schill?

Schill. I never saw them before in my life. What are they?

Both Blind Men. We've changed. We've changed.

Bobby. What were your names in your former life?

First Blind Man. I was Jacob Hueblein. Jacob Hueblein.

Second Blind Man. I was Ludwig Sparr. Ludwig Sparr.

Bobby (*To* SCHILL). Well?

Schill. These names mean nothing to me.

Bobby. Jacob Hueblein and Ludwig Sparr, do you recognize the defendant?

First Blind Man. We're blind.

Second Blind Man. We're blind.

Schill. Ha-ha-ha!

Bobby. By his voice?

Both Blind Men. By his voice. By his voice.

Bobby. At that trial, I was the judge. And you?

Both Blind Men. We were the witnesses.

Bobby. And what did you testify on that occasion?

First Blind Man. That we had slept with Clara Wäscher.

Second Blind Man. Both of us. Many times.

Bobby. And was it true?

First Blind Man. No.

Second Blind Man. We swore falsely.

Bobby. And why did you swear falsely?

First Blind Man. Anton Schill bribed us.

Second Blind Man. He bribed us.

Bobby. With what?

Both Blind Men. With a bottle of schnapps.

Bobby. And now tell the people what happened to you. (*They hesitate and whimper*) Speak!

First Blind Man (*In a low voice*). She tracked us down.

Bobby. Madame Zachanassian tracked them down. Jacob Hueblein was found in Canada. Ludwig Sparr in Australia. And when she found you, what did she do to you?

Second Blind Man. She handed us over to Mike and Max.

Bobby. And what did Mike and Max do to you?

First Blind Man. They made us what you see.

(*The* BLIND MEN *cover their faces.* MIKE *and* MAX *push them off*)

Bobby. And there you have it. We are all present in Güllen once again. The plaintiff. The defendant. The two false witnesses. The judge. Many years have passed. Does the plaintiff have anything further to add?

Claire. There is nothing to add.

Bobby. And the defendant?

Schill. Why are you doing this? It was all dead and buried.

Bobby. What happened to the child that was born?

Claire (*In a low voice*). It lived a year.

Bobby. And what happened to you?

Claire. I became a whore.

Bobby. Why?

Claire. The judgment of the court left me no alternative. No one would trust me. No one would give me work.

Bobby. So. And now, what is the nature of the reparation you demand?

Claire. I want the life of Schill.

(FRAU SCHILL *springs to Anton's side. She puts her arms around him.*

The children rush to him. He breaks away)

Frau Schill. Anton! No! No!

Schill. No— No— She's joking. That happened long ago. That's all forgotten.

Claire. Nothing is forgotten. Neither the mornings in the forest, nor the nights in the great barn, nor the bedroom in the cottage, nor your treachery at the end. You said this morning that you wished that time might be rolled back. Very well—I have rolled it back. And now it is I who will buy justice. You bought it with a bottle of schnapps. I am willing to pay one billion marks.

(*The* BURGOMASTER *stands up, very pale and dignified*)

Burgomaster. Madame Zachanassian, we are not in the jungle. We are in Europe. We may be poor, but we are not heathens. In the name of the town of Güllen, I decline your offer. In the name of humanity. We shall never accept.

(*All applaud wildly. The applause turns into a sinister rhythmic beat. As* CLAIRE *rises, it dies away. She looks at the crowd, then at the* BURGO-MASTER)

Claire. Thank you, Burgomaster. (*She stares at him a long moment*) I can wait.

(*She turns and walks off*)

Curtain

ACT TWO

*The façade of the Golden Apostle, with a balcony on which chairs and a table are set out. To the right of the inn is a sign which reads: "*ANTON SCHILL, HANDLUNG.*" Under the sign the* *shop is represented by a broken counter. Behind the counter are some shelves with tobacco, cigarettes and liquor bottles. There are two milk cans. The shop door is imaginary, but each entrance is indicated by a doorbell with a tinny sound.*

It is early morning.

SCHILL *is sweeping the shop. The* SON *has a pan and brush and also sweeps. The* DAUGHTER *is dusting. They are singing "The Happy Wanderer."*

Schill. Karl—

(KARL *crosses with a dustpan.* SCHILL *sweeps dust into the pan. The doorbell rings. The* THIRD MAN *appears, carrying a crate of eggs*)

Third Man. 'Morning.

Schill. Ah, good mornnig, Wechsler.

Third Man. Twelve dozen eggs, medium brown. Right?

Schill. Take them, Karl. (*The* SON *puts the crate in a corner*) Did they deliver the milk yet?

Son. Before you came down.

Third Man. Eggs are going up again, Herr Schill. First of the month.

(*He gives* SCHILL *a slip to sign*)

Schill. What? Again? And who's going to buy them?

Third Man. Fifty pfennig a dozen.

Schill. I'll have to cancel my order, that's all.

Third Man. That's up to you, Herr Schill.

(SCHILL *signs the slip*)

Schill. There's nothing else to do. (*He hands back the slip*) And how's the family?

Third Man. Oh, scraping along. Maybe now things will get better.

Schill. Maybe.

Third Man (*Going*). 'Morning.

Schill. Close the door. Don't let the flies in. (*The children resume their singing*) Now, listen to me, children. I have a little piece of good news for you. I didn't mean to speak of it yet awhile, but well, why not? Who do you suppose is going to be the next Burgomaster? Eh? (*They look up at him*) Yes, in spite of everything. It's settled. It's official. What an honor for the family, eh? Especially at a time like this. To say nothing of the salary and the rest of it.

Son. Burgomaster!

Schill. Burgomaster. (*The* SON *shakes him warmly by the hand. The* DAUGHTER *kisses him*) You see, you don't have to be entirely ashamed of your father. (*Silence*) Is your mother coming down to breakfast soon?

Daughter. Mother's tired. She's going to stay upstairs.

Schill. You have a good mother, at least. There you are lucky. Oh, well, if she wants to rest, let her rest. We'll have breakfast together, the three of us. I'll fry some eggs and open a tin of the American ham. This morning we're going to breakfast like kings.

Son. I'd like to, only—I can't.

Schill. You've got to eat, you know.

Son. I've got to run down to the station. One of the laborers is sick. They said they could use me.

Schill. You want to work on the rails in all this heat? That's no work for a son of mine.

Son. Look, Father, we can use the money.

Schill. Well, if you feel you have to.

(*The* SON *goes to the door. The* DAUGHTER *moves toward* SCHILL)

Daughter. I'm sorry, Father. I have to go too.

Schill. You too? And where is the young lady going, if I may be so bold?

Daughter. There may be something for me at the employment agency.

Schill. Employment agency?

Daughter. It's important to get there early.

Schill. All right. I'll have something nice for you when you get home.

Son and Daughter (*Salute*). Good day, Burgomaster.

(*The* SON *and* DAUGHTER *go out. The* FIRST MAN *comes into* SCHILL'S *shop. Mandolin and guitar music are heard offstage*)

Schill. Good morning, Hofbauer.

First Man. Cigarettes. (SCHILL *takes a pack from the shelf*) Not those. I'll have the green today.

Schill. They cost more.

First Man. Put it in the book.

Schill. What?

First Man. Charge it.

Schill. Well, all right, I'll make an exception this time—seeing it's you, Hofbauer.

(SCHILL *writes in his cash book*)

First Man (*Opening the pack of cigarettes*). Who's that playing out there?

Schill. The two blind men.

First Man. They play well.

Schill. To hell with them.

First Man. They make you nervous? (SCHILL *shrugs. The* FIRST MAN *lights a cigarette*) She's getting ready for the wedding, I hear.

Schill. Yes. So they say.

(*Enter the* FIRST *and* SECOND WOMAN. *They cross to the counter*)

First Woman. Good morning, good morning.

First Man. Good morning.

Second Woman. Good morning.

Schill. Good morning, ladies.

First Woman. Good morning, Herr Schill.

Second Woman. Good morning.

First Woman. Milk please, Herr Schill.

Schill. Milk.

Second Woman. And milk for me too.

Schill. A liter of milk each. Right away.

First Woman. Whole milk, please, Herr Schill.

Schill. Whole milk?

Second Woman. Yes. Whole milk, please.

Schill. Whole milk, I can only give you half a liter each of whole milk.

First Woman. All right.

Schill. Half a liter of whole milk here, and half a liter of whole milk here. There you are.

First Woman. And butter please, a quarter kilo.

Schill. Butter, I haven't any butter. I can give you some very nice lard?

First Woman. No. Butter.

Schill. Goose fat? (*The* FIRST WOMAN *shakes her head*) Chicken fat?

First Woman. Butter.

Schill. Butter. Now, wait a minute, though. I have a tin of imported butter here somewhere. Ah. There you are. No, sorry, she asked first, but I can order some for you from Kalberstadt tomorrow.

Second Woman. And white bread.

Schill. White bread.

(*He takes a loaf and a knife*)

Second Woman. The whole loaf.

Schill. But a whole loaf would cost . . .

Second Woman. Charge it.

Schill. Charge it?

First Woman. And a package of milk chocolate.

Schill. Package of milk chocolate—right away.

Second Woman. One for me, too, Herr Schill.

Schill. And a package of milk chocolate for you, too.

First Woman. We'll eat it here, if you don't mind.

Schill. Yes, please do.

Second Woman. It's so cool at the back of the shop.

Schill. Charge it?

Women. Of course.

Schill. All for one, one for all.

(*The* Second Man *enters*)

Second Man. Good morning.

The Two Women. Good morning.

Schill. Good morning, Helmesberger.

Second Man. It's going to be a hot day.

Schill. Phew!

Second Man. How's business?

Schill. Fabulous. For a while no one came, and now all of a sudden I'm running a luxury trade.

Second Man. Good!

Schill. Oh, I'll never forget the way you all stood by me at the Golden Apostle in spite of your need, in spite of everything. That was the finest hour of my life.

First Man. We're not heathens, you know.

Second Man. We're behind you, my boy; the whole town's behind you.

First Man. As firm as a rock.

First Woman (*Munching her chocolate*). As firm as a rock, Herr Schill.

Both Women. As firm as a rock.

Second Man. There's no denying it—you're the most popular man in town.

First Man. The most important.

Second Man. And in the spring, God willing, you will be our Burgomaster.

First Man. Sure as a gun.

All. Sure as a gun.

(*Enter* Pedro *with fishing equipment and a fish in his landing net*)

Pedro. Would you please weigh my fish for me?

Schill (*Weighs it*). Two kilos.

Pedro. Is that all?

Schill. Two kilos exactly.

Pedro. Two kilos!

(*He gives* Schill *a tip and exits*)

Second Woman. The fiancé.

First Woman. They're to be married this week. It will be a tremendous wedding.

Second Woman. I saw his picture in the paper.

First Woman (*Sighs*). Ah, what a man!

Second Man. Give me a bottle of schnapps.

Schill. The usual?

Second Man. No, cognac.

Schill. Cognac? But cognac costs twenty-two marks fifty.

Second Man. We all have to splurge a little now and again—

Schill. Here you are. Three Star.

Second Man. And a package of pipe tobacco.

Schill. Black or blond?

Second Man. English.

Schill. English! But that makes twenty-three marks eighty.

Second Man. Chalk it up.

Schill. Now, look. I'll make an exception this week. Only, you will have to pay me the moment your unemployment check comes in. I don't want to be kept waiting. (*Suddenly*) Helmesberger, are those new shoes you're wearing?

Second Man. Yes, what about it?

Schill. You too, Hofbauer. Yellow shoes! Brand new!

First Man. So?

Schill (*To the women*). And you. You all have new shoes! New shoes!

First Woman. A person can't walk around forever in the same old shoes.

Second Woman. Shoes wear out.

Schill. And the money. Where does the money come from?

First Woman. We got them on credit, Herr Schill.

Second Woman. On credit.

Schill. On credit? And where all of a sudden do you get credit?

Second Man. Everybody gives credit now.

First Woman. You gave us credit yourself.

Schill. And what are you going to pay with? Eh? (*They are all silent.* SCHILL *advances upon them threateningly*) With what? Eh? With what? With what?

(*Suddenly he understands. He takes his apron off quickly, flings it on the counter, gets his jacket, and walks off with an air of determination. Now the shop sign vanishes. The shelves are pushed off. The lights go up on the balcony of the Golden Apostle, and the balcony unit itself moves forward into the optical center.* CLAIRE *and* BOBBY *step out on the balcony.* CLAIRE *sits down.* BOBBY *serves coffee*)

Claire. A lovely autumn morning. A silver haze on the streets and a violet sky above. Count Holk would have liked this. Remember him, Bobby? My third husband?

Bobby. Yes, madame.

Claire. Horrible man!

Bobby. Yes, madame.

Claire. Where is Monsieur Pedro? Is he up yet?

Bobby. Yes, madame. He's fishing.

Claire. Already? What a singular passion!

(PEDRO *comes in with the fish*)

Pedro. Good morning, my love.

Claire. Pedro! There you are.

Pedro. Look, my darling. Four kilos!

Claire. A jewel! I'll have it grilled for your lunch. Give it to Bobby.

Pedro. Ah—it is so wonderful here! I like your little town.

Claire. Oh, do you?

Pedro. Yes. These people, they are all so—what is the word?

Claire. Simple, honest, hard-working, decent.

Pedro. But, my angel, you are a mind reader. That's just what I was going to say—however did you guess?

Claire. I know them.

Pedro. Yet when we arrived it was all so dirty, so—what is the word?

Claire. Shabby.

Pedro. Exactly. But now everywhere you go, you see them busy as bees, cleaning their streets—

Claire. Repairing their houses, sweeping—dusting—hanging new curtains in the windows—singing as they work.

Pedro. But you astonishing, wonderful woman! You can't see all that from here.

Claire. I know them. And in their gardens—I am sure that in their gardens they are manuring the soil for the spring.

Pedro. My angel, you know everything. This morning on my way fishing I said to myself, look at them all manuring their gardens. It is extraordinary—and it's all because of you.

Your return has given them a new—what is the word?

Claire. Lease on life?

Pedro. Precisely.

Claire. The town was dying, it's true. But a town doesn't have to die. I think they realize that now. People die, not towns. Bobby! (BOBBY *appears*) A cigar.

(*The lights fade on the balcony, which moves back upstage. Somewhat to the right, a sign descends. It reads: "Polizei." The* POLICEMAN *pushes a desk under it. This, with the bench, becomes the police station. He places a bottle of beer and a glass on the desk, and goes to hang up his coat offstage. The telephone rings*)

Policeman. Schultz speaking. Yes, we have a couple of rooms for the night. No, not for rent. This is not the hotel. This is the Güllen police station.

(*He laughs and hangs up.* SCHILL *comes in. He is evidently nervous*)

Schill. Schultz.

Policeman. Hello, Schill. Come in. Sit down. Beer?

Schill. Please.

(*He drinks thirstily*)

Policeman. What can I do for you?

Schill. I want you to arrest Madame Zachanassian.

Policeman. Eh?

Schill. I said I want you to arrest Madame Zachanassian.

Policeman. What the hell are you talking about?

Schill. I ask you to arrest this woman at once.

Policeman. What offense has the lady committed?

Schill. You know perfectly well. She offered a billion marks—

Policeman. And you want her arrested for that?

(*He pours beer into his glass*)

Schill. Schultz! It's your duty.

Schultz. Extraordinary! Extraordinary idea!

(*He drinks his beer*)

Schill. I'm speaking to you as your next Burgomaster.

Policeman. Schill, that's true. The lady offered us a billion marks. But that doesn't entitle us to take police action against her.

Schill. Why not?

Policeman. In order to be arrested, a person must first commit a crime.

Schill. Incitement to murder.

Policeman. Incitement to murder is a crime. I agree.

Schill. Well?

Policeman. And such a proposal—if serious—constitutes an assault.

Schill. That's what I mean.

Policeman. But her offer can't be serious.

Schill. Why?

Policeman. The price is too high. In a case like yours, one pays a thousand marks, at the most two thousand. But not a billion! That's ridiculous. And even if she meant it, that would only prove she was out of her mind. And that's not a matter for the police.

Schill. Whether she's out of her mind or not, the danger to me is the same. That's obvious.

Policeman. Look, Schill, you show us where anyone threatens your life in any way—say, for instance, a man points a gun at you—and we'll be there in a flash.

Schill (*Gets up*). So I'm to wait till someone points a gun at me?

Policeman. Pull yourself together, Schill. We're all for you in this town.

Schill. I wish I could believe it.

Policeman. You don't believe it?

Schill. No. No, I don't. All of a sudden my customers are buying white bread, whole milk, butter, imported tobacco. What does it mean?

Policeman. It means business is picking up.

Schill. Helmesberger lives on the dole; he hasn't earned anything in five years. Today he bought French cognac.

Policeman. I'll have to try your cognac one of these days.

Schill. And shoes. They all have new shoes.

Policeman. And what have you got against new shoes? I'm wearing a new pair myself.

(*He holds out his foot*)

Schill. You too?

Policeman. Why not?

(*He pours out the rest of his beer*)

Schill. Is that Pilsen you're drinking now?

Policeman. It's the only thing.

Schill. You used to drink the local beer.

Policeman. Hogwash.

(*Radio music is heard offstage*)

Schill. Listen. You hear?

Policeman. "The Merry Widow." Yes.

Schill. No. It's a radio.

Policeman. That's Bergholzer's radio.

Schill. Bergholzer!

Policeman. You're right. He should close his window when he plays it. I'll make a note to speak to him.

(*He makes a note in his notebook*)

Schill. And how can Bergholzer pay for a radio?

Policeman. That's his business.

Schill. And you, Schultz, with your new shoes and your imported beer—how are you going to pay for them?

Policeman. That's my business. (*His telephone rings. He picks it up*) Police Station, Güllen. What? What? Where? Where? How? Right, we'll deal with it.

(*He hangs up*)

Schill (*He speaks during the* POLICE- MAN's *telephone conversation*) Schultz, listen. No. Schultz, please— listen to me. Don't you see they're all . . . Listen, please. Look, Schultz. They're all running up debts. And out of these debts comes this sudden prosperity. And out of this prosperity comes the absolute need to kill me.

Policeman (*Putting on his jacket*) You're imagining things.

Schill. All she has to do is to sit on her balcony and wait.

Policeman. Don't be a child.

Schill. You're all waiting.

Policeman (*Snaps a loaded clip into the magazine of a rifle*). Look, Schill, you can relax. The police are here for your protection. They know their job. Let anyone, any time, make the slightest threat to your life, and all you have to do is let us know. We'll do the rest . . . Now, don't worry.

Schill. No, I won't.

Policeman. And don't upset yourself. All right?

Schill. Yes. I won't. (*Then suddenly, in a low tone*) You have a new gold tooth in your mouth!

Policeman. What are you talking about?

Schill (*Taking the* POLICEMAN's *head in his hands, and forcing his lips open*). A brand new, shining gold tooth.

Policeman (*Breaks away and involuntarily levels the gun at* Schill). Are you crazy? Look, I've no time to waste. Madame Zachanassian's panther's broken loose.

Schill. Panther?

Policeman. Yes, it's at large. I've got to hunt it down.

Schill. You're not hunting a panther and you know it. It's me you're hunting!

(*The* Policeman *clicks on the safety and lowers the gun*)

Policeman. Schill! Take my advice. Go home. Lock the door. Keep out of everyone's way. That way you'll be safe. Cheer up! Good times are just around the corner!

(*The lights dim in this area and light up on the balcony.* Pedro *is lounging in a chair.* Claire *is smoking*)

Pedro. Oh, this little town oppresses me.

Claire. Oh, does it? So you've changed your mind?

Pedro. It is true, I find it charming, delightful—

Claire. Picturesque.

Pedro. Yes. After all, it's the place where you were born. But it is too quiet for me. Too provincial. Too much like all small towns everywhere. These people—look at them. They fear nothing, they desire nothing, they strive for nothing. They have everything they want. They are asleep.

Claire. Perhaps one day they will come to life again.

Pedro. My God—do I have to wait for that?

Claire. Yes, you do. Why don't you go back to your fishing?

Pedro. I think I will.

(Pedro *turns to go*)

Claire. Pedro.

Pedro. Yes, my love?

Claire. Telephone the president of Hambro's Bank. Ask him to transfer a billion marks to my current account.

Pedro. A billion? Yes, my love.

(*He goes. The lights fade on the balcony. A sign is flown in. It reads: "Rathaus." The* Third Man *crosses the stage, right to left, wheeling a new television set on a hand truck. The counter of* Schill's *shop is transformed into the* Burgomaster's *office. The* Burgomaster *comes in. He takes a revolver from his pocket, examines it and sets it down on the desk. He sits down and starts writing.* Schill *knocks*)

Burgomaster. Come in.

Schill. I must have a word with you, Burgomaster.

Burgomaster. Ah, Schill. Sit down, my friend.

Schill. Man to man. As your successor.

Burgomaster. But of course. Naturally.

(Schill *remains standing. He looks at the revolver*)

Schill. Is that a gun?

Burgomaster. Madame Zachanassian's black panther's broken loose. It's been seen near the cathedral. It's as well to be prepared.

Schill. Oh, yes. Of course.

Burgomaster. I've sent out a call for all able-bodied men with firearms. The streets have been cleared. The children have been kept in school. We don't want any accidents.

Schill (*Suspiciously*). You're making quite a thing of it.

Burgomaster (*Shrugs*). Naturally. A panther is a dangerous beast. Well?

What's on your mind? Speak out. We're old friends.

Schill. That's a good cigar you're smoking, Burgomaster.

Burgomaster. Yes. Havana.

Schill. You used to smoke something else.

Burgomaster. Fortuna.

Schill. Cheaper.

Burgomaster. Too strong.

Schill. A new tie? Silk?

Burgomaster. Yes. Do you like it?

Schill. And have you also bought new shoes?

Burgomaster (*Brings his feet out from under the desk*). Why, yes. I ordered a new pair from Kalberstadt. Extraordinary! However did you guess?

Schill. That's why I'm here.

(*The* THIRD MAN *knocks*)

Burgomaster. Come in.

Third Man. The new typewriter, sir.

Burgomaster. Put it on the table. (*The* THIRD MAN *sets it down and goes*) What's the matter with you? My dear fellow, aren't you well?

Schill. It's you who don't seem well, Burgomaster.

Burgomaster. What do you mean?

Schill. You look pale.

Burgomaster. I?

Schill. Your hands are trembling. (*The* BURGOMASTER *involuntarily hides his hands*) Are you frightened?

Burgomaster. What have I to be afraid of?

Schill. Perhaps this sudden prosperity alarms you.

Burgomaster. Is prosperity a crime?

Schill. That depends on how you pay for it.

Burgomaster. You'll have to forgive me, Schill, but I really haven't the slightest idea what you're talking

about. Am I supposed to feel like a criminal every time I order a new typewriter?

Schill. Do you?

Burgomaster. Well, I hope you haven't come here to talk about a new typewriter. Now, what was it you wanted?

Schill. I have come to claim the protection of the authorities.

Burgomaster. Ei! Against whom?

Schill. You know against whom.

Burgomaster. You don't trust us?

Schill. That woman has put a price on my head.

Burgomaster. If you don't feel safe, why don't you go to the police?

Schill. I have just come from the police.

Burgomaster. And?

Schill. The chief has a new gold tooth in his mouth.

Burgomaster. A new—? Oh, Schill, really! You're forgetting. This is Güllen, the town of humane traditions. Goethe slept here. Brahms composed a quartet. You must have faith in us. This is a law-abiding community.

Schill. Then arrest this woman who wants to have me killed.

Burgomaster. Look here, Schill. God knows the lady has every right to be angry with you. What you did there wasn't very pretty. You forced two decent lads to perjure themselves and had a young girl thrown out on the streets.

Schill. That young girl owns half the world.

(*A moment's silence*)

Burgomaster. Very well, then, we'll speak frankly.

Schill. That's why I'm here.

Burgomaster. Man to man, just as you said. (*He clears his throat*) Now—

after what you did, you have no moral right to say a word against this lady. And I advise you not to try. Also—I regret to have to tell you this—there is no longer any question of your being elected Burgomaster.

Schill. Is that official?

Burgomaster. Official.

Schill. I see.

Burgomaster. The man who is chosen to exercise the high post of Burgomaster must have, obviously, certain moral qualifications. Qualifications which, unhappily, you no longer possess. Naturally, you may count on the esteem and friendship of the town, just as before. That goes without saying. The best thing will be to spread the mantle of silence over the whole miserable business.

Schill. So I'm to remain silent while they arrange my murder?

(*The* Burgomaster *gets up*)

Burgomaster (*Suddenly noble*). Now, who is arranging your murder? Give me the names and I will investigate the case at once. Unrelentingly. Well? The names?

Schill. You.

Burgomaster. I resent this. Do you think we want to kill you for money?

Schill. No. You don't want to kill me. But you want to have me killed.

(*The lights go down. The stage is filled with men prowling about with rifles, as if they were stalking a quarry. In the interval the* Police- man's *bench and the* Burgomaster's *desk are shifted somewhat, so that they will compose the setting for the sacristy. The stage empties. The lights come up on the balcony.* Claire *appears*)

Claire. Bobby, what's going on here?

What are all these men doing with guns? Whom are they hunting?

Bobby. The black panther has escaped, madame.

Claire. Who let him out?

Bobby. Kobby and Lobby, madame.

Claire. How excited they are! There may be shooting?

Bobby. It is possible, madame.

(*The lights fade on the balcony. The* Sacristan *comes in. He arranges the set, and puts the altar cloth on the altar. Then* Schill *comes on. He is looking for the* Pastor. *The* Pastor *enters, left. He is wearing his gown and carrying a rifle*)

Schill. Sorry to disturb you, Pastor.

Pastor. God's house is open to all. (*He sees that* Schill *is staring at the gun*) Oh, the gun? That's because of the panther. It's best to be prepared.

Schill. Pastor, help me.

Pastor. Of course. Sit down. (*He puts the rifle on the bench*) What's the trouble?

Schill (*Sits on the bench*). I'm frightened.

Pastor. Frightened? Of what?

Schill. Of everyone. They're hunting me down like a beast.

Pastor. Have no fear of man, Schill. Fear God. Fear not the death of the body. Fear the death of the soul. Zip up my gown behind, Sacristan.

Schill. I'm afraid, Pastor.

Pastor. Put your trust in heaven, my friend.

Schill. You see, I'm not well. I shake. I have pains around the heart. I sweat.

Pastor. I know. You're passing through a profound psychic experience.

Schill. I'm going through hell.

Pastor. The hell you are going through

exists only within yourself. Many years ago you betrayed a girl shamefully, for money. Now you think that we shall sell you just as you sold her. No, my friend, you are projecting your guilt upon others. It's quite natural. But remember, the root of our torment lies always within ourselves, in our hearts, in our sins. When you have understood this, you can conquer the fears that oppress you; you have weapons with which to destroy them.

Schill. Siemethofer has bought a new washing machine.

Pastor. Don't worry about the washing machine. Worry about your immortal soul.

Schill. Stockers has a television set.

Pastor. There is also great comfort in prayer. Sacristan, the bands. (SCHILL *crosses to the altar and kneels. The* SACRISTAN *ties on the* PASTOR's *bands*) Examine your conscience, Schill. Repent. Otherwise your fears will consume you. Believe me, this is the only way. We have no other. (*The church bell begins to peal.* SCHILL *seems relieved*) Now I must leave you. I have a baptism. You may stay as long as you like. Sacristan, the Bible, Liturgy and Psalter. The child is beginning to cry. I can hear it from here. It is frightened. Let us make haste to give it the only security which this world affords.

Schill. A new bell?

Pastor. Yes. Its tone is marvelous, don't you think? Full. Sonorous.

Schill (*Steps back in horror*). A new bell! You too, Pastor? You too?

(*The* PASTOR *clasps his hands in horror. Then he takes* SCHILL *into his arms*)

Pastor. Oh, God, God forgive me. We are poor, weak things, all of us. Do not tempt us further into the hell in which you are burning. Go, Schill, my friend, go, my brother, go while there is time.

(*The* PASTOR *goes.* SCHILL *picks up the rifle with a gesture of desperation. He goes out with it. As the lights fade, men appear with guns. Two shots are fired in the darkness. The lights come up on the balcony, which moves forward*)

Claire. Bobby! What was that shooting? Have they caught the panther?

Bobby. He is dead, madame.

Claire. There were two shots.

Bobby. The panther is dead, madame.

Claire. I loved him. (*Waves* BOBBY *away*) I shall miss him.

(*The* TEACHER *comes in with two little girls, singing. They stop under the balcony*)

Teacher. Gracious lady, be so good as to accept our heartfelt condolences. Your beautiful panther is no more. Believe me, we are deeply pained that so tragic an event should mar your visit here. But what could we do? The panther was savage, a beast. To him our human laws could not apply. There was no other way— (SCHILL *appears with the gun. He looks dangerous. The girls run off, frightened. The* TEACHER *follows the girls*) Children—children—children!

Claire. Anton, why are you frightening the children?

(*He works the bolt, loading the chamber, and raises the gun slowly*)

Schill. Go away, Claire—I warn you. Go away.

Claire. How strange it is, Anton! How

clearly it comes back to me! The day we saw one another for the first time, do you remember? I was on a balcony then. It was a day like today, a day in autumn without a breath of wind, warm as it is now—only lately I am always cold. You stood down there and stared at me without moving. I was embarrassed. I didn't know what to do. I wanted to go back into the darkness of the room, where it was safe, but I couldn't. You stared up at me darkly, almost angrily, as if you wished to hurt me, but your eyes were full of passion. (SCHILL *begins to lower the rifle involuntarily*) Then, I don't know why, I left the balcony and I came down and stood in the street beside you. You didn't greet me, you didn't say a word, but you took my hand and we walked together out of the town into the fields, and behind us came Kobby and Lobby, like two dogs, sniveling and giggling and snarling. Suddenly you picked up a stone and hurled it at them, and they ran yelping back into the town, and we were alone. (SCHILL *has lowered the rifle completely. He moves toward her, as close as he can come*) That was the beginning, and everything else had to follow. There is no escape.

(*She goes in and closes the shutters.* SCHILL *stands immobile. The* TEACHER *tiptoes in. He stares at* SCHILL, *who doesn't see him. Then he beckons to the children*)

Teacher. Come, children, sing. Sing.

(*They begin singing. He creeps behind* SCHILL *and snatches away the the rifle.* SCHILL *turns sharply. The* PASTOR *comes in*)

Pastor. Go, Schill—go!

(SCHILL *goes out. The children continue singing, moving across the stage and off. The Golden Apostle vanishes. The crossing bell is heard. The scene dissolves into the railway-station setting, as in Act One. But there are certain changes. The time-table marked "Fahrplan" is now new, the frame freshly painted. There is a new travel poster on the station wall. It has a yellow sun and the words: "Reist in den Süden." On the other side of the Fahrplan is another poster with the words: "Die Passionsspiele Oberammergau." The sound of passing trains covers the scene change.* SCHILL *appears with an old valise in his hand, dressed in a shabby trench coat, his hat on his head. He looks about with a furtive air, walking slowly to the platform. Slowly, as if by chance, the* TOWNS-PEOPLE *enter, from all sides.* SCHILL *hesitates, stops*)

Burgomaster (*From upstage, center*). Good evening, Schill.

Schill. Good evening.

Policeman. Good evening.

Schill. Good evening.

Painter (*Enters*). Good evening.

Schill. Good evening.

Doctor. Good evening.

Schill. Good evening.

Burgomaster. So you're taking a little trip?

Schill. Yes. A little trip.

Policeman. May one ask where to?

Schill. I don't know.

Painter. Don't know?

Schill. To Kalberstadt.

Burgomaster (*With disbelief, pointing to the valise*). Kalberstadt?

Schill. After that—somewhere else.

Painter. Ah. After that somewhere else.

(*The* Fourth Man *walks in*)

Schill. I thought maybe Australia.

Burgomaster. Australia!

All. Australia!

Schill. I'll raise the money somehow.

Burgomaster. But why Australia?

Policeman. What would you be doing in Australia?

Schill. One can't always live in the same town, year in, year out.

Painter. But Australia—

Doctor. It's a risky trip for a man of your age.

Burgomaster. One of the lady's little men ran off to Australia . . .

All. Yes.

Policeman. You'll be much safer here.

Painter. Much!

(Schill *looks about him in anguish, like a beast at bay*)

Schill (*Low voice*). I wrote a letter to the administration at Kaffigen.

Burgomaster. Yes? And?

(*They are all intent on the answer*)

Schill. They didn't answer.

(*All laugh*)

Doctor. Do you mean to say you don't trust your old friends? That's not very flattering, you know.

Burgomaster. No one's going to do you any harm here.

Doctor. No harm here.

Schill. They didn't answer because our postmaster held up my letter.

Painter. Our postmaster? What an idea.

Burgomaster. The postmaster is a member of the town council.

Policeman. A man of the utmost integrity.

Doctor. He doesn't hold up letters. What an idea!

(*The crossing bell starts ringing*)

Station Master (*Announces*). Local to Kalberstadt!

(*The* Townspeople *all cross down to see the train arrive. Then they turn, with their backs to the audience, in a line across the stage.* Schill *cannot get through to reach the train*)

Schill (*In a low voice*). What are you all doing here? What do you want of me?

Burgomaster. We don't like to see you go.

Doctor. We've come to see you off.

(*The sound of the approaching train grows louder*)

Schill. I didn't ask you to come.

Policeman. But we have come.

Doctor. As old friends.

All. As old friends.

(*The* Station Master *holds up his paddle. The train stops with a screech of brakes. We hear the engine panting offstage*)

Voice (*Offstage*). Güllen!

Burgomaster. A pleasant journey.

Doctor. And long life!

Painter. And good luck in Australia!

All. Yes, good luck in Australia.

(*They press around him jovially. He stands motionless and pale*)

Schill. Why are you crowding me?

Policeman. What's the matter now?

(*The* Station Master *blows a long blast on his whistle*)

Schill. Give me room.

Doctor. But you have plenty of room.

(*They all move away from him*)

Policeman. Better get aboard, Schill.

Schill. I see. I see. One of you is going to push me under the wheels.

Policeman. Oh, nonsense. Go on, get aboard.

Schill. Get away from me, all of you.

Burgomaster. I don't know what you want. Just get on the train.

Schill. No. One of you will push me under.

Doctor. You're being ridiculous. Now, go on, get on the train.

Schill. Why are you all so near me?

Doctor. The man's gone mad.

Station Master. 'Board!

(*He blows his whistle. The engine bell clangs. The train starts*)

Burgomaster. Get aboard, man. Quick.

(*The following speeches are spoken all together until the train noises fade away*)

Doctor. The train's starting.

All. Get aboard, man. Get aboard. The train's starting.

Schill. If I try to get aboard, one of you will hold me back.

All. No, no.

Burgomaster. Get on the train.

Schill (*In terror, crouches against the wall of the* Station Master's *office*). No—no—no. No. (*He falls on his knees. The others crowd around him. He cowers on the ground, abjectly.*

The train sounds fade away) Oh, no —no—don't push me, don't push me!

Policeman. There. It's gone off without you.

(*Slowly they leave him. He raises himself up to a sitting position, still trembling. A* Truck Driver *enters with an empty can*)

Truck Driver. Do you know where I can get some water? My truck's boiling over. (Schill *points to the station office*) Thanks. (*He enters the office, gets the water and comes out. By this time,* Schill *is erect*) Missed your train?

Schill. Yes.

Truck Driver. To Kalberstadt?

Schill. Yes.

Truck Driver. Well, come with me. I'm going that way.

Schill. This is my town. This is my home. (*With strange new dignity*) No, thank you. I've changed my mind. I'm staying.

Truck Driver (*Shrugs*). All right.

(*He goes out.* Schill *picks up his bag, looks right and left, and slowly walks off*)

Curtain

ACT THREE

Music is heard. Then the curtain rises on the interior of the old barn, a dim, cavernous structure. Bars of light fall across the shadowy forms, shafts of sunlight from the holes and cracks in the walls and roof. Overhead hang old rags, decaying sacks, great cobwebs. Extreme left is a ladder leading to the loft. Near it, an old haycart. Left, Claire Zachanassian *is sitting in her gilded sedan chair, motionless, in her magnificent bridal gown and veil. Near the chair stands an old keg.*

Bobby (*Comes in, treading carefully*). The doctor and the teacher from the high school to see you, madame.

Claire (*Impassive*). Show them in.

(BOBBY *ushers them in as if they were entering a hall of state. The two grope their way through the litter. At last they find the lady, and bow. They are both well dressed in new clothes, but are very dusty*)

Bobby. Dr. Nüsslin and Professor Müller.

Doctor. Madame.

Claire. You look dusty, gentlemen.

Doctor (*Dusts himself off vigorously*). Oh, forgive us. We had to climb over an old carriage.

Teacher. Our respects.

Doctor. A fabulous wedding.

Teacher. Beautiful occasion.

Claire. It's stifling here. But I love this old barn. The smell of hay and old straw and axle grease—it is the scent of my youth. Sit down. All this rubbish—the haycart, the old carriage, the cask, even the pitchfork—it was all here when I was a girl.

Teacher. Remarkable place.

(*He mops his brow*)

Claire. I thought the pastor's text was very appropriate. The lesson a trifle long.

Teacher. I Corinthians 13.

Claire. Your choristers sang beautifully, Professor.

Teacher. Bach. From the *St. Matthew Passion.*

Doctor. Güllen has never seen such magnificence! The flowers! The jewels! And the people.

Teacher. The theatrical world, the world of finance, the world of art, the world of science . . .

Claire. All these worlds are now back in their Cadillacs, speeding toward the capital for the wedding recep-

tion. But I'm sure you didn't come here to talk about them.

Doctor. Dear lady, we should not intrude on your valuable time. Your husband must be waiting impatiently.

Claire. No, no. I've packed him off to Brazil.

Doctor. To Brazil, madame?

Claire. Yes. For his honeymoon.

Teacher and Doctor. Oh! But your wedding guests?

Claire. I've planned a delightful dinner for them. They'll never miss me. Now what was it you wished to talk about?

Teacher. About Anton Schill, madame.

Claire. Is he dead?

Teacher. Madame, we may be poor. But we have our principles.

Claire. I see. Then what do you want?

Teacher (*He mops his brow again*). The fact is, madame, in anticipation of your well-known munificence, that is, feeling that you would give the town some sort of gift, we have all been buying things. Necessities . . .

Doctor. With money we don't have.

(*The* TEACHER *blows his nose*)

Claire. You've run into debt?

Doctor. Up to here.

Claire. In spite of your principles?

Teacher. We're human, madame.

Claire. I see

Teacher. We have been poor for a long time. A long, long time.

Doctor (*He rises*). The question is, how are we going to pay?

Claire. You already know.

Teacher (*Courageously*). I beg you, Madame Zachanassian, put yourself in our position for a moment. For twenty-two years I've been cudgeling my brains to plant a few seeds of knowledge in this wilderness. And all this time, my gallant colleague, Dr. Nüsslin, has been rattling around in his ancient Mercedes, from patient to patient, trying to keep these wretches alive. Why? Why have we spent our lives in this miserable hole? For money? Hardly. The pay is ridiculous.

Doctor. And yet, the professor here has declined an offer to head the high school in Kalberstadt.

Teacher. And Dr. Nüsslin has refused an important post at the University of Erlangen. Madame, the simple fact is, we love our town. We were born here. It is our life.

Doctor. That's true.

Teacher. What has kept us going all these years is the hope that one day the community will prosper again as it did in the days when we were young.

Claire. Good.

Teacher. Madame, there is no reason for our poverty. We suffer here from a mysterious blight. We have factories. They stand idle. There is oil in the valley of Pückenried.

Doctor. There is copper under the Konradsweil Forest. There is power in our streams, in our waterfalls.

Teacher. We are not poor, madame. If we had credit, if we had confidence, the factories would open, orders and commissions would pour in. And our economy would bloom together with our cultural life. We would become once again like the towns around us, healthy and prosperous.

Doctor. If the Wagonworks were put on its feet again—

Teacher. The Foundry.

Doctor. The Golden Eagle Pencil Factory.

Teacher. Buy these plants, madame. Put them in operation once more, and I swear to you, Güllen will flourish and it will bless you. We don't need a billion marks. Ten million, properly invested, would give us back our life, and incidentally return to the investor an excellent dividend. Save us, madame. Save us, and we will not only bless you, we will make money for you.

Claire. I don't need money.

Doctor. Madame, we are not asking for charity. This is business.

Claire. It's a good idea . . .

Doctor. Dear lady! I knew you wouldn't let us down.

Claire. But it's out of the question. I cannot buy the Wagonworks. I already own them.

Doctor. The Wagonworks?

Teacher. And the Foundry?

Claire. And the Foundry.

Doctor. And the Golden Eagle Pencil Factory?

Claire. Everything. The valley of Pückenried with its oil, the forest of Konradsweil with its ore, the barn, the town, the streets, the houses, the shops, everything. I had my agents buy up this rubbish over the years, bit by bit, piece by piece, until I had it all. Your hopes were an illusion, your vision empty, your self-sacrifice a stupidity, your whole life completely senseless.

Teacher. Then the mysterious blight—

Claire. The mysterious blight was I.

Doctor. But this is monstrous!

Claire. Monstrous. I was seventeen when I left this town. It was winter. I was dressed in a sailor suit and my red braids hung down my back. I was in my seventh month. As I walked down the street to the station, the boys whistled after me, and someone threw something. I sat freezing in my seat in the Hamburg Express. But before the roof of the great barn was lost behind the trees, I had made up my mind that one day I would come back . . .

Teacher. But, madame—

Claire (*She smiles*). And now I have. (*She claps her hands*) Mike. Max. Take me back to the Golden Apostle. I've been here long enough.

(MIKE *and* MAX *start to pick up the sedan chair. The* TEACHER *pushes* MIKE *away*)

Teacher. Madame. One moment. Please. I see it all now. I had thought of you as an avenging fury, a Medea, a Clytemnestra—but I was wrong. You are a warm-hearted woman who has suffered a terrible injustice, and now you have returned and taught us an unforgettable lesson. You have stripped us bare. But now that we stand before you naked, I know you will set aside these thoughts of vengeance. If we made you suffer, you too have put us through the fire. Have mercy, madame.

Claire. When I have had justice. Mike!

(*She signals to* MIKE *and* MAX *to pick up the sedan chair. They cross the stage. The* TEACHER *bars the way*)

Teacher. But, madame, one injustice cannot cure another. What good will it do to force us into crime? Horror succeeds horror, shame is piled on shame. It settles nothing.

Claire. It settles everything.

(*They move upstage toward the exit. The* TEACHER *follows*)

Teacher. Madame, this lesson you have taught us will never be forgotten. We will hand it down from father to son. It will be a monument more lasting than any vengeance. Whatever we have been, in the future we shall be better because of you. You have pushed us to the extreme. Now forgive us. Show us the way to a better life. Have pity, madame— pity. That is the highest justice.

(*The sedan chair stops*)

Claire. The highest justice has no pity. It is bright and pure and clear. The world made me into a whore; now I make the world into a brothel. Those who wish to go down, may go down. Those who wish to dance with me, may dance with me. (*To her porters*) Go.

(*She is carried off. The lights black out. Downstage, right, appears* SCHILL's *shop. It has a new sign, a new counter. The doorbell, when it rings, has an impressive sound. FRAU SCHILL stands behind the counter in a new dress. The FIRST MAN enters, left. He is dressed as a prosperous butcher, a few bloodstains on his snowy apron, a gold watch chain across his open vest*)

First Man. What a wedding! I'll swear the whole town was there. Cigarettes.

Frau Schill. Clara is entitled to a little happiness after all. I'm happy for her. Green or white?

First Man. Turkish. The bridesmaids! Dancers and opera singers. And the dresses! Down to here.

Frau Schill. It's the fashion nowadays.

First man. Reporters! Photographers! From all over the world! (*In a low voice*) They will be here any minute.

Frau Schill. What have reporters to do with us? We are simple people, Herr Hofbauer. There is nothing for them here.

First Man. They're questioning everybody. They're asking everything. (*The* FIRST MAN *lights a cigarette. He looks up at the ceiling*) Footsteps.

Frau Schill. He's pacing the room. Up and down. Day and night.

First Man. Haven't seen him all week.

Frau Schill. He never goes out.

First Man. It's his conscience. That was pretty mean, the way he treated poor Madame Zachanassian.

Frau Schill. That's true. I feel very badly about it myself.

First Man. To ruin a young girl like that—God doesn't forgive it. (FRAU SCHILL *nods solemnly with pursed lips. The butcher gives her a level glance*) Look, I hope he'll have sense enough to keep his mouth shut in front of the reporters.

Frau Schill. I certainly hope so.

First Man. You know his character.

Frau Schill. Only too well, Herr Hofbauer.

First Man. If he tries to throw dirt at our Clara and tell a lot of lies, how she tried to get us to kill him, which anyway she never meant—

Frau Schill. Of course not.

First Man. —Then we'll really have to do something! And not because of the money— (*He spits*) But out of ordinary human decency. God knows Madame Zachanassian has suffered enough through him already.

Frau Schill. She has indeed.

(*The* TEACHER *comes in. He is not quite sober*)

Teacher (*Looks about the shop*). Has the press been here yet?

First Man. No.

Teacher. It's not my custom, as you know, Frau Schill—but I wonder if I could have a strong alcoholic drink?

Frau Schill. It's an honor to serve you, Herr Professor. I have a good Steinhäger. Would you like to try a glass?

Teacher. A very small glass.

(FRAU SCHILL *serves bottle and glass. The* TEACHER *tosses off a glass*)

Frau Schill. Your hand is shaking, Herr Professor.

Teacher. To tell the truth, I have been drinking a little already.

Frau Schill. Have another glass. It will do you good.

(*He accepts another glass*)

Teacher. Is that he up there, walking?

Frau Schill. Up and down. Up and down.

First Man. It's God punishing him.

(*The* PAINTER *comes in with the* SON *and the* DAUGHTER)

Painter. Careful! A reporter just asked us the way to this shop.

First Man. I hope you didn't tell him.

Painter. I told him we were strangers here.

(*They all laugh. The door opens. The* SECOND MAN *darts into the shop*)

Second Man. Look out, everybody! The press! They are across the street in your shop, Hofbauer.

First Man. My boy will know how to deal with them.

Second Man. Make sure Schill doesn't come down, Hofbauer.

First Man. Leave that to me.

(*They group themselves about the shop*)

Teacher. Listen to me, all of you. When the reporters come I'm going to speak to them. I'm going to make a statement. A statement to the world on behalf of myself as Rector of Güllen High School and on behalf of you all, for all your sakes.

Painter. What are you going to say?

Teacher. I shall tell the truth about Claire Zachanassian.

Frau Schill. You're drunk, Herr Professor; you should be ashamed of yourself.

Teacher. I should be ashamed? You should all be ashamed!

Son. Shut your trap. You're drunk.

Daughter. Please, Professor—

Teacher. Girl, you disappoint me. It is your place to speak. But you are silent and you force your old teacher to raise his voice. I am going to speak the truth. It is my duty and I am not afraid. The world may not wish to listen, but no one can silence me. I'm not going to wait—I'm going over to Hofbauer's shop now.

All. No, you're not. Stop him. Stop him.

(*They all spring at the* TEACHER. *He defends himself. At this moment,* SCHILL *appears through the door upstage. In contrast to the others, he is dressed shabbily in an old black jacket, his best*)

Schill. What's going on in my shop? (*The* TOWNSMEN *let go of the* TEACHER *and turn to stare at* SCHILL) What's the trouble, Professor?

Teacher. Schill, I am speaking out at last! I am going to tell the press everything.

Schill. Be quiet, Professor.

Teacher. What did you say?

Schill. Be quiet.

Teacher. You want me to be quiet?

Schill. Please.

Teacher. But, Schill, if I keep quiet, if you miss this opportunity—they're over in Hofbauer's shop now . . .

Schill. Please.

Teacher. As you wish. If you too are on their side, I have no more to say.

(*The doorbell jingles. A* REPORTER *comes in*)

Reporter. Is Anton Schill here? (*Moves to* SCHILL) Are you Herr Schill?

Schill. What?

Reporter. Herr Schill.

Schill. Er—no. Herr Schill's gone to Kalberstadt for the day.

Reporter. Oh, thank you. Good day.

(*He goes out*)

Painter (*Mops his brow*). Whew! Close shave.

(*He follows the* REPORTER *out*)

Second Man (*Walking up to* SCHILL). That was pretty smart of you to keep your mouth shut. You know what to expect if you don't.

(*He goes*)

First Man. Give me a Havana. (SCHILL *serves him*) Charge it. You bastard!

(*He goes.* SCHILL *opens his account book*)

Frau Schill. Come along, children—

(FRAU SCHILL, *the* SON *and the* DAUGHTER *go off, upstage*)

Teacher. They're going to kill you. I've known it all along, and you too, you must have known it. The need is too strong, the temptation too great. And now perhaps I too will join against you. I belong to them and, like them, I can feel myself hardening into something that is not human —not beautiful.

Schill. It can't be helped.

Teacher. Pull yourself together, man. Speak to the reporters; you've no time to lose.

(SCHILL *looks up from his account book*)

Schill. No. I'm not going to fight any more.

Teacher. Are you so frightened that you don't dare open your mouth?

Schill. I made Claire what she is, I made myself what I am. What should I do? Should I pretend that I'm innocent?

Teacher. No, you can't. You are as guilty as hell.

Schill. Yes.

Teacher. You are a bastard.

Schill. Yes.

Teacher. But that does not justify your murder. (SCHILL *looks at him*) I wish I could believe that for what they're doing—for what they're going to do—they will suffer for the rest of their lives. But it's not true. In a little while they will have justified everything and forgotten everything.

Schill. Of course.

Teacher. Your name will never again be mentioned in this town. That's how it will be.

Schill. I don't hold it against you.

Teacher. But I do. I will hold it against myself all my life. That's why—

(*The doorbell jingles. The* BURGOMASTER *comes in. The* TEACHER *stares at him, then goes out without another word*)

Burgomaster. Good afternoon, Schill. Don't let me disturb you. I've just dropped in for a moment.

Schill. I'm just finishing my accounts for the week.

(*A moment's pause*)

Burgomaster. The town council meets tonight. At the Golden Apostle. In the auditorium.

Schill. I'll be there.

Burgomaster. The whole town will be there. Your case will be discussed and final action taken. You've put us in a pretty tight spot, you know.

Schill. Yes. I'm sorry.

Burgomaster. The lady's offer will be rejected.

Schill. Possibly.

Burgomaster. Of course, I may be wrong.

Schill. Of course.

Burgomaster. In that case—are you prepared to accept the judgment of the town? The meeting will be covered by the press, you know.

Schill. By the press?

Burgomaster. Yes, and the radio and the newsreel. It's a very ticklish situation. Not only for you—believe me, it's even worse for us. What with the wedding, and all the publicity, we've become famous. All of a sudden our ancient democratic institutions have become of interest to the world.

Schill. Are you going to make the lady's condition public?

Burgomaster. No, no, of course not. Not directly. We will have to put the matter to a vote—that is unavoidable. But only those involved will understand.

Schill. I see.

Burgomaster. As far as the press is concerned, you are simply the intermediary between us and Madame Zachanassian. I have whitewashed you completely.

Schill. That is very generous of you.

Burgomaster. Frankly, it's not for your sake, but for the sake of your family.

They are honest and decent people.

Schill. Oh—

Burgomaster. So far we've all played fair. You've kept your mouth shut and so have we. Now can we continue to depend on you? Because if you have any idea of opening your mouth at tonight's meeting, there won't be any meeting.

Schill. I'm glad to hear an open threat at last.

Burgomaster. We are not threatening you. You are threatening us. If you speak, you force us to act—in advance.

Schill. That won't be necessary.

Burgomaster. So if the town decides against you?

Schill. I will accept their decision.

Burgomaster. Good. (*A moment's pause*) I'm delighted to see there is still a spark of decency left in you. But—wouldn't it be better if we didn't have to call a meeting at all? (*He pauses. He takes a gun from his pocket and puts it on the counter*) I've brought you this.

Schill. Thank you.

Burgomaster. It's loaded.

Schill. I don't need a gun.

Burgomaster (*He clears his throat*). You see? We could tell the lady that we had condemned you in secret session and you had anticipated our decision. I've lost a lot of sleep getting to this point, believe me.

Schill. I believe you.

Burgomaster. Frankly, in your place, I myself would prefer to take the path of honor. Get it over with, once and for all. Don't you agree? For the sake of your friends! For the sake of our children, your own children —you have a daughter, a son—Schill, you know our need, our misery.

Schill. You've put me through hell, you and your town. You were my friends, you smiled and reassured me. But day by day I saw you change—your shoes, your ties, your suits—your hearts. If you had been honest with me then, perhaps I would feel differently toward you now. I might even use that gun you brought me. For the sake of my friends. But now I have conquered my fear. Alone. It was hard, but it's done. And now you will have to judge me. And I will accept your judgment. For me that will be justice. How it will be for you, I don't know. (*He turns away*) You may kill me if you like. I won't complain, I won't protest, I won't defend myself. But I won't do your job for you either.

Burgomaster (*Takes up his gun*). There it is. You've had your chance and you won't take it. Too bad. (*He takes out a cigarette*) I suppose it's more than we can expect of a man like you. (SCHILL *lights the* BURGOMASTER's *cigarette*) Good day.

Schill. Good day. (*The* BURGOMASTER *goes,* FRAU SCHILL *comes in, dressed in a fur coat. The* DAUGHTER *is in a new red dress. The* SON *has a new sports jacket*) What a beautiful coat, Mathilde!

Frau Schill. Real fur. You like it?

Schill. Should I? What a lovely dress, Ottilie!

Daughter. *C'est très chic, n'est-ce-pas?*

Schill. What?

Frau Schill. Ottilie is taking a course in French.

Schill. Very useful. Karl—whose automobile is that out there at the curb?

Son. Oh, it's only an Opel. They're not expensive.

Schill. You bought yourself a car?

Son. On credit. Easiest thing in the world.

Frau Schill. Everyone's buying on credit now, Anton. These fears of yours are ridiculous. You'll see. Clara has a good heart. She only means to teach you a lesson.

Daughter. She means to teach you a lesson, that's all.

Son. It's high time you got the point, Father.

Schill. I get the point. (*The church bells start ringing*) Listen. The bells of Güllen. Do you hear?

Son. Yes, we have four bells now. It sounds quite good.

Daughter. Just like Gray's Elegy.

Schill. What?

Frau Schill. Ottilie is taking a course in English literature.

Schill. Congratulations! It's Sunday. I should very much like to take a ride in your car. Our car.

Son. You want to ride in the car?

Schill. Why not? I want to ride through the Konradsweil Forest. I want to see the town where I've lived all my life.

Frau Schill. I don't think that will look very nice for any of us.

Schill. No—perhaps not. Well, I'll go for a walk by myself.

Frau Schill. Then take us to Kalberstadt, Karl, and we'll go to a cinema.

Schill. A cinema? It's a good idea.

Frau Schill. See you soon, Anton.

Schill. Good-bye, Ottilie. Good-bye, Karl. Good-bye, Mathilde.

Family. Good-bye.

(*They go out*)

Schill. Good-bye. (*The shop sign flies off. The lights black out. They come up at once on the forest scene*)

Autumn. Even the forest has turned to gold.

(Schill *wanders down to the bench in the forest. He sits.* Claire's *voice is heard*)

Claire (*Offstage*). Stop. Wait here. (Claire *comes in. She gazes slowly up at the trees, kicks at some leaves. Then she walks slowly down center. She stops before a tree, glances up the trunk*) Bark-borers. The old tree is dying.

Schill. Clara.

Claire. How pleasant to see you here. I was visiting my forest. May I sit by you?

Schill. Oh, yes. Please do. (*She sits next to him*) I've just been saying good-bye to my family. They've gone to the cinema. Karl has bought himself a car.

Claire. How nice.

Schill. Ottilie is taking French lessons. And a course in English literature.

Claire. You see? They're beginning to take an interest in higher things.

Schill. Listen. A finch. You hear?

Claire. Yes. It's a finch. And a cuckoo in the distance. Would you like some music?

Schill. Oh, yes. That would be very nice.

Claire. Anything special?

Schill. "Deep in the Forest."

Claire. Your favorite song. They know it.

(*She raises her hand. Offstage, the mandolin and guitar play the tune softly*)

Schill. We had a child?

Claire. Yes.

Schill. Boy or girl?

Claire. Girl.

Schill. What name did you give her?

Claire. I called her Genevieve.

Schill. That's a very pretty name.

Claire. Yes.

Schill. What was she like?

Claire. I saw her only once. When she was born. Then they took her away from me.

Schill. Her eyes?

Claire. They weren't open yet.

Schill. And her hair?

Claire. Black, I think. It's usually black at first.

Schill. Yes, of course. Where did she die, Clara?

Claire. In some family. I've forgotten their name. Meningitis, they said. The officials wrote me a letter.

Schill. Oh, I'm so very sorry, Clara.

Claire. I've told you about our child. Now tell me about myself.

Schill. About yourself?

Claire. Yes. How I was when I was seventeen in the days when you loved me.

Schill. I remember one day you waited for me in the great barn. I had to look all over the place for you. At last I found you lying in the haycart with nothing on and a long straw between your lips . . .

Claire. Yes. I was pretty in those days.

Schill. You were beautiful, Clara.

Claire. You were strong. The time you fought with those two railway men who were following me, I wiped the blood from your face with my red petticoat. (*The music ends*) They've stopped.

Schill. Tell them to play "Thoughts of Home."

Claire. They know that too.

(*The music plays*)

Schill. Here we are, Clara, sitting together in our forest for the last time.

The town council meets tonight. They will condemn me to death, and one of them will kill me. I don't know who and I don't know where. Clara, I only know that in a little while a useless life will come to an end.

(*He bows his head on her bosom. She takes him in her arms*)

Claire (*Tenderly*). I shall take you in your coffin to Capri. You will have your tomb in the park of my villa, where I can see you from my bedroom window. White marble and onyx in a grove of green cypress. With a beautiful view of the Mediterranean.

Schill. I've always wanted to see it.

Claire. Your love for me died years ago, Anton. But my love for you would not die. It turned into something strong, like the hidden roots of the forest; something evil, like white mushrooms that grow unseen in the darkness. And slowly it reached out for your life. Now I have you. You are mine. Alone. At last, and forever, a peaceful ghost in a silent house.

(*The music ends*)

Schill. The song is over.

Claire. Adieu, Anton.

(*CLAIRE kisses ANTON, a long kiss. Then she rises*)

Schill. Adieu.

(*She goes. SCHILL remains sitting on the bench. A row of lamps descends from the flies. The TOWNSMEN come in from both sides, each bearing his chair. A table and chairs are set upstage, center. On both sides sit the TOWNSMEN. The POLICEMAN, in a new uniform, sits on the bench behind SCHILL. All the TOWNSMEN are in new Sunday clothes. Around them are* TECHNICIANS *of all sorts, with lights, cameras and other equipment. The* TOWNSWOMEN *are absent. They do not vote. The* BURGOMASTER *takes his place at the table, center. The* DOCTOR *and the* PASTOR *sit at the same table, at his right, and the* TEACHER *in his academic gown, at his left*)

Burgomaster (*At a sign from the* RADIO TECHNICIAN, *he pounds the floor with his wand of office*). Fellow citizens of Güllen, I call this meeting to order. The agenda: there is only one matter before us. I have the honor to announce officially that Madame Claire Zachanassian, daughter of our beloved citizen, the famous architect Siegfried Wäscher, has decided to make a gift to the town of one billion marks. Five hundred million to the town, five hundred million to be divided per capita among the citizens. After certain necessary preliminaries, a vote will be taken, and you, as citizens of Güllen, will signify your will by a show of hands. Has anyone any objection to this mode of procedure? The pastor? (*Silence*) The police? (*Silence*) The town health official? (*Silence*) The Rector of Güllen High School? (*Silence*) The political opposition? (*Silence*) I shall then proceed to the vote—(*The* TEACHER *rises. The* BURGOMASTER *turns in surprise and irritation*) You wish to speak?

Teacher. Yes.

Burgomaster. Very well.

(*He takes his seat. The* TEACHER *advances. The movie camera starts running*)

Teacher. Fellow townsmen. (*The* PHOTOGRAPHER *flashes a bulb in his face*) Fellow townsmen. We all know that by means of this gift, Madame Claire Zachanassian intends to attain a certain object. What is this object? To enrich the town of her youth, yes. But more than that, she desires by means of this gift to re-establish justice among us. This desire expressed by our benefactress raises an all-important question. Is it true that our community harbors in its soul such a burden of guilt?

Burgomaster. Yes! True!

Second Man. Crimes are concealed among us.

Third Man (*He jumps up*). Sins!

Fourth Man (*He jumps up also*). Perjuries.

Painter. Justice!

Townsmen. Justice! Justice!

Teacher. Citizens of Güllen, this, then, is the simple fact of the case. We have participated in an injustice. I thoroughly recognize the material advantages which this gift opens to us —I do not overlook the fact that it is poverty which is the root of all this bitterness and evil. Nevertheless, there is no question here of money.

Townsmen. No! No!

Teacher. Here there is no question of our prosperity as a community, or our well-being as individuals— The question is—must be—whether or not we wish to live according to the principles of justice, those principles for which our forefathers lived and fought and for which they died, those principles which form the soul of our Western culture.

Townsmen. Hear! Hear!

(*Applause*)

Teacher (*Desperately, realizing that*

he is fighting a losing battle, and on the verge of hysteria). Wealth has meaning only when benevolence comes of it, but only he who hungers for grace will receive grace. Do you feel this hunger, my fellow citizens, this hunger of the spirit, or do you feel only that other profane hunger, the hunger of the body? That is the question which I, as Rector of your high school, now propound to you. Only if you can no longer tolerate the presence of evil among you, only if you can in no circumstances endure a world in which injustice exists, are you worthy to receive Madame Zachanassian's billion and fulfill the condition bound up with this gift. If not—(*Wild applause. He gestures desperately for silence*) If not, then God have mercy on us!

(*The* TOWNSMEN *crowd around him, ambiguously, in a mood somewhat between threat and congratulation. He takes his seat, utterly crushed, exhausted by his effort. The* BURGO-MASTER *advances and takes charge once again. Order is restored*)

Burgomaster. Anton Schill—(*The* PO-LICEMAN *gives* SCHILL *a shove.* SCHILL *gets up*) Anton Schill, it is through you that this gift is offered to the town. Are you willing that this offer should be accepted?

(SCHILL *mumbles something*)

Radio Reporter (*Steps to his side*). You'll have to speak up a little, Herr Schill.

Schill. Yes.

Burgomaster. Will you respect our decision in the matter before us?

Schill. I will respect your decision.

Burgomaster. Then I proceed to the vote. All those who are in accord with

the terms on which this gift is offered will signify the same by raising their right hands. (*After a moment, the* POLICEMAN *raises his hand. Then one by one the others. Last of all, very slowly, the* TEACHER) All against? The offer is accepted. I now solemnly call upon you, fellow townsmen, to declare in the face of all the world that you take this action, not out of love for worldly gain . . .

Townsmen (*In chorus*). Not out of love for worldly gain . . .

Burgomaster. But out of love for the right.

Townsmen. But out of love for the right.

Burgomaster (*Holds up his hand, as if taking an oath*). We join together, now, as brothers . . .

Townsmen (*Hold up their hands*). We join together, now, as brothers . . .

Burgomaster. To purify our town of guilt . . .

Townsmen. To purify our town of guilt . . .

Burgomaster. And to reaffirm our faith . . . .

Townsmen. And to reaffirm our faith . . .

Burgomaster. In the eternal power of justice.

Townsmen. In the eternal power of justice.

(*The lights go off suddenly*)

Schill (*A scream*). Oh, God!

Voice. I'm sorry, Herr Burgomaster. We seem to have blown a fuse. (*The lights go on*) Ah—there we are. Would you mind doing that last bit again?

Burgomaster. Again?

The Cameraman (*Walks forward*). Yes, for the newsreel.

Burgomaster. Oh, the newsreel. Certainly.

The Cameraman. Ready now? Right.

Burgomaster. And to reaffirm our faith . . .

Townsmen. And to reaffirm our faith . . .

Burgomaster. In the eternal power of justice.

Townsmen. In the eternal power of justice.

The Cameraman (*To his* ASSISTANT). It was better before, when he screamed "Oh, God."

(*The* ASSISTANT *shrugs*)

Burgomaster. Fellow citizens of Güllen, I declare this meeting adjourned. The ladies and gentlemen of the press will find refreshments served downstairs, with the compliments of the town council. The exits lead directly to the restaurant.

The Cameraman. Thank you.

(*The* NEWSMEN *go off with alacrity. The* TOWNSMEN *remain on the stage.* SCHILL *gets up*)

Policeman (*Pushes* SCHILL *down*). Sit down.

Schill. Is it to be now?

Policeman. Naturally, now.

Schill. I thought it might be best to have it at my house.

Policeman. It will be here.

Burgomaster. Lower the lights. (*The lights dim*) Are they all gone?

Voice. All gone.

Burgomaster. The gallery?

Second Voice. Empty.

Burgomaster. Lock the doors.

The Voice. Locked here.

Second Voice. Locked here.

Burgomaster. Form a lane. (*The men form a lane. At the end stands the* ATHLETE *in elegant white slacks, a red scarf around his singlet*) Pastor. Will you be so good?

(*The* PASTOR *walks slowly to* SCHILL)

Pastor. Anton Schill, your heavy hour has come.

Schill. May I have a cigarette?

Pastor. Cigarette, Burgomaster.

Burgomaster. Of course, With pleasure. And a good one.

(*He gives his case to the* PASTOR, *who offers it to* SCHILL. *The* POLICEMAN *lights the cigarette. The* PASTOR *returns the case*)

Pastor. In the words of the prophet Amos—

Schill. Please—

(*He shakes his head*)

Pastor. You're no longer afraid?

Schill. No. I'm not afraid.

Pastor. I will pray for you.

Schill. Pray for us all.

(*The* PASTOR *bows his head*)

Burgomaster. Anton Schill, stand up!

(SCHILL *hesitates*)

Policeman. Stand up, you swine!

Burgomaster. Schultz, please.

Policeman. I'm sorry. I was carried away. (SCHILL *gives the cigarette to the* POLICEMAN. *Then he walks slowly to the center of the stage and turns his back on the audience*) Enter the lane.

(SCHILL *hesitates a moment. He goes slowly into the lane of silent men. The* ATHLETE *stares at him from the opposite end.* SCHILL *looks in turn at the hard faces of those who surround him, and sinks slowly to his knees. The lane contracts silently into a knot as the men close in and crouch over. Complete silence. The knot of men pulls back slowly, coming down-*

stage. Then it opens. Only the Doc-
tor is left in the center of the stage,
kneeling by the corpse, over which
the Teacher's gown has been spread.
The Doctor rises and takes off his
stethoscope)

Pastor. Is it all over?

Doctor. Heart failure.

Burgomaster. Died of joy.

All. Died of joy.

(*The Townsmen turn their backs on*
the corpse and at once light ciga-
rettes. A cloud of smoke rises over
them. From the left comes Claire
Zachanassian, dressed in black, fol-
lowed by Bobby. She sees the corpse.
Then she walks slowly to center stage
and looks down at the body of
Schill)

Claire. Uncover him. (Bobby *uncovers*
Schill's face. She stares at it a long
moment. She sighs) Cover his face.

(Bobby *covers it. Claire goes out, up*
center. Bobby takes the check from
his wallet, holds it out peremptorily
to the Burgomaster, who walks over
from the knot of silent men. He holds
out his hand for the check. The lights
fade. At once the warning bell is
heard, and the scene dissolves into
the setting of the railway station. The
gradual transformation of the shabby
town into a thing of elegance and
beauty is now accomplished. The
railway station glitters with neon
lights and is surrounded with garlands, bright posters and flags. The
Townsfolk, men and women, now in
brand new clothes, form themselves
into a group in front of the station.
The sound of the approaching train
grows louder. The train stops*)

Station Master. Güllen-Rome Express.
All aboard, please. (*The church bells*
start pealing. Men appear with
trunks and boxes, a procession which
duplicates that of the lady's arrival,
but in inverse order. Then come the
Two Blind Men, then Bobby, and
Mike and Max carrying the coffin.
Lastly Claire. She is dressed in
modish black. Her head is high, her
face as impassive as that of an an-
cient idol. The procession crosses the
stage and goes off. The people bow
in silence as the coffin passes. When
Claire and her retinue have boarded
the train, the Station Master blows
a long blast) 'Bo—ard!

(*He holds up his paddle. The train*
starts and moves off slowly, picking
up speed. The crowd turns slowly,
gazing after the departing train in
complete silence. The train sounds
fade)

The curtain falls slowly

Index